KU-515-270

Time Out

Barcelona

Penguin Books

PENGUIN BOOKS

Published by the Penguin Group
Penguin Books Ltd, 27 Wrights Lane, London W8 5TZ, England
Penguin Books USA Inc., 375 Hudson Street, New York, New York 10014, USA
Penguin Books Australia Ltd, Ringwood, Victoria, Australia
Penguin Books Canada Ltd, 10 Alcorn Avenue, Toronto, Ontario, Canada M4V 3B2
Penguin Books (NZ) Ltd, 182-190 Wairau Road, Auckland 10, New Zealand

Penguin Books Ltd, Registered Offices: Harmondsworth, Middlesex, England

First published 1996
Second edition 1998
Third edition 2000
10 9 8 7 6 5 4 3 2 1

Copyright © Time Out Group Ltd, 1996, 1998, 2000
All rights reserved

Colour reprographics by Precise Litho, 34-35 Great Sutton Street, London EC1
Printed and bound by William Clowes Ltd, Beccles, Suffolk NR34 9QE

Edited and designed by

Time Out Guides Limited
Universal House
251 Tottenham Court Road
London W1P OAB
Tel + 44 (0)20 7813 3000
Fax + 44 (0)20 7813 6001
Email guides@timeout.com
www.timeout.com

Editorial

Editor Nick Rider
Deputy Editor Sophie Blacksell
Researchers Laia Oliver, Sheri Ahmed
Proofreader Alison Bravington
Indexer Jackie Brind

Editorial Director Peter Fiennes
Series Editor Caroline Taverne

Design

Art Director John Oakey
Art Editor Mandy Martin
Senior Designer Scott Moore
Designers Benjamin de Lotz, Lucy Grant
Scanning & Imaging Chris Quinn
Picture Editor Kerri Miles
Deputy Picture Editor Olivia Duncan-Jones
Picture Researcher Kit Burnet

Advertising

Group Advertisement Director Lesley Gill
Sales Director Mark Phillips
International Sales Manager Mary L Rega
Advertisement Sales (Barcelona) Barcelona Metropolitan
Advertising Assistant Daniel Heaf

Administration

Publisher Tony Elliott
Managing Director Mike Hardwick
Financial Director Kevin Ellis
Marketing Director Gillian Auld
General Manager Nichola Coulthard
Production Manager Mark Lamond
Accountant Bridget Carter

Features in this guide were written and updated by:

Introduction Nick Rider. **Barcelona by Season** Jonathan Bennett. **History** Nick Rider, Jeffrey Swartz, EM Butterfield. **Architecture** Jane Opher, David Howel Evans, Nick Rider. **Language** Matthew Tree. **Barcelona Today** Richard Schweid. **Sightseeing** EM Butterfield, Nick Rider, Jeffrey Swartz. **Museums** Jeffrey Swartz. **Art Galleries** Jeffrey Swartz. **Accommodation** Anne Heverin. **Restaurants** William Truini. **Cafés & Bars** William Truini. **Nightlife** William Truini, Marisol Grandón. **Shopping** Anne Heverin, Glòria Sallent. **Services** Anne Heverin. **Children** Esther Jones. **Dance** Richard Schweid. **Film** Richard Schweid. **Gay & Lesbian Barcelona** Eric Goode. **Media** Richard Schweid. **Music: Classical & Opera** Jonathan Bennett. **Music: Rock, Roots & Jazz** Robert Southon, Glòria Sallent. **Sport & Fitness** Stuart Goodsir. **Theatre** Jeffrey Swartz. **Trips Out of Town** William Truini. **Directory** Robert Southon.

The editors, writers and publisher would like to thank the following: Maria Lluïsa Albacar, Mònica Solès and the rest of the staff of Turisme de Barcelona; the staff of the Palau Robert; Alfons Blanco, Transports Metropolitans de Barcelona; RENFE; Institut de Cultura de Barcelona; Col.lecció Thyssen-Bornemisza; Museu Nacional de Catalunya; Claustra Rafart, Museu Picasso; Fundació la Caixa; Esther Jones and all at Metropolitan; Perejaume; Oliver Harris; Jeff King; Steven Guest; Jacqueline Minnett; Eamon Butterfield; Bettina Marten; Lily Dunn, Ruth Jarvis, Caroline Taverne; the Oliver family and Ethel Rimmer.

Maps by Mapworld, 71 Blandy Road, Henley-on-Thames, Oxon RG9 1QB.

Photography by Ingrid Morató **except**: page 7 Rafael Badia; page 26 AHCB-A; page 30 David "Chim" Seymour/Magnum Photos; page 33 Empics Ltd; pages 93 Fundacion Coleccion Thyssen-Bornemisza; pages 96 and 97 SPADEM 1989; page 111 Perejaume; page 223 Ros Ribas; pages 261 and 265 Turisme de Catalunya; pages 16, 21, 24, 25, 262, 264, 268, 269, 273, 274 Godo-Foto; page 243 Angel Holina; The following photographs were supplied by the featured establishments: pages 94, 95, 101 and 225

Contents

About the Guide

This is the third edition of the *Time Out Barcelona Guide*, one in a series of city guides that includes London, Paris, New York, Rome, Prague, Brussels, Las Vegas, Madrid and other cities around the world. For the new edition our team of resident writers has checked out and revisited museums and cafés, back-street shops and harbourside clubs, to give as complete a picture as possible of this fast-changing city as it is today.

We cover every aspect of Barcelona – from its history and traditions to current politics, fashions and alternative arts venues. We point you towards obscure clubs and hidden-away shops, and, if you're thinking of staying for a while, give tips on handling local bureaucracy and other aspects of living.

CHECKED & CORRECT

We've tried to make this guide as useful as possible. All addresses, phone numbers, transport details, opening times, admission prices and credit card details were correct at time of going to press. In any city, though, places can close and things can change at any time; in Barcelona, also, many places do not keep strictly to stated hours. Before going anywhere out of your way, it's a good idea to phone ahead to check on current times and dates.

LANGUAGE

Barcelona is a bilingual city; however, the majority language is Catalan, which is now the sole language used on street signs, and most maps. We have followed Catalan usage in all addresses and in most other parts of the guide. In many areas, Catalan and Spanish are frequently mixed, and you may hear Spanish equivalents that can be very different. Where both versions of a word or phrase can be useful we give both, with the Catalan first, as in *demà/mañana* (tomorrow). *See also pages 41-3*.

TELEPHONE NUMBERS

Since 1998 it has been necessary to dial provincial area codes with all Spanish phone numbers, even for local calls. Hence all normal Barcelona numbers (not mobiles, or special-rate numbers) have to begin with **93**, whether you are calling from outside the city or within it. From abroad, you must dial 34 (Spain) + 93. *See also page 286*.

MAP REFERENCES

Most places listed in this guide are within the area of the maps on *pages 309-19*. References in plain type (A2) refer to the city maps on *pages 309-15*; references in **bold (C4)** refer to the detailed map of the old city on *pages 316-7*.

PRICES

The prices listed should be regarded as guidelines, not gospel. Fluctuating exchange rates and inflation can cause prices to change unpredictably. However, if prices anywhere vary wildly from those we've quoted, ask if there's a reason. If there's not, go elsewhere, and then please let us know. We aim to give the best and most up-to-date advice, and always want to hear if you've been overcharged or badly treated.

CREDIT CARDS

The following abbreviations have been used for credit cards in this guide: **AmEx** – American Express; **DC** – Diners' Club; **EC** – Eurocheque card; **JCB** – Japanese credit bank card; **MC** – Mastercard; **TC** – travellers' cheques in any currency; **$TC**, **£TC** – travellers' cheques in US dollars or pounds sterling; **V** – Visa.

RIGHT TO REPLY

It should be stressed that the information we give is impartial. No organisation, venue or business has been included in this guide because its owner or manager has advertised in our publications. Their impartiality is one reason why *Time Out* guides are successful and well-respected. We hope you will enjoy the *Time Out Barcelona Guide*, but we'd also like to know if you don't. We welcome tips for places to be included in future editions, and take notice of your criticisms of any of our choices. You'll find a reader's reply card at the back of this book.

> There is an online version of this guide, as well as weekly events listings for several international cities, at http://www.timeout.co.com

Introduction

Barcelona is sometimes a very showy city. It always seems to be asking you to look at its new bridge, new gallery space, new parks, all-rebuilt state-of-the-art opera house or the perfectly-toned grey suits on the pretty staff at an exhibition, and stand up and admire the sheer style with which they were put together. And it's hard not to, which is why Barcelona basks in a near-unequalled aura of international acclaim. Hard on the heels of the Royal Institute of British Architects' Gold Medal, awarded for the first time ever to a single city, comes a survey by *National Geographic* rating Barcelona as one of the 50 Wonders of the Modern World – rare praise coming from Americans, who of all foreigners seem to have the greatest tendency to find the winding streets of the old city scuzzy and threatening rather than the concentrated urban experience they have always been.

It's possible to suffer from 'design stress' in Barcelona, a sensation of vague unease at everything around you having been so cleverly thought out. Recently, the ever-active city council has taken to removing the old wooden benches from streets and squares and replacing them with single seats with concrete legs, scattered at odd angles as if they'd been left behind after an outdoor party – most visibly in the Plaça Reial, where the benches used to be occupied all day by drunks and the lost having rambling conversations. This was apparently done at the behest of none other than Oriol Bohigas himself, the guru of Barcelona's urban renovations since the 1970s. Instead of something to sit on, you have an art object, which you can appreciate in solitary thought without the risk of an undesigned drunk sitting down beside you and slobbering on your sleeve.

Similarly, before the cement has set on any of the city's giant-scale urban renovation schemes – the Olympic buildings, the transformation of an old industrial harbour into the 'Port Vell' leisure zone – the Barcelona authorities are already announcing some new grand plan that is going to grab everybody's attention and redefine urban life as we know it for the next decade, or six months. Sometimes, one wonders if Barcelona is ever going to stop *projecting* and *becoming*, and just *be*.

And Barcelona has long been a great place just to be, even without the project-junkies tinkering with it. Its people have many other qualities, besides architectural ability. Catalans are contradictory. To take shopkeepers (iconic figures in Catalonia): many may seem positively lugubrious in style, dry and

ungiving, but go a little further, maybe ask for something specific, and you are served in a way that could not be more personal or concerned. The relationship between warmth and reserve is not an obvious one here. One very marked Catalan characteristic is a notably individualistic determination, if there's something that someone is interested in, to go about it, not in a showy way, but to its conclusion, however strange anyone else might find it. This is a city of obsessives, who pursue their interests – whether it be in design, in putting together a cool bar, in collecting spoons or producing fine food – with devotion. This makes it all the more interesting for visitors from outside, who reap the benefits. A relatively small city in world terms, Barcelona nevertheless has a very special, quirky – obsessive – variety.

Barcelona has for centuries lived with the tension of having the attributes and outlook of a capital city without officially being one. It has compensated for the absence of the pomp of state-capitalhood precisely through the creativity, imagination and sometimes intensity of its people, which is an essential reason why so many others like to come here. And this energy sometimes expresses itself in showy ways. It's an occupational hazard.

And showiness, and obsessiveness, have their very human side. One of the showiest things in Barcelona is the dancing fountain on Montjuïc, which is utterly silly and something that more workaday cities would never have even given street room, but is also somehow wonderful. Some of Barcelona's obsessives have reached the point of being deeply eccentric – Gaudí is the glaring example – but the city has given them room to live and even revered them. This all helps give the city it's special density, a concentrated sense of life. You never know what may be going on inside the head of the next person whose eyes cross with yours as you walk along the Rambla. *Nick Rider.*

In Context

book online at go-fly.com
the low cost airline from british airways

Barcelona by Season

Giants, fatheads and fire-runners, fashion shows and arts fests – a unique calendar of celebration.

Something is always happening, or due to happen, in Barcelona. The city's main holidays (*festes* in Catalan, *fiestas* in Spanish) are spread through the year, and at other times there are music, art, theatre and film festivals going on. Catalans have a strong sense of identity and civic pride, and many customs and traditions underline this feeling of community. There is a great sense of what should be done on a particular occasion, whether it's setting off fireworks on **Sant Joan**, eating the right cake for each saint's day (*pastisseries* play a major part in Catalan holidays) or visiting the cemetery on **Tots Sants**.

The city's biggest celebration, its *festa major*, is the **Mercè** in September, but each district also has its own local equivalent. Associated with them is a unique body of Catalan folklore (*see page 9*): human castles, giants, fatheads and the pyromaniac pandemonium of the *correfoc* (fire-running). Barcelona also hosts a myriad collection of conventions and trade fairs, at the **Fira de Barcelona** (*see page 296*). Most are trade-only, but some are open to the public, and the **Moda Barcelona/Espai Gaudí** fashion weeks in January and September create a buzz with many semi-public events.

Information

Good sources of information on what's going on are city tourist offices, the **Centre d'Informació de la Virreina**, the **010** phone line and city websites (for all, *see pages 294-5*). The local press also gives *festa* details, especially in weekend supplements (*see chapter* **Media**). For more on festivals for children, *see chapter* **Children**, and for music events *see chapters* **Music: Classical & Opera** *and* **Music: Rock, Roots & Jazz**. For some *festes* outside Barcelona, *see page 278*. In the listings below events that include public holidays are marked*.

*Don't try this at home... Playing with fire on **Sant Joan**. See page 8.*

Spring

Festes de Sant Medir de Gràcia

Gràcia to Sant Cugat and back, usually via Plaça Lesseps, Avda República Argentina & Carretera de l'Arrabassada. Metro Fontana/bus 22, 24, 28. **Information** tourist offices & 010. **Date** 3 Mar. **Map** D2-3

A celebration held since 1830, in which a procession of carriages and riders on horses leaves Gràcia in the morning after parading around Plaça Rius i Taulet with the banners of the *colles* (clubs) who organise the event. They head over Collserola by the winding Arrabassada road for the Hermitage of Sant Medir ('patron saint of broad beans') near Sant Cugat, to have a beany lunch. In the afternoon, as they return, they parade down Gran de Gràcia, throwing sweets into the crowd – a local version of the *Cavalcada dels Reis*.

Setmana Santa* (Holy Week)

Information tourist offices, Centre d'Informació de la Virreina & 010. **Dates** Easter (Mar-Apr).

Holy Week, most important festival of the year in southern Spain, is of much lesser importance here, although there are a few small-scale religious processions, and *L'Ou com Balla* (*see below*) is repeated in the Cathedral cloister. For most people Holy Week is simply a holiday when the city closes down – except for the pastry shops. Having made sweet cakes called *bunyols* every Wednesday and Friday through Lent, they sell *mones* (chocolate sculptures) for Easter. A run-of-the-mill *mona* is a rabbit or a figure of whichever cartoon character is the rage that year, but many *pastisseries* also make elaborate set-pieces, with reproductions of famous buildings, people or events. The most spectacular are usually in **Escribà** (*see chapter* **Shopping**).

Sant Jordi

La Rambla, and all over Barcelona. **Date** 23 Apr.

No one has a monopoly on Saint George, who as *Sant Jordi* is one of the patron saints of Catalonia, and can be found, with his dragon, all over Barcelona. His day has been celebrated here since 1667, and since 1923 has also been the Day of the Book (*Dia del Llibre*) in honour of Cervantes and Shakespeare, who both died on this same day in 1616. It used to be traditional for men to give their ladies a rose, in honour of Sant Jordi, and women to give their men a book, but nowadays you can give either to either. Or indeed both to both. What makes the day really special are the book stalls and spectacular rose stands that line the streets, in the Rambla, Passeig de Gràcia and all over the city. Every bookshop lays out a stall (with discount prices), and publishers wheel out their authors for marathon signing and meet-the-public sessions, while rose sellers, from florists to eager students, stand at every street corner. This is also, tradition-ally,the day of the year when the public go to visit the **Palau de la Generalitat**, to see the palace's own dazzling displays of red roses, arranged through its Gothic patios (queues are huge; *see p61*).

Feria de Abril

Diagonal-Mar, Sant Adrià del Besòs. Metro Besòs-Mar, then special buses. **Information** Federación de Entidades Culturales Andaluces en Cataluña (93 453 60 00). **Date** end Apr-early May.

For ten days each spring this satellite of the world-famous April *Feria* in Seville brings a breath of Andalusia to cool Catalonia, with song, dance, food, wine and a real taste of southern culture – a great chance to catch good flamenco and *sevillanas*. Begun as a migrant get-together in the '70s, it now draws some two million people, and looks set to be held for the time-being in the newly-developed Diagonal-Mar area near the Besòs river, with special buses for those who don't have a traditional horse and flower-cart.

Dia del Treball* (May Day)

Date 1 May.

The largest demonstration, by the mainstream trade unions, goes from Passeig de Gràcia to Plaça Sant Jaume; the anarchosyndicalist CNT meets at the Cotxeres de Sants on C/Sants before its march. For most people nowadays, though, it's just a day off.

Sant Ponç

C/Hospital. Metro Liceu/bus 14, 38, 59, 91. **Date** 11 May. **Map** C6/**A2-3**

Patron saint of beekeepers and herbalists, and on his day C/Hospital is lined with stalls selling honey, herbs, *fruta confitada* (very sweet candied fruit), perfumes, sweet wine and other natural products. It's a charming, colourful event, and the scents of the bunches of fresh herbs are exhilarating.

Andalusian antics at the **Feria de Abril***.*

Saló International del Còmic

*Estació de França (93 301 23 69). Metro Barceloneta/
bus 14, 39, 40, 51.* **Information** *Ficòmic, C/Palau 4*
(93 301 23 69). **Date** *May.* **Map** *E6/C4*
Barcelona's comic fair, one of the world's best, draws
crowds from across Europe, America and Japan.

Marató de l'Espectacle

Mercat de Les Flors, C/Lleida 59. **Information**
*Associació Marató de l'Espectacle, C/Trafalgar 78,
1er 1ª (93 268 18 68). Metro Espanya/bus all routes
to Plaça Espanya.* **Date** *late May/early June.* **Map** *B6*
Forty-eight hours of performance mayhem that go
some way to making up for the **Grec**'s lack of an
alternative element. Pieces, performed in the Mercat
de les Flors or the Teatre Grec, last from 30 seconds
to ten minutes, with a continuous flow of people as
members of the audience drift between spaces, go
up to perform their bits before returning to their
seats or head for the bar for a rest and some net-
working. With over 80 performances, amid dance,
theatre, comedy, music, puppets, installations and
film screenings, this is a great showcase for new
talent, albeit, inevitably, with peaks and troughs.

Festa de la Diversitat

*Moll de la Fusta. Metro Drassanes/bus 14, 36, 38,
57, 59, 64, 157, N4, N6, N9.* **Information** *SOS
Racisme, Passatge de la Pau 10 (93 301 05 97/fax 93
301 01 47).* **Date** *May/June.* **Map** *C-D7/A-B4*
Outside parts of the Raval or La Ribera, Barcelona's
non-Hispanic ethnic minorities keep a fairly low pro-
file most of the year. SOS Racisme's annual jamboree is one opportunity for the city to explore its
cultural and ethnic diversity. The three-day event
takes over the harbourside for a packed programme
of live music, exhibits, kid's activities and workshops, with stalls run by immigrant organisations
providing information, clothes, craftwork and food.

Festa de la Bicicleta

Information *Servei d'Informació Esportiva (93 402
30 00).* **Date** *One Sunday in May/June.*
Thanks largely to former 'Olympic' mayor Pasqual
Maragall, Barcelona has become switched on to the
importance of pedal power, with an expanding network of cycle routes, although the car is still king
and the Vespa court jester. The 'Day of the Bicycle'
attracts about 10,000 people, who ride en masse from
the centre (usually) to the Vila Olímpica and Glories.
Special cycle-hire services are available for the day.

Summer

L'Ou com Balla

Venues *Ateneu Barcelonès, C/Canuda 6; Casa de
l'Ardiaca, C/Santa Llúcia 1; Cathedral Cloister;
Museu Frederic Marès; Reial Academia de les Bones
Lletres, C/Bisbe Caçador 3. Metro Jaume I/bus 17,
19, 40, 45.* **Dates** *Corpus Christi (May or early June)*
and the following Sunday. **Map** *D6/B3*
L'Ou com Balla (roughly 'the Egg that Dances') is a
curious custom that traditionally took place only
during Corpus Christi, until the last century the most

important festival in Barcelona. A previously emp-
tied eggshell is left to bob on top of the jets of fountains in the cathedral cloister, the patio of the Casa
de l'Ardiaca in front of the cathedral, and other
patios of the Barri Gòtic, all wonderfully garlanded
with fragrant broom and carnations. This very old
tradition, reported in the sixteenth century, can also
be seen in the cathedral cloister in Easter week.

Trobada Castellera (Meeting of human-tower builders)

Plaça Sant Jaume. Metro Jaume I/bus 17, 19, 40, 45.
Information *tourist offices.* **Date** *June.* **Map** *D6/B3*
A non-competitive display of human-tower building
involving all the existing *casteller* groups in
Catalonia (for an explanation of *castells, see right*).

Festa de la Música

All over Barcelona. **Information** *Centre
d'Informació de la Virreina.* **Date** *around 21 June.*
'International Music Day' (21 June), initiated by then-
French Minister of Culture Jack Lang in 1982, has
been celebrated in Barcelona since 1996. Hundreds
of performances take place in squares, parks, museums and cultural centres all over the city, all for free.

Sant Joan*

All over Barcelona. **Date** *night of 23 & 24* June.*
One could argue that Catalans are a nation of pyro-
maniacs (witness the *correfoc*): there's no better
evidence for this than the night of 23 June, the eve or
verbena of *Sant Joan* (24 June), strictly speaking the
feast of Saint John the Baptist. This is *la Nit del Foc*,
the Night of Fire, throughout Catalonia and the
Balearics; marking the summer solstice (to which
Saint John is the nearest saint's day), it's clearly pagan
in origin, and the wildest night of the year. Nowadays
the huge bonfires that used to burn at every road junction in the city have been banned, but they still fill the
Ramblas of towns up and down the coast, and even
in the city there are still one or two 'private initiatives'.
For a week before Sant Joan the June air is ripped
apart by explosions, as every schoolkid in town
spends his or her pocket-money on terrifying bangers.
Come the night itself, the city sounds like a virtual
war zone, with impromptu firework displays explod-
ing from balconies and squares. There are big displays on Tibidabo, Montjuïc and, especially, by the
beach, with live bands to dance to – good places to
head for – smaller events in squares across the city,
and countless house- and terrace-parties.
 Marking the 'official' start of summer, this is the
night of the year when Catalans really let their hair
down, and the atmosphere is thick with excitement
and gunpowder as midsummer madness takes a
grip. *De rigueur* things to consume are *coca de Sant
Joan*, a shallow, bread-like cake decorated with very
sweet candied fruit, and loads of *cava* (sold from
improvised stalls along the Rambla). The best thing
to do is keep going all night, and a 'traditional' way
to end Sant Joan is to head for the beach at dawn, to
watch the sunrise. Afterwards, 24 June is a public
holiday, and nothing moves before mid-afternoon.

Festival del Grec

Teatre Grec, Mercat de les Flors and other venues.
Information Centre d'Informació de la Virreina.
Tickets available from Centre d'Informació de la
Virreina & Tel-entrada (*see p295, p215*). **Date** late
June-mid-Aug. **Map** (Grec theatre) B6
Barcelona's main performing arts festival takes its
name from the open-air Greek theatre on Montjuïc,
also the venue for many of the performances. The
programme is usually fairly mainstream. Most
theatre is in Catalan or Spanish, although there's
some in other languages; the dance offerings are
mainly contemporary. The music menu has something for most tastes – Van Morrison and Cesária
Evora headlined in 1999 – but is especially strong on
flamenco, salsa and jazz. Other recent elements have
been a short film festival (*Net*) and 'film and swim'
late-night sessions at the **Picornell** swimming pool
on Montjuïc (*see chapter* **Sports & Fitness**). For
the year 2000 the Grec has a new director, who has
promised a shorter, more selective festival.
Website: www.grecbcn.com

Here be dragons...

Festivals in Barcelona have in common a series
of very special popular traditions. Some hark
back to ancient pagan revels, and all are at least
four centuries old.

Gegants & capgrossos

The *gegants* or giants – lofty figures of wood and
papier-mâché, each supported by a person
peeping out through a mesh in the skirts – were
originally part of the festival of Corpus Christi,
instituted by the Church in 1264 partly in order to
incorporate pre-Christian figures into conventional ritual. There are many theories on their
origin – one that they are based on David and
Goliath – but they represent many folkloric
characters. In Barcelona two of the most historic
are the *Gegants del Pi*, kept in the church of Santa
Maria del Pi; more recent are the city's 'official'
giants, who represent King Jaume I and his queen,
Violant of Hungary. Equally popular are the *capgrossos* ('fatheads') who accompany the parade of
giants, wearing huge papier-mâché and wood
heads, usually with bizarre fixed smiles.
Mischievous, leprechaun-like figures, they once
represented the biblical tribes of Sem, Cam and
Japhet, but the heads can now resemble celebrities or all sorts of popular figures. One of the most
skilled makers of them is El Ingenio (*see chapter*
Shopping). Like the *correfoc* and other parts of
the *festa*, these parades are accompanied by special music played on traditional instruments. The
festival of Corpus went into decline, but the giants
and fatheads were incorporated into the *festa
major* in the nineteenth century. Like other *festa*
traditions giants and *capgrossos* have enjoyed a
boom in popularity since the 1980s, and *gegants*
and all their friends can be seen in every district
festa as well as in the city-wide **Mercè**.

Dracs, dimonis & the correfoc

If you see the giants and fatheads during the day,
you can be almost certain that at sunset you'll see
the *dracs* (dragons) and *dimonis* (devils) come out
to play, waving fireworks and scuttling after

crowds of screaming spectators. The dragon is a
constant feature in Catalan folklore, in contrast to
the bull-obsession of much of Iberia. The *festa*
dragons are big, wood-and-canvas monsters,
carried by teams, with fireworks in their snouts;
their attendant devils are men and women in
demon suits carrying powerful fireworks that
spin round on sticks. Their procession is called
the *correfoc* (literally 'fire-running'), the wild
climax of the *festa*, when the dragons spin and
swirl through a surging crowd amid a manic
atmosphere and clouds of smoke. If you aim to be
at the front of the crowd, it's advisable to cover as
much of your body as possible, with hoods and
handkerchiefs over the mouth, which is how
dedicated fire-runners dress, even in August.
Once the dragons are worn out, the party
continues with yet more fireworks, and dancing.

Castells

The formation of *castells*, or human towers,
possibly originated in medieval prowess games,
and in a popular dance from the seventeenth
century, the *moixiganga*. At the end of this dance,
men would form a human tower up to six people
high. Later, tower-building took precedence over
dancing, and tower-building clubs (*colles*) began
to form. In each *castell*, a large group links arms
at the bottom to form the base, the *pinya* (pine-
cone), with the crowd joining in around them for
extra support. Successive layers then climb on top
of them, the upper levels getting smaller until it
comes down to a single small boy or girl, who tops
the tower off with a wave. There are many
different formations of towers: the most difficult
are combinations like *5 de 8* (five people in each
level, eight levels) or anything with nine levels.
The completion of each level is accompanied by
its own music, and there's a tremendous sense of
suspense and excitement in the final, most precarious stages. Interest in *castells* was waning
until the 1980s, when a major revival began. And,
as with the dragons and other *colles*, *castells* are
now entirely open to women and girls.

Festa Major de Gràcia

All over Gràcia. Metro Fontana/bus 22, 24, 28, N4.
Information Centre d'Informació de la Virreina,
010, & 93 291 66 00. **Date** late Aug. **Map** D-E2-3
Held since the 1820s, Gràcia's *festa major* has now
almost outgrown the *barri* itself, attracting thousands
from all over the city, to an extent that can annoy true
locals. A unique feature is the competition between
streets for the best decoration: they are decked out to
represent elaborate fantasy scenarios, from desert-
islands to satires on current events. Each street also
has its own programme of entertainment, plus an
open-air meal for all the neighbours. District-wide
events are centred on Plaça Rius i Taulet, and there's
music nightly in Plaça de la Revolució, Plaça del Sol
and Plaça de la Virreina. The *festa* opens with *gegants*
and *castells* in Plaça Rius i Taulet, and climaxes on
the last night with a *correfoc* and more fireworks.

Festa Major de Sants

*All over Sants. Metro Plaça de Sants, Sants
Estació/bus all routes to Estació de Sants.*
Information Centre d'Informació de la
Virreina & 010. **Date** late Aug. **Map** A4
Following right after Gràcia, the smaller *festa major*
in Sants has not had the benefit of the same historical
continuity, and had to be revived after the dictator-
ship. Major events, such as the *correfoc,* are held in

The *Sardana*

The sedate Catalan round dance, the *sardana,* is
not limited to seasonal celebrations, since it can be
seen throughout the year, but it is also a part of
every local *festa*. Its origins are believed to go back
to ancient Greece; the name comes from the *ballo
sardo* of Sardinia, an island occupied by Catalans
for centuries, and the first written reference to it
is from 1587. It consists of a moving circle, whose
members hold hands and mark a set pattern of
paces that shift from left to right and back again.
Referring to it as 'dancing in the streets' doesn't
quite give the right idea: it's more like a folk dance
invented by mathematicians, as serious dancers
have to concentrate to follow the step sequences.
The *sardana* was already popular as a folk dance
in the Empordà before 1800, but was given its
modern form in the mid-nineteenth century by a
self-taught musician, Pep Ventura. He established
the line-up of the traditional *sardana* band, known
as the *cobla,* combining traditional and brass
instruments, and gave the dance a definitive
musical form, writing 400 scores himself. The
sardana spread across the country. Charged with
symbolic references to unity and equality, it was
adopted as Catalonia's national dance, and has
become one of its best-known symbols.

In Barcelona, as well as during *festes, sardanes*
are danced every Sunday in front of the cathedral
from about noon to 2pm, and in the Plaça Sant
Jaume from 7pm to 9pm. You don't have to be an
expert to join in, and anyone wanting to try just
has to enter a circle.

the Parc de L'Espanya Industrial; others are centred on Plaça del Centre, C/Sant Antoni, Plaça de la Farga and Plaça Joan Peiro, behind Sants station.

Diada National de Catalunya* (Catalan National Day)

All over Barcelona. **Date** 11 Sept

On 11 September 1714 Barcelona fell to the Castilian/French army in the War of the Spanish Succession, a national disaster that led to the loss of all Catalan institutions for 200 years (*see p20*). This heroic defeat is commemorated as Catalan National Day. In 1977, the first time it could be celebrated openly after the dictatorship, over a million people took to the streets. It's now lost its force a little, but is still a day for national reaffirmation and demonstrations, with flags displayed on balconies. At night, separatist groups have confrontations with the police.

La Diadeta de la Barceloneta

All over Barceloneta. Metro Barceloneta/bus 17, 36, 39, 40, 45, 57, 59, 64, 157, N6, N8.
Date weekend in mid-Sept.

Held shortly before the Barceloneta's full *festa major* (*see below*), the *Diadeta* (little day) is an unusual, very local celebration organised by *penyes* (local associations) connected to different bars or restaurants. Their male members, in an assortment of traditional regalia, disappear for a day, to come back – usually drunk – laden with rabbits and other animals they have 'hunted' for food; the rest of the district celebrates their return with a procession of emblems of guilds linked to fishing in this old fishermen's *barri*.

Festes de La Mercè*

All over Barcelona.
Information Centre d'Informació de la Virreina, 010 & tourist offices. **Date** one week around 23 Sept.

If Sant Joan celebrates the beginning of summer, La Mercè marks its end. *Nostra Senyora de la Mercè* (Our Lady of Mercy) joined Santa Eulàlia as one of the patron saints of Barcelona in 1637 after stamping out a plague of locusts; the city's biggest celebrations have been dedicated to her since 1871. The festivities combine the ingredients of a traditional Catalan town *festa major*, on a bigger scale: beginning with an early-morning clarion call, as drummers and musicians march around the Barri Gòtic, and Mass at the shrine of the Virgin in the Basílica de la Mercè, by the port. Later there are processions of *gegants*, who come to the Ajuntament to get the mayor's permission to party, human towers, and Barcelona's most spectacular *correfoc*, preceded the night before by a dry run for the faint-hearted as the dragons lumber through town without their attendant devils.

There are also *sardanes*, a parade, a hugely popular fun-run (the *Cursa de la Mercè*), a mass swim across the port and a giant firework display on Montjuïc. Added to which are dozens of free, mostly-open-air concerts, in Plaça Catalunya, the Moll de la Fusta and other venues, with flamenco, rock, rai, dance, salsa, classical and jazz music in the main programme, or associated events such as the

Festival de Músiques Contemporànies and **BAM** (*see pp236-45*). Museums have free-entry days, and there are craft and food shows, one of them the **Mostra de Vins i Caves**, a showcase for Catalan wines, usually held in or alongside Maremàgnum. A free programme booklet, listing all Mercè events, is available from early September.

Festa Major de la Barceloneta

All over Barceloneta. Metro Barceloneta/bus 17, 36, 39, 40, 45, 57, 59, 64, 157, N6, N8.
Date end Sept-early Oct. **Map** D-E7/C4

One of the liveliest of the smaller district *festes*, which runs on from the end of the Mercè. Activities centre around Plaça de la Barceloneta and Plaça de la Font. A grotesque – supposedly French – general, *General Bum Bum* (Boom Boom, possibly named after Prosper Verboom, the French army engineer who designed the *barri*), leads a procession of kids around the district firing off cannon – a tradition dating from 1881. There's dancing on the beach at night, and some people take to boats to eat, drink and watch the firework display from the sea.

Autumn

Tots Sants* (All Saints' Day)

All over Barcelona. **Date** 1 Nov.

All Saints' Day is the day to remember the dead, and traditional Barcelonans visit the city's cemeteries to pay their respects. Around this time, roast *moniatos* (sweet potatoes) and chestnuts – deemed the favourite food of the dead – are sold at street stalls, and *panellets* (almond cakes coated in pine-nuts) at pastry shops. People also hold All Saints' Eve parties, at which these traditional foods are washed down with sweet wines like *moscatell* or *malvasia*.

Fira del Disc de Col.leccionista

Fira de Barcelona, Avda Reina Maria Cristina 1 (93 233 20 00). Metro Espanya/bus all routes to Plaça d'Espanya.
Date usually first or second week Nov. **Map** A4

Curiously, Barcelona hosts the largest second-hand record fair in Europe: a vast array of vinyl LPs, 45s, tapes and CDs, ending in an auction of rock memorabilia that draws buyers from around the world.

Winter

Fira de Santa Llúcia

Pla de la Seu & Avda de la Catedral. Metro Jaume I/bus 17, 19, 40, 45. **Dates** usually 8-24 Dec.
Map D6/B2-3

Christmas in Barcelona begins with the Christmas fair in front of the cathedral, at which hand-made pieces are sold for the nativity scenes that Catalan and Spanish families build up year by year. They include not only the usual Josephs and Marys but also the exclusively Catalan figure of the *caganer*: a man, sometimes a woman, having a realistically sculpted crap within spitting distance of the King of Kings. It's by far the most popular figure in the

Catalan crib, and local artesans compete each year to create new *caganer* designs. As for the origins of the Catalans' scatalogical obsession (especially visible in Christmas traditions), it awaits full anthropological explanation. At the fair you can also find Christmas trees – a foreign but well-established import – and a range of craftwork.

Nadal* & Sant Esteve*
(Christmas Day & Boxing Day)
All over Barcelona. **Dates** 25*, 26* Dec.
Centrepiece of Barcelona's Christmas decorations is an extravagant life-size crib in Plaça Sant Jaume, surrounded by real palms. Some people have their main Christmas dinner late on Christmas Eve, as is the custom in the rest of Spain, but many Catalans have two big lunches, one on Christmas Day with the family of one parent and another on Boxing Day with the family of the other. Around Christmas children get to expend their energies in a ritual known as the *Caga Tió*, when the kids 'beat the crap' – more scatology – out of a wooden log with sticks, then run into an adjoining room. When they return, the log has crapped them out small presents.

Cap d'Any (New Year's Eve)
All over Barcelona. **Date** 31 Dec, 1 Jan*.
As on Sant Joan (*see p8*), discos and bars charge outrageous admission for New Year parties: the mass public celebrations around the city are cheaper. Wherever you are, at midnight – well announced on TV – you'll be expected to start stuffing 12 grapes into your mouth, one for every chime of the bell, without stopping until the New Year has been fully rung in. Otherwise, it's bad luck. Many taxi drivers take the night off, so it can be hard to get around.

Cavalcada dels Reis
(Three Kings' Parade)
Route *Kings normally arrive at Moll de la Fusta, then parade up the Rambla to Plaça Sant Jaume, and continue to Passeig de Gràcia; detailed route changes each year.* **Information** Centre d'Informació de la Virreina & 010. **Date** 5 Jan. **Map** C-D5-7/**A-B1-4**
Not to be missed by anyone with children. Epiphany, the Day of the Three Wise Men (Three Kings) on 6 January, is celebrated in many Latin countries, and until the recent advent of Father Christmas was the time when children, and often adults, received their main presents. On 5 January the 'Kings' arrive by sea (from across the harbour) and are formally welcomed by the mayor. They then parade around the city, with accompanying floats, and throw sweets to kids in the crowd along the route. Some hold umbrellas inside out to catch as many as they can. A toy fair is held on Gran Via (usually 2-6 Jan), which stays open through the night for late present-buyers. And, in case you'd forgotten the scatology, they also sell sugary coal and turd-lookalikes in fig-paste, for kids who have been naughty in the preceding year.

Festa dels Tres Tombs
District of Sant Antoni. Metro Sant Antoni/bus 20, 24, 38, 64, N6. **Date** 17 Jan. **Map** B-C5

Sant Antoni Abat (Saint Anthony the Abbot) is patron saint of domestic animals and muleteers. There may no longer be any members of this trade left, but a small procession of horsemen, dressed in tailcoats and top hats, still commemorates his day by riding three times (*Tres Tombs*, Three Turns) around a route from Ronda Sant Antoni, through Plaça Universitat, Pelai and Plaça Catalunya, down the Rambla and back along Nou de la Rambla. This coincides with the *festa major* of the *barri* of Sant Antoni, which continues for a week.

Carnestoltes (Carnival)
All over Barcelona. **Date** usually late Feb.
The opening event is a procession of figures in outrageous outfits, from Brazilian dancers to the usual Catalan monsters, led by *el Rei Carnestoltes* and *Don Carnal*, amid a confusion of confetti, blunderbuss salvos and fireworks. The origins of Carnival are in a once-traditional outburst of eating, drinking and fornicating prior to the limitations of Lent; King Carnestoltes – the masked personification of the carnival spirit – also used to criticise the authorities and reveal scandals, a tradition that unfortunately has died out. Other events in the city's ten-day modern carnival include dancing in Plaça Catalunya, concerts in different venues and a *Gran Botifarrada Popular* on the Rambla, when sausage is handed out. There are children's fancy-dress carnivals, so it's common to see kids in the street dressed up as bees or Marie Antoinettes, and Carnival is also a big show in the city's markets, where traders get dressed up. The end of Carnival on Ash Wednesday is marked by the *Enterrament de la Sardina*, the Burial of the Sardine, on Montjuïc or in Barceloneta, when a humble fish – symbol perhaps of the penis – is buried to emphasise even frugal fare will not be consumed for 40 days. More concentrated than Barcelona's Carnival are those in **Vilanova i la Geltrú** and **Sitges** (*see also pp258-9, 278*).

A Christmas crapper, **el caganer.**

History

Roman outpost, merchant capital, bourgeois paradise, heartland of revolution and modern style mecca – Barcelona is the city of transformations.

Origins

It was in the first thousand years of Barcelona's history that the foundations were laid of Catalan identity and language. Multiple invasions between periods of growth and decay left the isolated, self-reliant people of the city and the surrounding countryside with traditions and a character quite distinct from those of their neighbours in other parts of the Iberian peninsula.

The Romans founded Barcelona, in about 15 BC, on the *Mons Taber*, a small hill between two streams with a good view of the Mediterranean, today crowned by the cathedral. The plain around it was sparsely inhabited by the *Laetani*, an agrarian Celtiberian people known for producing grain and honey and gathering oysters. Named *Barcino*, the town was much smaller than the capital of the Roman province of *Hispania Citerior*, *Tarraco* (Tarragona), but had the only harbour, albeit a poor one, between there and Narbonne.

Like virtually every other Roman new town in Europe it was a fortified rectangle with a cross-roads at its centre, where the Plaça Sant Jaume is today. It was a decidedly unimportant, provincial town, but nonetheless the rich plain provided it with a produce garden, and the sea gave it an incipient maritime trade. It acquired a Jewish community very soon after its foundation, and was associated with some Christian martyrs, notably Barcelona's first patron saint Santa Eulàlia. She was supposedly executed at the end of the third century via a series of revolting tortures, including being rolled naked in a sealed barrel full of glass shards down the alley now called Baixada (descent) de Santa Eulàlia.

Nevertheless, Barcelona accepted Christianity shortly afterwards, in 312 AD, together with the rest of the Roman Empire, which by then was under growing threat of invasion. In the fourth century *Barcino*'s rough defences were replaced with massive stone walls, many sections of which

The **Temple of Augustus** *was at the centre of* Barcino.

Key Events

Origins

c15 BC *Barcino* founded by Roman soldiers.
Fourth century AD Roman stone city walls built.
415 Barcelona briefly capital of Visigoths under Ataülf.
719 Moslems attack and seize Barcelona.
801 Barcelona taken by Franks, under Louis the Pious.
878 Guifré *el Pilós* becomes Count of Barcelona.
985 Moslems under Al-Mansur sack Barcelona; Count Borrell II renounces Frankish sovereignty.

A medieval Golden Age

1035-76 Count Ramon Berenguer I of Barcelona extends his possessions into southern France.
1064-8 First Catalan *Usatges* or legal code written.
1137 Count Ramon Berenguer IV marries Petronella of Aragon, uniting the two states in the 'Crown of Aragon'.
1148-9 Lleida and Tortosa taken from the Moslems.
c1160 *Homilies d'Organyà*, first Catalan texts, written.
1213 Battle of Muret: Pere I is killed and virtually all his lands north of the Pyrenees are seized by France.
1229 Jaume I conquers Mallorca, then Ibiza (1235) and Valencia (1238); second city wall built in Barcelona.
1265 Ramon Llull devotes himself to thought and writing.
1274 *Consell de Cent* (Council of 100), municipal government of Barcelona, established.
1282 Pere II conquers Sicily.
1298 Gothic cathedral begun. Population of city c40,000.
1323-4 Conquest of Corsica and Sardinia.
1347-8 Black Death cuts population by half.
1391 Thousands of Jews massacred in Barcelona *Call*.
1401 *Taula de Canvi*, first deposit bank, founded.
1412 Crown of Aragon given to Fernando de Antequera.
1462-72 Catalan civil war.
1474 First book printed in Catalan, in Valencia.

The fall of Barcelona

1479 Ferran II (Ferdinand) inherits Crown of Aragon, and with his wife Isabella unites the Spanish kingdoms.
1492 Final expulsion of Jews, and discovery of America.
1516 Charles of Habsburg (Charles V), King of Spain.
1522 Catalans refused permission to trade in America.
1640 Catalan national revolt, the *Guerra dels Segadors*.
1652 Barcelona falls to Spanish army.
1659 Catalan territory of Roussillon is given to France.
1702 War of Spanish Succession begins.
1714 Barcelona falls to Franco-Spanish army after siege.
1715 *Nova Planta* decree abolishes Catalan institutions; new ramparts and citadel built around Barcelona. Population of the city c33,000.
1775 Paving of the Barcelona Rambla begun.
1808-13 French occupation.

Factories, poets & barricades

1814 Restoration of Ferdinand VII after French defeat.
1824 Building of Carrer Ferran begun on former church land; in 1827, route of the Passeig de Gràcia is laid.
1832 First steam-driven factory in Spain, in Barcelona.
1833 Aribau publishes *Oda a la Pàtria*, beginning of Catalan cultural renaissance. Carlist wars begin.

1836-7 Dissolution of most monasteries in Barcelona.
1839 First workers' associations formed in Barcelona.
1842-4 Barcelona bombarded for the last time from Montjuïc, to suppress a liberal revolt, the *Jamancia*.
1848 First railway line in Spain, between Barcelona and Mataró; Liceu opera house inaugurated.
1850 Population of Barcelona 175,331.
1854 Demolition of Barcelona city walls begins.
1855 First general strike is violently suppressed.
1859 Cerdà plan for the Barcelona *Eixample* approved.
1868 September: revolution overthrows Isabel II. November: first anarchist meetings held in Barcelona.
1873 First Spanish Republic.
1874 Bourbon monarchy restored under Alfonso XII.
1882 Work begins on the Sagrada Familia.
1888 Barcelona Universal Exhibition.

The city of the new century

1892 *Bases de Manresa*, demands for Catalan autonomy.
1897 Gràcia and Sants incorporated into Barcelona.
1898 Spain loses Cuba and Philippines in war with USA.
1899 FC Barcelona founded; first electric trams.
1900 Population of Barcelona 537,354.
1907 Via Laietana cut through old city of Barcelona.
1909 *Setmana Tràgica*, anti-church and anti-army riots.
1910 CNT anarchist workers' union founded.
1919 CNT general strike paralyses Barcelona.
1920 Spiral of violence in labour conflicts in Catalonia.
1921 First Barcelona Metro line opened.
1923 Primo de Rivera establishes dictatorship in Spain.
1929 Barcelona International Exhibition on Montjuïc.
1930 Population 1,005, 565. Fall of Primo de Rivera.
1931 14 April: Second Spanish Republic. Francesc Macià declares Catalan independence, then accepts autonomy.
1934 October: Generalitat attempts revolt against new right-wing government in Madrid, and is then suspended.
1936 February: Popular Front wins Spanish elections; Catalan Generalitat restored. 19 July: military uprising against left-wing government is defeated in Barcelona.
1937 May: fighting within the republican camp in Barcelona, mainly between anarchists and Communists.
1939 26 January: Barcelona taken by Franco's army.

Grey years

1951 Barcelona tram strike.
1953 Co-operation treaty between Spain and the USA.
1959 Stabilisation Plan opens up Spanish economy.
1975 20 November: death of Franco.

The new era

1977 First democratic general elections in Spain since 1936; provisional Catalan Generalitat re-established.
1978 First local elections in Barcelona won by Socialists.
1980 Generalitat fully re-established under Jordi Pujol.
1982 Pasqual Maragall becomes Mayor; urban spaces programme gains momentum.
1986 Barcelona awarded 1992 Olympic Games.
1992 Barcelona Olympics.
1996 *Partido Popular* wins Spanish national elections.
1997 Joan Clos replaces Pasqual Maragall as Mayor.

can still be seen today. It was these ramparts that ensured Barcelona's continuity, making it a stronghold much desired by later warlords (for more on relics of Roman Barcelona, *see page 56*).

These and other defences did not prevent the empire's disintegration. In 415, Barcelona briefly became capital of the kingdom of the Visigoths, under their chieftain Ataülf. He brought with him as a prisoner Gala Placidia, the 20-year-old daughter of a Roman emperor, who he forced to marry him. She is famous, though, as a woman of strong character, and is credited with converting the barbarian king to Christianity. She was also perhaps fortunate in that Ataülf died shortly afterwards, whereupon Gala Placidia left, married her relative the Emperor Constantius I, and for a time became the most powerful figure in the court of Byzantium. Back in Barcelona, meanwhile, the Visigoths soon moved on southwards to extend their control over the whole of the Iberian peninsula, and for the next 400 years the town was a neglected backwater.

It was in this state when the Moslems swept across the peninsula after 711, easily crushing Goth resistance. They made little attempt to settle Catalonia, but much of the Christian population retreated into the Pyrenees, the first Catalan heartland. Then, at the end of the eighth century, the Franks began to drive southwards against the Moslems from across the mountains. In 801 Charlemagne's son Louis the Pious took Barcelona and made it a bastion of the *Marca Hispanica* or 'Spanish March', the southern buffer of his father's empire. This gave Catalonia a trans-Pyrenean origin entirely different from that of the other Christian states in Spain; equally, it is for this reason that the closest relative of the Catalan language is Provençal, not Castilian.

When the Frankish princes returned to their main business further north, local counts were left behind with sections of the Catalan territories to rule, charged in exchange with defending the frontier against the Saracens. At the end of the ninth century one, Count Guifré *el Pilós*, 'Wilfred the Hairy' (approx 860-98), from his base in the Pyrenean valleys around Ripoll succeeded in gaining title to several of the Catalan counties. He united them under his rule, creating the basis for a future Catalan state and founding the dynasty of Counts of Barcelona that would reign in an unbroken line until 1410. He also made Barcelona his capital, and so set the seal on the city's future.

As a founding patriarch Wilfred is a semi-mythical figure, surrounded by legends, not the least of them that he was the source of the Catalan national flag, the *Quatre Barres* (Four Bars) of red on a yellow background, also known as *La Senyera*. The story goes that he was fighting against the Saracens alongside his lord, the Frankish emperor, when he was mortally wounded; in recognition of Wilfred's heroism, the emperor dipped his fingers into his friend's bloody wounds and ran them down the Count's golden shield. Whatever its mythical origins, the four-red-stripes-on-yellow symbol is first recorded on the tomb of Count Ramon Berenguer II in 1082, making the *Quatre Barres* the oldest national flag in Europe, predating its nearest competitor, that of Denmark, by a hundred years. What is not known is in what way Wilfred was so hairy, although he could perhaps be imagined as the prototype of every deep-voiced, barrel-chested Catalan man with a beard.

A century after Wilfred, in 985, the great minister of the Caliph of Córdoba, Al-Mansur, attacked and sacked Barcelona. The hairy Count's great-grandson, Count Borrell II, requested aid from his theoretical feudal lord, the Frankish king. He received no reply, and so repudiated all Frankish sovereignty over Catalonia. From then on – although the name was not yet in use – Catalonia was effectively independent, and the Counts of Barcelona were free to forge its destiny.

A medieval Golden Age

In the year 1000 Barcelona had a growing population of nearly 6,000, and was witnessing the first glimmerings of mercantile and artisan activity. During the first century of the new millennium Catalonia was consolidated as a political entity, and entered an era of great cultural richness.

The Catalan Counties retained from their Frankish origins a French system of aristocratic feudalism – another difference from the rest of Iberia – but also had a peasantry who were notably independent and resistant to noble demands. In the 1060s the *Usatges* ('Usages') were established, the country's distinctive legal code. The Counts of Barcelona and lesser nobles also endowed monasteries throughout Catalonia, consecrating the influence of a powerful clergy.

This provided the background to the years of glory of Romanesque art, with the building of the great monasteries and churches of northern Catalonia, such as **Sant Pere de Rodes** near Figueres, and the painting of the superb murals now in the **Museu Nacional** on Montjuïc. There was also a flowering of scholarship, reflecting contacts with Islamic and Carolingian cultures. In Barcelona, shipbuilding and commerce in grain and wine all expanded, and a new trade developed in textiles. The city grew both inside its old Roman walls and outside them, where *vilanoves* or 'new towns' appeared at Sant Pere and La Ribera.

Catalonia – a name that gained currency in Latin in the eleventh century – was also gaining more territory from the Moslems to the south, beyond the Penedès. For a long time, though, the realm of the Counts of Barcelona continued to look just as much to the north, across the Pyrenees, where the Provençal-speaking Languedoc was then the most sophisticated society in western Europe. After 1035, during the reigns of the four Counts Ramon Berenguer, large areas of what is now southern France were acquired through marriage or with Arab booty. In 1112 the union of Ramon Berenguer III 'the Great' (1093-1131) with Princess Dolça of Provence extended his authority as far as the Rhone.

A more significant marriage occurred in 1137, when Ramon Berenguer IV (1131-62) wed Petronella, heir to the throne of Aragon. This would, in the long term, bind Catalonia into Iberia. The uniting of the two dynasties created a powerful entity known as the 'Crown of Aragon', each element retaining its separate institutions, and ruled by monarchs known as the 'Count-Kings'. Since Aragon was already a kingdom, it was given precedence and its name was often used to refer to the state, but the court language was Catalan and the centre of government remained in Barcelona.

Ramon Berenguer IV also extended Catalan territory to its current frontiers in the Ebro valley, in a series of campaigns against the Moslem emirs. At the beginning of the next century, however, the dynasty lost virtually all of its lands north of the Pyrenees to France, when Count-King Pere I 'the Catholic' was killed at the battle of Muret in 1213. This was a blessing in disguise. In future, the Catalan-Aragonese state would be oriented decisively towards the Mediterranean and the

Queen Maria and Consellers *in the 1430s.*

south, and was able to embark on two centuries of imperialism equalled in vigour only by Barcelona's burgeoning commercial enterprise.

MEDITERRANEAN EMPIRE

Pere I's successor was the most expansionist of the Count-Kings. Jaume I 'the Conqueror' (1213-76) abandoned any idea of further adventures in Provence and joined decisively in the campaign against the Moslems to the south, taking Mallorca in 1229, Ibiza in 1235 and then, at much greater cost, Valencia in 1238. He made it another separate kingdom, the third part of the 'Crown of Aragon'.

Barcelona became the centre of an empire extending across the Mediterranean. The city grew tremendously under Jaume I, and in mid-century he ordered the building of a new, second wall, along the line of the Rambla and roughly encircling the area between there and the modern Parc de la Ciutadella, thus bringing La Ribera and the other *vilanoves* within the city. In 1274 he also gave Barcelona a form of representative self-government, the *Consell de Cent,* or Council of 100 chosen citizens, an institution that would last for over 400 years. In Catalonia as a whole, royal powers were limited by a parliament, the *Corts,* with a permanent standing committee, known as the *Generalitat.*

Catalan imperialism advanced by conquest and marriage well beyond the Balearic Islands. The Count-Kings commanded a sail-powered fleet, more flexible than oar-driven galleys, and a mercenary army, the 'Catalan Companies' (*Almogàvers*). For decades they were led by two great commanders, the fleet by Roger de Llúria and the army by Roger de Flor. The stuff of another set of heroic legends – such as their sword-in-hand battle cry '*desperta ferro!*' ('awaken, iron!') – the *Almogàvers* made themselves feared equally by Christians and Moslems, as they travelled the Mediterranean conquering, plundering and enslaving in the name of God and the Crown of Aragon.

In 1282 Pere II 'the Great' annexed Sicily, of vital strategic importance and a major source of grain. Catalan domination of the island would last for nearly 150 years. Shortly afterwards an episode occurred that has been depicted as a great military feat (by Catalan romantic historians) or as utterly discreditable (by most others). In 1302 Roger de Flor and his *Almogàvers* were sent to Greece to assist the Byzantine Emperor against the Turks. Finding he could not pay them adequately, they turned against the Emperor and carved out an independent dukedom for themselves in Athens that would last for 80 years.

The Catalan empire reached its greatest strength under Jaume II 'the Just' (1291-1327). Corsica (1323) and Sardinia (1324) were added to the possessions of the Crown of Aragon, although the latter would never submit to Catalan rule and would be a constant focus of revolt.

The Call: Jewish Barcelona

Barcelona's *Call* or Jewish quarter, occupying one remarkably cramped corner within the city's original Roman walls, was home to one of the most important Jewish populations in medieval Spain.

Recent researches and excavations have indicated that it may have been first established very shortly after the foundation of *Barcino*, reviving a (for some) controversial theory that there were actually Jews in Barcelona many years before there were Christians. Under the Visigoths, in 694, all Jews were decreed slaves. Later, the Count-Kings improved their status to that of serfs. Heavily taxed with no civil rights, Jews were required to wear special dress in order to be identifiable at all times by a law of Jaume I of 1243.

The Barcelona *Call* was nevertheless widely known as a very learned, religious community. Rabbi Benjamin of Tudela, a famous twelfth-century chronicler, wrote of the 'wise and learned men among the Jewish community in Barcelona'. Jewish women too were unusually well educated. The inhabitants of the *Call* were mostly artisans and farmers, but they were also known for their excellence as fiscal agents and money changers, and as doctors, Arabic translators, scholars and booksellers. Many worked for the Catalan nobility and as advisors to the Crown of Aragon. It was here that the famous 'Disputation of Barcelona' took place in 1263 between the Girona Jewish mystic Moshe ben Nahman (Nachmanides, known locally as Bonastruc da Porta) and Dominican monks, under the watchful eye of Jaume I. They debated the divinity of Christ and other great questions of faith for three whole days, and though the monks naturally did not accept defeat, the king was said to be so impressed by the rabbi's eloquence that he gave him a large reward.

By this time the community was enclosed from dusk to dawn behind the arches that once lined the Carrer del Call, the quarter's most prominent boundary, C/Banys Nous and the present wall of the Generalitat (extended after the *Call*'s abolition). Eventually their enemies had their way: the *Call*

was sacked in a pogrom of 6-8 August 1391, which spread to every Jewish quarter in Catalonia, Valencia and the Balearics. A Christian mob, incited by monks, massacred hundreds of its inhabitants. The *Call* never recovered, and no Jews were left in Barcelona when they were officially banned from the city in 1424, a prelude to the expulsion of all Jews from Spain in 1492.

Today, a walk around these silent, winding streets can still turn up fragments from this centuries-old past. Recent studies have identified a building at the intersection of C/Marlet and C/Sant Domenec del Call (**Map** D6/**B3**; the building opposite and to the left, if you walk up from C/Ferran) as the site of the *Sinagoga Major*; the dank half-basement seen through the windows at knee-level corresponds to the type of synagogue permitted under the Crown of Aragon, while the odd angle on C/Marlet suggests a wall oriented towards Jerusalem. A private project is under way to convert the site into a museum and information point. In the wall of Carrer Marlet 1, by the corner with C/Arc de Sant Ramon del Call, there is a twelfth-century Hebrew inscription (*pictured*), placed here in the last century; C/Arc de Sant Roman also once housed a Jewish women's school. A separate water fountain for the Jewish quarter was located in the middle of C/Sant Honorat, at the junction with C/Fruita, and a smaller synagogue (the *Sinagoga Poca*) stood on the site of the Sant Jordi chapel in the Generalitat.

After the 1391 pogrom, the Jewish cemetery was desecrated and tombstones were used as building materials. Hebrew inscriptions can be seen on stones on the eastern wall of Plaça Sant Iu, across from the Cathedral, and at ankle-level in the Plaça del Rei, near the north entry to the Museu d'Història de la Ciutat. Jewish archaeological remains can also be seen in the **Museu Militar** and the Gothic section of the **MNAC** (*see pages 95, 103*). Neither the Museu d'Història de la Ciutat and the Museu d'Història de Catalunya, though, have generally dealt with Jewish history adequately.

The adventures of Friar Anselm

For a people with such a strong collective identity Catalans also have a marked strain of quirky individuality, and there's no better example than poet-philosopher Anselm Turmeda, one of the great mavericks of the Middle Ages. He was born in Mallorca in about 1352. He stood out for his intellectual ability at an early age, becoming a Franciscan Friar at the age of 20. He then spent ten years as a wandering scholar around Europe, mainly in Bologna but also in Paris. He was especially renowned for his knowledge of the Greeks and the Islamic Andaluz scholar Averröes.

On his return to Catalonia in the 1380s he was in great demand from Church and state for his knowledge of many fields and languages, as well as being known for his sophisticated, worldly wit, which perhaps already put other churchmen on their guard. He kept moving, however, and next turned up in Sicily. Then, in about 1388, Anselm appeared in Tunis, and announced he had become a Moslem.

In that era, there was no greater heresy. Much about Turmeda's life and motives is clouded in mystery. He immediately became the target of a sustained attempt at character assassination, especially by his former Franciscan brothers, who put around the story that he had fled together with another errant monk and several 'fallen women', driven only by 'a desire for adventure and lustful passions'. Just how highly regarded he was by others, though, is shown by the fact that both King Martí I and Pope Benedict XIII

sent letters pleading with him to reconsider, and many years later Alfons IV offered the ageing Anselm safe conduct if he wished to make a visit home. In his new life, however, he soon won just as much prestige, serving the Bey of Tunis as diplomat and interpreter, travelling to many parts of the Islamic world, marrying a sultan's daughter and being appointed head of the Tunis customs house.

His verse dialogues were all written in Tunis, but in Catalan: corrosive, clever satires of the life of late-medieval Europe and the corruption of the Church, and no more orthodox in Islam than they were to Christians. In the *Disputa de l'Ase* ('Dispute with the Ass', 1418), the animals choose a donkey as their king, declaring their moral superiority over humans. Turmeda himself, as narrator, comes forward to defend humanity, but in the 'debate' he puts into the mouth of the ass a comprehensive, sarcastic demolition job of medieval society and its pervasive hypocrisy, until Anselm has to concede the beast has a point.

Despite its 'Islamic' origin the 'Dispute' was quite widely distributed for a book of its time, until it was banned absolutely by the Inquisition in 1583. Near the end of his life Anselm wrote his one book in Arabic, the anti-Christian polemic *Refutation of the Followers of the Cross*, which apparently is still in print in some Arab countries. He died in 1432 in Tunis, where (as Abdullah Al-taryuman) he has a street named after him.

THE CITY OF THE GOLDEN AGE

The Crown of Aragon was often at war with Arab rulers, but its capital flourished through commerce with every part of the Mediterranean, Christian and Moslem. Catalan ships also sailed into the Atlantic, to England and Flanders. Their ventures were actively supported by the Count-Kings and burghers of Barcelona, and regulated by the first-ever code of maritime law, the *Llibre del Consolat de Mar* (written 1258-72), an early example of Catalans' tendency to legalism, the influence of which extended far beyond their own territories. Barcelona had a lighthouse in place as early as 1094, and by the late thirteenth century nearly 130 consulates ringed the Mediterranean, engaged in a complex system of trade that involved spices, coral, grain, slaves, metals, wool and other textiles, olive oil, salt fish and leather goods.

Not surprisingly, this age of power and prestige was also the great era of building in medieval

Barcelona. The Catalan Gothic style reached its peak between the reigns of Jaume the Just and Pere III 'the Ceremonious' (1336-87). The Count-Kings' imperial conquests may have been ephemeral, but their talent for permanence in building can still be admired today. Between 1290 and 1340 the construction of most of Barcelona's major Gothic buildings was initiated. Religious edifices such as the **cathedral**, **Santa Maria del Mar** and **Santa Maria del Pi** were matched by civil buildings such as the **Saló de Tinell** and the **Llotja**, the old market and stock exchange. As a result, Barcelona today contains the most important nucleus of Gothic civil architecture in Europe.

The ships of the Catalan navy were built in the monumental **Drassanes** (shipyards), begun by Pere II and completed under Pere III, in 1378. In 1359 Pere III also built the third, final city wall, along the line of the modern Paral.lel, Ronda Sant Pau and Ronda Sant Antoni. This gave the 'old city' of Barcelona its definitive shape, although large areas of the Raval, between the second and third walls, would not be built up for centuries.

La Ribera, 'the waterfront', was the centre of trade and industry in fourteenth-century Barcelona. Once unloaded at the beach, wares were taken to the Llotja (the Lodge), the porticoed market place and exchange. Just inland, the Carrer Montcada was the street *par excellence* where newly enriched merchants could display their wealth in opulent Gothic palaces. All around were the workers of the various craft guilds, grouped together in their own streets – Agullers (needle-makers), Mirallers (mirror-makers) and many others (*see page 66* **Walk 2: La Ribera**).

Women's domains in this Barcelona were initially limited to home, market, convent or brothel, although in 1249 they gained the right to inherit property, and women were at one time the principal textile workers, even though the guilds still officially barred them from many trades. At the very top of society some women became very powerful, as it was quite common – unusually for that era – for Catalan Count-Kings to delegate their authority to their queens while they were away on imperial campaigns, as happened with Eleonor of Sicily, wife of Pere III.

The Catalan 'Golden Age' was also an era of cultural greatness. Catalonia was one of the first areas in Europe to use its vernacular language, as well as Latin, in written form and as a language of culture. The oldest written texts in Catalan are the *Homilies d'Organyà*, translations from the Bible dating from the twelfth century. Not just monks, but also the court and the aristocracy seem very early to have attained an unusual level of literacy, and Jaume I wrote his own autobiography, the *Llibre dels Feits* or 'Book of Deeds', dramatically recounting his achievements and conquests.

Incipient Catalan literature was given a vital thrust by the unique figure of Ramon Llull (1235-1316). After a debauched youth, he turned to more serious pursuits after a series of religious visions, and became the first man in post-Roman Europe to write philosophy in a vernacular language. Steeped in Arabic and Hebrew writings, he brought together Christian, Islamic, Jewish and Classical ideas, and also wrote a vast amount on other subjects – from theories of chivalry to poetry and visionary tales. In doing so he effectively created Catalan as a literary language. Catalan translations from Greek and Latin were also undertaken at this time; troubadours brought legends and tales of courtly love to Barcelona, while chroniclers such as Ramon Muntaner recorded the exploits of Count-Kings and *Almogàvers*. In the very twilight of the Golden Age, in 1490, the Valencian Joanot Martorell published *Tirant Lo Blanc*, the bawdy story that is considered the first true European novel.

CRISIS & DECLINE

Barcelona was not, though, a peaceful and harmonious place during its Golden Age, especially as the fourteenth century wore on. Social unrest and violence in the streets were common: grain riots, popular uprisings, attacks on Jews and gang warfare. An ongoing struggle took place between two political factions, the *Biga* (roughly representing the most established merchants) and the *Busca* (roughly composed of smaller tradesmen).

The extraordinary prosperity of the medieval period was not to last. The Count-Kings had over extended Barcelona's resources, and over-invested in far-off ports. By 1400 the effort to maintain their conquests by force, especially Sardinia, had exhausted the spirit and the coffers of the Catalan imperialist drive. The Black Death arrived in the 1340s, and had a devastating impact on Catalonia. This only intensified the bitterness of social conflicts, between the aristocracy, merchants, peasants and the urban poor.

In 1410 Martí I 'the Humane' died without an heir, bringing to an end the line of Counts of Barcelona unbroken since Guifré *el Pilós*. After much deliberation the Crown of Aragon was passed to a member of a Castilian noble family, the Trastámaras: Fernando de Antequera (1410-16).

His son, Alfons IV 'the Magnanimous' (1416-58), undertook one more conquest, of Naples, but the empire was under ever-greater pressure, and Barcelona merchants were unable to compete with the Genoese and Venetians. At home, in the 1460s, the effects of war and catastrophic famine led to a collapse into civil war and peasant revolt. The population was depleted to such an extent that Barcelona would not regain the numbers it had had in 1400, 40,000, until the eighteenth century.

The fall of Barcelona

In 1469 an important union for Spain initiated a woeful period in Barcelona's history, dubbed by some Catalan historians *la Decadència*, which would lead to the end of Catalonia as a separate entity. In that year Ferdinand of Aragon (reigned 1479-1516) married Isabella of Castile (1476-1506), and so united the different Spanish kingdoms, even though they would retain their separate institutions for another two centuries. It was theoretically a union of equals, but it soon became clear that the new monarchy would be dominated by Castile.

As Catalonia's fortunes had declined, those of Castile had risen. While Catalonia was impoverished and in chaos, Castile was larger, richer, had a bigger population and was on the crest of a wave of expansion. In 1492 Granada, last Moslem foothold in Spain, was conquered, Isabella decreed the expulsion of all Jews from Castile and Aragon, and Columbus discovered America.

It was Castile's seafaring orientation toward the Atlantic, rather than the Mediterranean, that confirmed Catalonia's decline. The discovery of the New World was an absolute disaster for Catalan commerce: trade shifted decisively away from the Mediterranean, and Catalans were officially barred from participating in the exploitation of the new empire until the 1770s. The weight of Castile in the monarchy was increased, and it became the clear seat of government.

In 1516 the Spanish crown passed to the House of Habsburg, in the shape of Ferdinand and Isabella's grandson the Emperor Charles V. His son Philip II of Spain established Madrid as the capital of all his dominions in 1561. Catalonia was managed by appointed Viceroys, the power of its institutions increasingly restricted, with a down-at-heel aristocracy and meagre cultural life. Instead of the kings and merchant-magnates of former years, the main patrons of new building in Barcelona were the Church and state governors, who built baroque churches and a few official buildings, many of them since demolished.

THE GREAT DEFEATS

While Castilian Spain went through its 'Golden Century', Catalonia was left more and more on the margins. Worse was to come, however, in the following century, with the two national revolts, both heroic defeats, that have since acquired a central role in Catalan nationalist mythology.

The problem for the Spanish monarchy was that, whereas Castile was an absolute monarchy and so could be taxed at will, in the former Aragonese territories, and especially Catalonia, royal authority kept coming up against a mass of local rights and privileges. As the empire became bogged down in endless wars – against the English, the Dutch, the Turks, the French – and expenses that not even American gold could meet, the Count-Duke of Olivares, the great minister of King Philip IV (1621-65), resolved to extract more money and troops from the non-Castilian dominions of the crown. The Catalans, however, felt they were taxed quite enough already.

In 1640 a mass of peasants, the 'Reapers', gathered on the Rambla in Barcelona, outside the Porta Ferrissa or 'Iron Gate' in the second wall. They rioted against royal authority, surged into the city and murdered the Viceroy, the Marqués de Santa Coloma. This began the general uprising known as the *Guerra dels Segadors*, the 'Reapers' War'. The authorities of the Generalitat, led by Pau Claris, were fearful of the violence of the poor and, lacking the confidence to declare Catalonia independent, appealed for protection from Louis XIII of France. French rule, however, created another, new set of problems, and French armies were in any case unable to defend Catalonia adequately. In 1652 a destitute Barcelona

capitulated to the equally exhausted army of Philip IV. Later, in 1659, France and Spain made peace with a treaty under which the Catalan territory of Roussillon, around Perpignan, was given to France. After the revolt, Philip IV and his ministers were surprisingly magnanimous, allowing the Catalans to retain what was left of their institutions despite their disloyalty. This war, however, provided the Catalan national anthem, *Els Segadors*, 'The Reapers'.

Fifty years later came the second of the great national rebellions, in the War of the Spanish Succession, the last time Catalonia sought to regain its national freedoms by force. In 1700 Charles II of Spain died without an heir. Castile accepted the grandson of Louis XIV of France, Philip of Anjou, as King Philip V of Spain (1700-46). However, the alternative candidate, the Archduke Charles of Austria, promised to restore the traditional rights of the former Aragonese territories, and so won their allegiance. He also had the support, against France, of Britain, Holland and Austria. Once again, though, Catalonia backed the wrong horse, and was let down in its choice of allies. In 1713 Britain and the Dutch made a separate peace and withdrew their aid, leaving the Catalans stranded with no possibility of victory. After a 13-month siege in which every citizen was called to arms, Barcelona fell to the French and Spanish armies on 11 September 1714.

The most heroic defeat of all, this date marked the most decisive political reverse in Barcelona's history, and is now commemorated as Catalan National Day, the *Diada*. Some of Barcelona's resisters were buried next to Santa Maria del Mar in the **Fossar de les Moreres** ('Mulberry Graveyard'), now a memorial (*see page 67*).

In 1715 Philip V issued his decree of *Nova Planta*, abolishing all the remaining separate institutions of the Crown of Aragon and so, in effect, creating 'Spain' as a single, unitary state. Barcelona's own institutions, such as the *Consell de Cent*, were also dismantled, and local authority was vested in the military commander, the Captain-General. Large-scale 'Castilianisation' of the country was initiated, and Castilian replaced the Catalan language in all official documents.

In Barcelona, extra measures were taken to keep the city under firm control. The crumbling medieval walls and the castle on Montjuïc were refurbished with new ramparts, and a massive new Citadel was built on the eastern side of the old city, where the Parc de la Ciutadella is today. To make space for it, thousands of people had to be expelled from La Ribera and forcibly rehoused in the Barceloneta, Barcelona's first-ever planned housing scheme, with its barrack-like street plan unmistakably provided by French military engineers. This citadel became the most hated symbol of Catalan subordination.

Generalitat President Rafael Casanova falls leading the defence of Barcelona, 1714.

BARCELONA BOUNCES BACK

Politically subjugated and without much of a native ruling class after the departure of many of its remaining aristocrats to serve the monarchy in Madrid, Catalonia nevertheless revived in the eighteenth century. Catalans continued speaking their language, and went about developing independent commercial initiatives. Barcelona began to grow again, as peasants flowed in from the war-devastated countryside.

Ironically, the Bourbons, by abolishing legal differences between Catalonia and the rest of Spain, also removed the earlier restrictions on Catalan trade, especially with the colonies. The strength of the guild system of Barcelona had enabled it to maintain its artisan industries, and the city revived particularly following the official authorisation to trade with the Americas by King Charles III in 1778.

Shipping picked up again, and in the last years of the eighteenth century Barcelona had a booming export trade to the New World in wines and spirits from Catalan vineyards and textiles, wool and silk. In 1780 a merchant called Erasme de Gómina opened Barcelona's first true factory, a hand-powered weaving mill in C/Riera Alta with 800 workers. In the next decade Catalan trade with Spanish America quadrupled; Barcelona's population had grown from around 30,000 in 1720 to close to 100,000 by the end of the century.

This prosperity was reflected in a new wave of building in the city. Neo-classical mansions appeared, notably on C/Ample and the Rambla. The greatest transformation, though, was in the Rambla itself. Until the 1770s it had been no more than a dusty, dry river-bed where country people came to sell their produce, lined on the Raval side mostly with giant religious houses and on the other with Jaume I's second wall. In 1775 the Captain-General, the Marqués de la Mina, embarked on an ambitious scheme to demolish the wall and turn the Rambla into a paved promenade, work that would continue into the next century. Beyond the Rambla, the previously semi-rural Raval was rapidly becoming densely populated.

Barcelona's expansion was briefly interrupted by the French invasion of 1808. Napoleon sought to appeal to Catalans by offering them national recognition within his empire, but, curiously, met with very little response. After six years of turmoil, Barcelona's growing business class resumed their projects in 1814, with the restoration of the Bourbon monarchy in the shape of Ferdinand VII.

Factories, poets & barricades

The upheaval of the Napoleonic occupation ushered in 60 years of conflict and political disorder in Spain, as new and traditional forces in society – reactionaries, conservatives, reformists and revolutionaries – struggled with each other to establish a viable system of government. Even so, during this same era Barcelona was still able to embark upon the transformations of the industrial revolution, Catalonia, with Lombardy, being one of only two areas in southern Europe to do so before the last years of the nineteenth century.

On his restoration Ferdinand VII (1808-33) attempted to reinstate the absolute monarchy of his youth and reimpose his authority over Spain's American colonies, and failed to do either. On his death he was succeeded by his three-year-old daughter Isabel II (1833-68), but the throne was also claimed by his brother Carlos, who was backed by the most reactionary sectors in the country. To defend Isabel's rights the Regent, Ferdinand's widow Queen Maria Cristina, was obliged to seek the support of liberals, and so granted a very limited form of constitution. Thus began Spain's Carlist Wars, which had a powerful impact in conservative rural Catalonia, where Don Carlos' faction won a considerable following, in part because of its support for traditional local rights and customs.

INDUSTRIAL REVOLUTION

While this see-saw struggle went on around the country, in Barcelona a liberal-minded local administration, freed from subordination to the military, was able to engage in some city planning, opening up the soon-to-be fashionable C/Ferran and Plaça Sant Jaume in the 1820s, and later adding the Plaça Reial. A fundamental change came in 1836, when the liberal government in Madrid decreed the *Desamortización*, or disentailment, of Spain's monasteries. In Barcelona, where convents and religious houses still took up great sections of the Raval and the Rambla, a huge area was freed for development.

The Rambla took on the appearance it roughly retains today, while the Raval, the main district for new industry in a Barcelona still contained within its walls, rapidly filled up with tenements and textile mills, built several storeys high to maximise space. In 1832 the first steam-driven factory in Spain was built on C/Tallers, sparking resistance from hand-spinners and weavers. Catalans who had made fortunes in the colonies invested back home, and industry developed apace.

Most of their factories, though, were still relatively small, and Catalan manufacturers were very aware that they were at a disadvantage with regard to the industries of Britain and other countries to the north. For decades, their political motto would not be anything to do with nationalism but protectionism, as they incessantly demanded of Madrid that the textile markets of Spain and its remaining colonies be sealed against all foreign competition.

Also, they did not have the city to themselves. Not only did the anti-industrial Carlists threaten from the countryside, but Barcelona soon became a centre of radical ideas. Its people were notably rebellious, and liberal, republican, free-thinking and even utopian socialist groups proliferated between sporadic bursts of repression. In 1842 a liberal revolt, the *Jamància*, took over Barcelona,

and barricades went up around the city. This was the last occasion Barcelona was bombarded from the castle on Montjuïc, as the army struggled to regain control.

The Catalan language, by this time, had been relegated to secondary status, spoken in every street but rarely written or used in cultured discourse. Then, in 1833 Bonaventura Carles Aribau published his *Oda a la Pàtria*, a romantic eulogy in Catalan of the country, its language and its past. This one poem had an extraordinary impact, and is traditionally credited with initiating the *Renaixença* or rebirth of Catalan heritage and culture. Early literature was lyrical and romantic rather than political, but reflected the underlying energies of a renascent culture. The year 1848 was a high point for Barcelona and Catalonia, with the inauguration of the first railway in Spain, from Barcelona to Mataró, and the opening of the Liceu opera. Improved transport increased Barcelona's contacts with Paris, the mecca for all new ideas, and so augmented the city's cosmopolitan patina.

BARCELONA BREAKS ITS BANKS

The optimism of Barcelona's new middle class was counterpointed by two persistent obstacles: the weakness of the Spanish economy as a whole, and the instability of their own society, reflected in atrocious labour relations. No consideration was given to the manpower behind the industrial surge, the underpaid, overworked men, women and children who lived in increasingly appalling conditions in high-rise slums within the cramped city. Epidemics were frequent, and unrest multiplied. In 1855 the first general strike took place in Barcelona. The Captain-General, Zapatero, inaugurating a long cycle of conflict, refused to permit any workers' organisations, and bloodily suppressed all resistance.

One response to the city's problems that had almost universal support in Barcelona was the demolition of the city walls, which had imposed a stifling restriction on its growth. For years, however, the Spanish state refused to relinquish this hold on the city. To find space, larger factories were established in villages around Barcelona, such as Sants and Poble Nou. In 1854 permission finally came for the demolition of the citadel and the walls. The work began with enthusiastic popular participation, crowds of volunteers joining in at weekends. Barcelona at last broke out of the space it had occupied since the fourteenth century and spread outward into its new *Eixample*, the 'Extension', to a plan by Ildefons Cerdà (*see right*).

In 1868 Isabel II, once a symbol of liberalism, was overthrown by a progressive revolt. During the six years of upheaval that followed, power in Madrid would be held by a provisional government, a constitutional monarchy under an Italian prince and then a federal republic. Workers were

The man with the ruler: Cerdà

Once Barcelona's walls came down (*see left*), a plan was needed to develop the land beyond them and connect the city with Gràcia and the outlying towns. The Ajuntament held a competition for projects in 1859. The councillors actually preferred a scheme presented by the prestigious architect Antoni Rovira i Trias, for long straight streets radiating fan-like from Plaça Catalunya. Controversially, however, and for reasons that have never been explained, orders came from Madrid that the plan to be adopted was that of another Catalan engineer, Ildefons Cerdà (1815-75).

Cerdà had surveyed and drawn the city's first accurate plans in 1855. He was also a radical influenced by utopian socialist ideas, concerned with the cramped, unhealthy conditions of workers' housing in the old city. With its love of straight lines and uniform grid, Cerdà's plan is very much related to visionary rationalist ideas of its time, as was the idea of placing two of its main avenues along a geographic parallel and a meridian. His central aim was to alleviate over-population problems while encouraging social equality by using quadrangular blocks of a standard size, with strict building controls to ensure that they were built up on only two sides, to a limited height, leaving a garden in between. Each district would be of 20 blocks, containing all community necessities.

In the event, though, this idealised use of urban space was scarcely ever achieved, for the private developers who actually built the Eixample regarded Cerdà's restrictions on their property as pointless interference. Buildings went up to much more than the planned heights, and in practice all the blocks from Plaça Catalunya to the Diagonal have been enclosed, with very few inner gardens withstanding the onslaught of construction.

The most enduring feature of Cerdà's plan is the *xamfrà*, the bevelled corner of each block, which makes each junction an open space. The Ajuntament had disliked the scheme because it seemed to disregard the old centre of the city, and *Modernista* architects, in love with curves, initially railed against the project as a horror. Nevertheless, it would become the primary showcase for their imaginative feats, and an essential part of Barcelona's identity.

free to organise, and in November 1868 Giuseppe Fanelli, an Italian emissary of Bakunin, brought the ideas of anarchism to Madrid and Barcelona, encountering a ready response in Catalonia. In 1870 the first Spanish workers' congress was held in Barcelona. The radical forces, however, were divided between multiple factions, while the established classes of society, increasingly threatened, called for the restoration of order. Carlist guerrillas reappeared in the countryside, sending refugees streaming into Barcelona. The Republic proclaimed in 1873 was unable to establish its authority, and succumbed to a military coup.

THE YANKEES OF EUROPE

In 1874 the Bourbon dynasty was restored to the Spanish throne in the shape of Alfonso XII, son of Isabel II. Workers' organisations were again suppressed. The middle classes, however, felt their confidence renewed. The 1870s saw a frenzied boom in stock speculation, the *Febre d'Or* or 'Gold Fever', and the real take-off of building in the *Eixample*. From the 1880s *Modernisme* (*see pages 36-7*) became the preferred style of the new district, the perfect expression for the self-confidence, romanticism and impetus of the industrial class. The first modern Catalanist political movement was founded by Valentí Almirall.

Barcelona felt it needed to show the world all that it had achieved, and that it was more than just a 'second city'. In 1885 an exhibition promoter named Eugenio Serrano de Casanova proposed to the city council the holding of an international exhibition, such as had been held successfully in London, Paris and Vienna. Serrano was actually a highly dubious character, who eventually made off with large amounts of public funds, but by the time this became clear the city fathers had fully committed themselves. The Universal Exhibition of 1888 was used as a pretext for the final conversion of the **Ciutadella** into a park; giant efforts had to be made to get everything ready in time, including the building of an 'International Hotel' for exhibition visitors designed by Domènech i Montaner (which did not have permanent foundations, and had to be demolished immediately after the exhibition) in only 100 days on the present-day Moll de la Fusta, a feat that led the mayor, Francesc Rius i Taulet, to exclaim that 'the Catalan people are the yankee people of Europe'. The first of Barcelona's three great efforts to demonstrate its status to the world, the 1888 Exhibition signified both the consecration of the Modernist style, and the end of provincial, dowdy Barcelona and its establishment as a modern-day city on the international map.

Barcelona in the 1900s: strollers on the Rambla, and demonstrators calling for an amnesty

The city of the new century

The 1888 Exhibition left Barcelona with huge debts, a new look and reasons to believe in itself as a paradigm of progress. The middle classes could see themselves as models of both taste and efficiency; radicals could feel they were at the centre of a hub of new ideas. As the year 1900 approached, in few cities was the new century regarded with greater anticipation than in Barcelona.

The Catalan *Renaixença* continued, and acquired a more political tone. In 1892 the *Bases de Manresa* were drawn up, a first draft plan for Catalan autonomy. Middle-class opinion was becoming more sympathetic to political Catalanism. A decisive moment came in 1898, when the underlying weakness of the Spanish state was abruptly made plain, despite the superficial prosperity of the first years of the Bourbon restoration.

Spain was manœuvred into a short war with the United States, in which it very quickly lost its remaining empire in Cuba, the Philippines and Puerto Rico. Catalan industrialists, horrified at losing the lucrative Cuban market, despaired of the ability of the state ever to reform itself. Many swung behind a conservative nationalist movement founded in 1901, the *Lliga Regionalista* or Regionalist League, led by Enric Prat de la Riba and the politician-financier Francesc Cambó. It promised both national revival and modern, efficient government.

Barcelona continued to grow, fuelling Catalanist optimism. The city incorporated most of the surrounding communities in 1897, reaching a population of over half a million, and in 1907 initiated the 'internal reform' of the old city with the cutting through it of the Via Laietana, intended to allow in more air and so make the streets less unhealthy.

Catalan letters were thriving: the *Institut d'Estudis Catalans* (Institute of Catalan Studies) was founded in 1906, and Pompeu Fabra set out to create the first Catalan dictionary. Literature had acquired a new maturity, and in 1905 Victor Català (a pseudonym for a woman, Caterina Albert) shocked the country with *Solitud*, a darkly modern novel of a woman's sexual awakening that predated DH Lawrence on the subject. Above all, Barcelona had a vibrant artistic community, centred on *Modernisme*, consisting of great architects and established, wealthy painters like Rusiñol and Casas, and the penniless bohemians who gathered round them, like the young Picasso.

Barcelona's bohemians were also drawn to the increasingly wild nightlife of the Raval. The area had already been known for very downmarket entertainments in the 1740s, but cabarets, bars and brothels multiplied at the end of the nineteenth century. Looking back many years later from exile, the writer Lluis Capdevila wrote that one thing he missed about the Barcelona of his youth was that he had never known another city where there were so many places to eat at three in the morning.

Around the cabarets, though, there were also the poorest of the working class, whose conditions had

after the Setmana Tràgica *riots of 1909.*

were summarily executed, as was anarchist educationalist Francesc Ferrer, accused of 'moral responsibility' even though he had not even been in Barcelona at the time.

These events dented the optimism of the Catalanists of the *Lliga*, but in 1914 they secured from Madrid the *Mancomunitat* or administrative union of the four Catalan provinces, the first joint government of any kind in Catalonia in 200 years. Its first President was Prat de la Riba, succeeded in 1917 by the architect Puig i Cadafalch. However, the *Lliga*'s further projects for respectable Catalonia were to be obstructed by a further inflammation of social tensions.

MAD YEARS, BAD YEARS, RED YEARS

Spain's neutral status during World War I gave a huge boost to the Spanish, and especially Catalan, economy. Exports soared, as Catalonia's manufacturers made millions supplying uniforms to the French army. The economy was able to diversify, from textiles into engineering, chemicals and other more modern sectors. This provided the background to an extraordinary drama.

Barcelona also became the most amenable place of refuge for anyone in Europe who wished to avoid the war. It acquired an international refugee community, among them avant-garde artists Sonia and Robert Delaunay, Francis Picabia, Marie Laurencin and Albert Gleizes, and was a bolt-hole for all kinds of low-life from around Europe. The nightlife of the lower Raval took on a newly exotic look, and a string of new cabarets and dance halls opened along the Rambla and C/Nou de la Rambla. All featured the required music of that era for a wild time, the tango. Gambling houses and drug dens appeared around the bars and brothels, and cocaine became widely available. Shortly afterwards this area would be dubbed the *Barrio Chino*, 'Chinatown', definitively identifying it as an area of sin and perdition, and the city acquired a reputation similar to that of Marseille in the 1970s, as the centre of drug trafficking and about every other kind of illegal trade in the Mediterranean.

Some of the most regular patrons of the lavish new cabarets were industrialists, for many of the war profits were spent immediately in very conspicuous consumption. This took place against a still more dramatic social background. The war also set off massive inflation, driving people in their thousands from rural Spain into the cities. Barcelona doubled in size in 20 years to become the largest city in Spain, and the fulcrum of Spanish politics.

Workers' wages, meanwhile, had lost half their real value. The chief channel of protest in Barcelona was the anarchist workers' union, the CNT, constituted in 1910, which gained half a million members in Catalonia by 1919. The CNT and the socialist UGT launched a joint general

continued to decline. Barcelona had some of the worst overcrowding and highest mortality rates of any city in Europe. Most exploited were women and children, toiling for a pittance 15 hours a day. A respectable feminist movement, led by such figures as the writer Dolors Monserdà, undertook philanthropic projects aimed at educating the female masses. Barcelona, however, was more associated internationally with revolutionary politics and violence than gradual reform.

In 1893 over 20 people were killed in a series of anarchist bombings, the most renowned of them when a bomb was thrown down into the stalls of the Liceu during a performance of *William Tell*. The perpetrators were individuals acting alone, but the authorities took the opportunity to carry out a general round-up of anarchists and radicals, several of whom, soon known as the 'Martyrs of Montjuïc', were tortured and executed in the castle above Barcelona. In retaliation, in 1906 a Catalan anarchist tried to assassinate King Alfonso XIII on his wedding day in Madrid.

Anarchism was still only a minority current among workers in Barcelona, but in general rebellious attitudes, growing republican sentiment and a fierce hatred of the Catholic Church united the underclasses and predisposed them to take to the barricades with little provocation. In 1909 came the explosive *Setmana Tràgica*, the Tragic Week. It began as a protest against the conscription of troops for the colonial war in Morocco, but degenerated into a general riot and the destruction of churches by excited mobs. Suspected culprits

A walk with ghosts

Barcelona has been famous for many things: Gaudí, the Rambla – and the *Barrio Chino*, for decades one of the legendary centres of low-life in Europe. The French in particular romanticised the *Chino* – Jean Genet's *The Thief's Journal* and André Pieyre de Mandiargues' *La Marge* are two classics of *Chino* literature – and right up until very recently visiting French literati, when asked what most impressed them in Barcelona, regularly used to say the *Chino*, with its Felliniesque whores and smell of piss. Their hosts often pursed their lips, detesting this idea of their city as a place for picturesque slumming.

Barcelona without its *Chino* used to be inconceiveable, but there is no preservation order on it, and today only lipstick traces of this lost world can be seen. This was a harsh, often overwhelming, desperate place, certainly; it was also one of the planet's rarer environments, and before it vanishes entirely it can be thought provoking to take a last look.

Unless otherwise indicated, all the places mentioned here have disappeared. Another leap of imagination is required to populate these streets with massed crowds of people, for photos from the '30s, when the Chino was at its peak, show its alleys packed from one side to the other, 24 hours a day. There were brothels, gambling dens, *tavernas*, pawnshops, music halls, drifters, ordinary workers and the very poor, all coexisting side by side, equally dedicated to the business of surviving. Today, although the streets may be far quieter, this is still a hard area, and this walk is not one to try after dark (it is shown in **orange** on **Map 5**, *page 314*).

Near the bottom of the Rambla, at the corner of C/Portal de Santa Madrona and Avda Drassanes, it's impossible not to see a 1960s skyscraper, the **Edifici Colom**, the product of Franco-era attempt at modernisation. It stands on the site of a celebrated brothel of the 1930s, **Can Manco** ('House of the One-Armed Man'), famous for specialising in cheap and quick *flautes* (flutes) or blow-jobs. Around the corner at C/Montserrat 20 stood the **Teatro Circo Barcelonés**, known for its *transformistas* or drag-queens. This street maintains its traditions, and the **Cangrejo** at No.9 is perhaps the most authentic survivor of old *Chino* nightlife.

Turning left into C/Cervelló and then right and across at Avda Drassanes you enter **C/del Cid**. **C/Peracamps**, on the left, was known as a street of ultra-cheap doss-houses. In the 1930s C/del Cid was the epicentre of the *Chino*: No.10,

now a more recent block of flats, was the site of **La Criolla**, most celebrated cabaret of the era, renowned for its drag and female performers and patronised by high and low society. Lesbians also met here in relative safety. It was a gambling joint too, and a centre for drugs and arms dealing; the owner, *Pepe el de la Criolla*, was shot down in the doorway in one of the *Chino*'s most famous murders, in April 1936.

A turn right into the Paral.lel and right again takes you into **C/Arc de Teatre**. On the present site of the **Mercat del Carme** was **La Mina**, a *taverna* that had – shades of Dickens – an *academia de lladres* (school for thieves) in its basement. At the junction with Avda Drassanes is Barcelona's memorial to its most famous rent boy, the tiny **Plaça Jean Genet**. Genet came to the *Chino* in the '30s, selling sex, thieving and begging. He robbed clients after servicing them, stole from churches and earned three pesetas a night in La Criolla, dressed as a girl. C/Arc de Teatre 6, now demolished, was the site of **Madame Petit**, an internationally-famous brothel known for answering every need, including sado-masochism and necrophilia.

C/Arc del Teatre, 1932.

Turn left into the Rambla and left again into **C/Nou de la Rambla**. This was the more public main avenue of the *Chino*, especially in the boom years of World War I. The **Hotel Gaudí** at No.12 – opposite the **Palau Güell** – occupies the site of the **Eden Concert**, Barcelona's most opulent *café concierto*, a combination of music hall, high-class restaurant, gambling den and strip club. Here textile millionaires and their mistresses rubbed shoulders with *pinxos* – the *Chino*'s hard men, part pimps, part bouncers, part gang-members.

On the left is **C/Lancaster**, where at No.2 the sign can still be read of the **Bar Bohemia**, a legendary venue where very aged performers of the old cabarets used to keep their acts going, and which only finally closed in 1997. On the right at C/Nou 34 is the 1910 **London Bar**, last of the *cafés concierto*, and now a foreigner's favourite (*see chapter* **Nightlife**). Further along C/Nou is C/Estel, which had at No.2 **La Suerte Loca**, a 1900s brothel frequented by Picasso. At the very end of C/Nou (No.103), was **El Pompeya**, a cheap cabaret for workers and students. It is now the **Bagdad**, where live porn is available and which currently offers 'interactive sex' by Internet.

Turning right into the Paral.lel again you find the **Arnau** music hall, and a little further on the **Bar Español**, now a nondescript modern bar but in its day (1910-30) a haunt of both revolutionaries and police informers. Next to the Arnau, turn back into C/Tàpies. Along this street heavily made-up old women used to sit on chairs in the street to sell their favours for the price of a sandwich, mostly to equally elderly clients. This was the most pathetic face of the *Chino*, and only came to an end just before the 1992 Olympics.

If you carry on going toward the Rambla, left at C/Sant Oleguer, right at C/Marqués de Barberà and then left at C/Sant Ramon you enter an area where street prostitution and squalor are still very visible. On the corner of C/Sant Ramon and C/Sant Pau there is the **Bar Marsella**, a bar that has survived all the district's renovations, and so fascinates young foreigners. Almost opposite is **Plaça Salvador Seguí**: he was the greatest of Barcelona's CNT union leaders, murdered in 1923 by a gunman hired by employers, at the nearby corner of C/Cadena-C/Sant Rafael. Along **C/Robador**, across the shabby square, there are still *bares de camareras*, shabby 'girly bars' used for prostitution. This last vestige of the *Chino*, though, is doomed, for these old, decrepit blocks will probably soon be swept away, and new apartments, as it were, erected.

strike in 1917, roughly co-ordinated with a campaign by the *Lliga* and other liberal politicians for political reform. However, the politicians quickly withdrew at the prospect of serious social unrest. Inflation continued to intensify, and in 1919 Barcelona was paralysed for two months by a CNT general strike over union recognition. Employers refused to recognise the CNT, and the most intransigent of them hired gunmen to get rid of union leaders, often using a gang organised by an ex-German spy known as the 'Baron de Koening'. Union activists replied in kind, and virtual guerrilla warfare developed between the CNT, the employers and the state. Over 800 people were killed on the city's streets in the space of five years.

In 1923, in response both to the chaos in Barcelona and a crisis in the war in Morocco, the Captain-General of Barcelona, Miguel Primo de Rivera, staged a coup and established a military dictatorship under King Alfonso XIII. The CNT, already exhausted, was suppressed. Conservative Catalanists, longing for an end to disorder and the revolutionary threat, initially supported the coup, but were rewarded by the abolition of the *Mancomunitat* and a vindictive campaign by the Primo regime against the Catalan language and national symbols.

This, however, achieved the contrary of the desired effect, helping to radicalise and popularise Catalan nationalism. After the terrible struggles of the previous years, the 1920s were actually a time of notable prosperity for many in Barcelona, as some of the wealth recently accumulated filtered through the economy. Economic changes brought greater numbers of office and shop workers, who enjoyed new kinds of leisure like jazz, football and the cinema. The first signs of a tourist industry were seen along the recently-named *Costa Brava*. This was also, though, a highly politicised society, in which new magazines and forums for discussion – despite the restrictions of the Dictatorship – found a ready audience.

A prime motor of Barcelona's prosperity during the 1920s was the International Exhibition of 1929, the second of the city's great showcase events. It had been proposed by Cambó and Catalan business groups, but Primo de Rivera saw that it could also serve as a propaganda event for his regime. A huge number of public projects were undertaken in association with the main event, including the post office in Via Laietana, the Estació de França and Barcelona's first Metro line, from Plaça Catalunya to Plaça d'Espanya. Thousands of migrant workers came from southern Spain to build them, many living in decrepit housing or shanties on the city fringes. By 1930, Barcelona was very different from the place it had been in 1910; it had over a million people, and its urban sprawl had crossed into neighbouring towns such as Hospitalet and Santa Coloma.

For the Exhibition itself Montjuïc and Plaça d'Espanya were comprehensively redeveloped, with grand halls by Puig i Cadafalch and other local architects in the style of the Catalan neo-classical movement *Noucentisme*, a backward-looking reaction to the excesses of Modernism. They contrasted strikingly, though, with the German pavilion by Mies van der Rohe (the **Pavelló Barcelona**), emphatically announcing the international trend toward rationalism.

THE REPUBLIC

Despite the Exhibition's success, in January 1930 Primo de Rivera resigned, exhausted. The King appointed another soldier, General Berenguer, as prime minister with the mission of restoring stability. The Dictatorship, though, had fatally discredited the old regime, and a protest movement spread across Catalonia against the monarchy. In early 1931 Berenguer called local elections, as a first step towards a restoration of constitutional rule. The outcome was a complete surprise, for republicans were elected in all of Spain's cities. Ecstatic crowds poured into the streets, and Alfonso XIII abdicated. On 14 April 1931, the Second Spanish Republic was proclaimed.

The Republic came in amid real euphoria. It was especially so in Catalonia, where it was associated with hopes for both social change and national reaffirmation. The clear winner of the elections in the country had been the *Esquerra Republicana*, a leftist Catalanist group led by Francesc Macià. A raffish, elderly figure, Macià was one of the first politicians in Spain to win genuine affection from ordinary people. He declared Catalonia independent, but later agreed to accept autonomy within the Spanish Republic.

The Generalitat was re-established as a government that would, potentially, acquire wide powers. All aspects of Catalan culture were then in expansion, and a popular press in Catalan achieved a wide readership. Barcelona was a small but notable centre of the avant-garde. Miró and Dalí had already made their mark in painting, and in 1928 a group of artists and critics – Dalí among them – had issued the *Manifest Groc* (Yellow Manifesto), which broke resoundingly with the traditions of *Modernisme* and most Catalan art by pouring scorn on all ornamentation. Under the Republic, the ADLAN (*Amics de l'Art Nou*, Friends of New Art) group worked to promote con-

Barcelona in red & black

One of Barcelona's many distinctions is that of being the only city in western Europe to have experienced a thoroughgoing social revolution within living memory. Another is that this revolution was to a very large extent inspired by anarchists. Anarchism arrived in the city in the 1860s, and attained greater influence here than anywhere else in the world. Over the next 70 years the Catalan anarchist movement hit the depths and scaled the heights, from crude violence to the highest idealism, from euphoria to defeat.

The individual terrorist attacks of the 1890s were very untypical of Catalan anarchism. Rather, anarchists believed that an entirely self-managed society could be achieved through constant collective organisation, and a pugnacious intransigence before the ruling classes and the law. Anarchists set up co-operatives and workers' societies, schools and social centres, and were among the first to introduce progressive ideas on education and sexuality into Spain. During the 1930s, anarchist housing campaigns ensured that many of the poorest of the poor paid no rent, a feminist group, *Mujeres Libres* (Free Women), gained momentum, and a group called the 'Practical Idealists' planned a self-managed health service.

Anarchism gained its greatest strength in the 1910s and 1930s, after the creation of the union confederation the CNT. If the Passeig de Gràcia was the heart of the respectable city, the centre of anarchist Barcelona was the Paral.lel. On a corner of the small *plaça* by Paral.lel Metro a Caixa bank office now occupies the site of the bar *La Tranquilidad*, which, as one veteran remembers, 'had nothing tranquil about it' – a meeting place of legendary militants such as Durruti and Ascaso, and frequently raided by the police. Nearby in Avda Mistral (at No.17) was the base of the *Agrupación Faros*, largest of the anarchist clubs of the 1930s, which at one time had over 2,000 members.

In the first months of the Civil War, factories, public services, cinemas, the phone system and food distribution were all collectivised. Some of the collectives, such as those that took over public transport, worked very well; others met with more and more difficulties, especially as the war ground on, and morale was steadily worn down. Today the CNT continues to keep the flame alive in union affairs, but this world can often seem to be just so many ghosts, less commemorated in modern Barcelona than events of the 1640s.

temporary art, and the GATCPAC architectural collective sought to work with the new authorities to bring rationalist architecture to Barcelona.

Prospects were still clouded by social conflicts. The CNT revived, and there were bitter strikes in some industries. By this time the anarchist Confederation was only one of many leftist tendencies in the city – albeit the largest – for this was a time of enormous political effervescence. The *Esquerra*, in power in the Generalitat and the Barcelona Ajuntament, tried to follow its own, reformist agenda. Its achievements in five years were more a matter of potential than realities, but tangible advances were made, particularly in primary education – a level of practical reform that contributed to social conflicts being slightly less intense in Catalonia than in the rest of Spain.

In Madrid, the Republic's first government was a coalition of republicans and socialists led by Manuel Azaña. Its goal was to modernise Spanish society through liberal-democratic reforms, but as social tensions intensified the coalition collapsed, and a conservative republican party, with support from the traditional Spanish right, secured power after new elections in 1933. For Catalonia, the prospect of a return to right-wing rule prompted fears that it would immediately abrogate the Generalitat's hard-won powers. On 6 October 1934, while a general strike was launched against the central government in Asturias and some other parts of Spain, Lluís Companys, leader of the Generalitat since Macià's death the previous year, declared Catalonia independent. This, however, turned out to be something of a farce, for the Generalitat had no means of resisting the army, and the 'Catalan Republic' was rapidly suppressed.

The Generalitat was suspended, its leaders imprisoned. Over the next year fascism seemed to become a real threat, as political positions became polarised throughout Spain. Then, in February 1936, fresh Spain-wide elections were won by the Popular Front of the left. The Generalitat was reinstated, and in Catalonia the next few months were, surprisingly, relatively peaceful. In the rest of Spain, though, tensions were reaching bursting point, and right-wing politicians, refusing to accept the loss of power, talked openly of the need for the military to intervene. In July, the 1929 stadium on Montjuïc was to be the site of the Popular Olympics, a leftist alternative to the main Olympics of that year in Nazi Germany. On the day of their inauguration, however, 18 July, army generals launched a coup against the Republic and its left-wing governments, expecting no resistance.

REVOLUTIONARY BARCELONA

In Barcelona, militants of the unions and leftist parties, on alert for weeks, poured into the streets to oppose the troops in fierce fighting. In the course of 19 July the military were gradually worn down,

and finally surrendered in the Hotel Colón on Plaça Catalunya (by the corner with Passeig de Gràcia, the site of which is now occupied by the Radio Nacional de España building). Opinions have always differed as to who could claim most credit for this remarkable popular victory: workers' militants have claimed it was the 'people in arms' who defeated the army, while others stress the importance of the police having remained loyal to the Generalitat. A likely answer is that they actually encouraged each other.

Tension released, the city was taken over by the revolution. People's militias of the CNT, different Marxist parties and other left-wing factions marched off to Aragon, led by streetfighters such as the anarchists Durruti and García Oliver, to continue the battle. The army rising had failed in Spain's major cities but won a foothold in Castile, Aragon and the south, although in the heady atmosphere of Barcelona in July 1936 it was often assumed that their resistance could not last long, and that the people's victory was near-inevitable.

Far from the front, Barcelona was the chief centre of the revolution in Republican Spain, the only truly proletarian city. Its middle class avoided the streets, where, as Orwell recorded in his *Homage to Catalonia*, workers' clothing was all there was to be seen. Barcelona became a magnet for leftists from around the world, including writers such as Malraux, Hemingway and Octavio Paz. Industries and public services were collectivised. Ad-hoc 'control patrols' of the revolutionary militias roamed the streets supposedly checking for suspected right-wing agents and sometimes carrying out summary executions, a practice that was condemned by many leftist leaders.

The alliance between the different left-wing groups was unstable and riddled with tensions. The Communists, who had extra leverage because the Soviet Union was the only country prepared to give the Spanish Republic arms, demanded the integration of the loosely-organised militias in a conventional army under a strong central authority. This was resisted by the anarchists and a radical-Marxist party, the POUM, as a dilution of the revolution, and a back-door Communist attempt to establish a monopoly of power. For weeks the Generalitat was inoperative before the *de facto* power of the workers' militias, but in September 1936 a new administration was formed with, remarkably, CNT ministers, who were also represented in the central republican government. The following months saw continual political infighting between the CNT, the POUM and the Communists, and co-operation broke down completely in May 1937, when republican and Communist troops seized the telephone building in Plaça Catalunya (on the corner of Portal de l'Angel) from a CNT committee, sparking off the confused war-within-the-civil-war witnessed by

After the bombing, 1938.

Orwell from the roof of the **Teatre Poliorama**. A temporary agreement was patched up, but shortly afterwards the POUM was banned, and the CNT excluded from power. A new republican central government was formed under Dr Juan Negrín, a Socialist allied to the Communists.

The war became more of a conventional conflict. This did little, however, to improve the Republic's position, for the Nationalists under General Francisco Franco and their German and Italian allies had been continually gaining ground. Madrid was under siege, and the capital of the Republic was moved to Valencia and then to Barcelona, in November 1937.

Catalonia received thousands of refugees, and food shortages and the lack of armaments ground down morale. Barcelona also had the sad distinction of being the first major city in Europe to be subjected to sustained intensive bombing, to an extent that has rarely been appreciated, with heavy raids throughout 1938, especially by Italian bombers based in Mallorca. The Basque Country and Asturias had already fallen to Franco, and in March 1938 his troops reached the Mediterranean near Castellón, cutting the main Republican zone in two. The Republic had one last throw of the dice, in the Battle of the Ebro in summer 1938, when for months the Popular Army struggled to retake control of the river. After that, the Republic was exhausted. Barcelona fell to the Francoist army on 26 January 1939. Half a million refugees fled to France, to be interned in barbed-wire camps along the beaches.

Grey years

In Catalonia the Franco regime was iron-fisted and especially vengeful. Thousands of Catalan republicans and leftists were executed, Generalitat President Lluís Companys among them; exile and deportation were the fate of thousands more. Publishing, teaching and any other public cultural expression in Catalan, including even speaking it in the street, were rigorously prohibited, and every Catalanist monument in the city was dismantled. All independent political activity was suspended: censorship and the secret police were a constant presence, and the resulting atmosphere of fear and suspicion was to mark many who lived through it. The entire political and cultural development of the country during the previous century and a half was thus brought to an abrupt halt.

The epic of the Spanish Civil War is known worldwide; more present in the collective memory of Barcelona, though, is the long *posguerra* or post-war period, which lasted nearly two decades after 1939. The Barcelona of these years is best recorded in the novels of Juan Marsé, a grimy, pinched city full of the smell of drains and casual cruelty, in which any high idealistic expectations had given way to a fatalistic concern for getting by from one day to the next. The memory of these dead years has without doubt fed through into the assertiveness – combined with a wariness of theoretical idealism – of Catalonia since 1975.

Barcelona was impoverished, and would not regain its standard of living of 1936 until the mid-

1950s; food and electricity were rationed. Nevertheless, migrants in flight from the still more brutal poverty of the south flowed into Barcelona, occupying precarious shanty towns around Montjuïc and other areas on the city's edge. Reconstruction of the nearly 2,000 buildings destroyed by bombing was slow, for the regime built little during its first few years other than monumental showpieces and the vulgarly ornate basilica on top of Tibidabo, completed to expiate Barcelona's 'sinful' role during the war. Later, cheap housing projects – standardised blocks – were undertaken to accommodate some of the city's mushrooming population.

Some underground political movements were able to operate. Anarchist urban guerrillas such as the Sabaté brothers attempted to carry on armed resistance, and March 1951 saw the last gasp of the pre-war labour movement in a general tram strike, the only major strike during the harshest years of the regime. It was fiercely repressed, but also achieved some of its goals. Clandestine Catalanist groups undertook small acts of resistance and rebellion, through underground publications or the performance in secret of a new Catalan play. Some Catalan high culture was tolerated: the poet Salvador Espriu promoted a certain resurgence of Catalan literature, and the young Antoni Tàpies held his first solo exhibition in 1949. For a great many people, though, the only remaining public focus of national sentiment – of any collective excitement – was Barcelona football club, which took on an extraordinary importance at this time, above all in its biannual meetings with the 'team of the regime', Real Madrid.

As a fascist survivor, the Franco regime was subject to a UN embargo after World War II. Years of international isolation and attempted self-sufficiency came to an end in 1953, when the United States and the Vatican saw to it that this anti-communist state was at least partially readmitted to the western fold. Even a limited opening to the outside world meant that foreign money began to enter the country, and the regime relaxed some control over its population. In 1959 the *Plan de Estabilización* (Stabilisation Plan), drawn up by Catholic technocrats of the Opus Dei, brought Spain definitively within the western economy, throwing its doors open to tourism and foreign investment. With tourist income the Europe-wide boom of the 1960s arrived in Spain, setting off change at a vertiginous pace.

Two years earlier in 1957 José María de Porcioles was appointed Mayor of Barcelona, a post he would retain until 1973. Porcioles has since been regarded as the personification of the damage inflicted on the city by the Franco regime during its 1960s boom, accused of covering it with drab high-rises and road schemes without any concern for its character. Barcelona grew chaotically,

stretching in every direction and surrounded by polluting factories. Many valuable historic buildings – such as the grand cafés of the Plaça Catalunya – were torn down to make way for bland modern business blocks, and minimal attention was paid to collective amenities.

After the years of repression and the years of development, 1966 marked the beginning of what became known as *tardofranquisme*, 'late Francoism'. Having made its opening to the outside world, the regime was losing its grip, and labour, youth and student movements began to emerge from beneath the shroud of repression. Nevertheless, the Franco regime never hesitated to show its strength. Strikes and demonstrations were dealt with savagely, and just months before the dictator's death the last person to be executed in Spain by the traditional method of the garrotte, a Catalan anarchist named Puig Antich, went to his death in Barcelona.

In 1973, however, Franco's closest follower, Admiral Carrero Blanco, had been blown into the sky by a bomb planted by the Basque terrorist group ETA, leaving no one to guard over the core values of the regime. Change was in the air. Agitation grew, the mood was feisty, and people did not have long to wait.

The new era

When Franco died on 20 November 1975, the people of Barcelona took to the streets in celebration, and not a bottle of *cava* was left in the city by evening. However, no one knew quite what was about to happen. The Bourbon monarchy was restored, under King Juan Carlos, but his attitudes and intentions were not clear. In 1976 he made a little-known Francoist bureaucrat, Adolfo Suárez, prime minister, charged with leading the country to democracy.

The first months and years of Spain's 'transition' were still a difficult period. Nationalist and other demonstrations continued to be repressed by the police with considerable brutality, and far-right groups threatened less open violence. However, political parties were legalised, and June 1977 saw the first democratic elections since 1936. They were won across Spain by Suárez' own new party, the UCD, and in Catalonia by a mixture of Socialists, Communists and nationalist groups.

It was, again, not clear how Suárez expected to deal with the demands of Catalonia, but shortly after the elections he surprised everyone by going to visit the President of the Generalitat in exile, a veteran pre-Civil War politician, Josep Tarradellas. His office was the only institution of the old Republic to be so recognised, perhaps because Suárez astutely identified in the old man a fellow conservative. Tarradellas was invited to return as provisional President of a restored Generalitat, and in October 1977 announced his arrival with the simple phrase *'Ja soc aquí'* ('Here I am!') from the balcony in the Plaça Sant Jaume.

The following year the first free local elections took place, won by the Socialist Party, with Narcís Serra as Mayor. They have retained control of the Barcelona Ajuntament ever since, presided over for most of the intervening years by Pasqual Maragall, who replaced Serra when the latter left to join the Madrid government in 1982. The year 1980 saw yet another set of elections, to the restored Generalitat, won by Jordi Pujol and his party *Convergència i Unió*. Again, they have kept power throughout the '80s and '90s. Imprisoned for Catalanist activities in 1960, Pujol represents a strain of conservative nationalism that goes back to Prat de la Riba. His multi-pronged platform covers the promotion, at home, of Catalan autonomy, language, culture and identity; the building up of an independent role for Catalonia in Spanish affairs; and the consolidation of Catalonia as an economic hub with a distinctive identity within the European Union. Facing each other across Plaça Sant Jaume, Generalitat and Ajuntament are the two constants of modern Catalan politics.

STYLE CITY

Inseparable from the restoration of democracy was a complete change in the city's atmosphere in the late 1970s. New freedoms – in culture, in sexuality, in work – were explored, newly-released energies expressed in a multitude of ways. Barcelona soon began to look different too, as the inherent dowdiness of the Franco years was swept away by a new Catalan style for the new Catalonia: postmodern, high-tech, punkish, comic strip, minimalist and tautly fashionable. For a time street culture was still highly politicised, but simultaneously it was also increasingly hedonistic. In the 1980s design mania struck the city, a product of unbottled energies, a rebirth of Barcelona's artistic, artisan and architectural traditions, and maybe another outbreak of that historic urge to remake the city in its own Catalan image, as in the preparations for the Exhibition of 1888. Innovative designers in all media began to add a new layer of sleek, chromed shine to a city whose Gothic and *Modernista* heritage had been fading from years of neglect.

This emphasis on slick, fresh style began on a street and underground level, but the special feature of Barcelona was the extent to which it was taken up by public authorities, and above all the Ajuntament, as a central part of their drive to reverse the policies of the previous regime. The highly-educated technocrats who led the Socialist city administration began, gradually at first, to 'recover' the city from its neglected state, and in doing so enlisted the elite of the Catalan intellectual and artistic community in their support. No one epitomises this more than Oriol Bohigas, the

architect and writer who was long the city's head of culture and chief planner. A rolling programme of urban renewal was initiated, beginning with the open spaces and public sculpture programme (*see chapter* **Art Galleries**) and low-level initiatives like the *'Barcelona, posa't guapa'* ('Barcelona, do yourself up') campaign, through which hundreds of historic façades were given an overdue facelift.

This ambitious and emphatically modern approach to urban problems and design acquired much greater focus after Barcelona's bid to host the 1992 Olympic Games was accepted, in 1986. It was not entirely appreciated just what the city wanted the Games for. Far more than just a sports event, the Games were to be Barcelona's third great effort to cast aside suggestions of second-city status and show the world its wares. The exhibitions of 1888 and 1929 had seen developments in the Ciutadella and on and around Montjuïc; the Olympics provided an opening to work on a city-wide scale. Taking advantage of the public and private investment they would attract, Barcelona planned an all-new orientation of itself toward the sea, in a programme of urban renovation of a scope scarcely seen in Europe since the years of reconstruction after World War II.

Along with the creation of the new Barcelona in bricks and mortar went the city-sponsored promotion of Barcelona-as-concept, a seductive cocktail of architecture, imagination, tradition, style, nightlife and primary colours. This was perhaps the most spectacular – certainly the most deliberate – of Barcelona's many reinventions of itself; it also succeeded in good part because this image of creativity and vivacity fitted an idea many of Barcelona's citizens had always had of their town, as if the drab decades had been just a bad dream.

Inseparable from all this was Mayor Maragall, a tireless 'Mr Barcelona' who appeared in every possible forum to expound his vision of the role of cities and intervened personally to set the guidelines for projects or secure the participation of major international architects. In the process Barcelona, like all Spanish cities a byword for modern blight only a few years before, became an international reference point in urban affairs. Maragall also established a personal popularity well beyond that of his Catalan Socialist Party.

BARCELON-AAH

When the Games were finally held in July-August 1992, after much of Barcelona had spent six years *en obres* (under construction), no one could quite say whether they were worth it, but all agreed they were a great success. Once the parade had gone by, the city held its breath to see what happened next, and 1993 was a difficult year. The citizens had been assured many times that the Games would cost them next to nothing, but the next year they were presented with the highest local tax

Not just any Olympics: theatre group La Fura dels Baus *in the 1992 opening ceremony.*

increases in Barcelona's history. Bringing this off with charisma scarcely blemished was perhaps a greater demonstration of Pasqual Maragall's political skills than anything he'd done before.

From 1994 onwards, moreover, confidence picked up again, the city's relentless self-promotion seemed actually to be working in attracting investment, and Barcelona and Catalonia rode out Spain's post-1992 recession better than any other part of the country. Far from calling a halt to its building plans, the Ajuntament announced still more large-scale projects, this time in areas little touched in the run-up to 1992 such as the Old Port and the Raval. Maragall's own popularity was such that he was able to stand aside from the corruption scandals that dragged down his Socialist allies in the central government of Felipe González after 13 years in office, and enabled the right-wing *Partido Popular* to take power in Madrid after the elections of 1996.

Since 1993 the support of the Catalan nationalists in the Madrid parliament has been essential to keep minority Socialist (till 1996) and then *Partido Popular* central governments in power, a situation that has enabled Jordi Pujol and his *Convergència* party to build up a pivotal role in all-Spanish affairs. In return for this support he has demanded more and more concessions for the Generalitat. Pujol's reputation as the most artful operator and power-

broker in Spanish politics has reinforced his popularity among his core support in Catalonia, while intensifying the aversion felt towards him in many other parts of the country. Parallel to this has been a growing ambiguity about the ultimate aims of Pujol's brand of nationalism, particularly with regard to the status of the Catalan language.

In the Barcelona Ajuntament, Pasqual Maragall caused general surprise by standing down in 1997, after winning a fifth term. He was succeeded as Mayor by his deputy Joan Clos, a previously rather anonymous figure who, however, held on to the post with an increased majority in the next city elections in June 1999. Maragall declared his intention to stand as the next Socialist candidate for President of the Generalitat, implying he could bring to the whole of Catalonia the same kind of modernising, projects-for-the-people policies he had applied in the city. Big changes seemed on the cards: then, in the October '99 elections the Socialists won more votes than *Convergència*, but fewer seats in the Catalan Parliament – a situation not supposed to happen in the PR system used in elections in Spain, but which did. To stay in power Pujol was obliged to call on the local *PP* to return the favour he had done their government in Madrid. Change was coming, but not fast enough to deny Jordi Pujol the twentieth year of his reign.

Architecture

Ingenuity, solidity, exuberant creativity, a unique mix of styles: even before it became a design showcase, Barcelona's architecture was a key to the city's identity.

Architecture has always had a very special importance among all the arts in Catalonia. It has frequently taken on the role of most appropriate medium – ahead of painting, music or any other art form – through which to express national identity. Periods when architecture flourished have paralleled eras of increased Catalan freedom of action and self-expression, greater wealth and a reinforcement of collective civic pride.

A clear line of continuity, of recurring characteristics, can be traced between generations of Catalan architects. Ideas, attitudes and trends are taken in from abroad, but are assimilated into this strong local culture. Catalan builders have always shown interest in decorating surfaces, and a concern with texture and the use of fine materials and finishes. This is combined with a simplicity of line and sense of sobriety often seen as distinguishing Catalan character from that of the rest of Spain. Other common elements are references to the traditional architecture of rural Catalonia – the large *masia* farmhouses, with chalet-type tile roofs, massive stone walls and round-arched doorways, a style maintained by anonymous builders for centuries – and to the powerful constructions of Catalan Romanesque and Gothic. There has also long been a close relationship between architects and craftsmen in the production of buildings, especially in the working of metal and wood.

The revival and renewed vigour of Catalan culture and the city of Barcelona since 1975 have once again been accompanied by dynamic expansion in architecture, as is now world-famous. Modern Catalans have a sense of contributing to their architectural heritage in the present day, rather than preserving it as a relic. Contemporary buildings are daringly constructed alongside (or even within) old ones, and this mix of old and new is a major characteristic of many spectacular projects seen in Barcelona over the last two decades.

The importance of architecture is also reflected in public attitudes. Barcelona's citizens cherish their buildings, and form a critical audience. A range of architectural guides is available, some in English (*see page 299* **Further Reading**). Informative leaflets on different styles are also provided (in English) at tourist offices (*see pages 294-5*). For details of buildings mentioned in this chapter, *see chapter* **Sightseeing**.

The old city

The old city of Barcelona, confined within its successive rings of walls, had by 1850 become one of the densest urban areas in Europe. Open space has been at a premium here, and largely still is today, despite recent clearances. Small squares and paved areas feel almost sculpted out of a solid mass of buildings. The Mediterranean sun, which rarely reaches some streets, fills these often modest spaces with light, giving an unequalled sense of drama. The spaces within buildings also sometimes seem hollowed out from the city fabric. The breathtaking beauty of **Santa Maria del Mar**, or the scale of the **Saló del Tinell**, contrast with the tightly packed streets around them. This gives a feeling of luxury to even the simplest square or church.

Roman to Romanesque

The Roman citadel of *Barcino* was founded on the hill of *Mons Taber*, just behind the cathedral, which to this day remains the religious and civic heart of the city. It left an important legacy in the shape of the fourth-century first city wall, fragments of which are visible at many points around the old city (*see page 56*).

Barcelona's next occupiers, the Visigoths, left little in the city, although a trio of fine Visigothic churches survives nearby in **Terrassa**. When the Catalan state began to form under the Counts of Barcelona from the ninth century, the dominant architecture of this new community was massive, simple Romanesque. In the Pyrenean valleys there are hundreds of fine Romanesque buildings,

*The cloistered calm of **Sant Pau del Camp**.*

*Simplicity is the essence of Catalan Gothic: the C/Ciutat entrance to the **Ajuntament**.*

notably at **Sant Pere de Rodes, Ripoll, Sant Joan de les Abadesses** and **Besalú** (*see chapter* **Trips Out of Town**). There is, however, relatively little in Barcelona. On the right-hand side of the cathedral, looking at the main façade, is the thirteenth-century chapel of **Santa Llúcia**, incorporated into the later building; tucked away near Plaça Catalunya is the church of **Santa Anna**; and in La Ribera there is the tiny travellers' chapel, the **Capella d'en Marcús**. The city's greatest Romanesque monument, though, is the beautifully plain twelfth-century church and cloister of **Sant Pau del Camp**, built as part of a larger monastery.

Catalan Gothic

By the thirteenth century, Barcelona was the capital of a trading empire, and growing rapidly. The settlements called *ravals* or *vilanoves* that had sprung up outside the Roman walls were brought within the city by the building of Jaume I's second set of walls, which extended Barcelona west to the Rambla, then just an often-dry river-bed.

This growth and political eminence formed the background to the great flowering of Catalan Gothic, and the construction of many of Barcelona's most important civic and religious buildings to replace Romanesque equivalents. The **cathedral** was begun in 1298, in place of an eleventh-century building. Work commenced on the **Ajuntament** (*Casa de la Ciutat*) and **Palau de la Generalitat** (later subject to extensive alteration) in 1372 and 1403 respectively. Major additions were made to the **Palau Reial** of the Catalan-Aragonese kings, especially the **Saló del Tinell** of 1359-62, and the

great hall of the **Llotja** or trading exchange was finished in 1380-92. Many of Barcelona's finest buildings were built or completed in these years, in the midst of the crisis that followed the Black Death.

Catalan Gothic has very particular characteristics that distinguish it clearly from more northern, classic Gothic. It is simpler, and gives more prominence to solid, plain walls between towers and columns rather than the empty spaces between intricate flying buttresses of the great French cathedrals. Buildings thus appear much more massive. In façades, as much emphasis is given to horizontals as to verticals, and the latter and their octagonal towers end in flat roofs, not spires. Decorative intricacies are mainly confined to windows, portals, arches and gargoyles. Many churches have no aisles but only a single nave, the classic example being the beautiful **Santa Maria del Pi** in Plaça del Pi, built from 1322 to 1453.

This style has provided the historic benchmark for Catalan architecture. It is simple and robust, yet elegant and practical. Innovative, sophisticated techniques were developed: the use of transverse arches supporting timber roofs allowed the spanning of great halls uninterrupted by columns, a system used in the **Saló del Tinell**. Designed by Pere III's court architect Guillem Carbonell, it has some of the largest pure masonry arches in Europe, the elegance and sheer scale of which gives the space tremendous splendour. The **Drassanes**, built from 1378 as the royal shipyards (and now the **Museu Marítim**), is really just a very beautiful shed, but the enormous parallel aisles make it one of the most exciting spaces in the city.

La Ribera, the *Vilanova del Mar*, was the commercial centre of the city, and gained the great masterpiece of Catalan Gothic, **Santa Maria del Mar**, built between 1329 and 1384. Its superb proportions are based on a series of squares imposed on one another, with three aisles of, unusually, almost equal height. The interior is staggering for its austerity and spareness of structure.

The domestic architecture of medieval Barcelona, at least that of its noble and merchant residences, can be seen at its best in the line of palaces along **Carrer Montcada**, next to Santa Maria. Built by the city's merchant élite at the height of their confidence and wealth, they conform to a very Mediterranean style of urban palace, making maximum use of space. A plain exterior is presented to the street, with heavy doors opening into an imposing patio, on one side of which a grand external staircase leads to the main rooms on the first floor (*planta noble*), which often have elegant open loggias. Humbler dwellings, while lacking the details, scale and fine carving of the Montcada palaces, often followed a similar layout. Many of these palaces now house some of Barcelona's most visited cultural institutions.

Forgotten centuries

By the beginning of the sixteenth century, political and economic decline meant there were far fewer patrons for new building in the city. In the next 300 years a good deal was still built in Barcelona, but rarely in any distinctively Catalan style, so that it has often been disregarded.

In the 1550s the **Palau del Lloctinent** was built for the royal viceroys on one side of Plaça del Rei, and in 1596 the present main façade was added to the **Generalitat**, in an Italian Renaissance style. The Church built lavishly, with baroque convents and churches along La Rambla, of which the **Betlem** from 1680-1729, at the corner of C/Carme, is the most important survivor. Later baroque churches include **Sant Felip Neri** (1721-52) and **La Mercè** (1765-75).

Another addition, after the siege of Barcelona in 1714, was new military architecture, since the city was encased in ramparts and fortresses. Examples remain in the **Castell de Montjuïc**, the buildings in the **Ciutadella** – one, curiously, the Catalan parliament – and the **Barceloneta**.

A more positive eighteenth-century alteration was the conversion of the Rambla into an urbanised promenade, begun in 1775 with the demolition of Jaume I's second wall. Neo-classical palaces were built alongside: **La Virreina** and the **Palau Moja** (at the corner of Portaferrisa) both date from the 1770s. Also from that time but in a less classical style is the **Gremial dels Velers** (Candlemakers' Guild) at Via Laietana 50, with its two-coloured stucco decoration.

It was not, however, until the closure of the monasteries in the 1820s and 1830s that major rebuilding on the Rambla could begin. Most of the first constructions that replaced them were still in international, neo-classical styles. The site that is now the **Mercat de la Boqueria** was first remodelled in 1836-40 as Plaça Sant Josep to a design by Francesc Daniel Molina based on the English Regency style of John Nash. It's now buried beneath the 1870s market building, but its Doric colonnade can still be detected.

Molina also designed the **Plaça Reial**, begun in 1848. Other fine examples from the same era are the collonaded **Porxos d'en Xifré**, the 1836 blocks opposite the Llotja on Passeig Isabel II.

In the 1850s, Barcelona was able to expand physically, with the demolition of the walls, and psychologically, with economic expansion and the cultural reawakening of the Catalan *Renaixença*. The stage was set for it to spread into the great grid of Ildefons Cerdà's **Eixample** (*see also page 23*).

Cerdà's most visionary ideas were largely lost; however, the construction of the Eixample saw the refinement of a specific type of building: the apartment block, with giant flats on the *principal* floor (first above the ground), often with large glassed-in galleries for the drawing room, and smaller flats above. The area's growth also provided perfect conditions for the pre-eminence of the most famous of Catalan architectural styles, *Modernisme*.

Modernisme

The late nineteenth century was a time of uncertainty in the arts and architecture across Europe. The huge expansion of cities, dramatic social upheavals and new political pressures all created special tensions, while the introduction of new materials such as iron and steel demanded a new architectural language. As the end of the century approached, the movement known in French and English as art nouveau emerged, encompassing some of these concerns and contradictions.

International interest in Gaudí has often eclipsed the fact that the branch of art nouveau seen in Catalonia, *Modernisme* (always confusing, since 'modernism' in English usually refers to twentieth-century functional styles), was quite distinct in its ideas and its products, and also that the style was perhaps more widely accepted in Barcelona than in any other city in Europe.

It developed out of the general renaissance of Catalan culture. Influenced, like other forms of art nouveau, by Ruskin, William Morris and the Arts and Crafts movement, French Symbolism and other international currents, *Modernisme* was also a self-consciously indigenous expression that made use of its own Catalan traditions of design and craftwork. *Modernista* architects, as the name suggests, sought to function entirely within the modern world – hence their experimental use of iron and glass – but also to revalue distinctly Catalan traditions – and so showed enormous interest in the Gothic of the Catalan Golden Age.

Modernisme was also a very wide-ranging and flexible movement. It admitted the coexistence of Gothic revivalism, floralising and decoration to the point of delirium, rationalist machine worship and the most advanced, revolutionary expressionism. *Modernistes* also sought to integrate fine and decorative arts, and so gave as much weight to furniture or glasswork as to painting, sculpture or architecture.

Modernista architecture was given a decisive boost by the buildings for the Universal Exhibition of 1888, most of which were by Lluís Domènech i Montaner (1850-1923). Most no longer exist, notably the 'International Hotel' on the Moll de la Fusta built in under 100 days, but one that remains is the 'Castle of the Three Dragons' in the Ciutadella, once the exhibition restaurant and now the **Museu de Zoologia**. It already showed many key features of Modernist style: the use of structural ironwork allowed greater freedom in the creation of openings, arches and windows, and plain brick, instead of the stucco previously applied to most buildings in Barcelona, was used in an exuberantly decorative manner. As further decoration there is an eclectic mix of neo-Moorish and medieval motifs in terracotta and glazed tiles.

Domènech was one of the first Modernist architects to develop the idea of the 'total work', working closely with craftsmen and designers on every aspect of a building – ornament, lighting, glass. His greatest creations are the **Hospital de Sant Pau**, built as small 'pavilions' within a garden to avoid the usual effect of a monolithic hospital, and the fabulous **Palau de la Música Catalana**, an extraordinary display of outrageous decoration.

After Domènech and Gaudí, third in the trio of leading Modernist architects was Josep Puig i Cadafalch (1867-1957), who showed a strong neo-Gothic influence in such buildings as his *Casa de les Punxes* ('House of Spikes', officially the **Casa Terrades**) in the Diagonal, combined with many traditional Catalan touches. These are the famous names of *Modernista* architecture, but there were many others, for the style caught on with extraordinary vigour throughout Catalonia. Some of the most engaging are the least known internationally, such as Gaudí's assistant Josep Maria Jujol, who in his own name built some remarkable, sinuous buildings in Sant Joan Despí, west of Barcelona.

Catalan Modernist creativity was at its peak for about 20 years, from 1888 to 1908, during which time an extraordinary amount of work was produced, large and small. The Eixample is the style's foremost display case, with the greatest concentration of art nouveau in Europe (the Ajuntament's *Quadrat d'Or* book is a good architectural guide), but *Modernista* buildings and details can be found in innumerable other locations around Barcelona and Catalonia: in streets behind the Paral.lel or villas on Tibidabo, in shop interiors or dark hallways, in country town halls or the *cava* cellars of the Penedès. For a walk taking in some of the lesser-known features of the *Modernista* Eixample, *see page 77*.

The twentieth century

By the 1900s *Modernisme* had become too extreme for the Barcelona middle class, and the later buildings of Gaudí, for example, were met with derision. The new 'proper' style for Catalan architecture was *Noucentisme*, which stressed the importance of classical proportions. However, it failed to produce anything of much note: the main buildings that survive are those of the 1929 Exhibition – also the excuse for the bizarre neo-baroque **Palau Nacional**.

The 1929 Exhibition also brought to Barcelona, though, one of the most important buildings of the century: Mies van der Rohe's German Pavilion, the **Pavelló Barcelona**. Even today it is modern in its challenge to conventional ideas of space, and its impact at the time was extraordinary. The famous Barcelona chair was designed for this building, which was rebuilt to its original design in 1986.

Mies had a strong influence on the main new trend in Catalan architecture of the 1930s, which, reacting against *Modernisme* and nearly all earlier Catalan styles, was emphatically functionalist. Its leading figures were Josep Lluis Sert and the GATCPAC collective, who struggled to introduce the ideas of their friend Le Corbusier and the 'International Style'. Under the Republic Sert built a sanatorium off C/Tallers, and the **Casa Bloc**, a workers' housing project at Passeig Torres i Bages 91-105 in Sant Andreu. In 1937 he also built the Spanish Republic's pavilion for that year's Paris Exhibition, since rebuilt in Barcelona as the **Pavelló de la República** in Vall d'Hebron. Sert's finest work, however, came much later, in the **Fundació Joan Miró**, built in the 1970s after he had spent years in exile in the USA.

Barcelona's third style

The Franco years had an enormous impact on the city: as the economy expanded at breakneck pace in the 1960s, Barcelona received a massive influx of migrants, in a context of unchecked property speculation and minimal planning controls. The city was thus surrounded by endless high-rise suburbs. Another legacy of the era are some ostentatiously tall office blocks, especially on the Diagonal and around Plaça Francesc Macià.

Saint Gaudí

Seen as the genius of the *Modernista* movement, Antoni Gaudí was really a one-off, an unclassifiable figure. His work was a product of the social and cultural context of the time, but also of his own unique perception of the world, together with a typically Catalan devotion to anything specifically Catalan. His two great colleagues in Modernism, Domènech and Puig, were public figures who took an active part in politics and many other fields; Gaudí, after being fairly sociable as a youth, became increasingly eccentric, leading a semi-monastic existence, enclosed in his own obsessions.

Born in Reus in 1852, he qualified as an architect in 1878. His first architectural work was as assistant to Josep Fontseré on the building of the **Parc de la Ciutadella** during the 1870s. The gates and fountain of the park are attributed to him, and around the same time he also designed the lamp-posts in the **Plaça Reial**. His first major commission was for the **Casa Vicens** in 1883-8. An orientalist fantasy, it is structurally fairly conventional, but his control of the use of surface material already stands out in its exuberant neo-Moorish decoration, multi-coloured tiling and superbly elaborate ironwork on the gates. The **Col.legi de les Teresianes** convent school, undertaken in 1888-9, is more restrained still, but the clarity and fluidity of the building, with its simple finishes and use of light, is very appealing.

An event of crucial importance in Gaudí's life came in 1878, when he met Eusebi Güell, heir to one of the largest industrial fortunes in Catalonia. Güell had been impressed by some of Gaudí's early furniture, and they also discovered they shared many religious ideas, on the socially redemptive role of architecture and (for Güell) philanthropy. Güell placed such utter confidence in his architect that he was able to work with complete liberty. He produced several buildings for his patron, beginning with the **Palau Güell** (1886-8), a darkly impressive, historicist building that established Gaudí's reputation, and including the crypt at **Colònia Güell**, one of his most structurally experimental and surprising buildings.

In 1883 Gaudí first became involved in the design of the temple of the **Sagrada Família**, begun the previous year. He would eventually devote himself entirely to this work. Gaudí was profoundly religious, and an extreme Catholic conservative; part of his obsession with the building was a belief that it would help redeem Barcelona from the sins of secularism and the modern era (some conservative Catalan Catholics are currently proposing that he should be made a saint). From 1908 until his death he worked on no other projects, often sleeping on site, a shabby, white-haired hermit, producing visionary ideas that his assistants had to 'interpret' into drawings (on show in the museum alongside). If most of his modern admirers were to meet him they would probably say he was mad, but this strange figure would have an immense effect on Barcelona.

The Sagrada Família became the testing ground for his ideas on structure and form. However, he would see built only the crypt, apse and nativity façade, with its representation of 30 different species of plants. As his work matured he abandoned historicism and developed free-flowing, sinuous expressionist forms. His boyhood interest in nature began to take over from more architectural references, and what had previously provided external decorative motifs became the inspiration for the actual structure of his buildings.

In his greatest years, Gaudí combined other commissions with his cathedral. **La Pedrera** or **Casa Milà**, begun in 1905, was his most complete project. In a prime location on a corner of Passeig de Gràcia, it has an aquatic feel about it: the balconies resemble seaweed, and the undulating façade the sea, or rocks washed by it. Interior patios are in blues and greens, and the roofscape is like an imaginary landscape inhabited by mysterious figures. The **Casa Batlló**, across Passeig de Gràcia, was an existing building remodelled by Gaudí in 1905-7, with a roof resembling a reptilian creature perched high above the street. An essential contribution was made by Gaudí's assistant Josep Maria Jujol, himself a very original *Modernista* architect, and more skilled than his master as a mosaicist.

Gaudí's later work has a dreamlike quality, which makes it unique and personal. His fascination with natural forms found full expression

*The powerful façade of the **Palau Güell**.*

Abstract chimneys: part of the fantastic roofscape of **La Pedrera.**

in the **Parc Güell** of 1900-14. Here he blurs the distinction between natural and built form in a series of colonnades winding up the hill. These seemingly informal paths lead to the surprisingly large central terrace projecting over the hall below, a forest of distorted Doric columns planned as the marketplace for Güell's proposed 'garden city'. The benches of the terrace are covered in some of the finest examples of *trencadís* or broken mosaic work, again mostly by Jujol.

In June 1926, Antoni Gaudí was run over by a tram on the Gran Via. Nobody recognised the down-at-heel old man, and he was taken to a public ward in the old Hospital de Santa Creu in the Raval. When it was discovered who he was, however, Barcelona gave its most famous architect almost a state funeral.

Gaudí in Barcelona

Gaudí left ten buildings in Barcelona. There are also buildings by him nearby at the **Colònia Güell** and **Garraf** (*see p257, p258*).

Casa Batlló *Passeig de Gràcia 43.*
Metro Passeig de Gràcia/bus 7, 16, 17, 22, 24, 28. See p80. **Map** D4
Casa Calvet *C/Casp 48. Metro Urquinaona/bus all routes to Plaça Urquinaona.* An apartment block from 1898-1900, relatively conventional from the outside, but with a more radical interior and fine details typical of Gaudí. **Map** D5/**B-C1**
Casa Vicens *C/Carolines 22.*
Metro Fontana/bus 22, 24, 25, 27, 28, 31, 32.
Not open to the public, but the exterior is very visible from the street. **Map** D2-3

Col.legi de les Teresianes *C/Ganduxer 86-105 (93 212 33 54). FGC Bonanova/bus 14, 16, 70, 72, 74.* **Open** (by appointment only)*Sept-June* 11am-1pm Sat. **Admission** free. **Map** B-C2
Palau Güell *C/Nou de la Rambla 3-5. Metro Liceu/bus 14, 38, 59, 91.* **Open** (guided visits only) 10am-7pm Mon-Fri. Closed public holidays. **Admission** 400ptas; 200ptas over-65s, students; free under-6s. *See p63.* **Map** C6/**A3**
Parc Güell *C/d'Olot. Bus 24, 25.* **Open** *Nov-Feb* 10am-6pm; *Mar, Oct* 10am-7pm; *Apr, Sept* 10am-8pm; *May-Aug* 10am-9pm, daily. *See p84.* **Map** E2
Pavellons de la Finca Güell
Avda Pedralbes 7. Metro Palau Reial/bus 7, 33, 63, 67, 68, 74, 75, 78. The spectacular dragon gates in wrought iron from 1884-7 and the gatehouses on either side were the only parts of the Güell estate built by Gaudí. **Map** A2
La Pedrera *Passeig de Gràcia 92 (93 487 36 13/box office 93 484 59 92). Metro Diagonal/bus 7, 16, 17, 22, 24, 28.* **Guided tours** (English) 6pm Mon-Fri; 11am Sat, Sun, public holidays. **Admission** 600ptas, 350ptas students, over-65s, free under-12s. *See p80.* **Map** D4
Temple Expiatori de la Sagrada Família
C/Mallorca 401 (93 207 30 31). Metro Sagrada Família/bus 10, 19, 33, 34, 43, 44, 50, 51, 101.
Open *Nov-Feb* 9am-6pm; *Mar, Sep-Oct* 9am-7pm; *Apr-Aug* 9am-8pm, daily. Closed pm 25 Dec, 1 Jan. **Admission** 800ptas, 600ptas students; group discounts. *See p81.* **Map** F4
Torre Bellesguard *C/Bellesguard 16-20. Bus 22, 64, 75.* A more than usually Gothic-looking fantasy house built in 1900-2, not open to visitors but visible from the street. To find it, follow C/Sant Joan de la Salle straight up from the Plaça Bonanova.

Hence, when an all-new democratic city administration finally took over the reins of Barcelona at the end of the 1970s, there was a great deal for them to do. Budgets were limited, so it was decided that resources should initially be concentrated not on buildings as such but the gaps in between, the public spaces, with a string of fresh, contemporary parks and squares, many of them incorporating original art work (*see also chapter* **Art Galleries**). From this beginning, Barcelona placed itself in the forefront of international urban design.

Barcelona's renewal programme took on a far more ambitious shape with the award of the 1992 Olympics, helped by a booming economy in the late 1980s. The Games were intended to be stylish and innovative, but most of all to provide a focus for a sweeping renovation of the city, with emblematic new buildings and infrastructure projects linked by clear strategic planning.

The three main Olympic sites – Vila Olímpica, Montjuïc and Vall d'Hebron – are quite different. The **Vila Olímpica** had the most comprehensive masterplan, which sought to extend Cerdà's grid down to the seafront. The main project on **Montjuïc** was the transformation of the existing 1929 stadium, but alongside it there is also Arata Isozaki's **Palau Sant Jordi**, with its space-frame roof. **Vall d'Hebron** is the least successful of the three sites, but Esteve Bonell's **Velòdrom** is one of the finest (and earliest) of the sports buildings, built before the Olympic bid in 1984.

Not content with all the projects completed up to 1992, the city has continued to expand its modern architecture collection ever since, as one major scheme has followed after another. Post-1992 the main focus of activity shifted to the **Raval** and the **Port Vell** (old port), and is now moving on to the Diagonal-Mar area in the north of the city. Many striking buildings are by local architects such as Helio Piñón and Albert Viaplana, whose work combines fluid, elegant lines with a strikingly modern use of materials, from the controversial 1983 **Plaça dels Països Catalans** through daring transformations of historic buildings such as the Casa de la Caritat, now the **Centre de Cultura Contemporània**, and on to all-new projects like **Maremàgnum** in the port. Others are by international names: Richard Meier's bold white **MACBA**, or Norman Foster's **Torre de Collserola** on Tibidabo, which, with the skyscrapers in the Vila Olímpica, has provided new emblems for Barcelona's skyline. One of the latest major acquisitions, the giant-box-like **Auditori**, is by a Madrid-based Spanish architect (a rare thing in Barcelona), Rafael Moneo. Barcelona's dynamic modern architecture has come to represent a 'third style' incorporated into the city's identity, alongside Gothic and *Modernisme* – but far more diffuse and eclectic than either.

The city's audacious approach to urban renewal has also won it unprecedented international praise, not least with the award of the Royal Institute of British Architects' Gold Medal in 1999. With all this acclaim, though, it's perhaps time to point out that amid the work carried out with real imagination and panache Barcelona has also acquired mediocre architecture in the 1990s, and that recently, especially, there has been a growing tendency to rely on an up-and-down 'beige-block' style – quick to build, with no expensive details, but easily forgettable – particularly for many lesser-profile projects: the tourist police station on the Rambla, health centres, the sports centre by Sant Pau del Camp, new hotels, many of the (sometimes even shoddy) new housing blocks in the Raval. Beige blocks also now loom over the Plaça Catalunya – stubbornly the city's centre despite all efforts by planners to displace it – with the dull 1999 **Triangle** mall facing the 1994 façade of the **Corte Inglés**. It could be time to draw breath.

Sleek new space: part of Piñón and Viaplana's **Maremàgnum** *complex.*

Language

Yes, there are two: Matthew Tree, English-born writer in Catalan, gives some reflections on the language of Barcelona.

Happens all the time: you ask a first time visitor from abroad if he or she likes Barcelona (which you pronounce *Bar-sell-owner*), and if this visitor has some knowledge or inkling of Spanish – as loads of people seem to do – chances are he or she will immediately say, 'aha, but isn't the correct pronunciation *Bartha-loner*?'… In Spanish, yes, you say, but you were pronouncing 'Barcelona' the Catalan way, *Bar-sell-owner* – very similar to English, as it happens, and more authentic, rooted and down-home than the Spanish version, to boot – upon hearing which he or she will (very probably) ask, 'So what's all this Catalan business about, then?'

He or she or just about anybody else: after all, Catalan – although still a majority language on its own territory – has not had anything like the lavish PR enjoyed by the transcontinental Spanish language, with the result that of the thirty-five million or so foreigners who visit the Catalan-speaking areas of Europe each year (Spanish Catalonia, French Catalonia, the Balearic Islands, Valencia, Andorra, part of Aragon and one town in Sardinia), a majority are either unaware of the existence of Catalan, or maybe have a vague idea of it as some kind of quaint Mediterranean gobbledegook best left in troll-like isolation. 'Ah', he or she may well go on, 'so it's a dialect, then?'

Nope, it's not a dialect, it's a Romance language (in other words, it is derived from early first millennium colonial Latin), which is closer to French and Provençal than to Spanish and has a strong lexical similarity (87 per cent) to Italian. Catalan has some dialects of its own, notably the western one, spoken in Lleida and Valencia, and the eastern one, spoken everywhere else (including *Bar-sell-owner*), and there are also small variations as you move from town to town, or from the mainland to the islands. This dialectal variety does not mean, though, contrary to what many people – including many Spaniards, unfortunately – seem to assume, that Catalan is a valley patois spoken by a handful of dozy swineherds.

Far from it: Catalan – though still unrecognised in the European Parliament – is spoken by more people than several of the official languages of the EU, such as Finnish and Danish, and Catalan speakers form the largest linguistic community in the whole of Europe without its own national state. The situation of Catalan is therefore a very

different kettle of fish from that of the many other minority languages it tends to be automatically compared to, like Scots Gaelic, Breton or Basque, which – with all due respect to the speakers of those languages – have largely been obliged to retreat to isolated rural areas. Instead, it is a fully-fledged modern tongue in normal daily use in cities, towns and at every level of society, in which conversations can be had about the weather or the latest developments in genetic engineering or whatever else people want to have them about, throughout the length and breadth of its territory (population 10 million, of whom 6.5 million speak Catalan and most of the rest understand it).

SOUNDS IN THE MOUTH

If your visitor is not stifling a chain of yawns – not yet, at least –, he/she may want to know something about what this language sounds like. One of the very few impressionistic descriptions of spoken Catalan in English fiction is to be found in PJ Kavanagh's autobiographical novel from 1966,

Vocabularies: Catalan...

Catalan is a Latin language that's readily comprehensible with a little knowledge of French or Spanish grammar. The extent to which Catalans expect visitors to speak it varies greatly, but it is certainly useful to have some recognition of the language to be able to read signs, understand what's said to you and pronounce place names correctly. Catalan phonetics are significantly different from those of Spanish, with a wider range of vowels and soft consonants. Catalans use the familiar (*tu*) rather than the polite (*vostè*) forms of the second person very freely, but for convenience verbs are given here in the polite form. For food and menu terms, *see pages 134-5*.

Catalan pronunciation: some basics

In Catalan, as in French but unlike in Spanish, words are run together, so *si us plau* (please) is more like *sees-plow*.
à at the end of a word (as in Francesc Macià) is an open **a** rather like when you say **ah**, but very clipped
ç, and **c** before an i or an e, are like a soft **s**, as in sit
c in all other cases is as in cat
unstressed **e**, in a plural such as cerveses (beers), and Jaume I, is a weak sound like centre or comfortable
g, before an i or an e, and **j** are pronounced like the **s** in pleasure; **tg** and **tj** are similar to the **dg** in badge
g after an i at the end of a word (Puig) is a hard **ch** sound, as in watch; **g** in all other cases is as in get
h beginning a word is normally silent
ll is like the **lli** in million
l.l the 'split double-l', most unusual feature of Catalan spelling, refers to a barely audible difference, a slightly stronger stress on a single l sound
o at the end of a word is like the **u** sound in flu;
ó at the end of a word is similar to the **o** in tomato;
ò is like the **o** in hot
A single **r** beginning a word and **rr** are heavily rolled; **r** at the end of a word strengthens the previous vowel but is almost silent, so *carrer* (street) sounds like *carr-ay*
s at the beginning and end of words and
ss between vowels are soft, as in sit
A single **s** between two vowels is a **z** sound, as in lazy
x is like the **sh** in shoe, except in the combination **tx**, which is like the **tch** in watch
y after an **n** at the end of a word or in **nys** is not a vowel but adds a nasal stress and a y-sound to the n

Things everyone here knows

please *si us plau;* **very good/great/OK** *molt bé*
hello *hola;* **goodbye** *adéu;* **open** *obert;* **closed** *tancat*
entrance *entrada;* **exit** *sortida*
nothing at all/zilch *res de res* (said with both s silent)
price *preu;* **free** *gratuït/de franc;* **change, exchange** *canvi;* **llogar** *to rent;* (de) **lloguer** (for) *rent, rental*
up with Barcelona FC *Visca el Barça* (corny, yes, but often good for a cheap laugh)

More expressions

hello (when answering the phone) *hola, digui'm*
good morning, good day *bon dia;* **good afternoon, good evening** *bona tarda;* **good night** *bona nit*
thank you (very much) *(moltes) gràcies*
you're welcome *de res*

do you speak English? *parla anglès?*
I'm sorry, I don't speak Catalan *ho sento, no parlo català;* **I don't understand** *no entenc*
can you say it to me in Spanish, please? *m'ho pot dir en castellà, si us plau?;* **how do you say that in Catalan?** *com se diu això en Català?*
what's your name? *com se diu?*
Sir/Mr *senyor (sr.);* **Madam/Mrs** *senyora (sra.);* **Miss** *senyoreta (srta.);*
excuse me/sorry *perdoni/disculpi;* **excuse me, please** *escolti* (literally 'listen to me'); **OK/fine** *val/d'acord*
enough *prou;* **how much is it** *quant és?*
why? *perquè?;* **when?** *quan?;* **who?** *qui?;* **what?** *què?;* **where?** *on?;* **how?** *com?;* **where is...?** *on és...?;* **who is it?** *qui és?;* **is/are there any...?** *hi ha...?/n'hi ha de...?*
very *molt;* **and** *i;* **or** *o;* **with** *amb;* **without** *sense*
I would like... *vull...* (literally, 'I want'); **how many would you like?** *quants en vol?;* **I don't want** *no vull*
I like *m'agrada;* **I don't like** *no m'agrada*
good *bo/bona;* **bad** *dolent/a;* **well/badly** *bé/malament;* **small** *petit/a;* **big** *gran;* **expensive** *car/a;* **cheap** *barat/a;* **hot** (food, drink) *calent/a;* **cold** *fred/a;* **something** *alguna cosa;* **nothing** *res;* **more** *més;* **less** *menys;* **more or less** *més o menys*
toilet *el bany/els serveis/el lavabo*

Getting around

a ticket *un bitllet;* **return** *d'anada i tornada*
card expired (on Metro cards) *títol esgotat*
left *esquerra;* **right** *dreta;* **here** *aquí;* **there** *allí;* **straight on** *recte;* **at the corner** *a la cantonada;* **as far as** *fins a;* **towards** *cap a;* **near** *a prop;* **far** *lluny;* **is it far?** *és lluny?*

Time

In Catalan quarter- and half-hours can be referred to as quarters of the next hour (so, 1.30 is two quarters of 2)
now *ara;* **later** *més tard;* **yesterday** *ahir;* **today** *avui;* **tomorrow** *demà;* **tomorrow morning** *demà pel matí*
morning *el matí;* **midday** *migdia;* **afternoon** *la tarda;* **evening** *el vespre;* **night** *la nit;* **late night** (roughly 1-6am) *la matinada;* **at what time...?** *a quina hora...?*
in an hour *en una hora;* **the bus will take two hours** (to get there) *l'autobús trigarà dues hores (en arribar)*
at 2 *a les dues;* **at 8pm** *a les vuit del vespre;* **at 1.30** *a dos quarts de dues/a la una i mitja;* **at 5.15** *a un quart de sis/a les cinc i quart;* **at 22.30** *a vint-i-dos-trenta*

Numbers

0 *zero;* **1** *u, un,una;* **2** *dos, dues;* **3** *tres;* **4** *quatre;* **5** *cinc;* **6** *sis;* **7** *set;* **8** *vuit;* **9** *nou;* **10** *deu;* **11** *onze;* **12** *dotze;* **13** *tretze;* **14** *catorze;* **15** *quinze;* **16** *setze;* **17** *disset;* **18** *divuit;* **19** *dinou;* **20** *vint;* **21** *vint-i-u;* **22** *vint-i-dos, vint-i-dues;* **30** *trenta;* **40** *quaranta;* **50** *cinquanta;* **60** *seixanta;* **70** *setanta;* **80** *vuitanta;* **90** *noranta;* **100** *cent;* **200** *dos-cents, dues-centes,* **1,000** *mil;* **1,000,000** *un milló*

Days, months & seasons

Monday *dilluns;* **Tuesday** *dimarts;* **Wednesday** *dimecres;* **Thursday** *dijous;* **Friday** *divendres;* **Saturday** *dissabte;* **Sunday** *diumenge*
January *gener;* **February** *febrer;* **March** *març;* **April** *abril;* **May** *maig;* **June** *juny;* **July** *juliol;* **August** *agost;* **September** *setembre;* **October** *octobre;* **November** *novembre;* **December** *desembre*
spring *primavera;* **summer** *estiu;* **autumn/fall** *tardor;* **winter** *hivern*

…and Spanish

Note that in Catalonia, still more than in the rest of Spain, this language is generally referred to as *castellano* (Castilian), rather than *español*. Like other Latin languages it has different familiar and polite forms of the second person (you). Many young people now use the familiar *tú* most of the time; for foreigners, though, it's always advisable to use the more polite *usted* with anyone you do not know, especially older people. All verbs here are given in the *usted* form. For help in making your way through menus, *see pages 134-5*.

Spanish pronunciation

c, before an i or an e, and **z** are like **th** in thin
c in all other cases is as in cat
g, before an i or an e, and **j** are pronounced with a guttural h-sound that doesn't exist in English – like **ch** in Scottish lo**ch**, but much harder
g in all other cases is as in get
h at the beginning of a word is normally silent
ll is pronounced almost like a **y**
ñ is like **ny** in canyon
A single **r** at the beginning of a word and **rr** elsewhere are heavily rolled

Useful expressions

hello *hola;* **hello** (when answering the phone) *hola, diga*
good morning, good day *buenos días;* **good afternoon, good evening** *buenas tardes;* **good evening** (after dark), **good night** *buenas noches*
goodbye/see you later *adios/hasta luego*
please *por favor;* **thank you (very much)** *(muchas) gracias;* **you're welcome** *de nada*
do you speak English? *¿habla inglés?*
I don't speak Spanish *no hablo castellano*
I don't understand *no entiendo*
can you say that to me in Catalan, please? *¿me lo puede decir en Catalán, por favor?*
what's your name? *¿cómo se llama?*
speak more slowly, please *hable más despacio, por favor;* **wait a moment** *espere un momento*
Sir/Mr *señor (sr.);* **Madam/Mrs** *señora (sra.);* **Miss** *señorita (srta.)*
excuse me/sorry *perdón*
excuse me, please *oiga* (the standard way to attract someone's attention, politely; literally 'hear me')
OK/fine/(or to a waiter) **that's enough** *vale*
where is…? *¿dónde está…?*
why? *¿porqué?;* **when?** *¿cuándo?;* **who?** *¿quién?;* **what?** *¿qué?;* **where?** *¿dónde?;* **how?** *¿cómo?*
who is it? *¿quién es?;* **is/are there any…?** *¿hay…?*
very *muy;* **and** *y;* **or** *o;* **with** *con;* **without** *sin*
open *abierto;* **closed** *cerrado;* **what time does it open/close?** *¿a qué hora abre/cierra?*
pull (on signs) *tirar;* **push** *empujar*
I would like… *quiero…*(literally, 'I want')
how many would you like? *¿cuántos quiere?*
how much is it *¿cuánto es?*
I like *me gusta;* **I don't like** *no me gusta*
good *bueno/a;* **bad** *malo/a;* **well/badly** *bien/mal;*
small *pequeño/a;* **big** *gran, grande;* **expensive** *caro/a;* **cheap** *barato/a;* **hot** (food, drink) *caliente;* **cold** *frío/a.*
something *algo;* **nothing** *nada*
more/less *más/menos;* **more or less** *más o menos*

do you have any change? *¿tiene cambio?*
price *precio;* **free** *gratis;* **discount** *descuento;* **bank** *banco;* **alquilar** to rent; **(en) alquiler** (for) *rent, rental;* **post office** *correos;* **stamp** *sello;* **postcard** *postal;* **toilet** *los servicios*

Getting around

airport *aeropuerto;* **railway station** *estación de ferrocarril/estación de RENFE* (Spanish railways)
Metro station *estación de Metro*
entrance *entrada;* **exit** *salida*
car *coche;* **bus** *autobus;* **train** *tren*
a ticket *un billete;* **return** *de ida y vuelta;* **bus stop** *parada de autobus;* **the next stop** *la próxima parada*
excuse me, do you know the way to…? *¿oiga, señor/señora/etc, sabe cómo llegar a…?*
left *izquierda;* **right** *derecha*
here *aquí;* **there** *allí;* **straight on** *recto;*
to the end of the street *al final de la calle;*
as far as *hasta;* **towards** *hacia;* **near** *cerca;* **far** *lejos*

Accommodation

do you have a double/single room for tonight/one week? *¿tiene una habitación doble/para una persona para esta noche/una semana?*
we have a reservation *tenemos reserva;* **an inside/outside room** *una habitación interior/exterior* **with/without bathroom** *con/sin baño;* **shower** *ducha;* **double bed** *cama de matrimonio;* **with twin beds** *con dos camas;* **breakfast included** *desayuno incluido;* **air-conditioning** *aire acondicionado;* **lift** *ascensor;* **swimming pool** *piscina*

Time

now *ahora;* **later** *más tarde*
yesterday *ayer;* **today** *hoy;* **tomorrow** *mañana;*
tomorrow morning *mañana por la mañana*
morning *la mañana;* **midday** *mediodia;*
afternoon/evening *la tarde;* **night** *la noche;* **late night** (roughly 1-6am) *la madrugada*
at what time…? *¿a qué hora…?;* **at 2** *a las dos;* **at 8pm** *a las ocho de la tarde;* **at 1.30** *a la una y media;* **at 5.15** *a las cinco y cuarto;* **at 22.30** *a veintidos treinta*
in an hour *en una hora;* **the bus will take 2 hours** (to get there) *el autobus tardará dos horas (en llegar)*

Numbers

0 *cero;* **1** *un, uno,una;* **2** *dos;* **3** *tres;* **4** *cuatro;* **5** *cinco;* **6** *seis;* **7** *siete;* **8** *ocho;* **9** *nueve;* **10** *diez;* **11** *once;* **12** *doce;* **13** *trece;* **14** *catorce;* **15** *quince;* **16** *dieciséis;* **17** *diecisiete;* **18** *dieciocho;* **19** *diecinueve;* **20** *veinte;* **21** *veintiuno;* **30** *treinta;* **40** *cuarenta;* **50** *cincuenta;* **60** *sesenta;* **70** *setenta;* **80** *ochenta;* **90** *noventa;* **100** *cien;* **200** *doscientos;* **1,000** *mil;* **1,000,000** *un millón*

Days, months & seasons

Monday *lunes;* **Tuesday** *martes;* **Wednesday** *miércoles;* **Thursday** *jueves;* **Friday** *viernes;* **Saturday** *sábado;* **Sunday** *domingo*
January *enero;* **February** *febrero;* **March** *marzo;* **April** *abril;* **May** *mayo;* **June** *junio;* **July** *julio;* **August** *agosto;* **September** *septiembre;* **October** *octubre;* **November** *noviembre;* **December** *diciembre*
spring *primavera;* **summer** *verano;* **autumn/fall** *otoño;* **winter** *invierno*

The Perfect Stranger: '...the strange, monosyllabic language that twanged around us, sounding as though it consisted of abbreviations...' Spot on, indeed it does, not least because of its short present-tense verb forms (*moc, coc, fot, puc, sap, cloc*; I move, I cook, he/she fucks, I can, he/she knows, I close up) not to mention a plethora of short nouns (*pou, gos, nit, prat, clot*; a well, a dog, night, meadow, a dip in the ground) as well as frequent brusque adjectival endings (*tancat, barat, xop, boig, fotut, inclòs*; closed, cheap, soaked, mad, fucked, included).

It's also true that the common –*ny* ending in Catalan makes a bouncy donging sound that could well be described as a twang (*bony, any, company, empeny, parany*; a bump on the head, a year, companion, effort, a trap), but Kavanagh didn't pick up for some reason on the softer shushing sound of so many Catalan words, such as *xarxa* ('shar-shah': a fishnet, a rail network, or the Internet) or, lord be praised, *xiuxiueig* ('shee-oo-shee-oo-aydge': a whisper). Neither did he mention the clickety-clack sound of many common words (*mica, bonica, pica, recerca*; a little, pretty, a sink, research), nor its unique double-l feature that sounds as if the speakers are flapping their tongues in honey (*lluna, poll, ventall, Lluís, crioll*; moon, a baby chicken, a fan, a man's name, creole).

COMMUNITY RELATIONS

Everything has been pretty simple so far, but it's only a matter of time before your visitor asks the FAQ of Catalan FAQs: 'How do Spanish and Catalan speakers get on together? Isn't there conflict over the issue?' To which the most accurate answer is: amazingly little. Take the capital, which is where the linguistic mix is most in evidence: almost all Barcelonans now understand Catalan and over half speak it, with the result that the monolingual use of Catalan (without Spanish translation) is accepted on or in street signs, road signs, 12,000 new books per year, two daily newspapers, three TV stations, fifteen theatres, most art galleries, most gas and electricity bills and an overwhelming majority of toilet doors. What's more, while a minority of Spanish-speaking parents have resisted the establishment, by the Catalan autonomous government, of Catalan as the main language of instruction in primary schools, surveys have also shown that a clear majority of the area's non-Spanish speakers now regard Catalan as a socially and economically useful language, which they wish to learn. The support of non-Catalan parents was of crucial importance in the passing of local decrees in 1984 and 1992 to ensure that the language would be taught efficiently throughout the school system.

All of which is pretty good going considering that a process of systematic oppression of Catalan that began in the 1700s had been brought to a climax only recently by a Spanish nationalist dictator who ostensibly created the perfect conditions for a major conflict between the original Catalan population and the 1.5 million economic migrants – mainly Spanish-speakers – who turned up in Barcelona in the 1960s. Twenty-five years after the reedy-voiced despot finally breathed his last, however, an area that could have turned into a linguistic Bosnia has instead ended up as an open, fluid, bilingual culture, which nevertheless still has the Catalan language as its prime emblem.

If the visitor is still around, he/she might then ask one last, logical question: how come Catalan has survived so successfully? Italian sociologist Daniele Conversi has dedicated pretty much a whole book to this question (*The Basques, The Catalans, and Spain*, 1997). He concludes that the key factor is Catalans' lack of an ethnic – as opposed to a linguistic – sense of identity. Whereas in some parts of Europe groups of people who speak the same language are capable of murdering each other because the other person's great-grandfather had the wrong surname, Catalans in general hold out the main factor that differentiates them – their language – as the key to integration: learn it (or at least learn to live with it) and you're in. This attitude makes mincemeat of any attempts at creating ethnic divisions and, according to Professor Conversi, is an example the rest of Europe – rotten with racism, as we all know – should consider following.

Catalan is no local code, then, no private lingo for the natives only, no exclusive barrier. Anybody can use it: a few years ago a Canadian friend of this writer, a first-time visitor with more than an inkling of Spanish but just a few phrases of Catalan, had his doubts, but eventually decided to give it a try, just for jolly; he went into a bar and said, loudly and clearly: *Un cafè amb llet, si us plau.* When a large white coffee appeared in front of him a couple of minutes later, he looked up, dumbfounded, and yelled, 'Hey, it works!', as if being able to order something as useful and everyday as a drink in Catalan was some kind of miracle. Which, of course – given the sheaves of centralist laws under which it was supposed to have been stifled long ago – it is.

Barcelona Today

Welcome to utopia?

Barcelona was particularly well-treated by the British in 1999. For the first time in its 150-year history, the Gold Medal of the Royal Institute of British Architects (RIBA) was awarded to a city – Barcelona – rather than an individual architect. And the Blair government's 'Urban Task Force', chaired by Richard Rogers, issued a report recommending that ten British cities be designated to follow 'the Barcelona model' of urban regeneration and sell themselves as exciting, stylish places to live and work.

The RIBA award praised the city for maintaining its historic façades while implementing creative urban design policies. Special mention was made of the commitment of resources by successive Socialist administrations in Barcelona's Ajuntament (City Hall) to work with architects and city planners. The planners were lauded for the attention they paid to urban public spaces, to parks and plazas, to letting in air and light.

'Over the past 20 years the quality of work in Barcelona has successfully married modern interventions and working with the old buildings of the city, so you have many good old and new buildings', said RIBA president David Rock, 'There has been an integration of political imperative with urban design… There's a lesson here for other cities'. For the international architectural and design community, especially, Barcelona has established itself as the number-one city, and this is not only because architects elsewhere would dearly love to see their cities hand out the kind of juicy commissions that have been current in the capital of Catalonia.

MEMORIES

Some of the people most surprised to find Barcelona being held up as a model city are the Catalans who live here, and whose families have been here for generations. For them, memories are still fresh of Barcelona as it was for most of the twentieth century: serious, industrial, a grimy worker's city where the sea was hidden away behind railroad tracks and port facilities, and where the temperature of political life and class struggle often ran high. Barcelona was many kinds of things to many people in the past 100 years – focus of the hopes of the cultured Catalan middle classes who patronised *Modernista* architects, the revolutionary mecca of the anarchists and 1930s idealists – but an internationally

recognised 'model city' was not one of them. Least of all in the previous 40 years, under the iron-fisted rule of the Franco dictatorship.

It was an urban planner named Oriol Bohigas who initiated Barcelona's contemporary renovation with an apparently modest policy of creating new public open spaces, neighbourhood by neighbourhood. As the first post-Franco democratic city administration's head of urban affairs, he slowly began to transform the urban topography. Bohigas understood the exigencies of a limited budget, and his open spaces are almost all cement. They have air and light, but not much green or shade. Perhaps a palm tree or two, and a few bushes. Still, his programme created scores of pocket parks, and – most importantly – enlisted imaginative contemporary architects to give them visual class. There are dirt *petanca* courts for older people who like to bowl, *pipi-cans* where dogs relieve themselves, and bits of playground equipment for kids, like swings and climbing bars. This increase in public space was of immediate, tangible benefit in a city that is one of the most concentrated in the world, crammed in between the hills of Collserola and the sea, packed with cars, and noise, and people.

ONWARD AND ONWARD

At the same time, Bohigas' friend and boss Mayor Pasqual Maragall pursued Barcelona's bid to host the 1992 Olympic Games. When it was announced in 1986 that the city had won the prize, many locals were convinced the whole thing would fall flat on its face, that neither Barcelona nor Spain were up to it. Things worked here then, but slowly. After all, in 1986, it could still take a year to get a phone put in your flat. Nevertheless, all the stops were pulled out, billions were invested in the city and the Games, and Barcelona was remade, opened up to the sea. Barcelona-style-town was born.

The Olympic echo has faded, but the reborn city continues to promote itself without stopping, almost as if it were an addiction. And it's worked, not least in that Barcelona has become colossally popular – with a visible leap at the end of the '90s – as a place to visit. The city received almost three million visitors in 1998, a popularity that has fuelled a rise in hotel prices – by an average of 21 per cent in 1998 – and sometimes made it hard to find a room at all. One reason for the sudden jump in tourist numbers is the result of another piece of determined planning, Barcelona's emphatic effort

to carve out a position as foremost cruise port of the Mediterranean, with all-new harbour terminals. This has brought a new kind of traveller into the throngs on Barcelona's streets, who fly in, stay one night, spend a couple of hours shopping before they board the boat, and then return briefly at the end of the cruise to catch a flight home.

The city's days as a dingy manufacturing centre are history. It still has plenty of large-scale industry, but you'll find it in well-organised locations around the new container terminals and the Zona Franca, near the airport, or in suburban towns. Increasingly, this is a city of service industries and tourism, conferences and conventions.

For those who live here, these changes are a two-edged sword. It's good to have the city open to the sea, to light and air, but the old Barcelona, too, had its charm. As Manuel Vázquez Montalbán, perhaps Barcelona's best-known modern writer, whose Pepe Carvalho detective novels have been translated into 25 languages, has put it, 'until very recently this was a city of contrasts, of layers, almost an archaeological museum. It was a city of workers, of whores in the *Barrio Chino*. A city of the gentlemen of Pedralbes and Passeig de Gràcia, and the horrible city built for immigrants in Bellvitge, and a belt of poverty around the city. Now, more and more, it's a city like a city in Germany or France, somewhere easy to do business'.

One thing that hasn't changed, thankfully, is the tolerance of Catalans for people different to themselves. This has always made the city more open than the rest of Spain. It still is a tolerant city – overall – even though it has its groups of bulletheads who would like things otherwise, and who carry out racist attacks against the growing numbers of North African or Pakistani immigrants. Despite all the political energy expended around Catalan language and identity, the bilingualism of

Barcelona most often enforces a certain admirable civility between its residents. As well as being a visually beautiful city, it's one in which people can live the life they choose. People are even still remarkably tolerant of hordes of tourists.

NOBODY'S PERFECT
Barcelona has its problems. One of the principal points made by the city's foreign admirers is that, by determined, active regeneration of old central districts, it has avoided suburbanisation, the conversion of the city centre into a business, tourist and fun area that's vacated after the last bar closes. It hasn't, not completely. Districts of the old city such as La Ribera or the Raval have ageing, thinning, populations. The objectives of the urban regeneration schemes have to some extent been contradicted by the results of another goal, economic growth: the centre of Barcelona is now an expensive place to live for many young families, unless they move into the unimproved, poverty-row flats that are increasingly taken over by immigrants or young foreigners experiencing the Barcelona life. Where city communities remain in place, incidents have been reported of tenants being offered one-off cash payments to vacate their Barri Gòtic flats, so that the building can be sold and converted into offices or a hotel. More people living out of town adds to the problem of traffic, which, despite a public transport system that's the envy of many cities elsewhere in Europe, is horrendous. Barcelona is one of the most densely populated cities in the world, with an oppressive quantity of cars and motor scooters, and consistently ranks as one of the noisiest.

Nevertheless, Barcelona's way is to fix things rather than just look at them, and the coming years are still full of projects. Economically, Barcelona increasingly begins to look almost unstoppable. And as before, it has a 'big event' to showcase its next stage of growth, the **Fòrum Global de les Cultures**, to be held in 2004, described as an international, non-governmental gathering of the world's cultures, a locally-conceived project of rather questionable usefulness – from the point of view of the rest of the world, not Barcelona's – but which nevertheless seems to be gaining ground. Mayor Joan Clos, Pasqual Maragall's successor, was re-elected in 1999 with a stronger-than-expected showing. He has declared his intention to address the traffic problem, and make further big improvements in public transport. Historically, Barcelona has been a city where not much changes for a long time, and then the city erupts in a fever of big projects and great changes. Its current fever has been going on for quite a while, but, judging by the last elections, its people are not yet ready to settle down with the city they have remade, and want the city's institutions to go on creating, transforming, experimenting and imagining. Stay tuned.

Sightseeing

WISH YOU WERE HERE...
You won´t want to go home. Waiting for you in the port of Barcelona, surrounded by the Mediterranean, full of shops open 365 days a year from 11:00 AM til 11:00 PM. Plus cinemas, restaurants, games, bars and discos. Come and see. Day and night in Maremagnum, the city of the sea.
MAREMAGNUM
OPEN 365 DAYS A YEAR
www.maremagnum.es
MAREMAGNUM®
SHOPS • DRINKS • RESTAURANTS • CINEMAS • GAMES
ODISEA 2000 SL
MAREMAGNUM PLANT
MOLL D'ESPANYA S/
08039 BARCELONA
TEL. 93 225 81 00
FAX 93 225 80 96

Sightseeing

Medieval squares to beaches via spectacular modern projects, sinuous Modernista details and a unique street life – Barcelona has many, many layers.

Time was when the only visitors who came to Barcelona were most likely business people arriving for trade shows, or day trippers in on a rainy day from the beaches to the north and south. This all changed in the 1980s, with the rise of Barcelona as a fashion city – and fashionable city – and all the pre-Olympic promotion of the town. Today, the city's popularity is nothing short of a phenomenon, and in the late '90s, above all, visitor numbers shot up almost by the month.

Barcelona's emphatic self-promotion aside, it's not hard to see why the city has become such a worldwide draw, with its mix of tradition, modernity and style, unique architecture and vivid streetlife. Its compactness makes it an easy city to explore, with many sights within easy walking distance of each other. When places are further afield, an excellent transport system makes them easy to reach (*see pages 282-3*).

Pick up any map of Barcelona and you will see a tightly-packed mass of narrow streets bordered by Avda Paral.lel, the Ciutadella park, Plaça Catalunya and the sea. This is the area that fell within the medieval walls and, until 150 years ago, made up the entire city. At its heart is the **Barri Gòtic** (Gothic Quarter), a body of interconnecting streets and buildings from Barcelona's Golden Age. Its twisting streets grew inside the original Roman wall; then, as Barcelona grew wealthy in the Middle Ages, new communities developed around the Roman perimeter. These areas, La Mercè, **Sant Pere** and **La Ribera**, were brought within the city with the building of the second wall in the thirteenth century. The area south of this wall, on the other side of the river bed later to become the **Rambla**, was the **Raval**, the 'city outside the walls', but enclosed within a third city wall built in the fourteenth century. All of Barcelona's great medieval buildings are within this old walled city, except for a very few – most notably the superb Gothic monastery of **Pedralbes** (*see page 86*) – which when built were in open countryside.

Barcelona grew little between 1450 and 1800. The old walls remained standing, and the city's first modern industries developed inside them. Factories also appeared in small towns on the surrounding plain such as **Gràcia, Sants, Sant Martí** and **Sant Andreu**. The walls finally came down in the 1850s, and Barcelona extended across the plain following Ildefons Cerdà's plan for the **Eixample** (*see also page 23*). With its long, straight streets, this became Barcelona's second great characteristic district, and the location for many of the greatest works of *Modernista* creativity between 1880 and 1914 – although there are others to be found in many parts of the city. Beyond that are the city's traditional green lungs, the mountains of **Montjuïc** and, at the centre of the great ridge of the Serra de Collserola, **Tibidabo**, both towering above Barcelona and providing wonderful views.

Each of Barcelona's traditional districts (*barris*) has its own resilient, often idiosyncratic character. However, since the 1970s the city has undergone an unprecedented physical transformation, in a burst of urban renovation unequalled in Europe. Areas such as **Montjuïc** – with the main stadium

Relaxing Gothic: **Plaça del Pi**. *See page 57.*

Street theatre: La Rambla

One of the first things any visitor to Barcelona does – it's all but inevitable – is to stroll along **La Rambla**, the magnificent mile-long walkway that cuts through the middle of the old city and leads down to the port. This is perhaps Barcelona's most original contribution to urban design, although there has never been anything planned about it. Neatly reversing the modern urban relationship between pedestrian and vehicle, it has often been described as the world's greatest street, and is certainly the definitive stroller's boulevard.

A *rambla* is an urban feature virtually unique to Catalonia, and there is one in most Catalan towns. Originally, the Rambla of Barcelona, like most of its smaller equivalents, was a seasonal river-bed, running along the western edge of the thirteenth-century city, the name deriving from an Arabic word for river-bed, *ramla*. From the Middle Ages to the baroque era a great many churches and convents were built on the other side of this riverbed, some of which have given their names to sections of it: as one descends from Plaça Catalunya, it is successively called Rambla de Canaletes, Rambla dels Estudis (or dels Ocells), Rambla de Sant Josep (or de les Flors), Rambla dels Caputxins and Rambla de Santa Mònica. Hence, the plural is often used – *Rambles*, or **Ramblas** in Spanish and English.

The Rambla also served as the meeting ground for city and country dwellers, for on the other side of these church buildings lay the still scarcely-built-up Raval, 'the city outside the walls', and rural Catalonia. At the fountain on the corner with C/Portaferrissa, once a city gateway, there is an artist's impression in tiles of this space beside the wall, which became a natural market-place. From these beginnings sprang **La Boqueria**, the city's largest market, still on the Rambla today.

The Rambla took on its recognisable present form roughly between 1770 and 1860. The second city wall came down in 1775, and the Rambla was gradually paved and turned into a boulevard. Seats were available to strollers for rent in the late eighteenth century. The avenue acquired its definitive shape after the closure of the monasteries in the 1830s, which made swathes of land available for new building. No longer on the city's edge, the Rambla became a wide path through its heart.

It used to be said it was an obligation for every true Barcelona citizen to walk down the Rambla and back at least once a day. Nowadays, many locals are blasé about the place, and it could well do with fewer multi-national fast-food outlets. The growth in tourist numbers has been met by a positive overdose of human statues – Julius Caesars, Chinese warriors – working at turning the Rambla into a cliché (another growth area has been in pickpockets, so that you need to be at least a little streetwise, and not wander along with open bags dangling at your back). Nevertheless, the avenue remains one of Barcelona's essential attractions. There are many ways of *ramblejant*, going along the Rambla (a specific verb), from a saunter to a purposeful stride, but the best way to get a feel for the place is to take one of the seats at the top of the avenue (for which you pay a few coins) or, more expensively, in a café, and watch the parade go by. An eternal feature of the Rambla is eye contact: people look you in the eye, see what's what, and glance away. It may be personal, or it may not.

As well as having five names, the Rambla is divided into territories. The first part – at the top, by Plaça Catalunya – has belonged by unwritten agreement to groups of men perpetually engaged in a *tertulia*, a classic Iberian half-conversation, half-argument about anything from politics to football. The **Font de Canaletes** drinking fountain is beside them; if you drink from it, the legend goes, you'll return to Barcelona. Here too is where *Barça* fans converge to celebrate their triumphs.

Below this, heading downhill, there are kiosks divided between those selling fauna and those selling flora. Keep walking, past the **Poliorama**

theatre, and on the left is C/Portaferrissa, now a fashionable shopping street, which leads to the cathedral and the Barri Gòtic; to the right, C/Bonsuccès or C/Carme will take you towards the **MACBA** and other attractions of the Raval.

Next comes perhaps the best-loved section of the boulevard, known as *Rambla de les Flors* because of its line of magnificent flower-stalls, open into the night. To the right are the **Virreina** exhibition and information centre, and the superb **Boqueria** market. A little further is the **Pla de l'Os** (or **Pla de la Boqueria**), centre-point of the Rambla, with Liceu Metro and a pavement mosaic created in 1976 by Joan Miró. On the left, where more streets run off into the Barri Gòtic, is the extraordinary **Bruno Quadros** building (1883), with umbrellas on the wall and a Chinese dragon protruding over the street. Almost opposite is the **Liceu** opera, finally reopened after its 1994 fire. Behind it lies

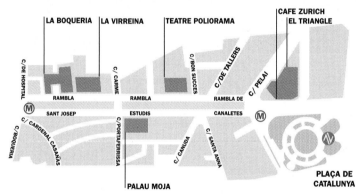

the *Barrio Chino*, traditional home of Barcelona low-life, but now much changed (*see pages 62-3*).

The Rambla de Caputxins is lined with mostly-expensive cafés. The **Café de l'Opera**, opposite the Liceu, is the best (*see page 158*). Further down on the left are C/Ferran, the most direct route to **Plaça Sant Jaume**, and the **Plaça Reial**, with its cafés, restaurants, budget hotels and drunks.

A detour to the right on C/Nou de la Rambla will take you to Gaudí's **Palau Güell**, before the promenade widens into the Rambla de Santa Mònica. Here you hit the stretch that was a thriving prostitution belt. You may still see a few lycra-and-furred transvestites, but official clean-up efforts have greatly reduced the visibility (if not the existence) of street soliciting. A series of renovations, including a 1980s arts centre (the **Centre d'Art Santa Mònica**), have diluted the sleaziness of this part of the Rambla, although this is still one of the areas where you need to be most wary of pick-

pockets and bag-snatchers. Further towards the port and the **Colom** column are the **Museu de Cera** wax museum and, at weekends, stalls selling bric-a-brac and craftwork, alongside fortune-tellers and tarot-readers catering to an incorrigible local interest in all things astrological.

Other 'sights' of the Rambla are the 24-hour newsstands, offering the Spanish and world press and huge amounts of porn. This is where you come to buy a paper late-night or on Sundays. As well as the human statues there will be buskers, clowns, puppeteers, dancers and musicians. There's street theatre of another kind in the shape of the three-card sharpers or hustlers with three walnut shells and a pea under one of them, challenging you to a bet. There's the portrait painter and the caricature painter and the poet selling his wares. In short, all human life is there – along what García Lorca called 'the very spirit of a city'.

When you think this human statue business is getting out of hand...

– the **Port Olímpic** and the **beach** were rebuilt or created from next to nothing for the 1992 Olympics; since then the pace of renovation has not let up, with the spectacular reinvention of the old harbour or **Port Vell**, and attention has now moved on to the Diagonal-Mar project, in the very north of the city. In the process the identities of individual *barris* have been altered, pushed and pulled in many directions, and sometimes changed beyond recognition.

Barcelona has entered squarely into the post-industrial age, as a city with big ambitions, and change is one of its prime characteristics. Most of its factories are now in the **Zona Franca**, the industrial zone between Montjuïc and the airport. Within the city, old factories that had still not moved out have been encouraged to, while the shells of those that did have become art spaces, sports centres, studios, clubs or restaurants. The ultimate aim, according to former Mayor Maragall, has been 'for Barcelona to become a city of services'. Time will tell if it does.

Tourist tickets & discount schemes

Barcelona offers a variety of tour facilities and discount schemes for admission to many attractions: for details of the **Barcelona Card**, **Bus Turístic** and other tours, *see page 58*; for the **Articket**, *see page 90, in chapter* **Museums**. Where discounts apply this is indicated in the listings below with the abbreviations **BC**, **BT** and **Articket**. For more on museums and galleries mentioned in this chapter, *see chapters* **Museums** *and* **Art Galleries**.

Hubs of the city

Plaça Catalunya & Passeig de Gràcia

Map D5/B1. The Plaça Catalunya is the city's centre – despite many plans to replace it – and the point at which the old, once-walled city meets Cerdà's nineteenth-century **Eixample**, the 525 square blocks above it. Most of the Plaça's statues and fountains date from the 1920s, but since the 1980s the square has been repeatedly dug up and relaid to accommodate new traffic patterns. Of late it has also begun to be surrounded by rather monolithic beige-block buildings such as the early-'90s façade of the **Corte Inglés** department store and, opposite, a big new mall, **El Triangle**, opened in 1999. On the Rambla side there is also a giant new **Marks & Spencer's** store, installed in a former bank. The Plaça Catalunya is an obvious city focal point, in that it's a transport hub: many bus routes stop here, including the airport bus; two Metro lines meet; the FGC lines to Tibidabo, Sarrià and the suburbs begin; and it has a mainline (RENFE) railway station serving the airport, the coast to the north and the Montseny and Pyrenees mountains. **Bus Turístic** routes start here (*see p58*), and the *plaça* contains (underground) the very useful main city **tourist office** (*see p294*), on the Corte Inglés side and identified by large red signs with a white *i* on them. Around the *plaça* are plenty of pavement cafés, with their attendant buskers. The most strategically-sited is the **Cafè Zurich**, at the top of the Rambla in one corner of the Triangle building. It's really a simulation of the historic café that until 1997

...there's always flower stalls to admire. Life on **La Rambla**. *See pages 50-1.*

stood on this site, built within the new mall, but has quickly become a magnet for tourists and locals.

Stretching away from the square down towards the sea are Barcelona's most famous avenue, the **Rambla**, and the **Portal de l'Angel**, a popular shopping street and another gateway to the **Barri Gòtic**. On the inland side is the **Passeig de Gràcia**, main thoroughfare of the Eixample. Along it are two of Gaudí's greatest works, **La Pedrera** and the **Casa Batlló**, and on either side the long, straight streets are full of *Modernista* gems. Parallel to Passeig de Gràcia is **Rambla Catalunya**, the *Rambla* of the Eixample, with more cafés. Back on the Passeig itself, halfway up, is Passeig de Gràcia RENFE station, stopping-point for long-distance trains and services to Castelldefels and Sitges. At the top, Passeig de Gràcia crosses the great avenue of the **Diagonal** to disappear into the attractive old town of **Gràcia**. From here the Diagonal, longest single street in Europe, runs left up to **Plaça Francesc Macià**, the modern business centre of Barcelona and a fashionable shopping area, and to the right down to Plaça de les Glòries and the sea.

Plaça d'Espanya

Map A-B5. The Plaça d'Espanya is the main entrance route to the park of **Montjuïc** and the **Palau Nacional,** home of the **Museu Nacional d'Art de Catalunya (MNAC)** (*see pp94-5*). Like the Palau the *plaça* itself was created for Barcelona's last great international jamboree before the Games of 1992, the Exhibition of 1929. Today most of the original Exhibition area is occupied by the **Fira de Barcelona**, the city's Trade Fair. Montjuïc also

provided the most important of the Olympic sites for 1992, the '**Olympic Ring**', with the **Estadi Olímpic** and **Palau Sant Jordi** indoor sports hall, and is the location of several more museums and cultural venues. From Plaça d'Espanya a 61 bus will take you up the hill to the Olympic Ring, the **Fundació Miró**, or, nearer the bottom, the **Poble Espanyol** and the **Casaramona**, a *Modernista* factory from 1911 under conversion into a cultural centre. Giant escalators have also been installed alongside the steps up to the Palau Nacional, giving easy access to the top of the hill, and another way up is to take the **Funicular** from another side of Montjuïc, by Paral.lel Metro. Not to be missed is a summer evening visit, when the **Font Màgica**, the giant illuminated fountain, dances elegantly to sometimes-cheesy music (*see p75*).

The Plaça d'Espanya also has a train station, for the FGC line to western Catalonia and Montserrat, and the airport bus stops here. Along the foot of Montjuïc, Avda Paral.lel leads back to the port area, while on the opposite side of the Plaça C/Tarragona – with, on one side, the **Parc de l'Escorxador**, containing an obelisk by Miró (*see p83*) – runs up to Barcelona's main rail station in Sants, and C/Creu Coberta leads straight into the *barri* of Sants.

Plaça de les Glòries

Map F5. In Ildefons Cerdà's original 1859 plan for the Eixample it was intended that this square should eventually become the centre of Barcelona. For most of the time since then it's been a hub more in potential than reality, an unlovely traffic junction; only in the last few years, almost semi-accidentally,

Visit us at the Palau Robert, the best place in Barcelona for getting to know **Catalonia**

Exhibitions, bookshop, interactive information terminals, staffed information desk, etc.

Palau Robert

Catalan Tourism

Information Centre

Passeig de Gràcia, 107

08008 Barcelona

Tel. 93 238 40 00

Fax 93 238 40 10

www.gencat.es/probert

Opening times

From Monday to Saturday

from 10 a.m. to 7.30 p.m.

Sundays from 10 a.m. to 2.30 p.m.

How to arrive:

Underground: lines 3 & 5

(Diagonal Station)

Ferrocarrils de la Generalitat:

(Railway) Provença Station

Bus: 6, 7, 15, 16, 17, 22, 24,

28, 33, 34, 68 & T1

Generalitat de Catalunya
Government of Catalonia

The rapid tour

If you've only a short time in Barcelona, these highlights could be enjoyed in a (very intensive) two-day tour. Any selection is, of course, a personal matter – this one provides several options. To get around quickly, the **Bus Turístic** (*see page 58*) is very helpful.

Day 1

• **La Rambla**. A natural starting point.
• From the Miró mosaic, walk into the **Barri Gòtic** via **Plaça del Pi**. Wander on to Avda Catedral, and through the Roman gate in Plaça Nova. Take a look at the **cathedral cloister** and go on to **Plaça del Rei**. Visit the **Museu d'Història de la Ciutat** for its subterranean Roman excavations, and the medieval **Palau Reial**. Continue to **Plaça Sant Jaume**.
• Down C/Llibreteria and across Via Laietana to explore **La Ribera** and **C/Montcada**, with the **Museu Picasso**, its medieval palaces and other museums; **Santa Maria del Mar**, the finest single building in Barcelona; and the district's bars, on Montcada, the **Passeig del Born** or in front of the church on **Plaça Santa Maria**.
• Metro from Jaume I to the **Port Olímpic** (great for a waterside lunch) and the **beaches**.
• Suitably rested, wander back through **Barceloneta** to join the evening crowds around **Port Vell** and **Maremàgnum**. Kids and others love the **Aquàrium**. If that's not enough, go to a concert at the **Palau de la Música Catalana**.

Day 2

There are too many architectural and artistic highlights for one day, so choices are involved.
• Contemporary art fans should wander into the Upper Raval to the **MACBA**, and the **CCCB** alongside. The area also has more funky bars.
• Essential: from Plaça Catalunya, walk up **Passeig de Gràcia**. Take a look at the **Mansana de la Discòrdia**, with **Casa Morera** and Gaudí's **Casa Batlló**. Visit **La Pedrera**.
• Metro from Diagonal to the **Sagrada Família**
• Cab or Bus Turístic to the **Parc Güell**.
• Cab or Bus Turístic to Av Tibidabo FGC stop, and **Tramvia Blau** up **Tibidabo**, for breathtaking views from its bars and restaurants. Or continue up on the **funicular** to the **funfair** and **Torre de Collserola**, for still wider views.
• Options: for historic art and architecture lovers, the **Monestir de Pedralbes** and **Col.lecció Thyssen**; for sports fans, the **Nou Camp**.
• **Plaça d'Espanya**, to climb **Montjuïc**. More options: the **MNAC** for Romanesque murals, **Fundació Miró** for contemporary art. Then the **Anella Olímpica** buildings, and **Miramar** for more views, especially at sunset. Bus back to Plaça d'Espanya to be awestruck by the **Font Màgica**. And to have a rest in a bar alongside.

have some of Cerdà's ideas for it finally begun to take shape. Next to it there are now several newly-built major cultural projects, the **Teatre Nacional**, the **Auditori** concert-hall and a historical archive, the **Arxiu de la Corona d'Aragó**; there is also the vast **Barcelona Glòries** shopping mall. The extension of the Diagonal to the sea and development of the Diagonal-Mar area will increase this area's importance in future. More traditionally, Glòries is the location of **Els Encants** flea market, and is already of interest to drivers, as the site of the **Metro-Park** park-and-ride car park (*see p285*).

Barri Gòtic

In the first century BC Roman soldiers established a colony on a small hill called the *Mons Taber*, the precise centre of which was long believed to have been marked by a round millstone set into the paving of the Carrer Paradis, between the cathedral and the Plaça Sant Jaume. The real centre of the Roman city, however, was a road junction that occupied one part of the modern Plaça Sant Jaume. Large sections of the Roman wall can still be seen (*see page 56* **Walk 1:** *Barcino*).

When Barcelona began to revive under the Catalan Counts, its social and political core stayed where it had been under the Romans. As a result, it became the site of what is now one of the most complete surviving ensembles of medieval buildings – from churches to private residences – in Europe.

The Gothic **cathedral** is the third one built on the same site; the first was in the sixth century. Many buildings around here represent history written in stone. In C/Santa Llúcia, just in front of the cathedral, is **Ca de l'Ardiaca**, a fifteenth-century residence, with superb tiled patio, which now houses the city archives. It was renovated recently, and before that in the 1870s, when it acquired its curious letterbox by the *Modernista* architect Domènech i Montaner showing swallows and a tortoise, said to symbolise the contrast between the swiftness of truth and 'the law's delay'. On the north side of the cathedral in Plaça Sant Iu is the **Museu Frederic Marès**, with a Gothic courtyard hosting a café in summer that's one of the best places in the city on a hot day, the massive stone having a wonderfully cooling effect.

Alongside the cathedral the Catalan monarchs built the various sections of their Royal Palace, clustered around the **Plaça del Rei**. Most of them now form part of the **Museu d'Història de la Ciutat**. Even after Catalonia lost its indigenous monarchy in the fifteenth century, this complex was still the seat of the Viceroys who governed the country. Local civil administration, meanwhile, was centred in the nearby **Generalitat** and **Ajuntament**, which before the opening of **Plaça Sant Jaume** in the 1820s faced onto the Carrers Bisbe and Ciutat.

Walk 1: *Barcino*

Medieval Barcelona and all subsequent buildings in the Barri Gòtic were constructed on top of Roman *Barcino*, founded in 15 BC, and many a local resident has set out to makeover a bathroom and turned up a bit of ancient masonry. The original Roman city was only a second-rank outpost, covering just 10 hectares (24 acres). Some of its street plan can be seen in the extraordinary remains beneath the **Museu d'Història de la Ciutat** (*see pages 60, 102*), the largest underground excavation of a Roman site in Europe. *Barcino* has had an unappreciated impact on every subsequent era: many of Barcelona's most familiar streets – C/Hospital, even Passeig de Gràcia – follow the line of Roman roads. The best way to get an idea of the Roman town is to walk the line of its walls, where all kinds of Roman remains can be found, poking out from where they were re-used or

built over by medieval and later builders (this walk is marked in **red** on Maps 7-8, *pages 316-7*).

Barcino's central axis was the junction of C/Llibreteria and C/Bisbe, now a corner of Plaça Sant Jaume. **Llibreteria** began life as the *Cardus Maximus*, the main road to Rome; walk down it, and at **C/Tapineria** turn left to reach **Plaça Ramon Berenguer el Gran** and the largest surviving stretch of ancient wall, incorporated into the medieval Palau Reial. Continue on along Tapineria, where there are many sections of Roman building, to **Avda Catedral**. The massive twin-drum gate on C/Bisbe, when often retouched, in its basic shape has not changed since it was the main gate of the Roman town. To its left are fragments of aqueduct. If you take a detour up C/Capellans to **C/Duran i Bas**, you can see another four arches of an aqueduct; nearby in **Plaça Vila de Madrid** are tombs from the ancient cemetery, which in accordance with Roman custom had to be outside the city walls.

Returning to the cathedral, turn right into **C/de la Palla**. A little way along a large chunk of wall is visible, only discovered when a building was demolished in the 1980s. Palla runs into **C/Banys Nous**, where at No.16 there is a centre for disabled children that has inside it a piece of wall with a relief of legs and feet (try to phone ahead, 93 318 14 81, for a viewing time). Beyond there is the junction with **C/Call**, the other end of the *Cardus*,

and so the opposite side of the Roman town from Llibreteria-Tapineria. The owners of the shoe shop at C/Call 1 are used to people wandering in to examine their piece of Roman tower. Carry on across C/Ferran and down **C/Avinyó**, next continuation of the perimeter. At the back of the Pakistani restaurant at No.19 there is a cave-like space that once again incorporates portions of Roman wall. At Plaça Milans, turn left onto **C/Gignás**: by the junction with **C/Regomir** there are remains of the fourth sea gate of the town, which would have faced the beach, and the Roman shipyard. On Regomir there is also one of the most important relics of *Barcino*, the **Pati Llimona**. After visiting there, walk up **C/Correu Vell**, with more fragments of wall, to reach one of the most impressive relics of Roman Barcelona in the small, shady **Plaça Traginers** (*pictured*) – a Roman tower, one corner of the ancient wall, in a remarkable state of preservation, despite having had a medieval house built on top of it. Turn up **C/Sots-Tinent Navarro** – with a massive stretch of Roman rampart – to complete the circuit back at Llibreteria, and maybe head back to *Barcino*'s centre and the **Temple of Augustus**.

Pati Llimona

C/Regomir 3 (93 268 47 00). Metro Jaume I/bus 17, 40, 45. **Open** 8am-10pm Mon-Fri; 10am-2pm Sat, Sun; *exhibitions* 10am-2pm, 4-8pm, Mon-Fri; 10am-2pm Sat, Sun. **Admission** free. **Map** D5
One of the oldest continually-occupied sites in Barcelona, incorporating part of a round tower that dates from the first Roman settlement, and later Roman baths. The excavated foundations are visible from the street, through large windows. Most of the building above is a fifteenth-century aristocratic residence, converted into a social centre in 1988.

Temple d'August
(Temple of Augustus)

C/Paradis 10 (Information Museu d'Història de la Ciutat, 93 315 11 11). Metro Jaume I/bus 17, 40, 45. **Open** 10am-2pm, 4-8pm, Tue-Sat; 10am-2pm Sun, public holidays. **Admission** free. **Map** D5
The Centre Excursionista de Catalunya (a hiking club) contains four fluted Corinthian columns that formed the rear corner of this temple, built in the first century BC as the hub of the town's Forum.

*Essence of Gothic: from the **Generalitat**, and the **Cathedral** cloister. See pages 60-1.*

The district's ancientness is very genuine, but the idea of it as a 'Gothic Quarter' is a fairly recent invention, from the 1920s. To help the image stick, a few touches were made to enhance the area's Gothic-ness. One of the most-photographed features of the Barri Gòtic, the 'Bridge of Sighs' across C/Bisbe from the Generalitat, was actually a completely new addition, from 1928.

A great part of the charm of the Barri Gòtic and areas around it lies in the way in which you can discover some of their ancient corners almost by accident, apparently half-forgotten amid later building. Right next to the noise of Plaça Catalunya is the marvellous little Romanesque church of **Santa Anna**, begun in 1141 as part of a monastery then outside the walls, and with an exquisite fourteenth-century cloister; nearby, in the sorely mistreated **Plaça Vila de Madrid**, there are some excavated Roman tombs (*see left*). If you walk from Plaça Sant Jaume up C/Ciutat, to the left of the Ajuntament, and turn down the narrow alley of C/Hércules you will come to **Plaça Sant Just**, a fascinating old square with a Gothic water fountain from 1367 and the grand church of **Sants Just i Pastor**, built in the fourteenth century on the site of a chapel founded by Charlemagne's son Louis the Pious.

The narrow streets bounded by Carrers Banys Nous, Call and Bisbe once housed a rich Jewish

Call or ghetto (*see page 17*). Today the area is best known for its antique shops. To walk around this area is to delight in what is perhaps the most satisfying and peaceful part of the Barri Gòtic. Near the centre of the Call is the beautiful little square of **Sant Felip Neri**, with a fine baroque church and a soothing fountain in the centre. On C/Banys Nous, the old **Portalón** *bodega* still offers cheap meals in an increasingly expensive area.

Close by are the leafily attractive **Plaça del Pi** and **Plaça Sant Josep Oriol**, where there are some great pavement bars, and painters exhibit work at weekends. The squares are separated by **Santa Maria del Pi**, one of Barcelona's most distinguished – but least visited – Gothic churches, with a magnificent rose window. Another attraction of the streets between the Rambla and Via Laietana is the wonderful variety of their shops, from the oldest in Barcelona to smart modern arcades. The **C/Portaferrissa** is one of the city's most popular shopping streets, with street-trendy shops in places like the **Gralla Hall** mini-mall.

Despite the expansion of Barcelona into the Eixample, the old centre has remained a hub of cultural, social and political life. In a narrow street off Portal de l'Angel, C/Montsió, is the **Quatre Gats** café, legendary haunt of Picasso and other artists and bohemians. Between C/Portaferrissa and Plaça del Pi lies C/Petritxol, one of the most

Ways to see the city

Transport & discount schemes

Another scheme, the **Articket**, is a joint entry ticket for seven major arts centres (*see page 90*). For tourist offices, *see pages 294-5*; for regular city transport, *see pages 282-4*.

Barcelona Card

Rates *Adults* 2,500ptas 24 hours; 3,000ptas 48 hours; 3,500ptas 72 hours. *Children aged 6-15* 2,000ptas 24 hours; 2,500ptas 48 hours; 3,000ptas 72 hours.
Discount scheme run by the city tourist authority: for the time stipulated the card gives you unlimited transport on Metro and buses, and discounts on the airport bus, entry to a wide variety of attractions and at some shops and restaurants (a current list comes with the card). It is sold at city **tourist offices** or via **Tel-entrada** (*see p215*). When Barcelona Card discounts are available at museums or other attractions this is indicated in this Guide with the letters **BC**. Another scheme, **Barcelona Pass**, must be ordered via travel agents. Inquire when booking.

Bus Turístic (Tourist Bus)

Dates Mar-Jan. **Frequency** *Mar-June, Oct-Jan* every 30 min, *June-Sept* every 15min, 9am-7.40pm daily. **Tickets** *1 day* 1,800ptas, 1,100ptas 4-12s; *2 days* 2,300ptas; free under-4s. **No credit cards**.
A special sightseeing bus service with two circular routes, both running through Plaça Catalunya: the northern (red) route passes La Pedrera, Sagrada Família, Parc Güell, Tibidabo and Pedralbes; the southern (blue) route takes in Montjuïc, Port Vell, Vila Olímpica and the Barri Gòtic. With one ticket you can get on and off buses on either route as many times as you like the same day. Buses have multilingual guides, and most are adapted for wheelchairs. Tickets are bought at city **tourist offices**, transport offices (*see p283*) or on the buses themselves. Ticket-holders have discount vouchers for another big range of attractions (which need not be used the same day). Where these discounts apply this is shown in this Guide with the letters **BT**.

Barcelona Moon Express

Dates & times *July-Sept* 10pm-2am daily.
Tickets 700ptas. **No credit cards. Map** D5/B1
A night-time tour from Plaça Catalunya past Passeig de Gràcia, the Rambla, Port Vell and Barri Gòtic. You can get on and off the trolleys – pulled by a truck disguised as a steam loco – as many times as you like the same night.

Rodamolls

Dates & times *Easter-21 June, 14 Sept-Oct/Nov* 11am-11pm Sat, Sun; *22 June-13 Sept* 11am-11pm daily. **Tickets** 400ptas; 300ptas under-11s.
Discounts BT. **No credit cards.**

The 'quay-wanderer' is another special bus service that follows a route around the port area, from Colom to Port Olímpic and back.

Tours

Barcelona by Bicycle

C/Esparteria 3 (93 268 21 05). Metro Barceloneta/ bus 14, 17, 39, 40, 45, 51. **Tours** 10am Sat, Sun; 8.30pm Tue, Sat. Group tours also available.
Prices *day tours* 2,500ptas; *evening tours* 5,500ptas. **No credit cards. Map** D-E6/**C3-4**
Un Cotxe Menys cycle shop (*see p285*) offers tours of the city, bike hire included, with English-speaking guides: day tours (snack included) last 2½ hours, evening trips (meal included) 3½. Booking essential.

Bus tours

Julià Tours *Ronda Universitat 5 (93 317 64 54). Metro Universitat/bus all routes to Plaça Universitat.* **Open** 9.30am-1pm, 3.30-7pm, daily. **Tickets** 4,750ptas. **No credit cards. Map** C5/**A1**
Pullman Tours *Gran Via de les Corts Catalanes 635 (93 317 12 97). Metro Passeig de Gràcia/bus 7, 18, 50, 54, 56.* **Open** 9.30am-1pm, 3.30-7pm, daily. **Tickets** 4,750ptas. **No credit cards. Map** D5
Classic coach tours with multilingual guides.

Museu d'Història tours

Information: Museu d'Història de la Ciutat *C/Veguer 2 (93 315 11 11). Metro Jaume I/bus 17, 19, 40, 45.* **Tours** *Nit al Museu* 9pm, 9.30pm, Tue, Wed; *Ruta del Gòtic* (phone to confirm) 10am Thur, Sat. **Tickets** *Nit al Museu* 1,000ptas; *Ruta del Gòtic* 1,000ptas; discounts students, 6-12s, over-65s. **No credit cards. Map** D6/**B3**
One of the most enterprising of Barcelona museums is the focus for several interesting tours, especially *Una Nit al Museu*, a great night tour around the buildings of Plaça del Rei. Timings and programmes change, so always check at the museum.

Ruta del Modernisme

Information & sales: *Centre del Modernisme, Casa Morera, Passeig de Gràcia 35 (93 488 01 39). Metro Passeig de Gràcia/bus all routes to Passeig de Gràcia.* **Open** 10am-7pm Mon-Sat; 10am-3pm Sun. **Tickets** 600ptas; 400ptas students, over-65s; free under-10s. **No credit cards. Map** D5
Multi-access ticket giving discounts on entry to *Modernista* buildings (and at some restaurants); a guidebook is available, and guided tours are often included. Tickets are valid 30 days. The starting point, **Casa Morera**, is a Modernist gem (*see p80*).

Walking tours

Information: *Plaça Catalunya tourist office (906 30 12 82).* **Tours** 10am (English), noon (Catalan/ Spanish), Sat, Sun. **Tickets** 950ptas; 500ptas 4-12s.
Discounts BC, BT. **No credit cards. Map** D5/**B1**
Every weekend professional English-speaking guides take visitors around the Barri Gòtic on foot in an informative tour of about two hours. Numbers are limited, so booking is necessary.

All aboard: rides

Most of Barcelona's special rides offer ways of getting around, up or down the city's three great fun-areas, the Port, Montjuïc and Tibidabo.

Horse-drawn carriages

Plaça Portal de la Pau. Metro Drassanes/bus 14, 20, 36, 38, 57, 59, 64, 91, 157. **Services** *Mar-Nov* 11am-dark daily. **Charge** 6,000ptas per hour; groups negotiable. **No credit cards. Map** C7/A4

You don't mind looking silly? Ask a man for a ride up and down the Rambla behind his tired old nags.

The Port

Golondrines (swallow boats)

Moll de la Fusta (93 442 31 06). Metro Drassanes/ bus 14, 36, 38, 57, 59, 64, 157. **Map** C7 **Drassanes-breakwater & return** (35min): **Departures** *late Sept-Mar* 11am-1pm Mon-Fri, 11am-4pm Sat, Sun; *April-Sept* 11am-5/6pm daily, till 8pm in July-Sept. *Late-Sept-June* no stop at the breakwater Mon-Fri. Closed 16 Dec-1 Jan. **Frequency** normally hourly Mon-Fri, every 35 mins Sat, Sun; *July-Sept* every 35-45mins daily. **Tickets** 485ptas; 250ptas 4-10s; free under-4s. **Drassanes-Port Olímpic & return** (1½hrs): **Departures** *Oct-Mar* two daily; *Apr-June* three daily; *July-late-Sept* four/five daily. **Tickets** 1,275ptas; 900ptas 11-18s, over-65s; 550ptas 4-10s; free under-4s; group discounts. **Discounts** BC, BT. **Credit** MC, V.

The double-decker 'Swallow boats' take you around the harbour to the end of the breakwater, where you can eat out, take in the sea air, go fishing, or come straight back. More solid, sea-going boats run on a longer trip round to the Port Olímpic.

Transbordador Aeri (port cable cars)

Miramar, Parc de Montjuïc–Torre de Jaume I–Torre de Sant Sebastià, Barceloneta (93 441 48 20). Metro Paral.lel & Funicular de Montjuïc/bus 61, or bus 17, 64 to Barceloneta. **Open** *mid-Oct-Feb* noon-5.30pm; *Mar-mid-June, mid-Sept-mid-Oct* 10.30am-7pm; *mid-June-mid Sept* 10.30am-8pm. **Tickets** 1,200ptas round trip; 1,000ptas one way; 800ptas one way Barceloneta–Jaume I or Jaume I–Miramar. **No credit cards. Map** C-D7

The 1929 cable car rattles its way across the harbour from Miramar on Montjuïc to Barceloneta, with a stop in the middle by the World Trade Center. Views of Barceloneta and the Port are spectacular; however, the WTC project will likely lead to its closure, so catch it while you can.

Montjuïc

Funicular de Montjuïc

Metro Paral.lel-Avda Miramar (93 443 08 59). Metro Paral.lel/bus 20, 36, 57, 64, 91, 157. **Open** *Nov-June* 10.45am-8pm Sat, Sun, public holidays; *June-Oct* 11am-10pm daily. **Tickets** *single* 225ptas; *return* 375ptas. **Discounts** BT. **No credit cards. Map** B-C6

Mostly underground, so not much sightseeing, but it brings you out well placed for the Fundació Miró and Miramar. Connects with the **Teleferic**.

Montjuïc Tourist Train

Departs from Plaça d'Espanya. Metro Espanya/bus all routes to Plaça d'Espanya. **Dates** *April-Sept* 11am-10pm daily. **Tickets** 300ptas; 225ptas under-16s; *all day ticket* 500ptas, 400ptas under-16s. **Discounts** BT. **No credit cards. Map** A-B5

Not a train but an open trolley pulled by a truck, which goes up Montjuïc to Miramar.

Teleferic de Montjuïc (cable cars)

Estació Funicular, Avda Miramar (93 443 08 59). Metro Paral.lel, Funicular de Montjuic/bus 61. **Open** *Nov-Mar* 11.30am-2.45pm, 4-7.30pm, Sat, Sun, public holidays; *April-May, mid-Sept-Oct* 11.15am-2.45pm, 4-7.30pm, daily; *June-mid-Sept* 11.15am-8pm Mon-Fri, 11.15am-9pm Sat, Sun. **Tickets** *single* 450ptas; *return* 650ptas, 500ptas under-12s; group discounts. **Discounts** BT. **No credit cards. Map** B6

From outside the funicular station, the Montjuïc cable cars run up to the castle at the top. Vertigo sufferers might not enjoy the trip, but there are superb views over Montjuïc and the port.

Tibidabo

Funicular de Tibidabo

Plaça Doctor Andreu–Plaça Tibidabo (93 211 79 42). FGC Avda Tibidabo/bus 17, 22, 58, 73, N8, then Tramvia Blau. **Open** *end-Mar-June, late Sept-early Oct* noon-early eve Sat, Sun, public holidays; plus *May* 10am-6pm Thur, Fri; *June* 10am-6pm Wed-Fri. *July, Aug* noon-10pm Mon-Thur, Sun, public holidays; noon-1am Fri, Sat; *early Sept* noon-8pm Mon-Thur; noon-10pm Fri-Sun, public holidays. **Tickets** *single* 300ptas; *return* 400ptas. **No credit cards.**

The funicular that takes you from the end of the tramline to the very top of the mountain is art deco-esque, like much of the funfair. Each train has two halves, one pointing down and one up, and from the 'down' end you get a panoramic view of the city.

Tramvia Blau (Blue Tram)

Avda Tibidabo–Plaça Doctor Andreu (93 318 70 74). FGC Avda Tibidabo/bus 17, 22, 58, 73, N8. **Services** *mid Sept-22 June* 9.05am-9.35pm Sat, Sun, public holidays; (bus 7.05am-9.45pm Mon-Fri); *23 June-mid-Sept* 9.05am-9.35pm daily. **Tickets** *single* 250ptas; *return* 375ptas. **No credit cards.**

The Blue Trams, beautiful old machines in service since 1902, clank their way up Avda Tibidabo between the FGC station and Plaça Doctor Andreu. Once there, you can take in the view, have a meal or a drink, or catch the funicular to the funfair. Except in summer there's a plain bus service on weekdays.

charming streets of the Barri Gòtic, known for its traditional *granges* offering coffee and cakes (*see page 160*), but which also has the **Sala Parés**, the city's oldest art gallery, where Rusiñol, Casas and the young Picasso all exhibited.

Properly called **La Mercè**, the area between C/Ferran and the port has a different atmosphere from the Barri Gòtic proper, shabbier and with less prosperous shops. Its heart is the **Plaça Reial**, known for bars and cheap hotels, and a favourite spot for a drink or an outdoor meal, provided you don't mind the odd drunk or other strange human fauna who might also be around. An addition from the 1840s, the *plaça* has the **Tres Gràcies** fountain in the centre and lamp-posts designed by the young Gaudí. On Sunday mornings a coin and stamp market is held here. Plaça Reial has had a dangerous reputation in the past, but has been made safer by heavy policing, and its revival in popularity, seen in the opening or revamping of restaurants such as **Les Quinze Nits** and clubs like the **Jamboree**. Such are the fickle ways of Barcelona fashion that **C/Escudellers**, the next street towards the port, once a deeply dubious and shabby prostitutes' alley, is now a trendy place for grungy, hip socialising, with a string of cheap, studenty bars.

It's hard to imagine, but the streets nearest the port, particularly C/Ample, were until the building of the Eixample the most fashionable in the city. The grand porticoes of some buildings – once wealthy merchants' mansions – still give evidence of former glories. Here too is the church of the **Mercè**, home of Barcelona's patron Virgin, where *Barça* football club has to come properly to dedicate its victories. There are also the lively *tasca* tapas bars on C/de la Mercè. Most of this area, though, has been becoming steadily more run down throughout the twentieth century. The city authorities, as elsewhere, have been making efforts to change the district's character, opening up new squares: **Plaça George Orwell** on Escudellers, and **Plaça Joaquim Xirau**, off the Rambla. Another tactic is the siting of parts of the Universitat Pompeu Fabra on the lower Rambla, using students as guinea pigs in urban renewal. Flats in run-down areas of the old city are also popular with young foreigners, who don't object to their condition as much as local families do.

Beyond C/Ample and the Mercè you emerge from narrow alleys onto the Passeig de Colom, where a few shipping offices and ships' chandlers still recall the dockside atmosphere of former decades (*see also page 68*). **Plaça Medinaceli**, where Almodóvar shot some scenes in his *Todo Sobre Mi Madre*, has in the **Paulino** one of the oldest bars in the city. Monolithic on Passeig de Colom is the army headquarters, the **Capitanía General**, with a façade that has the distinction of being the one construction in Barcelona directly attributable to the Dictatorship of Primo de Rivera.

Catedral de Barcelona

Pla de la Seu (93 315 15 54). Metro Liceu, Jaume I/ bus 17, 19, 40, 45. **Open** 8am-1.30pm, 4-7.30pm, Mon-Fri; 8am-1.30pm, 5-7.30pm, Sat, Sun. *Cloister* 9am-1.15pm, 4-7pm, daily. *Museum* 10am-1pm daily. **Admission** *Cathedral/cloister* free; *choir* 125ptas, groups 100ptas; *museum* 100ptas. **No credit cards. Map D6/B3**

The first cathedral on this site was founded in the sixth century, but the present one dates from between 1298 and 1430, except for its façade, only completed in a rather un-Catalan Gothic-revival style in 1913 during the 'rediscovery' of medieval Barcelona. Not all is Gothic: in the far right corner of the cathedral, looking at the façade, is the older and simpler Romanesque chapel of **Santa Llúcia**. The most striking aspect of the cathedral is its volume: it has three naves of near-equal width. It contains many images, paintings and sculptures, and an intricately-carved choir built in the 1390s. The cathedral museum, in the seventeenth-century Chapter House, has paintings and sculptures with works by the Gothic masters Jaume Huguet, Bernat Martorell and Bartolomé Bermejo. In the crypt is the alabaster tomb of Santa Eulàlia, local Christian martyr and first patron saint of Barcelona. The cloister, bathed in light filtered through arches, palms and fountains, is the most attractive section of the cathedral, and an atmospheric retreat from the city. It contains some white geese, said to represent the purity of Santa Eulàlia. Inside there is also a lift to the roof, for a magnificent view of the old city. *Wheelchair access.*

Plaça del Rei
& Museu d'Història de la Ciutat

Plaça del Rei. Metro Liceu, Jaume I/bus 17, 19, 40, 45. **Museum** *C/Veguer 2 (93 315 11 11).* **Open** *1 Oct-31 May* 10am-2pm, 4-8pm, Tue-Sat; 10am-2pm Sun, public holidays. *1 June-30 Sept* 10am-8pm Tue-Sat; 10am-2pm Sun, public holidays. *Guided tours* by appointment. **Admission** 500ptas; 300ptas under-16s, students, over-65s; free under-12s & first Sat of month. **Discounts** BC. **No credit cards. Map D6/B3**

This wholly-preserved medieval square is flanked on two sides by the **Palau Reial** (Royal Palace), most of which was built in the thirteenth and fourteenth centuries for the Catalano-Aragonese 'Count-Kings', and is now part of the Museu d'Història de la Ciutat. With additions from different periods piled on top of each other, the *plaça* gives a vivid impression of the nature of life in the medieval city, particularly since the square, as well as receiving all the traffic of the court, also served as the main flour and fodder market. It has been fairly well-established that Ferdinand and Isabella received Columbus on his first return from America either on the palace steps or in the **Saló del Tinell** behind, although miserable sceptics still place the story in doubt. To the left, looking into the *plaça*, is the sixteenth-century Viceroys' palace, with its five-tiered watchtower, the Mirador del Rei Martí. The square, magnificently floodlit, is an important venue for summer concerts in the **Grec** festival (*see p9*).

The interest of the City History Museum lies as much in the buildings it occupies as in the collections it holds. The basements of the fifteenth-century main building contain excavations of a huge area of the Roman city, which extend like a giant, complex cavern under the adjoining square (*see also p56* **Walk 1: *Barcino***). The main sections of the Palau Reial are the chapel of **Santa Agata** and the extraordinary Great Hall or **Saló del Tinell** – its massive, unadorned arches a classic example of Catalan Gothic. The chapel has a fifteenth-century altarpiece by Jaume Huguet, one of the greatest Catalan medieval paintings. From the upper floors, there is access to the inside of the **Roman wall**, and from the chapel you can climb up the **Mirador del Rei Martí** watchtower. Another section, the Casa Padellàs, houses excellent temporary exhibitions. The museum has recently added to its attractions *Barcelona: Una Història Virtual*, an impressive state-of-the-art virtual reality presentation on the city's history (with English commentary; shows last approx 30min; book for a time when you arrive at the museum). There's a well-stocked bookshop and information centre with informative leaflets in English, and the museum is also a jumping-off point for city tours, and opens for special late-night visits (*see p58*). *See also chapter* **Museums**. *Shop.*

Plaça Sant Jaume

Metro Liceu, Jaume I/bus 17, 19, 40, 45, N8.
Map D6/B3
The main square of the old city and still the administrative centre of modern Barcelona, the Plaça Sant Jaume contains both the City Hall (**Ajuntament**) and the seat of the Catalan regional government (**Palau de la Generalitat**), standing opposite each other in occasional rivalry. They have not always done so: the square was only opened up in 1823, after which the present neo-classical façade was added to the Ajuntament. That of the Generalitat is older, from 1598-1602. The greater part of both buildings, however, was built in the early fifteenth century, and both of their original main entrances open onto the street now called Bisbe Irurita on one side of the *plaça*, and Ciutat on the other.
Ajuntament de Barcelona *Plaça Sant Jaume (93 402 70 00/special visits 93 402 73 64).*
Open *office* 8am-3pm Mon-Fri; *visits* 10am-2pm Sat, Sun. **Admission** free.
Contrasting completely with the main façade, the old C/Ciutat entrance to the City Hall is entirely a work of Catalan Gothic. The centrepiece of the Ajuntament is the fifteenth-century **Saló de Cent** (Hall of One Hundred), site of all major municipal ceremonies. Visitors can see the main rooms at weekends. The entrance to the tourist information office and gift shop is on the C/Ciutat side. *Wheelchair access.*
Palau de la Generalitat *Plaça Sant Jaume (93 402 46 00).* **Open** *guided tours second & fourth Sundays of each month* 10.30am-1.30pm Sun. **Admission** free.

Like the City Hall, the Generalitat has a Gothic side entrance, with above it a beautiful relief of Saint George, patron saint of Catalonia, made by master carver Pere Johan in 1418. Inside, the finest features are the raised patio the **Pati de Tarongers** (Orange-Tree Patio, because it is planted with orange trees), and the magnificent chapel of **Sant Jordi** of 1432-4, the masterpiece of Catalan architect Marc Safont. The Generalitat is traditionally open to the public on Sant Jordi, 23 April, when its patios are spectacularly decorated with red roses (and queues are huge); it also opens its doors on 11 September (Catalan National Day) and 24 September (La Mercè) and on some other holidays each year (*see pp5-12* **Barcelona by Season**). Tours are also run on two Sundays each month, and on other Saturdays and Sundays can be booked by prior reservation.

The Raval

If, from the Rambla, instead of going into the Barri Gòtic you turn right, looking towards the sea, you will enter the Raval. This is the name currently used for the area bounded by the Rambla, Paral.lel, Ronda Sant Pau and Ronda Sant Antoni, but it has been known by many different names in the past. 'Raval' is the original medieval name, referring to the part of the city outside the walls. The trades and institutions then confined here were those too dangerous or noxious to be allowed inside the city, such as brickmaking or slaughtering, or the huge **Antic Hospital de la Santa Creu**, which served the needs of the city from the fifteenth century until it finally closed in 1926. Other institutions located here were those that demanded too much space, such as the line of monasteries that once ran down one side of the Rambla. In the corner of the Raval next to the sea were the **Drassanes** or shipyards, now the **Museu Marítim.**
On the Paral.lel, near the port, there is still a large section of Barcelona's third **city wall**, which brought the Raval within the city in the fourteenth century. However, Barcelona largely stagnated in the following centuries, and in 1800 much of the Raval had still not been built up, but consisted of small fruit and vegetable gardens, or sometimes even vineyards. A trace of this earlier Raval can still be seen in the name of one of the most beautiful pockets of peace in the district, the ancient Romanesque church of **Sant Pau del Camp** (Saint Paul in the Field).
Hence, when industry began to develop, it was in this area that most land was available. A great deal more land also came into use when liberal governments dissolved the monasteries in 1836, especially in the area around one of the great hubs of the district, the **Boqueria** market, built on the site of the former convent of Sant Josep. Barcelona's first industry, mainly textile mills, thus had to grow within the cramped confines of

Hey, no traffic... so let's retake the streets. An average day in the Raval.

the still-walled Raval, making use of every particle of space. Some of the strange, barrack-like factories from that time can still be seen in places, despite recent demolitions. Their workers lived alongside them, often in appalling conditions.

Then known to most people as the *Quinto* or 'Fifth District', this was the area where the dangerous classes of society took refuge, and it became the great centre of revolutionary Barcelona, a perennial breeding ground for anarchist and other radical groups. Conspiracies galore were hatched here, riots and revolts began on innumerable occasions, and whole streets became no-go areas for the police after dark.

The other aspect of the area (or of that part of it between C/Sant Pau and the port) that made it notorious was its situation as a centre of low-life, drug trafficking and the sex industry, with high-class brothels for the rich and cheap dives for the poor in the so-called *Barrio Chino* (*Xino*, in Catalan) or Chinatown. This label was given to the area (which had no Chinese connections) in the 1920s by a journalist, Francesc Madrid, after he saw a film about vice in San Francisco's Chinatown, and swiftly caught on. Barcelona had always had an underworld, centred in the Raval, but it really took off during World War I (*see page 25*). The heyday of the *Barrio Chino* was in the '20s and '30s, but it managed to survive to a certain extent under Franco. Hundreds of bars and cheap *hostals* lined streets like Nou de la Rambla, catering to a floating population (for a walk around some relics of the area, *see pages 26-7*).

Today the whole district has changed enormously, perhaps more comprehensively than anywhere else in Barcelona. Its surviving industry consists of a dwindling number of old-fashioned workshops in trades like printing, bookbinding, furniture repair or building supplies. The hospital now houses cultural and academic institutions. In the new Euro-Spain radical politics is but a shadow of its pre-Franco self. The biggest change of all has been in the *Chino*, a prime target of the Ajuntament's urban renewal schemes.

In the late 1970s serious problems were caused in the *Chino* by the arrival of heroin. The old, semi-tolerated petty criminality became much more threatening, affecting the morale of Barcelona residents and the tourist trade. The authorities set about the problem with their customary clean-sweep approach. Between 1988 and 1992 the cheapest *hostals* were closed, and whole blocks associated with drug dealers or prostitution demolished to make way for new squares. The people displaced were often transferred to newer flats on the outskirts of town, out of sight and so perhaps out of mind. Another element in the *esponjament* (mopping up) of the Raval has been gentrification, with the construction of a students' residence, a new police station and office blocks. Well in progress is a sweeping *Pla* (plan) *General del Raval*, to create a '*Raval obert al cel*' – 'a Raval open to the sky', with far more open space. The Avinguda Drassanes, by Colom, was actually created in an earlier attempt to 'open up' the Raval, under Franco's mayor Porcioles in the '60s (one thing

Franco's administrators and modern planners could agree on is that the *Chino* has to go), but only got as far as C/Nou de la Rambla. It has now been extended far into the district, bulldozing all before it up to C/Hospital, and the plan is to lay it out as a new *Rambla del Raval*. Entire streets have already disappeared in its wake.

Some of these changes have undeniably been for the best, but their cumulative effect has been to leave one of the more unique parts of the city looking rather empty. It still has a hard edge, though, and it's an area where it's advisable to be wary of thieves and avoid acting the dumb tourist, especially between Sant Pau and the port. Another, unpredicted change in the Raval has been the appearance of a sizeable Moslem community, mostly from Pakistan and the Maghreb countries, who have taken over flats no longer wanted by Spaniards. This is now one of the city's most multi-cultural areas, where Moslem *halal* butcher shops serving North Africans sit alongside *carnisseries* selling every part of the pig to Catalans.

The main thoroughfare of the lower Raval, **C/Nou de la Rambla**, today has only a fraction of its earlier animation, but retains a sometimes surreal selection of shops. It also contains a peculiar addition from the 1880s, the **Palau Güell**, built by Gaudí for Eusebi Güell. It was a very eccentric decision by Güell to have his new residence located in what was a deeply unfashionable area, and he often had trouble persuading dinner guests to take up their invitations. Nearby in C/Sant Pau is another *Modernista* landmark, the **Hotel España** (*see page 123*).

The upper Raval, towards Plaça Catalunya, has seen the largest-scale official projects for the rejuvenation of the area, in the giant cultural complex that includes the **Museu d'Art Contemporani (MACBA)** and the **Centre de Cultura Contemporània (CCCB)**, built in what was once the workhouse, the *Casa de la Caritat*. A clutch of galleries has sprung up around them, although a failure to attract wealthier art-buyers has led to some moving back to more traditional gallery areas in the Eixample (*see chapter* **Art Galleries**). C/Riera Baixa is now Barcelona's liveliest street for innovative club and street fashion.

Alongside the new association with sophisticated culture, parts of the old Raval are also enjoying a new lease of life thanks to their being (re)discovered as hip places to be. There are laid-back restaurants like **Silenus**, cool bars like **Muebles Navarro** or **Rita Blue** on Plaça Sant Agustí, and open-air bars like the **Kasparo** on Plaça Vicenç Martorell. At one end of the Raval the **Pastis** on C/Santa Mònica remains interestingly French, and a great night out can be had in **La Paloma** on C/Tigre. The grungy **London Bar** on C/Nou de la Rambla and **Marsella** on C/Sant Pau are forever popular with the local foreign commu-

nity. One of the area's newer popular watering holes is the Irish **Quiet Man** on C/Marqués de Barberà (*see chapter* **Cafés & Bars**).

Antic Hospital de la Santa Creu

C/Carme 47-C/Hospital 56 (no phone).
Metro Liceu/bus 14, 18, 38, 59. **Open** 9am-8pm Mon-Fri; 9am-2pm Sat. **Map** C6/A2

A hospital was founded on this site in 1024: the buildings combine a fifteenth-century Gothic core – including a beautifully shady collonaded courtyard – with baroque and classical additions. It remained the city's main hospital until 1926, and Gaudí died here. Today it houses Catalonia's main library, an arts school and **La Capella** exhibition space, in the chapel (*see chapter* **Art Galleries**).

Palau Güell

C/Nou de la Rambla 3-5 (93 317 39 74). Metro Liceu/bus 14, 38, 59, 91. **Open** *guided tours only* 10am-1pm, 4-7pm, Mon-Fri. Opening hours are subject to change. Closed public holidays.
Admission 400ptas; 200ptas students, over-65s; free under-6s. **No credit cards. Map** A3/C6

This vaguely medievalist palace was built in 1886-8 as a residence for Gaudí's patron Eusebi Güell. It was Gaudí's first major commission for Güell, and one of the first buildings in which he revealed the originality of his ideas. Once past the fortress-like facade, one finds an interior in impeccable condition, with lavish wooden ceilings, dozens of snake-eye stone pillars, and original furniture – like a dressing table whose mirror looks like it's about to fall off. The roof terrace is a garden of decorated chimneys, each one different from the other. Queues are often long for the guided tours, so try to get there early; mornings are better than afternoons.

Sant Pau del Camp

C/Sant Pau 101 (93 441 00 01). Metro Paral.lel/bus 20, 36, 57, 64, 91. **Open** 11.30am-1pm, 6-7.30pm, Mon, Wed-Sun; 11.30am-12.30pm Tue. **Admission** free. **Map** C6

Barcelona's oldest church was built in the twelfth century, when the surrounding Raval was just open fields, as part of a monastery. The Romanesque structure has none of the towering grandeur of the cathedral or Santa Maria del Mar: it is a squat, hulking building, rounded in on itself to give a sense of intimacy and protection to worshippers. On either side of the portal are columns made from material from seventh- and eighth-century buildings.

Sant Pere, La Ribera & the Born

Back on the east side of the Rambla, the Barri Gótic is now effectively limited on its eastern flank by the long, straight Via Laietana. This is a twentieth-century addition, cut through the old city in 1907. The *barris* to the right of it on the map were contained, like the Barri Gòtic, within the second, thirteenth-century city wall, and include some of the most fascinating parts of the medieval city.

Below Plaça Urquinaona lies the district of **Sant Pere**, originally centred around the monastery of **Sant Pere de les Puelles**, which still stands, if greatly altered, in Plaça de Sant Pere. This was Barcelona's main centre of textile production for centuries, and to this day streets like Sant Pere Més Baix and Sant Pere Més Alt contain many textile wholesalers and retailers. The area may be medieval in origin, but its finest monument is one of the most extraordinary works of *Modernisme*, the **Palau de la Música Catalana**, facing C/Sant Pere Més Alt. Less noticed on the same street is a curious feature, unique in Barcelona, the **Passatge de la Indústria**, a long narrow arcade between C/ Sant Pere Més Alt and C/Ortigosa.

Like other parts of the old city Sant Pere looks very run down in places, but as elsewhere is undergoing renovation. The district market, **Mercat de Santa Catalina** – one of Barcelona's oldest – is being completely rebuilt, and in the meantime its stallholders have been relocated along Passeig Lluís Companys, by the park. As with the Raval, the district's neglected state is an obvious explanation of why it has become home to many recent immigrants, the most prominent of whom are black Latin Americans from the Dominican Republic – you can often hear salsa or merengue wafting out across medieval alleys like C/Fonollar.

The name of the area below Sant Pere, **La Ribera** (the waterfront), recalls the time before permanent quays were built, when the shoreline reached much further inland. One of the most engaging districts of the old city, it has, though, fallen victim to two historic acts of urban vandalism. The first took place after the 1714 siege, when the victors razed one whole corner of the Ribera in order to construct the fortress of the Ciutadella, now the **Parc de la Ciutadella**. The second occurred when the Via Laietana was struck through the *barri* in the 1900s, in line with the contemporary theory of 'ventilating' insanitary city districts by driving wide avenues through them.

In Barcelona's Golden Age, from the twelfth century onwards, La Ribera was both the favourite residential area of the city's merchant élite and the principal centre of commerce and trade. The **Plaça de l'Angel**, now a rather nondescript space on Via Laietana by Jaume I Metro station, is all that remains of the Plaça del Blat, the 'wheat square', where all grain brought into the city was traded. If the Royal Palace, Generalitat and Ajuntament were the 'official' centre of the medieval city, this was its commercial and popular heart, where virtually everybody had to come at least once a day. The main street of La Ribera is still **Carrer Montcada**, one of the unmissable parts of old Barcelona. It is lined with an extraordinary succession of medieval palaces, the greatest of which house museums such as the **Museu Tèxtil**, the **Museu Barbier-Mueller** of Pre-Colombian art and, above all, the **Museu Picasso** (*for all, see chapter* **Museums**). Montcada also has a unique selection of bars for settling into (*see page 166*). The surrounding streets were once filled with workshops supplying anything the merchant owners might need (*see page 66* **Walk 2: La Ribera**).

So find a better view from a pavement café... Outside **Santa Maria del Mar**. *See page 67.*

Walk 2: La Ribera

Centuries of Barcelona life, work and wealth are reflected in the medieval streets of La Ribera. This walk is marked in **green** on Maps 7-8 on *pages 316-7*; it begins, like that around the Roman city (*see page 56*), on Plaça Sant Jaume. From there, walk down **C/Llibreteria**, as important in the Middle Ages as it had been as the Roman *Cardus*, and still the main north road. Cross **Plaça de l'Angel**, site of the *Plaça del Blat*, the grain market. The continuation of the Roman road across Via Laietana is **C/Bòria**, a name that probably means 'outskirts' or 'suburbs', since it was outside the original city.

C/Bòria continues into the extraordinarily evocative **Plaça de la Llana** (wool), old centre of wool trading in the city, now with a clutch of Dominican-owned bars. Alleys to the left were associated with food trades: **C/Mercaders** (traders, probably in grain), **C/de l'Oli** (olive oil); **C/Semoleres**, where semolina was made. To the right on Bòria is **C/Pou de la Cadena** (well with a chain), a reminder that water was essential for textile working.

After Plaça de la Llana the Roman road's name becomes **C/Corders** (rope-makers), and then **C/Carders** (carders, or combers of wool). Where the name changes there is a tiny square, Placeta Marcús, with a smaller Romanesque chapel, the **Capella d'en Marcús**, built in the early twelfth century to give shelter to travellers on the road who arrived after the city gates had closed for the night. Bernat Marcús, who paid for it, is also said to have organised the first postal service in Europe, and it was from here that his riders set off north. The chapel is rarely open (for worship only).

Carry on a little way along C/Carders to **Plaça Sant Agustí Vell**, different bits of which hail from many centuries, from medieval to nineteenth: in **C/Basses de Sant Pere**, leading away to the left, there is an intact fourteenth-century house.

Retrace your steps down C/Carders, to turn left into **C/Blanqueria** (bleaching). Here wool was fulled and washed before being spun. Inside its giant doorways are smaller versions of the patios seen on C/Montcada. At **C/Assaonadors** (tanners), turn right. At the end of this street, behind the Marcús chapel, is a statue of Saint John the Baptist, patron saint of the tanners' guild.

Here you are at the top of **C/Montcada**. In La Ribera's Golden Age this beautiful street was the broadest thoroughfare in the district, and its busiest.

Its merchant residences conform to a typical style of Mediterranean urban palace – elegant entrance patios with the main rooms on the first floor – and are closely packed together. Most have features from several periods. Today this is one of Barcelona's great museum centres. The first palace you reach after crossing C/Princesa is the **Palau Berenguer d'Aguilar** (*pictured*), home of the **Museu Picasso**, which has also taken over four more palaces (*see pages 96-7*). Opposite is one of the finest and largest palaces, the **Palau dels Marquesos de Lló**, now the **Museu Tèxtil**, with a fine café; nearby is another great Montcada feature, the **Xampanyet** *cava* bar. A relative newcomer is the bar in the seventeenth-century **Palau Dalmases**.

To the right is **C/Sombrerers**, where hat makers wrought their craft; opposite it is Barcelona's narrowest street, **Carrer de les Mosques** (Street of Flies), not even wide enough for an adult to lie across. It has been closed because too many people were pissing in it at night.

Montcada ends at **Passeig del Born**, a hub of the city's trades for 400 years. Turn left, and on the left there is **C/Flassaders** (blanket makers), and to the right **C/del Rec**, the irrigation canal. Go down Rec to turn right into **C/Esparteria**, where *espart* (hemp) was woven. Turnings off it include **C/Calders**, where smelting furnaces would have been found, and **C/Formatgeria**, where one would have gone to buy cheese. After that is **C/Vidrieria**, where glass was stored and sold; **Vidrieria Grau** at No.6 (*see chapter* **Shopping**) is the last survivor of this centuries-old trade in the street .

Esparteria runs into C/Ases, which crosses **C/Malcuinat** ('badly-cooked'), so there must have been evil smells nearby. Turn left into **C/Espaseria** (sword-making) to emerge out of ancient alleys onto the open space of Pla del Palau. Turn right, and right again into **C/Canvis Vells** (old exchange). A tiny street to the left, C/Panses, has an archway above it, with a stone sculpture of a face over the second floor. This face, called a *carabassa*, indicated the existence of a legalised brothel. At the end of Canvis Vells you come to **Plaça Santa Maria** and La Ribera's superb parish church: on the left is **C/Abaixadors** (unloaders), where porters would unload goods, and from the square **C/Argenteria** (silverware) leads back to the Plaça de l'Angel.

On the corner of Montcada and C/Assaonadors is the small chapel the **Capella d'en Marcús** (*see also left*), which when built, in the twelfth century, was surrounded by fields and gardens. Close by was the main route through the district, along Carrers Corders and Carders. C/Princesa is a much more recent addition, created in the 1850s.

From C/Carders, C/Montcada leads across C/Princesa to the centre of the Ribera, the **Passeig del Born**. Its name originally meant 'joust' or 'list', and in the Middle Ages and for many centuries thereafter this was the centre for the city's festivals, processions, tournaments, carnivals and the burning of heretics by the Inquisition. At one end of the square is the old **Born** market, a magnificent 1870s wrought-iron structure that used to be Barcelona's main wholesale food market. It closed in the 1970s, when the market was transferred to the other side of Montjuïc. The building was saved from demolition, and current plans are that it should house an arts centre.

At the other end of the Passeig from the market stands the greatest of all Catalan Gothic buildings, the magnificent church of **Santa Maria del Mar**. On one side of a rather ugly new square was opened in 1989 on the site where it is believed the last defenders of the city were executed after the fall of Barcelona to the Spanish army in 1714. Called the **Fossar de les Moreres**, the 'Mulberry Graveyard', the square is inscribed with emphatic patriotic poetry, and nationalist demonstrations converge here on Catalan National Day, 11 September. It is now undergoing renovation, sponsored by, of all people, Marks & Spencer.

The closure of the Born market led initially to a certain decline in this area, but it has survived as the home of an old-established community, and thanks to its inherent attractions for tourism and nightlife. As a nightlife haunt the Born tends to go in and out of fashion, with booms and slumps every few years; currently it seems to be ending the Millennium on a roll, as the once-quiet Passeig and its bars are packed with wandering crowds on weekend nights. The area is full of great bars, and has an ever-expanding number of restaurants. Since the 1980s it has also been a hub of the city's alternative art scene. Around C/Banys Vells, parallel to Montcada, there is now an interesting selection of independent textile and craft workshops, set up by young designers (*see chapter* **Shopping**).

From the Born and Santa Maria, tiny streets lead through precarious-looking, centuries-old arches to the harbourside avenue and another symbol of the Ribera, the **Llotja** (Exchange). Its outer shell is neoclassical, added in the eighteenth century, but its core is a superb 1380's Gothic hall which, until the exchange moved to Passeig de Gràcia in 1994, was the oldest continuously-functioning stock exchange in Europe. It once housed the *Consolat del Mar*, the 'Consulate of the Sea', established to arbitrate in commercial disputes throughout the Mediterranean, and since then has equally accommodated a Customs Post and a School of Fine Arts, at which Picasso and many other artists studied. Unfortunately it can (usually) only be visited if you attend a function organised through its owners, the Chamber of Commerce (*see page 296*).

Palau de la Música Catalana

*C/Sant Francesc de Paula 2 (93 268 10 00).
Metro Urquinaona/bus 17, 19, 40, 45.*
Guided tours 10am-3pm daily. **Admission** 700ptas; 500ptas over-65, students, groups.
No credit cards. Map D5/B-C2
Gaudí may be the best-known of Barcelona's turn-of-the-century architects, but the building that most truly represents the pure *Modernista* style is Domènech i Montaner's 'Palace of Catalan Music'. Built in 1905-8, it's still the most prestigious concert hall in the city, despite the inauguration of the all-modern **Auditori**. The façade, with its combination of bare brick, busts and mosaic friezes representing Catalan musical traditions alongside the great composers, is impressive enough, but it is surpassed by the building's staggering interior. Decoration erupts everywhere: the ceiling centrepiece is of multi-coloured stained glass; 18 half-mosaic, half-relief figures representing the musical muses appear out of the back of the stage; and on one side, massive Wagnerian carved horses ride out to accompany a bust of Beethoven. The old Palau has been bursting under the pressure of the musical activity going on inside it, and an extension and renovation programme by Oscar Tusquets in the 1980s is being followed by yet more alterations by the same architect.

The best way to see the Palau is to go to a concert, but now that the opening of the Auditori and re-opening of the **Liceu** have relieved concert pressure in the hall it is easier to visit it with a guided tour. Tours are available in English, Catalan or Spanish, last 50 minutes and leave every half-hour or so. They begin with a 20-minute video, which can make the remaining tour a bit rushed, and parts of the building (such as the exterior decoration) are not touched upon. Don't feel shy about asking questions: it's the best way to get to interesting information beyond the basics. Photography and filming are forbidden during tours. The Palau also has an attractive shop, **Les Muses del Palau** (*see chapter* **Shopping**). *See also chapter* **Music: Classical & Opera**. *Wheelchair access.*

Santa Maria del Mar

Plaça de Santa Maria (93 310 23 90). Metro Jaume I/bus 17, 19, 40, 45. **Open** 9am-1.30pm, 4.30-8pm, daily. **Admission** free. **Map D6/C3**
The cathedral may attract more attention, but Santa Maria del Mar, known as 'the people's cathedral' because of its traditionally greater popularity, is undoubtedly the city's finest church, the summit of Catalan Gothic. Built remarkably quickly for a medieval building, between 1329 and 1384, it has an unusual unity of style. Inside, two ranks of slim,

perfectly proportioned columns soar up to fan vaults, creating a wonderful atmosphere of space and peace. It's not so much a historical artefact as simply a marvellous building, somehow outside of time. There's also superb stained glass, particularly the great fifteenth-century rose window above the main door. Our ability to appreciate it is helped greatly by the fact that revolutionaries set fire to it in 1936, clearing out the wooden baroque images that clutter so many Spanish churches, and allowing the simplicity of its lines to emerge. From the outside, especially Plaça Santa Maria with its delightful pavement cafés (*see pp 165-6*), the church is equally impressive.

The Port Vell

At the foot of the Rambla, Columbus, **Colom** in Catalan, points out to sea from atop his column, confusingly enough towards Italy. To his right are the fourteenth-century shipyards or **Drassanes**, now the **Museu Marítim**, and from near the foot of his column you can cross the harbour on the **Golondrines** boat trips (*see page 59*). These are features that have been in place for years. However, had you made the ride up to the crown at Columbus' feet in, say, 1980, you would have seen the harbour beneath you thronged with cargo ships waiting to load or unload. Today, they have disappeared, and the scene has changed utterly. Commercial traffic has moved away to container terminals outside the main port, in the Zona Franca. Simultaneously, Barcelona's inner harbour, rechristened the **Port Vell** or Old Port, has undergone an extraordinary overhaul to turn it into a waterside leisure area, so much so that 20 years on a visitor simply would not know it. In just a few years since the mid-1990s, the former dockside has become one of Barcelona's foremost party zones.

At the end of the Rambla, if you make your way through the traffic of the Passeig de Colom to the waterfront, you will come to the **Rambla de Mar**, a swivel-section wooden footbridge (which opens to let boats enter and leave) that leads to the **Moll d'Espanya** quay. The quay is dominated by the **Maremàgnum** complex, a trademark work by ever-active architects Helio Piñón and Albert Viaplana (*see also chapters* **Nightlife** *and* **Shopping**). As much an entertainment as a shopping centre, it contains 50 shops, 25 restaurants and a dozen clubs and bars. Slow to gain momentum when first opened in 1995, Maremàgnum has become spectacularly successful, packed with young crowds on weekend evenings throughout the year. Further along the same quay there's also an eight-screen cinema, the **IMAX** giant-format movie-house and Barcelona's **Aquàrium**, one of the best of its kind in the world.

If you've had enough of the mall and come back across the footbridge and turn right, you will come to the **Moll de la Fusta** or Wood Quay, which was the first part of the port to be redeveloped. When inaugurated in 1987 it contained a string of pavement bars and restaurants in glass kiosks, among them Gambrinus, topped by a giant fibre-

Columbus strives to make himself heard amid the new architecture of the Port Vell.

glass lobster by designer Javier Mariscal that became a real symbol of 1980s, pre-Olympic Barcelona. Today, Gambrinus has closed – even though the lobster's still there – and several of the bars are looking rather shabby, but some have also been reborn late-night as happening harbourside club venues such as **Distrito Marítimo** and **Octopussy** (*see chapter* **Nightlife**). Impossible to miss at the north end of the Moll de la Fusta, by the borders of La Ribera, is the giant 14-metre (46-foot) high mosaic sculpture *Barcelona Head*, by the late Roy Lichtenstein (*see page 71*).

If you carry on round the port to the right, you will reach the marina – with some very luxurious yachts – and a line of waterside restaurants. The *tinglados*, the huge dock storage sheds that once dominated Passeig Joan de Borbó, have nearly all been pulled down to open up an entirely new, positively gracious harbourside promenade on this side of Barceloneta. One exception is the **Palau de Mar**, a converted warehouse that now hosts a clutch of restaurants and cafés and the **Museu d'Història de Catalunya**. The only remaining commercial section is a small area for fishermen. Beyond there, if you continue walking you can go through the Barceloneta district to the Port Olímpic and the city's beaches.

Returning to Columbus' feet, if, instead of walking across to Maremàgnum or along the Moll de la Fusta you head to the right, looking out to sea, you will come to the **Moll de Barcelona**, the view of which is dominated by the giant metal tower that (for the time being) supports the **Transbordador Aeri** cable cars. This is a working quay, the departure point for Balearics ferries (*see page 266*). At the end of the quay, though, there is another giant building scheme labelled (in English) the **World Trade Center (WTC)**. Stalled for years for lack of finance, this finally opened – even though it was not really finished – amid great fanfare in July 1999. Currently semi-circular, the WTC is to have 13,000 square metres (15,550 square yards) of floor space, between offices, a concert hall, a conference centre, and shops. On either side of it will be cruise terminals, which will round off Barcelona's – – already hugely successful – drive to become the dominant cruise port of the Mediterranean. To serve the cruise passengers there will be a giant hotel making up the landward side of the complex, still unbuilt but due to be in place by 2002.

The World Trade Center is also intended to play a wider role in post-Millennium Barcelona. South of Montjuïc work is under way on extending the Zona Franca industrial area to create a new 'Logistics Park' with optimum port, road, rail and air links. The objective is to consolidate Barcelona as the foremost freight port and distribution centre in the western Mediterranean, ahead of eternal rivals Marseilles and Genoa. The WTC will be the administrative centre of this operation, and the

hope of Barcelona's ever-ambitious planners is that multinationals will soon be banging at its doors, all eager to make the building their Mediterranean headquarters.

Colom (Columbus Monument)

Plaça Portal de la Pau (93 302 52 24). Metro Drassanes/bus 14, 20, 36, 38, 57, 59, 64, 91, 157. **Open** *late-Sept-Mar* 10am-1pm, 3.30-6.30pm, Mon-Fri; 10am-6.30pm Sat, Sun, public holidays. *April, May* 10am-1pm, 3.30-7.30pm, Mon-Fri; 10am-7.30pm Sat, Sun, public holidays. *1 June-late-Sept* 9am-8.30pm daily. **Admission** 250ptas; 150ptas over-65s, 4-12s; free under-4s; group discounts. **Discounts** BC, BT. **No credit cards**. **Map** C7/A4
Ride to the top of the Columbus column, built for the Exhibition of 1888, for a panoramic view of the old city and the port from within the crown at the explorer's feet. The lift only holds four people plus an attendant at a time, so there may be a big queue. In addition, the column is undergoing repairs (complicated by the discovery of medieval remains beneath its base), and so is often shrouded in scaffolding; nevertheless, the lift remains open for business.

Barceloneta

The triangular district known as Barceloneta ('Little Barcelona'), the part of the city between the harbour and the sea, was the product of an early example of authoritarian town planning. When after 1714 a large section of the Ribera (*see pages 20, 65*) was razed to the ground to make way for the new Citadel, the people thus displaced lived for many years in makeshift shelters on the beach, until in the 1750s the authorities decided to rehouse them in line with a plan drawn up by a French army engineer, Prosper Verboom.

The new district was built on land reclaimed from the sea. The street plan of Barceloneta, with long, narrow blocks, reveals its military origins. In the nineteenth century this became the dockers' and fishermen's district, and a massive road and rail barrier was built cutting Barceloneta off from the rest of the city right up until the transformations of the 1990s. This helped the area retain a distinctive atmosphere and identity; the local **Festa Major** in September is a riot of colour (*see page 11*).

Barceloneta has also traditionally been the city's gateway to the beach. Until the last few years this was of interest only to a few devotees of sunbathing rather than seabathing. Some may cavil at the water quality even today, but since the comprehensive reconstruction of the city's beaches they have become far more pleasant. Consequently Barceloneta has become still more crowded on summer weekends, as throngs make their way through its streets for a meal or a swim.

Barceloneta has also been long associated with fine fish and seafood restaurants. There are any number of them in the district, but among the best

On the beach

A key slogan of Barcelona's whole pre/post-Olympic project was that it should create a *Barcelona Oberta al Mar*, a 'Barcelona Open to the Sea'. As a major port it had obviously always been open to the sea in a grimy, workaday sort of way; most of the sea frontage northeast of the harbour was an industrial dump. What was meant now, though, was that the city should take on board, and enjoy, the fact that it lies on the Mediterranean. In a few years the seafront was changed beyond recognition: over four kilometres of new beaches were created, with thousands of tons of fresh sand, stylish parks and palm-lined promenades; special measures were taken to improve water cleanliness; and, as a centrepiece, the **Port Olímpic** was built, one of Barcelona's most popular new amenities. This is perhaps the most spectacular of all the city's transformations.

Barcelona's people have caught on to their new beaches in a big way, and on any summer's day can be found in huge numbers along the sand, or rollerblading along the prom. Since 1994 a **Festa de la Platja** has been held every April by the Ajuntament. All the beaches have gained the EU's Blue Flag certificate of cleanliness, and all have permanent lifeguards, ramps for wheelchair access and other high-standard facilities. A section of the **Mar Bella** beach is reserved for nudists (who are mostly men), although it's not very clearly indicated.

Sun, sea and sand aren't the only attractions of the beachfront, for there's an enjoyable, leisurely walk between there and Colom. Centrepiece is the **Port Olímpic**, with its bars and restaurants for when you come off the beach (*see chapter* **Restaurants**). Beyond it, looking towards the city, you'll see gleaming in the sunshine Frank Gehry's huge copper *Fish* sculpture, next to which there's a footbridge that will take you past other pleasant, clean beaches to Barceloneta.

Beaches *Beaches of Sant Sebastià, Barceloneta, Nova Icària, Mar Bella & Nova Mar Bella. Metro Barceloneta-Selva de Mar, yellow line/bus 10, 36, 41, 45, 57, 59, 71, 92, 100, 157.*

are **Can Ros** and **Can Ramonet**. Away from the beach and the city, at its 'tip' Barceloneta leads into Passeig de l'Escullera, the long road along the breakwater at the end of which is another restaurant and a landing point for the **Golondrines** boat trips. A plan has also been proposed for this area, by the often-controversial Ricard Bofill, involving the creation of a leisure area on reclaimed land, but this has yet to get the go-ahead from City Hall.

A famous feature of Barceloneta was that it used to be possible to combine the district's two pleasures in the traditional paella and seafood restaurants that lined the beach. These basic *chiringuitos* were closed down by city edict in 1991, but have (slightly) revived in smarter form. For Barceloneta, the city's massive reworking of the old port – and the transformation of Passeig Joan de Borbó from dockyard service road to waterside promenade – has in effect meant a complete re-orientation of the area through 180°, from looking out to sea to overlooking the port. Some former *chiringuito*-owners have therefore been encouraged to reopen, alongside all-new restaurants, on the new harbourside *passeig* and in the **Palau de Mar**, while other dock buildings have been torn down to open up a view of the harbour and Montjuïc that most Barceloneta residents had been unaware of all their lives.

The Vila Olímpica

In 1986 Barcelona was elected Olympic City for 1992, and the whole population seemed to pour into the streets to celebrate. Then the job began of preparing to build what would soon be called the city's newest *barri*, the Olympic Village, most ambitious of all the 1992 projects. It was a local cliché to say that Barcelona had turned its back to the sea, with barriers of railways, factories and dirty industrial roads that since the 1850s had cut its citizens off from their abandoned, refuse-strewn beaches. Now, the plan was to open out.

Not since Cerdà or Gaudí has anyone had such an impact on the face of Barcelona as the architects Oriol Bohigas, Josep Martorell, long-time English resident David Mackay and Albert Puigdomènech, who were entrusted with the overall design of the all-new district, to be built on reclaimed industrial land. Constructed in just two years, it was initially named *Nova Icària* to recall the utopian socialist community that briefly existed in this area in the last century, but the name has never stuck. As well as a range of services some 2,000 apartments were built, which it was hoped would provide low-cost housing once the athletes had vacated them after the Games. However, economic realities have since dictated otherwise.

Those who have paid the relatively high prices and acquired flats in the village have at their disposal an impressive range of new leisure areas and seafront parks. Taken as a whole the project is spectacular. By far the most successful part of the Vila is the **Port Olímpic,** the 743-mooring space leisure marina built from nothing since 1988, now lined with bars and restaurants packed with crowds of all ages every weekend night of the year (*see chapters* **Restaurants** *and* **Nightlife**). By day, the Port Olímpic is also the place to go to hire sailing boats (*see chapter* **Sports & Fitness**).

Further inland, Cerdà's original concept for the Eixample was taken as an inspiration, with semi-open blocks built around services and garden areas. Every stop had to be pulled out to get things ready for July 1992 – some sections, such as the skyscraper **Hotel Arts,** missed the date and were not inaugurated until a good while later.

The final effect, however, is of a rather cold, un-Mediterranean suburb, although the waterway parallel to C/Moscou and the red brick of **Plaça Tirant lo Blanc** soften the harshness. The glass and stone gateway buildings to the *barri* create a forbidding impression; there are few corner shops or cafés; the spiky metal pergolas on Avda Icària look like a grim parody of trees. Even the jokey sculpture in Parc de Carles I, *David i Goliat*, leaves one with the feeling that this is a world in which the Goliaths usually slay the Davids. However a touch of humour can be found in the same park, in the enormous six-metre (20-foot) sculpture of the lower half of a human body. By Basque artist Eduardo Úrculo, it has inevitably become known as *el culo de Úrculo,* Úrculo's arse. And, as in many suburbs, the Vila's open spaces are colonised by cyclists and rollerbladers at weekends.

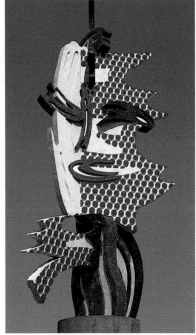

*Lichtenstein/*Barcelona Head. *See page 69.*

Dazzling glass in the Casa Morera, *part of the* **Mansana de la Discòrdia**. *See page 80.*

EL TRIANGLE

ALL YOUR SHOPPING
WITHOUT MOVING FROM THE CENTRE

DISCOVER THE NEW HEART OF OUR CITY.
RIGHT IN THE CENTRE OF BARCELONA,
YOU'LL FIND IT AT THE TOP OF THE RAMBLAS
AND ALONGSIDE PLAÇA CATALUNYA.

MUCH MORE THAN A SHOPPING CENTRE, EL
TRIANGLE IS THE BEST WAY OF STARTING
YOUR STAY IN BARCELONA.

COME AND DISCOVER EL TRIANGLE.

YOU'LL FIND EVERYTHING WITHOUT MOVING
FROM THE CENTRE.

HOW TO GET THERE?

CAR PARK ENTRANCES

METRO LINES: L2, L3 AND CATALAN TRAINS

BUS ROUTES: 9, 14, 16, 17, 22, 24, 28, 38, 41,
42, 47, 55, 58, 59, 62, 66, 67, 68, 91, 141, AND
TOURISTIC BUS.

TAXI RANKS: FONTANELLA ST.

C/ PELAI, 39
08001 BARCELONA
TEL. 93 318 01 08

OPENING HOURS:
MONDAY TO SATURDAY
WINTER: 10 A.M. - 9.30 P.M.
SUMMER: 10 A.M. - 10 P.M.

 LUCES DE BOHEMIA

 LOVE STORE

 Bernat Picbi

 TOSCANA

 L'ESCRIBA

 GRUS WATCH

 TEA SHOP

 AGATHA

 fnac

 GUESS

habitat

 DOCKERS

Massimo Dutti

 CAMPER

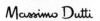 SEPHORA

 DESIGUAL

 GRAND OPTICAL

 TRUCCO

WE ARE IN THE HEART OF BARCELONA

EL**T**RIANGLE

THE CENTRE OF THE CENTRE

PLAÇA CATALUNYA

RECORDS / DECORATION / BOOKS / CLOTHES / COMPLEMENTS / OPTICIANS / PERFUMES

Magic mountain: Montjuïc

Whether the name means mountain of the Jews or the mountain of Jupiter, the huge, sprawling mass of Montjuïc, rising over the city from beside the port, is one of Barcelona's most loved features. This hill of 200 hectares (494 acres) is a world of its own, encompassing any number of quite different areas. It's not a district, for hardly anyone lives there, but it is a delightful place for a stroll. From all over the hill you get wonderful views: they're particularly spectacular by the **Palau Nacional** and at **Miramar**, overlooking the harbour.

According to one legend of the origins of Barcelona, it was founded by Hercules and populated by the crew of the ninth ship (*Barca nona*) that went with him on his labours. Hercules then sat on Montjuïc to admire his creation. But it also has other associations. The **Castell de Montjuïc**, built in the seventeenth century, became a symbol of the suppression of Catalan liberties after 1714. As a prison and torture centre for rebels and radicals – or those deemed such – it inspired fear and loathing for two centuries. The castle was finally handed over to Barcelona by the army in 1960, but it still houses the **Museu Militar**.

At the same time the rest of Montjuïc, wild and empty, was the city's favourite park, and when Barcelona was still confined in its walls people used to climb the hill to spend a day in the country. The military refused to allow much building on the mountain until well into this century, and it was not until the run-up to the 1929 Exhibition that Montjuïc was landscaped.

Today Montjuïc, like so many parts of Barcelona, has been earmarked for some big changes, especially on its still semi-wild, mysterious southern flank. A 'macropark', with lake included, is projected between Miramar and the vast cemetery on the mountain's south side. The old Montjuïc funfair has already closed, perhaps because it was a bit vulgar and shabby for the

planners. As in Poble Nou, it is hoped everything will be ready for the new magical year, 2004.

Despite all the activity on the mountain, and its proximity to the city centre, it's surprisingly easy to find peaceful, shaded places among the many park areas. Below the castle, on the steep flank nearest the port, are the **Jardins Costa i Llobera**, which abound in exotic plants such as a Mexican cactus popularly known as *el seient de la sogra*, 'mother-in-law's seat'. Not far above, on the Montjuïc road, Avda Miramar, are the **Jardins del Mirador**, from where there is a spectacular view over the harbour. Carry on along this road away from the sea and you will reach the **Jardins Cinto Verdaguer**, with a beautiful pond, flowers and more views; a little further on are the municipal swimming pool, spectacularly rebuilt for the 1992 diving events, and the **Fundació Miró**. Continue uphill to reach the **Anella Olímpica**, with the main Olympic buildings and the **Bernat Picornell** swimming pool. If you want to cut the walk short, Montjuïc has several fun means of transport to help you up the hill (*see page 59*).

If on the other hand from the Fundació Miró you turn right and head downhill you will come upon a veritable orgy of monumentalist and *Noucentista* architecture from 1929, which now contain the area's other main cultural centres. There are museums (the **MNAC**, the **Museu d'Arqueologia**, the **Museu Etnològic**), and the **Mercat de les Flors** and **Teatre Grec** theatres. Plans are underway to integrate these venues into a *Ciutat del Teatre*, a complete theatre complex (*see chapter* **Theatre**). Further down are the **Mies van der Rohe Pavilion** and the ineffable **Poble Espanyol**, and next to Plaça d'Espanya are the Trade Fair buildings (the **Fira**). Across the road from the Mies Pavilion, a *Modernista* factory, the **Casaramona**, is being made into yet another new cultural centre, by the Fundació la Caixa (*see chapter* **Art Galleries**). As you approach Plaça

d'Espanya, Carles Buigas' water-and-light spectacular the **Font Màgica**, however corny, never fails to round off a memorable walk.

L' Anella Olímpica (The Olympic Ring)

Passeig Olímpic (93 426 20 89). Metro Espanya, or Paral.lel, then Funicular de Montjuïc/bus 50. **Information** *Estadi Olímpic (Catalan 93 481 00 92/Spanish 93 481 10 92); Palau Sant Jordi (Catalan 93 481 00 92/Spanish 93 481 11 92); Palau d'Esports (Catalan 93 481 00 93/Spanish 93 481 10 93).* **Map** A6.

The core area from the 1992 Games consists of a compact hub of buildings in contrasting

styles. The **Estadi Olímpic** – now home to the city's 'second' football team, Espanyol – although entirely new, was built within the façade of an existing 1929 stadium by a design team led by Federico Correa and Alfonso Milà. Next to it is the most original and attractive of the Olympic facilities, Arata Isozaki's **Palau Sant Jordi** indoor hall, with a vast metal roof built on the ground and raised into place by hydraulic jacks. It now regularly serves as a concert venue. In the plaça in front locals gather on Sundays for family walks and picnics, next to Santiago Calatrava's remarkable bow-like **Telefònica** tower; further along is Barcelona's best swimming pool, the **Bernat Picornell** – predating the Games, but rebuilt for them – and the Sports University, designed by Ricard Bofill and Peter Hodgkinson in their neo-classical style. At the foot of the hill by Plaça d'Espanya is another sports hall, the **Palau d'Esports,** built in the 1960s but rebuilt for 1992.

Font Màgica de Montjuïc

Plaça d'Espanya. Metro Espanya/ bus all routes to Plaça d'Espanya. **Fountains** *23 June-23 Sept* 8pm-midnight; *music* 9.30-11.30pm, Thur-Sun, public holidays. **Map** A5 Outrageously over-the-top but not to be missed, the 1929 'magic fountain' swells and dances to Tchaikovsky's *Nutcracker*, Abba hits and other favourites, showing off its kaleidoscope of pastel colours, while searchlights play in a giant fan pattern over the palace dome. Fantastic.

Pavelló Barcelona (Pavelló Mies van der Rohe)

Avda Marqués de Comillas (93 423 40 16). Metro Espanya/bus 13, 50, 100. **Open** *Nov-Mar* 10am-6.30pm, *Apr-Oct* 10am-8pm, daily. **Admission** 400ptas; 250ptas students; free under-18s. **Credit** (shop only) MC, V. **Map** A5

The German Pavilion for the 1929 Exhibition, by Ludwig Mies van der Rohe, was also home to the *Barcelona chair*, copied worldwide in millions of office waiting rooms. The Pavilion was a founding monument of modern rationalist architecture, with a revolutionary use of stone, glass and space. It was demolished after the Exhibition, but in 1986 a replica was built on the same site. Purists may think of it as a synthetic inferior of the original, but the elegance and simplicity of the design are still a striking demonstration of what rationalist architecture could do before it was reduced to production-line clichés.

Poble Espanyol

Avda del Marquès de Comillas (93 325 78 66). Metro Espanya/bus 13, 50, 61. **Open** *Sept-June* 9am-8pm Mon; 9am-2am Tue-Sat; 9am-midnight Sun. *July, Aug* 9am-8pm Mon; 9am-2am Tue-Thur; 9am-4am Fri, Sat; 9am-midnight Sun. **Admission** 950ptas; 500ptas 7-14s, students, over-65s; free under-7s; group discounts. **Discounts** BC, BT. **Credit** MC, V. **Map** A5 As part of the preparations for the 1929 Exhibition, someone had the bright idea of building, in one enclosed area, examples of traditional architecture from every region in Spain. The result was the *Poble Espanyol*, or Spanish Village. Inside it, a Castilian square leads to an Andalusian church, then to replicas of village houses from Aragon, and so on. There are bars and restaurants of all kinds, including vegetarian, and over 60 shops. Many of its businesses are workshops in which craftspeople hand-make and sell Spanish folk artefacts – ceramics, embroidery, fans, metalwork, candles and so on. Some of the work is quite attractive, some tacky, and prices are generally high. Outside, street performers re-create bits of Catalan and Spanish folklore, and there are special children's shows, and the 'Barcelona Experience', an audio-visual history presentation (available in English). The Poble has an unmistakeable tourist-trap air, but it does have its fun side, and many of its buildings and squares are genuinely attractive. It also tries hard to promote itself as a night-spot, with karaoke bars, Cuban dinner-and-dance restaurants, discos and a flamenco show, and dance bands and music groups perform regularly in the main square. Attached to the village is the bar that was once the pinnacle of Barcelona design-bar-dom, **Torres de Avila**, and lately one of the city's most hip clubs, **La Terrrazza/Discothèque**, has opened up at the back of the *Poble* (*see chapter* **Nightlife**).

Curves of the Casa Batlló. *See page 80.*

Paral.lel & Poble Sec

Back in the old city, on the south side of the Raval near the Drassanes, if you stand by the surviving stretch of fourteenth-century city wall at Santa Madrona and look across the broad street towards Montjuïc, you will see a *barri* lining the side of the hill. The street is Avinguda Paral.lel, a curious name that derives from the fact that it coincides exactly with 41° 44' latitude north, one of Ildefons Cerdà's more eccentric conceits. The district is Poble Sec. The avenue was the prime centre of Barcelona nightlife – often called its 'Montmartre' – in the first half of the twentieth century, full of theatres, night clubs and music halls. A statue on the corner with C/Nou de la Rambla commemorates Raquel Meller, a legendary star of the street who went on to equal celebrity around the world. She stands outside Barcelona's notorious modern live-porn venue, the Bagdad. Apart from this, while there are still theatres and cinemas along the Paral.lel, most of its cabarets have disappeared. A real end of an era came in 1997 when El Molino, most celebrated of the avenue's traditional, ultra-vulgar old music halls, suddenly shut up shop (although some Russian investors apparently have a plan to reopen it).

The name *Poble Sec* means 'dry village', fitting testimony to the fact that as late as 1894 this *barri*

of poor workers celebrated with dancing the installation of the area's first street fountain, which still stands, in C/Margarit. By 1914 some 5,000 people lived in shanties up where the district meets Montjuïc. During the *Setmana Tràgica* in 1909, more religious buildings were destroyed here than in any other part of the city (*see page 25*).

On the stretch of the Paral.lel opposite the city walls three tall chimneys stand incongruously in the middle of modern office blocks. They are all that remains of the Anglo-Canadian-owned power station known locally as *La Canadenca* ('The Canadian'), centre of the city's largest general strike, in 1919. Beside the chimneys an open space has been created – the **Parc de les Tres Xemeneies**, now popular with rollerbladers.

Today Poble Sec remains a friendly, working class area of quiet, relaxed streets and squares. It has plenty of cheap bars, some more eccentric bars (*see page 167*) and several reasonable restaurants. Towards the Paral.lel there are some distinguished *Modernista* buildings, which local legend has maintained were built for *artistas* from the cabarets by rich sugar-daddies. At C/Tapioles 12 there is a beautiful, extremely narrow wooden Modernist door with typically writhing ironwork, while at C/Elkano 4 don't miss **La Casa de les Rajoles**, with a strange white mosaic façade that gives an impression of weightlessness. Poble Sec is also one of the most characterful access points to Montjuïc, and as you penetrate further into the densely populated *barri* the streets grow steeper, some becoming narrow lanes of steps climbing up the mountain that eventually provide a superb view of the city.

The Eixample

A fateful decision was taken in the 1850s when, after Barcelona was finally given permission to expand beyond its medieval walls, the plan chosen (by the government in Madrid) was the regular gridiron of Ildefons Cerdà. Opinion in Barcelona was much more favourable to the fan-shaped design of the municipal architect Antoni Rovira i Trias, a reproduction of which can be seen at the foot of a sculpture of the man in Plaça Rovira i Trias, in Gràcia (*see also page 23*).

With time, though, the 'Extension' (*Eixample/ Ensanche*) has become as much – if not more – of a distinctive feature of Barcelona as the medieval city. With its love of straight lines, parallels, diagonals and meridians, Cerdà's plan is a monumental example of nineteenth-century rationalism. The more utopian features of the plan, however – building on only two sides of each block, height limits of just two or three storeys, and gardens in the middle of the blocks – were quickly discarded. Today, most of the interior courtyards are car parks, workshops or shopping centres. The garden

Walk 3: the details of *Modernisme*

The grander (or more outrageous) *Modernista* buildings are easy to find; however, one of the most striking things about the style is the way it appears at so many points in the city's fabric, often in unexpected places. This route (shown in **blue** on Maps 2-3, 5-6, *pages 310-1, 314-5*) covers a selection of lesser-known *Modernista* creations. The buildings are nearly all private, but it's often possible to look in the entrances; however, most also require repair work, so there's always a risk they may be under scaffolding.

The walk begins at Plaça Urquinaona (**Map** D5). From there, go along C/Ausiàs Marc. At No.20 is **Casa Manuel Felip**, designed by an otherwise little-known architect, Telmo Fernández, in 1901, with tall graceful galleries to left and right connecting the first and second floors. At No.31 is the **Farmàcia Nordbeck** (1905), with a rich dark wood exterior. *Modernisme* and pharmacies were peculiarly closely associated in the Eixample.

At the next corner, with C/Girona, is **Casa Antoni Roger** (1890), at C/Ausiàs Marc 33-5, by one of the more prominent (and bombastic) *Modernista* architects, Enric Sagnier. Further along Ausiàs Marc, on the next block at Nos.42-6, is **Casa Antonia Burés** (1906), a truly extraordinary building by another forgotten architect, Juli Batllevell. Two magnificent stone columns in the shape of trees seem to be holding up the building, anticipating the same motif in the Parc Güell.

Turn left at C/Bailen, then left again into C/Casp, and walk back two blocks. At No.48 is **Casa Calvet** (1900), Gaudí's first commissioned apartment block. The symmetrical façade seems very un-Gaudí-like, but the interlacing wrought iron strips around the gallery – with mushroom motifs – and immense iron door-knockers betray the 'master's touch'. On the next block, still on Casp at No.22, is **Casa Llorenç Camprubí** (1901). The long, narrow windows in its (huge) first-floor gallery and very neo-Gothic windows give a superb impression of verticality.

Turn right up C/Pau Claris, past **Laie** bookshop. On the next corner, at Gran Via 650, is another extravagant *Modernista* pharmacy, **Farmàcia Vilardell** (1914). From there, walk along Gran Via three blocks, cross over and turn left into C/Girona.

Casa Jacinta Ruiz, designed by Ramon Viñolas in 1909, is at No.54. Glassed-in *galeries* characterise most *Modernista* houses, but here the spectacular four-storey gallery takes up the entire façade, and is almost Modern rather than *Modernista* in the cleanness of its lines. The wrought iron of the balconies is also especially delicate.

Another block up, at the corner of C/Consell de Cent, is **Forn Serrat**, C/Girona 73. This bakery looks a little rundown; outside, though, it has curving woodwork framing a picture of a girl with bales of wheat and ears of corn – a classic example of the *Modernista* tendency to round off work with a grand flourish.

At C/Girona 86, in the next block, is **Casa Isabel Pomar** (1906), an almost bizarrely narrow building by Joan Rubió i Bellver. Its neo-Gothic roof and pinnacle, like a church in the sky, may have been an architect's joke. Cross C/Aragó, and continue to C/València. Turn right to go to the next corner (C/Bailen) and the marvellous **Casa Manuel Llopis** (1902), No.339, by Antoni Gallissà and Gaudí's collaborator Josep Maria Jujol. It has angular galleries running almost the whole height of the building, together with very elaborate thin brickwork and lovely inlaid tilework.

If you retrace your steps along C/València and continue another three blocks, at the corner with C/Roger de Llúria you will come upon a veritable explosion of *Modernista* architecture. At No.312 (Llúria 80) is **Casa Villanueva** (1909), with graceful thin columns, elaborate glass galleries and a needle-topped tower. Opposite at No.285, **Casa Jaume Forn** (1909) has beautiful stained glass and a magnificent carved door. On this crossing is **Queviures Murrià** grocery, with its tiled advertising posters, from designs by Ramon Casas, still in place (*see chapter* **Shopping**), and down the street at C/Roger de Llúria 74 is one more pharmacy, **Farmàcia Argelaguet** (1904), with fine stained glass and floral decoration on the walls.

At the next junction uphill, C/Roger de Llúria-C/Mallorca, there are two major buildings by Domènech i Montaner. To the left, at Mallorca 278, is the **Palau Montaner** (1893), built for his own family and now government offices. Close by at Mallorca 291 is **Casa Thomas** (1905), now, fittingly, home to the **BD** design company and store (*see chapter* **Shopping**). Much less known is the elegant **Casa Dolors Xiró** (1913), C/Mallorca 302, by Josep Barenys. To finish, go up just another block and a half to Puig i Cadafalch's neo-Gothic fantasy house the **Casa Terrades**, or *Casa de les Punxes* (*see page 79*).

Art**ICKET**

Visit 6 art centers **in Barcelona for 15 €**

Fundació Joan Miró

FUNDACIÓ ANTONI TÀPIES
BARCELONA

Centre de Cultura Contemporània de Barcelona

Centre Cultural CAIXA CATALUNYA

Ticket valid for three months
www.telentrada.com
From abroad (+34) 934 799 920
Ticket offices at the art centers.

902 10 12 12 **TEL·ENTRADA** CAIXA CATALUNYA

around the **Torre de les Aigües** water tower at C/Llúria 56 is one of the few courtyards where one can get a glimpse of how attractive Cerdà's plan could have been.

The Eixample was built up between 1860 and the 1920s, mostly after 1890. This coincided with – and vitally encouraged – the great flowering of *Modernisme*, the distinctive Catalan variant of art nouveau. The equal weight *Modernistes* gave to decorative and fine arts is reflected throughout the district, in countless shop fronts, hallways, and small gems of panelling or stained glass.

The Eixample is the economic and commercial core of Barcelona, with banks and insurance companies, fashion shops and arcades, any number of restaurants, good cinemas and the best art galleries and bookshops, as well as its world-famous architecture. However, the fabric is showing its age, to the extent that people have been killed in the last ten years by crumbling pieces of façades falling into the streets. Some 3,000 have undergone face-lifts, but about another tenth of all the façades in the Eixample still require urgent repairs. As a residential area the district also has an ageing population. Traffic, which has become more and more dominant in the long one-way streets, is a major source of problems. The city council has set up a *Pro-Eixample* project to revitalise the area, one aim of which is to re-humanise its streets by recovering for communal use the inner courtyard of each block.

When the Eixample was first built and until the 1920s the rail line to Sarrià (now the FGC) went above ground up C/Balmes, effectively cutting the district in two. Ever since, the grid has been regarded as having two halves. The *Dreta* (right – to the right of Balmes looking uphill) contains the most distinguished architecture, the main museums and main shopping avenues. The *Esquerra* (left – to the left of Balmes) was built slightly later. Together they have formed the centre of Catalan middle-class life for most of the last hundred years, and to some extent, despite a certain migration to quieter areas out of town, still do. To newcomers unused to such straight lines they can be disorientating, but they form a very special urban environment, with an atmosphere all of its own.

The Dreta

The great avenue of the **Passeig de Gràcia** is the centre of the district. It is famous for its architectural masterpieces, built as elegant residences, such as Gaudí's **La Pedrera** and the **Mansana de la Discòrdia**, with buildings by Gaudí, Puig i Cadafalch and Domènech i Montaner. The Passeig and parallel Rambla Catalunya are fashionable shopping streets, a centre for both stylish arcades like **Bulevard Rosa** and design emporia like **Vinçon**. Window shopping for art has tradi-

tionally been concentrated close by in C/Consell de Cent between Balmes and Rambla Catalunya, and nearby there is too one of the most impressive of all Barcelona's art spaces, the **Fundació Tàpies**.

The cafés on Rambla Catalunya are pleasant, but pricey, and a favourite meeting place for affluent local residents on summer evenings. Cheaper possibilities for a stopover on a walk around the area are **La Bodegueta** and the **Bracafé**. This part of the Eixample is also the place to find some of the city's famed 1980s' design bars and clubs, which, though, have been sliding down the pinnacle of fashion for years. Notable from a design point of view are **Nick Havanna** and **Zsa Zsa**, both near the corner of Balmes and Rosselló.

As well as the most renowned *Modernista* buildings, the streets around Passeig de Gràcia are full of other extraordinary examples of work from that time, whether whole buildings or details. The section of the Eixample between C/Muntaner and C/Roger de Flor has been labelled the *Quadrat d'Or* or 'Golden Square' of *Modernisme*, and plaques have been placed on 150 protected buildings. A guide to them is available (with an English edition) from city bookshops. For a walk taking in some lesser-known features of the area, *see page 77* **Walk 3: the details of *Modernisme.***

Particularly of note are the hallway and exuberant decoration of **Casa Comalat**, designed by Salvador Valeri in 1906 (Avda Diagonal 442-C/Còrsega 316). On Avda Diagonal are two characteristic buildings by Puig i Cadafalch, the **Casa Vidal Quadras** (number 373), now the **Museu de la Música**, and the **Casa Terrades** (416-420), an extraordinary neo-Gothic fantasy with pointed towers that gained it the alternative name of *Casa de les Punxes* (House of Spikes). Not far away – in the block on the corner of C/València and C/Bruc – there is a market by Rovira i Trias, the **Mercat de la Concepció**, reopened after extensive repair work that has saved the lovely tilework of its roof. This is the market where it is possible to buy flowers 24 hours a day, although its flower stalls are now inside the building, rather than in the street.

The outer Eixample above the Diagonal is a mainly residential area, for the most part built after 1910, but with some striking Modernist buildings such as Puig i Cadafalch's 1901 **Casa Macaya,** now the cultural centre of the **Fundació La Caixa** (*see chapter* **Art Galleries**). The area is dominated, though, by the towering mass of the **Sagrada Família**. Not far away is another great *Modernista* project, Domènech i Montaner's **Hospital de Sant Pau**. This and Gaudí's creation stand at opposite ends of Avda Gaudí, made into a pleasant walkway in 1985.

Hospital de la Santa Creu i Sant Pau

C/Sant Antoni Maria Claret 167 (93 291 90 00).
Metro Hospital de Sant Pau/bus 15, 19, 20, 35, 45,
47, 50, 51, 92, N1, N4. **Map** F4

*Up the ladder to the roof of the world: the **Sagrada Família**.*

Influenced by garden-city ideas, Domènech's hospital became the most useful of *Modernista* projects, as well as one of the most beautiful. Begun in 1901 as a long-overdue replacement for the old hospital in the Raval, it was not finished until 1930, by the architect's son. It consists of 48 pavilions, separated by gardens and linked by underground tunnels. A wealth of sculptures, murals and mosaics strikes the eye everywhere, each pavilion having its own ornamental identity. As a place for a patient suffering from a not-too-distressing illness, it is wonderful – though not, alas, for much longer: Domènech's design is considered unsuitable for modern medicine, and plans are afoot to move some of its services elsewhere. While it is a working hospital visitors are free to wander through the courtyards and gardens.

La 'Mansana de la Discòrdia'

Passeig de Gràcia 35-45. Metro Passeig de Gràcia/ bus all routes to Passeig de Gràcia. **Open** (Casa Morera) 10am-7pm Mon-Sat; 10am-3pm Sun. **Map** D4
The 'Block of Discord', on Passeig de Gràcia between Carrers Consell de Cent and Aragó, is so-called because on it, almost alongside each other, stand buildings by the three greatest figures of Catalan Modernist architecture, all constructed between 1900 and 1907 in wildly clashing styles. On the corner of C/Consell de Cent at number 35 is Domènech i Muntaner's **Casa Lleó Morera**, a classic *Modernista* building of exuberantly convoluted, decorative forms. Three doors up at number 41 is Puig i Cadafalch's Gothic-influenced **Casa Amatller**, and next to that is Gaudí's **Casa Batlló,** rising like a giant fish out of the pavement

(*see also chapter* **Architecture**). The Casa Morera is now a **Centre del Modernisme**, with a small exhibition on the style, and the hub of the *Ruta del Modernisme* tour (*see p58*). Visitors to the centre also get to see the first floor of the building, with a superb Modernist interior, and fabulous stained glass (if you don't get a *Ruta* ticket, tours cost 200ptas).

La Pedrera

Passeig de Gràcia 92-C/Provença 261-5 (93 484 59 95/93 484 59 00). Metro Diagonal/bus 7, 16, 17, 22, 24, 28. **Open** 10am-8pm daily; *mid-June-mid-Sept also 9pm-1am Fri, Sat. Guided tours (in English)* 6pm Mon-Fri; 11am Sat, Sun, public holidays.
Admission 600ptas; 350ptas students, over-65s; free under-12s. **Discounts** BC, BT, Articket.
Credit MC, V. **Map** D4
The last non-religious building Gaudí worked on represents his most radical departure from a recognisably *Modernista* style. Built entirely on columns and parabolic arches, with no supporting walls, and supposedly without a single straight line or right-angled corner, this curving, globular apartment block, also known as the Casa Milà, contrasts strikingly with the angularity of much of the Eixample. Its revolutionary features were not appreciated by the Milà family – who paid for it – nor by contemporary opinion, which christened it *La Pedrera* ('The Stone Quarry') as a joke. It is now owned by the **Fundació Caixa de Catalunya**, which has restored the building beautifully. One floor is an exhibition space, while in another is a permanent exhibition, the **Espai Gaudí** (*see chapters* **Museums** *and* **Art Galleries**), and the fourth floor contains the recently-inaugurated **Pis de la Pedrera**, a reconstruction of a

Modernista apartment interior of the 1900s. Informative guided tours (in English, Catalan or Spanish) allow you to see more of the Pedrera's main features and especially the roof, with its extraordinary semi-abstract sculptures (actually ventilation shafts and chimneys). In winter tours may not continue after dark, even though the exhibition space stays open; in summer, however, the roof is opened as **La Pedrera de nit**, a very special terrace bar (*see chapter* **Nightlife**). *Shop.*

Temple Expiatori de la Sagrada Família

Plaça Sagrada Família-C/Mallorca 401 (93 207 30 31). Metro Sagrada Família/bus 10, 19, 33, 34, 43, 44, 50, 51, 101. **Open** *Nov-Feb* 9am-6pm; *Mar, Sept-Oct* 9am-7pm; *April-Aug* 9am-8pm, daily. Closed pm Christmas Day and New Year's Day. **Admission** 800ptas; 600ptas students, over 65s; free under-10s; group discounts. Lifts to the spires 200ptas. **Discounts** BC, BT.
Credit (groups only) MC, V. **Map** F4
It is a supreme irony that this emblematic symbol of the city and Gaudí's masterpiece (or monsterpiece) was neither begun nor finished by the great man. The project was initiated in 1882 by another architect, Francisco del Villar, and Gaudí's involvement did not begin until 1891, but he did transform the design completely and dedicate over 40 years of his life to the building – the last 18 years exclusively – often sleeping on the site. Only the crypt, the apse and the four towers of the Façade of the Nativity, along C/Marina, were completed in his lifetime. Every element in the decoration, much of it carved from life, was conceived by Gaudí as having a precise symbolic meaning, and he was deeply opposed to the idea of anyone appreciating the building outside of its religious context. An essential part of any visit is an attempt to climb the towers beyond the level that can be reached by lift: this gives an extraordinary sensation of walking out into space. Descent via the spiral staircase is not recommended for those suffering from vertigo.

The **museum** in the crypt contains models and a history of the project and other information on Gaudí (*see p92*). The architect himself is buried beneath the nave of the basilica, and steps toward his canonisation have been taken by Catalan bishops. Work on the temple was resumed in 1952 by some of Gaudí's assistants, who drew up plans based on some of his sketches and what they remembered of the great man's ideas (he never used detailed plans). It has accelerated considerably since the 1980s. Josep Maria Subirachs has completed the new towers of the Façade of the Passion along C/Sardenya – with sculptures that horrify many Gaudí admirers – and is now sculpting the apostles on the bronze entrance to the cathedral. The second sculptor working on the building is Japanese, Etsuro Sotoo, who seems to be adhering more faithfully to Gaudí's intentions, with six flowing, modest musicians, at the rear of the temple. Among the next parts due for completion are the vaults of the principal nave, which would for the first time give the Sagrada Família a substantial roof, but (as is often the case) work has been nowhere near advanced enough to meet the ambitious published schedule. Work has also begun on the construction of four massive columns made of porphyry – the hardest stone in existence – to support the great dome, which will make the temple once again the tallest building in Barcelona. No one would hazard a guess when it will be finished.
Museum. Shop.

The Esquerra

This side of the Eixample quickly became the new area for some activities of the city that the middle classes did not want to see on their doorsteps. A huge slaughterhouse was built in the extreme left of the area, knocked down and replaced by the **Parc Joan Miró** in 1979. The functional **Hospital Clínic** was sited on two blocks between C/Còrsega and C/Provença, and further out still on C/Entença is the city's 1905 **Modelo** prison. There are two great markets, the **Ninot**, by the hospital, and the **Mercat de Sant Antoni**, on the edge of the Raval, which is taken over by a great **second-hand book market** every Sunday morning. This is also an area for academic institutions, from the vast **Escola Industrial** on C/Comte d'Urgell to the original **Universitat** central building on Plaça Universitat, constructed in 1842.

Bull-business

Plaza de Toros Monumental

Gran Via de les Corts Catalanes 743 (93 245 58 04). Metro Monumental/bus 6, 7, 18, 56, 62. **Open** *Apr-Sept only: museum* 10.30am-2pm, 4-7pm, Mon-Sat; 10.30am-1pm Sun; *bullfights* approx 5-6pm Sun. **Admission** *museum* 375ptas; *bullfights* 1,500-12,000ptas. **No credit cards**. **Map** F5
If you're set on seeing a bullfight, carry on to Madrid or Seville – this archetypal Spanish activity has never had a strong following in Barcelona, and one of the city's two bullrings has closed. The other, the Monumental, still holds fights on Sundays in season, and has a small museum; the rest of the year it hosts circuses or concerts, which usually draw bigger audiences. Also, the Catalan government dislikes bullfighting, and among new restrictive regulations on the *corrida* is a minimum age limit of 14 for seeing a fight.
Ticket office: *C/Muntaner 24 (93 453 38 21). Metro Universitat/bus all routes to Plaça Universitat.* **Open** *Apr-Sept only* 11am-2pm, 4-8pm, Wed-Sat. Closed public holidays.
No credit cards. **Map** C5

Parklife

This is an intensely urban city, but fortunately there are green areas and even near-virgin woodland a short way from the centre, and Barcelona has also acquired many spectacular modern open spaces. A series of concerts is held in parks (*see chapter* **Music: Classical & Opera**).

All city parks are open *Nov-Feb* 10am-6pm, *Mar, Oct* 10am-7pm, *Apr, Sept* 10am-8pm, *May-Aug* 10am-9pm, daily. **Admission** is free to all except the **Parc del Laberint**.

Parc de Cervantes
Avda Diagonal/Carretera d'Esplugues. Metro Zona Universitària/bus 7, 33, 54, 60, 67, 75, 78.
On the very edge of the city, this is nevertheless one of Barcelona's most beautiful parks. The grass is always green, and it has a kids' play area, a picnic site and a lovely shaded area for when it's very hot. Above all it has a magnificent rose garden, an explosion of colours and smells, especially in late spring. In the centre is Andreu Alfaro's sculpture *Dos Rombs*, aluminium spikes that always look rhomboid, from wherever you see them. From 2000 an annual rose competition will be held here.

Parc de la Ciutadella
Metro Arc de Triomf, Barceloneta/bus 14, 39, 40, 41, 42, 51, 100, 141. **Map** E6
Barcelona's most historic park, the Ciutadella occupies the site of the eighteenth-century Citadel. It was created as the site of the 1888 Exhibition, and just outside it is the **Arc de Triomf** (Triumphal Arch), which formed the main Exhibition entrance. In the middle of the park is a lake where boats can be hired (200ptas per person, per half-hour); beside it is the **Cascade**, or ornamental fountain, on which the young Gaudí worked as assistant to Josep Fontseré, architect of the park. Although formally laid out, the Ciutadella makes an attractive change from the surrounding streets. Surprisingly extensive, it also has specific attractions: the **Museu d'Art Modern**, sharing the surviving buildings of the Citadel with the Catalan Parliament, the **Museu de Geologia** and **Museu de Zoologia**. The **Zoo**, due to move to the Diagonal-Mar area at some point, currently takes up over half the park's space. Not to be missed are the **Umbracle** or greenhouse, also from the 1880s, beautifully restored to provide a mysterious pocket of tropical forest in the city, and the **Hivernacle** or winter garden, with a fine café (*see p165*). Near the Ciutadella bikes can be hired to ride in the park.

Parc del Clot
C/Escultors Claperós. Metro Glòries/bus 56, 60, 92.
A few streets from the flea market at Glòries, a park built on the site of an old RENFE warehouse, full of palms and pines. Curving sections of the old brick walls are imaginatively integrated into the space.

Parc de la Creueta del Coll
C/Mare de Déu del Coll. Metro Vallcarca/ bus 19, 25, 28, 87.
An impressive park created from an old quarry by Josep Martorell and David Mackay in 1987. At its centre is a large lake with artificial beach, and like other '80s parks it has modern sculpture: an Ellsworth Kelly, and a monumental piece by Eduardo Chillida, *In Praise of Water*, hanging from cables. In 1998 one snapped and the massive block came crashing down, injuring three people. It has been restored, but people tend to give it a wide berth.

Parc de l'Espanya Industrial & Plaça dels Països Catalans
Metro Sants-Estació/bus all routes to Sants-Estació. **Map** A4
The Espanya Industrial, by Basque architect Luis Peña Ganchegui, is the most post-modern of Barcelona's new parks. Ten watchtowers, like ship superstructures, look out over the boating lake: at

---

Modernista architecture does extend over into the Esquerra (as the *Quadrat d'Or* concept recognises), with superb examples such as the **Casa Societat Torres Germans** (C/París 180-2) from 1905. There are also fine bars, like the **Velòdrom** on C/ Muntaner, and Barcelona's biggest concentration of gay nightlife in the streets around the crossing of C/Consell de Cent and C/Muntaner – lately tagged *Gayxample* (*see chapter* **Gay & Lesbian Barcelona**). Beyond the hospital the outer Eixample has no great sights, but leads up to **Plaça Francesc Macià**, developed since the 1960s as the centre of the new business district, and the main crossroads of affluent Barcelona. Beyond the office blocks of the *plaça* lie the fashionable business, shopping and residential areas of the Zona Alta.

Gràcia

'Gràcia – independència' and even 'Freedom for Gràcia' can sometimes be seen on T-shirts here. This isn't a demand for the district to become one of the smallest states in the world but rather a half-serious petition to be separated from Barcelona, to which it was annexed in 1897. Fiercely protective of their own identity, *Graciencs* still sometimes refer to outsiders from other parts of town as *'barcelonins'*, as if they did not really belong here.

Little more than a village in 1820, with about 2,500 inhabitants, Gràcia had become the ninth-largest city in Spain by 1897, when it had 61,000 people. It was also known as a radical centre of Catalanism, republicanism, anarchism and, to a

night, lit up, they create the impression that some strange warship has managed to dock by Sants rail station. This is one of the 1980s parks most liked by the public: boats can be hired on the lake, and kids play on Andrés Nagel's *Gran Drac de Sant Jordi* dragon sculpture. Another sculpture is by Anthony Caro. On the other side of the station is the ferociously modern Plaça dels Països Catalans, created by Helio Piñón and Albert Viaplana in 1983 on a site where, they claimed, nothing could be planted due to the amount of industrial detritus in the soil. It's an open, concreted space, with shelter provided not by trees but steel ramps and canopies, the kind of architecture you either find totally hostile or consider to have great monumental strength.

Parc de l'Estació del Nord

C/Nàpols. Metro Arc de Triomf/bus 40, 42, 54, 141. Map E-F5-6

Behind the Estació de Nord bus station is this very striking park from 1988. It's an open, grassy crescent with few trees or benches, just flat ceramic forms in turquoise and cobalt, swooping and curving through the park: an earthwork sculpture by Beverly Pepper.

Parc Joan Miró (Parc de l'Escorxador)

Metro Tarragona, Espanya/bus all routes to Plaça d'Espanya. Map B4-5

This park takes up four city blocks but feels like much more. Built on the site of a slaughterhouse, it's all stubby *palmera* trees, but there's a surprising tranquillity to the large dirt space, helped by Miró's huge phallic sculpture *Dona i Ocell* (Woman and Bird), rising out of the pool for which it was designed.

Parc del Laberint

C/Germans Desvalls (nr Passeig Vall d'Hebron). Metro Montbau/bus 27, 60, 73, 76, 85, 173. **Admission** Mon, Tue, Thur-Sat 275ptas; free under-6s, over-65s. Wed, Sun free.

One of the most atmospheric (and leafiest) parks is also the most out-of-the-way, in Vall d'Hebron. Originally the grounds of a mansion (long demolished), it is densely wooded with pines, and in the centre there is an eighteenth-century formal garden with a deliberately-picturesque fantasy element, including a romantic stream and waterfall. The maze that gives the park its name has often proved a match for cynics who thought it was only for children.

certain extent, feminism. Place names such as Mercat de la Llibertat, Plaça de la Revolució and C/Fraternitat tell their own story.

As you enter the district, and the rigid blocks of Cerdà's grid give way to narrow streets arranged haphazardly, the change in atmosphere is striking. Some streets consist of small, two-storey buildings, and a series of attractive small squares provide space to pause and talk. The most important of them are **Plaça Rius i Taulet**, site of the pre-1897 town hall and a magnificent clock tower designed by Rovira i Trias, **Plaça de la Virreina**, with its village-like church, the peaceful and relaxing **Plaça Rovira i Trias**, with an appealing bronze statue of this great-but-unappreciated architect himself, and **Plaça del Sol**. In **Plaça del Diamant**, the setting

of one of the most popular of modern Catalan novels, a Civil War air-raid shelter has recently been discovered, which it is hoped will be made into a peace museum. Gràcia also acquired a new square in 1993, not elegant but unpretentious and designed for kids, the **Plaça John Lennon**.

Gràcia contains one of Gaudí's earliest and most fascinating works, the **Casa Vicens** of 1883-8, hidden away in C/Carolines (not open to visitors, but the exterior is impressive enough). And of course the most visited place in the whole municipal district is his **Parc Güell**, on the Tibidabo side of the area above Plaça Lesseps, across the busy Travessera de Dalt. *Modernisme* is also represented by Domènech's **Can Fuster** (1908-11) at C/Gran de Gràcia 2-4, and above all by the work

Plaça-life and Gràcia go together: in the **Plaça de la Virreina**.

of Francesc Berenguer, one of Gaudí's assistants, who designed the **Mercat de la Llibertat.**

Gràcia's independent attitude is also reflected in a strong attachment to traditions like the **Festa Major**, the biggest in Barcelona, which for a few days in August makes the *barri* a centre for the whole city (*see page 10*). The district contains many small factories and workshops, and has a sizeable Catalan-speaking gypsy community. Gràcia is also home to a large number of students, and a substantial creative community of artists, actors, photographers and designers, all of whom contribute to its bohemian flavour.

Coffee in Plaça del Sol is a relaxing alternative to busier places in the centre of the city, though the area is at its best after dark. The **Café del Sol** itself is an old favourite but the streets below are full of other cafés. Gràcia had its turn as the city's most in-vogue area for night-time wandering during the 1980s, when many bars opened; since then it's settled into a comfortable position neither at the top nor the bottom of the fashion league, but remaining enduringly popular.

The educated nature of local residents is seen in the number of cultural venues in the district, such as the **Centre Artesà Tradicionarius** for folk music and dance, theatres such as the innovative **Sala Beckett** and two of the most enterprising cinemas in the city, the **Verdi** and **Verdi Park**. The district is also home to the **Gràcia Territori Sonor** experimental music collective, who perform at **Sonar** and other festivals.

Parc Güell

C/d'Olot. Bus 24, 25. **Open** *Nov-Feb* 10am-6pm; *Mar, Oct* 10am-7pm; *April, Sept* 10am-8pm; *May-Aug* 10am-9pm. **Map** E2

In 1900 Gaudí's patron Eusebi Güell commissioned him to oversee the design of a garden city development on a hill on the edge of the city, which he envisaged would become a fashionable residential area. Gaudí was to design the basic structure and main public areas; the houses were to be designed by other architects. The wealthy families of the time, however, did not appreciate Gaudí's wilder ideas, scarcely any plots were sold, and eventually the estate was taken over by the city as a park. Its most complete part is the entrance, with its Disneylandish gatehouses and the mosaic dragon that's become another of Barcelona's favourite symbols. The park has a wonderfully playful quality, with its twisted pathways and avenues of columns intertwined with the natural structure of the hillside. At the centre is the great esplanade, with an undulating bench covered in *trencadís*, broken mosaic – much of it not the work of Gaudí but of his assistant Josep Maria Jujol. Gaudí lived for several years in one of the two houses built on the site (not designed by himself); it is now the **Casa-Museu Gaudí** (*see p91*). The park stretches well beyond the area designed by Gaudí, away into the wooded hillside. Guided tours are available, sometimes in English. Note: the best way to get to the park is with the 24 bus; if you go via Lesseps Metro, be ready for a steep uphill walk. *Café-restaurants.*

Sants

The official city district of Sants, meaning 'Saints', includes three *barris*, Sants proper, La Bordeta and Hostafrancs. When Barcelona's gates shut at 9pm every night, hostels, inns and smithies grew up around the city to cater for latecomers. Such was the origin of Sants, but by the 1850s it had also become a major industrial centre.

Centred around an old Roman road called for centuries *Camí d'Espanya* ('the Road to Spain') and now C/Creu Coberta-C/de Sants, Sants became the site for giant textile factories such as Joan Güell's *Vapor Vell*, the Muntades brothers' *L'Espanya Industrial* and Can Batlló. Few of the people who admire Gaudí's work in the Casa Batlló, the Palau

Güell or Parc Güell give much attention to the fact that it was these factories and the workers in them that produced the wealth necessary to support such projects. It was also a centre of labour militancy, and in 1855 the first-ever general strike in Catalonia broke out here.

Today Sants remains, like Gràcia, one of the areas of Barcelona with a strongest sense of its own identity, and like Gràcia also has a significant Catalan-speaking gypsy community. Practically all its industrial centres, though, have disappeared. The huge **Espanya Industrial** site became a futuristic park in 1985 after a long neighbourhood campaign for more open spaces, and after a 20-year struggle by residents, **El Vapor Vell** is being converted into one of the city's biggest libraries.

The **Estació de Sants**, alongside the Espanya Industrial, also dominates the *barri*. In front of it is the **Plaça dels Països Catalans**, a square of granite and grim metal as much loathed by local residents as it is admired by design critics. On the other side of the station are the more appealing *places* of **Sants** and **Peiró**. In the latter the first-ever Catalan film was shot, '*Baralla en un café*' ('Cafe Brawl'), in 1898. Near the Plaça de Sants is a complex called **Les Cotxeres**, an old tram depot, now converted into a multi-functional community and arts centre. From there, C/Creu Coberta runs to Plaça d'Espanya, where C/Tarragona, to the left, sharply marks the end of Sants and the beginning of the Eixample. This street has been changed totally by pre- and post-Olympic projects, with high-rise office towers that have led it to be dubbed – perhaps in hope – the 'Wall Street' of Barcelona.

Tibidabo & the Zona Alta

Local dignitaries have customarily taken official visitors to the top of **Tibidabo**, the giant peak towering up behind the city, for an overview of Barcelona. The name *Tibi dabo* comes from the Latin, 'to thee I shall give', the words used by the Devil during his temptation of Christ. The view is certainly magnificent, even when there's smog

down below, and the clean air a welcome change. Since it was made accessible by the building of the rail line to Avinguda Tibidabo and the wonderful **Tramvia Blau** ('Blue Tram') in the 1900s Tibidabo has joined Montjuïc as one of Barcelona's two 'pleasure mountains', visited at least a few times each year by just about everyone in town.

Getting there, by train, Tramvia Blau and **Funicular**, is part of the fun (*see page 59*). The square between the tram and the funicular is one of the best places in the city for an al fresco drink or meal: try the **Mirablau** or **La Venta** (*see chapters* **Restaurants** *and* **Cafés & Bars**). From the square, tracks lead along the city-side of the Serra de Collserola that are great for jogging. Further down the flanks of the hill there are more elegant, airy bars (*see chapter* **Nightlife**), and the **Museu de la Ciència**. At the very top of the funicular is a great **funfair** (*see chapter* **Children**), and, for a completely limitless view, the giant needle of Norman Foster's **Torre de Collserola**. Next to the funfair is a church, built in an extravagantly bombastic style and completed in 1940 to 'atone' for Barcelona's revolutionary role in the Spanish Civil War. To the left of it, on the other side of the ridge, there are stunning views over the Vallès to the north, while down the hillside are tracks where you can easily lose yourself for an afternoon among near-virgin pinewoods. For more on walks nearby, *see page 87* **Exploring Collserola**.

Below Tibidabo are the districts of the **Zona Alta** (literally 'Upper Zone', or simply Uptown). This is the name collectively given to a series of *barris* including Sant Gervasi, Sarrià, Pedralbes and Putxet that fan out across the area above the Diagonal and to the left of Gràcia on the map. They are 'upper' both literally (in that they are at a higher elevation than most of the city and so enjoy cleaner air) and in social standing (these are the most expensive residential areas of Barcelona). In the Zona Alta streets are cleaner, quieter, and have markedly fewer small shops and businesses than in other areas of the city.

This is the home of the *pijos* and *pijas*, the city's pampered upper-middle-class youth, who throng the area's many bars and cafés. As well as luxury apartment blocks it is common to see large, individual houses with gardens, some of which have also been turned into elegant restaurants and bars. These areas have few major sights other than the remarkable **Museu-Monestir de Pedralbes**, now home of the Barcelona branch of the **Col.lecció Thyssen**. However, the centre of **Sarrià** and the little web of streets of old **Pedralbes** around the monastery still retain an appreciable flavour of what were quite sleepy country towns until well into this century.

The Zona Alta has dotted around it several works by Gaudi. From wealthy Pedralbes a walk down Avda de Pedralbes leads to his wonderful

More curves: the **Parc Güell**.

gatehouse and gates, the **Pavellons de la Finca Güell** at No.15, with a bizarre wrought-iron dragon. In the garden of the **Palau de Pedralbes** on Avda Diagonal, a former Güell residence, there is a delightful Gaudí fountain, and back on the other side of the Zona Alta off the Plaça Bonanova, near Tibidabo FGC station, is the remarkable Gothic-influenced **Torre Figueres**, or **Bellesguard**. Further into town near Putxet is one of his larger but more sober designs, the **Col.legi de les Teresianes** (C/Ganduxer 85-105) from 1888-9.

The Palau de Pedralbes contains two interesting museums, the **Museu de Ceràmica** and **Museu de les Arts Decoratives.** Around it, on either side of the Diagonal, is the bleakly functional Zona Universitària, chosen as the area for the expansion of Barcelona's main university in the 1950s. On the very fringes of the city, at the very end of the Diagonal, is the **Parc de Cervantes** (*see page 82*), with a magnificent rose garden.

From there, turn back along the Diagonal toward Plaça Maria Cristina and Plaça Francesc Macià to enter Barcelona's fast-growing modern business district. It is just as fast-growing a shopping area, with stores, fashion malls and the 'horizontal skyscraper', **L'Illa**. Close to Plaça Francesc Macià itself there is a small, popular park, the **Turó Parc**. To the right of it on the map is **Sant Gervasi**. This area had its moment of glory as the most fashionable night-time meeting-point in early-'90s Barcelona, especially the streets around the junction of C/Marià Cubí and C/Santaló, site of bars and clubs such as **Mas i Mas** and **Universal**. Also in Sant Gervasi, but closer to Gràcia, is one of the great survivors of the Barcelona club scene, the **Otto Zutz**.

Monestir de Pedralbes (Col.lecció Thyssen-Bornemisza)

Baixada del Monestir 9 (93 280 14 34). FGC Reina Elisenda/bus 22, 63, 64, 75, 78. **Open** 10am-2pm Tue-Sun. **Admission** *Monastery only* 400ptas; 250ptas students under 25, over-65s; group discounts; free under-12s. *Col.lecció Thyssen only* 400ptas; 250ptas students under 25, over-65s; group discounts; free under-12s. *Monastery & Col.lecció Thyssen* 700ptas; 400ptas students under 25, over-65s; group discounts; free under-12s. **Discounts** BC, BT. **Credit** (shop only) AmEx, MC, V. **Map** A1
Founded in 1326 by Queen Elisenda, wife of Jaume II of Aragon, this monastery is still home to a community of 24 nuns. With the installation of the Thyssen-Bornemisza art collection in part of the cloister the rest of the monastery that is on view has also been thoroughly reorganised. A tour of the building now provides a fascinating glimpse of life in a medieval cloister: visitors can see the pharmacy, the kitchens, and the huge refectory with its vaulted ceiling. The main attraction, though, is the convent itself, and above all its magnificent, entirely intact three-storey Gothic cloister. To one side is the tiny chapel of Sant Miquel, covered with

striking murals from 1343 by Ferrer Bassa, a Catalan painter who was a student of Giotto. The Thyssen collection occupies an all-white former nuns' dormitory on one of the upper floors (*see also p92, in chapter* **Museums**).
Disabled: wheelchair access to art collection only. Shop.

Torre de Collserola

(93 406 93 54). FGC Avda Tibidabo/bus 17, 22, 58, 73, 85 then Tramvia Blau and Funicular, then bus 211. **Open** *(subject to confirmation) Sept-May* 11am-2.30pm, 3.30-7pm, Wed-Fri; 11am-8pm Sat, Sun, public holidays. *June-Aug* 11am-2.30pm, 3.30-8pm, Wed-Fri; 11am-8pm Sat, Sun, public holidays. **Admission** 500ptas; free under-3s; group discounts. **Credit** MC, V.
Norman Foster's 288-metre (800-ft) communications tower, built to take TV signals to the world in 1992, stands atop Collserola like some mutant insect poised to swoop on the city. A glass lift takes you to an observation deck 115m (377ft) up, which means you are 560m (1,838ft) above sea level. On a decent day, it's a staggering eagle's-eye view of Barcelona: a couple of times a year, it's also clear enough to see Mallorca; at other times, you might just see an endless haze.

Les Corts

The rural origin of this *barri* can still be heard in the name, 'The Farmsheds', although there rarely seems much that's rustic in it any more. In among its apartment blocks, though, there is **Plaça del Carme**, the surviving core of the old village of Les Corts, annexed to Barcelona in 1867, which still evokes the atmosphere of a very different era.

For most Barcelona residents, though, Les Corts means **Fútbol Club Barcelona**, whose massive sports complex takes up a great deal of the district's space. Curiously, at night the surrounding area becomes the haunt of prostitutes, transvestites and cruising drivers. *Barça*, though, like every other institution in Barcelona, has development plans, and has proposed the construction of a vast all-purpose leisure complex called **Barça 2000** around the existing stadium. However, the plan has been severely criticised by architects and locals, and may not win approval from the Ajuntament.

Nou Camp – FC Barcelona

Avda Aristides Maillol, access 7&9 (93 330 94 11/ 93 496 36 00). Metro Collblanc/bus 15, 54, 56, 57, 75, 101, 157. **Open** *Nov-Mar* 10am-1pm, 3-6pm, Tue-Fri; 10am-2pm Sat, Sun, public holidays. Closed Mon. *April-Oct* 10am-1pm, 3-6pm, Mon-Sat; 10am-2pm public holidays. Closed Sun. **Admission** 500ptas; 350ptas under-13s; group discounts. **Discounts** BC, BT. **No credit cards. Map** A3
The largest football stadium in Europe, shrine of Barcelona FC. First built in 1954, the Nou Camp has since been extended to accommodate nearly all of the club's 100,000-plus members. It also contains the club museum, visitors to which also get to tour the stadium (*see also p105 and chapter* **Sport & Fitness**).

Poble Nou, Clot, Sagrera

These three districts, north of the old city along the coast, once formed part of one large independent municipality, **Sant Martí de Provençals**. Originally a farming and fishing community, it was, like Sants, one of the areas chosen by manufacturers as they sought to expand, and became the great centre of heavy industry in Barcelona, disputing with Sabadell the title of *la Manchester Catalana*. This brought the usual problems – child labour, diseases, overcrowding, noise, smells, smoke – and the usual responses: cooperatives, unions, strikes and other conflicts. In 1897 it was absorbed into Barcelona, and split into three districts, Poble Nou, Clot and La Sagrera.

Poble Nou contained the greater part of Sant Martí's industry, and so continued to be a centre of radicalism and conflict. As a result it would pay dearly after 1939. Then, in the 1960s, the *barri* began to change its character as entire factories folded, moved to the Zona Franca or got out of the city altogether. The departure of the most historic, Can Girona, in 1992, marked the end of an epoch.

Today Poble Nou has become a laboratory for post-industrial experiments. Old factories are now schools, civic centres, workshops and open spaces. In the early '90s many artists moved in, drawn by greater working space and lower rents compared with Ciutat Vella. For a while Poble Nou gained a reputation as a new centre for contemporary creation, but more recently many artists have moved out again, as the cheap old buildings they occupied have been replaced by new blocks of flats.

One entire section of the *barri* is now the Vila Olímpica; once a hive of dirty industry, it is now one of the gateways to the beach. In the middle of the district there are still parts of the old Poble Nou, and even earlier Sant Martí: lovely **Rambla del Poble Nou** compares favourably with the one in the city centre, and the area around **Plaça Prim** has kept its village atmosphere. Some disused factories have been recycled as clubs and music venues, the best known **Zeleste**. And Poble Nou still has (looking odd amid recent developments) Barcelona's oldest, most atmospheric cemetery, the **Cementiri de l'Est**, with the extraordinary sculpture *El bes de la mort* (Kiss of Death) to remind us of the brevity of human existence.

Clot and **La Sagrera**, both small *barris*, experienced much the same history as Poble Nou. Clot boasts a very intimate and friendly food market in the **Plaça Font i Sagué**, and a striking piece of urban design, the **Parc del Clot**. Nearby is **Plaça de les Glòries** (*see page 53*), centrepiece of plans to upgrade this incorrigibly shabby area.

Exploring Collserola

With the exception of Tibidabo, for decades Barcelona cold-shouldered the long Collserola mountain chain to its north and west. Now, things have changed. **Tibidabo**, with its funfair, tram, bars, restaurants and fabulous views, especially from the huge **Torre de Collserola**, is at the centre of the ridge. The 6,550-hectare (16,000-acre) park of the Serra de Collserola proper is, however, more easily reached by FGC trains on the Terrassa-Sabadell line from Plaça Catalunya, getting off at **Baixador de Vallvidrera** station.

A ten-minute walk from the station up into the woods along Carretera de l'Església will take you to the **Museu Verdaguer** (*see page 105*) and the park's **Centre d'Informació** (93 280 35 52), where maps can be bought. Some information about the mountain is also available in English. This very helpful centre also has an exhibition area and bar. There are five suggested itineraries, ranging from a walk of a mere 20 minutes to an excursion to the Serra d'en Cardona of two hours-plus. Other, longer hikes are also signposted. The great thing however is to explore for oneself, because the Collserola is a wonderful natural reserve, with the trees providing delicious shade on a hot day. Walking is easy, as paths and climbs are well maintained. You occasionally come upon abandoned *masies*, traditional farmhouses. Picnic spaces are clearly indicated, but it is strictly forbidden to light fires. Holm oak and pines predominate among the trees, squirrels and rabbits are everywhere, and the scents and colours of herbs and wild flowers are exhilarating. For bird-watchers there is scarcely a better place in Catalonia, and it's also excellent for mountain-biking.

One easy itinerary is to walk the 2km (1.2 miles) from the Information Centre to the quiet hilltop town of **Vallvidrera**, stopping on the way at the **Font de la Budellera**, a spring and picnic site. In Vallvidrera's main *plaça* there are two bar-restaurants to provide rest and refreshment for the traveller, **Can Trampa** and **Can Josean** – the latter has a superb view down over Barcelona. The Torre de Collserola is a short walk away, or a ride down the funicular – with another panoramic view – will take you to **Peu del Funicular** station, from where FGC trains run back to Plaça Catalunya.

In La Sagrera, meanwhile, the huge Pegaso truck factory has been recycled into a school and the **Parc Pegaso**, with a boating lake, and the area has one of the finest pieces of recent architecture in Barcelona, the supremely elegant **Pont de Calatrava** bridge, linking it to Poble Nou via C/Bac de Roda, about the only new construction in the city to be popularly known by the name of its architect, Santiago Calatrava. La Sagrera has also been provisionally chosen as the site for another 'project', an all-new main station for the high-speed train line linking Madrid, Barcelona and France, due to come into service early in the new century.

Diagonal-Mar

It is, however, the area on the north side of Poble Nou along the coast that is undergoing the greatest changes, for this is the part of Barcelona that, with the transformation of the Port Vell complete, has become the latest focus of attention of the city planners. Starting-point of the scheme, carried out in 1999, has been the extension all the way to the sea of Avda Diagonal, which – contrary to the Cerdà plan – used to fizzle out just east of Glòries. The area where the avenue now meets the sea by the mouth of the Besòs, previously known as a Franco-era slum, has been re-christened *Diagonal-Mar*, and work has begun on reshaping it into an all-new, landscaped district, with more new beach, a lake, a multi-media business park and a new site for Barcelona's zoo, removing it from its cramped location in the Ciutadella. The site is already used as a venue for the **Feria de Abril** (*see page 7*).

As in 1929 and 1992, though, Barcelona hopes to underpin its infrastructural schemes with an attention-grabbing international event, in this case the highly controversial **Fòrum Universal de les Cultures** or 'Universal Forum of Cultures', scheduled for 2004 (*see also chapter* **Barcelona Today**). The idea for this 'worldwide forum' has actually been conceived entirely in Barcelona (and with Barcelona's own ends in mind), and how much interest (and so money) it will ultimately generate internationally is a very open question. If it all comes to fruition, this will be one more part of Barcelona changed out of all recognition.

Guinardó, Horta, Vall d'Hebron

The area north of Gràcia, above and to the right of it on the map, is made up of contrasting districts, traditionally of rich and poor, the former in valleys and the latter on hillsides. Until the building of the **Túnel de la Rovira**, which begins near the Plaça d'Alfons el Savi, many of these areas were relatively isolated from the city.

Joined to Gràcia by the long Avda Mare de Déu de Montserrat, **Guinardó** above all consists of two big parks. One, the **Parc de les Aigües**, contains a fun sculpture of a buried submarine by Josep Maria Riera, and Barcelona's most eccentrically beautiful municipal district headquarters, the **Casa de les Altures**, a neo-Arabic fantasy from 1890. The other, **Parc del Guinardó**, is one of the city's older parks, opened in 1920. The *barri* of **El Carmel** has its own **Parc del Carmel**, but also the extraordinary **Parc de la Creueta del Coll**, an old quarry turned into a swimming pool. Escalators have been installed in some of the district's (very) steep streets to make climbing easier.

Incorporated into Barcelona in 1904, the aptly-named **Horta**, 'market garden', has retained many rural features, including some very well-preserved *masia* traditional farmhouses. The medieval **Can Cortada**, in C/Campoamor, shows at a glance that these houses also served as fortresses, while **Can Mariner** in C/d'Horta is said to date back to 1050. Another now houses a great restaurant, **Can Travi Nou**. Horta's abundant water supply once made it the laundry centre for respectable Barcelona, with a whole community of *bugaderes* or washerwomen, as the open-air stone tanks along the lovely C/Aiguafreda attest.

The **Vall d'Hebron**, just above Horta along the Ronda de Dalt ring road on the flanks of Collserola, was one of the city's four main venues for Olympic events, and so has inherited centres for tennis, archery and cycling, at the **Velòdrom**. Around the sports venues there are very striking examples of street sculpture, such as Claes Oldenburg's spectacular *Matches*, near the tennis centre, and Joan Brossa's *Visual Poem*, by the Velòdrom. There is also a reconstruction of the **Pavelló de la República**. One of the area's most distinctive assets is much older, the delightful, semi-concealed **Parc del Laberint** from 1791 (*see page 83*) – testimony to this hillside's much earlier role as a site for aristocratic country residences. For many locals, though, the Vall d'Hebron means above all the **Ciutat Sanitària**, largest hospital in the city and the place where many first saw the light of day.

Pavelló de la República

Avda Cardenal Vidal i Barraquer (93 428 54 57). Metro Montbau/bus 10, 27, 60, 73, 76, 85, 173. **Open** 9am-8pm Mon-Fri. Closed public holidays. **Admission** free.

The Spanish Republic's pavilion for the 1937 Paris Exhibition, designed by Josep Lluís Sert, was the building in which Picasso's Guernica was first exhibited, and an emblematic work of rationalist architecture. It was demolished after the exhibition, but in 1992, following the recreation of that other flagship building the **Pavelló Barcelona** (*see p75*), the controversial decision was taken to create a facsimile of Sert's building, even though it had no direct connection with Barcelona. Austerely functionalist, it forms a curious pair with Oldenberg's *Matches* across the street. It houses a research library, but visitors can see most of the building.

The most elegant creation of Barcelona's new architecture, Sagrera's **Pont de Calatrava**.

Sant Andreu & Nou Barris

On the way out of Barcelona along the Meridiana, which like the Paral.lel derives its name from solar coordinates, **Sant Andreu** is to the right, and **Nou Barris** to the left. Sant Andreu was another of the industrial and working class hubs of the city. Much altered in the 1960s, it has seen some recent renovations: on Passeig Torres i Bages, at Nos. 91-105, Sert's **Casa Bloc**, a rationalist block of flats that was one of the main contributions of the brieft Republican era to Barcelona, has been restored, and, just off the Meridiana, a lovely wine press has been installed in Plaça d'en Xandri.

Nou Barris (Nine Neighbourhoods) has a different make-up. In the 1950s, when the flow of migration into the city was at its height, ramshackle settlements were built here, followed by tower blocks. The price is now being paid, as flats scarcely 40 years old have fallen into ruins and are being demolished. Services of all kinds are deficient; **Vallbona** does not have a single pharmacy; in **Roquetas** some streets are still dirt tracks. The city has now provided parks, sculptures and services – the **Can Dragó** sports complex has the biggest public swimming pool in Barcelona, and a new **Parc Central** was completed in 1999 – but overall these areas represent very much the 'other side' of the new Barcelona.

The outer limits

As well as Barcelona proper, the city's *Area Metropolitana* is made up of a ring of smaller cities. Until this century, all were still rural, but beginning in the 1920s they have acquired industrial estates and large migrant populations from the rest of Spain, and in many cases become virtual dormitory towns for Barcelona.

Due north of the city and spanning both banks of the Besòs river, **Sant Adrià del Besòs** is famous for two things. The first is the district of **La Mina**, notorious as a hotbed of crime and poverty, although it is hoped it will benefit from the Fòrum 2004 to be staged nearby. The second is that for the next few years the **Feria de Abril** is likely to be held there, in the Diagonal-Mar development zone (*see left and page 7*). North of Sant Adrià, **Badalona** is famous for its basketball team, **Joventut** (currently unfortunately renamed by its sponsors **Pinturas Bruguera**), which has won the European Basketball Cup, something its rival FC Barcelona has never managed. It also has its own traditions, with a great **Festa Major** in May, climaxing with the *Cremada del Dimoni*, when a huge devil is burnt on the beach.

On some cars in Barcelona you may see the sticker *'L'H'*. This assertion of identity is a reminder that **L'Hospitalet de Llobregat**, just south west, is the second city of Catalonia, even though it is completely integrated into Barcelona's transport network. With a big Andalusian-born population, it is also Catalonia's main centre for flamenco. There are several flamenco *peñas*, or clubs, in the town, among them **ACA**, C/Clavells 2-4 (93 437 55 02), for dancing, and **Tertulia Flamenca**, C/Calderon de la Barca 12 (93 437 20 44), which runs guitar classes. A special flamenco festival is held on the Saturday before Christmas at **Teatre Joventut**, C/Joventut 10, Hospitalet, when *villancicos*, strange flamenco carols, are sung. Equally, Hospitalet has plenty of bars and restaurants with good Andalusian specialities – try **Andalucía Chiquita,** Avda Isabel la Catòlica 89 (93 438 12 67). In summer, the area around C/Severo Ochoa becomes a huge outdoor café, offering tapas of all types at much more reasonable prices than in Barcelona.

Museums

Stylish, refined, erotic, esoteric – Barcelona's museums are a reflection of the city's character.

Barcelona has numerous fascinating, high-quality museums, but only a few that can really be considered world class. The chief reason is historical. State capitals like London, Paris or Madrid have had responsibility for creating representative national collections; Barcelona, with its much more ambiguous political status, has had to piece its museums together by other means. The fruit of private initiatives and individual energies, Barcelona's museums tend to be more partial than comprehensive, more idiosyncratic than conventional, full of wonderful objects, but with only a handful of recognised masterworks.

Barcelona awoke late to the pleasures of museum culture. Its first public museum – now the **Museu de Geologia** – was set up just before the 1888 Universal Exhibition, and more were born following the 1929 Exhibition on Montjuïc. Only since the most recent restoration of the Catalan government, the Generalitat, in 1980 has there been a drive to create 'national' museums, with the aim of representing historical and contemporary art (the **MNAC** and **MACBA** respectively), Catalan history (the **Museu d'Història de Catalunya**) or Catalonia's scientific legacy, in the **Museu Nacional de la Ciència i la Tècnica** in Terrassa (*see page 257*).

Apart from these official projects, the richness of Barcelona's museums is largely the result of an impressive level of individual effort, especially in the early part of this century. Scientists and academics gathered material for research purposes (as in the older science museums). Wealthy specialised collectors like Rocamora (in the **Museu Tèxtil**) or Plandiura and Cambó (most of whose holdings are now in the **MNAC**) accumulated fine art and objects for pure pleasure, later ceding or selling them to public institutions. Equally, artists such as Picasso and Miró, late in life, favoured the city with legacies of their work, while the sculptor Frederic Marès was given an entire building not for his own work but to display an incredible collection of sculpture and other oddities (the **Museu Frederic Marès**). In most cases these holdings have passed into public ownership.

Barcelona has had the good sense to house its collections in the best of its architecture, from the **Museu d'Història de la Ciutat** (the city history museum), literally within the ruins of the Roman city and a medieval royal palace, to the **Museu Picasso** with its Gothic patio and the **Museu Marítim** in the inspiring fourteenth-century shipyard of the Drassanes. Purpose-built and equally impressive are Josep Lluís Sert's impeccable **Fundació Miró**, and the luminous **MACBA**, by Richard Meier. The extraordinary settings of many museums can be sufficient compensation for the limitations they might have in other areas.

In contrast to these more spectacular examples, there's a rambling selection of private, small museums hidden away in the oddest of places, like the **Museu d'Autòmates** on Tibidabo, the **Museu del Perfum** with its thousands of scent bottles, the **Museu de Carrosses Fúnebres** with its old hearses or the **Museu del Calçat**, the shoe museum. Plans have also been underway for some time to create a motorcycle museum in Poble Nou, and the pastrycooks' guild is due to open a museum of chocolate in the old Sant Agustí convent on C/Comerç, near the Ciutadella, which hopefully will be at least a little interactive.

Opening days & information

Most museums, and all public ones except the MACBA, are closed on Mondays. They are open, with Sunday hours, on most public holidays, but there are days when virtually all museums close: Christmas Day; 26 December; New Year's Day; 6 January. When it comes to working out what is being shown, most labelling is in Catalan, Spanish or both. A small (if slowly growing) number of museums now provide some labelling in English, or offer free brochures or translations to be consulted while touring the galleries. Some museums also offer guided tours, but, again, they are rarely in English.

The Articket & other discounts

The **Articket** is a joint entry ticket for seven major arts centres – **MNAC** (which includes the **Museu d'Art Modern**), **MACBA**, the **Fundació Miró**, **Espai Gaudí/La Pedrera**, the **Fundació Tàpies** and the **CCCB** (for the last two, *see chapter* **Art Galleries**). It has the distinction of being the first product in Barcelona priced from the outset in euros: 12 euros, or an awkward 1,997ptas (so each centre is roughly half-price). You can visit them at any time within three months of the date of purchase; the ticket is available from participating venues and via **Tel-entrada** (*see p215*). Many museums also give discounts to holders of the **Barcelona Card** and/or **Bus Turístic** tickets (*see p58*); where this is so it is indicated in listings with the letters **BC** and **BT**.

Gaudí & Miró

Casa-Museu Gaudí

Parc Güell, Carretera del Carmel (93 219 38 11).
Bus 24, 25. **Open** *Oct-May* 10am-6pm,
June-Sept 10am-7pm, daily. **Admission** 300ptas;
free under 10s; group discounts.
Credit (shop only) MC, V. **Map** E2
One of only a few houses completed in the **Parc
Güell**, this modest residence was designed by
Gaudí's colleague Francesc Berenguer. Gaudí himself designed the graceful pergola in the garden, and
lived here from 1906 to 1926, although in his last
years he mostly slept in the workshop at the Sagrada
Família. The simple interior, in tune with Gaudí's
spartan religiosity, offers examples of the beautiful
and outlandish furniture designed by him and by
disciples such as Josep Maria Jujol. Also on show are
memorabilia of Gaudí and his collaborators, and
drawings for some of his wilder, unfinished projects.

Espai Gaudí – La Pedrera

*Passeig de Gràcia 92-C/Provença 261-5 (93 484 59
95/93 484 59 00). Metro Diagonal/bus 7, 16, 17, 22,
24, 28.* **Open** 10am-8pm daily; *mid-June-mid-Sept*
also 9pm-1am Fri, Sat. *Guided tours (in English)* 6pm
Mon-Fri; 11am Sat, Sun, public holidays.
Admission 600ptas; 350ptas students, over-65s;
free under-12s. **Discounts** Articket, BC, BT.
Credit MC, V. **Map** D4
In the large attic of Gaudí's **La Pedrera** (*see also
p80*), beneath an inspiring sequence of brick arches,
is the city's only systematic overview of Gaudí's
œuvre. Drawings, photographs, models and audio-
visual displays give a simple yet thorough idea of

the master's creative evolution, with special emphasis on La Pedrera itself. The recently restored space
was once used to hang residents' washing, and at
one time there were even some small apartments in
part of the floor. Above is the building's marvellous
roof terrace. Admission now also allows you to see
the **Pis de la Pedrera**, on the fourth floor, a reconstruction of a *Modernista* apartment interior (not by
Gaudí) and lower down there is the (free) **Centre
Cultural Caixa Catalunya**, the temporary exhibition space of the savings bank foundation that
owns the building (*see also chapter* **Art Galleries**).
Shop.
Website: www.caixacat.es/fundcat.html

Fundació Joan Miró

*Plaça Neptú, Parc de Montjuïc (93 329 19 08/
fjmiro@bcn.fjmiro.es). Metro Paral.lel, then
Funicular de Montjuïc/bus 61.* **Open** *Oct-June* 10am-
7pm Tue, Wed, Fri, Sat; 10am-9.30pm Thur; 10am-
2.30pm Sun, public holidays. *July-Sept* 10am-8pm
Tue, Wed, Fri, Sat; 10am-9.30pm Thur; 10am-2.30pm
Sun, public holidays. *Guided tours* 12.30pm Sat, Sun.
Admission 800ptas; 450ptas students, over-65s; free
under-14s; group discounts. **Discounts** Articket,
BC, BT. **Credit** (shop only) MC, V. **Map** B6
Joan Miró died in 1983, but not before creating the
foundation that bears his name, open to the public
since 1975. Designed by his friend Josep Lluís Sert,
this is one of the world's great museum buildings:
white walls, rustic tile floors, open airy galleries, and
an elegant system of roof arches to let in natural
light. Expanded in the 1980s, it houses a collection
of over 200 paintings, 150 sculptures – including two
recently-added large outdoor pieces – and all of

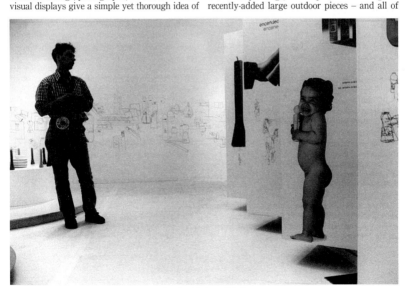

The founder's spirit lives on at the **Fundació Joan Miró**.

Miró's graphic work, a huge legacy of some 5,000 drawings, plus notebooks and other material. Some of the graphic work is always on show in a windowless gallery upstairs, although not all can be shown at once. The permanent collection occupies over half the museum's exhibition space; it begins with large paintings from Miró's late period, giving an idea of his trademark use of primary colours and simplified organic forms symbolising stars, the moon and women. There is also a huge tapestry. On the way to the sculpture gallery is the reconstructed *Mercury Fountain* by Miró's great friend Alexander Calder, originally created for the Spanish Republic's pavi-lion at the 1937 Paris Exhibition; a number of other Calder works, including a mobile, are dotted about the building. Next there are some of Miró's sculptures, made with great technical virtuosity, such as the bronze *Man and Woman in the Night* (1969). His transition from youth to maturity is seen in donations from his wife, Pilar Juncosa, and his dealer, Joan Prats. The **Sala Joan Prats** shows Miró as a cubist (*Street in Pedralbes*, 1917), naïve (*Portrait of a Young Girl*, 1919) or surrealist, culminating in the ominous *Man and Woman in Front of a Pile of Excrements* (1935). From the **Sala Pilar Juncosa** upstairs a ramp leads to newer paintings. Larger and simpler in form, many use thick black outlining, like *Catalan Peasant by Moonlight* (1968). The large *Sunbird* (1968) sculpture is of Carrara marble, and more sculpture is found on the roof terrace, which has a fabulous view of the city. The collection ends with works by other twentieth-century masters – Moore, Léger, Balthus, Ernst, Oldenburg – donated to the foundation. The Miró is also an important venue for temporary shows, in the galleries nearest the entrance, hosting an all-sorts, deliberately varied menu of contemporary art and other exhibits that's very uneven, but also often very interesting. One gallery, **Espai 13** in the basement, is given over to young contemporary artists. The Foundation hosts other activities as well, especially contemporary music (*see chapter* **Music: Classical & Opera**) and has a fine research library.
Café-restaurant. Children's theatre, weekends Oct-May. Concerts. Disabled: toilets, wheelchair access. Library. Shop.
Website: www.bcn.fjmiro.es

Museu del Temple Expiatori de la Sagrada Família

C/Mallorca 401 (93 207 30 31). Metro Sagrada Família/bus all routes to Sagrada Família. **Open** *Nov-Feb 9am-6pm daily; Mar, Sept, Oct 9am-7pm daily; Apr-Aug 9am-8pm daily. Closed pm 25 Dec, 1 Jan.* **Admission** 800ptas; 600ptas students, over-65s; free under-10s. *Lifts to spires* 200ptas. **Discounts** BC, BT.**Credit** (groups & shop only) MC, V. **Map** F4
In the crypt of the Sagrada Família is a rather piecemeal display on the design and the ongoing construction of Gaudí's interminable cathedral. Perhaps the most fascinating discovery is that Gaudí's drawings for the project were largely creative expressions of his ideas, rather than any kind of detailed plan that could be followed; another is the imaginary drawing of the finished cathedral, showing the immense size of the temple if it is ever completed. Photos trace the temple's long history, while models and decorative details bring the construction process closer. There are also images from other Gaudí buildings. *See also p81.*

Art museums

Col.lecció Thyssen-Bornemisza – Monestir de Pedralbes

Baixada del Monestir 9 (93 280 14 34). FGC Reina Elisenda/bus 22, 63, 64, 75, 78. **Open** 10am-2pm Tue-Sun. **Admission** *monastery only* 400ptas; 250ptas students under 25, over-65s; free under-12s. *Col.lecció Thyssen only* 400ptas; 250ptas students under 25, over-65s; free under-12s. *Combined ticket* 700ptas; 400ptas students under 25, over-65s; free under-12s. Group discounts to monastery & museum. **Discounts** BC, BT. **Credit** (shop only) AmEx, MC, V. **Map** A1
The Pedralbes Monastery was a fascinating place to visit even before the Thyssen Collection moved in, and together they make medieval religious life all the more vivid. Much the greater part of Baron Hans-Heinrich von Thyssen-Bornemisza's remarkable art collection, acquired for Spain in 1993, is in the Museo Thyssen in Madrid, but the 90 works brought to Barcelona were chosen to harmonise with the setting, with religious images such as the Virgin predominant. Occupying a former nuns' dormitory on one side of the convent's magnificent fourteenth-century cloister, the collection specialises in Italian painting from the thirteenth to the seventeenth century – an important influence in Catalonia – and European baroque works. There is one true masterpiece, Fra Angelico's *Madonna of Humility*, painted in Florence in the 1430s. Other notable works include a small *Nativity* (c1325) by Taddeo Gaddi, several works by the Ferraran painter Francesco del Cossa (*Saint Catherine*, from 1470-2, *pictured left*) and a subtle *Madonna and Child* by Titian (1545). German painting is well represented, with a series of saints by Lucas Cranach the Older, and there is a Rubens *Virgin with Child* from 1618. Spanish baroque works include a Velázquez portrait of Mariana of Austria, Queen of Spain (1655-7); getting further away from religious themes, there are also eighteenth-century Italian paintings by Canaletto, Guardi and Pietro Longhi. Selected paintings from the Madrid museum are regularly shown in Pedralbes, generally, again, early and religious works chosen to match the setting. Still a convent of the 'Poor Clares', the monastery, with its three-level cloister, is one of the best-preserved in Europe. In one of the day cells there are extraordinary mural paintings attributed to the Catalan master Ferrer Bassa (1346), influenced by the school of Siena. It's also possible to visit the chapterhouse, refectory and many other parts of the convent (*see p86*). *Disabled: wheelchair access to art collection only. Shop.*

Museu d'Art Contemporani de Barcelona (MACBA)

Plaça dels Àngels 1 (93 412 08 10/group enquiries 93 412 14 13/fax 93 412 46 02/macba@macba.es). Metro Catalunya/bus all routes to Plaça Catalunya. **Open** *26 Sept-24 June* 11am-7.30pm Mon, Wed-Fri; 10am-8pm Sat; 10am-3pm Sun, public holidays. *25 June-25 Sept* 11am-8pm Mon, Wed, Fri; 11am-9pm Thur; 10am-8pm Sat; 10am-3pm Sun, public holidays. *Guided tours* (26 Sept-24 June only) 6pm Sat; 11am Sun, public holidays; group tours by appointment. Closed Tue. **Admission** 750ptas; 550ptas students, over-65s; free under-16s. *Wed only* 375ptas. **Discounts** Articket, BC, BT. **Credit** AmEx (shop only), MC, V. **Map C5/A1**

The pristine white MACBA, obstreperously landed in the middle of the old Raval, is more than a museum: it is the shiniest symbol of the ongoing project to revitalise this historically shabby working-class quarter with culture. While all around it the city is tearing down large tracts of housing, speculators have been pouncing on what's left, and this contemporary art museum, designed by fashionable US architect Richard Meier and opened in late 1995, stands out on its own, as if dropped from the sky. Meier has associated the whiteness of the building with Mediterranean light and sensibility, although this doesn't explain why he used the same white in Des Moines, Iowa, and the City Hall in The Hague as well. Like many of his buildings, the MACBA has a perky geometry: horizontal sun screens break the glass façade; the entrance, marked by a jutting balcony, is like a constructivist puzzle. Most Barcelonans were quite happy with the results, until Frank Gehry's stunning Guggenheim in Bilbao came along to awaken all their old insecurities about cultural inferiority; more to the point, in its first years general dissatisfaction was also expressed with the MACBA's content, especially the unfocussed permanent collection. Barcelona's Leviathan-like art bureaucracy, eager to find someone to be held responsible for such mediocrity, devoured two directors between '95 and '98. Today, however, people are having to recognise that the MACBA is at last coming together, after years of backbiting and polemic, and that under its able current director Manuel Borja-Villel the museum has a much more coherent direction. He has added new, fresh content to the collection – in areas such as socially-conscious art of the '60s and '70s, Latin American art, and contemporary conceptualists – and has imaginatively opened up the roster of temporary shows, with a noticeably international focus in place of the localism often shown by Barcelona museums.

Like the Raval's other major cultural acquistion, the neighbouring **CCCB** (*see chapter* **Art Galleries**), the MACBA has a lot of excess space, with an entrance hall, lobby, interminable hallways and long ramps eventually leading to the shows, which are hidden away behind free-standing walls. The museum normally shows a part of its permanent collection in combination with temporary

The MNAC

In the late 1980s work began on creating the **Museu Nacional d'Art de Catalunya**, the National Museum of Catalan Art or MNAC, which is intended to bring together work from every era of the country's rich visual heritage up to the early twentieth century in one comprehensive museum, housed in the giant **Palau Nacional** on Montjuïc. This project still has years to run, but since the reopening of the Romanesque collections at the end of 1995, and the addition of the Gothic sections in 1997, its main elements have taken shape. When the renovation of the building is finally complete the idea is to install the rest of the national collections century by century, perhaps even moving the works of *Modernisme* up the hill from the **Museu d'Art Modern** (*see page 97*).

The museum's beginnings

In the first decades of this century a handful of art historians realised that scores of solitary churches in the Pyrenees were falling into ruin, and with them the extraordinary Romanesque mural paintings that adorned their interiors. Entire chunks of some buildings were 'saved' by private collectors to be set up elsewhere (as in the Cloisters in New York), but in Catalonia the laborious task was begun of removing murals intact from church apses and remounting them on new supports. Since the 1930s, the Palau Nacional has been the haven for this rare legacy, unique in the world, now shown in an updated installation from 1995.

The Palau looks down over the city from a regal perch on Montjuïc, presiding over the long boulevard leading up from Plaça Espanya. Although it may look like the baroque palace of some absolute monarch, it was built only as a 'temporary pavilion' for the 1929 Exhibition. If that clash of times and styles does not make it enough of a pastiche, then its renovation under architect Gae Aulenti, famous for the Musée d'Orsay in Paris, helps provide the ultimate postmodern touch. Underneath the dome is the **Sala Oval**, an enormous hall that is used for occasional public and corporate events.

Some proud locals call the MNAC the 'Catalan Louvre', but its only resemblance to the Parisian museum is in square metres of galleries. Where the collection really stands out – in its collection of Romanesque murals – neither the Louvre nor any other museum can compare. Yet the MNAC makes absolutely no attempt to represent major

international tendencies in art as truly great world museums like the Louvre, New York's Metropolitan or the National Gallery in London do. The Gothic section, however superb, presents exclusively Catalan art and its influences. Not even the large private collection left to Catalonia by the Cambó family, which includes a few non-Spanish masters (Tintoretto, Rubens, De la Tour) mixed in with national figures (Zurbarán and Goya), can make up for this.

The Romanesque murals

None of this takes anything away from the undisputed star of the MNAC, the Romanesque, a style long disdained as rough and primitive, lacking the perspective and masterly technique of Renaissance art. Curiously enough, if the Romanesque is now admired, it is partly due to the avant-garde, with its search for abstract forms and eagerness to shake up classical harmony. Whatever our reasons for enjoying it today, though, the Catalan Romanesque was developed in other times and for quite other motives. As eleventh-century Christendom pushed the Moors southward out of Catalonia, small churches and monasteries were founded along the way, serving as beacons for beleaguered pilgrims and monks. Inside, unsophisticated depictions of the *Pantocrator* (Christ in Majesty), the Virgin, biblical stories and the sufferings of the saints served to instruct doubting villagers in the basics of the faith, turning church walls into a picture book.

The result is a series of images of extraordinary and timeless power. The new display comprises 21 sections in loose chronological order, with the murals set into free-standing wood supports or reconstructed church interiors. For each group there is a photo and model of the original church, and a map of its location. One of the highlights is the tremendous *Crist de Taüll*, from the twelfth-century church of Sant Climent de Taüll in the Pyrenean valley of Boí, in section five (*pictured right*). The massive figure of the Pantocrator holds a book with the words *Ego Sum Lux Mundi*, 'I am the Light of the World'. On the left, near a smaller apse, there is a figure of a monk meditating. Section seven reveals another treasure, from the church of Santa Maria de Taüll (in the same village as Sant Climent), with an apse of the Epiphany and Three Kings and a wall of the Last Judgement, packed with images of demons and the unrighteous being tossed into the flames of Purgatory. On some columns original 'graffiti' has been preserved, scratchings – probably by monks – of animals, crosses and labyrinths.

Other sections, including carvings and sculptures, focus thematically on dramatic angels, strange seraphim with wings covered in eyes (from the apse of Santa Maria d'Aneu), the Lamb of God, or the transition from the expressionless early figures of the Virgin and Child to the more tender renderings that emerged later. After 1200 (section 13) greater fluidity and sophistication was evident in painting, with personalised details for each particular figure, their eyes more alive. The last section, 21, has some non-Catalan murals, saved from the burning-out during the Civil War of the monastery of Sigena in Aragon, and displaying a remarkable mix of thirteenth-century influences from across Europe.

Gothic & Renaissance galleries

The Gothic collection is also impressive, although the strong Italian and Flemish influences that can be traced in the different works make it clear that the styles on display were not unique to Catalonia. Visitors can follow the evolution of Catalan Gothic painting, with altarpieces on wood panels and alabaster sculptures pulled out of parish churches in Barcelona itself. Section three even points out how anti-Semitic iconography made its way into some painting.

The highlights are the works of the indisputable Catalan masters from the Golden Age, such as Bernat Martorell (section 11), and the tremendously subtle Jaume Huguet (section 12), including a series on Saint Vincent and a lovely *Saint George Escorting a Princess* (*pictured left*). The MNAC's Renaissance and baroque holdings come predominantly from the personal collection of the politician-financier Francesc Cambó, and are an international mix of works from the fifteenth to the eighteenth centuries, from Sebastiano del Piombo to Fragonard. High-quality temporary shows are presented at the MNAC, including some with works lent by the Prado in Madrid. There is also good labelling in English, and a helpful English guidebook.

Museu Nacional d'Art de Catalunya

Palau Nacional, Parc de Montjuïc (93 423 71 99/93 325 57 73/mnac@correu.gencat.es). Metro Espanya/bus all routes to Plaça d'Espanya, then escalator. **Open** 10am-7pm Tue, Wed, Fri, Sat; 10am-9pm Thur; 10am-2.30pm Sun, public holidays. **Admission** 800ptas; *temporary exhibitions* 500ptas; *combined ticket* 900ptas; 30% discount under-21s, over-65s, after 6pm Thur; group, family discounts; free under-7s. *Romanesque & Gothic* free first Thur of month. **Discounts** Articket, BC, BT. **Credit** (shop only) V. **Map** A6 *Café. Disabled: toilets, wheelchair access. Shop. Website: www.gencat.es/mnac*

The Picasso Museum

When his father José Ruiz Blasco was hired to teach at Barcelona's art school in 1895, 13-year-old Pablo Ruíz Picasso was a budding young artist whose drawings suggested a firm academic training. By the time of his definitive move to Paris in 1904 he had already painted his greatest Blue Period works, and was on his way to becoming the most acclaimed artist of the century. Barcelona's Picasso Museum is testimony to these vital formative years, spent in the city in the company of Catalonia's nascent avant-garde; it is above all a wonderful place to appreciate the formation of a genius, rather than to see him at his peak.

The museum arose out of a donation to the city by Picasso's secretary and friend Jaume Sabartès, complemented by holdings from the artist's family. It graces a row of elegant medieval courtyard-palaces on C/Montcada, beginning with the mostly fifteenth-century Palau Berenguer d'Aguilar, with a courtyard almost certainly by Marc Safont, architect of the patios of the Generalitat. Since it opened in 1963 it has expanded to incorporate two adjacent mansions, the later but also impressive Palaus Meca and Castellet, and in 1999 it spread into two more, the baroque Casa Mauri and early-

Gothic Casa Finestres (Nos.21 and 23), and a large courtyard behind them. All to show as much of the collection of over 3,000 paintings, drawings and other work as possible, together with temporary shows on Picasso-related themes and other twentieth-century masters, which will probably now be housed in the newly-acquired spaces.

Two things stand out in the museum. The seamless presentation of Picasso's development from 1890 to 1904, from schoolboy doodlings – he was a constant, and very skilful, doodler – to art school copies to intense innovations in blue, is unbeatable. Then, in a flash, one jumps to a gallery of mature cubist paintings from 1917, and completes the hopscotch with a leap to oils from the late 1950s, based on Velázquez' famous *Las Meninas* in the Prado in Madrid. This veritable *vistus interruptus* could leave the visitor itching for more. The culmination of Picasso's early genius in *Les Demoiselles d'Avignon* and the first cubist paintings (1907 and beyond) is completely absent.

So, there's nothing one can do but accept the collection's gaps as twists of history, and enjoy its many strengths. After some wonderful ceramics – donated by his widow Jacqueline – the chronological galleries begin in 1890, when young Pablo still lived in his native Málaga, sketching pigeons like his father (who painted them incessantly). Already at the age of nine his drawing was sure and inventive. After he had painted some perceptive portraits of old people and sailors in La Coruña (1895), Picasso and his family came to Barcelona, living on the nearby C/de la Mercè. Work from Picasso's student years includes life drawings, portraits of his family, and landscapes, including some of Barceloneta beach. Under pressure from his father to attract patrons, he did some large realist paintings, one of which, *Science and Charity* (1897), won a prize in Madrid. Only in the late 1890s did he begin to sign his bawdy nightlife scenes and caricatures with Picasso, his mother's last name. There are fascinating sketches of Barcelona 'decadents', letters-in-cartoons done on his first trip to Paris, and his menu cover from **Els Quatre Gats**, his first paid commission (*see page 161*).

As he gained in artistic independence, Picasso's taste for marginal types intensified, with perversely beautiful paintings like *Margot* and *La Nana* (1901). The intense Blue Period is well represented by *Dead Woman* (1903) and

El Loco (1904, *above*), as well as an azure oil of Barcelona rooftops recently donated to the museum by the Picasso heirs. The chronology is broken with the works from 1917 – the last extended period Picasso spent in Barcelona – including one titled *Passeig de Colom*, before you arrive at the many works inspired by *Las Meninas* and a series done in Cannes in 1957. Finally, the museum has an extensive collection of his impressive limited-edition lithographs and lino cuts.

Museu Picasso

C/Montcada 15-19 (93 319 63 10).
Metro Jaume I/bus 17, 19, 40, 45. **Open** 10am-7.30pm Tue-Sat, public holidays; 10am-3pm Sun. **Admission** *museum only* 700ptas; 400ptas students under 25, over-65s; 250ptas student groups (by appointment); *temporary exhibitions* prices vary; free under-12s, 1st Sun of month, 3-7.30pm Wed for student groups by appointment. **Discounts** BC. **Credit** (shop only) AmEx, MC, V. **Map** D6/**C3**
Café-restaurant. Library. Shop.

exhibits. Since the MNAC and Museu d'Art Modern are supposed to take us up to the Civil War, the MACBA begins with the 1940s, although earlier works by Paul Klee, Alexander Calder and Catalan sculptor Leandre Cristòfol can be seen. The work from the 1940s to the 1960s is mostly painting, with Spanish artists of the *art informel* style (Millares, Tàpies, Guinovart), a sister movement to abstract expressionism. Holdings from the last 30 years feature more international artists, with work by Rauschenberg, Beuys, Dubuffet, Anselm Kiefer, Mario Merz, Christian Boltanski and photographer Hannah Collins complementing a Spanish collection that includes a thorough review of Catalan painting (Ràfols Casamada, Xavier Grau, Miquel Barceló) and Spanish sculpture (Miquel Navarro, Susana Solano, Sergi Aguilar), with fine Basque abstract work (Oteiza and Chillida). Temporary shows run from small solo shows to large-scale collaborations with other museums. The MACBA also has a very good gift-and-design shop (*see chapter* **Shopping**).
Café-restaurant. Disabled: toilets, wheelchair access. Library. Shop.
Website: www.macba.es

Museu d'Art Modern

Edifici del Parlament, Parc de la Ciutadella (93 319 57 28). Metro Ciutadella/bus 14, 39, 40, 41, 42, 51, 100, 141. **Open** 10am-7pm Tue-Sat; 10am-2.30pm Sun. *Guided tours* by appointment. **Admission** 500ptas; 350ptas 7-21s, over-65s; free under-7s; group discounts; *temporary exhibitions* 400ptas; 300ptas 7-21s, over-65s; free under-7s; *combined ticket* 600ptas, 400ptas 7-21s, over-65s; free under-7s. **Discounts** Articket, BC. **Credit** (shop only) V. **Map** E6

Sharing one of the eighteenth-century citadel buildings in the Parc de la Ciutadella with the Catalan Parliament, this museum should not be confused with most 'museums of modern art' in other countries. Its theme is not contemporary art, but Catalan art from the early nineteenth century to the 1930s. It is therefore the prime showcase for the great burst of creativity – leaving aside architecture – associated with *Modernisme*, Catalan art nouveau. It is now administratively part of the MNAC, and it could end up being moved into the Palau Nacional, but it's hard to imagine it all fitting. The galleries begin with the Romantic painter Marià Fortuny, whose liking for oriental exoticism and ostentatious detail led to his *Odalisque* (1861) and telling *La Vicaria* (1870). After the realism of the Olot school (the Vayreda brothers) there is some impressionist-influenced work by the main *Modernista* painters, Ramon Casas and Santiago Rusiñol. Casas' beloved image painted for the **Quatre Gats** café (*see p161*), of himself and the café's owner Pere Romeu riding a tandem, gives a vivid sense of the vibrant spirit of the close of the last century, and there is a large collection of drawings and graphic work. *Modernisme* always sought not to discriminate between fine and decorative arts, and a major attraction here is the superb selection of furniture and decorative objects in different media, as fine a demonstration as the

All glass and dazzling whiteness: Richard Meier's **MACBA**. *See page 93.*

movement's painting and architecture of the creative freedom and new-found wealth of the time. There is masterful work by Gaudí and Puig i Cadafalch, and exquisite marquetry tables and other pieces by the superb furniture-maker Gaspar Homar. Figurative sculpture is represented by Josep Llimona and the neo-classicist Josep Clarà. In painting, the collection carries on with the dark, intense gypsy portraits by Isidre Nonell, which influenced Picasso's Blue Period, the blurry, lavishly coloured landscapes of Joaquim Mir, and the eerie tones of Josep de Togores. The collection trickles off at the end with just two paintings by Dalí – one a 1925 portrait of his father – and work by two avant-garde sculptors from the 1930s, Julio González and Pau Gargallo. González' welded head (*The Tunnel*, 1932-3) points to the roots of contemporary abstract sculpture. There is also a gallery for very well-done temporary exhibits on themes related to the museum's period.
Disabled: toilets, wheelchair access (permanent exhibition only). Shop.

Museu Diocesà (Diocesan Museum)
Avda de la Catedral, Pla de la Seu (93 315 22 13). Metro Jaume I/bus 17, 19, 40, 45. **Open** 10am-2pm, 4-8pm Tue-Sat; 10am-2pm Sun, public holidays. **Admission** 300ptas (varies, depending on exhibition). **Credit** (shop only) V. **Map D6/B2**
The best of Catalan religious art is in the MNAC on Montjuïc, but this space run by the Diocese of Barcelona has a few strong works, such as a group of sculpted virgins on the top floor, altarpieces by the Gothic master Bernat Martorell and some other fine paintings. The display is rather confusing and disorganised, but a visit here is interesting for the building itself, which includes the *Pia Almoina*, a former almshouse, stuck on to a Renaissance canon's residence, which in turn was built inside a Roman tower. This architectural mishmash, so typical of Barcelona, is topped off by the effects of recent renovation. The museum also hosts temporary shows, which tend to have nothing to do with the main exhibit.
Shop.

Museu Frederic Marès
Plaça Sant Iu 5-6 (93 310 58 00). Metro Jaume I/bus 17, 19, 40, 45. **Open** 10am-5pm Tue, Thur; 10am-7pm Wed, Fri, Sat; 10am-3pm Sun, public holidays. **Admission** 300ptas; 150ptas students under 25, 12-16s, over-65s; free under-12s and for all from 4pm Wed, first Sun of month; 250ptas groups (by appointment). **Discounts** BC. **Credit** (shop only) AmEx, MC, V. **Map D6/B3**
The son of a customs agent in Port Bou on the French border, Frederic Marès possibly began his career in the arts by 'collecting' from travellers unable to pay import duties in cash. Trained as a sculptor (his figurative bronzes and marbles are found all over Barcelona), Marès dedicated his 97-year-long life to gathering every imaginable type of object. Created for him by the city in the 1940s, his museum contains his personal collection of religious sculpture, and the stunning 'Sentimental Museum'.

Legions of sculpted virgins, crucifixions and saints on the lower floors testify to an intense interest in the history of his own profession. Marès even collected clothing for saints. The *Museu Sentimental* on the top floor contains his more extraordinary collections: everything from iron keys, ceramics and old carpenters' tools to Havana cigar labels, pocket watches, early Daguerrotypes, Torah pointers … Especially beautiful is the *Sala Femenina*, in a room once belonging to the medieval royal palace: fans, sewing scissors, nutcrackers, and perfume flasks give a charming image of nineteenth-century bourgeois taste. The museum has completed the first part of a well-thought-out renovation programme, which is bringing some coherence to Marès kleptomaniac collecting and making it possible to appreciate the real quality of the collection rather than just its bizarre quantity. In future, religious sculpture from different periods will be more clearly organised by floors (Romanesque, Gothic, Renaissance, baroque), and the renovation has also included the opening of Marès own study and library. The reorganised Marès also hosts an interesting and unusual range of temporary shows, in its delicious, deep-arched medieval patio; other pluses include unusually good labelling in English for a Barcelona museum, and that (in summer only) the patio contains a great open-air café, the **Cafè d'Estiu** (*see p164*).
Café (mid-Mar-late Sept). Shop.

Decorative & performing arts

Museu de Ceràmica/ Museu de les Arts Decoratives
Palau Reial de Pedralbes, Avda Diagonal 686 (Ceràmica 93 280 16 21/Arts Decoratives 93 280 50 24). Metro Palau Reial/bus 7, 33, 67, 68, 74, 75. **Open** 10am-6pm Tue-Sat; 10am-3pm Sun, public holidays. **Admission** *both museums* 700ptas; 400ptas students under 25, over-65s; free under-12s; *one museum* 400ptas; 250ptas students under 25, over-65s. **Discounts** BC, BT. **No credit cards**. **Map A2**
The Palau Reial on the Diagonal was originally built as a residence for the family of Gaudí's patron Eusebi Güell, and in one corner of the gardens is a famous iron gate designed by Gaudí. It became a royal palace and was greatly expanded in the 1920s, when it was ceded to King Alfonso XIII (the building briefly returned to royal use in 1997, when it was used for the wedding banquet of King Juan Carlos' daughter Cristina). The rest of the time it houses two separate museums, which can both be entered on the same ticket. The **Ceramics Museum**, another museum that has recently been attractively reorganised, has an exceptionally fine collection of Spanish ceramics stretching back several centuries, organised by regional styles, which vary sharply. Especially beautiful are the medieval dishes, mostly for everyday use, particularly from Manises near Valencia. Catalan holdings include two wonderful tile murals from the eighteenth century: *la xocolatada* depicts

chocolate-drinking at a garden party, while the other gives a graphic image of a chaotic baroque bullfight. An entire section is dedicated to the famous Valencian manufacture of Alcora, which from 1727 to 1895 satisfied the tastes of the world's aristocracies. Upstairs there is an equally impressive collection of twentieth-century work – highlights include the refined simplicity of Catalan master Josep Llorens Artigas, and pieces by Picasso and Miró – and a space used for excellent temporary exhibits of contemporary ceramics. The **Decorative Arts Museum** occupies the other wing of the building. The palace's original painted walls provide a handsome setting for furniture and decorative objects from the Middle Ages onward, with styles from Gothic through to romanticism and Catalan *Modernisme*, ending with art deco. Quality is high, although not a lot of the museum's first-class holdings of decorative clocks, Catalan glasswork and other artefacts can be shown at any one time. Visitors can also look down into the palace's sumptuously decorated oval throne room. A special section is dedicated to twentieth-century Catalan industrial design. Key works from the 1950s and '60s include Antoni Bonet's BKF chair, and designs by Barba Corsini and André Ricard; the 1980s are represented by Oscar Tusquets' and Javier Mariscal's 'duplex stool'. In one building in the gardens there is also a collection of old carriages, which, though, has been closed up for some time.

Disabled: wheelchair access to Decorative Arts Museum only. Shop.

Museu del Calçat (Shoe Museum)

Plaça Sant Felip Neri 5 (93 301 45 33).
Metro Liceu, Jaume I/bus 17, 19, 40, 45.
Open 11am-2pm Tue-Sun. **Admission** 200ptas; 100ptas students, over-65s; free under-7s; group discounts. **No credit cards**. **Map** D6/**B3**
Run by a shoemakers' guild founded in 1203, this museum is in a tiny building on one of the city's most enigmatic squares. On view is only a small part of a collection that goes from original Roman sandals to present-day footwear: especially fine are the women's embroidered satin dress shoes from the last century. Shoes worn by the famous include pairs donated by cellist Pau Casals and celebrated Catalan clown Charlie Rivel, or the boots of the first Catalan on Everest. There's also seamless footwear, baby booties, traditional shepherds' shoes, and an enormous shoe made from the mould for the Columbus statue at the foot (where else) of La Rambla.

Museu de la Música

Avda Diagonal 373 (93 416 11 57). Metro Diagonal/bus all routes to Passeig de Gràcia/Diagonal. **Open** *mid-June-mid-Sept* 10am-2pm Tue-Sun; *mid-Sept-mid-June* 10am-2pm Tue, Thur-Sun; 10am-8pm Wed. **Admission** 400ptas; 250ptas students under 25, over-65s; free under-12s. **Discounts** BC. **No credit cards**. **Map** D4
The museum occupies the beautiful *Modernista* Casa Vidal-Quadras, completed by Puig i Cadafalch

on the basis of an existing building in 1902. Its collection of historic guitars, tracing the instrument's development from its origins 200 years ago in Andalusia, is one of the best in the world, and the museum does a good job of contrasting European instruments with parallel versions from other continents. An excellent example is a display linking African percussion with jazz drumming, while the cross-cultural mix of instruments as diverse as wood flutes, bagpipes and sitars is fascinating. The collection also testifies to the work of an instrument industry in Barcelona dating back two centuries. Temporary shows are held on the top floor. *Shop.*

Museu Tèxtil i de la Indumentària (Textile & Fashion Museum)

C/Montcada 12 (93 319 76 03/93 310 45 16). Metro Jaume I/bus 17, 19, 40, 45. **Open** 10am-8pm Tue-Sat; 10am-3pm Sun. *Guided tours* by appointment. **Admission** 400ptas; 250ptas students under 25, over-65s; group discounts; free under-12s, 3-8pm 1st Sat, student groups by appointment on third Wed of month. *Combined ticket* with Museu Barbier-Mueller 700ptas; 400ptas students under 25. **Discounts** BC. **Credit** (shop only) AmEx, MC, V. **Map** D6/**C3**
Even if clothing is not your thing, the sight of café tables might draw you into the handsome courtyard of this C/Montcada palace, across from the Picasso Museum. It occupies two side-by-side buildings, the Palau Nadal and Palau dels Marquesos de Lló; the latter retains some of its thirteenth-century wooden ceilings. It brings together items from a number of collections, including medieval Hispano-Arab textiles and the city's lace and embroidery collection. The real highlight is the collection of historic fashions – from baroque to twentieth century – that Manuel Rocamora donated in the 1960s, one of the finest of its kind. Recently the museum has also expanded its collections through some important donations, including one from Spanish designer Cristóbal Balenciaga, famous for the 1958 'baby doll' dress, just the thing for breakfast at Tiffany's. Contemporary textile art and a very smart selection of small temporary shows also feature, and there is also one of the city's best museum shops (*see chapter* **Shopping**). For the very popular café, *see p166. Café-restaurant. Shop.*

History & archaeology

Museu d'Arqueologia de Catalunya

Passeig de Santa Madrona 39-41 (93 423 21 49/93 423 56 01). Metro Poble Sec/bus 55. **Open** 9.30am-7pm Tue-Sat; 10am-2.30pm Sun. **Admission** 400ptas; 300ptas students, over-65s; free under-16s; group discounts. **No credit cards**. **Map** B6
In the Palace of Decorative Arts, built for the 1929 Exhibition on Montjuïc, this is one of the city's better scientific museums, and the art deco centre section has been imaginatively refurbished. Its artefacts come mostly from digs in Catalonia and Mediterranean Spain, starting with the palaeolithic

From the **Museu Barbier-Mueller**.

period and moving on through subsequent eras, with relics of Greek, Punic, Roman and Visigoth colonisers, to take us right up to the early Middle Ages. There are curious objects related to early metallurgy, along with models of neolithic and Iron Age burial sites. A few galleries are dedicated to the Mallorcan Talaiotic cave culture, and there is a very good display (expanded with the results of several digs-in-progress) on the Iberians, the pre-Hellenic, pre-Roman inhabitants of western Spain, whose importance and level of sophistication has been significantly re-evaluated in recent years. The Carthaginian presence in the Balearics is recalled by lovely terracotta goddesses and beautiful jewellery from a huge dig on Ibiza, and a large gallery is dedicated to Greek Empúries, a source of extensive holdings (for Empúries itself, *see pp264-5*). Roman work includes original floor mosaics (curators argue they are better preserved when walked upon), and a reconstructed Pompeian palace room. The centre section has monumental Greek and Roman pieces, including a sarcophagus showing the rape of Proserpine, and upstairs there are Roman funerary stiles and fine mosaics, one of a woman wearing a grotesque comic mask. For some reason an enormous statue of a sexually charged Priapus cannot be visited up close (it was formerly hidden from view completely, and they are still unsure what to do with it). The museum also hosts some temporary shows.
Disabled: toilets, wheelchair access. Library. Shop.

Museu Barbier-Mueller d'Art Precolombí

C/Montcada 14 (93 319 76 03). Metro Jaume I/bus 17, 19, 40, 45. **Open** 10am-8pm Tue-Sat; 10am-3pm Sun. **Admission** 400ptas; 250ptas students under 25, over-65s; group discounts; free under-12s, 3-8pm

1st Sat, student groups by appointment on third Wed of month. *Combined ticket* with Museu Tèxtil 700ptas; 400ptas students under 25. **Discounts** BC. **Credit** (shop only) AmEx, MC, V. **Map** D6/**C3**

Though Columbus' famed voyage took place in 1492, this museum makes clear that the 'pre-Columbian' era extended well beyond that date, as the subjugation of indigenous cultures by the *conquistadores* lasted for decades. In 1996 the Barbier-Mueller museum in Geneva agreed to show around 170 pieces from its collection of ancient American art in Barcelona, carefully selected and displayed on a rotating basis. To house them, the city spent several million pesetas renovating a medieval palace next to the Textile Museum. A minus is its overly theatrical lighting, a cliché of 'tribal art' presentation, but nevertheless the museum treats us to many extraordinary pieces from Mexico, Central America, the Andes and the lower Amazon, some of which date from the second millennium BC. Among its treasures are a large, hollow, ceramic female figure from the pre-Mayan Olmec period, an expressive sculpture of the fire god Huehueteotl (Veracruz, AD 500-800) and rare holdings from the little-known Caviana and Marajó islands at the mouth of the Amazon, stylistically close to present-day Brazilian indigenous patterns. Gold and silver objects from Peru and Bolivia complete this good introduction to pre-Columbian art. The museum also hosts an innovative range of temporary shows, some from the parent museum in Switzerland, others more off-the-wall, such as a recent one on the image of indigenous Americans in Spanish comics.
Café. Shop.

Museu Egipci (Egyptian Museum)

Rambla Catalunya 57-9 (93 488 01 88). Metro Passeig de Gràcia/bus 7, 16, 17, 22, 24, 28. **Open** 10am-2pm, 4-8pm Mon-Sat; 10am-2pm Sun. **Admission** 700ptas; 500ptas under-15s, students, over-65s; free under-5s. **Discounts** BC. **Credit** (shop only) MC, V. **Map** D4

This private museum is run by the Fundació Arqueològica Clos, whose founder Jordi Clos owns a hotel chain that includes the nearby Hotel Claris (*see p117*). Clos has collected Egyptian artefacts since he was a young man, and his foundation is reputable enough to do official digs in Egypt. Almost all finds from these excavations stay in Egypt, but Clos also buys pieces from auctions and museums. Most of the objects in the museum, from pre-dynastic ceramics (3,500 BC) to a sarcophagus from the 'decadent' Ptolemaic period (third century BC), are related to burial rites. A small ancient-empire carved goods carrier and a lower-epoch mummy are among the most important items, and there are dramatic re-creations of tombs, beautiful examples of ornamentation and impressive x-rays of mummified animals. **Note** that for some time the museum has been due to move to a new, larger space at C/València 284, between Passeig de Gràcia and C/Pau Claris; construction problems have caused delays, but the move will probably be completed at

some time in the first half of 2000. The phone number will remain the same, but opening times may change. The new space will also house temporary exhibits organised in collaboration with major world museums in the field, and will have a terrace café.
Library. Shop.

Museu Etnològic

Passeig de Santa Madrona (93 424 68 07).
Metro Poble Sec/bus 55. **Open** 10am-7pm Tue, Thur; 10am-2pm Wed, Fri-Sun, public holidays.
Admission 400ptas; 250ptas students under 25, over-65s; group discounts; free under-12s.
Discounts BC. **No credit cards. Map** A6
Extensive holdings from non-European cultures, totalling over 30,000 pieces, are shown in Montjuïc's Ethnology Museum on a rotating basis. Shows change every few years, and are designed to give an idea of different cultures and not just display objects out of context. The museum is strong in certain areas: pre-Columbian artefacts, Afghan carpets, religious sculpture from India and Nepal, Australian Aboriginal bark painting. Partly to attract Japanese visitors it has also acquired a fine collection of *Mingei*, Japanese popular crafts, and Japan-related shows and activities are also organised.
Library. Shop.

Museu d'Història de Catalunya

Plaça Pau Vila 3 (93 225 47 00). Metro Barceloneta/ bus all routes to Barceloneta. **Open** 10am-7pm Tue, Thur-Sat; 10am-8pm Wed; 10am-2.30pm Sun, public holidays. **Admission** 500ptas; 350ptas under-15s, students under 25, over-65s; group discounts; free under-7s, disabled. *Temporary exhibitions & combined ticket prices vary.* **Discounts** BC, BT.
Credit (shop only) MC, V. **Map** D7/C4
This is the only example in Barcelona of a museum that consciously sets out to explain something thoroughly – Catalan history – from start to finish. Opened in 1996 in the Palau de Mar by the old port, its relative shortage of museum-quality objects has led detractors to call it a theme park, but the visually dynamic displays offer a pretty complete overview of Catalan history from pre-history to the restoration of the Generalitat in the 1980s. All kinds of materials are used to keep us alert and entertained– texts, photos, real objects, reproductions, videos, animated models and re-creations of domestic scenes. There are hands-on exhibits, such as a waterwheel and wearable armour. The eight sections have titles like 'Roots', 'Birth of a Nation' (the consolidation of Catalonia in the Middle Ages) and so on, coming into the contemporary era with 'The Electric Years', including the Civil War (with a recreated bomb shelter), and 'Undoing and New Beginnings' on life under Franco and beyond. Large temporary shows deal with just about everything imaginable, from the history of the Liceu opera to different Catalan regions. Despite being a Generalitat project, the museum manages to avoid overbearing flag-waving, although a drawback for visitors can be that the exhibits are labelled only in Catalan, with just a guidebook in English. A

The **Museu Marítim**'s spectacular setting.

Mediateca on an upper floor has photos, texts and videos on screen, consultable in English, and the top-floor restaurant has a great view over the port and Barceloneta. From June to September, the museum is open 10pm-midnight on Wednesdays for night-time guided tours (in Catalan).
Café. Disabled: wheelchair access. Shop.

Museu d'Història de la Ciutat

C/Veguer 2 (93 315 11 11). Metro Jaume I/bus 17, 19, 40, 45. **Open** *1 Oct-31 May* 10am-2pm, 4-8pm, Tue-Sat; 10am-2pm Sun, public holidays. *1 June-30 Sept* 10am-8pm Tue-Sat; 10am-2pm Sun, public holidays. *Guided tours* by appointment.
Admission 500ptas; 300ptas under-16s, students, over-65s; free under-12s & first Sat of month.
Discounts BC. **No credit cards. Map** D6/B3
The City History Museum had a chance beginning: when the medieval Casa Padellàs was being transferred to this site in 1931, remains of the Roman city of *Barcino* were uncovered while digging the new foundations. They now form a giant labyrinthine cellar beneath the museum, with Roman streets and villas still visible. A visit to the remains takes you right underneath the Plaça del Rei and winds as far as the cathedral itself, beneath which there is a fourth-century baptistery. Busts, monuments and other sculpture found in the excavations are also on display. The admission fee, as well as giving you access to wonderful medieval buildings around the Plaça del Rei, allows you to see the 'Virtual History' audio-visual exhibit and the excellent large-scale exhibitions on different aspects of Barcelona's long history presented in the Casa Padellàs (recent examples have been a superb show on the aftermath of the Civil War, and another on Gothic Barcelona). The bookshop and information centre are useful too.
See also pp60-1.
Shop.

Museu Marítim

Avda de les Drassanes (93 342 99 29). Metro Drassanes/bus 14, 20, 36, 38, 57, 59, 64, 91, 157. **Open** 10am-7pm daily. **Admission** 800ptas; 400ptas students, over-65s, under-16s; free under-7s. **Discounts** BC, BT. **Credit** MC, V. **Map** C6/A4

The oft-stated remark that Barcelona has lived with its back to the sea is belied by the building this museum occupies – the giant *Drassanes* or medieval shipyards, the finest of their kind in the world. Since a 1990s facelift, the museum has also become one of the most visited in the city. The highlight is the full-scale reproduction of the Royal Galley that was the flagship of Don Juan de Austria at the battle of Lepanto against the Turks in 1571. This battle and the subsequent history of Barcelona's port are now presented in 'The Great Sea Adventure', a series of unashamedly audience-pleasing historical simulations, with headphone commentaries (also in English). Visitors get caught in a storm on a nineteenth-century trade ship, take a steamer to Buenos Aires, and go underwater in the *Ictineo*, the prototype submarine of Catalan inventor Narcis Monturiol. Another display, 'From the Boat to the Company', recreates dockside-life scenes from the last century. There is lots of space for temporary shows under the Gothic arches, on entertaining nautical themes. The museum has a prolific collection of paintings and drawings that show you how the port of Barcelona has changed, as well as pleasure boats, traditional fishing craft, fishing paraphernalia, explanations of boat-building techniques and a section on map-making and navigation. A full visit takes a good hour and a half. Attached to the museum there is also an unusually excellent café-restaurant, **La Llotja** (*see chapters* **Restaurants** *and* **Cafés & Bars**). *Café-restaurant. Library. Shop.*

Museu Militar

Castell de Montjuïc, Parc de Montjuïc (93 329 86 13). Metro Paral.lel then Funicular and Teleféric de Montjuïc. **Open** 9.30am-8pm Tue-Sun, public holidays. **Admission** 200ptas; group discounts. **Discounts** BC. **No credit cards. Map** B7

The museum occupies the eighteenth-century fortress overlooking the city on the top of Montjuïc. Used to bombard Barcelona in past conflicts, and as a prison and place of execution after the Civil War (a monument in the moat to Catalan President Lluís Companys recalls his death here in 1940), the castle has strong repressive associations, and is the only place in Barcelona where there is still a statue of Franco. However, its selection of historic weapons – including non-European – is quite special: armour, swords and lances; muskets (beautiful Moroccan *moukhala*), rifles and pistols; and menacing crossbows. Other highlights include 23,000 lead soldiers representing a Spanish division of the 1920s, a room of Scottish uniforms, and, very strangely, a display of Jewish tombstones from the desecrated medieval cemetery that were discovered nearby, the only direct reminder of death in the entire museum. *Bar. Library. Shop.*

Science & natural history

Museu de la Ciència

C/Teodor Roviralta 55-C/Cister 64 (93 212 60 50). FGC Tibidabo then Tramvia Blau/bus 17, 22, 73, 85, 158. **Open** 10am-8pm Tue-Sun, public holidays. **Admission** 500ptas; 350ptas students under 25, over-65s; group discounts; free under-7s and 1st Sun of month. *Additional exhibits* 250ptas extra; 200ptas extra students under 25, over-65s. **Discounts** BC. **Credit** (shop only) MC, V.

Barcelona's Science Museum – fitted into a restored factory building near the foot of Tibidabo – is run by the ever-active La Caixa cultural foundation. Oriented especially towards school groups and young people, the museum is designed to teach basic scientific principles in the most engaging way possible. The quality of the displays is such that there's plenty to interest visitors of all ages, although some of the museums's hands-on exhibits, highly innovative when it opened in the 1980s, are beginning to look a little 'mechanical' and dated now that many state-of-the-art museums are electronics-based. The permanent section uses lively interactive apparatus to explain optical phenomena, quirks of perception, mechanical principles, meteorology, the solar system – there's a planetarium – and many other topics. For very small children there's a special *Clik dels Nens* interactive section. Temporary exhibits are also presented. It's quite out of the way, so a packed lunch is a good idea. *See also chapter* **Children**. *Café. Disabled: wheelchair access. Shop.*

Museu de Geologia

Passeig dels Tilers/Passeig Picasso, Parc de la Ciutadella (93 319 68 95). Metro Arc de Triomf/bus 14, 39, 40, 41, 42, 51, 141. **Open** 10am-2pm Tue, Wed, Fri-Sun, public holidays; 10am-6.30pm Thur. *Guided tours* by appointment. **Admission** 400ptas; 250ptas under-16s, students under 25, over-65s; free under-12s, 1st Sun of month; group discounts. **Discounts** BC. **No credit cards. Map** E6

Once known as the Museu Martorell, the oldest museum in Barcelona was opened in 1882 in this same building to house the private holdings of Francesc Martorell. In one wing there is a rather dry display of minerals, painstakingly classified, alongside explanations of geological phenomena found in Catalonia. More interesting is the other wing, with a selection from the museum's collection of over 300,000 fossils, including imprints of flora and fauna – even dinosaurs – and fossilised bones from all geological periods. Many fossils were found locally on Montjuïc or inside caves on the site of the Parc Güell. *Library.*

Museu de Zoologia

Passeig Picasso, Parc de la Ciutadella (93 319 69 12). Metro Arc de Triomf/bus 14, 39, 40, 41, 42, 51, 141. **Open** 10am-2pm Tue, Wed, Fri-Sun, public holidays; 10am-6pm Thur. **Admission** 400ptas; 250ptas under-16s, students under 25, over-65s; free under-12s, 1st Sun of month; group discounts. **Discounts** BC. **No credit cards. Map** E6

Another of the city's older museums in the Ciutadella, the Zoology Museum occupies the much-loved 'Castle of the Three Dragons', built by Domènech i Muntaner as the café-restaurant for the 1888 Exhibition. In the basement, there's a Whale Room with, yes, a whale skeleton, where popular temporary shows are organised, such as one on bats and another on endangered species. The upper floor has a big collection of dissected and preserved animals, displayed just as they were at the turn of the century. The museum is trying to shift to a more modern, ecological approach, and a very thorough guidebook is available in English.
Disabled: wheelchair access.

Strange days: the **Museu d'Autòmates**.

Specialities & oddities

Galeria Olímpica

Estadi Olímpic, Parc de Montjuïc (93 426 06 60). Metro Paral.lel, then Funicular de Montjuïc/bus 61. **Open** *Oct-Mar* 10am-1pm, 4-6pm, Mon-Fri; 10am-2pm Sat, Sun, public holidays. *Apr-June* 10am-2pm, 4-7pm, Mon-Sat; 10am-2pm Sun, public holidays. *July-Sept* 10am-2pm, 4-8pm, Mon-Sat; 10am-2pm Sun, public holidays. **Admission** 400ptas; 350ptas students; 170ptas over-65s, under-12s; group discounts. **Discounts** BC, BT. **Credit** AmEx, MC, V. **Map** A6

Barcelona's great event of 1992 deserves a better monument than this, for it has little of the kind of thing real sports fans want to see. It would not really be so difficult to get 1,500m-winner Fermín Cacho's shoes, a Michael Jordan Dream Team kit, or the swimsuit of some gold-medal Australian crawler, but instead the small space is chock-full of photos and video fragments, and a lot of peripheral paraphernalia: a huge inflatable Cobi mascot, a recreation of an Olympic Village room, designer volleyball holders. There is a large video library, but it's open only to researchers, a shame for anyone who'd like to relive their favourite event. The best part is a section of costumes, props and scenery – some by theatre group Fura dels Baus – from the opening and closing ceremonies. A spectacular big-screen film on the Games is uninformative but gives you some feel of the event.
Disabled: wheelchair access. Library (Mon-Fri only). Shop.

Museu d'Autòmates del Tibidabo (Tibidabo Automata Museum)

Parc d'Atraccions del Tibidabo (93 211 79 42). FGC Av Tibidabo/bus 17, 22, 73, 85 then Tramvia Blau and Funicular de Tibidabo. **Open** as funfair *(see chapter* **Children***)*. **Admission** included in funfair ticket. **Credit** MC, V.

The first automata belonged to the mechanical age, operating without the constant intervention of external energy. In contrast, this collection of electrified toys from the early twentieth century, inside the funfair on Tibidabo, contains some of the finest examples of coin-operated fairground machines in the world. Still in working order, some

date from as far back as 1909. The entertaining scenarios include a 1924 mechanic's workshop and the saucy *La Monyos* (1913), named after a famed eccentric who cruised the Rambla: she claps her hands, shakes her shoulders and winks, her pigtails flying. Best of all is the depiction of hell (*El Infierno*): look through a small glass hole into a fireball and, to the sound of roaring flames, repentant maidens slide slowly into the pit prodded by naked devils. Admission is pricey if you don't tour the amusement park as well.

Museu de Carrosses Fúnebres (Hearse Museum)

C/Sancho de Avila 2 (93 484 17 00). Metro Marina/bus 6, 10, 40, 42, 141. **Open** 10am-1pm, 4-6pm, daily. **Admission** free. **Map** F5

Mysteriously invisible from the street (ask the security guard at the desk to see it), this incredible collection of historic funeral carriages definitely counts as one of Barcelona's more bizarre cultural assets. The unquestionable charm of these 20 horse-drawn carriages and three motorised vehicles is that they actually were used in Barcelona, from the eighteenth century up to the 1970s. Carriages vary from delicately ornate white hearses for children and 'single people' (presumably virgins), to a window-less black velour mourning carriage that carried the unfortunate 'second wife' (mistress) to the cemetery gates. Dummy horses and funeral officials in costume complete the scene, with images of the carriages as originally used. The Studebaker used to bury Generalitat President Francesc Macià in 1933 and a hefty Buick Special round off the collection.

Museu del Clavegueram (Sewer Museum)

Passeig de Sant Joan, corner Avda Diagonal (93 457 65 50). Metro Verdaguer/bus 6, 15, 19, 33, 34, 50, 51, 55. **Open** *museum* 9am-2pm Tue-Sun; *sewers* 10am-1pm Sat, Sun. **Admission** 200ptas. **No credit cards. Map** E4

The olfactory antipode of the Perfume Museum. The aromas of the sewer museum waft all the way up to the entrance, in a small glass box-like structure in the middle of the pavement just off the Diagonal. A sequence of ramps takes you well below street level

to rooms full of photos, drawings, plans and texts tracing the history of sewers from early examples in ancient Babylonia, Rome and Crete through the centuries to modern versions in London, Paris and Barcelona. An excessively detailed section on the present-day Barcelona system closes the exhibition. Only at weekends are visitors taken in to see the monumental water collectors and sewers below, accompanied by the flow of thousands of rushing flushes and, sometimes, the sound of some of the city's six million rats.
Disabled: wheelchair access (museum only).

Museu de l'Eròtica

La Rambla 96 bis (93 318 98 65). Metro Liceu/bus 14, 38, 59, N6, N9. **Open** 10am-midnight daily. **Admission** 975ptas; 775ptas students, over-65s; free under-16s (only accompanied by an adult). **Discounts** BT. **Credit** MC, V. **Map** D6/**A3**
When this private museum first opened in a more spacious location off Plaça Catalunya in 1997 it seemed to be trying to be a sex museum with, if not a deeply serious approach, at least a bit of class and sophistication. It combined large doses of appropriate kitsch (a section on Barcelona's 'T & A' music-hall tradition, intimidating replicas of antique S & M contraptions) with a genuinely rare collection of erotic art – Kama Sutra illustrations and Japanese erotic drawings, images from 1900s French girly magazines, nineteenth-century engravings by German Peter Fendi and extraordinary photos of brothels and transvestites in Barcelona's *Barrio Chino* in the decadent 1930s. In its new setting up a shady-looking staircase on the Rambla it seems to have gone the other way: the décor looks as though it has been made almost deliberately as tacky and shabby as possible, and the display is just as messy, with no visible concern for anything distinctive in the collection. All right, if you like things tawdry.

Museu del FC Barcelona

Nou Camp, Avda Aristides Maillol, access 7 & 9 (93 496 36 00/93 496 36 08). Metro Collblanc/bus 15, 54, 56, 57, 75, 101, 157. **Open** 10am-6.30pm Mon-Sat; 10am-2pm Sun, public holidays. **Admission** 500ptas; 350ptas under-13s; group discounts. **Discounts** BC, BT. **No credit cards. Map** A3
A must-see for soccer fans, Museu de FC Barcelona vies with the slightly higher-brow Picasso as Barcelona's most visited museum. Even visiting non-fanatics might find a certain charm in the paraphernalia and photos that have accumulated since the club was founded in 1899. The shiniest silver in the trophy case belongs to the European Cup Winners' Cups of 1979, 1982, 1989 and 1997, and the club's greatest treasure, the 1992 European Cup, won at Wembley against Sampdoria. Anything goes in the chronologically-arranged collection – old entrance tickets, players' boots, models of former stadiums, a ref's whistle – and there's also sports memorabilia given to the club but with no real connection with *Barça*, such as a pair of basketball ace Scottie Pippen's shoes. We discover the origin of

Barça fans' nickname, *culés* ('bums', as in rear-ends): spectators used to sit on the high perimeter wall surrounding the old field, their overhanging backsides offering a singular view to those outside. A visit to the museum also gives you a chance to look around the cavernous and legendary Nou Camp, a partial substitute if you can't get to a game. Upstairs there is *Barça's* rather embarrassing art collection. 1999 being *Barça's* centenary year, a huge special exhibition is being presented in the **Fundació la Caixa**'s new *Casaramona* building on Montjuïc (*see chapter* **Art Galleries**), which will run until at least mid-2000. Afterwards parts of the exhibition will probably be preserved in the *Barça* museum. For general information about **FC Barcelona**, *see also chapter* **Sports & Fitness**.
Café (Apr-Oct). Shop.

Museu del Perfum

Passeig de Gràcia 39 (93 215 72 38). Metro Passeig de Gràcia/bus 7, 16, 17, 22, 24, 28. **Open** 10.30am-1.30pm, 4.30-7.30pm Mon-Fri; 11am-1.30pm Sat. **Admission** free. **Map** D4
Thousands of people walk past the Regia perfumery (*see chapter* **Shopping**) every day without realising that the 'Museu del Perfum' sign is no promotional gimmick. Entering through a narrow corridor at the back, one comes into a room full of thousands of scent bottles, dating from pre-dynastic Egypt to the present. The museum began when owner Ramon Planas moved his shop here in 1960, and began gathering what is now one of the world's finest collections. Hundreds of bottles trace the period before perfumes were labelled, including Egyptian, Greek, Roman and baroque examples. The rest are shown by brands: examples from the late eighteenth century onwards (Guerlain, Dior and 4711 limited-edition bottles, such as a Dali creation for Schiaparelli and a prized art nouveau flask by René Lalique for the Coty Cyclamen brand. The bottled aromas of many other lands – India, Turkey, Iran, even countries in the former Soviet Union – can also be seen, if not sniffed.

Museu Verdaguer

Vil.la Joana, Carretera de les Planes, Vallvidrera (93 204 78 05). By train FGC from Plaça Catalunya to Baixador de Vallvidrera. **Open** 10am-2pm Tue-Sun, public holidays. **Admission** free.
Jacint Verdaguer (1845-1902) was the foremost poet of the nineteenth-century Catalan *Renaixença*. His neo-romantic poetry, often on nature or spiritual themes, was enormously popular at the time, and even though he was a priest his funeral brought thousands onto the streets in anti-clerical Barcelona. This old stone farmhouse where he spent his last days has a sparse collection of his belongings, but even if you can't understand the nuances of Catalan poetry, its setting in the hills above the city makes this an attractive outing, with particularly enticing views. A visit to Museu Verdaguer can be combined with a walk around Collserola (*see p87*).
Library. Shop.

Art Galleries

Despite the allure of past glories, Barcelona's art scene is always producing vibrant – and ever more international – new initiatives.

Barcelona's art scene lives a perpetual tug-of-war between the vivid memory of past grandeur and the compulsive need to get on with being a seedbed of contemporary art in the here and now. Names such as Picasso, Miró, Dalí and Gaudí all testify to the vitality of visual culture in the city in the first decades of the twentieth century. Living up to such standards in the present is no easy task.

If Barcelona was a minor hot spot of the early twentieth-century avant-garde, it was in great part because it had a liberal bourgeoisie willing to tolerate and even promote the radical ideas of artists and architects. This spirit was knocked back under the Franco regime, and attempts to revive it had to be made semi-clandestinely. In the 1940s the *Dau al Set* (Dice on Seven) group, among them painter Antoni Tàpies, published their surrealistic magazine virtually underground. Tàpies was the only internationally relevant artist to emerge at this time, his abstract style – still highly influential – evolving from surrealism to *art informel*, a continental version of abstract expressionism.

When democracy returned, the Barcelona art world was convinced that simply by invoking the mood of the pre-war years, and adding in a hefty dose of chauvinistic self-promotion, the city would be able to offer another generation of top-flight artists to the world. Some who fitted the art-star formula – like the spectacular Mallorcan-born painter Miquel Barceló – were hyped to the heavens, while other excellent artists, including some successful elsewhere, were virtually ignored.

Only now is the city beginning to grasp the difference between quality culture within its midst and mere hyperbole. At the same time, Barcelona is finally starting to shake off the pressure of former glories, as a new generation of artists come to share in the benefits of globalised culture, with all that it entails: stylistic homogenisation, a certain nonchalant cosmopolitanism, and – almost for the first time ever in Catalonia – indifference to local artistic traditions.

If Barcelona art is coming back to its creative senses, it is in large part due to the vision and long term planning of public institutions and private foundations. The **MACBA**, after years of floundering, is finally assuming its role as the flagship of Catalan contemporary art (*see page 93*). In contrast, even prestigious private commercial galleries are losing their reputation as trendsetters,

descending into caprice and at times plain bad taste. The weakness of the contemporary market – odd in such an economically buoyant city – may be a factor, with the result that many commercially viable artists are playing gallery hopscotch, jumping from dealer to dealer or spending years without showing in their home town.

FRINGE ADVENTURES

With so many big institutions patronising contemporary art, the Catalan art scene has a tendency to get 'top-heavy'. Post-Olympic Barcelona was inundated by a wave of fresh alternative projects, but many of these have petered out or been assimilated into larger cultural programmes, losing much of their edge. The projects that have managed to survive provide respite from the staid nature of official shows, and much of the commercial gallery scene. Finding what's on offer in this alternative art world can be difficult, but it has given Barcelona a much more varied and enjoyable art scene (*see page 111*).

There is no definitive guide to galleries and artistic activities. Listings appear in the *Guía de Ocio* and some papers, but are rarely comprehensive (*see chapter* **Media**). It can be just as easy to go to a gallery district and do the rounds. All galleries are closed on Sundays and Mondays and for the whole of August. Show openings typically take place around 8pm midweek, and are open to anyone.

Public spaces & foundations

Many museums, particularly the **Fundació Miró** and the **MACBA**, also host temporary exhibitions. For these, *see chapter* **Museums**.

La Capella (Capella de l'Antic Hospital de la Santa Creu)

C/Hospital 56 (93 442 71 71). Metro Liceu/ bus 14, 38, 59. **Open** noon-2pm, 4-8pm, Tue-Sat; 11am-2pm Sun. **Admission** free.
Map C6/A2

Curators at this Ajuntament-administered space seek out younger artists to create new work. The impressive Gothic building was the chapel of the medieval hospital next door, and the choir balcony and side chapels add character to the space. As well as showing Barcelona-based artists, the gallery displays work from local art schools and exchanges exhibits with foreign art academies.

Centre d'Art Santa Mònica

La Rambla 7 (93 316 28 10). Metro Drassanes/bus 14, 38, 59, 91. **Open** 11am-2pm, 5-8pm, Mon-Sat; 11am-3pm Sun. **Admission** normally free. **Map** C6/A4

In the 1980s the Catalan government undertook the renovation of this seventeenth-century monastery as a centre for contemporary art. The polemical result, by Maremàgnum-architects Piñón and Viaplana, is hard enough for installation artists to work with, and almost unusable when it comes to showing paintings (observe the extravagantly tiled lower cloister, or the ridiculously narrow corridors that pass for galleries upstairs). After hosting fine shows in the mid-1990s (Joseph Beuys, Antoni Muntadas), it has taken a nose dive, as the Generalitat's art budget is absorbed by the MACBA. *Bookshop. Disabled: wheelchair access.*

Centre de Cultura Contemporània de Barcelona (CCCB)

C/Montalegre 5 (93 306 41 00). Metro Catalunya/bus all routes to Plaça Catalunya. **Open** *mid-June-mid-Sept* 11am-8pm Tue-Sat; 11am-7pm Sun, public holidays; *mid-Sept-mid-June* 11am-2pm, 4-8pm, Tue, Thur, Fri; 11am-8pm Wed, Sat; 11am-7pm Sun, public holidays. **Admission** (prices vary) *One exhibition* 600ptas; 400ptas students under 25, over-65s, Wed only 400ptas; *two exhibitions* 900ptas; 700ptas students under 25, over-65s; *three exhibitions* 1,200ptas; 1,000ptas students under 25, over-65s; free under-12s. **Discounts** Articket, BC, BT. **Credit** MC, V. **Map** C5/A1

This lavishly equipped centre makes a duo of recent major cultural projects in the Raval with the adjacent **MACBA**. It occupies part of the Casa de la Caritat, built in 1802 on the site of a medieval monastery to serve as the city's main workhouse. The massive façade and courtyard remain from the old building, but beginning in 1988 the rest was rebuilt wholesale (by Piñón and Viaplana) to transform it into a 'multi-disciplinary, multi-functional' cultural centre. The result is a dramatic combination of the original building with Piñón and Viaplana's favoured glass curtain walls. The guiding focus of the centre is on cities in all their aspects, including an excellent series linking writers with their cities (Joyce's Dublin, Kafka's Prague). The CCCB offers very solid exhibitions on twentieth-century art, architecture and urban themes, and a whole gamut of other activities: a festival of video art, an alternative cinema festival, the **Sonar** music festival (*see p242*), dance performances, concerts, film screenings and inter-disciplinary urban studies courses. Visitors are obliged to descend a ramp on one side of the courtyard, pass through a wide hall, pay, and then take escalators up to the galleries – a circuitous route that shows off the architecture while associating 'contemporary culture' with long, vacuous preludes. *Bookshop. Café. Disabled: toilets, wheelchair access.*

Centre Cultural Caixa Catalunya - La Pedrera

Passeig de Gràcia 92-C/Provença 261-5 (93 484 59 95/93 489 59 00). Metro Diagonal/bus 7, 16, 17, 22,

La Capella, *a Gothic beauty.*

24, 28. **Open** 10am-8pm daily; *mid-June-mid Sept* also 9pm-1am Fri, Sat. **Admission** 600ptas; 350ptas students, over-65s; free under-12s; *exhibitions* free. **Credit** (shop only) MC, V. **Discounts** Articket, BC, BT. **Map** D4

This Caixa foundation has the advantage of owning Gaudí's masterpiece the **Casa Milà** (La Pedrera, *see page 80*) which it has been restoring as a cultural centre. Access to the gallery space is via the spectacular main entrance and staircase. The gallery itself is an excellent example of a Gaudí interior: plaster reliefs in the ceiling recall the building's marine-life themes, and none of the walls are straight. Shows mainly feature high-quality international twentieth-century art and modern Barcelona artists, but are worth visiting just to get a full look at Gaudí's work. On floors above are the **Pis de Pedrera**, a reconstructed *Modernista* apartment from the 1900s, and **Espai Gaudí** (*see p91*).

Col.legi d'Arquitectes

Plaça Nova 5 (93 301 50 00). Metro Jaume I/bus 17, 19, 40, 45. **Open** 10am-9pm Mon-Fri; 10am-2pm Sat. **Admission** free. **Map** D6/B2

The College of Architects, opposite the Cathedral, hosts interesting exhibitions on twentieth-century architecture. The façade murals were designed by Picasso in the 1950s, but executed by other artists, since he was not then able to enter Spain. *Bookshop. Café. Disabled: wheelchair access.*

Foment de les Arts Decoratives (FAD)

Plaça dels Àngels 5-6 (93 443 75 20). Metro Catalunya/bus all routes to Plaça Catalunya. **Open** 9.30am-8pm Mon-Thur; 9.30am-1.30pm Fri. **Map** C5/A1

This 100-year-old foundation uniting designers, crafts people, artists and architects is undergoing a notable revival, spurred on by a recent move to this Gothic convent opposite the MACBA. Its annual prizes are very prestigious. Besides organising exhibits of contemporary art, architecture and design, the FAD has assumed responsibility for an open-studio project to be held each June in Ciutat Vella.

Street art

At the end of the 1970s the new, democratic socialist administration of Barcelona set out with a will to renovate their long-neglected city, to an extent that few citizens could then imagine. Beginning before the 1992 Olympics were even a vague project, they embarked on a remarkably ambitious programme to develop new public space in the city, with nearly 100 entirely new squares and parks.

Typified by hard surfaces and creatively designed benches and lamp-posts, these squares were also conceived to incorporate dozens of public sculptures specially commissioned by the city, in the largest programme of its kind in the world. Artists were offered a modest flat fee, with costs born by the Ajuntament; many major Spanish and international artists – Joan Miró, Antoni Tàpies, Eduardo Chillida, Richard Serra, Roy Lichtenstein, Jannis Kounellis, Rebecca Horn – responded. A special effort was made to establish visual landmarks in outlying neighbourhoods that had sprung up chaotically in the 1950s and 1960s. The result is truly impressive. The initiative was stalled in 1993, but recently some new pieces have been done by Lawrence Weiner on Avda Mistral.

Sculpture around the city

Barceloneta & Port Vell *Metro Barceloneta or Drassanes/bus 14, 17, 36, 39, 45, 57, 59, 64, 157.* **Map** D-E7. Sculptures related to harbour themes by Rebecca Horn (Barceloneta beach), Jannis Kounellis (C/Almirall Cervera), Lothar Baumgarten (the names of the winds of the Catalan coast, set into the paving of Passeig Joan de Borbó), and Juan Muñoz (end of Passeig Joan de Borbó). Roy Lichtenstein's unmissable *Barcelona Head* is on Passeig de Colom.
Parc de la Creueta del Coll *Metro*

The innovative work of **Rebecca Horn**.

Penitents/bus 19, 25, 28, 87. Giant sculptures by Ellsworth Kelly and Eduardo Chillida.
Parc de l'Espanya Industrial *Metro Sants-Estació/bus all routes to Estació Sants.* **Map** A4. Small sculptures by Anthony Caro, Pablo Palazuelo and others.
Parc de l'Estació del Nord *Metro Arc de Triomf/bus 40, 42, 141.* **Map** E-F5-6. A large landscape sculpture by Beverly Pepper.
Plaça de les Palmeres *Metro La Pau/bus 11, 12, 34, 35, 36, 40.* Richard Serra's *Wall*, a brilliantly conceived double-curving wall, divides this square in the east of Barcelona, created out of a factory site.
Vall d'Hebron *Metro Montbau/bus 27, 60, 73, 76, 85, 173.* Near the former Olympic tennis site are works by Susanna Solano and Claes Oldenburg (his giant *Matches*). Joan Brossa's disintegrating *Visual Poem* is nearby, by the Horta Velodrome. Much older, but also fascinating, is the Parc del Laberint.
Via Júlia *Metro Roquetes/bus 11, 32, 50, 51, 76, 81.* Sculptures by Sergi Aguilar and Jaume Plensa.
Vila Olímpica *Metro Ciutadella-Vila Olímpica/bus 36, 41.* **Map** F7. Sculptures including Frank Gehry's *Fish* (at the Hotel Arts) and Antoni Llena's kite-like *David* (Parc de les Cascades).

Fundació Antoni Tàpies

C/Aragó 255 (93 487 03 15). Metro Passeig de Gràcia/bus 7, 16, 17, 22, 24, 28. **Open** 10am-8pm Tue-Sun. **Admission** 350ptas-700ptas. **Discounts** Articket, BC. **No credit cards. Map** D4
Antoni Tàpies is Catalonia's best-known living artist, and his foundation in the Eixample is a must-see, if not for obvious reasons. Tàpies had the sense to do more than simply create a shrine to himself: he set up a foundation, with solid exhibition programming in a handsome, idiosyncratic gallery. It is housed in a renovated *Modernista* publishing house built in the 1880s by Domènech i Muntaner. Opened in 1990, it has presented some of the best (if often overly specialised) shows in the city: thematic shows (the idea of the museum, the Fluxus movement)

alternate with retrospectives of artists such as Hans Haacke or Brazilian Lygia Clark. A selection of Tàpies' own work can usually be seen on the upper floor, and sometimes throughout the entire space. The incredible winding tube sculpture on the roof, titled *Núvol i Cadira* (Cloud and Chair), reflects his fascination with eastern mysticism. The library contains a fine collection of books on oriental art.
Disabled: wheelchair access. Library (restricted access).

Fundació la Caixa

Centre Cultural de la Fundació la Caixa, Passeig de Sant Joan 108 (93 458 89 07). Metro Verdaguer/bus 6, 15, 19, 33, 34, 43, 44, 50, 51, 55. **Open** 11am-8pm Tue-Sat; 11am-3pm Sun, public holidays. Closed Aug. **Admission** free. **Discount** BC. **Credit** AmEx, DC, MC, V. **Map** E4

All Spain's *caixes* (*cajas*, in Spanish), or savings banks, are obliged to spend part of their earnings on social and cultural activities. The foundation set up by the largest, the Caixa de Pensions or just *la Caixa*, has since the 1980s built up one of the most important collections of international contemporary art in Spain. More recently the foundation has been shifting its focus towards other fields, but it still presents some of the best art exhibits in Barcelona. The main centre has been at this address, the Palau Macaya, a magnificent *Modernista* building by Puig i Cadafalch from 1901 that creatively mixes Moorish and Gothic styles; however, *la Caixa* is in the process of converting another *Modernista* edifice, the **Casaramona** textile factory near Plaça d'Espanya, into a still larger cultural centre, the better to be able to display the Caixa's art collection. This transfer will probably not take place until 2002, but for much of 2000 the half-complete Casaramona will house the centenary exhibition of Barcelona football club. In the meantime, the Macaya centre usually offers one large or two smaller exhibits, one of them often of photography. The same building houses the **Mediateca** arts library (*see p292*), and an excellent bookshop. *La Caixa* also runs one of Barcelona's best spaces for more daring contemporary art, the **Sala Montcada** by the Picasso Museum.

Bookshop. Café. Library.

Branch: Sala Montcada C/Montcada 14 (93 310 06 99).

Palau de la Virreina

La Rambla 99 (93 301 77 75) Metro Liceu/bus 14, 38, 59, 91. **Open** 11am-8.30pm Tue-Sat; 11am-2.30pm Sun. **Admission** 500ptas; 250ptas students, over-65s; free under-16s. **No credit cards.**

Map D6/**A2**

This neo-classical palace takes its name from the wife of a Viceroy of Peru, who lived there after it was built in the 1770s. Once the city's main exhibition space, the Virreina is suffering a similar fate as the Centre d'Art Santa Monica, mishmashing crowd-pleasing shows, such as one on erotic art, with veritable duds dedicated to obscure designers or photographers of little renown. The lower floor is used mostly to show the work of mid-career Catalan artists, but it has been suggested to turn it into a restaurant. The courtyard is often used for installations. In the same building is the city's cultural information centre and bookshop (*see pages 191, 295*). *Disabled: wheelchair access.*

Tecla Sala Centre Cultural

Avda Josep Tarradellas 44, Hospitalet de Llobregat (93 338 57 71). Metro La Torrassa/bus L12 from Plaça Maria Cristina. **Open** 11am-2pm, 5-8pm, Tue-Sat; 11am-2pm Sun, public holidays. Closed sometimes Aug. **Admission** normally free.

The magnetism of Barcelona tends to mean that suburban artistic endeavours are condemned to obscurity. In Hospitalet, Tecla Sala, one of the most attractive gallery spaces in the city, has been making dents in the metropolitan cultural scene. It pre-

sents its own shows of top-level Spanish artists, such as Rogelio López Cuenca, and important international figures (sculptor Barry Flanagan, or avant-garde photographer Emmanuel Sougez).

Commercial galleries

C/Consell de Cent and the Barri Gòtic are Barcelona's longest-established gallery areas, but in recent years new clusters of contemporary galleries have developed around the **MACBA** in the Raval and in La Ribera, near the Born market.

Barri Gòtic

The Gothic Quarter has held its own in spite of the fuss made about MACBA across the Rambla. Its galleries are very varied: on C/Petritxol and C/Portaferrissa you'll find mostly figurative painting; Palla and Banys Nous are the home of historic painting, antiques and book dealers; below Plaça Sant Jaume is mainly for contemporary art. Also interesting are **Galeria Miguel Marcos**, C/Jonqueres 10, 1º 1ª (93 319 07 57), and **Galeria Segovia Isaacs**, C/Palla 8 (93 302 29 80), with a good selection of contemporary figuration.

Antonio de Barnola

C/Palau 4 (93 412 22 14). Metro Liceu, Jaume I/bus 14, 17, 19, 38, 40, 45, 59, 91. **Open** 5-9pm Tue-Fri; noon-2pm, 5-9pm, Sat. Closed Aug. **Credit** AmEx, MC, TC, V. **Map** D6/**B3**

This handsome gallery presents impeccable shows of the best of Spanish contemporary art. Dozens of artists – young Catalan painter Mireya Masó, sculptor Begoña Montalbán, national photography prize-winner Humberto Rivas – have shown here.

Sala d'Art Artur Ramon

C/Palla 23 (93 302 59 70). Metro Liceu/bus 14, 17, 19, 38, 40, 45, 59. **Open** 5-8pm Mon; 10am-1.30pm, 5-8pm, Tue-Sat. Closed Aug, some Sats June-Sept. **No credit cards**. **Map** D6/**B2-3**

The best of the local dealers in historic art, Artur Ramon puts together intelligent exhibits of Catalan and European painters and thematic shows (from Chinese snuff bottles to Catalan ceramics), spending years searching through private collections.

Sala Parés

C/Petritxol 5 (93 318 70 08). Metro Liceu/bus 14, 38, 59. **Open** 10.30am-2pm, 4.30-8.30pm, Mon-Sat; *Oct-June* only 11.30am-2pm Sun. Closed 3 weeks Aug. **Credit** MC, V. **Map** D6/**A2**

The Sala Parés opened in 1840 and is now owned by a branch of former Mayor Pasqual Maragall's family. It promoted *Modernista* painters (Rusiñol, Mir, Nonell) and it was here that Picasso had his first one-man show. Now renovated, the spacious gallery specialises in figurative and historical painting. Across the street, the associated **Galeria Trama** offers more contemporary work.

Branch: Galeria Trama C/Petritxol 8 (93 317 48 77).

The upper Raval/MACBA area

Since the opening of the MACBA galleries have sprouted up around the upper Raval, in anticipation of an art boom. Some are new, others have moved in from elsewhere, and the quality of only a few is proven. Others, dismayed by the results, have already closed shop. Other venues worth a look are **Galeria dels Àngels**, C/Àngels 16 (93 412 54 54), New York-based **BAI**, C/Ferlandina 25 (93 443 22 25) and **Cotthem Gallery**, C/Dr Dou 15 (93 270 16 69).

Galeria Ferran Cano

Plaça dels Àngels 4 (93 310 15 48). Metro Catalunya/bus all routes to Plaça Catalunya. noon-2pm, 5-8pm, Mon-Sat; *Aug* 5-8pm only. **No credit cards. Map** C5/A1
One of the most successful dealers in Spain, Mallorca-based Ferran Cano has opened a small gallery on the square facing the MACBA. He shows lots of different artists, often young, commercially viable painters.

Urània

C/Dr Dou 19 (93 412 23 45). Metro Plaça Catalunya/bus all routes to Plaça Catalunya. **Open** 11am-1.30pm, 5-8.30pm, Tue-Sat. **Credit** MC, V. **Map** C5/A2
A showcase for a range of projects in graphic design, architecture and photography. Regular artists include Cuban photographer Juan Pablo Ballester and Madrid-based Amparo Garrido.

La Ribera & the Born

The Born district was the hub of Barcelona's 1980s art boom, but the last few years have seen many galleries close. However, the proximity of the **Museu Picasso** and reopening of **Metrònom** have assured the district's continuity. Also worth a look is **Tristan Barberà**, C/Fusina 11 (93 319 46 69), for limited-edition prints.

Galeria Berini

Plaça Comercial 3 (93 310 54 43). Metro Jaume I/bus 14, 39, 51. **Open** *Sept-June* 10.30am-2pm, 5-8.30pm, Tue-Sat; *July* closed Sat. Closed Aug. **Credit** MC, V. **Map** E6/**C3**

Galeria Maeght, *a first-class space.*

One of few prestige Born galleries to have resisted the MACBA fanfare. Berini showcases the work of sculptors and painters from Spain and the USA, and Latin American figurative painters. *Disabled: wheelchair access.*

Galeria Maeght

C/Montcada 25 (93 310 42 45). Metro Jaume I/bus 17, 19, 40, 45. **Open** 10am-2pm, 4-8pm, Tue-Sat. **Credit** AmEx, MC, V. **Map** D6/**C3**
The Paris-based Maeght gallery opened this extraordinary space in the 1970s. In a Renaissance palace on C/Montcada with a lovely courtyard and staircase, it shows hot Spanish and European painters and sculptors, and has the work of many first-class artists in its holdings. It also promotes and sells the fine prints and books of Éditions Maeght. *Disabled: wheelchair access.*

Metrònom

C/Fusina 9 (93 268 42 98). Metro Jaume I/bus 39, 51. **Open** 10am-2pm, 4.30-8.30pm, Tue-Sat. Closed Aug, plus some days July, Sept. **Map** E6/**C3**
Run by collector Rafael Tous, this was Barcelona's most vital art space in the 1980s. After closing briefly, it was now back with original impetus, focusing on photography and multimedia installations. Beneath a glorious *belle époque* domed ceiling, Tous also organises concerts of experimental music, and upstairs there is a performance and video space. *Bookshop. Disabled: wheelchair access.*

The Eixample

The C/Consell de Cent is historically Barcelona's most prestigious gallery district. Recently, the area has undergone a minor revival as many dealers abandon the Raval. Not all of these new spaces are of real calibre. Other galleries of interest are **Galeria María José Castellví**, C/Consell de Cent 278 (93 216 04 82), **Galeria Joan Gaspar**, Plaça Dr Letamendi 1 (93 323 07 48) and **Ignacio de Lassaletta**, Rambla de Catalunya 47, pral (93 488 00 06), with a stunning *Modernista* interior.

Galeria Carles Taché

C/Consell de Cent 290 (93 487 88 36). Metro Passeig de Gràcia/bus 7, 16, 17, 63, 67, 68. **Open** 10am-2pm, 4-8.30pm, Tue-Sat. Closed Aug. **No credit cards. Map** D5
One of the few dealers to emphasise Spanish artists. Taché has the good fortune to represent some of the best, including senior painters Eduardo Arroyo and Miguel Angel Campano and the young Barcelona sculptor Jordi Colomer. The prices are pretty steep. *Disabled: wheelchair access.*

Galeria Estrany-de la Mota

Passatge Mercader 18 (93 215 70 51). FGC Provença/bus 7, 16, 17, 20, 31, 43, 44, 67, 68. **Open** *Sept-June* 10.30am-1.30pm, 4.30-8.30pm, Tue-Sat; *July* 10.30am-1.30pm, 4.30-8.30pm, Mon-Fri. Closed Aug. **No credit cards. Map** D4
Formerly Gràcia-based dealer Àngels de la Mota has teamed up with prestigious dealer Antoni Estrany.

They use this iron-columned basement to show Spanish neo-conceptualists such as Pep Agut, photographer Montserrat Soto and foreign artists such as Thomas Grunfeld. Good for serious collectors.

Galeria Joan Prats

Rambla Catalunya 54 (93 216 02 84). Metro Passeig de Gràcia/bus 7, 16, 17, 22, 24, 28, 63, 67, 68. **Open** 10.30am-1.30pm, 5-8.30pm, Tue-Sat. Closed Aug. **Credit** V. **Map** D4-5

This gallery has its origins in an encounter in the 1920s between Joan Prats, son of a fashionable hatmaker, and Joan Miró. The only remnant of the original business is the name and the hat motifs on the façade – Prats' collection of Miró is now in the **Fundació Miró**. 'La Prats' represents senior Catalan painters such as Ràfols Casamada and Hernández Pijoan, and also shows important mid-career artists, including Catalonia's most original creator, Perejaume. A wide selection of prints by renowned artists can be viewed and bought at the **Joan Prats-Artgràfic** space, a block away. **Branch**: **Joan Prats-Artgràfic** C/Balmes 54 (93 488 13 98).

Galeria Senda

C/Consell de Cent 337 (93 487 67 59). Metro Passeig de Gràcia/bus 7, 16, 17, 22, 24, 28. **Open** 11am-2pm, 5-8.30pm, Tue-Sun. Closed Aug. **Credit** MC, V. **Map** D4-5

Dealer Carles Duran shows Spanish and international painting, as well as organising specialised shows on historic figures of modern art. A second space is used for younger artists and riskier projects. **Branch: Galeria S-292** C/Consell de Cent 292.

Galeria Toni Tàpies/Edicions T

C/Consell de Cent 282 (93 487 64 02). Metro Passeig de Gràcia/bus 7, 16, 17, 63, 67, 68. **Open** 10am-2pm, 4-8pm, Tue-Fri; 11am-2pm, 5-8.30pm, Sat. Closed Aug. **Credit** MC, V. **Map** D5

Owned by a son of the illustrious painter, this gallery was founded to produce fine art prints. It now shows some of the best of Spanish and foreign art, including Catalan Antoni Llena and Czech-born Jana Sterbak. Prints by Tàpies, Arnulf Rainer and Sol Lewitt are available, among others.

Zona Alta & Gràcia

There is no defined gallery district in the city's Zona Alta, but a few good spaces are dotted around the areas above and below Diagonal.

Galeria Alejandro Sales

C/Julián Romea 16 (93 415 20 54). FGC Gràcia/bus 16, 17, 22, 24, 27, 28, 31, 32. **Open** 11am-2pm, 5-8.30pm, Tue-Sat. Closed Aug. **No credit cards.** **Map** D3

Alejandro Sales is one of the city's most successful young dealers. As well as hosting impeccable shows by name artists in his main space, he has 'Blackspace', a room where young Spanish and foreign artists present small-scale exhibitions – often installations – with little commercial pressure.

Back into Barcelona's **BAI.**

Galeria H₂0

C/Verdi 152 (93 415 18 01). Bus 24, 31, 32, 74. **Open** 11am-1pm, 5.30-8pm, Tue-Fri; 11am-1pm Sat. Closed Aug. **No credit cards.** **Map** E2

A space run by industrial designers on one floor of a small Gràcia house, showing design, photography, architectural projects and contemporary art. Performance art and literary readings are often presented in the charming back garden.

Galeria Metropolitana de Barcelona

C/Torrijos 44 (93 284 31 83). Metro Fontana/bus 39. **Open** 11am-1.30pm, 5-9pm, Mon-Fri. Closed last half July, 1st half Aug. **No credit cards.** **Map** E3

This small gallery on a lively Gràcia street has come up with some of the city's freshest, most innovative recent shows. A show on painting and the cinema and a visiting exhibit of Japanese artists are examples of the mixed bag offered here.

Website: www.galeria-metropolitana.com

The fringe scene

Perhaps the oddest aspect of the Barcelona art scene before the 1992 Olympics was the scarcity of independent initiatives by artists. The speculative international art market of the 1980s, and the bonanza of official patronage available in pre-Olympic Barcelona seduced many artists into an aggressive quest for commercial success.

A new type of politicised art activism has been striving to emerge since 1992. Some initiatives imitate 1970s models (art parties, performance art, open studios), while others hook up with the city's squatters' movement. In some fields – performance, video art – there is a distinctly iconoclastic Catalan style. Venues that welcome the best work include **Metrònom**, the **Mediateca** at Fundació La Caixa, and the **CCCB**, which hosts the **Mostra de Vídeo Independent** in the **Sonar** music festival in June (*see chapter* **Music: Rock, Roots & Jazz**). On a smaller scale, there are places that stage art parties and performance

Perejaume: all the world's a Liceu

When the Liceu opera house burned down in early 1994, the leading families of Barcelona's historical opera house rose in nostalgia at the memory of their private boxes to insist that it be restored as a faithful reproduction of its nineteenth-century opulence. Hence the inside of the new theatre, reopened in October 1999, looks a great deal like its predecessor, thanks to meticulous copying of the elaborate gilt mouldings and the plush seating – only much cleaner, and in fireproof material.

If the lighting systems and sightlines have been altered for the better, they do nothing to break the illusion of the past. Which makes it all the more extraordinary that the commission to replace the traditional ceiling paintings consumed in the flames was won by Catalan artist Perejaume. Perejaume's eight circular images surrounding the central ceiling light (*pictured*) and the large paintings above the stage are, with fashion designer Toni Miró's richly draped curtain, the only suggestions of anything contemporary within the Liceu's performance hall.

Perejaume is an idiosyncratic and very original artist who has dedicated his painting, installation, and photography to question the way we limit and define what is art – what is found inside the picture frame, the theatre proscenium, the book's covers – and what is not. Not surprisingly, the Liceu itself, Catalonia's preeminent place for representation, has been a source for many of his pieces.

The Liceu work takes as its starting point a familiar element: the theatre's trademark red velour seat. Perejaume took a photo of a single seat, and repeated it thousand-fold with the help of digital computer graphics. The result on each round ceiling image is an improbable panorama: an extensive mountain landscape covered by rows and rows of Liceu seating, the contours rolling as far as the turbulent horizon. By setting these points of reflection and fantasy high in the Liceu's upper reaches, he imagines the drama of the universe itself as the opera, and the whole earth a theatre from where we can view it.

evenings. This kind of thing blends into frontier Barcelona nightlife, and semi-legal venues that come and go. For more on all this, and more venues, *see chapter* **Nightlife**.

22A
C/Margarit 70, baixos (93 319 51 31). Metro Paral.lel/bus 20, 57, 64, 157. **Open** 5-8pm Thur, Fri; 11am-2pm Sat. **Map** B6
After the demolition crews wiped out their Poble Nou space, this artist-run gallery relocated to the upper reaches of Poble Sec. European and North American artists are invited to do solo shows, complementing exhibits by prestigious Catalan artists.

Centro Cultural La Santa
C/Rec 58, corner of C/Guillem (93 268 11 56). Metro Barceloneta/bus 14, 39, 51. **Open** 5-8pm Tue-Thur. **Map** E6/C4
In a ramshackle old workshop just off the Born, this is the 'showcase' for an international association of over 100 artists. As much a part of the exhibit is the place itself, with its kitsch/surreal décor. There are also extravagant chairs, jewellery and other items for sale. The Tuesday and Thursday events have a party atmosphere; there may be something going on there at other times, but it's best to check first.

Hangar
Passatge del Marqués de Santa Isabel 40 (tel/fax 93 308 40 41). Metro Poble Nou/ bus 40, 42. **Open** *information* 9am-2pm Mon-Fri. Closed Aug.
Besides being a multi-disciplinary production centre with studios, a small gallery and other services for artists, Hangar is the headquarters of the influential Catalan visual artists' association. Other artist-run spaces in Poble Nou include the gallery of the **Centre Cívic Can Felipa**, C/Pallars 277 (93 266 44 41). Poble Nou artists also organise an open studio project in the summer.

Eat, Drink, Sleep, Shop

Accommodation

They're always opening more hotels in Barcelona – but they just as soon fill up.

The 1992 Olympic Games provided the first big catalyst for recent hotel building in Barcelona, with some 30 all-new places opening in just a couple of years. New construction and improvements, modernisations or complete makeovers of older hotels have not ceased ever since, as Barcelona has grown massively – above all in the late '90s – in popularity as a city to visit. Even with all this building activity, demand has still moved faster. Barcelona no longer has a true low season as such (although January and February are perhaps relatively slack), and in 1999, for the first time, it actually became hard to find a room of any kind in the city at some times in midsummer.

This unprecedented worldwide exposure may do much for Barcelonese pride, but to the rest of us it means that **it is always advisable to book a room well in advance**. This rapid growth in numbers has also pushed up prices very noticeably: mid-range hotel rates, especially, shot up in '98-9, and there has been an almost total disappearance of the once-traditional cheaper weekend rates. However, since this situation has arisen quite

suddenly, while some hotels have jacked up their prices, others have shown a welcome reluctance to squeeze their clients, so that there are now wide disparities in rates, and good deals can still be had.

Another side of post-'92 Barcelona hotels is that many, above all the ranks of mid-range hotels with uniform beige marble lobbies, can seem strangely similar, functionally comfortable but without any noticeable character. Hotels with individual appeal are surprisingly – given the idiosyncrasies of Catalan design in every other area – scarce. Those that do stand out from the crowd – from the **Arts** or the **Ritz** through the new **Urquinaona** to pleasant budget options – are to be treasured.

Barcelona's first real hotels were all built along the Rambla, and a great many places are still concentrated in the old city, which is also still the best area to find cheaper accommodation. Hotels on or very near the Rambla itself are naturally convenient, but have tended to bring in the most swingeing price hikes; they're also often noisy, and this is where you most need to be streetwise about petty crime (*see pages 293-4*). The other

*Top of the line: cool comfort at the **Hotel Arts**. See page 115.*

main hotel area is the Eixample, with many mid-range places and some good-value *hostals*. This is the best place to stay if you have a car, in a hotel with its own parking, as on-street parking is very inconvenient (*see page 285*). As the centre has filled up, mid-range and budget hotels have also been opening up in districts a bit further afield such as Poble Sec or Vall d'Hebron, which are worth considering: they offer greater tranquillity, and thanks to Barcelona's compactness and good transport links, are never more than a half-hour or so from the centre.

STARS, HOTELS, *HOSTALS*, PRICES

All accommodation in Catalonia is regulated by the regional government, the Generalitat. There are now only two official categories, hotels (H) and *hostals* (HS), although many places still use older names (*fondes, residències, pensions*), which can be confusing. To be a hotel, star-rated one to five, a place must have bathrooms in every room. Ratings are given on the basis of general quality and services rather than price. *Hostals*, rated one to three and usually cheaper, do not have to have en suite bathrooms throughout, nor do many have restaurants. Most, though, have also been renovated in the last few years, and many now have bathrooms in at least some rooms. In short, star ratings are not an automatic guide to cost or facilities.

All hotel bills are subject to seven per cent IVA (value added tax) on top of the basic price, which is normally quoted separately on bills. Hotels and *hostals* listed here are divided according to the **basic price of a double room without IVA**, according to the official weekday rates in high season. They should be taken as **guidelines** only, though, for prices can still vary by sizeable amounts at different times of year. Also, although far fewer hotels now offer weekend and other short-term discounts, it's still worth asking whether any such deals may be available. Breakfast is not included in rates given below unless stated. Hotel breakfasts are often poor and overpriced, and you frequently do better to go to a café. If you make use of a hotel car park this will also add to the bill, and you should reserve a space when booking the room.

If you arrive in Barcelona without a room, the **tourist offices** in Plaça Catalunya and Plaça Sant Jaume (*see page 294*) have hotel booking desks that can usually find somewhere. There's no commission, but a deposit is requested against the bill. Two private services are listed below. None of their lists are exhaustive of all accommodation in Barcelona, but tourist offices can provide a complete local hotel booklet. When booking, to be sure of light or a view, ask for an outside room (*habitación exterior*); many Barcelona buildings are built around a central patio or air shaft, which can be gloomy. Inside (*interior*) rooms, though,

often gain in quietness what they lack in light. For flat rental agencies, *see page 131*; for student and youth accommodation services, *see page 297*.

Halcón Viajes

C/Aribau 34 (93 454 59 95/902 30 06 00).
Metro Universitat/bus all routes to Plaça Universitat.
Open 9.30am-1.30pm, 4.30-8pm, Mon-Fri; 10am-1.30pm Sat. **Credit** AmEx, DC, MC, V. **Map** C5
This giant travel agency with 500 offices across Spain can also book rooms in many hotels (often with car rental deals included). Commission is paid.

Ultramar Express

Vestibule, Estació de Sants (93 491 44 63).
Metro Sants-Estació/bus all routes to Estació de Sants. **Open** 8am-10pm daily. Closed 26 Dec & some public holidays. **Map** A4
An office in the vestibule at Sants train station: when booking you will be asked to pay a deposit (around 2,000ptas), which will be incorporated into your final hotel bill, plus a small fee of about 100ptas. You will be given a map and directions to the hotel.

Real luxury (over 30,000ptas)

Barcelona Hilton

Avda Diagonal 589-91, 08014 (93 495 77 77/fax 93 495 77 00/hilton@lix.intercom.es). Metro Maria Cristina/bus 6, 7, 33, 34, 63, 66, 67, 68, N12.
Rates *single* 32,000-36,000ptas; *double* 36,500-40,500ptas; *suites* 75,000-95,000ptas.
Credit AmEx, DC, JCB, MC, TC, V. **Map** B2-3
Opened in 1990, the steel-and-glass 286-room Hilton lacks the range of facilities of some of its competitors, but its rooms are a little more intimate. Located in the heart of Barcelona's main business district, the Hilton concentrates on providing a comprehensive range of business services.
Hotel services *Air-conditioning. Babysitting. Bar. Conference facilities. Car park. Disabled: rooms (4) adapted for the disabled, toilets, wheelchair access. E-mail. Fax. Gym. Interpreters. Laundry. Limousine. Multilingual staff. Non-smoking rooms. Restaurants. Safe. Terrace.* **Room services** *Hairdryer. Minibar. Radio. Room service (24hrs). Telephone. TV (satellite).*
Website: www.hilton.com

Hotel Arts

C/Marina 19-21, 08005 (93 221 10 00/ fax 93 221 10 70/info@harts.es/reservations from UK freephone 0800 234 0000/from US freephone 0800 2241 3333). Metro Ciutadella/bus 10, 36, 71, 92, N6, N8. **Rates** *standard room* 40,000-45,000ptas; *suites* 65,000ptas.
Credit AmEx, DC, JCB, MC, V. **Map** F7
Designed by US architects Skidmore, Owings and Merrill, the first Ritz-Carlton hotel in Europe towers 44 storeys above the beachfront and Port Olímpic. Fountains play by the entrance, and palm-fringed gardens surround modern sculptures and the city's only beach-front pool. The Arts offers matchless service, stunning interiors – specially-commissioned artwork is scattered throughout the hotel – and

*A real pool with a view, at the **Barcelona Plaza Hotel**. See page 118.*

staggering views, and the hotel has impressed even seasoned world travellers. Three upper floors form 'The Club' for guests desiring still more comfort and service, and the top six floors house magnificent luxury duplex apartments with contemporary décor by Catalan designer Jaume Treserra.

Hotel services *Air-conditioning. Babysitting. Bar. Beauty salon. Car park. Conference facilities. Disabled: rooms (3) adapted for the disabled, toilets, wheelchair access. E-mail. Fax. Fitness centre (gym/sauna/massage). Garden. Hairdresser. Interpreters. Laundry. Lifts. Limousine. Multilingual staff. Non-smoking floor. Restaurants. Shops. Swimming pool (outdoor). Ticket agency.* **Room services** *CD player. Hairdryer. Minibar. Radio. Room service (24hrs). Safe. Telephone. TV (satellite).*
Website: www.harts.es

Cool pools

Swimming pools are a fairly recent feature in many Barcelona hotels, and some of those offered are truly tiny. Below we list the best.
Hotel Arts – Barcelona's only seafront pool.
Barcelona Plaza (*above*) – Unbeatable views, a real, full-size pool, and the world at your feet.
Hotel Ambassador – Rooftop pool *and* whirlpool.
Hotel Balmes – Ground floor patio pool, for those with no head for heights.
Hotel Regente – Not a big pool, but the rooftop bar at sunset makes up for it.

Hotel Claris
C/Pau Claris 150, 08009 (93 487 62 62/fax 93 215 79 70/claris@derbyhotels.es). Metro Passeig de Gràcia/bus all routes to Passeig de Gràcia. **Rates** *single* 32,000ptas; *double* 32,700-40,900ptas; *suites* 50,000-110,000ptas; *breakfast* 2,700ptas. **Credit** AmEx, DC, EC, JCB, MC, TC, V. **Map** D4
This discreet, refined 120-room Eixample hotel is well suited to lovers of ancient art, modern design, new technology and *la dolce vita*. The Claris reflects the archaeological interests of owner Jordi Clos, who maintains the private **Museu Egipci** of Egyptian relics (*see p101*); artefacts from his wide-ranging collections (Roman, Egyptian, Asian and American), are distributed around the hotel, some in a small museum, others in the public areas and bedrooms. In 2000 the Egyptian relics in the hotel will all be transferred to the museum, and be replaced by Pre-Columbian American art. A drawback is the staff, who can be strangely unhelpful for a hotel of this class.

Hotel services *Air-conditioning. Bar. Business services. Car park. Child-minding service. Conference facilities. Disabled: rooms (4) adapted for the disabled, wheelchair access. E-mail. Fax. Fitness centre (gym/sauna). Interpreters. Laundry. Lifts. Limousine. Multilingual staff. Non-smoking floor. Restaurants. Swimming pool (outdoor). Ticket agency.* **Room services** *Hairdryer. Minibar. Room service (24hrs). Safe. Telephone. TV (satellite). Video (on request).*
Website: www.derbyhotels.es

Hotel Le Meridien Barcelona
La Rambla 111, 08002 (93 318 62 00/fax 93 301 77 76). Metro Liceu/bus 14, 38, 59, 91, N9, N12. **Rates** *single* 30,000ptas; *double* 36,000ptas; *suite* 58,000-80,000ptas; *breakfast* 2,250ptas. **Credit** AmEx, DC, JCB, MC, TC, V. **Map** D5/A2

An ultra-central location right on the Rambla and luxurious accommodation have often made this 206-room hotel a first choice for celebs such as Bruce Springsteen, Michael Jackson, the Stones and Oasis (although lately the Arts has stolen its thunder). It has a fine restaurant, Le Patio, with Mediterranean cuisine. Good rates have been available December-February and July-August.

Hotel services *Air-conditioning. Babysitting. Bar. Car park. Conference facilities. Disabled: rooms (4) adapted for the disabled, toilets, wheelchair access. E-mail. Fax. Fitness centre (gym). Interpreters. Laundry. Lifts. Limousine. Multilingual staff. Non-smoking rooms. Restaurant. Safe. Ticket agency.* **Room services** *Hairdryer. Minibar. Radio. Room service (24hrs). Telephone. TV (satellite). Video. Website: www.meridienbarcelona.com*

Ritz Hotel

Gran Via de les Corts Catalanes 668, 08010 (93 318 52 00/fax 93 318 01 48/ritz@ritzbcn.com). Metro Passeig de Gràcia/bus 7, 39, 45, 47, 50, 54, 56, 62. **Rates** *single* 30,000ptas; *double* 38,000ptas; *suites* 85,000-133,000ptas; *breakfast* 2,450ptas. **Credit** AmEx, DC, EC, JCB, MC, TC, V. **Map** D5
After an interlude as the Husa Palace, Barcelona's Ritz has now regained its original emblematic title. The nineteenth-century building has been finely renovated, and it still qualifies as the most elegant hotel in town, offering old-fashioned style in quantities its rivals can only envy. The celebrity guest list has included Woody Allen, Orson Welles and especially Salvador Dali, who spent months here at a stretch; suite 108 is the one to go for. The sumptuous restaurant is open to non-guests.

Hotel services *Air-conditioning. Babysitting. Bar. Conference facilities. E-mail. Fax. Garden. Interpreters. Laundry. Lifts. Limousine. Multilingual staff. Non-smoking floor. Restaurant. Ticket agency.* **Room services** *Hairdryer. Minibar. Room service (24hrs). Safe. Telephone. TV. Website: www.ritzbcn.com*

Smooth comfort (20-30,000ptas)

Barcelona Plaza Hotel

Plaça Espanya 6-8, 08014 (93 426 26 00/fax 93 426 04 00/plaza@hoteles-catalonia.es). Metro Plaça Espanya/bus all routes to Plaça Espanya. **Rates** *single* 19,900-28,900ptas; *double* 24,900-32,900ptas; *suites* 40,000-50,000ptas; *breakfast* 1,500ptas. **Credit** AmEx, DC, EC, JCB, MC, TC, V. **Map** A5
The bunker-like façade of this 347-room hotel, looming up like a great monolith beside the Plaça d'Espanya, hides a splendid and charming interior. Guest rooms at the front and the nine tower suites have breathtaking views over the plaça, Montjuïc and its fountains, the ornate breakfast room is magnificently over-the-top, and its many leisure facilities include a truly stunning rooftop pool. The Plaza is often booked up, with business and holiday travellers; November-December and July-August are the easiest times to get in, when lower rates may (still) be available.

Hotel services *Air-conditioning. Babysitting. Bar. Car park. Conference facilities. Disabled: rooms (4) adapted for the disabled, wheelchair access. E-mail. Fax. Fitness centre (gym/massage/sauna). Interpreters. Laundry. Lifts. Limousine. Multilingual staff. Restaurant. Swimming pool (outdoor). Terrace.* **Room services** *Hairdryer. Minibar. Room service (24hrs). Safe. Telephone. TV (satellite). Website: www.hoteles-catalonia.es*

Hotel Allegro

Avda Portal de l'Angel 17, 08002 (93 318 41 41/fax 93 301 26 31/cataloni@hoteles-catalonia.es). Metro Catalunya/bus all routes to Plaça Catalunya. **Rates** *single* 20,900ptas; *double* 22,900ptas; *triple* 25,000ptas. **Credit** AmEx, DC, MC, TC, V. **Map** D5/**B2**
This very elegant 74-room hotel opened in 1998. Built in 1872, the former mansion of the Rocamora family retains a great deal of its original structure. The spacious and comfortable guest rooms are completely new; several have terraces over the gracious courtyard, or balconies overlooking a pedestrian street. Breakfast is served in a marquee structure (with heat or a/c) in the courtyard. A treat.

Hotel services *Air-conditioning. Bar. Disabled: rooms (2) adapted for the disabled, toilets, wheelchair access. Fax. Garden. Interpreters. Laundry. Lift. Multilingual staff. Ticket agency.* **Room services** *Hairdryer. Minibar. Room service. Safe. Telephone. TV (satellite).*

Hotel Ambassador

C/Pintor Fortuny 13, 08001 (93 412 05 30/ reservations 93 301 34 75/fax 93 302 79 77/ rivoli@alba.mssl.es). Metro Liceu/bus 14, 38, 59, 91, N9, N12. **Rates** *single* 15,500-24,000ptas; *double* 17,500-30,000ptas; *suite* 35,000-42,000ptas. **Credit** AmEx, DC, EC, JCB, MC, TC, V. **Map** D5/**A2**
The slightly shabby street off the Rambla gives no clue to the smart, stylish interior of this modern hotel. Drinks are served from a turn-of-the-century newspaper kiosk in the lounge bar; other highlights include a rooftop pool, jacuzzi and sun lounge with panoramic views. Upper-floor rooms at the back benefit from direct sunlight, but others lower down can be a bit gloomy. Prices vary accordingly.

Hotel services *Air-conditioning. Bar. Car park. Conference facilities. Disabled: rooms (4) adapted for the disabled, toilets, wheelchair access. E-mail. Fax. Fitness centre (gym/massage/sauna). Interpreters. Laundry. Lifts. Limousine. Multilingual staff. Non-smoking rooms. Restaurant. Swimming pool (outdoor). Terrace. Ticket agency.* **Room services** *Hairdryer. Minibar. Room service (7am-11pm daily). Safe. Telephone. TV (satellite).*

Hotel Balmes

C/Mallorca 216, 08008 (93 451 19 14/fax 93 451 00 49/balmes@derbyhotels.es). FGC Provença/bus 7, 16, 17, 20, 43, 44, 67, 68, N7. **Rates** *single* 13,500ptas; *double* 22,200ptas; *suite* 25,000ptas; *breakfast* 1,600ptas. **Credit** AmEx, DC, EC, MC, TC, V. **Map** C4
A pleasant 1990-vintage 100-room hotel in the middle of the Eixample offering all-round comfort and a high standard of service. Rooms at the rear get the morning sun, and look onto the interior garden,

solarium and pool; some ground-floor rooms have outside terraces. The peace of the patio contrasts greatly with the bustle of the street outside.
Hotel services *Air-conditioning. Babysitting (24hrs' notice). Bar (Mon-Fri). Car park. Conference facilities. E-mail. Fax. Garden. Interpreters. Laundry. Lifts. Limousine. Multilingual staff. Restaurant (Mon-Fri). Swimming pool (outdoor). Ticket agency.*
Room services *Hairdryer (some rooms). Minibar. Radio. Room service (8am-11pm Mon-Fri). Safe. Telephone. TV (satellite).*
Website: www.derbyhotels.es

Hotel Colón

Avda de la Catedral 7, 08002 (93 301 14 04/fax 93 317 29 15/colon@ncsa.es/colon@nexus.es). Metro Jaume I/bus 17, 19, 40, 45. **Rates** *single 17,000-21,500ptas; double 25,500-40,000ptas; suites 45,000ptas; breakfast 1,800ptas.* **Credit** AmEx, DC, EC, JCB, MC, TC, V. **Map** D6/**B2**
With touches of old-world luxury, this 147-room hotel has a superb location opposite the cathedral, with matchless views of the Sunday *sardana* dancing or Thursday's antique market. There's a relaxing piano bar and good restaurant; staff are friendly and efficient. Guests at a sister hotel around the corner, the cheaper **Regencia Colón** (14,500ptas, double), can use the Colón's facilities.
Hotel services *Air-conditioning. Babysitting. Bar. Conference facilities. Disabled: rooms (2) adapted for the disabled, wheelchair access. E-mail. Fax. Laundry. Lifts. Limousine. Multilingual staff. Restaurant.*

*Open doors at the **Hotel Regente**.*

Room services *Hairdryer. Minibar. Radio. Room service (24hrs). Safe. Telephone. TV (satellite).*
Website: www.hotelcolon.es
Branch: Hotel Regencia Colón C/Sagristans 13-17, 08002 (93 318 98 58/fax 93 317 28 22).

Hotel Duques de Bergara

C/Bergara 11, 08002 (93 301 51 51/fax 93 317 34 42/cataloni@hoteles-catalonia.es). Metro Catalunya/bus all routes to Plaça Catalunya. **Rates** *single 19,900-28,900ptas; double 24,900-32,900ptas; triple 27,900-35,900ptas; suites 40,500ptas; breakfast 1,500ptas.* **Credit** AmEx, DC, MC, TC, V.
Map D5/**A1**
An elegant hotel just off Plaça Catalunya, created in the 1980s within an 1898 Modernist edifice by Gaudí's professor Emili Sala. The original style remains in the hall and stairways, while the communal areas and 151 guest rooms are modern, spacious and well furnished. In the courtyard there is a medium-sized swimming pool. Check when booking to avoid the hotel's few dark rooms.
Hotel services *Air-conditioning. Babysitting. Conference facilities. Disabled: rooms (7) adapted for the disabled, toilets, wheelchair access. Fax. Laundry. Lifts. Limousine. Multilingual staff. Swimming pool (outdoor). Terrace. Ticket agency.*
Room services *Hairdryer. Minibar. Radio. Room service (24hrs). Safe. Telephone. TV (satellite).*
Website: www.hoteles-catalonia.es

Hotel Inglaterra

C/Pelai 14, 08001 (93 505 11 00/fax 93 505 11 09/hi@hotelinglaterra.com). Metro Universitat/bus all routes to Plaça Universitat. **Rates** *single 12,000-20,000ptas; double 25,000ptas.* **Credit** AmEx, DC, MC, V. **Map** C5/**A1**
The Inglaterra opened only in 1999, and everything in the building except the façade and tiled staircase is entirely new. It's aimed mainly at a business clientele – so still offers weekend rates – but the hotel couldn't be better located for seeing the sights. The rooms offer refined comfort, and as well as a rooftop terrace the sixth floor contains an extra-large guest room that will be excellent for anyone looking for extra space and privacy.
Hotel services *Air-conditioning. Bar. Conference facilities. Disabled: room (1) adapted for the disabled, toilets, wheelchair access. Fax. Interpreters. Laundry. Lifts. Multilingual staff. Safe. Ticket agency.*
Room services *Hairdryer. Minibar. Room service. Telephone. TV (satellite).*

Hotel Regente

Rambla Catalunya 76, 08008 (93 487 59 89/fax 93 487 32 27/regente@inf.entorno.es). Metro Passeig de Gràcia, FGC Provença/bus all routes to Passeig de Gràcia. **Rates** *single 16,900-21,400ptas; double 19,900-26,800ptas; breakfast 1,850-1,950ptas.*
Credit AmEx, DC, JCB, MC, TC, V. **Map** D4
The Regente occupies a renovated 1913 Evarist Juncosa *Modernista* mansion with a finely restored façade. Stained-glass decoration imparts distinctive charm, while double glazing shields guests from the Eixample's street noise; sixth- and seventh-floor

rooms have terraces with stunning views, many lower rooms open onto grand wrought-iron balconies, and there's a rooftop pool that's a perfect place to enjoy the sunset.
Hotel services *Air-conditioning. Babysitting. Bar. Conference facilities. Disabled: rooms (2) adapted for the disabled, wheelchair access. Fax. Fitness facilities. Interpreters. Laundry. Lifts. Limousine. Multilingual staff. Swimming pool (outdoor). Ticket agency.*
Room services *Fitness cycles (in some rooms). Hairdryer. Minibar. Radio. Room service (7am-11pm daily). Safe. Telephone. TV (satellite). Website: www.hoteles-centro-ciudad.es*

Hotel Rivoli Ramblas

La Rambla 128, 08002 (93 302 66 43/reservations 93 412 09 88/fax 93 317 50 53/rivoli@mssl.es). Metro Catalunya/bus all routes to Plaça Catalunya. **Rates** *single* 16,500-25,000ptas; *double* 18,500-31,500ptas; *suite* 31,500-85,000ptas. **Credit** AmEx, DC, JCB, MC, TC, V. **Map** D5-6/**A2**
Rebuilt in the early '90s, the Rivoli is a world apart from the bustle on the Rambla outside. The 89 rooms have interesting colour schemes, and the Blue Moon piano bar is a relaxing place to end the evening. A popular choice for tourists and business people.
Hotel services *Air-conditioning. Babysitting. Bar. Car park. Conference facilities. Fax. Fitness centre (gym/sauna/solarium). Interpreters. Laundry. Lifts. Limousine. Multilingual staff. Restaurant. Terrace. Ticket agency.* **Room services** *Hairdryer. Minibar. Room service (7am-11pm). Safe. Telephone. TV (satellite).*

Upper-mid (14-20,000ptas)

Hotel Alimara

C/Berruguete 126, 08035 (tel/fax 93 427 00 00/fax 93 427 92 92/hotel.alimara@cett.es) Metro Montbau/bus 10, 27, 60, 73, 76, 85, 173, N4. **Rates** *single* 17,200ptas; *double* 19,800ptas; *suite* 28,000ptas. **Credit** AmEx, DC, V.

Rooms with views

Hotel Arts – Hard to beat.
Barcelona Plaza – Hypnotising – you might never leave your room.
Hotel Colón – Prime site to view the cathedral.
Hotel Rubens – A different slant on Barcelona, from the hills near Parc Güell.
Hotel San Agustín – Romantic views of the old city and Plaça Sant Agusti.
Hostal Jardí – Medieval architecture, and perfect for people-watching.
Hostal-Residencia Oliva – Good views are not only found in luxury hotels.

In an unusual location in the hills of Vall d'Hebron, the Alimara is still only 15 minutes from Passeig de Gràcia. It was built in 1992 near the Olympic velodrome and tennis courts, but unlike many hotels of the same vintage has elegant decoration and a comfortable, airy atmosphere to go with its modern exterior. The junior suites on the third floor have large terraces with wonderful views; more spectacular still are those from the glass lift, and La Ronda restaurant. Good weekend rates are offered, and it's also handy for anyone coming to Barcelona by car.
Hotel services *Air-conditioning. Bar. Business services. Car park. Conference facilities. Disabled: rooms (3) adapted for the disabled, toilets, wheelchair access. Fax. Garden. Interpreters. Laundry. Lift. Limousine. Multilingual staff. Non-smoking rooms. Restaurant. Ticket agency.* **Room services** *Hairdryer. Minibar. Radio. Room service (24 hrs). Safe. Telephone. TV. Video.*

Hotel Gaudí

C/Nou de la Rambla 12, 08001 (93 317 90 32/fax 93 412 26 36/gaudi@hotelgaudi.es). Metro Liceu/bus 14, 38, 59, 91, N9, N12. **Rates** *single* 10,500ptas; *double* 14,000ptas; *triple* 18,000ptas; *quad* 20,000ptas. **Credit** AmEx, DC, JCB, MC, V. **Map** C6/**A3**
The Gaudí's great selling point is its convenience as the main mid-level hotel in a central, much-visited area, directly opposite Gaudí's **Palau Güell** (*see p63*). True to its name, it has a Gaudí-inspired lobby; the 73 rooms contrast with the shabbiness of the surrounding *Barrio Chino* and are good for the area, but staff make little effort to be welcoming.
Hotel services *Air-conditioning. Babysitting. Bar (noon-midnight). Car park. Conference facilities. Disabled: rooms (2) adapted for the disabled, wheelchair access. E-mail. Fax. Fitness centre (gym). Interpreters. Lifts. Multilingual staff. Restaurant.* **Room services** *Hairdryer. Radio. Room service (noon-midnight). Safe (for hire). Telephone. TV (satellite). Website: www.hotelgaudi.es*

Hotel Onix

C/Llançà 30, 08015 (93 426 00 87/fax 93 426 19 81). Metro Espanya/bus all routes to Plaça d'Espanya. **Rates** *single* 11,600-13,600ptas; *double* 14,500-17,000ptas; *triple* 18,500-21,000ptas; *breakfast* 1,200ptas. **Credit** AmEx, DC, MC, V. **Map** B5
A comfortable if functional business hotel off Plaça d'Espanya, close to Sants rail station and with easy access to the airport. The quiet outside rooms have views of the old Arenas bullring on one side, and **Parc Joan Miró** (*see p83*) on the other. All rooms have balconies. The Onix also has the (albeit small) luxury of a tiny rooftop pool and sun deck.
Hotel services *Air-conditioning. Bar. Babysitting (24hrs' notice). Conference facilities. Car park. Disabled: rooms (3) adapted for the disabled, wheelchair access. Fax. Laundry. Lifts. Multilingual staff. Restaurant (for groups only). Swimming pool (outdoor). Ticket agency.* **Room services** *Hairdryer. Minibar. Radio. Refrigerator. Room service (8am-11pm). Safe. Telephone. TV (satellite).*

The ornate **Hotel Granvia**. *See page 123.*

Hotel Oriente

La Rambla 45-7, 08002 (93 302 25 58/fax 93 412 38 19/horiente@husa.es). Metro Drassanes/bus 14, 38, 59, 91, N9, N12. **Rates** *single* 13,600ptas; *double* 17,000ptas; *breakfast* 850-900ptas. **Credit** AmEx, DC, EC, MC, TC, V. **Map** C-D6/**A3**

Inaugurated in 1842 as Barcelona's first ever 'grand hotel', the Oriente is undeniably atmospheric. It was built incorporating parts of an old Franciscan monastery – remnants of the pillars of which are just visible in the ballroom – and long played host to the illustrious musicians – Toscanini, Maria Callas and others – who performed in the Liceu next door. Hans Christian Andersen, General Grant and Errol Flynn also put up here. The old-world dining room and elegant ballroom are a reminder of this glorious past, but the hotel is now a far cry from the glamour of its heyday. Its 142 rooms are spacious but rather spartan, and those with a view of the Rambla have the downside of being quite noisy. Service is also distinctly patchy; on the up-side, there are often still decent weekend rates and low-season offers.
Hotel services *Bar. Conference facilities. Fax. Lifts. Multilingual staff. Restaurant.* **Room services** *Room service (7am-10pm). Safe. Telephone. TV. Website: www.husa.es*

Hotel Rubens

Passeig de la Mare de Déu del Coll 10, 08023 (93 219 12 04/fax 93 219 12 69/cataloni@hoteles-catalonia.es). Metro Vallcarca/bus 25, 28, N4.

Rates *single* 15,900ptas; *double* 17,900ptas; *triple* 20,900ptas; *quad* 23,900ptas; *quintuple* 25,900ptas. **Credit** AmEx, DC, JCB, MC, TC, V.

The three-star, modern Rubens stands in a hilly residential area above Gràcia, between the Parc Güell and the Crueta del Coll park. As an alternative to city centre hotels, it offers cleaner air, panoramic views, and the chance to go walking in the parks nearby. Upper-floor rooms have private terraces, and there is a large sun deck on the sixth floor. The city centre is ten minutes away by Metro.
Hotel services *Air-conditioning. Bar. Car park. Conference facilities. Disabled: rooms (2) adapted for the disabled, toilets, wheelchair access. Fax. Laundry. Lifts. Restaurant.* **Room services** *Radio. Safe. Telephone. TV (Satellite). Website: www.hoteles-catalonia.es*

Hotel San Agustín

Plaça Sant Agustí 3, 08001 (93 318 16 58/ fax 93 317 29 28). Metro Liceu/bus 14, 38, 59, 91, N9, N12. **Rates** *single* 10,500-12,500ptas; *double* 14,000-17,500ptas; *triple* 17,500-22,000ptas. **Credit** AmEx, DC, MC, V. **Map** C6/**A3**

One of the oldest continually-functioning hotels in Barcelona, the San Agustín has been welcoming guests for well over 100 years, but has had two major facelifts in the last decade. It now offers an all-new reception, lifts, modern bathrooms, air-con and TVs in every room. Some say it's lost its character, but the rooms are comfortable, and retain a bit of old-world charm: top-floor rooms have oak-beamed ceilings and romantic views, while some of the lower rooms have balconies over the *plaça*, which has been under renovation itself. Three big rooms (with two bathrooms each) sleep up to six. The hotel has also retained a very pleasant lounge bar, and it remains one of the most attractive options in the Rambla area.
Hotel services *Air-conditioning. Babysitting. Bar. Conference facilities. Disabled: rooms (5) adapted for the disabled, wheelchair access. Fax. Laundry. Lifts. Multilingual staff. Restaurant.* **Room services** *Hairdryer. Safe. Telephone. TV.*

Hotel Splendid

C/Muntaner 2, 08011 (93 451 21 42/fax 93 323 16 84/splendid@smc.es) Metro Universitat/bus 24, 41, 55, 64, 91, 141, N6. **Rates** *single* 12,500-15,000ptas; *double* 18,000ptas; *triple* 21,000ptas; *junior suite* 20,000ptas. **Credit** AmEx, DC, MC, V. **Map** C5

Small and functional, this brand new hotel just beside Plaça Universitat opened in 1999. It's been created with the business world in mind, but its central location is also ideal for sightseeing. Each room has a minibar, desk and direct Net access, and a very generous hot, buffet breakfast is served for 1,000ptas. Weekend rates are offered.
Hotel services *Air-conditioning. Bar. Car park. Conference facilities. Disabled: room (1) adapted for the disabled, toilet, wheelchair access. Fax. Interpreters. Laundry. Lift. Multilingual staff. Non-smoking rooms.* **Room services** *Hairdryer. Minibar. Modem points. Room service. Safe. Telephone. TV (satellite). Video.*

Ramblas Hotel

*La Rambla 33, 08002 (93 301 57 00/
fax 93 412 25 07). Metro Drassanes/bus 14, 38, 59,
91, N9, N12.* **Rates** *single* 14-18,000ptas; *double* 14-
20,000ptas; *triple* 18-24,000ptas; *quad* 22-28,000ptas.
Credit AmEx, MC, V. **Map** C6/**A3-4**
The simply-named Ramblas occupies an attractive
eighteenth-century building with tiled *Modernista*
façade, but is another very recent conversion.
Rooms are spacious and comfortable; those on the
eighth and ninth floors have large terraces, and
while front rooms have views of the Rambla and the
port, those at the back have an outlook taking in
Montjuïc and the roof of Gaudí's Palau Güell. If you
stay here, though, be prepared to be in the busiest
part of the Rambla.
Hotel services *Air-conditioning. Bar. Laundry.
Lift.* **Room services** *Minibar. Room service
(breakfast only). Safe. Telephone. TV (satellite).*

Lower-mid (7-14,000ptas)

Hostal Ciudad Condal

*C/Mallorca 255, pral., 08008 (93 215 10 40).
Metro Passeig de Gràcia, FGC Provença/bus 20, 21,
28, 43, 44, N7.* **Rates** *single* 6,000ptas; *double*
9,500ptas. **Credit** MC, V. **Map** D4
The Ciudad Condal occupies part of the Casa Angel
Batlló, an 1891 *Modernista* block of three houses
with one single façade that was designed by Josep
Vilaseca i Casanovas (not, though, the same building as Gaudí's Casa Batlló). The 15 rooms are a little
spartan, but those one the outside have high ceilings
and balconies.
Hotel services *Air-conditioning.* **Room services**
Telephone. TV.

Hostal Opera

*C/Sant Pau 20, 08001 (tel/fax 93 318 82 01).
Metro Liceu/bus 14, 38, 59, 91, N9, N12.* **Rates**
single 4,000ptas; *double* 7,000ptas; *triple* 9,000ptas.
No credit cards. Map C6/**A3**
As the name hints this hostal is right beside the
Liceu opera house, just off the Rambla. All 69 rooms
are newly decorated, and most have new bathrooms
and air-conditioning. The complete renovation is
due to be finished by early 2000.
Hotel services *Disabled: rooms (6) adapted for the
disabled. Lift. Multilingual staff. Non-smoking rooms.
Safe.* **Room services** *Air-conditioning (some).*

Hostal Plaza

*C/Fontanella 18, 08010 (tel/fax 93 301 01 39/
plazahostal@mx3.redestb.es). Metro Urquinaona/bus
all routes to Plaça Catalunya, Plaça Urquinaona.*
Rates *single* 4,500-5,000ptas; *double* 7,000-8,000ptas.
Credit AmEx, DC, MC, V. **Map** D5/**B1**
Run by eager-to-please Hispanic Americans, the
Plaza is an unusual, fun hotel. It offers a glut of services rarely found in lower-bracket Spanish hotels,
including laundry (5kg, 1,000ptas), TV room, fridge,
freezer and microwave, loads of information on the
city and even, they say, discounts at local restaurants
and clubs. All 14 rooms have showers and fans.

Hotel services *E-mail. Fax. Laundry. Lift.
Microwave. Multilingual staff. Safe. TV room
(satellite). Vending machine.* **Room services** *Fan.
Radio (some).*

Hostal-Residencia Ramos

*C/Hospital 36, 08001 (93 302 07 23/
fax 93 302 04 30). Metro Liceu/bus 14, 38, 59, 91,
N9, N12.* **Rates** *single* 4,000-5,000ptas; *double* 7,000-
8,000ptas; *triple* 9,600-10,500ptas.
Credit AmEx, DC, EC, MC, TC, V. **Map** C6/**A2-3**
Another off-Rambla hotel, the Ramos occupies the
first and second floors of a charming old building
with a tiled entrance and elegant wide staircase. All
rooms have bathrooms; those at the front overlook
the church and trees of Plaça San Agustí.
Hotel services *Air-conditioning. Fax. Lift.
Multilingual staff. Refreshments available. Safe.
Terrace.* **Room services** *Room service (10am-
6pm). Telephone. TV.*

Hostal Rey Don Jaime I

*C/Jaume I 11, 08002 (tel/fax 93 310 62 08/
r.d.jaime@atriumhotels.com). Metro Jaume I/bus 17,
19, 40, 45, N8.* **Rates** *single* 4,950ptas; *double*
7,250ptas; *triple* 9,975ptas. **Credit** AmEx, DC, EC,
MC, V. **Map** D6/**B3**
The Don Jaime sits on the noisy main artery through
the centre of the old city, but is therefore handy for
both the Barri Gòtic and La Ribera, and it's popular
with a mostly-young clientele. Basic but clean, the
30 rooms all have balconies and bathrooms.
Hotel services *Disabled: toilets. Fax. Lift.
Lounge. Multilingual staff. Safe. TV.*
Room services *Telephone.*
Website: www.atriumhotels.com

Hotel España

*C/Sant Pau 9-11, 08001 (93 318 17 58/fax 93 317
11 34/hotelespanya@tresnet.com). Metro
Liceu/bus14, 38, 59, 91, N9, N12.* **Rates** *single*
5,600ptas; *double* 10,700ptas; *triple* 14,600ptas.
Credit AmEx, DC, MC, V. **Map** D6/**A3**
The España is a *Modernista* landmark, with lower
floors designed by Domènech i Montaner in 1902.
The main restaurant (good for lunch) is decorated
with floral motifs in tile and elaborate woodwork,
the larger dining room beyond it features extravagant tiled murals of river-nymphs by Ramon Casas,
and the huge fireplace in the bar was sculpted by
Eusebi Arnau. After all this the more modern guest
rooms can come as a disappointment, but several
open onto a bright interior patio. Book well in
advance, as it's regularly full; however, prices have
risen less than at many nearby hotels.
Hotel services *Conference facilities. E-mail. Fax.
Lifts. Multilingual staff. Restaurant. Safe. TV.*
Room services *Safe (some). Telephone.*

Hotel Granvía

*Gran Via de les Corts Catalanes 642, 08007 (93 318
19 00/fax 93 318 99 97). Metro Passeig de
Gràcia/bus 7, 16, 17, 22, 24, 28, 42, 47, 50, 54, 56,
62, N1, N2, N3, N9.* **Rates** *single* 9,000ptas; *double*
12,500ptas; *triple* 16,000ptas; *breakfast* 650ptas.
Credit AmEx, DC, JCB, MC, TC, V. **Map** D5

Amid the renovation fever of '90s Barcelona, the Granvía with its splendid Victorian-rococo interiors counts as a remarkable survivor. The mansion was built for a wealthy banker in 1873, and has been a hotel since 1936. The bedrooms have now been modernised, but no changes have marred the lounge area and mirrored breakfast room with their paintings, chandeliers and gilt frames. To go with this look of fading grandeur the atmosphere is suitably old-fashioned and sedate, but the hotel has real charm. There's also a pleasant outdoor patio.
Hotel services *Air-conditioning. Bar. Conference facilities. Garden. Lift.* **Room Services** *Minibar. Room service. Safe. Telephone. TV.*

Hotel Internacional

La Rambla 78-80, 08002 (93 302 25 66/fax 93 317 61 90). Metro Liceu/bus 14, 38, 59, 91, N9, N12. **Rates** (incl breakfast) *single* 7,500ptas; *double* 13,900ptas; *triple* 17,650ptas. **Credit** AmEx, DC, MC, V. **Map** D6/**A3**
An institution on the Rambla, presiding over the Pla de la Boquería, and ever-popular with visiting foreign football fans, who drape their colours along the balconies that provide ideal vantage points for taking in all the movement on the walkway below. Built in 1894, the 60-room hotel has been fully refurbished. It's always full, so book way ahead; it's also noisy, and note that this hotel has brought in some of the biggest recent price hikes of any Barcelona hotel.
Hotel services *Bar. Fax. Lift (from 1st floor). Meals for groups. Multilingual staff. TV.* **Room services** *Safe (for hire). Telephone.*

Hotel Mesón Castilla

C/Valldonzella 5, 08001 (93 318 21 82/fax 93 412 40 20). Metro Universitat/bus all routes to Plaça Catalunya, Plaça Universitat. **Rates** (incl breakfast) *single* 10,600ptas; *double* 13,600ptas; *triple* 18,500ptas. **Credit** AmEx, DC, EC, MC, TC, V. **Map** C5/**A1**
A favourite with British and North American visitors, who enjoy the hearty buffet breakfasts served in the cosy dining room or on the patio terrace. This old-world-style hotel has 56 impeccably clean, quiet rooms, some furnished with antiques, and some rear

Added value

With prices climbing all the time, places that offer an above-average deal are even more appreciated.
Hotel Mesón Castilla – Very central, but quiet, relaxing, friendly and reasonable.
Hotel Granvía – Old-world charm and a little grandeur at surprisingly low prices.
Hotel Urquinaona – A range of services well beyond what you expect in this price bracket.
Hostal Eden – Good extras, and some quirky features, at economic rates.
Hostal Maldà – No frills, but lots of charm.

rooms have balconies. Three large rooms with up to four beds are great for families with children. A pleasant central option that has kept its prices down.
Hotel services *Air-conditioning. Car park. Disabled: wheelchair access. Fax. Laundry. Lifts. Multilingual staff. Safe. Terrace.* **Room services** *Minibar (most rooms). Telephone. TV (satellite).*

Hotel Metropol

C/Ample 31, 08002 (93 310 51 00/ fax 93 319 12 76). Metro Jaume I/bus 14, 17, 19, 36, 40, 45, 57, 59, 64, 157, N6, N8. **Rates** *single* 9,700ptas; *double* 13,200ptas; *triple* 15,200ptas; *breakfast* 1,100ptas. **Credit** AmEx, DC, EC, MC, TC, V. **Map** D6/**B4**
Another nineteenth-century hotel that was given a makeover in 1992, although the reception area still has its old charm. Half the 71 rooms look on to C/Ample, which is surprisingly quiet and tranquil for an old-city street very near the port. The Metropol also offers good weekend deals.
Hotel services *Air-conditioning. Disabled: rooms currently being adapted, toilets, wheelchair access. Fax. Laundry. Lifts. Multilingual staff.* **Room services** *Minibar. Safe. Telephone. TV (satellite).*

Hotel Oasis

Pla del Palau 17, 08003 (93 319 43 96/fax 93 310 48 74). Metro Barceloneta/bus all routes to Pla del Palau. **Rates** *single* 6,400-6,950ptas; *double* 7,800-8,400ptas; *triple* 10,700ptas; *breakfast* 500ptas. **Credit** AmEx, DC, MC, V. **Map** D6/**C4**
This unusually well-equipped near-budget hotel is handily located between La Ribera and the Port Vell. All rooms have bathrooms and TV; exterior rooms also have balconies, but can be noisy. On the ground floor, there's also a handy bar-restaurant.
Hotel services *Bar. Lift (from first floor). Multilingual staff. Restaurant. Safe.* **Room services** *Air-conditioning (some rooms). Safe (some rooms). Telephone. TV.*

Hotel Pelayo

C/Pelai 9, 08001 (93 302 37 27/fax 93 412 31 68). Metro Universitat/bus all routes to Plaça Universitat. **Rates** *single* 5,000ptas; *double* 9,000ptas; *triple* 12,000ptas; *quad* 14,000ptas; *quintuple* 16,000ptas. **Credit** MC, V. **Map** D5/**A1**
The Pelayo occupies the first and second floors of a building in an ultra-central location by Plaça Universitat. Personal touches in the decoration give it warmth and character, and the owner appreciates it if her guests respond with equal courtesy. All 15 rooms have bathrooms, air-con and central heating; coffee and breakfast are available in reception.
Hotel services *Air-conditioning. Laundry. Lift. Multilingual staff. Safe.* **Room services** *Telephone. TV.*

Hotel Peninsular

C/Sant Pau 34-6, 08001 (93 302 31 38/fax 93 412 36 99). Metro Liceu/bus 14, 38, 59, 91, N9, N12. **Rates** *single* 5,000ptas; *double* 7,000ptas; *triple* 10,000ptas; *quad* 12,000ptas; *quintuple* 14,000ptas. **Credit** EC, MC, TC, V. **Map** C6/**A3**
Like the **Oriente** (*see p122*), the Peninsular was built inside the shell of a former monastery, and the

*Hidden in the Raval, the **Hotel Peninsular**.*

semi-subterranean room that's now the TV lounge once had a passageway connecting it to Sant Agusti church. The hotel was modernised in the early '90s, but wicker furniture imparts a colonial feel to its plant-lined patio. All 85 rooms are clean and comfortable, and most have en suite baths or showers, and air-conditioning.
Hotel services *Air-conditioning (partial).*
Fax. Lift. Multilingual staff. Patio. Safe. TV lounge.
Room services *Telephone.*

Hotel Principal
C/Junta de Comerç 8, 08001 (93 318 89 74/fax 93 412 08 19/hotel@hotelprincipal.es). Metro Liceu/bus 14, 38, 59, 91, N9, N12. **Rates** (incl breakfast) *double* 10,300ptas; *triple* 13,900ptas; *quad* 16,200ptas.
Credit AmEx, DC, EC, MC, TC, V. **Map** C6/**A3**
One of a few hotels and *hostals* on this quiet street near the Rambla, the Principal is distinguished by the ornate furniture in its 60 bedrooms, all of which have modernised bathrooms. The same owners also have the slightly cheaper **Joventut**, along the street, which has recently been thoroughly renovated.
Hotel services *Air-conditioning. Babysitting. Bar. Disabled: rooms (3) adapted for the disabled, toilets. E-mail. Fax. Lifts. Multilingual staff. Restaurant.*
Room services *Safe. Telephone. TV.*
Branch: Hotel Joventut
C/Junta de Comerç 12 (93 301 84 99).
Website: www.hotelprincipal.es

Hotel Urquinaona
Ronda de Sant Pere 24, 08010 (93 268 13 36/fax 93 295 41 37). Metro Urquinaona/bus all routes to Plaça Urquinaona. **Rates** *single* 7,900ptas; *double* 10,900ptas; *triple* 13,900ptas; *breakfast* 590ptas.
Credit MC, V. **Map** D5/**B1**
A former old-style *hostal* very recently transformed by enterprising management into a spik and span modern hotel, offering comforts that normally cost a lot more – air-con, satellite TV, phones, minibars and safes in all rooms – plus a pleasant breakfast room, and Internet access. A welcome departure from the norm in Barcelona hotels.
Hotel services *Air-conditioning. Beauty salon. Business services. Currency exchange. Disabled: wheelchair access. E-mail. Fax. Interpreting service. Laundry service. Multilingual staff.* **Room services** *Hairdryer. Minibar. Refrigerator. Room service (breakfast only). Safe. Telephone. TV (satellite). Website: www.barcelonahotel.com/urquinaona*

Hotel Via Augusta
Via Augusta 63, 08006 (93 217 92 50/fax 93 237 77 14). FGC Gràcia/bus 16,17, 22, 24, 25, 28, 31, 32, N4. **Rates** *single* 6,900-8,400ptas; *double* 10,500-11,000ptas; *triple* 13,000ptas; *cot* 1,500ptas; *breakfast* 950ptas. **Credit** AmEx, DC. MC, TC, V. **Map** D3
A pleasant hotel with superior facilities in an elegant building in Sant Gervasi, on the edge of Gràcia and well-communicated with the centre. The atmosphere is friendly, and the 56 rooms modern and bright, all with bathrooms; those facing Via Augusta can be a bit noisy. Generous buffet breakfasts.
Hotel services *Air-conditioning. Disabled: room (1) adapted for the disabled. Interpreting services. Laundry. Lift. Multilingual staff. Safe. Ticket agency.* **Room services** *Telephone. TV.*

Budget (7,000ptas and under)

In general, budget-bracket hotels have raised prices a bit less than mid-range places. Plaça Reial, just off the Rambla, is the long-established favourite for those in search of an inexpensive room in Barcelona, despite its seediness. Other good areas to look are the rest of the Barri Gòtic, and the Raval, on the opposite side of the Rambla. The Eixample also has some more tranquil, good-value accommodation, and, again, it's also worth considering areas a little further from the centre. Some budget hotels do not have someone on the door 24-hours a day, so check before going out.

Hostal Béjar
C/Béjar 36-8, 1°, 08014 (93 325 59 53). Metro Espanya, Tarragona/bus 27, 127, 109. **Rates** *single* 3,000ptas; *double* 5,000-6,000ptas. **Credit** MC, V. **Map** A4
In the Hostafrancs district, the Béjar is only a five-minute walk from Sants station or the Plaça d'Espanya. Its 22 rooms are spread between two buildings, with one reception area; six have bathrooms, and guests have use of a fridge. The owners speak English.
Hotel services *Laundry, Lift.*

Hostal Eden

C/Balmes 55, 08007 (tel/fax 93 454 73 63) Metro Passeig de Gràcia/bus 7, 16, 17, 63, 67, 68. **Rates** *single* 4,000-4,500ptas; *double* 5,500-6,000ptas; *triple* 7,500ptas. **Credit** EC, MC, TC, V. **Map** D4

One of the most interesting places in this price slot, the Eden occupies two floors of an old Eixample building. José and Dani, who run it, speak four languages and seem to have a good idea of what budget travellers are looking for. All of its 15 rooms are pleasant, but some enjoy unusual added facilities such as whirlpool baths and fridges, and still more extras are planned. Guests also have (coin-operated) Net access, and there's a 24-hour porter. A bright, friendly *hostal.*

Hotel services *Currency exchange. Fax. Internet access. Multilingual staff. Safe. Ticket agency. TV.* **Room services** *Fan. Safe. TV.*

Hostal Fontanella

Via Laietana 71, 2n (tel/fax 93 317 59 43). Metro Urquinaona/bus all routes to Plaça Urquinaona. **Rates** *single* 2,900-3,800ptas; *double* 4,800-5,500ptas; *triple* 6,700-7,700ptas. **Credit** AmEx, DC, MC, V. **Map** D5/B1

This *hostal* benefits from the personal touches of its owner, Encarna, who supervises everything down to the dried flower arrangements and 'weekend kits' (comb, soap and toothpaste) in each room. The Fontanella is clean, cosy and centrally located, and is particularly popular with young women.

Hotel services *Laundry. Lift. Safe.*

Hostal Girona

C/Girona 24, 1º 1ª, 08010 (93 265 02 59). Metro Urquinaona/bus all routes to Plaça Urquinaona. **Rates** *single* 3,000ptas; *double* 6,000ptas. **No credit cards. Map** E5/C1

A white marble stairway leads up to this cosy, family-run eight-room *pensión* in the Eixample. All bedrooms have central heating and TV; the four doubles also boast new en suite bathrooms. Refreshments are served in a tiny breakfast area. In the reception area there is some grand original *Modernista* furniture, and the streets nearby, off any of the main tourist routes, are full of fine Modernist architecture.

Hotel services *Telephone.* **Room services** *TV.*

Hostal Jardí

Plaça Sant Josep Oriol 1, 08002 (93 301 59 00/fax 93 318 36 64). Metro Liceu/bus 14, 38, 59, 91, N9, N12. **Rates** *interior rooms single* 4,000ptas; *double* 5,500ptas; *exterior rooms single or double* 6,600-7,500ptas. **Credit** DC, MC, V. **Map** D6/A3

Always one of the most popular budget options in Barcelona, the Jardí has a wonderful situation overlooking the leafy Plaça del Pi, central but peaceful. The rooms to go for are those with an outside view; interior rooms are more basic, and the patio can be noisy. All rooms have bathrooms, but facilities vary. To get in here, book well in advance.

Hotel services *Refreshments available from reception (24hrs). Safety deposit box.* **Room service** *Telephone. TV (some).*

Hostal Lausanne

Avda Portal de l'Àngel 24, 08002 (93 302 11 39). Metro Catalunya/bus all routes to Plaça Catalunya. **Rates** *double* 4,500-5,500ptas; *(with shower)* 6,000ptas; *(with bath)* 7,500ptas; *triple* 6,500ptas; *(with shower)* 8,500ptas; *(with bath)* 9,600ptas. **No credit cards. Map** D5/B2

This 17-room family-run *hostal* is on the first floor of a fine old building with high ceilings and ample rooms, some with balconies overlooking the Portal de l'Angel. It's clean and bright, with a big sitting room, and the owners are helpful and friendly.

Hotel services *24hr reception. Lift. Lounge. Multilingual staff. Safe. Telephone. TV. Terrace.*

Hostal Layetana

Plaça Ramon Berenguer el Gran 2, 08002 (tel/fax 93 319 20 12). Metro Jaume I/bus 17, 19, 40, 45, N8. **Rates** *single* 2,600ptas; *double* 4,200ptas; *triple* 5,850ptas. **Credit** DC, MC, V. **Map** D6/B3

A view right along the Roman wall and a stunning hall and lift give this *hostal* loads of character. Service is friendly, most of its 20 rooms have bathrooms, and the communal areas are well-kept. Noise from Via Laietana is the major drawback.

Hotel services *Lift. Refreshments available (24hrs). Safe. TV. Terrace.*

Hostal Malda

C/del Pi 5, 1º1ª. Metro Liceu/bus 14, 38, 59, 91, N9, N12. **Rates** *single* 1,500ptas; *double* 2,500-3,000ptas; *triple* 3,500ptas. **No credit cards. Map** D6/B2

*An ideal view from the **Hostal Jardí.***

*Climb up one of the canyons of the Barri Gòtic to **Hostal Maldà**. It's worth it. See page 127.*

This small, bright, comfortable *hostal* in the heart of the Barri Gòtic is a find in every sense: access is through one of the entrances to the Galeries Maldà shopping arcade, but even the hike up the stairs (no lift) is forgotten when you meet the friendly lady who runs it. No en suite facilities, but the communal bathrooms are impeccably clean. The entrance to the Galeries is open until 12.30am, when a porter comes on duty. A great bargain. **Hotel services** *Laundry. Lounge. Refrigerator. Telephone. TV (satellite).*

Hostal Noya

La Rambla 133, 1°, 08002 (93 301 48 31). Metro Catalunya/bus all routes to Plaça Catalunya. **Rates** *single* 1,800-2,200ptas; *double* 3,400-4,200ptas. **No credit cards. Map D5/A2**
This modest *hostal* is in an excellent position on the Rambla, and is decent value for its location. All 15 rooms have balconies overlooking the crowds, but bathrooms are communal. No breakfast either, but there is a good café-restaurant below. **Hotel services** *Telephone.*

Hostal Orleans

Avda Marquès de L'Argentera 13, 08003 (93 319 73 82/fax 93 319 22 19). Metro Barceloneta/ bus 14, 39, 51. **Rates** *single* 3,000-4,500ptas; *double* 5,600-6,500ptas. **Credit** AmEx, DC, MC, V. **Map E6/C4**
This family-run *hostal* near the Port and the Ciutadella has 17 good-sized rooms with en suite facilities, and some have balconies (which can be noisy). All are clean, but upper-floor rooms are more modern. There are special rates for triple or quadruple occupancy; weekly rates can also be negotiated. **Hotel services** *Fax. Laundry. Multilingual staff. Telephone. Vending machine.*
Room services *Telephone (some). TV.*

Hostal Palermo

C/Boqueria 21, 08002 (tel/fax 93 302 40 02). Metro Liceu/bus 14, 38, 59, 91, N9, N12. **Rates** *single* 3,400-5,000ptas; *double* 5,600-6,600ptas; *triple* 8,100-9,300ptas. **Credit** DC, MC, V. **Map D6/A3**
A cheerful place with 34 impeccably clean, recently-refurbished rooms. Some have baths, some don't. **Hotel services** *Lounge. Safe. Telephone. TV.*

Hostal Paris

C/Cardenal Casañas 4, 08002 (93 301 37 85/fax 93 412 70 96). Metro Liceu/bus 14, 38, 59, 91, N9, N12. **Rates** *single* 2,675ptas; *double* 4,300ptas; *(with shower)* 5,300ptas; *(with bath)* 6,500ptas. **Credit** DC, MC, V. **Map D6/A3**
This 45-room *hostal* has a pleasant reception area and large sitting room looking onto the Pla de la Boqueria. Exterior rooms are fine, but interior ones, while quieter, face a narrow air shaft – not for claustrophobics. **Hotel services** *Multilingual staff. Telephone. TV.*
Room services *Safe (some). TV.*

Hostal Parisien

La Rambla 114, 08002 (93 301 62 83). Metro Liceu/bus 14, 38, 59, 91, N9, N12. **Rates** *single* 2,000ptas; *double* 3,500ptas; *(with shower)* 4,000-4,500ptas. **No credit cards. Map D6/A2**
Run by a friendly young couple, the Parisien has a great mid-Rambla location opposite the Virreina. The 12 rooms at this student favourite are well-kept; eight have bathrooms. Those above the Rambla are noisy but atmospheric; others are darker but quieter. **Hotel services** *Lounge. Multilingual staff. Safe. Telephone. TV (satellite).*

Hostal Rembrandt

C/Portaferrisa 23, 08002 (tel/fax 93 318 10 11). Metro Liceu/bus 14, 38, 59, 91, N9, N12. **Rates** *single* 2,800ptas; *(with bath)* 3,800ptas; *double*

4,500ptas; *(with bath)* 5,500-6,300ptas; *triple* 7,000-7,500ptas; *(with bath)* 7,500-10,000ptas; *breakfast* 400ptas. **No credit cards. Map** D6/**B2**
Popular with backpackers, the cheerful 29-room Rembrandt is spotlessly clean with pleasantly decorated rooms, and the foyer opens onto a pleasant communal patio. The owners will accommodate up to five people in a room at reasonable prices.
Hotel services *Multilingual staff. Safe. Telephone. TV.*

Hostal-Residencia Barcelona

C/Roser 40, 08004 (tel/fax 93 443 27 06). Metro Paral.lel/bus 20, 57, 64, 91, 157, N6. **Rates** *single* 3,500ptas; *double* 6,400ptas; *triple* 8,400ptas; *quad* 10,400ptas. **Credit** AmEx, MC, V. **Map** B6
A *hostal* in the pleasant *barri* of Poble Sec, just off the Paral.lel – still only a walk from the centre. Its 60 rooms are basic but clean; most have bathrooms. Guests have use of a fridge in the reception area.
Hotel services *Lift. Multilingual staff. Safe. Ticket agency.* **Room services** *Air-conditioning (some), TV.*

Hostal-Residencia Oliva

Passeig de Gràcia 32, 4°, 08007 (93 488 01 62). Metro Catalunya, Passeig de Gràcia/bus 7, 16, 17, 22, 24, 28, N4, N6. **Rates** *single* 3,200ptas; *double* 6,000-7,000ptas. **No credit cards. Map** D5
The relaxed, family-run Oliva occupies the fourth floor of an old Eixample apartment block with two lifts – one a museum piece much photographed by Japanese guests. Most rooms are light and well-aired, and doubles with bathrooms are especially comfortable. The six rooms facing Passeig de Gràcia have splendid views, but can be noisy in summer.
Hotel services *Lounge. Lifts. Telephone.* **Room services** *TV (some).*

Hostal San Remo

C/Ausiàs Marc 19-C/Bruc 20, 1° 1ª, 08010 (93 302 19 89/fax 93 301 07 74). Metro Urquinaona/bus all routes to Plaça Urquinaona. **Rates** *single* 4,000-5,000ptas; *double* 5,500-6,000ptas; *triple* 7,500-8,000ptas. **Credit** MC, V. **Map** D-E5/**C1**
This friendly, family-run *hostal* on the first floor of an Eixample building offers pleasant rooms with new bathrooms en suite; outside rooms have sunny balconies. Breakfast is served in a bright sitting-room with TV and piano, and guests are given front-door keys. The attentive owner and her son speak some English.
Hotel services *Air-conditioning. Coffee machine. Lift. Safe. Telephone. TV.*

Hostal La Terrassa

C/Junta de Comerç 11, 08001 (93 302 51 74/fax 93 301 21 88). Metro Liceu/bus 14, 38, 59, 91, N9, N12. **Rates** *single* 2,200ptas; *double* 3,600ptas; *(with shower)* 4,400ptas; *triple* 4,800ptas; *(with shower)* 5,700ptas. **Credit** DC, MC, V. **Map** C6/**A3**
Under the same ownership as the hugely popular **Jardí** (*see above*), La Terrassa is one of Barcelona's most likeable cheap *hostals*, and great value. Around half the rooms have bathrooms, and the best have

Best for kids

Barcelona hotels rarely ever refuse to admit children, but there are few that offer special facilities or play areas.
Hotel Arts – Expensive, but there's all-day child-minding, a ground-level pool and the beach.
Hotel Balmes – A safe, ground-level pool and small garden patio.
Hotel Colón – Extra childminding facilities.
Hotel Mesón Castilla – Big family rooms, well-protected terraces and a delightful breakfast patio.
Hotel San Agustín – Adjoining rooms with room for six and two bathrooms that are ideal for families.

balconies overlooking the street or an attractive interior patio, where breakfast is served in summer.
Hotel services *Lounge. Multilingual staff. Safe. Telephone. TV. Terrace.*

Hostal Victòria

C/Comtal 9, 1° 1ª, 08002 (93 318 07 60/93 317 45 97). Metro Catalunya/bus all routes to Plaça Catalunya. **Rates** *single* 2,500-3,000ptas; *double* 4,500-5,000ptas; *(with bath)* 6,000ptas. **No credit cards. Map** D5/**B2**
This spacious 30-room *hostal* in the heart of the old city offers communal cooking and washing facilities. The owner is a bit authoritarian and rooms are basic, but they're clean and light, and most have balconies. Another feature is that discounts are available in winter (Nov-Mar) for stays of over a month.
Hotel services *Dining room. Kitchen. Laundry. Lift. Lounge. Refreshments available (24hrs). Telephone. TV. Terrace.*

Hosteria Grau

C/Ramelleres 27, 08001 (93 301 81 35/ fax 93 317 68 25). Metro Catalunya/bus all routes to Plaça Catalunya. **Rates** *single* 3,500-4,000ptas; *double* 5,000ptas; *(with shower)* 6,000ptas; *(with bath)* 7,000ptas; *triple* 7,500ptas; *(with shower)* 9,000ptas; *(with bath)* 10,000ptas. **Credit** AmEx, DC, EC, MC, TC, V. **Map** D5/**A1**
This pleasant *hostal* has a charming café downstairs (open until 9pm), and serves breakfast until noon in the tiny first-floor sitting room. Rooms are clean and pleasant, but inside singles are dark. City information is provided in reception.
Hotel services *24-hour reception. Bar. Fax. Multilingual staff. Telephone. TV lounge.*

Hotel Call

C/Arc de Sant Ramon del Call 4, 08002 (93 302 11 23/fax 93 301 34 86). Metro Liceu/bus 14, 38, 59, 91, N9, N12. **Rates** *single* 3,960ptas; *double* 5,245ptas; *triple* 7,275ptas; *quad* 8,025ptas. **Credit** MC, V. **Map** D6/**B3**

On a spectacularly narrow street in what was the medieval Jewish quarter – the Call – around the corner from Plaça Sant Jaume, this hotel (rebuilt in 1992) is a clean, modern, rather functional place that's nevertheless very good value. Rooms overlook quiet pedestrian streets or a dark-ish interior patio. All have air-conditioning and modern bathrooms.
Hotel services *Air-conditioning. Fax. Lift. Lounge. Multilingual staff. TV.* **Room services** *Telephone.*

Hotel Toledano

La Rambla 138, 08002 (93 301 08 72/fax 93 412 31 42). Metro Catalunya/bus all routes to Plaça Catalunya. **Rates** *single* 2,900-3,900ptas; *double* 4,600-6,900ptas. **Credit** AmEx, DC, MC, V. **Map** D5/**A2**
Very near Plaça Catalunya, the Toledano may be handily placed, but it can be noisy – interior rooms, with views of the cathedral, are the quietest. Its 28 rooms are basic but all have bathrooms, and there is a chintzy lounge area overlooking the Rambla.
Hotel services *Lift. Multilingual staff. Safe.* **Room services** *Telephone. TV (satellite).*

Pensión Ambos Mundos

Plaça Reial 10, 08002 (93 318 79 70/fax 93 412 23 63). Metro Drassanes/bus 14, 38, 59, 91, N9, N12. **Rates** *double* 4,000ptas; *triple* 6,000ptas.
Credit AmEx, DC, MC, V. **Map** D6/**A3**
A very popular Plaça Reial *hostal*, the Ambos Mundos is above a bar of the same name. The 12 simple tiled rooms all have baths; outside rooms have balconies overlooking the action. Guests can play pool or watch TV in the cavernous reception.
Hotel services *Bar-restaurant. Safe.* **Room services** *Telephone.*

Pensión-Hostal Mari-Luz

C/Palau 4, 2º 1a, 08002 (tel/fax 93 317 34 63). Metro Jaume I/bus 17, 19, 40, 45, N8. **Rates** *per person* 1,700-1,900ptas. **No credit cards. Map** D6/**B3**
Mari-Luz takes great care of her lodgers in this spotlessly clean *hostal*, a few streets' walk from the main Plaça Reial-drag. The 15 rooms, five of which have showers, are plain but quiet, and the old building is atmospheric and affordable. The family also own the similarly-cheap **Fernando** nearby.
Hotel services *Kitchen. Laundry. Multilingual staff. Refreshments available (24 hrs). Safe. TV.*
Branch: Pensión Fernando
C/Ferran 31 (93 301 79 93).

Pensión Rondas

C/Girona 4, 08010 (tel/fax 93 232 51 02) Metro Urquinaona/bus 19, 39, 40, 41, 42, 55, 141, N4, N11. **Rates** *single* 2,500ptas; *double* 4,000-4,500ptas; *(with shower)* 4,500-5,000ptas; *(with bath)* 5,500-6,000ptas. **No credit cards. Map** E5/**C1**
Nine basic, clean rooms, on the third floor of an old Eixample building in a central but unusually quiet location. The young sister and brother who run it are exceptionally friendly and helpful, and the atmosphere is pleasantly relaxed. The lift looks like a museum piece and is actually under an official preservation order, but it's recently been overhauled.
Hotel services *Lift.*

Pensión Vitoria

C/de la Palla 8, pral, 08002 (tel/fax93 302 08 34). Metro Liceu/bus 14, 38, 59, 91, N9, N12. **Rates** *single* 1,500-2,000ptas; *double* 2,500-4,000ptas; *(with shower)* 3,000-5,000ptas; *triple* 3,500-5,000ptas. **Credit** MC, V. **Map** D6/**B2-3**
Close to Plaça del Pi, the Vitoria has 11 clean, light, airy rooms, with balconies. Nine rooms share one bathroom, while two doubles have en suite showers and toilets. Despite the basic facilities, the *pensión* has a loyal bunch of repeat guests, so book early.
Hotel services *Multilingual staff. Telephone. TV.*

Apartment hotels

Apartment hotels are made up of self-contained small flats, with kitchen facilities, plus maid service. They are good for slightly longer stays, and usually offer reduced monthly or longer-term rates.

Apartaments Calàbria

C/Calàbria 129, 08015 (93 426 42 28/fax 93 426 76 40). Metro Rocafort/bus 9, 41, 50, 56, N1, N2, N13, N14, N15. **Apartment rates per night** *one person* 9,500ptas; *two* 11,500ptas; *each additional person* 3,250ptas. **Per month** 160,000ptas; *two months or more* 145,000ptas/month.
Credit AmEx, EC, MC, TC, V. **Map** B5
This Eixample apartment block houses 72 functional short-term apartments with good kitchen and bathroom facilities and separate lounge areas. Office services are available. Rates are competitive, so apartments need to be booked well in advance.
Hotel services *Air-conditioning. Disabled: wheelchair access. Fax. Laundry. Lifts. Multilingual staff.* **Room services** *Room service (not 24-hr). Safe. Telephone. TV (satellite).*

Aparthotel Bertran

C/Bertran 150, 08023 (93 212 75 50/fax 93 418 71 03). FGC Putxet/bus 16, 17, 74. **Apartment rates per night** *single* 8,400ptas; *double* 10,500ptas. **Per week** *single* 50,000ptas; *double* 63,000ptas. **Per month** *single/double* 190,000ptas. **Credit** AmEx, DC, EC, MC, TC, V.
In the residential Putxet area, near Tibidabo and with good vehicle access to the *rondes*, these 30 apartments are spacious and bright, with good facilities. Most have balconies, some have larger terraces, and there are more extras than at most aparthotels: a gym, cycle rental, rooftop terrace and a pool.
Hotel services *Air-conditioning. Car park. Conference facilities. Gym. Interpreters. Laundry. Lifts. Multilingual staff. Safe. Swimming pool (outdoor). Ticket agency.* **Room services** *Radio. Telephone. TV (satellite). Video (on request).*

Aparthotel Senator

Via Augusta 167, 08021 (93 201 14 05/fax 93 202 00 97/senator@city-hotels.es). FGC Muntaner/bus 58, 64, N8. **Apartment rates per night** *one person* 13,500ptas; *two* 15,500ptas; *three* 17,500ptas; *four* 19,500ptas. **Per month** *one person* 235,000ptas; *two* 265,000ptas; *three* 280,000ptas.
Credit AmEx, DC, MC, V. **Map** C2

Straightforward but comfortable apartments, with a few individual touches such as bamboo furniture and plants in each flat, in the Sant Gervasi district. There is no restaurant or bar, but the apartment kitchens are fine for preparing light meals.
Hotel services *Air-conditioning. Fax. Laundry. Lift. Multilingual staff. Safe.* **Room services** *Minibar. Telephone. TV.*
Website: www.city-hotel.es

Atenea Aparthotel

C/Joan Güell 207-11, 08028 (93 490 66 40/fax 93 490 64 20/atenea@city-hotels.es). Metro Les Corts/bus all routes to Plaça Maria Cristina.
Apartment rates per night *single studio or apartment* 15,800ptas; *double studio or apartment* 18,500ptas; *third person supplement* 4,000ptas; *breakfast* 1,500ptas; *group discounts.*
Per month *single* 300,000ptas; *double* 315,000ptas.
Credit AmEx, DC, EC, JCB, MC, TC, V. **Map** A3
A big (105 apartments) 1990s aparthotel offering four-star facilities including bar, restaurant and conference rooms, in the heart of the business district. Apartments are highly efficiently organised with first-rate technology, without having any great character. If you're really busy, a food shopping service is available on request.
Hotel services *Air-conditioning. Bar. Car park. Conference facilities. Disabled: rooms (4) adapted for the disabled, wheelchair access. E-mail. Fax. Lift. Multilingual staff. Photocopiers. Restaurant.*
Room services *Hairdryer. Room service (7am-11pm). Safe. Telephone. TV (satellite). Video (on request).*
Website: www.city-hotels.es

Apartment/room rentals

Barcelona Allotjament

C/Pelai 12, pral B (tel/fax 93 268 43 57/ bcnacom@ibernet.com). Metro Universitat/bus all routes to Plaça Universitat. **Open** 10am-2pm, 5-7pm, Mon-Thur; 10am-2pm Fri. Closed Aug. **Map** D5/A1
Rooms with local families (b&b, half-board or full-board), in shared student flats, in aparthotels and hotels or whole apartments can be booked through this agency, aimed at student, business and individual travellers. Short-term rates from 2,800ptas per day, b&b; long-term (course-length) stays cost around 50,000ptas per month, b&b, plus a 15,000ptas agency fee. Courses (in languages, dance, cookery) are also offered.
Website: www.barcelona-allotjament.com

B&B Norma Agency

C/Ali Bei 11, 3º 2ª (tel/fax 93 232 37 66). Metro Arc de Triomf/bus 19, 39, 40, 41, 42, 55, 141. **Open** 24-hour answerphone. **Map** E5/C1
Rooms booked on a bed-and-breakfast basis in private homes, or whole apartments, in Barcelona and along the coast, for short or longer-term stays. B&B rates begin at around 5,000ptas per night for a single room, or 7,500-10,000ptas for doubles.

Habit Servei

C/Muntaner 200, 2n 3a (93 209 50 45/ fax 93 414 54 25/habit_servei@seker.es). FGC Provença/bus 58, 64, 66, 67, 68. **Open** 9am-8pm Mon-Fri. **Credit** DC, MC, V. **Map** C3
This agency can find rooms in flats for anyone staying in Barcelona for at least two weeks. Rates are about

Beach-day today, so tomorrow we should do Gaudí… Hostal rooms in the Plaça Reial.

50,000ptas a month for a flat-share, or 40,000ptas for a room in a private house. Whole flats are also available. The agency fee (17,400ptas) is payable only when a suitable place is found, and a 40,000ptas deposit is returned at the end of the stay. English is spoken, and it's popular with Erasmus students.
Website: bbs.seker.es/~habit_servei

Youth hostels

Rates can vary by season. For student and youth services and websites that can take reservations for hostels, *see page 297*.

Albergue Kabul

Plaça Reial 17, 08002 (93 318 51 90/fax 93 301 40 34/kabul@kabul-hostel.com). Metro Liceu/bus 14, 38, 59, 91, N9, N12. **Open** 24 hours daily. **Rates** *per person* 1,200-2,500ptas. **No credit cards. Map** D6/A3
Rooms in this welcoming private hostel vary from cramped dormitories with mattresses on the floor to airy doubles with views of Plaça Reial. No private bathrooms, but communal facilities are clean. There's a TV and a drinks dispenser in reception.
Hostel services *Billiard table. Kitchen. Laundry. Lift. Lounge. Multilingual staff. Refreshments. Safe. Telephone. TV (satellite). Video.*
Website: www.kabul-hostel.com

Alberg Mare de Déu de Montserrat

Passeig de la Mare de Déu del Coll 41-51, 08023 (93 210 51 51/fax 93 210 07 98) Metro Vallcarca/bus 25, 28, 87, N4. **Open** *hostel* 8am-midnight (ring for entry after hours); *reception* 8am-4pm, 4.30-11pm, daily. **Rates** *under-25s* 1,800-2,775ptas; *over-25s* 2,325-3,650ptas. *Sheet/towel hire* 350ptas. **Credit** V.
This 183-bed hostel in a pleasant old house with garden is some way from the centre, but not far from a Metro station. Rooms sleep two to eight people, and there are lots of facilities. IYHF cards are required.
Hostel services *Auditorium. Car park. Dining room. Disabled: room (1) adapted for the disabled, toilets, wheelchair access. Fax & copy service. Internet access. Laundry. Multilingual staff. Refreshments available. Safe. TV (satellite)/video room.*

Alberg Pere Tarres

C/Numància 149-151, 08029 (93 410 23 09/fax 93 419 62 68/alberg@peretarres.org). Metro Les Corts/ bus all routes to C/Numància. **Rates** (incl breakfast) 1,600ptas; *sheet hire* 350ptas. **Credit** MC, V. **Map** B3
This hostel has 94 places, five shared bathrooms and an attractive roof terrace. Regulations are strict: no cigarettes or alcohol in dorms; no eating or drinking outside the dining room. IYHF cards are required, and you need to book in summer.
Hostel services *Car park. Kitchen. Laundry. Meals cooked for groups. Multilingual staff. Patio. Refreshments. TV lounge.*
Website: www.peretarres.org

Hostal de Joves de la Ciutadella

Passeig Pujades 29, 08018 (tel/fax 93 300 31 04). Metro Arc de Triomf/bus 40, 41, 42, 141, N6. **Open** 7-10am, 3pm-midnight, daily.

Rates (incl breakfast) *under-26s* 1,500ptas; *over-26s* 1,700ptas. **No credit cards. Map** E6
A renovated hostel by the Ciutadella. Most of the 68 beds are in non-smoking dorms, but there are a few double rooms. Rooms are allocated on a first-come-first-serve basis from 10.30 am each day. IYHF cards are needed, and five nights is the maximum stay.
Hostel services *Dining room. Fridge. Laundry. Lockers. Microwave. Multilingual staff. Refreshments available.*

Campsites

For more information on the 13 campsites not far from the city, get the *Catalunya Campings* brochure from the Palau Robert (*see page 295*).

Cala Gogó

Carretera de la Platja, 08820, El Prat de Llobregat (93 379 46 00/fax 93 379 47 11). Bus 65 from Plaça d'Espanya/by car C246 to Castelldefels, then Airport exit to Prat beach. **Open** *15 Mar-15 Oct* 9am-10pm daily. **Rates** (per person per night) *15 Mar-mid-June, mid-Sept-15 Oct* 430ptas; *under-10s* 330ptas; **plus** *plot* 1,120-1,435ptas. *Mid-June-mid-Sept* 620ptas; *under-10s* 470ptas; **plus** *plot* 1,600-2,050ptas. Lower rates for single tents. **Credit** EC, MC, TC, V.
The nearest campsite to Barcelona, 7km (4 miles) to the south near the beach and the airport, Cala Gogó is large and well-equipped, with a supermarket, restaurant, bar and swimming pool on-site.

Masnou

Carretera N11, km 633, 08320 El Masnou (tel/fax 93 555 15 03). Bus CASAS from Passeig Sant Joan/by car N11 to Masnou (11km/7 miles)/by train RENFE to Masnou from Plaça Catalunya. **Open** (reception) *winter* 8am-1pm, 2.30-8pm; *summer* 8am-1pm, 2.30pm-10pm, daily; (campsite) 7am-11.30pm daily. **Rates** (per person per night) 675ptas; *under-10s* 540ptas; plus extra charges for cars, motorbikes, caravans, tents, & light. **No credit cards.**
Tucked under an attractive range of hills near the coast north of Barcelona, this small site, open year-round, has a bar, restaurant and supermarket (open June-Sept only), kids' playground and pools. There's a sandy beach nearby, with diving and sailing facilities. Bungalows (2,500ptas per person per day) or rooms (4,100ptas, double) can also be rented.

El Toro Bravo

Autovia de Castelldefels, km 11, 08840 Viladecans (93 637 34 62/fax 93 637 21 15). Bus L95 from Barcelona (Ronda Universitat)/by car C246 to Viladecans (11km/7 miles). **Open** *mid-June-Aug* 8am-8pm; *Sept-mid-June* 8.30am-7pm. **Rates** (per person per night) *1 Sept-14 June* 650ptas; *under-9s* 485ptas; *15 June-31 Aug* 700ptas; *under-9s* 510ptas; plus extra charges for vehicles, tents, caravans & light. **Credit** AmEx, EC, MC, TC. V.
The site is 10km (6 miles) from the main road bus stop, but lifts are often given to puffed-out campers. This large seaside site is open all year, and has swimming pools, tennis courts and lots of shade. Bungalows (from 5,000ptas per day) can be rented.

Restaurants

Fine Catalan cuisine, gutsy country meats with rich all i oli, superb seafood, and hip new restaurants with global menus: Barcelona's food scene is getting more varied all the time.

The Mediterranean diet may be a buzzword to be fashionably hyped in other parts of the world, but here in Barcelona it's normal everyday fare – and people love it to such an extent that this can seem to be a city of restaurants. There are nearly 2,700 eating establishments in town, which by the law of averages means there's at least one place to eat on every other street.

Out of this huge selection, most places serve one form or another of Catalonia's own rich and varied cuisine (*see pages 134-5* **The Catalan Menu**). Contrary to what foreigners often assume, there is no such thing as a generic 'Spanish national' cuisine, once you get away from a few universal basics such as potato omelette and grilled hake. In Barcelona, as well as Catalan restaurants, there are many serving the mainly seafood-based cooking of Galicia in the north-west, plus others offering the food of the Basque Country, Andalusia, Castile or other regions. Foreign restaurants have also multiplied in the last few years (*see page 147*). Non-meat-eaters fare less well, but there are decent vegetarian options to choose from (*see page 151*).

As well as the restaurants listed here, many bars also provide food, from snacks to full meals, so for more places to eat, *see chapter* **Cafés & Bars**. For places to eat in the small hours, *see chapter* **Nightlife**, and for places with a mainly gay clientele, *see chapter* **Gay & Lesbian Barcelona**.

Eating habits

When to set your clock, and book Catalans eat late. Lunchtime is at what they call 'midday' – around 2pm. In the evening you won't get a full meal before 8.30pm in most places; 9-9.30pm is the average time for dinner. It's always a good idea to book in restaurants from mid-range upwards, and in every kind of restaurant on Fridays and Saturdays. **Children** Most restaurants welcome children, but few have specific children's menus, and they're not often seen in top-flight dining rooms (*see also chapter* **Children**).

Prices, tips & taxes The lunchtime *menú del dia* set meal is one of Barcelona's great bargains, and it's best to make this your main meal if you want to eat cheaply (for a selection of *menús, see p153*). Some budget restaurants open for lunch only. Evening prices are usually higher, although some restaurants offer a menu for dinner as well. There is no percentage rule for tipping: it's common in mid- or

upper-range restaurants to leave 200-300ptas – rarely over 500ptas – but many locals leave nothing, or just a nominal 25ptas. Bills include 7% IVA tax (VAT), which is usually, but not always, incorporated into the prices shown on the menu.

Sundays & holidays Despite growing flexibility in opening times, there are relatively few places open on Sunday evenings, and these are often very full. Many restaurants close for Easter (usually Good Friday to Easter Monday, sometimes longer) and for some time during August; we've listed annual dates where possible, but at holiday times it's a good idea to phone first to avoid a wasted journey.

Average prices listed are based on the average cost of a starter, a main course and dessert, without drink. Set menus, though, often include beer, wine or water.

The Rambla

Amaya

La Rambla 20-4 (93 302 10 37).
Metro Liceu/bus 14, 38, 59, 91, N9, N12. **Open** 1-5pm, 8.30pm-midnight, daily. **Average** 4,000ptas.
Set menu 950ptas Mon-Fri. **Credit** AmEx, DC, JCB, MC, V. **Map** C-D6/A4
A big, central Basque restaurant, traditionally popular with actors, writers, opera singers and politicians. Specialities include *angulas* (elvers, baby eels), *lubina* (sea bass) and *besugo* (sea bream), cooked several different ways. The extensive wine list includes Txakoli, a light and dry Basque white wine. Livelier for lunch than dinner.
Air-conditioning. Car park. Tables outdoors (Apr-Nov).

Barri Gòtic

Agut

C/Gignàs 16 (93 315 17 09). Metro Jaume I/bus 17, 40, 45. **Open** 1.30-4pm, 9pm-midnight, Tue-Sat; 1.30-4pm Sun. Closed some weeks July-Aug, 25 Dec.
Average 2,500ptas. **Set lunch** 1,275ptas Tue-Fri. **Credit** MC, V. **Map** D6/B4
This long-established, comfortable family-run restaurant is well known for appetising traditional Catalan food. Despite its location in a narrow old street near the port it has always drawn a very varied clientele, although recent price rises may augur a (perhaps regrettable) move upmarket. Agut is applauded for its cannelloni, steaks and home-made profiteroles.
Air-conditioning. Booking advisable.

The Catalan menu

Catalan food is not just a matter of a few regional dishes, but a complete cuisine easily distinguishable from its neighbours in France and the rest of Spain. Much use is made of four basic elements: the *sofregit*, chopped tomato and onion lightly fried together in olive oil; *samfaina*, a mixture of onion, peppers, ripe tomatoes, aubergines and garlic similar to ratatouille, used as an ingredient and an accompaniment; and most distinctive of all the *picada*, for thickening and seasoning, a variable combination of ingredients mixed in a mortar, perhaps garlic, parsley, saffron, ham, bread and crushed nuts. Last is *all i oli*, garlic mayonnaise, best of all made fresh just with wild garlic pounded together with olive oil (and occasionally an egg yolk), and served on the side with meats or seafood.

Grilled meat (with *all i oli*) is a mainstay of traditional Catalan country cooking, especially lamb, pork, sausages and rabbit, usually prepared on an open charcoal grill (*a la brasa*). There's also a vegetarian variant, *escalivada*, of aubergines, red peppers and onions grilled almost black, then peeled and cut into strips. Catalan cuisine is not afraid to mix flavours, such as meat, fruit and nuts. Casserole-like dishes, cooked in a broad earthenware bowl (a *cassola*), include fairly conventional things such as chicken with *samfaina*, but also surprises such as the *mar i muntanya* ('sea and mountain') dishes from the Empordà region around Figueres, mixing meat and seafood surf-and-turf style in subtle combinations such as a stew of prawns, chicken and wild mushrooms, or pork with crayfish. The many fish and seafood dishes include several made with the big frying pan called a paella. The world-famous rice paella hails from Valencia, but there are plenty of similar Catalan variants such as *arròs negre* and *fideuà*.

Other characteristic features of Catalan cuisine include its rich variety of salads, and other interesting vegetable-based dishes such as the beautifully simple *espinacs a la catalana*. Cannelloni (*canelons*), introduced from Italy in the last century, are surprisingly another standard, used in sufficiently distinctive ways (with no tomatoes in the sauce) to count as a real local speciality. Catalan cooking, moreover, has not stood still, and many restaurants present inventive modern Catalan food, incorporating a range of international influences and lighter, more subtle ingredients. For a note on wines, *see chapter* **Shopping**; for drinks and types of coffee, *see chapter* **Cafés & Bars**.

Words and phrases below are given in **Catalan**, *Spanish and* English, *respectively.*

Essential terminology

una cullera	*una cuchara*	a spoon
una forquilla	*un tenedor*	a fork
un ganivet	*un cuchillo*	a knife
un tovalló	*una servilleta*	a napkin
una ampolla de	*una botella de*	a bottle of
una altra	*otra*	another (one)
més	*más*	more
pa	*pan*	bread
oli d'oliva	*aceite de oliva*	olive oil
sal i pebre	*sal y pimienta*	salt and pepper
amanida	*ensalada*	salad
truita	*tortilla*	omelette
(note: *truita* can also mean trout)		
la nota	*la cuenta*	the bill
un cendrer	*un cenicero*	an ashtray
vinagre	*vinagre*	vinegar
vi negre/rosat/	*vino tinto/rosado/*	red/rosé/
blanc	*blanco*	white wine
bon profit	*aproveche*	Enjoy your meal
sóc vegetarià/ana	*soy vegetariano/a*	I'm a vegetarian
sóc diabètic/a	*soy diabético/a*	I'm a diabetic

Cooking terms

a la brasa	*a la brasa*	charcoal-grilled
a la graella/planxa	*a la plancha*	grilled on a hot metal plate
a la romana	*a la romana*	fried in batter
al forn	*al horno*	baked
al vapor	*al vapor*	steamed
fregit	*frito*	fried
rostit	*asado*	roast
ben fet	*bien hecho*	well-done
a punt	*medio hecho*	medium
poc fet	*poco hecho*	rare

Catalan specialities

amanida catalana/ensalada catalana mixed salad with a selection of cold meats

arròs negre/arroz negro 'black rice', rice cooked in squid ink, with other seafood usually included

bacallà a la llauna/bacalao 'a la llauna' salt cod baked in garlic, tomato, paprika and wine

botifarra/butifarra Catalan sausage: variants include *botifarra negre*, blood sausage; *blanca*, mixed with egg

botifarra amb mongetes/butifarra con judias sausage with haricot beans

calçots a specially sweet variety of large spring onion (scallion), available only from Nov to spring, and eaten char-grilled, with *romesco* sauce

carn d'olla traditional Christmas dish of various meats stewed with *escudella*, then served separately
***conill amb cargols/*conejo con caracoles** rabbit with snails
crema catalana cinnamon-flavoured custard dessert with burnt sugar topping, similar to crème brûlée
***escalivada/*escalibada** grilled and peeled peppers, onions and aubergine
escudella thick winter stew of meat and vegetables
***espinacs a la catalana/*espinacas a la catalana** spinach quick-fried in olive oil with garlic, raisins and pine kernels
esqueixada summer salad of marinated salt cod with onions, olives and tomato
***fideuà/*fideuá** paella made with noodles
***pa amb tomàquet/*pan con tomate** bread prepared with tomato, oil and salt (*see p156*)
***peus de porc/*pies de cerdo** pigs' trotters
romesco a spicy sauce from the coast south of Barcelona, made with crushed almonds and hazelnuts, tomatoes, oil and a special type of red pepper (the *nyora*)
***sarsuela/*zarzuela** fish and seafood stew
***sípia amb mandonguilles/*sepia con albóndigas** cuttlefish with meatballs
***suquet de peix/*suquet de pescado** fish and potato soup
***torrades/*tostadas** toasted *pa amb tomàquet*

Carn i aviram/Carne y aves/ Meat & poultry

ànec	*pato*	duck
bou	*buey*	beef
cabrit	*cabrito*	kid
conill	*conejo*	rabbit
faisà	*faisán*	pheasant
fetge	*higado*	liver
embotits	*embotidos*	cold cuts of sausage
llebre	*liebre*	hare
llengua	*lengua*	tongue
llom	*lomo*	loin of pork
ous	*huevos*	eggs
perdiu	*perdiz*	partridge
pernil	*jamón serrano*	dry-cured ham
pernil dolç	*jamón york*	cooked ham
pollastre	*pollo*	chicken
porc	*cerdo*	pork
porc senglar	*jabalí*	wild boar
ronyons	*riñones*	kidneys
vedella	*ternera*	veal
xai/be	*cordero*	lamb

Peix i marisc/Pescado y mariscos/ Fish & seafood

anxoves	*anchoas*	anchovies
bacallà	*bacalao*	salt cod
besuc	*besugo*	sea bream
calamarsos	*calamares*	squid
cloïsses	*almejas*	clams
cranc	*cangrejo*	crab
escamarlans	*cigalas*	crayfish
escopinyes	*berberechos*	cockles
gambes	*gambas*	prawns
llagosta	*langosta*	spiny lobster
llagostins	*langostinos*	langoustines
llenguado	*lenguado*	sole
llobarro	*lubina*	sea bass
lluç	*merluza*	hake
musclos	*mejillones*	mussels
pop	*pulpo*	octopus
rap	*rape*	monkfish
salmó	*salmón*	salmon
sardines	*sardinas*	sardines
sípia	*sepia*	cuttlefish
tonyina	*atún*	tuna
truita	*trucha*	trout
(*note:* **truita** *can also mean an omelette*)		

Verdures/Legumbres/Vegetables

all	*ajo*	garlic
alvocat	*aguacate*	avocado
bolets	*setas*	wild mushrooms
ceba	*cebolla*	onion
cigrons	*garbanzos*	chickpeas
col	*col*	cabbage
enciam	*lechuga*	lettuce
endivies	*endivias*	chicory
espinacs	*espinacas*	spinach
faves	*habas*	broad beans
mongetes blanques	*judias blancas*	haricot beans
mongetes verdes	*judias verdes*	French beans
pastanagues	*zanahorias*	carrots
patates	*patatas*	potatoes
pebrots	*pimientos*	peppers
pèsols	*guisantes*	peas
tomàquets	*tomates*	tomatoes
xampinyons	*champiñones*	mushrooms

Postres/Postres/Desserts

flam	*flan*	crème caramel
formatge	*queso*	cheese
gelat	*helado*	ice-cream
iogur	*yogur*	yoghurt
mel i mató	*miel y mató*	cottage cheese with honey
pastís	*pastel*	cake
postre de músic	*postre de músico*	nuts and raisins with muscatel
tarta	*tarta*	tart

Fruïta/Fruta/Fruit

figues	*higos*	figs
maduixes	*fresas*	strawberries
pera	*pear*	pear
plàtan	*plátano*	banana
poma	*manzana*	apple
préssec	*melocotón*	peach
raïm	*uvas*	grapes
taronja	*naranja*	orange

Agut d'Avignon

*C/Trinitat 3/Avinyo 8 (93 302 60 34). Metro Liceu/
bus 14, 38, 59, 91, N9, N12.* **Open**
9-11.30pm, daily. **Average** 4,000-4,500ptas. **Credit**
AmEx, DC, EC, JCB, MC, TC, V. **Map** D6/**B3**

In a small alleyway, one of Barcelona's most prestigious restaurants offers comfort and service belying
the shabbiness of much of the surrounding area.
Menus are based on classic Catalan dishes (excellent
farcellets de col, stuffed cabbage leaves), with others
from various Spanish regions, such as Castilian
roasts, and creations of their own like wild boar with
strawberry sauce, duck with figs, or oyster soup.
Air-conditioning. Booking essential.

Café de l'Acadèmia

*C/Lledó 1 (93 319 82 53/93 315 00 26).
Metro Jaume I/bus 17, 19, 40, 45, N8.*
Open 9am-noon, 1.30-4pm, 9pm-midnight, Mon-Fri.
Closed public holidays, two weeks Aug. **Average**
3,000ptas. **Set lunch** 1,000-1,275ptas. **Credit** AmEx,
MC, V. **Map** D6/**B3**

Perhaps the best of a clutch of quality restaurants
near the Catalan government and City Hall, the
Acadèmia serves some 50-odd dishes that range
from Catalan classics such as *rossejat* (rice cooked
in a fish broth) with prawns to a delicious chicken
brochette or quail with sesame and soy sauce. On
the floor above, there are magnificent rooms for
larger group dinners, offering beautiful views of the
medieval Plaça Sant Just.
*Air-conditioning. Booking essential. Tables outdoors
(Easter-Oct).*

Can Culleretes

*C/Quintana 5 (93 317 30 22). Metro Liceu/bus 14,
18, 38, 59.* **Open** 1.30-4pm, 9-11pm, Tue-Sat; 1.30-
4pm Sun. Closed three weeks July, 25 Dec. **Average**
3,000ptas. **Set menus** 1,600ptas Tue-Thur;
2,100ptas Tue-Fri. **Seafood menu** 3,000ptas.
Credit MC, V. **Map** D6/**A3**

Can Culleretes is the oldest restaurant in Barcelona.
It was founded in 1786, and has a rambling interior
covered in old photos of local celebrities. The
lengthy main menu includes rich traditional dishes
like *civet de porc senglar* (wild boar stew) and *cuixa
d'oca amb pomes* (goose leg with apples); there's also
a lighter seafood menu, which can be highly recommended. Culleretes undercharges for wine, and there
are good Raïmats at 1,100ptas. This is a popular
place, so go early to avoid queuing.
Air-conditioning. Booking essential (Fri-Sun).

Cervantes

*C/Cervantes 7 (93 317 33 84). Metro Jaume I/bus
14, 18, 38, 59, N6, N9.* **Open** 1.30-4.30pm Mon-Fri.
Closed Easter, three weeks Aug, public holidays. **Set
lunch** 1,100ptas. **No credit cards. Map** D6/**B3**

This friendly, low-priced lunch restaurant is run by
three sisters. The food is Catalan, including traditional classics such as *botifarra*, paella and *escudella*, and is especially popular with tie-wearing
city-hall workers and green-haired students from a
nearby art school.

Los Caracoles

*C/Escudellers 14 (93 302 31 85).
Metro Liceu/bus 14, 38, 59, 91, N9, N12.* **Open**
1pm-midnight daily. **Average** 3,500ptas. **Credit**
AmEx, DC, JCB, MC, V. **Map** D6/**A3**

With chickens roasting on spits outside, the
Caracoles has been in every guidebook to Barcelona
for about 50 years, and is consequently always
packed with tourists. Very few locals eat here,
though; why should that be?
Air-conditioning.

Govinda

*Plaça Vila de Madrid 4-5 (93 318 77 29).
Metro Catalunya/bus all routes to Plaça Catalunya.*
Open 1-4pm, 8.30-11.45pm, Tue-Sat; 1-4pm Mon,
Sun. Closed pm some public holidays.
Average 2,500ptas. **Set lunch** 1,275ptas Mon-Fri.
Set menu 1,740 Fri pm-Sun. **Credit** AmEx, DC, MC,
V. **Map** D5-6/**B2**

This Indian vegetarian restaurant is in a handy
location, in a square just off the Rambla. An excellent salad bar, a choice of two hot dishes and home-
made bread and desserts make up a great-value
lunch menu. There's no alcohol or coffee, though.
Air-conditioning. Booking advisable.

Juicy Jones

*C/Cardenal Casañas 7 (93 302 43 30). Metro
Liceu/bus 14, 38, 59, 91, N9, N12.* **Open** 1pm-
midnight daily. **Set menu** 1,000ptas. **No credit
cards. Map** D6/**A3**

With its island-hippy paint job, this could be the
original veggie voodoo lounge. At least 17 different
fresh juices are served from the long thin bar. For
something more substantial, the well-prepared all-
vegetarian food is decent, and is served all through
the day until midnight.

Top of the range

Fine cuisine in Barcelona is based above all on
subtle, imaginative interpretations of Catalan
cooking, with measured doses of other
influences – especially French, Basque and
from the rest of the Mediterranean. The ambience in these restaurants is a little formal –with
exceptions, such as **Passadís del Pep** and **Ot**
– but none follow any strict dress code.

Agut d'Avignon *Barri Gòtic, see left.*
Ca l'Isidre *The Raval, see p141.*
Passadis del Pep *Sant Pere, La Ribera & the
Born, see p147.*
Beltxenea; La Dama; Jaume de Provença
All in The Eixample, see pp152-4.
**Botafumeiro; Jean-Luc Figueras; Ot; Roig
Robí** *All in Gràcia, see pp154-6.*
La Balsa; Neichel *Both in Tibidabo & Zona
Alta, see pp156-7.*
Gaig *Horta, see p157.*

Mastroqué

C/Codols 29 (93 301 79 42). Metro Drassanes/bus 14, 36, 38, 57, 59, 64, 91, 157, N6, N9, N12. **Open** 1.30-3.30pm, 9-11.30pm, Mon-Fri; 9-11.30pm Sat. Closed Aug, some public holidays. **Average** 3,000ptas. **Set lunch** 1,200ptas. **Credit** MC, V. **Map** D6/**A-B4**

One thing Catalan restaurateurs might learn from their French neighbours is the art of mellow lighting. Many places in Barcelona are over-lit, but this is not the case with French-run Mastroqué. Despite being located on one of the narrowest streets in the city, this is a surprisingly roomy restaurant. It offers an interesting selection of regional dishes from France, Catalonia and other parts of Spain, such as a hot goat cheese starter with cooked peppers and tomatoes or a candied aubergine 'caviar'. The good value set lunch is generous and excellent.

Air-conditioning. Booking advisable (Thur-Sun).

Mercè Vins

C/Amargós 1 (93 302 60 56). Metro Urquinaona/ bus 17, 19, 40, 45, N8. **Open** 1.30-4pm Mon, Tue, Thur; 1.30-4pm, 8-11pm, Wed, Fri; 8am-noon, 8-11pm Sat. Closed public holidays, some days Aug. **Set lunch** 1,150ptas. **Credit** V. **Map** A5/**B2**

Mercè Vins offers short set menus (no à la carte) with interesting dishes such as *llom amb ametlles i prunes* (pork with almonds and prunes) or *estofat* (beef stew). It's tiny, opening times are eccentric, but it's always packed. In the evenings, there's a *llesqueria* service (*see p157*) only.

Air-conditioning (upstairs). Booking advisable.

Mesón Jesús

C/Cecs de la Boqueria 4 (93 317 46 98). Metro Liceu/bus 14, 38, 59, 91, N9, N12. **Open** 1-4pm, 8-11.30pm, Mon-Fri; 8-11.30pm Sat. Closed Easter, Aug-early Sept, public holidays. **Average** 2,500-3,000ptas. **Set lunch** 1,100ptas. **Set dinner** 1,250ptas. **Credit** MC, V. **Map** D6/**A3**

Small and cosy, this restaurant off Plaça del Pi feels like it hasn't changed much in 100 years. The hard-working team provide good Catalan and Spanish dishes, and it's popular with locals and foreigners.

Air-conditioning.

Oolong

C/Gignás 25 (93 315 12 59). Metro Jaume I/bus 17, 40, 45. **Open** 8.30am-2.30am Mon-Sat; 6pm-2am Sun. **Average** 2,500ptas. **Set menu** 1,000ptas. **Credit** AmEx, DC, MC, V. **Map** D6/**B4**

Worth the trip

A short journey by road or rail will take you to three of the most memorable restaurants in Catalonia. For transport information, *see page 256.*

El Bulli

Cala Montjoi (7km/4.5 miles from Roses) (972 15 04 57). By car A7 or N11/by train & bus RENFE from Sants or Passeig de Gràcia to Figueres, then bus to Roses, then taxi. **Open** *July-early Oct* 1-3pm, 8-10pm, daily; *mid-Mar-June* 1-3pm, 8-10pm, Wed-Sun. Closed mid-Oct-early Mar. **Average** 14,500ptas. **Credit** AmEx, DC, MC, V.

A privileged hideaway overlooking a small cove outside Roses on the Costa Brava, El Bulli has become known as one of the finest restaurants in Europe through the skill and imagination of chef Ferran Adrià. The long, set gourmet menu includes a parade of nine aperitifs, seven starters, three main dishes and two desserts, with such striking culinary events as candied trout eggs and duck tongues with pears and oysters; a real experience. For more on Roses, *see pp264-6.*

Air-conditioning. Disabled: wheelchair access. Tables outdoors.

Fonda Europa

C/Anselm Clavé 1, Granollers (93 870 03 12). By car A7 or N-152 (35km/22 miles)/by train RENFE to Granollers. **Open** 1-3.30pm, 9-11pm, daily. Closed 25 Dec. **Average** 4,000ptas. **Credit** AmEx, DC, JCB, MC, V.

First opened in 1714, and perhaps the best-preserved historic inn in Catalonia, the Europa serves very traditional Catalan food such as pork *a la llauna*, *cap i pota* (tripe, cheeks and trotters), cod with *samfaina* and equally hearty desserts. A 'cart-driver's breakfast' (smoked herring, wine and *torrades*) is served on market days (Thur).

Air-conditioning. Booking essential.

El Racó de Can Fabes

C/Sant Joan 6, Sant Celoni (93 867 28 51/fax 93 867 38 61). By car A7 or C-251 (60km/37 miles)/by train RENFE to Sant Celoni. **Open** 1.30-3.30pm, 8.30-10.30pm, Tue-Sat; 1.30-3.30pm Sun. Closed first two weeks Feb, end June-first week July, 25 Dec, 6 Jan. **Average** 12,500ptas. **Set menu** 12,500ptas. **Credit** AmEx, DC, EC, JCB, MC, TC, V.

In a small town at the foot of the Montseny mountains, the Racó has all of three Michelin stars, and presiding figure Santi Santamaria is acclaimed as one of the greatest Catalan chefs. Specialities include scallop salad, cold truffle stews and a superlative grill of Mediterranean seafood. Desserts and cheeses are as fine. A gourmet pilgrimage, and for all its prestige service El Racó is unpretentiously welcoming; those who make the trip don't regret it.

Air-conditioning. Booking essential. Car park. Disabled: wheelchair access.

*Recover from the MACBA at friendly **Silenus**. See page 146.*

Oolong's small but roomy space reveals some cool architectural details, such as cable-suspended stairs and overhead fans projecting from oak barrels. Friendly and relaxed, it emphasises vegetarian food, but white meat is also served, and the innovative 'fun cuisine' features a changing roster of Thai, Japanese or Spanish dishes. Its music is good too, from jazz to laidback boogie and ethnic beat.

Peimong

C/Templaris 6-10 (93 318 28 73). Metro Jaume I/bus 17, 19, 40, 45, N8. **Open** 1-4.30pm, 8pm-midnight, Tue-Sun. Closed (sometimes) Aug. **Average** 1,500ptas. **Credit** MC, V. **Map** D6/**B3**
If there's another Peruvian restaurant in town, it hasn't had the success of this small place. No-frills décor is made up for by the food, mainly from northern Peru – such things as *ceviche*, grouper marinated in lemon and spices, or *pato en ají*, duck stewed with peas, potatoes and white rice. It's popular with a mixed local and foreign crowd.
Air-conditioning. Booking essential (Fri-Sun).

La Poste

C/Gignàs 23 (93 315 15 04). Metro Jaume I/bus 17, 19, 40, 45, N8. **Open** 1-4.30pm, 8-11.30pm, Mon-Fri; 1-4.30pm Sat, Sun. Closed Christmas, Easter, late Aug-early Sept. **Average** 1,500ptas. **Set menus** 975ptas Mon-Sat; 1,100ptas Sun, public holidays. **No credit cards. Map** D6/**B4**
Faithful provider to postal workers from the nearby *Correus*, a cheap, enjoyable restaurant with time-honoured Spanish and Catalan dishes such as *botifarra amb mongetes*, paella, *faves a la catalana* (broad beans and blood sausage in white wine) and *empanadillas* (tuna pies). The three-course menu (for lunch or dinner) is one of the best deals in town.

Les Quinze Nits

Plaça Reial 6 (93 317 30 75). Metro Liceu/bus 14, 38, 59, 91, N9, N12. **Open** 1-3.30pm, 8.30-11.30pm, daily. Closed 25 Dec. **Average** 2,000ptas. **Set lunch** 995ptas Mon-Fri. **Credit** AmEx, DC, MC, V. **Map** D6/**A3**

This small (but growing) chain caused a minor sensation in the local restaurant world by offering a combination of sophisticated modern Catalan food in light, elegant surroundings at prices lower than the norm, and, in the case of its first two branches, in formerly down-at-heel locations in Plaça Reial and C/Escudellers where nobody thought restaurants like this could work. Defying the doubters, they are hugely successful. Menus are all similar: try the *civet de conill* (rabbit stew), *parillada de peix* (seafood mixed grill) or succulent *arrós negre*. Their popularity is such that food quality and service can get pressured at busy times, and they have an annoying no-bookings policy, which means lengthy queues. This sometimes favours foreigners, who tend to eat earlier than locals – but even if you arrive as it opens you may still have to wait.
Branches: La Dolça Herminia C/Magdalenes 27 (93 317 06 76); **La Fonda** C/Escudellers 10 (93 301 75 15); **Hostal de Rita** C/Aragó 279 (93 487 23 76); **L'Hostalet de la Mamasita** Avda Sarrià (93 321 92 96).
Air-conditioning. Disabled: wheelchair access. Tables outdoors (Quinze Nits only).

Restaurante Pakistani

C/Carabassa 3 (93 302 60 25). Metro Drassanes/bus 14, 36, 57, 59, 64, 157, N6. **Open** 1pm-1am daily. **Average** 750ptas. **No credit cards. Map** D6/**B3-4**
Central, just off Plaça George Orwell, this clean, green-walled little place serves good cheap dishes such as chicken with couscous (550ptas) or veggies with rice (425ptas). The branch down the street is a little bigger, but similar.
Branch: Cuatro Hermanos C/Carabassa 19 (93 302 60 25).

El Salón

C/Hostal d'en Sol 6-8 (93 315 21 59). Metro Jaume I/bus 17, 19, 40, 45, N8. **Open** 2-5pm, 8.30pm-midnight, Mon-Sat. Closed two weeks Aug, Christmas. **Average** 2,500ptas. **Credit** AmEx, MC, V. **Map** D6/**B4**

With antique couches, mirrors and high-backed chairs, El Salón has the feel of an elegant bohemian living room. The cuisine has French overtones, with a fair amount of creamy sauces, but the base is Catalan and very good. Try roast guinea-fowl with chestnut comfit and creamy clove sauce, or aubergine tart with goat's cheese and pesto.
Air-conditioning. Booking advisable. Disabled: wheelchair access.

Self Naturista
C/Santa Anna 11-17 (93 318 23 88/93 318 26 84). Metro Catalunya/bus all routes to Plaça Catalunya. **Open** 11.30am-10pm Mon-Sat. Closed public holidays. **Average** 1,250ptas. **Set menu** 930ptas. **No credit cards. Map** D5/B2
Barcelona's best-known vegetarian restaurant looks like a college self-service canteen, only cleaner. The good-value set menu includes stews and soups, most made without dairy products, and Catalan dishes such as *escalivada*. It's popular, so be prepared for long queues for lunch.
Air-conditioning.

Slokai
C/Palau 5 (93 317 90 94). Metro Liceu, Jaume I/ bus 14, 17, 19, 38, 40, 45, 49, N8, N9, N12. **Open** 1-4pm, 9pm-midnight, Mon-Fri; 9pm-midnight Sat. **Average** 2,300ptas. **Set lunch** (self service) 1,200ptas. **No credit cards. Map** D6/B3
White-walled and spacious, with only a few tables, this trendy spot is run by a young crowd who serve unabashedly modern dishes such as a terrine of salmon and prawns, or truffle-stuffed duck flan. Portions are nouvelle cuisine-small, but the food is well realised, and prices are within sampling range. For dessert, try tiramisú with strawberry sauce.

Sushi-ya
C/Quintana 4 (93 412 72 49). Metro Liceu/bus 14, 18, 38, 59, N6, N9. **Open** 1-4pm, 8.30-11.30pm, daily. **Average** 1,500ptas. **Set menus** 795-1,195ptas. **No credit cards. Map** D6/A3
A small, friendly sushi bar with bargain menus, which can include salad, miso soup, *gryndon* (beef and rice) or a choice of sushi, and exotic ice creams for dessert, such as one of sweet red beans.

Taxidermista
Plaça Reial 8 (93 412 45 36). Metro Liceu/bus 14, 38, 59, 91, N9, N12. **Open** meals served 1.30-4pm, 8.30-11.30pm, Tue-Sun; *tapas* 1.30pm-1am Tue-Sun. **Average** 3,000ptas. **Credit** AmEx, MC, V. **Map** D6/A3
As its name implies, this airy and elegant recent arrival was once a shop for stuffed animals, patronised by the likes of Dalí and Miró. The newly designed interior, by star architect Beth Gali achieves a calm, precise balance of old and new (minus the animals), while the well-staffed kitchen serves high quality Catalan and international cuisine, with some vegetarian dishes. It's easier to get into than its Plaça Reial neighbour the **Quinze Nits** (*see p139*); one drawback, though, can be its quite eccentrically bad service.

The Raval

L'Antic
C/Riereta 8 (93 442 81 79). Metro Sant Antoni/bus 20, 24, 64, 91, N6. **Open** 1-4pm, 8.30pm-midnight, Mon-Sat. Closed public holidays & one week Aug. **Average** 2,000ptas. **Set lunch** 1,000ptas Mon-Fri. **Set dinner** 1,500ptas Mon-Thur; 2,000ptas Fri, Sat. **Credit** DC, MC, V. **Map** C6
A small, comfortable restaurant in the old *Barrio Chino*, run by a Catalan-Argentinian couple who serve up grilled meats *al estilo argentino*. Other specialities include varied *torrades* (*see p156*).
Air-conditioning. Booking essential.

Biocenter
C/Pintor Fortuny 25 (93 301 45 83). Metro Liceu/ bus 14, 38, 59, 91, N9, N12. **Open** 9am-5pm Mon-Sat. Closed public holidays. **Average** 1,500ptas. **Set menu** 1,125ptas Mon-Fri; 1,500ptas Sat. **No credit cards. Map** C-D5/A2
This vegetarian café is across the street from a health-food shop of the same name, and serves a big range of salads, a filling set menu, and organic beer.
Air-conditioning. Vegan dishes.

El Cafetí
C/Hospital 99, end of passage (93 329 24 19). Metro Liceu/bus 14, 38, 59, 91, N9, N12. **Open** 1.30-3.30pm, 9-11.30pm, Tue-Sat; 1.30-3.30pm Sun. Closed Easter weekend, mid Aug. **Average** 2,500ptas. **Set menu** 1,100ptas Tue-Fri, Sat lunch (not public holidays). **Credit** AmEx, DC, MC, TC, V. **Map** C6
This small restaurant has perfected a series of Catalan-French dishes in the last 15-or-so years, and built up a regular clientele. Specialities include house paté, salt-cod dishes and home-made desserts. Staff speak English, French and German, and there is a function room for up to 30 people.
Air-conditioning. Booking essential weekends. Disabled: wheelchair access. Vegetarian dishes.

Ca l'Isidre
C/les Flors 12 (93 441 11 39/93 442 57 20). Metro Paral.lel/bus 20, 36, 57, 64, 91, 157, N6. **Open** 1.30-4pm, 8.30-11.30pm, Mon-Sat. Closed public holidays, Easter, four weeks July/Aug. **Average** 6,000ptas. **Credit** AmEx, DC, MC, V. **Map** C6

Special places

A selection of restaurants where the location can make the difference for that special meal...
La Llotja *The Raval, see p144.*
La Oficina *Port Vell & Barceloneta, see p151.*
Agua *Vila Olímpica, p151.*
Jean-Luc Figueras *Gràcia, p155.*
La Balsa; La Venta *Both in Tibidabo & Zona Alta, see pp156-7.*
Els Pescadors *Poble Nou, see p157.*
Can Travi Nou *Horta, see p157.*

A small family-run restaurant near the Paral.lel that receives regular visits from King Juan Carlos. Chef César Pastor's regular dishes include artichoke hearts stuffed with wild mushrooms and duck liver, and loin of lamb broiled English-style. Desserts are made by the daughter of the family, master *pastissera* Núria Gironès. English and French are spoken. *Air-conditioning. Booking essential.*

El Convent

C/Jerusalem 3 (93 317 10 52). Metro Liceu/bus 14, 18, 38, 59, 91, N4, N6, NS. **Open** 1-4pm, 8pm-midnight, daily. Closed 25 Dec.
Average 2,800ptas. **Set lunch** 990ptas Mon-Sat.
Credit AmEx, DC, EC, JCB, MC, V. **Map** C-D6/**A2**
Until 1998 this rambling old four-storey building housed the Egipte, many people's favourite Barcelona restaurant. When its owners retired they sold it to their former staff, who fortunately have kept it much as it was, with just a name change. It has almost exactly the same long menu of traditional Catalan dishes, and with its antique fittings, bustling atmosphere and enjoyable food it remains a convivial standby. As before, it's very crowded at peak times, when things can seem a bit chaotic.
Air-conditioning. Booking essential weekends.

Elisabets

C/Elisabets 2-4 (93 317 58 26).
Metro Catalunya/bus all routes to Plaça Catalunya.
Open 1-4pm Mon-Thur, Sat; 1-4pm, 9-11.30pm, Fri.
Closed three weeks Aug, public holidays.
Set lunch 995ptas. **Set dinner** 1,500-2,000ptas.
No credit cards. Map C-D5/**A2**
Classic little lunchtime eating house with a long history of serving good, cheap Catalan food to the neighbourhood and anyone else who wanders in. The menu gives a wider-than-average choice, often with good lamb with *all i oli*.
Air-conditioning. Booking advisable.

Escondite del Pirata

C/de la Cera 23 (93 443 04 34). Metro Sant Antoni/ bus 20, 24, 64, 91, N6. **Open** 1pm-1am Tue-Sat.
Average 2,500ptas. **Set menu** 1,000ptas.
No credit cards. Map C6
The 'Pirate's Hideout' serves decent versions of Catalan dishes such as rabbit stew or grilled fresh tuna, and a variety of original salads. The clientele is a mixture of noisy, alternative-ish locals, chain-smoking artists, and the odd foreigner.
Booking essential (Fri, Sat).

Estevet

C/Valldonzella 46 (93 302 41 86). Metro Universitat/ bus all routes to Plaça Universitat. **Open** 1.30-4pm, 9pm-midnight, Mon-Sat. Closed public holidays, two weeks Aug. **Average** 2,500ptas. **Set lunch** 1,200ptas. **Credit** AmEx, DC, MC, V. **Map** C5/**A1**
Estevet is one of the oldest restaurants in town, run for many years by Jordi Suñé. The food is enjoyable and carefully prepared – the langoustines, grilled asparagus and *filet Café de París* are especially good – but it's worth coming here almost as much for the uniquely warm atmosphere, with striking paintings,

Dinner grooves

The link-up of nightlife and restaurant-life didn't happen all that quickly in Barcelona. Somebody, though, must have got hungry, for a recent phenomenon has been the appearance of cool, fresh places where you can drink, hang out, and also eat from (usually) eclectic menus; a mix of music, ambience and food to get you grooved up for a night of fun. Some club-bar-restaurants are currently among the most popular places in town.

In the big car park/square behind the Boqueria market is **Bar Ra** (*pictured top right*), with tables outdoors and food from tapas to Mexican, West Indian and Thai dishes. Music covers the bases, from jazz to jesus rock, with ambient and light drum'n' bass the sounds of choice. On the back wall a tantric mural depicts a moon goddess smiling down on an orgy of sexy abundance – healthy inspiration, perhaps, for the clientele. A short walk from there is **Mama Café**, with pillow benches in its big, colourful space. The innovative food has fine offerings such as a chilled melon soup, or good stir-fried veggies. Music is digestive too, tending to acid jazz and ethnic beat.

Across the Rambla in the Barri Gòtic is **Xocoa**, a *granja* (*see page 160*) run by the friendly Marc, well-connected among DJ's, designers and artists. On Friday and Saturday nights the vaulted back room is transformed into a lounge-ambient club with high romantic potential. Being a *granja*, it's not so much dinner as desserts that stand out here. On Plaça George Orwell, **Ovisos** (*pictured bottom right; see also chapter* **Nightlife**), the slummer's paradise, offers surprisingly fine dinners. You have to push through young drunks to get to the less-crowded dining area, but once there you can savour dishes such as *llobarro amb ceba i tomàquet* (sea bass with onion and tomato). The menu changes according to the stylish chef's shopping habits; prices fluctuate too, and be warned: the food is not as cheap as the surrounding might suggest.

Over by the Born, **Suborn** plays rock-'n'roll, sliding into happy house as the night progresses. Facing the Ciutadella, it has an outdoor terrace and sometimes hosts live music. Food is straightforward – paellas, own-made tapas – and it's a popular leap-off point for the Moll de la Fusta or **Woman Caballero** (*see chapter* **Nightlife**).

Barbarella in the Eixample is right out of a movie; the dim, red-lit space has furry white walls, and mod-'60s lamps that hang over tables like giant eyeballs fascinated by what's happening on your plate – the work of a very good French chef. The cool music is attended to by DJ Lady B, who spins deep house and some hard-edged ambient tracks in case you start feeling too comfortable.

Finally, back in the Raval is **Salsitas**, a huge palace of whiteness. White feathered arches lead you into the dining hall, where white pillars in the form of palm trees surround tables and white cushioned chairs made of iron fish forms. The food is just about right for this camped-up Hollywood heaven, with salads, pizzas and main dishes such as chicken breast with sun-dried tomatoes, asparagus and wild mushrooms. Resident DJ Bass keeps the whiteness warm until 3am, spinning all kinds of contemporary dinner music, but with an emphasis on experimental, light (white?) house.

Locations

Barbarella *C/Calabria 142-4 (93 423 18 78). Metro Rocafort/bus 9, 41, 50, 56, N1, N2, N13, N14, N15.* **Open** 9pm-2am daily. Closed 24 Dec. **Average** 2,000ptas. **Credit** V. **Map** B5

Bar Ra *Plaça de la Garduña 7 (93 301 41 63). Metro Liceu/bus 14, 38, 59, N9, N12.*

Open 1-4pm, 8pm-12.30am, Mon-Sat. Closed 25, 31 Dec. **Average** 1,500ptas. **Set menu** 995ptas. **Credit** AmEx, DC, MC, V. **Map** C6/**A2**
Disabled: toilet, wheelchair access. Tables outdoors.
Mama Café *C/Doctor Dou 10 (93 412 63 16). Metro Catalunya/bus all routes to Plaça Catalunya.* **Open** 9am-5pm Mon; 9am-1am Tue-Fri; 1pm-1am Sat. Closed third week Aug. **Average** 1,500ptas. **Set menu** 1,100ptas. **Credit** DC, MC, V. **Map** C5/**A2**
Disabled: toilets.
Ovisos *C/Arai 5 (607 26 47 26). Metro Liceu/bus 14, 38, 59, N9, N12.* **Open** 10pm-12.30am Mon-Thur, Sun; 10pm-3am Fri-Sat. **Average** 2,000ptas. **No credit cards. Map** D6/**B3**
Suborn *C/de la Ribera 18 (93 310 11 10). Metro Barceloneta/bus 14, 39, 51.* **Open** 9am-1am Tue-Fri; noon-1am Sat, Sun; *tapas* 9am-1pm Tue-Fri. **Average** 1,200ptas. **Set menu** 1,100ptas Tue-Fri. **Credit** MC, V. **Map** E6/**C4**
Disabled: toilet, wheelchair access. Tables outdoors.
Salsitas *C/Nou de la Rambla 22 (93 318 08 40). Metro Liceu/bus 14, 38, 59, N9, N12.* **Open** noon-4pm, 8pm-midnight, Mon-Fri; 9am-midnight Sat, Sun. **Average** 2,500ptas. **Set menu** 1,200ptas. **Credit** MC, V. **Map** C6/**A3**
Xocoa *C/Petritxol 11 (93 301 11 97). Metro Liceu/bus 14, 38, 59, N9, N12.* **Open** *Croissanterie* 9am-9pm daily; *restaurant* 9am-10pm Fri, Sat. **Average** 1,200ptas. **Set menu** 1,000ptas. **No credit cards. Map** D6/**A2**

*Vegetarian relief at **Juicy Jones**. See page 137.*

photos of celebrity diners such as Maradona and Gary Lineker and regulars who treat it a bit like a family dining room.
Air-conditioning. Booking advisable. Disabled: wheelchair access.

Garduña

C/Morera 17-19 (93 302 43 23).
Metro Liceu/bus 14, 38, 59, 91, N9, N12.
Open 1-4pm, 8pm-midnight, Mon-Sat; 1-4pm Sun.
Average 3,000ptas. **Set menus** 1,075ptas (lunch, incl 1 drink); 1,475ptas (lunch & dinner, no drink).
Credit AmEx, DC, JCB, MC, V. **Map** D6/**A2**
Located inside the Boqueria market (near the back, the opposite side from the Rambla), the Garduña preserves a good deal of the atmosphere of the nineteenth-century inn it once was; it became a strictly eating establishment in the 1970s. With the superb market right on the doorstep, the Catalan menu guarantees the freshest ingredients. Try to get a table on the quieter upstairs floor better to appreciate the charm of the place.
Air-conditioning.

L'Hortet

C/Pintor Fortuny 32 (93 317 61 89).
Metro Liceu/bus 14, 38, 59, 91, N9, N12.
Open 1.15-4pm Mon-Thur, Sun; 1.15-4pm, 9-11pm, Fri, Sat. **Set dinner** 1,200ptas. **No credit cards**.
Map C5/**A2**
This homey little place is one of Barcelona's more imaginative vegetarian restaurants. L'Hortet offers a different set menu every day and is cheap, too. It doesn't serve alcohol, but there are good juices.
Disabled: wheelchair access.

La Llotja

Museu Marítim, Avda Drassanes (93 302 64 02).
Metro Drassanes/bus 14, 20, 36, 38, 57, 59, 64, 91, 157, N6, N9. **Open** *Oct-June* 2-3.45pm Mon-Thur, Sun; 2-3.45pm, 9pm-11.30pm, Fri, Sat. *July-Sept* 2-3.45pm Mon, Wed, Thur, Sun; 2-3.45pm, 9pm-11.30pm, Tue, Fri, Sat. Closed 25 Dec, 1 Jan.
Average 3,000ptas. **Set lunch** 1,250ptas.
Credit MC, V. **Map** C5/**A4**
The setting alone is wonderful: La Llotja, the recent creation of gourmet and food critic Josep Maria Blasi, sits beneath the lofty, perfectly rounded arches of the magnificent fourteenth-century Drassanes, home of the Museu Marítim. The excellent selection of Catalan food includes a medieval dish or two, such as roast chicken with saffron, in homage to the ancient stone edifice. At midday, there's an interesting two-course set menu. The restaurant and the equally-attractive café are entered from the garden beside the museum entrance, and are not very visible from the street.
See also p103, p164.
Air-conditioning. Disabled: wheelchair access.

Els Ocellets

Ronda Sant Pau 55 (93 441 10 46). Metro Sant Antoni or Paral.lel/bus 20, 24, 64, 91, N6. **Open** 1.30-4pm, 8.30-11.30pm, Tue-Sat; 1.30-4pm Sun. Closed Easter (sometimes). **Average** 2,000ptas. **Set lunch** 950ptas Tue-Fri (not holidays). **Credit** AmEx, DC, JCB, MC, V. **Map** C6
This comfortable restaurant, on the Ronda on the edge of the Raval, and its older, more picturesque parent Can Lluís, a little way up a narrow street opposite, share the same menu and popularity, but

lately the Ocellets has had the edge in cooking. Try the spicy *romescada*, the *esqueixada* or the *filet de vedella al cabrales* (veal fillet with a powerful goat's cheese sauce). Bookings are only taken for groups, so get there early. Menu prices do not include tax.
Branch: Can Lluís C/de la Cera 49 (93 441 11 87). *Air-conditioning (Els Ocellets only). Booking advisable.*

Pla dels Angels

C/Ferlandina 23 (93 443 31 03). Metro Universitat/ bus 24, 41, 55, 64, 91, 141, N6. **Open** 1.15-4pm Mon; 1.15-4pm, 9pm-midnight, Tue-Sat. **Average** 2,500ptas. **Set menus** 950-1,350ptas.
Credit DC, MC, V. **Map** C5
On the square right in front of the MACBA, this place is frequented by all sorts, from local toughs to softie artists and everyone in between. With the same owners as **Pla de la Garsa** (*see p148*), it serves fresh, simple dishes: pastas, salads, meat, fish, and there are good-value *menus* on offer for lunch or dinner.
Tables outdoors (Easter-Oct).

Punjab Restaurante

C/Joaquín Costa 1b (93 443 38 99). Metro Liceu/bus 14, 38, 59, N9, N12. **Open** 11am-5pm, 7pm-midnight, Mon, Wed-Sun; 7pm-midnight Tue. **Average** 2,000ptas.
Set lunch 500ptas. **Set dinner** 750ptas.
No credit cards. Map C5
When this small Pakistani restaurant first opened it put up a sign daringly offering 25,000ptas to anyone who found a cheaper place to eat. A couple of years later most of the sign remains, but the figure of 25,000ptas has been blanked out. Has someone actually come up with somewhere cheaper than the Punjab? Not that we know of. The menu features basics like chicken tikka or samosas, and the food is good for the price.
Air-conditioning. Booking advisable.

Around Spain

While Catalan cuisine takes centre stage in Barcelona's restaurant scene, the city also has a broad range of eating places offering specialities of other parts of the Spanish subcontinent. There is also a large number of Basque and Galician bars (*see chapter* **Cafés & Bars**).
Andalusian: Casi Casi *Gràcia, see p155.*
Asturian: Centro Asturiano de Barcelona *The Eixample, see p152.*
Basque: Amaya *The Rambla, see p133;*
Beltxenea *The Eixample, see p152.*
Castilian: El Asador de Burgos *The Eixample, see p152.*
Galician: Restaurante Xironda Orense *The Raval, see right;* **Marcelino 2000** *The Eixample, see p153;* **Botafumeiro** *Gràcia, see p154.*
Mallorcan: El Mallorquí *Gràcia, see p155.*

'Come and get it!' – **L'Hortet**. *See left.*

Restaurant Riera

C/Joaquín Costa 30 (93 443 32 93). Metro Universitat/bus 24, 41, 55, 64, 91, 141, N6. **Open** 1-4pm, 8-11pm, daily. **Average** 1,000ptas.
Set menus 750ptas, 800ptas.
No credit cards. Map C5
In perennial half-light despite the overhead florescent tubes, this is a budget traveller's classic, with menus day and night at ultra-low prices. For 750ptas you get three courses of ordinary local grub: soups, salads, paellas, meat or fish. Drinks are extra, unless you go for the 800ptas menu. The cook is from Bangladesh, and sometimes prepares curries and similar things. Vegetarian dishes always available.

Restaurante Romesco

C/Sant Pau 28 (93 318 93 81). Metro Liceu/bus 14, 38, 59, 91, N9, N12. **Open** 1pm-12.30am Mon-Sat. Closed Mon public holidays, Christmas, Aug.
Average 1,000ptas. **No credit cards. Map** C6/A3
Just off the Rambla, and nearly always full, the Romesco is enshrined as a favourite with young foreigners, and many locals too. House speciality is *fríjoles*, a Spanish-Caribbean dish of black beans, mince, rice and fried banana, a hearty and satisfying bargain at just over 500ptas. Noisy and convivial, this is one of the city's best cheap eating houses. To find it, just head down C/Sant Pau and look to the right.

Restaurante Xironda Orense

C/Roig 19 (93 442 30 91). Metro Liceu/bus 14, 38, 59, 91, N9, N12. **Open** 1-4pm, 8.30pm-2am, Mon-Sat. Closed Aug, some public holidays. **Average** 1,000ptas. **No credit cards. Map** C6
Walk past the narrow, crowded bar to the narrow, crowded dining room, where you can choose from a decent variety of salads and mainly meat-based Galician dishes, in surprisingly generous quantities. A Catalan salad costs 350ptas, a plate of lamb chops just 500ptas. There is no set menu.

Shalimar

C/Carme 71 (93 329 34 96). Metro Liceu/bus 17, 38, 59, 91, N9, N12. **Open** 1-4pm, 8-11.30pm Mon, Wed-Sun; 8-11.30pm Tue. Closed 25 Dec. **Average** 1,500ptas. **Credit** DC, MC, V. **Map** C6
One of the best mid-price Pakistani restaurants in town, the Shalimar serves a selection of South Asian

Cheap and cheerful, **Restaurante Romesco** *is a favourite with everyone. See page 145.*

standards, with good tandoori dishes, in pleasant and relaxed surroundings.
Air-conditioning. Booking essential (Fri, Sat).

Silenus

C/dels Angels 8 (93 302 26 80).
Metro Catalunya/bus 14, 38, 59, 91, N9, N12.
Open 1-4pm Mon; 1-4pm, 9-11.30pm, Tue-Thur;
1-4pm, 9-11.45pm Fri, Sat. Closed 25 Dec, 1 Jan.
Average 3,000ptas. **Set lunch** 1,200ptas Mon-Fri;
1,500ptas Sat. **Credit** DC, MC, V.
Map C5/A2
A short walk from the MACBA, and a meeting place for local artists, Silenus is laid-back and fresh, with comfy sofas lining the walls and minimalist décor that highlights the open, high-ceilinged space. The food is a creative mix of contemporary Catalan and Spanish dishes including a *crocantí de bacallà amb caviar d'alberginia i reducció de fórum* (salt cod in almond batter with aubergine caviar simmered in a sweet/sour vinegar) or a *terrina cremosa de formatge i tofona amb mel de flors* (a creamy cheese and truffle terrine with honey). Service is friendly, and there are regular art exhibits on the walls.
Booking advisable for dinner. Disabled: wheelchair access. Tables outdoors (May-Oct).

Sushi & News

C/Santa Mònica 2 bis (93 318 58 57).
Metro Drassanes/bus 14, 38, 59, 91, N9, N12.
Open 1.30-4.30pm, 8.30pm-12.30am, Tue-Sun. Closed Christmas.
Set menus 1,350ptas, 1,750ptas, Tue-Fri.
Gourmet menu 3,200ptas. **Credit** V. **Map** C6/A4
Stylish and relaxed, with bare brick walls and a sloping bar, Sushi & News is a 'Japanese tapas'

restaurant serving very good maki, sushi and sashimi, as well as decent salads and soups. If that's not enough for you, there's great blackberry sorbet for dessert.
Disabled: wheelchair access.

Los Toreros

C/Xuclà 3-5 (93 318 23 25). Metro Catalunya/bus 14, 38, 59, 91, N9, N12. **Open** 1-4pm, 8pm-midnight, Tue-Sat; 1-4pm Sun. Closed some public holidays. **Average** 1,200ptas. **Set lunch** 900ptas Tue-Fri; 1,100ptas Sat; 1,200ptas Sun. **Set dinner** 1,750-2,000ptas. **No credit cards. Map** D6/A2
This is a long-established low-price restaurant that serves *ternera* and chips, potato tortilla, salads and other standards. The walls are plastered with bullfight photos.
Air-conditioning. Booking essential (Thur-Sat).

Sant Pere, La Ribera & the Born

Bar Mundial

Plaça Sant Agustí Vell 1 (93 319 90 56).
Metro Arc de Triomf/bus 39, 40, 41, 42, 51, 141.
Open *bar* 9am-11pm Mon, Wed, Thur; 9am-11.30pm Fri, Sat; 9am-5pm Sun. *Restaurant* 1.30pm till close.
Closed last two weeks Aug. **Average** 2,500ptas.
No credit cards. Map E6/C2
Mundial is a small, unpretentious bar-restaurant specialising in freshly cooked seafood, mainly plain-grilled. A single *parrillada* (mixed seafood grill) is ample for two, and costs just 2,200ptas. The standard dishes can have their ups and downs, but on a good day it's a great bargain.
Air-conditioning. Booking essential (evenings).

Café de la Ribera

*Plaça de les Olles 6 (93 319 50 72). Metro
Barceloneta/bus 14, 17, 40, 45, 51.* **Open** *Apr-Oct*
8am-2am; *Nov-Mar* 8am-1am; *meals served* 1-4pm,
8pm-midnight, Mon-Sat. **Set lunch** 1,250ptas Mon-
Fri; 1,500ptas Sat. **Set dinner** 1,500ptas (not every
day). **Credit** DC, MC, V. **Map** D-E6/**C4**
Dishes at this very popular, ever-crowded place
include *revueltos de espinaca* (scrambled eggs with
spinach), veal with goat's cheese, and fish soups.
The set lunch menu changes daily, with salads,
pizzas and fresh juices available all day. From
spring to autumn you can also eat alfresco at the
outside tables.
Air-conditioning. Tables outdoors (April-Oct).

Cal Pep

*Plaça de les Olles 8 (93 310 79 61). Metro
Barceloneta/bus 14, 17, 40, 45, 51.* **Open** 8pm-
midnight Mon; 1.15-4.15pm, 8pm-midnight, Tue-Sat.
Closed Easter, Aug, public holidays. **Average** *bar*
3,500ptas; *restaurant* (groups only) 5,500ptas.
Credit AmEx, DC, MC, V. **Map** D-E6/**C4**
Most people choose to eat at the bar, although there's
also a restaurant – a brick-lined room decorated with
a boar's head and antique cash registers. At the bar,
Pep himself grills most of the exceptional fish and
seafood, while keeping customers amused with a
constant stream of chat. He also runs the costlier
Passadís del Pep (*see below*).
Air-conditioning. Booking essential for restaurant.

Classic Catalan escalivada. *See page 135.*

Globetrotting

Barcelona may not have the international
restaurant range of a London or a Paris, but the
days when the only non-Iberian food available
was mediocre Chinese have long gone.
**Brazilian: Conducta Ejemplar – El
Rodizio** *The Eixample, see p153.*
Chinese: Fu Li Yuan *The Eixample, see p153.*
Indian/Pakistani: Restaurante Pakistani
Barri Gòtic, see p139; **Punjab Restaurante;**
Shalimar *Both in The Raval, see p145.*
Italian: Al Passatore
Sant Pere, La Ribera & the Born, see p148.
Japanese: Sushi-ya *Barri Gòtic, see p141;*
Sushi & News *The Raval, see left.*
Mexican: Cantina Mexicana I & II
Gràcia, see p154.
Peruvian: Peimong *Barri Gòtic, see p139.*

Comme Bio

*Via Laietana 28 (93 319 89 68).
Metro Jaume I/bus 17, 19, 40, 45, N8.*
Open 1-4pm, 8-11pm, daily. **Average** 2,500ptas.
Set lunch & dinner 1,125ptas Mon-Fri; 1,545ptas
Sat, Sun. **Credit** AmEx, DC, MC, V. **Map** D6/**B3**
An ambitiously large, stylish place that combines a
health-food shop and boutique of artist-made prod-
ucts with a vegetarian restaurant. Maybe it's a vision
of the future; at any rate the food is good and rea-
sonably priced, with a varied mix of 40-odd dishes.
Branch: Gran Via de les Corts Catalanes 603
(93 301 03 76).
Air-conditioning. Booking essential.

El Foro

*C/Princesa 52 (93 487 01 96). Metro Jaume I/bus
17, 39, 40, 45, 51, N8.* **Open** 1-4pm, 9pm-midnight,
Tue, Wed, Sun; 1-4pm, 10.30pm-2am, Thur-Sat.
Average 2,000ptas. **Credit** MC, V. **Map** E6/**C3**
Big, new, and busy, El Foro is the kind of place that
gives you an appetite the minute you walk in. The
satisfying food shows Argentinian/Italian influences
in specialities like gnocchi, lasagne and pizza, but
many Catalan dishes are also served. Downstairs
there's a performance space that turns into **Galaxy**
(*see chapter* **Nightlife**) on Saturday night.

Passadís del Pep

*Pla del Palau 2 (93 310 10 21). Metro Barceloneta/
bus all routes to Pla del Palau.* **Lunch served** 1.30-
3.30pm, 9-11.30pm, Mon-Sat. Closed public holidays,
three weeks Aug. **Average** 9,500ptas (incl drink).
Credit AmEx, DC, MC, V. **Map** D6/**C4**
An eccentric restaurant that's impossible to find
unless you know where to look (go down a long,
unmarked corridor next door to a Caixa office).
There is no menu, just some of the best seafood in
Barcelona, with a superb first-course buffet and *cava*
included in the price. *Fideus amb llamàntol* (noodles

with lobster) are particularly recommended. If this place is too pricey, a cheaper alternative is **Cal Pep** (*see p147*), run by the same family.
Air-conditioning. Booking advisable.

Al Passatore
Pla del Palau 8 (93 319 78 51). Metro Barceloneta/ bus all routes to Pla del Palau. **Open** 1pm-1am daily. Closed 25, 30, 31 Dec. **Pizza** 750-1,300ptas. **Set lunch** 975ptas Mon-Fri. **Set dinner** 1,500-2,000ptas. **Credit** MC, V. **Map** D6/**C4**
An Italian restaurant very popular for its excellent, wood-fired oven pizzas, Al Passatore also offers a big choice of pasta dishes – *linguini al cartoccio* (linguini with a rich mix of seafood) is recommended – salads and meat and fish dishes. There's also a good lunch menu.
Branches: **Al Passatore** (Port Olímpic) Moll de Gregal 25 (93 225 00 47). **Montello** Via Laietana 42 (93 310 35 26).
Air conditioning. Disabled: wheelchair access. Tables outdoors (Easter-Oct).

Pla de la Garsa
C/Assaonadors 13 (93 315 24 13). Metro Jaume I/bus 17, 19, 40, 45, N8. **Open** 1.15-3.45pm, 8pm-1am, Mon-Fri; 1.30-4pm, 8pm-1am, Sat. Closed midday 25 Dec, 1 Jan. **Average** 2,500ptas. **Set lunch** 1,050-1,200ptas. **Set dinner** 1,100ptas (*summer only*) & 1,750ptas. **Credit** AmEx, MC, V. **Map** D-E6/**C3**

Sunny seclusion: **La Llotja**. *See page 144.*

Antique-dealer Ignasi Soler transformed a sixteenth-century stables and dairy near C/Montcada into this beautiful restaurant, serving high-quality cheeses, patés and cold meats. At midday there's an excellent, good-value set menu, with larger dishes as well as *torrades*.
Air-conditioning. Booking essential weekends. Disabled: wheelchair access.

Restaurante Económico – Borrás
Plaça Sant Agustí Vell 13 (93 319 64 94). Metro Arc de Triomf/bus 39, 40, 41, 42, 51, 141. **Open** 12.30-4.30pm Mon-Fri. Closed public holidays, Easter, Aug. **Average** 1,500ptas. **Set lunch** 1,000ptas. **No credit cards. Map** E6/**C2**
A pretty restaurant looking onto a centuries-old square. The set lunch gives a choice of around nine first courses and ten seconds, regularly including *fideuà*, baked potatoes, macaroni and *arroz a la Cubana*, rice with tomato sauce, a fried egg, and a fried banana, if you ask for one.

Rodrigo
C/Argenteria 67 (93 310 30 20). Metro Jaume I/bus 17, 19, 40, 45, N8. **Open** 8am-5pm, 8.30pm-1am, Mon, Tue, Fri-Sun; 8am-5pm Wed. Closed Aug. **Average** 2,000ptas. **Set lunch** 1,100ptas; 1,400ptas Sun, public holidays. **Set dinner** 1,400ptas. **Credit** MC, V. **Map** D6/**B-C3**
Home cooking and bargain prices attract huge crowds to Rodrigo's jumble of tables, especially on Sundays. Full meals are not served in the evening, but there is a wide choice of hot and cold sandwiches. Note the unusual closing day.

Salero
C/Rec 60 (93 319 80 22). Metro Jaume I/bus 14, 39, 51. **Open** 1-4pm, 9pm-midnight, Mon-Thur; 1-4pm, 9pm-1am, Fri, Sat; 9pm-midnight public holidays. Closed second week Aug. **Average** 3,000ptas. **Set menu** 1,100ptas Mon-Fri. **Credit** V. **Map** E6/**C3**
With its white interior and candlelit tables, Salero is a casually elegant spot serving an eclectic range of dishes at decent prices. Among the 20-odd offerings are Mediterranean-Japanese mixes such as *kakiage* (sautéed squid, onion, courgettes and carrot). Other treats include an excellent magret of duck with mango, or a beef fillet with foie-gras.
Air conditioning. Disabled: wheelchair access.

Senyor Parellada
C/Argenteria 37 (93 310 50 94). Metro Jaume I/bus 17, 19, 40, 45, N8. **Open** 1-3.30pm, 9-11.30pm, Mon-Sat. Closed public holidays. **Average** 3,000ptas. **Credit** AmEx, DC, JCB, MC, V. **Map** D6/**B3**
The atmosphere is relaxed, and the décor stylishly combines modern touches with the centuries-old stone walls of this old La Ribera building. As well as the pillared main room there are attractive spaces upstairs. Specialities include thyme soup, cod with honey, delicious variations on Catalan standards such as *escalivada* and, to finish, great cinnamon ice cream and *crema catalana*. Service is courteous, and it's a place where it's easy to settle in for a few hours.
Air-conditioning. Booking essential.

Waterside dining

Once upon a time it was possible to sit with your toes in the sand and sample a paella at a string of slightly ramshackle seafood restaurants on the beach in the Barceloneta. The Olympic revamp and EU regulations did away with those places, but one of the foremost themes of Barcelona's great reconstruction has been to 'open up the city to the sea', and so new places have been created where you can dine al fresco with a seafront view.

Within the **Port Vell**, by the new marina at the eastern end of the port, there is the well-restored **Palau de Mar**, lined with restaurants with outside tables such as **Emperador** (93 221 02 20) and the **Merendero de la Mari** (93 221 31 41). On a warm evening you get a superb view of the city back across the harbour. Behind the Palau, Barceloneta may have lost its beach-front paella-bars, but it still has the city's largest concentration of good seafood restaurants. It's possible to find a table outdoors all year long at the many places along Passeig Joan de Borbó, such as the low-priced **La Oficina** (*see page 151*) or **El Rey de la Gamba** (93 221 75 98).

When you reach the sea at the end of the Passeig, from April to November you'll find a handful of *chiringuitos*, temporary stands, on the beach. They serve an assortment of tapas and paellas, some more elaborate than others, such as those offered by **Chiringuito Silvestre Salamanca**, run by the nearby **Salamanca** restaurant (93 221 50 33). The furthest out, **Havana Beach Club** (619 04 43 86), also fires up a barbecue and offers grilled fish and meats.

Follow the sea northwards and you come to the **Port Olímpic**, most attractive of the Olympic areas (*see also page 70*). It's big, modern, and surrounded by the parasoled terraces of some 200 bars and restaurants. Some are overpriced, but it's also by the sea, busy, smells of fresh-cooked fish, democratic – with fast-food chains vying for space with luxury restaurants – and open late, with plenty of places serving until 2am. It can even have some of the atmosphere of the old Barceloneta beach.

There's a whole range of fast food on offer, from Mexican to, still surviving, the local satellite of **Planet Hollywood** (93 221 11 11). Nearby, **Agua**, (*pictured, and see page 151*), offers a much more elegant setting and eclectic food, (almost) on the beach. It's fish restaurants that predominate, though, and a wander around the Port leaves you spoilt for choice. For cheap seafood, try the branch of **El Rey de la Gamba** (93 221 00 12) or **La Taverna del Cel Ros** (*see page 151*). **Tinglado Moncho's** (93 221 83 83) and **El Cangrejo Loco** (93 221 05 33) are pricier but serve superb fresh seafood, and for summer the Cangrejo has an upper terrace with a sea view. More upmarket is **La Galerna** (93 221 27 74; average 3,500ptas), while **El Celler del Rocxi** (93 225 19 65) is most refined of all, with excellent food at 5,000ptas. Leaving the Port, a longish walk along the beach will take you to **Catamaran** (93 221 01 75), a good-quality, low-priced fish restaurant with a choice of self-service or (more expensive) table service.

Port Vell & Barceloneta

Can Ramonet

*C/Maquinista 17 (93 319 30 64). Metro Barceloneta/
bus 17, 36, 39, 45, 57, 59, 64, 157, N6, N8.* **Open**
10am-4pm, 8pm-midnight, Mon-Sat; 10am-4pm Sun.
Closed two weeks Aug. **Average** 3,500-4,500ptas.
Credit AmEx, DC, JCB, MC, V. **Map** E7
Reportedly the oldest building in Barceloneta,
opened as a tavern in 1763 and run since 1956 by the
Ballarín family. A spectacular display of fresh
seafood greets you at the entrance, and if you're not
sure what anything is called you can just point to it.
Eat tapas at the bar, or larger *racións* at a table,
perhaps lobster with clams, cod with *romesco*,
serrano ham or some of the best anchovies in town.
*Air-conditioning. Booking advisable. Car park.
Disabled: wheelchair access. Tables outdoors.*

Can Ros

*C/Almirall Aixada 7 (93 221 45 79). Metro
Barceloneta/bus 17, 39, 45, 57, 59, 64, 157, N8.*
Open 1-5pm, 8pm-midnight Mon, Tue, Thur-Sun; 1-
5pm Wed. **Average** 2,500ptas. **Set lunch** 1,025ptas
Mon-Fri. **Gourmet menu** 1,800ptas Mon-Fri.
Credit AmEx, MC, V. **Map** D7
The best value in Barcelona. A good way to order
is to pick a mixture of mussels, clams, *peixets* (white-
bait in batter), salted prawns and so on while you
wait for the main course, which can take up to 40
minutes for freshly-prepared paella or *arrós negre*.
Branch: La Marsalada Passeig Joan de Borbó 58
(93 221 21 27).
Air-conditioning. Booking advisable weekends.

La Oficina

*Passeig Don Joan de Borbó 30 (93 221 40 05).
Metro Barceloneta/bus 17, 39, 45, 57, 59, 64, 157,
N8.* **Open** 1-4.30pm, 8.30-11.30pm, Mon, Wed-Sun.
Closed some weeks Aug-Sept, midday 25 Dec.
Average 2,000ptas. **Set menus** 1,150ptas Mon-Sat;
1,300ptas Sun. **Credit** AmEx, DC, MC, V. **Map** D7
With tables outside all year round, and views of the
city and Port Vell, La Oficina provides one of the
best deals on this harbourside strip. Set menus give
a wide choice of dishes, usually including paella.
Air-conditioning. Tables outdoors.

Set Portes

*Passeig Isabel II 14 (93 319 29 50).
Metro Barceloneta/bus 14, 17, 40, 45, 51, 100.*
Open 1pm-1am daily. **Average** 4,000ptas.
Credit AmEx, DC, MC, TC, V. **Map** D6/C4
Founded in 1836 and a historic institution in itself,
the huge 'Seven Doors' is another restaurant that's
on every tourist list. It's regularly packed with
foreigners, but also manages to maintain standards,
and despite the frilly fittings and the piano player,
prices are generally reasonable. The speciality is
paella de peix: for maximum flavour ask for the
shells to be left on the seafood. Bookings are taken
only for meals at 1.30-2.30pm and 8-9.30pm; you can
expect long queues at most times, especially on
Sunday evenings.
Air-conditioning. Booking advisable.

Vegetarians

Vegetarian eating-places have traditionally
been few and far between in Barcelona, but the
number has been growing, and those that do
exist are generally of decent standard, and very
popular. A recent trend, also, is in restaurants
that serve a few meat or fish dishes, but which
emphasise vegetarian food as their main attraction. Note: visitors ordering 'vegetarian' sandwiches in non-vegetarian restaurants here
should not be surprised to find they include ham
or tuna, and that bean or lentil stews may
contain meat stock, so check when ordering (ask
¿lleva tocino? to see if it's made with pork fat).
**Govinda; Juicy Jones; Oolong; Self
Naturista** *All in Barri Gòtic, see pp133-41.*
Biocenter; L'Hortet
Both in The Raval, see p141, 144.
Comme Bio
Sant Pere, La Ribera & the Born, see p147.
L'Atzavara *The Eixample, see p152.*
La Buena Tierra; L'Illa de Gracia
Both in Gràcia, see pp154-5.

Vila Olímpica – Port Olímpic

Agua

*Passeig Marítim de la Barceloneta 30
(93 225 12 72). Metro Barceloneta/bus 45, 57, 59,
157, N8.* **Open** 1.30-4pm, 8.30pm-midnight, Mon-
Thur; 1.30-4pm, 8.30pm-1am, Fri; 1.30-5pm, 8.30pm-
1am, Sat; 1.30-5pm Sun. Closed eve 31 Dec.
Average 3,000ptas. **Credit** AmEx, MC, V.
Map F7
Bonafide beachfront tables and a warm, modern
interior make Agua a reliable bet for an enjoyable
meal. Dishes range from quirky starters such as
Montadito de la cecallà amb tomaquet sec (layered cod
cake with sun-dried tomatoes) to pasta or rice dishes such as *arròs salvatgte amb verdures i gingebre*
(wild rice with greens and ginger) and very good
meat and fish. Plus, you can watch the soothing
Mediterranean waves while you eat.
*Air-conditioning. Tables outdoors (all day summer;
lunch only winter).*

La Taverna del Cel Ros

*Moll del Mestral 26 (93 221 00 33).
Metro Ciutadella-Vila Olímpica/bus 36, N6, N8.*
Open 1-5pm, 8pm-midnight, Mon-Wed, Fri-Sun.
Closed Dec. **Average** 1,500ptas. **Set lunch**
1,100ptas. **Credit** AmEx, DC, JCB, MC, V. **Map** F7
Near the main entrance of the Port Olímpic, this is
one of just a few inexpensive, 'normal' places among
the Port's mass of quayside eateries, and so is
favoured by port workers, sailors and other regulars. The lunch menu is short, but good.
*Air-conditioning. Disabled: wheelchair access. Tables
outdoors.*

Budget eats

With a city as full of restaurants as Barcelona, competition is stiff, and finding a cheap place to eat is not hard. Many restaurants offer bargain set menus at lunchtime (*see right*). In addition, the cheap-food zone is increasingly being occupied by Pakistani and Asian places. **Cervantes; Mesón Jesús; La Poste; Restaurante Pakistani** *All in Barri Gòtic, see pp133-41.* **Elisabets; Punjab Restaurante; Restaurant Riera; Restaurante Romesco; Restaurante Xironda Orense; Los Toreros** *All in The Raval, see pp141-6.* **Restaurante Económico-Borrás; Rodrigo** *Sant Pere, La Ribera & the Born, see p148.* **Marcelino 2000** *The Eixample, see right.* **Ca l'Abuelo** *Gràcia, see p155.*

Poble Sec

La Bodegueta
C/Blai 47 (93 442 08 46).
Metro Poble Sec/bus 20, 57, 64, 157, N16.
Open 1.30-4pm, 8.30pm-midnight, Tue-Sun. Closed Easter, two weeks Aug, some public holidays.
Average 2,000ptas. **Credit** AmEx, DC, MC, V.
Map B6
A pleasant local *llesqueria* with enjoyable *escalivada* with anchovies and *bacallà amb samfaina*. Decent house wine, fast service and reasonable prices.
Air-conditioning. Booking essential weekends. Disabled: wheelchair access.

La Tomaquera
C/Margarit 58 (no phone).
Metro Paral.lel/bus 20, 36, 57, 64, N6, N9.
Open 2-4.30pm, 8.30-11.30pm, Tue-Sat; 2-4.30pm Sun. Closed eve public holidays, Easter, Aug, 25 Dec.
Average 2,500ptas. **No credit cards. Map** B6
Despite the owner's refusal to have a phone or put an entry into local listings guides, people from all over town visit this enjoyable Poble Sec restaurant, above all for its specialities: *caracoles* (snails) and *a la brasa* meat, with fabulous *all i oli*. In quality, quantity and preparation the meat is the best in town, and there are also good salads and desserts.

The Eixample

El Asador de Burgos
C/Bruc 118 (93 207 31 60).
Metro Verdaguer/bus 20, 39, 43, 44, 45, 47, N6, N7. **Open** 1-4pm, 8.30/9-11pm, Mon-Thur; 1-4pm, 9-11.30pm, Fri-Sat. Closed some weeks Aug. **Average** 5,000ptas. **Credit** AmEx, DC, MC, V. **Map** D4
Castilian food is for confirmed carnivores, with only very little vegetable relief. First courses here include

morcilla blood sausage, roast *chorizo*, sliced marinated pork, and baby peppers. Main courses are typically roast lamb, roast piglet, grilled ribs of lamb, and a veal steak that looks like it could kick sand in the face of any standard entrecôte. Booking is essential, as roasts are prepared three hours in advance, in a traditional tiled oven.
Air-conditioning. Booking essential. Disabled: wheelchair access.

L'Atzavara
C/Muntaner 109 (93 454 59 25).
Metro Diagonal, Hospital Clínic/bus 20, 43, 44, 54, 58, 64, 66, N3, N7. **Open** 1-4pm Mon-Thur; 1-4pm, 8.30-11.30pm, Fri, Sat. **Average** 1,500ptas. **Set lunches** 1,050-1,500ptas. **Credit** V. **Map** C4
As the queues of expectant *Eixampleros* indicates, this all-veggie restaurant is very popular, and for good reason. The three-course lunch menu offers generous salads and homemade soups, including gazpacho, while the second main dish might be a delicious vegetarian paella. A great bargain.

Beltxenea
C/Mallorca 275 (93 215 30 24).
Metro Diagonal, Passeig de Gràcia/bus 7, 16, 17, 20, 22, 24, 28, 43, 44, N4, N6, N7. **Open** 1.30-3.30pm, 8.30-11.30pm, Mon-Fri; 8.30-11.30pm Sat. Closed four weeks Aug. **Average** 7,500ptas.
Credit AmEx, DC, MC, V. **Map** D4
A first-floor Eixample flat with a pretty interior garden houses the foremost outpost of new Basque cuisine in Barcelona. It's very discreet; a small brass plaque is the only sign of the restaurant's existence from the street. As in all Basque cooking, the basis is seafood: specialities include a melon and lobster salad, and *tronc de lluç Ondarroa* (hake).
Air-conditioning. Booking essential. Tables outdoors (interior patio).

Café del Centre
C/Girona 69 (93 488 11 01).
Metro Girona/bus 7, 50, 54, 56, 62, N1, N2, N3, N9. **Open** 8am-2am Mon-Fri; 7.30pm-2am Sat. Closed public holidays, three weeks Aug. **Average** 1,500ptas. **Credit** MC, V. **Map** E5
This turn-of-the-century marble and wood *llesqueria*-style bar offers fine cheeses (try the Maó), patés, cold meats, smoked fish and ten different salads into the small hours, with live (and untacky) piano music on Thursday, Friday and Saturday nights. A genuine local bar that's well worth a visit.

Centro Asturiano de Barcelona
Passeig de Gràcia 78, pral. (93 215 30 10).
Metro Diagonal, Passeig de Gràcia/bus 7, 16, 17, 22, 24, 28, N4, N6. **Open** 1-4pm, 8.30-11.30pm, Mon-Thur; 1-4pm, 8.30pm-12.30am, Fri, Sat; 1-4pm Sun; *tapas only* 5-11.30pm Sun. Closed 25 Dec. **Average** 2,500ptas. **Set menus** 1,100ptas Mon-Fri; 1,300ptas Sat. **No credit cards. Map** D4
Rather hidden away on the city's swankiest street, the restaurant of the Asturian cultural center is a surprisingly relaxed, spacious place, with a big outdoor terrace and room for all who may wander in

(on a first floor, so walk up). The decently-priced lunch menu offers two courses of five or so choices each, featuring such Asturian specialities as salt cod with haricot beans or knuckle of pork with potatoes. In the evenings, the choice may be more limited.
Air-conditioning. Tables outdoors (summer).

Conducta Ejemplar – El Rodizio

C/Consell de Cent 403 (93 265 51 12).
Metro Girona/bus 6, 19, 47, 50, 51, 55, N1, N4.
Open 1-4pm, 8.30pm-midnight, Mon-Thur; 1-4pm, 8.30pm-1am, Fri, Sat; 1-4pm Sun. **Lunch buffet** 1,090ptas Mon-Fri; 2,300ptas Sat. **Evening buffet** 2,300ptas. **Credit** DC, MC, V. **Map** E4-5
An original; one of very few places in Barcelona to offer a *rodizio*, a Brazilian meat buffet. Eat as much as you like from a hot and cold buffet followed by 12 different types of meat including Castilian sausage, steak, turkey, lamb, Brazilian-cut beef, veal and marinated pork. Vegetarians beware.
Air-conditioning. Disabled: wheelchair access.

La Dama

Avda Diagonal 423 (93 202 06 86/93 202 03 22).
Metro Diagonal, FGC Provença/bus 6, 7, 15, 27, 32, 33, 34. **Open** 1-3.30pm, 8.30-11.30pm, daily. Closed eve 25 Dec. **Average** 7,000ptas.
Gourmet menus 6,250ptas, 9,275ptas.
Credit AmEx, DC, EC, MC, TC, V. **Map** C3
On the first floor of a *Modernista* building from 1915 by Manuel Sayrach, this is one of Barcelona's dining power-houses, serving a well-dressed clientele that includes wielders of the expense account. It maintains its status with superbly prepared classic and contemporary dishes, including such delicacies as gratinated sea urchins with *cava*, grilled goat's kidneys with herbs or loin of venison seasoned with five kinds of peppers. The only hitch is, it's also one of the most expensive in town. The wine list is ample, service utterly smooth.
Air-conditioning. Booking essential.

Fu Li Yuan

C/Viladomat 73 (93 325 10 48). Metro Sant Antoni/ bus 13, 20, 41, 55, 64, 91, 141, N6. **Open** noon-4.30pm, 8pm-midnight, daily. **Average** 1,500ptas.
Set lunches 825ptas, 1,050ptas. **Set dinner** 1,500ptas. **Credit** MC, V. **Map** B5
One of the few good budget Chinese restaurants, with some dishes such as Beijing duck normally only found in more upmarket competitors. Popular with locals, and service is friendly and fast.
Air-conditioning. Booking advisable.

Jaume de Provença

C/Provença 88 (93 430 00 29).
Metro Entença/bus 41, 43, 44, N7. **Open** 1-4pm, 9-11.30pm, Tue-Sat; 1-4pm Sun. Closed Easter, Aug, Christmas. **Average** 7,500ptas. **Gourmet menu** 6,500ptas. **Credit** AmEx, DC, MC, V. **Map** B4
This small restaurant tucked away in the Eixample is one of the most prestigious in Barcelona. Its excellent reputation is due entirely to the quality and originality of the cuisine of chef Jaume Barguès: menus are a mixture of traditional Catalan recipes and ideas

of his own, such as crab lasagne, or a salad of wild mushrooms with prawns and clams. The wine list is truly superlative.
Air-conditioning. Disabled: wheelchair access.

Madrid-Barcelona

C/Aragó 282 (93 215 70 26). Metro Passeig de Gràcia/bus 7, 16, 17, 22, 24, 28, N4, N6. **Open** 1-3.30pm, 8.30-11.30pm, Mon-Sat. **Average** 1,500ptas. **Credit** AmEx, DC, MC, V. **Map** D4
This café-restaurant opened in the 1940s as a station café, in the days when the railway line from Madrid ran as an open trench along C/Aragó – hence the name built into its stylish façade. A takeover has transformed it into a somewhat cute, trendy hangout for pretty young Catalans. The menus feature modern Catalan and international dishes.
Air-conditioning. Disabled: wheelchair access.

Marcelino 2000

C/Consell de Cent 236 (93 453 10 72).
Metro Universitat/bus 14, 54, 58, 59, 64, 66, N3, N8. **Open** 1-5pm, 8pm-midnight, Mon-Sat. Closed two weeks Aug, Christmas and Easter (phone to check). **Average** 1,500ptas. **Set menu** 1,000ptas Mon-Fri; 1,125ptas Sat, public holidays. **Credit** AmEx, MC, V. **Map** C5
The Bodegas Marcelino are a chain of bar-restaurants found right across the Eixample, offering a straightforward Galician-oriented menu consisting of first-course stews, soups and salads,

Star menus

If you want to eat well and cheaply, then the midday *menú del día* is your friend. Most bars and restaurants advertise them by a sign at the door with the price and a list of what's on that day. Menus nearly always include two courses, a drink, bread and dessert; increasingly, they can be divided into two groups: traditional – generous portions but straightforward food (*bistec amb patates* and the like); and modern versions with more elaborate cuisine but skimping a bit on quantity. The search for top menus is an elusive quest, but here are some favourites.
Cervantes; **Mastroqué**; **La Poste**
All in Barri Gòtic, see pp133-41.
L'Antic; **El Cafetí**; **El Convent**; **Elisabets**; **Estevet**; **Pla dels Angels**; **Restaurant Riera**; **Silenus** *All in The Raval, see pp141-6.*
Al Passatore; **Café de la Ribera**; **Pla de la Garsa**; **Restaurante Económico-Borrás**
All in Sant Pere, La Ribera & the Born, see pp146-8.
La Taverna del Cel Ros
Port Olímpic, see p151.
Centro Asturiano de Barcelona;
Marcelino 2000 *Both in The Eixample, see left and above.*

and mainly meat and seafood grills. The best way to find other branches is to visit one and pick up a napkin, which gives a full list.
Air-conditioning. Tables outdoors.

Qu Qu (Quasi Queviures)

Passeig de Gràcia 24 (93 317 45 12).
Metro Passeig de Gràcia/bus 7, 16, 17, 22, 24,
28, N4, N6. **Open** 8am-1am daily. Closed from 10pm 24, 31 Dec. **Average** 2,000ptas.
Credit AmEx, DC, MC, V. **Map** D5
One of a crop of new-style snack restaurants that have opened on Passeig de Gràcia, the Qu Qu is ahead of the rest, with a big range of high-quality salads, cheeses and Catalan charcuterie, including *llonganisses, bull, secallona, somaia* and other varieties that are otherwise hard to find in Barcelona. There's also a delicatessen counter selling the same food to take away.
Air-conditioning. Disabled: wheelchair access. Tables outdoors (Easter-Oct).

Tragaluz

Passatge de la Concepció 5 (93 487 01 96).
Metro Diagonal/bus 7, 16, 17, 31, 67, 68, N4, N7.
Open 1.30-4pm, 8.30pm-midnight, Mon-Wed, Sun; 1.30-4pm, 8.30pm-1am, Thur-Sat. **Average** 4,000ptas. **Set lunch** 2,500ptas.
AmEx, DC, MC, V. **Map** D4
Tragaluz's light, refreshing and hip interior – by '80s design star Javier Mariscal – includes a top floor and roof that have been made into a wonderfully airy, glass-covered dining room. To go with the stylish and very mellow surroundings there's a fashionably eclectic menu of Catalan/Mediterranean themes, with such things as *lluç al vapor amb esparrecs verds i salsa de poma àcida* (steamed hake with fresh asparagus and apple sauce) or *filet de porc amb figues i formatge de cabra* (porc fillet with figs and goat's cheese). Below there's a comfortable cocktail lounge, and across the street there's a spacious and very good Japanese restaurant, **El Japonés**, run by the same crowd.
Branches: Acontraluz C/Milanesat 19 (93 203 06 58); **Agua** (see p151); **Casi Negro** Avda Diagonal 640 (93 405 92 00); **El Japonés** Passatge de la Concepció 2 (93 487 25 92).

One of Mariscal's best: **Tragaluz**.

La Buena Tierra

C/Encarnació 56 (93 219 82 13). Metro Joanic/bus 25, 39, 55, N6. **Open** 1-4pm, 8pm-midnight, Mon-Sat. Closed Easter, Jul/Aug (phone to check).
Average 2,000ptas. **Set lunch** 900ptas Mon-Fri.
Credit MC, V. **Map** E3
A pleasant restaurant in a little old house in Gràcia, with a pretty garden at the back, which has some of the best vegetarian food in town. Specialities include *canelons de bosc* (cannelloni and wild mushrooms), vol-au-vent with cream of asparagus and refreshing gazpacho and melon soups in summer.
Branch: La Llar de Foc C/Ramon y Cajal 13 (93 284 10 25).
Booking essential (Fri, Sat). Tables outdoors (garden).

Cantina Mexicana I & II

C/Encarnació 51 (93 210 68 05) & C/Torrent de les Flors 53 (93 213 10 18). Metro Joanic/bus 39, 55, N6. **Open** 1-4pm, 8pm-12.30am, Mon-Sat; 8pm-12.30am Sun. Closed Easter week, part of Aug (phone to check), 24-26 & 31 Dec, 1 Jan. **Average** 2,500ptas.
Credit DC, MC, V. **Map** E3
Both Cantinas, very close to each other on a street corner, offer the same food – *enchiladas, machaca, guacamole, frijoles* – but CM II, in Torrent de les Flors, has a larger, more comfortable space. Ingredients are imported from Mexico, and dishes much more authentic than standard Tex-Mex. If one closes for a holiday, the other one will be open.
Air-conditioning. Booking advisable.

Botafumeiro

C/Gran de Gràcia 81 (93 218 42 30). Metro Fontana/bus 22, 24, 28, N4. **Open** 1pm-1am daily. Closed three weeks Aug. **Average** 6,000ptas.
Credit AmEx, DC, JCB, MC, TC, V. **Map** D3
This spacious restaurant specialises in the best of Galician food, which means, above all, quality seafood. The lobster, langoustines, scallops, oysters and other shellfish selected by chef-proprietor Moncho Neiras are unbeatable. Botafumeiro stays open late, and entertains its clientele with two singers, one with guitar. They only play if you want them to, or so they claim.
Air-conditioning. Booking essential.

Ca l'Abuelo

*C/Providència 44 (93 284 44 94). Metro Fontana,
Joanic/bus 39, N6.* **Open** 1.15-4pm Mon-Thur; 1.15-
4pm, 9-11.30pm, Fri, Sat. Closed Aug, Sept (phone to
check), Easter, Christmas. **Set lunch** 1,050ptas Mon-
Fri; 1,295ptas Sat. **Set dinner** 1,295ptas Fri, Sat.
Credit AmEx, DC, MC, V. **Map** E3
This well-run place offers a great deal: an open buf-
fet of over 40 different dishes for just over 1,000ptas.
Gorge yourself silly on prawns, chicken, veal, pork,
fish, stews or salads, and a good choice of desserts.
Air-conditioning. Booking essential (Fri, Sat).

Casi Casi

*C/Laforja 8 (93 415 81 94). FGC Gràcia/bus 16, 17,
22, 24, 25, 28, N4.* **Open** 1-4pm, 8pm-midnight,
daily. **Average** 2,500ptas. **Set lunch** 1,000ptas. **Set
dinner** 1,200ptas. **Credit** AmEx, DC, MC, V. **Map** D3
With nearly 70 dishes on its main menu, Casi Casi
mixes purely Andalusian food – fish or chickpeas *a
la andaluza*, or, in summer, cold soups like *gazpacho*
and *ajoblanco* (white garlic soup) – with more
Catalan-orientated cannelloni, pigs' trotters or *pa
amb tomàquet* with cheese or ham.

Flash Flash

*C/La Granada del Penedès 25 (93 237 09 90).
FGC Gràcia/bus 16, 17, 27, 31, 32.*
Open 1pm-1.30am daily. Closed 25 Dec. **Average**
2,500ptas. **Credit** AmEx, DC, MC, V. **Map** D3
This 'sandwicheria', opened in 1970, was Barcelona's
first-ever design bar. It's '60s-cool through and
through, all white with photos of Twiggy-esque
models around the walls. House speciality is tortilla,
in many varieties, and there are good burgers and
sandwiches, with lots of vegetarian options. Just
control those bad Austin Powers impersonations.
Air-conditioning. Disabled: wheelchair access.

El Glop

*C/Montmany 46 (93 213 70 58).
Metro Joanic/bus 39, 55, N6.* **Open** 1-4pm, 8pm-
1am, Tue-Sun. **Average** 2,000ptas. Set lunch
1,100ptas Tue-Fri. **Credit** MC, V. **Map** E3
El Glop ('The Sip') is a long-running success, serving
traditional chargrilled meat and seasonal vegetables
at good prices. Specialities include snails cooked *a la
llauna* and *xoriço al vi* (chorizo in wine), washed down
with powerful red *vi de Gandesa*, from the Ebro. In
summer the ceiling opens up to create a kind of indoor
patio. It's often crowded, but the more spacious **Nou
Glop** is only a few streets away.
*Air-conditioning. Booking essential. Disabled:
wheelchair access.*
Branches: El Nou Glop C/Montmany 49, torre (93
219 70 59). **El Glop de la Rambla** Rambla
Catalunya 65 (93 487 00 97).

L'Illa de Gràcia

*C/Sant Domènec 19 (93 238 02 29). Metro Fontana/
bus 22, 24, 28, N4, N6.* **Open** 1-4pm, 9pm-midnight,
Tue-Fri; 2-4pm, 9pm-midnight, Sat, Sun. Closed
Easter, late Aug, some public holidays. **Average**
1,500ptas. **Set lunch** 850ptas Mon-Fri. **Credit** DC,
MC, V. **Map** D3

An unusual place – while serving solely vegetarian
food, L'Illa allows smoking and serves beer, wine
and coffee. Specialities include *crep illa de Gràcia*
(pancake with mushrooms, cream and pepper), and
home-made cakes. Prices are very reasonable, with
the most expensive dish on the menu at just 675ptas,
and the set lunch is excellent value.
Air-conditioning. Booking essential (Fri, Sat)

Jean-Luc Figueras

*C/Santa Teresa 10 (93 415 28 77).
Metro Diagonal/bus 6, 15, 22, 24, 28, 33, 34, N4.*
Open 1.30-3.30pm, 8.30-11.30pm, Mon-Fri; 8.30-
11.30pm Sat. Closed two weeks Aug.
Average 8,500ptas. **Gourmet menu** 9,500ptas.
Credit AmEx, MC, V. **Map** D4
A nineteenth-century neo-classical palace houses
this award-winning restaurant, one of the city's finer
culinary jewels. The interior is spacious and under-
statedly refined, and perfect lighting gives one and
all the best of appearances. A Frenchman of Catalan
descent, Figueras is an exceptionally skilful and
inventive chef, who boasts the traditional French
ability with sauces. House delicacies include his
prawn salad with cream of summer squash, ginger,
a dab of orange mousse, and soy sauce; or leg of Les
Landes duck prepared with pears and liquorice. To
finish in style, desserts – such as cold rhubarb soup
with cream of pistachio and lemon sorbet – are just
as outstanding.
Air-conditioning. Disabled: toilet, wheelchair access.

El Mallorquí

*C/Francisco Giner 21 (93 217 06 05). Metro
Diagonal/bus 22, 24, 28, 39, N4.* **Open** 1-4pm, 8.30-
11pm, Mon-Fri; 8.30-11pm Sat. Closed Easter,
Christmas week. **Average** 1,500-2,000ptas. **Set
lunch** 975ptas Mon-Fri. **Credit** EC, MC, V. **Map** D3
A taste of the islands: an interesting assortment of
Mallorcan dishes such as *sobrassada*, a spicy
sausage meat, sometimes served with honey, or
tumbet, aubergine, potato, and red pepper baked in
tomato sauce and served with lamb (or without, for
vegetarians). There are also excellent cheeses from
Menorca and island goods for sale. For summer,
there's a pleasant outdoor dining area.
Booking advisable. Tables outdoors (garden, May-Sept).

Ot

*C/Torres 25 (93 284 77 52). Metro Joanic/bus 39,
45, N6.* **Open** 2-3.30pm, 9-10.30pm, Mon-Fri; 9-
10.30pm Sat. Closed Easter, two weeks July-Aug, 25
Dec. **Set menu** 5,100ptas. **Credit** MC, V. **Map** D-E3
This small restaurant on a quiet street has been
praised by gourmets as one of the Spanish culinary
surprises of recent years. Run by two young chefs,
it serves daringly original variations on classic
Catalan/Mediterranean cuisine; the finely tuned
ingredients in their version of *carn d'olla*, the traditional Catalan Christmas dish, are a real treat. Ot
offers a set menu of five courses, served in a coquet-
tishly modest manner and changed once a fortnight.
Wines and cheeses are also excellent.
Air-conditioning. Booking essential.

Roig Robí

C/Sèneca 20 (93 218 92 22/93 217 97 38).
Metro Diagonal/bus 6, 7, 15, 16, 17, 22, 24, 28, 33,
34, N4. **Open** 1.30-4pm, 9-11.30pm, Mon-Fri; 9-
11.30pm Sat. Closed public holidays, two weeks Aug.
Average 6,500ptas. **Gourmet menu** 6,800ptas.
Credit AmEx, DC, MC, V. **Map** D3
Roig Robí is run by self-taught chef Mercè Navarro
and two of her children – an unusual set-up for a top
restaurant that counts politicians, writers and artists
as regulars (Tàpies designed the menu). Specialities
include *amanida de foie* (foie gras salad), lobster
with rice, and prawns with leeks and garlic sauce.
Air-conditioning. Booking essential. Tables outside
(June-Sept). Vegetarian dishes on request.

Tábata

C/Torrent de l'Olla 27 (93 237 84 96). Metro
Diagonal/bus 39. **Open** 1-4pm Mon, Sat; 1-4pm, 9pm-
midnight, Tue-Thur. Closed two weeks Aug; 25, 26
Dec. **Average** 3,000ptas. **Set lunch** 950-1,500ptas.
Set dinner 2,300ptas Tue, Thur; 2,600ptas Fri, Sat.
Credit AmEx, DC, JCB, MC, TC, V. **Map** D3
An elegant space that specialises in meats and fish
prepared on searing hot *tabas*, slabs of talcum stone.
Midday there are various menus to choose from;
night-time menus are more expensive, but worth it.
Service is friendly and excellent.
Air-conditioning. Disabled: toilet, wheelchair access.

Sants

La Parra

C/Joanot Martorell 3 (93 332 51 34).
Metro Hostafrancs/bus 30, 56, 57, 157, N2, N14.
Open 8.30pm-12.30am Tue-Fri; 2-4.30pm, 8.30pm-
midnight, Sat; 2-4.30pm Sun. Closed public holidays,
Easter, Aug (phone to check). **Average** 3,500ptas.
Credit MC, V. **Map** A4
A great outlet for stout Catalan country cooking *a la*
brasa within the city asphalt. You pass a giant wood-

fired grill as you enter this 180-year-old ex-coaching
inn, offering one of the best *escalivades* in town and
hefty portions of lamb, rabbit, pork, beef and spare
ribs, served on wooden slabs with fresh *all i oli*. Other
specialities include roast duck and an unbeatable
orada a la sal (gilt-head bream baked in salt), and
from November to March there are *calçots*, specially
cultivated spring onions from the Valls area (*see*
p134 **The Catalan Menu**), eaten on their own, char-
coal-grilled, with *romesco* sauce. Well-priced wines
are served, and rare *orujos* (fierce Galician spirits),
but happily, they refuse to stock Coca-Cola.
Air-conditioning. Booking advisable. Disabled:
wheelchair access. Tables outdoors.

El Peixerot

C/Tarragona 177 (93 424 69 69).
Metro Sants Estacio/bus 27, 30, 109, 215, N0, N7.
Open 1-4pm, 8.30-11.30pm, Mon-Sat; 1-4pm Sun.
Closed Sat eve & Sun Aug, 31 Dec. **Average**
5,000ptas. **Credit** AmEx, DC, MC, V. **Map** A-B4
A branch of the excellent seafood restaurant in
Vilanova i la Geltrú, El Peixerot serves a great *arrós*
a la marinera (rice in a fish broth with seafood), pael-
la, *arròs negre* and fresh fish. There is also a very
good list of local wines – try Hermita d'Espiells, a
semi-dry white from the Penedès.
Air conditioning.

Tibidabo & Zona Alta

La Balsa

C/Infanta Isabel 4 (93 211 50 48).
FGC Avda Tibidabo/bus 22, 58, 73, 75, 85.
Open 9-11.30pm Mon; 2-3.30pm, 9-11.30pm, Tue-Sat.
Closed Easter, midday Aug.
Average 6,500ptas. **Credit** AmEx, MC, V.
Surrounded by lush gardens and with an equally
airy interior in an award-winning wooden building
designed by Oscar Tusquets and Lluís Clotets, La
Balsa is one of Barcelona's top-notch restaurants

Bread + tomato + oil

According to the head chef of **Set Portes** (*see*
page 151) *pa amb tomàquet* (bread with tomato,
pan con tomate in Castilian) is made as follows:
'Rub the open side of a very ripe tomato, cut in
half, against the surface of the bread, so that the
tomato pulp is evenly spread over the bread. Add
salt and a drop of oil.' If the slices of bread have
been toasted, they're called *torrades*. It may be
very simple, but this basic invention has become
one of the most universally appreciated creations
of Catalan cooking.

Tomatoes first appeared in Catalonia in the
sixteenth century, but didn't become well known
until the eighteenth. Leopold Pomés, author of

the definitive *Theory and Practice of Bread with*
Tomato (1984), claims *pa amb tomàquet* was
invented by a painter who wanted to combine
the colours of the sunset on an edible base, but
it most probably originated as a way of using
up the previous day's bread. The 'secret' is that
the tomatoes have to be good, and very ripe.
Both sweet and savoury, tomato bread is delicious with just about anything, but goes
especially well with strong hams, cold meats,
anchovies, roast vegetables (*escalivada*) and
cheeses. For Catalans it's an immediate, strong
symbol of home, especially, perhaps, because it's
perversely ignored in the rest of Iberia.

and a regular haunt of the city's élite. The food is an impressive array of sophisticated Mediterranean dishes, with regulars such as superb prawn and salt cod croquettes with tarragon sauce, and in August there's an open buffet at the bargain price of 3,500ptas. It is, though, above all the garden setting that makes eating here a delicious experience. *Tables outdoors.*

Neichel

C/Beltrán i Rózpide 16 bis (93 203 84 08).
Metro Maria Cristina/bus 7, 33, 63, 67, 68, 74, 75, 78, N12. **Open** 1.30-3.30pm, 8.30-11.30pm, Mon-Fri; 8.30-11.30pm Sat. Closed Easter, Aug, first week Sept, 25 Dec, 1-7 Jan, public holidays.
Average 9,500ptas. **Gourmet menu** 8,000ptas.
Credit AmEx, DC, MC, V.
In a modern block in the best part of town, Neichel serves an exquisite array of Mediterranean dishes, meticulously prepared and presented in high style. Owner-chef Jean-Louis Neichel, from Alsace, is the foremost representative of classic French culinary tradition in Barcelona, and his Michelin-starred restaurant is one of the city's very best. As well as a six-course gourmet menu there is a separate menu, also of six courses, devoted entirely to dishes made with black truffles. Wine list, cheeses and desserts are all equally remarkable.
Air-conditioning. Booking essential.

La Venta

Plaça Dr Andreu (93 212 64 55). FGC Avda Tibidabo/bus 17, 22, 58, 73, 75, 85, 101, then Tramvia Blau. **Open** 1.30-3.15pm, 9-11.15pm, Mon-Sat. Closed 25 Dec, 1 Jan. **Average** 5,000ptas.
Credit AmEx, DC, MC, V.
In the square at the foot of the funicular on Tibidabo, La Venta has an outside terrace that's a lovely place to enjoy a meal in the fresh mountain air. It's also attractive indoors, and in winter a glass conservatory maintains the open-air atmosphere. Regulars on the imaginative menu include sea urchins au gratin and cod tail with vegetables, and there are also morish desserts. Service is friendly and efficient.
Air-conditioning. Booking essential. Disabled: wheelchair access. Tables outdoors.

Poble Nou

Els Pescadors

Plaça Prim 1 (93 225 20 18).
Metro Poble Nou/bus 41. **Open** 1-3.45pm, 8pm-midnight, daily. Closed Easter, 24-26, 31 Dec, 1 Jan (phone to check), public holidays. **Average** 5,000ptas. **Credit** AmEx, DC, JCB, MC, V.
A very attractive restaurant in a small square in the old village of Poble Nou, back from the beach area, with a beautiful outside terrace. The specialities are refined Catalan fish and seafood dishes, and oven-cooked fish specials, using the pick of the same day's catch from ports on the coast, are superb. There are also interesting vegetarian options.
Air-conditioning. Booking essential. Disabled: wheelchair access. Tables outdoors (Apr-Oct).

Llesqueries

In Barcelona, traditional Spanish tapas bars have a local competitor – *llesqueries*, places that serve slices (*llesques*) of *torrades,* toasted Catalan tomato bread (*see left*), with a wide range of toppings – assortments of cheeses, cold meats, serrano ham, sliced peppers, anchovies and so on, usually accompanied by gutsy, strong red wine served in an earthenware jug.

Restaurants serving food *a la brasa* such as **La Parra** (*see left*) or **La Tomaquera** (*see p152*) and **El Glop** (*see p155*) offer similar dishes, as first courses or on their own. This can be a cheap or expensive way of eating, depending on the quality of the main ingredients – fine quality dry-cured ham is a very expensive commodity.
Mercè Vins *Barri Gòtic, see p138.*
Pla de la Garsa
Sant Pere, La Ribera & the Born, see p148.
La Bodegueta *Poble Sec, see p152.*
Café del Centre; Qu Qu (Queviures)
Both in The Eixample, see p152, 154.

Horta

Can Travi Nou

C/Jorge Manrique (93 428 03 01). Metro Horta/bus 10, 45, 102. **Open** 1.30-4pm, 8.30pm-midnight, Mon-Sat; 1.30-4pm Sun. **Average** 3,500ptas.
Credit AmEx, DC, JCB, MC, TC, V.
Occupying a huge, beautiful old *masia* or traditional Catalan farmhouse, with garden, on a hill above Horta, this feels more like a country restaurant than somewhere within a city. Food is traditional Catalan, with speciality *mar i muntanya* dishes such as *sípia amb mandonguilles* and *cueta de rap amb all torrat* (monkfish tail with toasted garlic). Difficult to reach by public transport, so take a cab, but worth finding.
Air-conditioning. Booking advisable. Disabled: wheelchair access. Tables outdoors (Easter-Sept).

Gaig

Passeig Maragall 402 (93 429 10 17). Metro Horta/bus 19, 45, N4. **Open** 1.30-4pm, 9pm-11pm, Tue-Sat; 1.30-4pm Sun, public holidays. Closed Easter, Aug, 25, 26 Dec. **Average** 6,500ptas. **Gourmet menu** 6,200ptas (no drinks); 9,200ptas (includes wine).
Credit AmEx, DC, EC, MC, V.
Founded in 1869 as a café for cart drivers, this renowned restaurant has been in the Gaig family for four generations. Specialities include *arròs de colomí amb ceps* (young pigeon in rice with wild mushrooms) and stuffed pigs' trotters. A favourite dessert is the *pecat de xocolata* ('chocolate sin', a thick mousse). The wine cellar is a sight in itself.
Air-conditioning. Booking essential. Disabled: wheelchair access. Tables outdoors (summer).

Cafés & Bars

Cocktails, beer, breakfast coffee, hot chocolate, lemon with crushed ice or cava with a tortilla tapa – having a drink can mean many things.

One reason why the Internet may never reach the same degree of saturation in Barcelona as it does everywhere else: people here truly enjoy spending time in the physical presence of others, and there's no better evidence for this than the city's huge number of bars and cafés. Some are meeting points around which neighbourhood life turns, others old *bodegas* with an ageing clientele sampling wine from the barrel; there are outdoor cafés on sunny squares, designer spots with imported beer, and small *granges* for afternoon coffee and cakes. Without paying a few of them a visit, you won't really get to know what Barcelona is about.

Tapas in Barcelona are generally not as varied as in some parts of Spain, but great examples can be found, and most bars offer food of some kind, from sandwiches to a full lunch menu. The listing that follows can only be one selection from all the (uncategorisable) cafés and drinking-holes around the city. For bars more clearly oriented to night-time socialising, *see chapter* **Nightlife**, and for more bar-restaurants, *see chapter* **Restaurants**.

Opening times, especially in traditional cafés, can be variable (many close earlier or later at night, according to trade), and those listed should be taken as guidelines rather than fixed hours. Except where indicated, bars listed do not accept **credit cards***.*

The Rambla

There is one main drawback to taking a table on the most famous café-pavement in town: the cost. There are exceptions: the new **Zurich** and **Cava Universal** still maintain reasonable prices. The **Opera** has an unchallenged claim to the most class.

Boadas
C/Tallers 1 (93 318 95 92). Metro Catalunya/bus all routes to Plaça Catalunya. **Open** noon-2am Mon-Thur; noon-3am Fri-Sat. **Map** D5/A2
One of Barcelona's institutions, a genuine 1933 art deco cocktail bar opened by Miquel Boadas after he learned his trade in the famed Floridita Bar in Havana. The barmen can mix a huge variety of cocktails, and the wood-lined walls are strung with mementos of its many famous patrons – including a sketch or two by Miró.

Cafè de l'Opera
La Rambla 74 (93 317 75 85/93 302 41 80). Metro Liceu/bus 14, 38, 59, N6, N9. **Open** 8am-2.15am Mon-Thur; 8am-3am Fri-Sun. Closed 25 Dec. **Map** D6/A3
And another institution, the last real nineteenth-century grand café in the city, and far the best of the cafés on the Rambla. With genuine *Modernista*-era décor, L'Opera remains enormously popular, with a contentedly mixed clientele – elderly locals, foreigners, a big gay contingent and anyone else. Unbeatable for people-watching on the Rambla. *Tables outdoors.*

Cafè Zurich
Plaça Catalunya 1/Pelai 39 (93 317 91 53). Metro Catalunya/bus all routes to Plaça Catalunya. **Open** *June-end Oct* 8am-1am Mon-Fri; 10am-1am Sat; 10am-11pm Sun. *End Oct-May* 8am-11pm Mon-Fri; 10am-11pm Sat, Sun. **No credit cards**. **Map** D5/B1
Not so much on the Rambla as staring down it from the corner of Plaça Catalunya, and with one of Barcelona's largest café terraces, the 1920s Zurich was for decades one of the city's universally recognised meeting-points. Hence it was a controversial

Webcaffs

Of the city's Net cafés, **Interlight** is among the best, with sleek décor and a good mix of pleasant atmosphere, low prices and plenty of ready computers. Staff are very friendly and helpful. **El Café de Internet** is a less individual venue. For places to send e-mail without a café attached, *see page 286.*

Locations
El Café de Internet *Gran Via de les Corts Catalanes 656 (93 412 19 15/cafe@ cafeinternet.es). Metro Passeig de Gràcia/ bus all routes to Passeig de Gràcia.* **Open** 9am-midnight daily. **Rates** from 600ptas per half-hour. **Map** D5
Interlight *C/Pau Claris 106 (93 301 11 80/ interlight@bcn.servicom.es). Metro Passeig de Gràcia/bus all routes to Passeig de Gràcia.* **Open** 11am-10pm Mon-Thur; 11am-midnight Fri, Sat; 5-10pm Sun. **Rates** from 500ptas per half-hour. **Map** D5

Café culture

Basic etiquette

The civilised system of pay-as-you-leave is the norm in Barcelona bars, except in busy night bars and some outdoor terraces, such as those in the Plaça Reial, where you are often asked to pay as soon as drinks are served. If you have trouble getting a waiter's attention, a loud but polite *'Oiga'* (literally, 'hear me'), or, in Catalan, *'Escolti'* should do the trick. Tipping is entirely discretionary, but it's common to leave something if you've had table service, and food as well as a drink. Most people just round up a bill to the nearest 100ptas, or leave some of the change. Some people also leave a few coins (rarely over 25ptas) when served at the bar, more an old-fashioned courtesy than a real tip.

In many old-fashioned bars paper napkins (*servilletas*), olive stones, toothpicks, cigarette butts and so on are customarily dropped on the floor, but this is not done in smarter places. One other point: Spaniards are the biggest consumers of low-alcohol drinks in the world. Catalans, in particular, do not drink to get drunk, and it's not unusual for people to sit on a drink for an hour or more.

Coffee & tea

A large, milky coffee is a *cafè amb llet* (Catalan) or *café con leche* (Spanish), which locals usually only have with breakfast, although you can order it at any time of day. After mid-morning people are more likely to have a small coffee with a dash of milk, a *tallat* (Catalan)/*cortado* (Spanish), or a black espresso (*cafè sol/café solo*). A *café americano* is a *solo* diluted with twice the normal amount of water, and a *carajillo* is a *solo* with a shot of spirits. It will normally be with brandy (*carajillo de coñac*), but you can also order a *carajillo de ron* (rum), whisky or whatever else may take your fancy. Decaffeinated coffee (*descafeinado*) is widely available, but if you don't want just instant decaf with hot milk, ask for it *de máquina* (espresso).

Tea, except from places that specialise in it, is a bit of a dead loss in Barcelona, but herbal teas (*infusiones*) such as *menta* (mint) or *manzanilla* (camomile) are always available.

Beer

Damm beer reigns supreme in Catalonia. The most popular is Estrella, a good, standard lager; Voll-Damm is stronger and heavier, and Bock-Damm is an interesting, but not widely distributed, dark beer. Bottled beers can be ordered in standard *mitjanes/medianas* (third of a litre) or smaller *quintos* (a quarter-litre). Draught beer is served in *cañas* (about the same as a mediana) or *jarras* (about half a litre). Imported beers are increasingly available, but are pricier than local brands.

Wines, spirits & other drinks

All bars stock a basic red (*negro* or *tinto*), white (*blanco*) or rosé (*rosado*). If a red wine is a bit acidic, try it with lemonade (*gaseosa*). Except in bars that are wine specialists, good wines tend to be expensive, and the range limited: for a wider choice, go to a *bodega*. Most bars stock popular brands of *cava*, but 'champagne bars' have a wider variety.

Spirit mixes such as *gin-tonic, vodka-tónica* or a *cuba-libre* (rum and coke) are very popular for night-time drinking. Both Catalonia and Andalusia produce high-quality brandies, more full-bodied than French brandies but still subtle; of Catalan labels, Torres 5 and 10 are two of the best. Fruit-flavoured schnapps drinks (peach, apple, hazelnut) are also popular, drunk icy-cold, as chasers to finish a meal.

Non-alcoholic drinks

Very popular alternatives to alcohol are the Campari-like but booze-free Bitter Kas, and tonic water (*una tónica*), drunk with just ice and lemon. Mineral water is *aigua/agua mineral:* ask for it *amb gas/con gas* (fizzy), or *sense gas/sin gas* (still).

Food

Most bars have some kind of *bocadillos*, hefty, crusty bread rolls filled with *llom/lomo* (pork), *jamón serrano*, potato tortilla, tuna, cheese and other fillings; some bars use long, thin rolls called *flautes*. When you order a *bocadillo* the waiter will usually check that you want it '*amb tomàquet?*' or '*con tomate?*', spread with tomato Catalan-style (*see p156*). A *sandwich* is made with white sliced bread, and a *bikini* is a toasted ham and cheese sandwich.

Most Barcelona tapas bars offer a fairly standard choice, although there are several Basque bars that have a wider range. Some Catalan bars have a different, *llesqueria* selection (*see chapter* **Restaurants**). Below are some of the most common tapas (in Spanish only).

Albóndigas meatballs; **Anchoas** salted anchovies; **Berberechos** cockles; **Boquerones** pickled fresh anchovies; **Chipirones en su tinta** small squid cooked in their ink; **Croquetas (de pollo, de bacalao,** etc) croquettes (with chicken, salt-cod, etc); **Empanadas** large flat pie, usually with tuna filling; **Empanadillas (de atún)** small fried pastries, usually with tuna filling; **Ensaladilla Rusa** mixed 'Russian' salad; **Gambas al ajillo** prawns fried with garlic; **Habas a la Catalana** broad beans, onions and **botifarra** blood sausage cooked in white wine; **Mejillones** mussels; **Olivas** olives; **Patatas bravas** deep-fried potatoes with hot pepper sauce; **Pincho moruno** peppered pork brochette; **Pulpo a la gallega** octopus with paprika and olive oil.

step when it was swept away in 1997, in another redevelopment scheme. To make amends, the shiny, new mall built on the site, El Triangle, has included a new version of the café, opened in 1999. The new-model Zurich has generically-old-style décor instead of the quirkiness of the original, with rather over-shiny woodwork, but nonetheless quickly regained its status as meet-up spot par excellence for locals, backpackers and other urban wanderers, and the tables outside are great for watching the parade of humanity flowing in and out of the Rambla.
Tables outdoors.

Cava Universal

Plaça Portal de la Pau 4 (93 302 61 84).
Metro Drassanes/bus 14, 20, 36, 38, 57, 59, 64, 91,
157, N6, N9. **Open** 7am-9pm daily. **Map** C6/A4
A landmark bar, oblivious to fashions and more than usually resistant to rising prices. Have a coffee, beer or *bocadillo* (it's not actually a *cava* bar) at the foot of the Rambla, beneath the statue of Columbus pointing the way to the New World, and enjoy the optimum view of the crowds heading back and forth from the new new world of Maremàgnum.
Tables outdoors.

Cool & sweet

One of Barcelona's symbolic links to the country-side is the *granja* – literally 'farm' – small family-run, slightly quaint cafés. Originally direct outlets for fresh dairy produce in the city, they developed into a genre of café/shop all their own. Most serve alcohol, but that's not the point of going there. Instead, they specialise in coffee, cakes, pastries, dairy products and such things as *suizos* (thick hot chocolate topped by a mountain of whipped cream) and *batidos* (milkshakes). Built to satisfy Catalans' traditional sweet tooth, they're especially popular for afternoon call-ins while shopping.

Some of the best are in C/Petritxol, between Plaça del Pi and C/Portaferrisa. The **Granja Dulcinea** boasts traditional wooden fittings and white-jacketed waiters who cater swiftly for Saturday evening crowds. **La Pallaresa** nearby has a more antiseptic 1960s look, but its *suizos* are rated among the best. **La Granja** on C/Banys Nous ran for years by two gentle old ladies, and then passed to a younger crew who have expanded it a bit – there's a room in the back with a section of Roman wall – but otherwise kept the same *granja* mentality. In a narrow street on the Raval side of the Rambla, **Granja M Viader** has done a roaring trade since 1870. In the Eixample, try the 1960s **Granja Camps**.

Swigging down thick chocolate can seem pretty heavy in the summer heat, but then other drinks are available. *Orxateries/horchaterías* serve *Orxata* (in Spanish, *horchata*), a delicious milky drink made by crushing a nut called a *chufa*. Many don't appreciate it on first tasting, but once you're used to it it's wonderfully refreshing on a hot day. *Orxata* curdles once made, and so has to be bought fresh from a specialised *orxateria*. They also sell home-made ice-creams and *granis-sats/granizados* (fruit or coffee drinks sipped through crushed ice). Two fine *horchaterías* very close to one another share the same name, although they rigorously deny any connection: the **Orxateria-Gelateria Sirvent** has outside tables that are a great place to sit out late,

while **Horchatería Sirvent** has none – but on summer nights, crowds of people drink standing around the door. Poble Nou boasts the famous **El Tío Che**, open since 1912, and the only place in town that still does a malt-flavoured *granizado*.
*See also page 169, **La Valenciana**.*

Locations

La Granja *C/Banys Nous 4 (93 302 6728).*
Metro Liceu/bus 14, 38, 59, 91. **Open** 8am-2pm, 5-9.30pm, Mon-Fri; 9am-2pm, 5-9.30pm, Sat; 10am-2pm, 5-9.30pm, Sun. Closed sometimes Sun. **Map** D6/B3
Granja Camps *Rambla Catalunya 113 (93 215 10 09). Metro Diagonal, FGC Provença/bus 7, 16, 17, 31, 67, 68.* **Open** *Sept-Apr* 7.15am-9pm Mon-Fri; 7.15am-2pm, 5-9pm, Sat. *May-Sept* 7.15am-10pm Mon-Fri; 7.15am-2pm, 5-9pm, Sat; Closed after 2pm Sat in Aug. **Map** D4
Granja Dulcinea *C/Petritxol 2 (93 302 68 24). Metro Liceu/bus 14, 38, 59, 91.* **Open** 9am-1pm, 4.30-9pm, Mon-Fri; 9am-1pm, 4.30-9.15pm, Sat, Sun, public holidays **Map** D6/A2
Granja La Pallaresa *C/Petritxol 11 (93 302 20 36). Metro Liceu/bus 14, 38, 59, 91.* **Open** 9am-1pm, 4-9pm Mon-Fri; 9am-1pm, 4-10pm, Sat, Sun. **Map** D6/A2
Granja M Viader *C/Xuclà 4-6 (93 318 34 86). Metro Liceu/bus 14, 38, 59, 91.* **Open** 5-8.45pm Mon; 9am-1.45pm, 5-8.45pm, Tue-Sat. Closed one week Aug. **Map** D6/A2
Horchatería Sirvent *C/Parlament 56 (93 441 27 20). Metro Poble Sec/bus 20, 24, 38, 64, 91, N6.* **Open** *Easter-early Nov* 9am-1.30am daily; *mid-Nov-Jan* 9am-9pm daily. **Map** C6
Orxateria-Gelateria Sirvent *Ronda Sant Pau 3 (93 441 76 16). Metro Paral.lel/bus 20, 36, 57, 64, 91, 157, N6.* **Open** 9am-1am daily. **Map** C6
El Tío Che *Rambla del Poble Nou 44-6 (93 309 18 72). Metro Poble Nou/bus 36, 71, 141, N6.* **Open** *Oct-May* 9am-2pm, 5-9pm, Mon, Tue, Thur-Sun; *May-mid-Sept* 9/10am-1am Mon-Thur, Sun; 9/10am-3am Fri, Sat.
Closing times for all the above places vary as the summer season progresses.

Barri Gòtic

L'Ascensor
*C/Bellafila 3 (93 318 53 47). Metro Jaume I/bus 17,
19, 40, 45, N8.* **Open** 6.30pm-3am daily. **Map D6/B3**
An old wooden *ascensor* (lift) forms the entrance to
this relaxed, comfortable bar near the Ajuntament.
Inside there's always an up-for-it, friendly crowd.

Cafè La Cereria
*C/Baixada Sant Miquel 3-5 (no phone).
Metro Liceu/bus 14, 38, 59, 91, N9, N12.*
Open 9am-10pm daily. Closing times may be earlier
Mon-Thur in winter. **Map D6/B3**
Amid the invasion of multinational 'Italian' coffee-
shop chains, this quiet, friendly café is very welcome.
In a *Modernista* former wax shop, run as a co-op, La
Cereria offers home-made cakes, tarts and a big
range of teas, herbal and traditional. Its wooden
tables are home-made too, as are, of course, the
varied *bocadillos* you can order when sitting at them.

Margarita Blue
*C/Josep Anselm Clavé 6 (93 317 71 76). Metro
Drassanes/bus 14, 18, 38, 59, N6, N9.* **Open** 11am-
2am Mon-Wed; 11am-3am Thur, Fri; 6pm-3am Sat;
6pm-2am Sun. **Credit** MC, V. **Map D6/A4**
A roomy, colourful bar/restaurant that serves very
good Mexican food at all hours at moderate prices.
On Thursday and Sunday evenings, short performances are held; on Friday and Saturday nights
a varied crowd gathers for drinks, nachos and
guacamole. As you sip your blue drink, observe the
weird, winged lightbulbs that serve as lamps, and
the tiled artwork of nude, flying women. If you're in
need of a pick-me-up, try the Ibizan energy cocktail,
the *turbital*. The latest branch of the Blue empire,
Rita Blue, has a more varied menu, similarly hip
décor, a big terrace and a subterranean party area.
Branches: **El Taco de Margarita** Plaça Duc de
Medinaceli 1 (93 318 63 21); **Rita Blue** Plaça Sant
Agustí 3 (93 412 34 38).

Mesón del Café
*C/Llibreteria 16 (93 315 07 54).
Metro Jaume I/bus 17, 19, 40, 45, N8.*
Open 7am-11pm Mon-Sat. **Map D6/B3**
A charming hole-in-the-wall café that's regularly
packed. It's reckoned to have the best coffee in town,
served by some of the city's fastest moving waiters.

Món Obert
*Passatge Escudellers 5 (93 301 72 73). Metro Liceu/
bus 14, 38, 59, N6, N9.* **Open** *mid-Sept-mid-May*
9am-9pm Mon-Thur; 9am-midnight Fri-Sat; *mid-
May-mid-Sept* 9am-10pm Mon, Tue; 9am-midnight
Wed-Sat. **Credit** MC, V. **Map D6/A4**
Large and tranquil, this space is a co-op organised
by six women. It combines a café (with full midday
menu, home-made bread and pastries, and sandwiches and light dishes until closing time), bookshop, library, art gallery, kid's area, music room and
private room for parties and special dinners. Check
out flyers announcing poetry readings, art openings,
tango classes, and other events.

Nostromo
*C/Ripoll 16 (93 412 24 55). Metro Urquinaona/bus
17, 19, 40, 45, N8.* **Open** 1.30pm-2.30am Mon-Thur;
1.30pm-3am Fri; 8pm-3am Sat, public holidays.
Closed 25 & 26 Dec. **Credit** V. **Map D6/B2**
Named after the Conrad novel and run by a retired
sailor, this is a relaxed haven for landlubbers and
mariners alike. The literary nature of the place is not
just a matter of a name: shelf-loads of books about
the sea, exotic parts and similar topics are
distributed about the bar, ready for browsing and/or
sale. There's an excellent lunch menu, and dinners
are cooked to order: ask for anything you like (within reason) and the chef will prepare it for you.

Els Quatre Gats
*C/Montsió 3-bis (93 302 41 40). Metro Catalunya/
bus all routes to Plaça Catalunya.* **Open** 9am-2am
Mon-Sat; 5pm-2am Sun. Closed three weeks Aug.
Credit AmEx, DC, JCB, MC, V. **Map D5/B2**
Not so much an institution as a monument. In 1897
a figure-about-town called Pere Romeu opened this
café in a *Modernista* building by Puig i Cadafalch,
and for a few years it was the great meeting-point
of bohemian Barcelona. Major artists of the day such
as Rusiñol and Casas painted pictures especially for
it, and the menu cover was Picasso's first paid commission. It closed in 1903, and was used for decades
as a textile warehouse, until in the 1980s it was
finally restored and reopened, with reproductions
by contemporary artists of the original paintings.
Under its current management it's much more smart
than bohemian, but it's an attractive place for a coffee, with good if pricey tapas. In the room at the
back, where Pere Romeu once presented avant-garde
performances, there is a restaurant, with a good set
lunch menu.

Schilling
*C/Ferran 23 (93 317 67 87). Metro Liceu/bus 14,
38, 59, N9, N12.* **Open** 10am-2.30am Mon-Sat; noon-
2.30am Sun. **Credit** V. **Map D6/A3**
Proof of Barcelona's membership of European café
society, Schilling could almost be a sleek modern
heir to the sort of grand café that thrived in the days
when the Habsburg empire was still intact (even
though the place only opened up in 1997). Spacious,
elegant, hip and popular – with a particularly large
gay clientele – Schilling serves a variety of enjoyable *bocadillos*, desserts and teas, as well as other
refreshments and alcohol.

Sotto Zero
*Plaça Duc de Medinaceli (607 83 97 27).
Metro Drassanes/bus 14, 36, 57, 64, 157, N6.*
Open *Sept-May* 10am-2.30am; *June-Aug* noon-4am,
daily. **No credit cards. Map D6/A4**
A laid-back juice bar for those in search of something besides alcohol to slake a thirst. Some 15 different fresh juices are available, as well as sorbets
and *gelati, orxatas,* teas and coffees and, alright,
beer. Books and magazines can be found next to the
comfy chairs, and plans for the future include the
possibility of checking e-mail accounts.

Les Tapes
*Plaça Regomir 4 (93 302 48 40). Metro Jaume I/
bus 17, 19, 40, 45, N8.* **Open** 9am-11pm Mon-Sat.
Closed some weeks Aug. **Map** D6/B3
The sign 'We rip off drunks and tourists' above the
bar shouldn't worry you, for this place is especially
welcoming to English-speakers. Run by Santi, who
worked in Birmingham as a chef, and his English
wife, it has UK football on the TV, shelves of English

books to browse through and a noticeboard for
foreigners looking for contacts, rooms, jobs and so on.

Tascas: Bar Celta & La Plata
*C/Mercè 16 (93 315 00 06) & C/Mercè 28 (93 315
10 09). Metro Drassanes/bus 14, 36, 57, 59, 64,
157, N6.* **Map** D6/B4
Among the survivors of old Barcelona is the line of
tascas along C/Mercè, near the port, small traditional

Down at the old *bodega*

As long as wine has been poured and stored in
cities in Spain, there have been *bodegas* (or
bodegues in Catalan). Originally warehouses for
wine, with time they came to be meeting places
– the prototype of the modern-day bar – for
sampling what the local vineyards had to offer,
and food began to accompany the tasting.

In Barcelona these traditional places, with
their oak barrels and sweet smell of wine, are a
vanishing breed. Foreigners love them, but
they're often sadly unappreciated by modernity-
oriented Catalans. Precisely because of their
aged charm, though, some still thrive. Such is
the case with the brick-arched **Portalón**
(*pictured*) on C/Banys Nous in the Barri Gòtic,
dating from the 1860s and perhaps the city's
most typical old-style *bodega*. Bargain food and
wine are served from a long wooden bar on to
marble tables, while regulars chat and play
dominoes. In a still more ancient street, C/Palma
de Sant Just, there is the tranquil **La Palma**,
suitably aged and with a curious collection of
paintings. It serves great *torrades* (slabs of toast
and tomato) with hams and cheeses.

Some attempts have been made to revive the
bodega idea. In La Ribera is **La Tinaja**, in the
entrance of a medieval palace, a tasteful place
with fine wines that, despite appearances,
opened only recently. To compare it with somewhere very authentically old, try **Can Paixano**
in the *bazares*, the streets of cheap electrical
shops by the port. The one hole-in-the-wall
Barcelona bar that so many travellers claim to
have 'discovered' first, it serves very drinkable

no-label *cava* and a huge range of dead-cheap
toasted *bocadillos*, and is nearly always packed
with local workers and young foreigners.

In the Eixample, you'll find **La Bodegueta**,
an unpretentious place in the middle of chic-dom
on the Rambla Catalunya. It has plenty of tapas
at reasonable prices, and good lunch menus.
Bar Canigó, on C/Verdi in Gràcia, has long
resisted thoughtless modernisation, preserving
its wooden bar and yellowing mirrors. No tapas,
but great *bocadillos* and *flautas* can be had, and
there are tables outside on the wonderfully-
named Plaça de la Revolució. **Bodega Manolo**
is another weathered Gràcia *bodega*, with
peeling paint as well as the requisite wall of
barrels. The speciality, apart from wine, is fine
anchovies from Cantabria. There are also good-
value (900ptas) lunch menus.

Locations

Bar Canigó *C/Verdi 2 (93 213 30 49).
Metro Fontana/bus 22, 24, 28, 39, N4.*
Open noon-2am Mon-Sat. Closed Sept. **Map** D3
Bodega Manolo *C/Torrent de les Flors 101
(93 284 43 77). Metro Joanic/bus 39, 55, N6.*
Open *bar* 9am-9pm Tue, Wed; 9am-11pm Thur-
Sat; 10.30am-3pm Sun. *Dinner served* 9-11.30pm
Thur-Sat. **Map** E3
La Bodegueta *Rambla de Catalunya 100
(93 215 48 94). FGC Provença/bus 7, 16, 17, 20,
22, 24, 28, 43, 44, N4, N7.* **Open** 8am-2am Mon-
Sat; 6.30pm-1am Sun. **Map** D4
Can Paixano *C/Reina Cristina 7 (93 310 08 39).
Metro Barceloneta/bus 14, 36, 39, 51, 57, 59, 64,
157.* **Open** 9am-10.30pm Mon-Sat. **Map** D6/C4
La Palma *C/Palma de Sant Just 7 (93 315 06 56).
Metro Jaume I/bus 17, 19, 40, 45, N8.* **Open** 8am-
3.30pm, 7-10pm Mon-Thur; 8am-3.30pm, 7-11pm
Fri, Sat. Closed three weeks Aug. **Map** D6/B3
El Portalón *C/Banys Nous 20 (93 302 11 87).
Metro Liceu/bus 14, 38, 59, N9, N12.*
Open 9.30am-midnight Mon-Sat. Closed Aug.
Map D6/B3
La Tinaja *C/Esparteria 9 (93 310 22 50).
Metro Barceloneta/bus 14, 17, 39, 40, 45, 51,
100.* **Open** 5pm-2am Mon-Sat. **Credit** AmEx, DC,
MC, V. **Map** D-E6/C3-4

bars ever-popular for a drinks-and-tapas crawl. One of the best is the Galician **Bar Celta** at No.16. Huge trays of (mostly) seafood line the bar: particularly recommended are the *patatas bravas* and *rabas* (deep-fried chunks of squid), washed down with Galician white wine served, as is traditional, in white ceramic cups. At No.28 is **La Plata**, a tiny tile-lined bar that serves only deep-fried whitebait, tomato and onion salads, anchovies and wines from the barrel. Hours are erratic (they tend to pull their shutters down once the night-time crowds have poured in). Both are open Mon-Sat; the Celta also opens on Sunday nights.

Taverna Basca Irati

C/Cardenal Casañas 17 (93 302 30 84).
Metro Liceu/bus 14, 38, 59, N9, N12.
Open noon-midnight Tue-Sat; noon-4.30pm Sun.
Closed three weeks Aug, two weeks Christmas.
Credit AmEx, MC, V. **Map** D6/A3
A very busy place serving excellent Basque-style tapas, with a long, long bar displaying the wealth of Basque imagination when it comes to designing delicious bite-size combinations. Note: the selection dwindles dramatically the later it gets, so don't miss out. There's also a good, full-service restaurant at the back of the bar.

Thiossan

C/Vidre 5 (93 317 10 31). Metro Liceu/bus 14, 38,
59, 91, N9, N12. **Open** *mid-Sept-July* 6pm-2am Tue-
Sun; *July-mid-Sept* 7.30pm-2.30am Tue-Thur, Sun;
7.30pm-3am Fri, Sat. **Map** D6/A3

A comfortable, laid-back African bar-cum-cultural-centre off Plaça Reial. It features exhibitions, light West African edibles, and regular music sessions.

Venus Delicatessen

C/Avinyó 25 (93 301 15 85). Metro Jaume I/
bus 17, 19, 40, 45, N8. **Open** noon-midnight Mon-
Sat. Closed two weeks Nov. **Map** D6/B3
Two sisters run this innovative place, serving decent deli-style food with a wide choice of pâtés and cheeses, nine different salads, numerous types of *bocadillos*, and dishes such as vegetable lasagne and chilli. The atmosphere is relaxed and international.

The Raval

Bar Almirall

C/Joaquín Costa 33 (93 412 15 35). Metro
Universitat/bus 24, 41, 55, 64, 91, 141, N6. **Open**
7pm-2.30am daily. **Map** C5
Opened in 1860, the Almirall has the distinction of being the oldest continuously functioning bar in the city, and still has its elegant early *Modernista* woodwork, although for some years it's been charmingly unkempt. At the end of '99 a city regulation forced its closure for renovation, but it's hoped this won't lead to drastic changes, or the loss of its big, soft sofas.

Bar Fortuny

C/Pintor Fortuny 31 (93 317 98 92).
Metro Catalunya/bus 14, 38, 59, N9, N12.
Open 10am-midnight Tue-Sun. Closed two weeks
Aug. **Map** C-D5/A2

Pub life BCN

In step with the world-wide mix of cultures, Catalans have opened their arms, wallets, and tastebuds to an ever-growing contingent of 'authentic' Irish, Scottish and English pubs – places to eat pub grub, knock down beers with local expats, catch English or Scottish football on satellite TV and, often, hear live Irish or other music. Some pubs, such as the huge, multi-purpose **Robin Hood**, also have dance floors. We could easily add a dozen more…

Locations

The Black Horse
C/Allada Vermell 16 (93 268 33 38). Metro Jaume
I/bus 39, 51. **Open** 6pm-3am daily. **Map** E6/C3
The Clansman *C/Vigatans 13 (93 319 71 69).*
Metro Jaume I/bus 17, 19, 40, 45, N8. **Open** *Sept-*
May 6pm-2.30am Mon-Thur; 6pm-3am Fri; 3pm-
3am Sat; 3pm-2.30am Sun. *June-Aug* 6pm-2.30am
Mon-Thur, Sun; 6pm-3am Fri, Sat. **Map** D6/B-C3
Flann O'Brien's *C/Casanova 264 (93 201 16 06).*
Bus 6, 7, 14, 15, 33, 34, 58, 59, 63, 64, 66, 67, 68,
N8. **Open** 6pm-3am daily. **Map** C3

George & Dragon *C/Diputació 269 (93 488 17*
65). Metro Passeig de Gràcia/bus all routes to
Passeig de Gràcia. **Open** 9am-2.30am Mon-Wed;
9am-3am Thur-Sun. **Map** D5
Irish Winds *Maremàgnum, Moll d'Espanya (93*
225 81 87). Metro Drassanes/bus 14, 36, 57, 59,
64, 157, N6, N9. **Open** 1.30pm-4.30am Mon-Thur,
Sun; 1.30pm-5am Fri, Sat. **Credit** V. **Map** D7
Kitty O'Shea's *C/Nau Santa Maria 5 (93 280 36*
75). Metro Maria Cristina/bus all routes to Maria
Cristina. **Open** 11am-2am Mon-Thur; 11am-3am
Fri; noon-3am Sat; noon-2am Sun. **Map** B2
Michael Collins Irish Pub *Plaça Sagrada*
Família 4 (93 459 19 64). Metro Sagrada
Família/bus all routes to Sagrada Família.
Open noon-3am daily. **Map** E-F4
The Quiet Man
C/Marquès de Barberà 11 (93 412 12 19). Metro
Liceu/bus 14, 38, 59, 91, N9, N12. **Open** 3pm-
3am Mon-Sat; 6pm-3am Sun. **Map** C6/A3
Robin Hood *La Rambla 31 (93 301 88 81).*
Metro Drassanes/bus 14, 38, 59, 91, N9, N12.
Open 9.30am-3.30am Sun-Thur; 9.30am-5am Fri,
Sat. **Credit** AmEx, DC, EC, MC, V. **Map** C6/A4

Tables in the shade

It's often debatable whether it's thirst that draws you to Barcelona's shaded outdoor café *terrazas* or just a desire to stop and admire the world around you. No matter, they make great places in which to write a postcard, read a book, meditate on the scenery, or just join in the great Mediterranean sport of people-watching.

Barri Gòtic & La Ribera

Several of Barcelona's older museums have realised that their stone courtyards make ideal locations for cafés. One is the **Tèxtil Cafè** (*see page 166*); another the delightful **Cafè d'Estiu** ('Summer Café' – as it's only open part of the year) in the Gothic courtyard of the Museu Frederic Marès. Also nearby is **L'Antiquari** in Plaça del Rei, with an excellent view of one of the area's finest medieval squares.

On a different note, in the Plaça Reial the **Glaciar** is a perennially hip spot from which to observe the *plaça*'s melting-pot of streetlife, while in the more peaceful and leafy Plaça Sant Josep Oriol **Bar del Pi** offers a front-row seat for the art market and buskers that appear there. Since 1999, too, a modern version of the most bustling of all Barcelona *terrazas*, the **Zurich** (*see page*

158), is once again serving drinks to the world from the top of the Rambla.

At the other end of the promenade, and far less widely known, is **La Llotja**, beneath the soaring arches of the vast old shipyard that houses the Museu Marítim (*see also pxxx*). Staying in the medieval world, in La Ribera **La Vinya del Senyor** (*see page 166*) and **Vascelum** are perfect places from which to contemplate the majestic counterposition of verticals and plain space in the façade of Santa Maria del Mar.

L'Antiquari de la Plaça del Rei *C/Veguer 13 (93 310 04 35). Metro Jaume I/bus 17, 19, 40, 45, N8.* **Open** *mid-Sept-July* 5pm-3am daily; *July-mid-Sept* 10.30am-2am daily. **Map** D6/**B3**

Bar del Pi *Plaça Sant Josep Oriol 1 (93 302 21 23). Metro Liceu/bus 14, 38, 59, N9, N12.* **Open** 9am-11pm Mon-Fri; 9.30am-11pm Sat; 10am-3pm, 5-10pm Sun. **Map** D6/**A3**

Cafè d'Estiu *Museu F Marés, Plaça Sant Iu 5 (93 310 30 14). Metro Jaume I/bus 17, 19, 40, 45, N8.* **Open** *Easter-Sept* 10am-10pm Tue-Sun. **Map** D6/**B3**

Glaciar *Plaça Reial 3 (93 302 11 63). Metro Liceu/bus 14, 38, 59, 91, N9, N12.* **Open** 4pm-2.15am Mon-Fri; 4pm-2.45am Sat; 9am-2.15am Sun. **Map** D6/**A3**

A subtle stroke of genius transformed this one-time neighbourhood hangout for chess-playing elderly men into a science-fiction-tinged arena where generations of the culturally hip now sit and smoke together. The former *bodega's* wine barrels are still in place, as are a few of the chess players, now overseen by a collection of toy robots. It's also popular with gay women. Good, wholesome home-cooking is available throughout the day and evening.

Bar Kasparo

Plaça Vicenç Martorell 4 (93 302 20 72). Metro Catalunya/bus all routes to Plaça Catalunya. **Open** *winter* 9am-10pm, *summer* 9am-midnight, daily. Closed Jan. **Map** D5/**A1-2**

A small bar in the arcades of one of the city's more peaceful squares, taken over (and renovated) by three Australian sisters, and offering more varied fare than basic tapas. The terrace is a great spot for sitting out on a sunny day.
Tables outdoors.

Bar Pastís

C/Santa Mònica 4 (93 318 79 80). Metro Drassanes/ bus 14, 38, 59, 91, N9, N12. **Open** 7.30pm-2.30am Mon-Thur, Sun; 7.30pm-3.30am Fri-Sat. **Map** C6/**A4**

Down a tiny alley off the bottom end of La Rambla, this is another of Barcelona's 'bar-institutions'. It was opened in the 1940s by Quimet and Carme, a Catalan

couple who'd lived in Marseilles, and the pictures around the walls were painted by Quimet himself, apparently always when drunk. They began the tradition of playing exclusively French music, and serving only pastis, and the bar became a favourite of boxers, French sailors, *Barrio Chino*-types and the Franco-era intelligentsia. Quimet died in 1963, and for years the bar became more eccentric still, as his wife made it a monument to his memory. Under its current management the drinks list has expanded, and there's now live music, 11pm-1.30am Sun, but the essence remains unchanged. Small, dark, quirky, and, with Piaf, Montand or Charles Trenet in the background, a unique atmosphere.

Buenas Migas

Plaça Bonsuccès 6 (93 412 16 86). Metro Catalunya/bus all routes to Plaça Catalunya. **Open** 10am-10pm Mon-Wed, Sun; 10am-midnight Thur-Sat. Closed 11 Sept-11 Oct; 25 Dec. **Credit** AmEx, MC, V. **Map** D5/**A2**

An Italian-run *focacceria* that serves tasty pizza squares and scrumptious desserts (the chocolate cake is particularly recommended). The unassuming rustic design, with pale wood furniture, is well in tune with the simple and delicious *focaccia* that comes out of the oven. In summer, the terrace is nicely shaded by acacia trees.
Tables outdoors (May-Sept only).

La Llotja *Museu Marítim, Avda Drassanes (93 302 64 02). Metro Drassanes/bus all routes to Colom.* **Open** *café* 12.30pm-2am Tue-Wed; 12.30pm-5am Thur-Sun, *terrace Easter-Sept* 9am-8pm Mon-Fri; 10am-8pm Sat; 10am-7.30pm Sun. **Map C6/A4**

Vascelum *Plaça Santa Maria del Mar (93 319 01 67). Metro Jaume I/bus 17, 19, 40, 45, N8.* **Open** 9.30am-1am Tue-Fri; 10.30am-1am Sat, Sun. **Map D6/C4**

Gràcia

The human-sized, interconnecting squares of the old town of Gràcia make ideal locations for pavement cafés. Plaça del Sol is lined with bars with tables outside, but **Cafè del Sol** is perennially the most popular – a fine place to spend a warm evening, watching the ebb and flow of mildly inebriated crowds. In a villagey square, beneath a huge old church, the **Virreina Bar** is a

friendly meeting place serving imported beers, as well as good *bocadillos* and sandwiches.

Cafè del Sol *Plaça del Sol 16 (93 415 56 63). Metro Fontana/bus 22, 24, 28, N4.* **Open** 1pm-2am Mon-Thur, Sun; 1pm-2.30am Fri, Sat. **Map D3**

Virreina Bar *Plaça de la Virreina 1 (93 237 98 80). Metro Fontana/bus 21, 39, N4.* **Open** 10am-2.30am Mon-Sat; 10am-midnight Sun. **Map E3**

Montjuïc & Tibidabo

For a real view, though, the best places are the mountains that overlook the city. The oddly little-known **Miramar** on Montjuïc, at the end of the road from the Fundació Miró, offers a sweeping vista over the port and Mediterranean. The most breathtaking panorama of all is the one from the **Mirablau**, at the end of the tram line on Tibidabo. It has both an outside garden terrace and, inside the bar, floor-to-ceiling windows seemingly suspended in space, from where you can admire Barcelona laid out below you by day and by night.

Mirablau *Plaça Doctor Andreu (93 418 58 79). FGC Tibidabo/bus 17, 22, 58, 73, 75, 85, 101, then Tramvia Blau.* **Open** 11am-4.30am Mon-Thur, Sun; 11am-5am Fri, Sat.

Miramar *Avda Miramar (93 442 31 00). Metro Paral.lel, then Funicular de Montjuïc/ bus 61.* **Open** *Dec-May* 10am-midnight Mon, Tue, Thur-Sun; *June-Nov* 10am-2am Mon, Tue, Thur-Sun. Closed some weeks in Nov. **Map B6**

(El bar que pone) Muebles Navarro
C/Riera Alta 4-6 (607 18 80 96). Metro Sant Antoni/bus 20, 24, 38, 41, 55, 64, 141, N6. **Open** 5pm-midnight Tue-Thur; 5pm-2am Fri, Sat; 5pm-midnight Sun, public holidays. *May-Sept* open from 6pm. Closed 25 Dec. **Map C6**
Once a furniture show-room, now a big, elegantly informal café with excellent, if pricey sandwiches, including New York lox with onion spread. In fact, the place could make you swear you were in New York: the studied effect of high ceilings, ventilation tubes and an abstract-minimalist paint job. An amalgam of armchairs, sofas and other furniture allows you to sit in comfort and style while at the same time being on display in the large front windows. Popular with the hip gay crowd, and yet more proof of the old Raval's inevitable lurch towards the good life.

Els Tres Tombs

Ronda Sant Antoni 2 (93 443 41 11/93 442 29 98). Metro Sant Antoni/bus 20, 24, 38, 41, 55, 64. **Open** 6am-12.30am daily. **Map C5**
A perennially busy bar/restaurant bordering Raval and Eixample, with year-round outdoor tables perfectly oriented to the sun. The bar is especially crowded midday on Sunday, after the book market at the Mercat de Sant Antoni, and is also an early morning fuelling stop for after-hours clubbers. *Tables outdoors.*

Sant Pere, La Ribera & the Born

Bar Hivernacle

Parc de la Ciutadella (93 295 40 17). Metro Arc de Triomf/bus 39, 40, 41, 42, 51, 141. **Open** 10am-1am daily. **Credit** AmEx, DC, MC, V. **Map E6**
A bar inside the beautiful iron-and-glass *Hivernacle*, or greenhouse, of the Ciutadella park, built by Josep Amargós in 1884. With three parts (one shaded room, one unshaded and a terrace), it hosts exhibitions and occasional jazz and classical concerts, as well as plants around the bar there's a display of tropical plants in one of the rooms alongside. *Tables outdoors.*

Cafè del Born Nou

Plaça Comercial 10 (93 268 32 72). Metro Jaume I/bus 14, 16, 17, 39, 45, 51. **Open** 9am-10pm Mon, Sun; 9am-3am Tue-Sat. Closed two weeks Aug. **Map E6/C3**
A big, airy café opposite the old Born market. With a soothing interior and music, an interesting food selection, papers to read and the odd exhibition from a local artist, this café makes one of the most relaxing places in the area to enjoy a coffee or two. *Tables outdoors (May-Sept).*

La Estrella de Plata

Pla del Palau 9 (93 319 60 07). Metro Barceloneta/ bus all routes to Pla del Palau. **Open** 1-4pm, 7pm-2am ,daily. **No credit cards. Map D6/C4**

Once a hangout for workers from the port, this long, thin bar has been tastefully re-hauled, and is now known for its 'designer' tapas, among the city's very best. Along with an excellent selection of seafood, such as Cantabrian anchovies served on *requesón* (junket) and superb fresh prawns, there are such offerings as an astounding *foie gras* simmered in port wine, or spicy lamb meatballs with a mayonnaise and pickle sauce. Though unpretentious in style, the place isn't cheap, as the BMWs often double-parked outside may indicate.

Euskal Etxea

C/Montcada 1-3 (93 310 21 85). Metro Jaume I/ bus 17, 19, 40, 45, N8. **Open** *restaurant* 1-3.30pm, 9-11.30pm, Tue-Sat; *bar* 8.30am-11.30pm Tue-Sat; 12.45-3.30pm Sun. Closed Aug, Easter, Christmas. **Credit** MC, V. **Map** D6/**C3**
Catalonia may not be famous for tapas, but the Basque Country certainly is, and this bar has the best Basque tapas in Barcelona, a mouth-watering array of small *pinchos* (from chunks of tuna and pickles to deep-fried crab claws and complicated mixed tapas) that make a grand entrance at midday and at 7pm. Get there early for the best selection, and be prepared to stand. At the back there's a full restaurant with a Basque menu, and the Barceloneta branch, Txakolín, has a larger dining room and bar. **Branch**: **Txakolín** C/Marquès de l'Argentera 19 (93 268 17 81).

Palau Dalmases

C/Montcada 20 (93 310 06 73). Metro Jaume I/ bus 17, 19, 40, 45, N8. **Open** 8pm-2am Tue-Sat; 6-10pm Sun. **Credit** MC, V. **Map** D6/**C3**
Not a bar, they say, but a 'baroque space' on the ground floor of one of the most beautiful courtyard palaces of C/Montcada, the seventeenth-century Palau Dalmases. Its promoters aim to provide an 'aesthetic experience' to 'satisfy all five senses': walls are adorned with period paintings, the ornate furniture and semi-religious accoutrements are to match; spectacular displays of flowers, fruit and aromatic herbs give it the look of an Italian still life, and suitably baroque music plays in the background. Fresh fruit drinks are provided as well as alcohol, and there are occasional music recitals. Deeply eccentric, decadent, a tad pretentious, but soothing to ear, nose and eye, and worth the elevated prices.
Tables outdoors (July, Aug).

Tèxtil Cafè

C/Montcada 12-14 (93 268 25 98). Metro Jaume I/ bus 17, 19, 40, 45, N8. **Open** 10am-midnight Tue-Sun. **Credit** MC, V. **Map** D6/**C3**
Another special bar on C/Montcada, in the tranquil courtyard of the fourteenth-century Palau dels Marquesos de Llió, now home to the Museu Tèxtil and Museu Barbier-Mueller (*see chapter* **Museums**). Good for lunch or a drink in special surroundings, the 'Textile Café' is popular with tourists, locals, a sizeable gay clientele and many others round about, and a great place to stop over while sightseeing.
Tables outdoors.

La Vinya del Senyor

Plaça Santa Maria 5 (93 310 33 79).
Metro Jaume I/bus 17, 19, 40, 45, 100, N8. **Open** noon-1.30am Tue-Sat; noon-midnight Sun. **Credit** AmEx, DC, MC, V. **Map** D6/**C3-4**
A wine taster's café with a front-row view of the glorious façade of Santa Maria del Mar. Wooden chairs and tables distinguish it from nearby competition, as does a superb list of over 300 wines. There's also a listing of selected wines, *cavas*, sherries and moscatels, changed every 15 days. Fine Iberian ham and other delicacies can accompany your sips.

El Xampanyet

C/Montcada 22 (93 319 70 03). Metro Jaume I/ bus 17, 19, 40, 45, N8. **Open** noon-4pm, 6.30-11.30pm, Tue-Sat; noon-4pm Sun. Closed Aug. **Credit** V. **Map** D6/**C3**
Forget art and museums for a while, this 'little champagne bar' is one of the eternal attractions of C/Montcada. It's lined with coloured tiles, barrels and antique curios, has a few marble tables, and there are three specialities: anchovies, cider and 'Champagne' (a pretty plain *cava*, if truth be told, but very refreshing), served by the glass or bottle. Other good tapas – particularly good tortilla – are available, too. Owner Sr Esteve – born above the shop in 1930, one year after his father opened the bar – and his family are unfailingly welcoming, and it's one of the best places on the entire planet to while away an afternoon, or a day, or a week. Opening times can vary unpredictably.

Port Vell & Barceloneta

Jai-ca

C/Ginebra 13 (93 319 50 02). Metro Barceloneta/ bus 17, 36, 39, 45, 57, 59, 64, 157, N6, N8. **Open** 10am-midnight daily. **Credit** V. **Map** E7
High-quality, no-nonsense Basque tapas bar in the heart of the Barceloneta, specialising in seafood. *Tables outdoors (May-Oct).*

Tapas Bar Maremàgnum

Space 10, Maremàgnum, Moll d'Espanya (93 225 81 80). Metro Drassanes/bus all routes to Colom. **Open** 11am-1am Mon-Thur, Sun; 11am-2am Fri, Sat. Closed 25 Dec. **Credit** AmEx, MC, V. **Map** D7
The best views of port and city that Maremàgnum can offer, with good if pricey tapas of every class: in exchange you get to watch the spectacle of a thousand bobbing heads passing over the Rambla de Mar, or boats slipping through its swing bridge.

El Vaso de Oro

C/Balboa 6 (93 319 30 98). Metro Barceloneta/bus 17, 39, 40, 45, 57, 59, 64, 157, N8. **Open** 8.30am-midnight daily. Closed Sept. **Map** E7
A very narrow *cerveceria* (beer-bar), one of few in Barcelona that makes their own (excellent) brew. Don't go expecting a table (there aren't any); there is, though, a long, often crowded bar that will test your dexterity as you try not to elbow your neighbour's *patatas bravas*. Tapas-lovers' heaven.

*Stolen glances at **Café La Cereria**. See page 161.*

Vila Olímpica – Port Olímpic

Port Olimpic has bars one after the other (*see also* chapter **Restaurants**), but worth singling out is:

Cafè & Cafè
Moll del Mestral 30 (93 221 00 19).
Metro Ciutadella/bus 36, 41, 71, 92, 100, N6, N8.
Open 4pm-3am Mon-Thur, Sun; 4pm-5am Fri, Sat.
Credit MC, V. **Map** F7
Relaxed coffee house/cocktail bar in the Port Olímpic with a mind-boggling range of coffees. Particularly good is the 'Royal', sweetened with cane sugar.
Tables outdoors.

Poble Sec

Bar Primavera
C/Nou de la Rambla 192 (93 329 30 62).
Metro Paral.lel/bus 20, 36, 57, 64, 91, 157, N6.
Open 10am-10pm Mon; 8am-10pm Tue-Sun; *Nov-Apr* until 5pm only. **Map** B6
At the very end of Nou de la Rambla, halfway up Montjuïc, this peaceful outdoor bar/café feels well away from the urban activity bubbling down below. In the summer grapevines provide shade, there's always a dog lying around, and it's a great place to stop on the way up or down the hill. Rudimentary *bocadillos* are served as well as drinks.
Tables outdoors (Easter-Sept).

Cervecería Jazz
C/Margarit 43 (no phone).
Metro Paral.lel/bus 20, 57, 64, 157, N0, N16.
Open 6pm-2am Mon-Sat. **Map** B6

German and Belgian beers, a long wooden bar and a rustic-meets-baroque interior make this one of the more original bars in the area. The sandwiches are great – from a standard 'club' to *frankfurt a la cerveza* (Frankfurter in beer) – and the music (mixed jazz) is never so loud as to inhibit conversation.

Quimet & Quimet
C/Poeta Cabanyes 25 (93 442 31 42). Metro Paral.lel/bus 20, 57, 64, 157, N6, N16. **Open** 11.30am-4pm, 7-10.30pm Tue-Sat; 11.30am-4pm Sun. Closed Aug. **Credit** MC, V. **Map** B6
A small, top-quality *bodega* with wines stacked behind the bar and a very healthy selection of tapas. Overwhelmingly crowded around mealtimes.

*Colourful **Margarita Blue**. See page 161.*

The Eixample

See also **Zona Alta** *for* **Mas i Mas Cafè**.

Bracafé

C/Casp 2 (93 302 30 82).
Metro Catalunya/bus all routes to Plaça Catalunya.
Open 7am-10.30pm daily. **Map** D5/**B1**
A bustling, popular café just off the Plaça Catalunya, patronised by Passeig de Gràcia shoppers and known for its Brazilian coffee, which has made it onto the 'best in Barcelona' list.
Tables outdoors.

La Gran Bodega

C/València 193 (93 453 10 53). Metro Universitat,
Passeig de Gràcia/bus 20, 43, 44, 54, 58, 63, 64, 66,
67, 68, N3, N7, N8. **Open** 8.30am-1am daily.
Credit MC, V. **Map** C4
Bustling tapas bar, a first stop for students and office workers before a night out. Adventurous tourists acquaint themselves here with the *porrón* (the Catalan drinking jug that has you pour wine down your throat from a long glass spout). It takes several goes to master the art – but it's fun trying.
Tables outdoors (May-end Sept).

Happy Café

C/Provença 286 (93 487 30 01). Metro Diagonal,
FGC Provença/bus 7, 16, 17, 20, 22, 24, 28, 43, 44,
100, 101, N4, N7. **Open** 9.30am-9pm Mon-Sat.
Credit AmEx, DC, MC, V. **Map** D4
A relaxed garden café in the patio of the **Happy Books** bookstore (*see chapter* **Shopping**). Excellent pastries accompany the bargain basement novel you just picked up while browsing the shelves.

Laie Llibreria Cafè

C/Pau Claris 85 (93 302 73 10). Metro
Urquinaona/bus all routes to Plaça Urquinaona.
Open *café* 9am-1am Mon-Fri; 10.30am-1am Sat;
bookshop 10am-9pm Mon-Fri; 10.30am-9pm Sat.
Credit AmEx, DC, MC, V. **Map** D5/**B1**
Barcelona's original bookshop-café, a hugely successful concept. The upstairs café has its own entrance, but is popular with a literary set and anyone looking for a comfortable bar in which to sit and read. It has great cakes and coffees, magazines for browsing and a good lunch menu for 1,650ptas; there are also outside tables on a patio, and live jazz some evenings. *See also chapter* **Shopping**.
Tables outdoors (May-Oct).

La Valenciana

C/Aribau 1 (93 453 11 38). Metro Universitat/bus all
routes to Plaça Universitat. **Open** *Sept-June* 8.30am-
10.30pm Mon-Thurs; 8.30am-2am Fri; 9am-2am Sat;
9am-2.30pm, 5-10.30pm Sun. *July, Aug* 8.30am-2am
daily. Closed 25, 26 Dec, 1 Jan. **Map** C5
A big, well-run and long-established *orxateria* and *torroneria* (nougat shop) that serves excellent homemade ice creams and sorbets, as well as other sweet things and savoury café standards. Upstairs there's a good-sized area to sit and read, chat or have lunch, served daily with a drink and dessert for 825ptas.
Tables outdoors.

El Velòdrom

C/Muntaner 213 (93 430 51 98). Metro Hospital
Clínic/bus 6, 7, 15, 27, 32, 33, 34, 58, 64, N8.
Open 6am-2am Mon-Wed; 6am-2.30am Thur; 6am-
3am Fri-Sat. Closed Aug, Easter, Christmas. **Map** C3

A golden oldie: **Bar Almirall**. *See page 163.*

'Focaccia, or pizza,... or chocolate cake?' Bar talk at **Buenas Migas**. See page 164.

A much-loved two-storey art deco bar from 1933 that attracts a complete mix of people, from office workers during the day to a younger crowd at night. (Several) billiard tables, long leather sofas and an upper balcony all help to give it a real 'café society' feel. A great café to visit with a group, or just for writing a letter alone in one of its many comfortable corners. Good sandwiches too.

Gràcia

Casa Quimet
Rambla del Prat 9 (93 217 53 27). Metro Fontana/ bus 22, 24, 25, 28, N4. **Open** 6.30pm-2am Tue-Sun, Mon if public holiday. Closed Feb, Aug. **Map** D3
Strange but true: also known as the 'guitar bar', Casa Quimet is just that: over 200 guitars line the walls and ceiling of this faded old bar, and you're welcome to grab one and join in the ongoing 'jam session'. You might be able to distinguish a song, or you might just hear a lot of people playing and singing at once, and you can also wear one of their very large stock of silly hats. Don't expect a friendly chat with the owner, for his detachment as he presides over the scene is legendary, adding one more surreal touch to the place.

La Fronda
C/Verdi 15 (93 415 20 55).
Metro Joanic, Fontana/bus 39, N4.
Open 7.30pm-1am Mon, Wed, Thur, Sun; 7.30pm-3am Fri, Sat. **Credit** AmEx, DC, MC, V. **Map** D3
A small sandwich and *bocata* spot conveniently located very near the Verdi cinema. The wide range

of *bocadillos* includes a great one with camembert and *xorissets* (spicy, small Catalan chorizo), and another of *botifarra* (sausage) with succulent red peppers and cheese.

El Roble
C/Lluís Antúnez 7 (93 218 73 87).
Metro Diagonal/bus 16, 17, 22, 24, 28, N4.
Open 7am-1am Mon-Sat. Closed Aug. **Map** D3
Large, bright, old-style tapas bar, with a great fresh seafood tapas, well-filled Galician *empanadas* and a wide range of *tortillas*. One of the better places to eat tapas in Barcelona, and often bustling.

Salambó
C/Torrijos 51 (93 218 69 66).
Metro Joanic/bus 39. **Open** noon-2am Mon-Thur, Sun; noon-3am Fri, Sat. **Credit** V. **Map** E3
An elegant two-storey café, opened in 1992 but which deliberately echoes the large literary cafés of the 1930s, with plenty of tables, billiard tables and an unusual selection of fragrant teas, sandwiches and salads. Extremely popular, especially with the crowds from the Verdi cinemas.
Tables outdoors (May-Oct).

Sol Solet
Plaça del Sol 21 (93 217 44 40). Metro Fontana/ bus 22, 24, 28, N4. **Open** 7pm-3am daily. **Map** D3
The only bar in town with wholefood tapas – tabouleh, guacamole, feta and tomato salads, and a selection of tortillas – and so a Godsend for vegetarians. Marble tables, wood-lined walls and intimate lighting also add to its appeal. Plus the fact that it's cheap.
Tables outdoors.

Muebles Navarro: *New York style comes to the Raval. See page 165.*

Tetería Jazmín

C/Maspons 11 (93 218 71 84). Metro Fontana/
bus 22, 24, 28, N4. **Open** 7pm-2am Tue-Thur; 7pm-
2.30am Fri-Sat; 7pm-midnight Sun. Closed three
weeks Aug/Sept. **Map** D3
A relaxed, comfortable, North African-style tea
room, with low tables and pillowed sofas conducive
to extended evenings of chat. Along with tea, you
can order light North African dinners of couscous
with a variety of vegetarian accompaniments.

Zona Alta

Bar Aula 'O'

Passeig de Santa Eulàlia 25 (93 204 13 45).
Bus 60, 66, N8. **Open** 8.30am-6pm Mon-Fri;
11am-7pm Sat, Sun.
In the romantic gardens of the former palace of the
Marqués de Sentmenat, high up on Tibidabo above
Sarrià, this slickly contemporary bar is shaped like
a shipping container, with one side opening onto a
garden terrace. Popular with students from the
nearby Eina design school, it has a fresh, original
feel and great views down onto the city. Its *bocadillos* and *platos combinados* are also well priced.
Tables outdoors.

Casa Fernández

C/Santaló 46 (93 201 93 08). FGC Muntaner/
bus 14, 58, 64, N8. **Open** *restaurant* 1pm-1.30am
Mon-Thur, Sun; 1pm-2am Fri, Sat; *bar* noon-2.30am
Mon-Thur, Sun; noon-3am Fri, Sat.
Credit AmEx, DC, MC, V. **Map** C3
An elegant variation on the tapas bar, and a regular
stop-off on the uptown bar circuit around C/Santaló,
Casa Fernández serves a fine array of tapas, desserts
and home-made soups, and their (very good) own-

brand beer as well as imported beers. A rather
expensive full restaurant menu is also available: particularly good are the meats and steaks.
Tables outdoors (May-Oct).

Mas i Mas

C/Marià Cubí 199 (93 209 45 02). FGC Muntaner/
bus 14, 58, 64, N8. **Open** 7.30pm-2.30am Mon-Thur,
Sun; 7.30pm-3am Fri, Sat. **Map** C3
The Mas family have made a splash throughout the
'90s with their music/club venues (La Boîte,
Jamboree, Moog: *see chapters* **Nightlife** *and*
Music: Rock, Roots & Jazz). They began with
this tapas bar-café on the Santaló route, an evergreen
favourite with the young uptown set. Defying the
upmarket image, the tapas are very good, and reasonably priced. In the Eixample, on C/Còrsega near
the junction of Passeig de Gràcia and Diagonal, the
Mases have a similarly stylish café-restaurant, with
fine tapas and a good, fair-value lunch menu.
Branch: C/Còrsega 300 (93 237 57 31).

Els Tres Tombs. *See page 165.*

Time Out Barcelona Guide **173**

Nightlife

House, salsa, lounge and paso doble, drinks on a Gaudí roof terrace and chocolate croissants at dawn. Just another night out.

Barcelona's fame as a party city grows year by year, and with good reason. Roving bands of revellers, post-midnight traffic jams and an array of crowded bars give the impression of a city in the throes of a major celebration. But no, it's simply that in this town people like to go out, they like to go out in groups, and they like to go out late.

Many of the city's hotspots have been the same for years, but the nocturnal terrain is also continually evolving. The scene encompasses huge entertainment zones in the **Port Vell** and the **Port Olímpic** – with no sleeping neighbours to worry about, these areas, especially in summer, are heaving with gleeful revellers until dawn.

There are several other recognisable night-time zones. The old town, the **Ciutat Vella**, has regained its popularity for the end of the millennium. The **Plaça Reial** is always full of activity, and nearby, **C/Escudellers** (which now has an open space, Plaça George Orwell), once the domain of Felliniesque tarts, now draws hordes of students, attracted by its old-world grunginess (and cheapness). Across Via Laietana, **La Ribera**

– around **Passeig del Born** – is enjoying one of its periodic moments in vogue, with elegant bars, deep-house hang-outs and local dives all within a stone's throw of one another. Another area of interest is **Poble Nou**, inland from Vila Olímpica, which like many *barris*, is very much party to its own scene.

The no-man's land of the **Eixample** is worth a visit, for a glance at its famous but now very passé design bars, or to visit some rejuvenated clubs. The area near Plaça Francesc Macià and C/Santaló has a slew of bars and clubs that cater to a young, affluent crowd. In **Gràcia**, the atmosphere is more relaxed: the two main squares, Plaça del Sol and Plaça Rius i Taulet, are great places in which to orientate yourself before exploring the area. Many of Barcelona's wealthy folk, meanwhile, live on or near **Tibidabo**, and the hill is where you'll find some of the most elegant bars and clubs, often with staggering vistas.

The Anglo-Saxon concept of a 'club', based on restrictive licencing laws, doesn't entirely apply here. Obviously, there are places that are very

*There's no mistaking the **Mojito Bar**, part of the **Maremàgnum** complex. See page 182.*

much clubs, with a door policy and so on, but there are also loads of places that are really just bars, don't charge admission (except maybe at peak times) but do have a dance floor. It is also worth noting that bars and clubs naturally open and close all the time, so look out for flyers, and check the local press for new arrivals (*see chapter* **Media**). Below is a sample of what to expect as you make a journey through to the end of night. *Unless otherwise stated, admission is free to the places listed, and they do not accept credit cards.*

Barri Gòtic

Les Artistes

C/Correu Vell 8 (617 80 81 85). Metro Jaume I/bus 17, 19, 40, 45, N8. **Open** 8pm-2.30am Tue-Thur, Sun; 8pm-3am Fri, Sat. **Map** D6/**B4**

Marcel from Marseille, a one-time resident of London and lively conversationalist, runs this hip little hideaway on a very narrow street near the post office. The fine selection of music ranges from mellow French hip-hop to drum'n'bass and romantic soul, while on tap there's Jamaican beer.

Dot

C/Nou de Sant Francesc 7 (93 302 70 26). Metro Drassanes/bus 14, 38, 59, 91, N9, N12. **Open** 10pm-2.30am Mon-Thur, Sun; 10pm-3am Fri, Sat. Closed some days Aug. **Map** D6/**A4**

Dot is a dance-bar in the dark and alley-like back streets around the Plaça Reial, with a coolness that has made it one of the most popular in the old city. Calling itself a 'light club', Dot consists of two spaces, a red-lit bar area for chat, and a small but functional dancefloor, through a futuristic door to the back. The sound system is top, as is the music – drum'n'bass, lounge, space funk and club/dance.

Heaven

C/Escudellers 20 (93 412 25 36). Metro Drassanes/bus 14, 38, 59, 91, N9, N12. **Open** 10pm-3am daily. **Credit** AmEx, DC, MC, V. **Map** D6/**A3**

This large, renovated Escudellers bar may not be everyone's vision of the eternal reward, but as a place to drink and slouch around on a couch it's fine. The crowd tends towards college age; the music is predominantly Britpop and trip-hop, and in the back room there's a pool table – a welcome sight for those in need of redemption.

Hook

C/Ample 35 (600 61 58 29). Metro Jaume I/bus 17, 19, 40, 45, N8. **Open** 7pm-2am Tue-Fri; 7pm-3am Sat; 6pm-1am Sun. **Map** D6/**B4**

The eccentric collection of clocks and other antique doo-dads that clutter this warm, cosy place are just this side of authenticity, and for an instant here, it's possible to believe Peter Pan might actually enjoy beer. The clientele consists of young foreigners and Catalans getting to know each other, as well as the occasional serious drinker mumbling to one of the clocks in the corner.

Jamboree

Plaça Reial 17 (93 301 75 64). Metro Liceu/bus 14, 38, 59, N9, N12. **Open** 10.30pm-5.30am daily; *gigs* 11pm-12.30am daily. **Admission** (incl one drink) 1,500ptas. **Map** D6/**A3**

Live acts end around 1am, and the club, famed for soul, R&B and low-grade swinger sounds, begins. This subterranean brick vault is hugely popular, and gets very cramped. Total gridlock is averted by a steady stream of people going upstairs (for free) to **Tarantos**, to chill to Latin and Spanish music. *See also chapter* **Music: Roots, Rock & Jazz.**

Karma

Plaça Reial 10 (93 302 56 80). Metro Liceu/bus 14, 38, 59, N9, N12. **Open** 11.30pm-5am Tue-Sun; *bar* 8.30pm-2.30am Tue-Sun. **Admission** free-1,000ptas (incl 1 drink). **Map** D6/**A3**

Right on Plaça Reial and with guard-boys at the door, Karma is impossible to miss. It has long served tourists and a cross-section of locals, although the young student crowd dominates. Intense competition from clubs nearby has lowered attendances, but this bomb-shelter of a club remains crammed at weekends. The doormen let you walk in if they like the look of you; if not, you pay. Music is mainstream rock with lapses into electronika.

Al Limón Negro

C/Escudellers Blancs 3 (93 318 97 70). Metro Liceu/bus 14, 38, 59, N9, N12. **Open** 11pm-3am Tue-Sun; *live shows* Fri, Sat. **Map** D6/**A3**

World music, contemporary art and pastel orange paint on 100-year-old walls give this bar a cheerful modern feel. It calls itself a 'multi-bar' and hosts exhibitions, live music and theatre. Food is served upstairs.

Malpaso

C/Rauric 20 (93 412 60 05). Metro Liceu/bus 14, 38, 59, N9, N12. **Open** *Sept-June* 9.30pm-2.30am Mon-Thur, Sun; 9.30pm-3am Fri, Sat, eves of public holidays. *July, Aug* 10pm-2.30am Mon-Thur, Sun; 10pm-3am Fri, Sat. **Map** D6/**A3**

Down a back alley from Plaça Reial is this busy little bar, replete with decks and a buzzy, young crowd. A good warm-up for **Moog**, the music flits unpredictably from indie to jungle to French touch disco all in one evening, but is consistently lively. As you sip your Carlsberg, check out the model train that runs the length of the glass-covered bar counter.

New York

C/Escudellers 5 (93 318 87 30). Metro Liceu/bus 14, 38, 59, N9, N12. **Open** 11pm-5am Thur-Sat. **Admission** midnight-1.15am 500ptas; 1.15am-close (incl one drink) 1,000ptas. **Map** D6/**A3**

Students and teenagers thrash it out to Britpop in this former sex club, which metamorphosed overnight into a hang-out for Barcelona's own version of Generation Z. It's big, with a mezzanine above the dancefloor and couches dating from the club's licentious origins in the 1970s, but with no air-conditioning, the air becomes a sweaty soup. **Panams**, at La Rambla 27, is a similar sex-club venue (which still has a live show) also hosting club nights.

Chilling out at **Ovisos'** stylish little sister, **Shanghai**. See also page 178.

Ovisos

C/Arai 5 (607 26 47 26). Metro Liceu/bus 14, 18,
38, 59, N9, N12. **Open** 10pm-12.30am Mon-Thur,
Sun; 10pm-3am Fri, Sat. **Map** D6/**B3**
A deep recess of a grunge bar in Plaça George
Orwell on C/Escudellers that attracts a young, hip,
down-and-out crowd. The music, though excellent
in range (ambient, garage, sip-hop) is often barely
audible, coming as it does from an old and battered
cassette deck placed on one corner of the main bar.
Surprisingly sophisticated (and surprisingly pricey)
food is also available (*see pp142-3*). Nearby on the
narrow C/Aglà, Ovisos has a sister bar, **Shanghai**,
which is smaller, more refined, but still packed at
weekends (*see p178,* **One lost weekend in BCN**).

Paradis

C/Paradis 4 (93 310 72 43). Metro Jaume I/bus 17,
19, 40, 45, N8. **Open** 11pm-3am Mon-Thur; 11pm-
4.30am Fri, Sat. **Map** D6/**B3**
A reggae, Afro-Latin music club, Paradís occupies
a vaulted basement, next door to the local government palaces. The place doesn't get going until
after 2 or 3am, when other places have closed.
Occasionally, live gigs are held, and there are also
reggae-dub rap sessions.

La Pilarica

C/Dagueria 20 (600 06 50 23). Metro Jaume I/bus
17, 19, 40, 45, N8. **Open** 8pm-2am Mon-Thur, Sun;
8pm-3am Fri, Sat. **Map** D6/**B3**
A pocket-size grotto of a bar run by a friendly
Englishman and always full of resident ex-pats. It
has a bulletin board by the door with useful information, things for sale or rent and jobs to be had.

Sidecar Factory Club

C/Heures 4-6 (93 302 15 86). Metro Liceu/bus 14,
38, 59, N9, N12. **Open** 10pm-3am Tue-Sat. Closed
Aug. **Map** D6/**A3**
In a corner of the Plaça Reial, Sidecar has been going
for years. Early evening it's a quiet place to play pool
or read comics; later it gets livelier, mostly with a
student crowd, and it can be difficult to move on the
dancefloor, let alone see bits of memorabilia such as
a petrol pump and yes, a sidecar. There's a terrace
bar in summer, and it's also a music venue (*see chapter* **Music: Rock, Roots & Jazz**).

The Raval

Aurora

C/Aurora 7 (93 442 30 44). Metro Paral.lel, Liceu/
bus 14, 20, 24, 38, 59, 64, N6, N9, N12.
Open 8pm-2.30am daily; also 6am-noon Sat, Sun,
public holidays. **Map** C6
A small, red-walled bar in the *Barrio Chino* with
eclectic music that attracts the perkier, more artistic elements of the neighbourhood. On Fridays and
Saturdays it's not clear if the bar ever shuts; on
Sunday at any rate, it's open at dawn, and steadily
fills up with restless types until about noon.

Benidorm

C/Joaquín Costa 39 (93 317 80 52). Metro
Universitat/bus all routes to Plaça Universitat. **Open**
6pm-2am Mon-Thur; 7pm-2.30am Fri, Sat; 7pm-2am
Sun. **Map** C5
Eye-catching proof of what can be achieved with a
little money and a lot of imagination. This new

One lost weekend in BCN

When it comes to dance culture in Spain, Barcelona is a hugely influential city. Many trends begin here and only later filter through to the other clubbing hubs of the country – Madrid, Valencia, the Basque Country. The massive **Sonar** festival in June, for example, has no real equivalent anywhere else in Europe (*see page 242*). Barcelona is a city that likes to be at the cutting edge in many things, and the club scene is no exception.

When all is said and done, though, this is still a relatively small city, and this is bound to affect diversity. The community responsible for club nights here is a fairly tight-knit bunch, and it's not unusual to find DJs such as Tres Manos, Omar, Angel Molina or Professor Angel Dust repeating sets all over town. Equally, there seems to be an established set of global DJs who return to the **Apolo** every couple of months.

Even so, new places and new promoters open up every year. The puzzling penchant for electro in many venues can surprise newcomers to Barcelona, but elements of techno and hard house are never far away. Variations of house have been infiltrating venues across the city, while a craze for lounge music has gripped smaller DJ bars. Pure drum'n'bass nights, not to mention jungle, are pretty much non-existent, but smatterings of the dreamy, melodic variety are popular in bars. If there's one thing to anticipate, it's the capacity of clubs to change their tune, dramatically, in the same evening or between rooms; **Moog** recently hosted a stunning set by Richie Hawtin, with Van Morrison's *Brown-eyed girl* playing in room two.

AB, the cooler-than-cool free monthly, *Micro* and *Mondo Sonoro* are definitive sources of information on clubs and bars in Barcelona, and can be picked up with stacks of flyers in shops on C/Riera Baixa (*see page 203*). Record-shop owners can also tell you all you need to know about upcoming events. The best bet is **La Casa** (*see page 212*).

The roster of places to check out can change at any time, but here's one way to make the most of a weekend in Barcelona. Sadly, there are no clubs in Gaudi buildings, but in summer you can start a night on top of **La Pedrera** (*see page 185*).

Thursday night-Friday morning
11.30pm After an innovative dinner in the **Mama Café** (*see p142*), make your way past the MACBA to **Bar Almirall** (*see p163*) for a laid-back *cava*.
12.30am Shift across to **Benidorm** for some smooth grooves, strong vodkas and people-watching.

1.15am Meander down the Rambla and see what oddities are taking place in Plaça Reial on your way to **Shanghai**, where the intimate, funky sound system and fresh cocktails get you ready for dancing.
2am Walk over to **Malpaso** for a final cheap drink and a blast of disco.
3am Get chucked out of Malpaso with your beer in a plastic cup, which you drink on a bench in Plaça Reial. When the sixth vagabond asks if he can have a sip, decide it's time to go to a club.
3.10am Arrive at **Moog**, knock back a vodka-Red Bull and attack the techno.
5.30am Amble round the corner to the **Pastelería** to buy fresh chocolate croissants. Make a gooey mess of yourself.
6.30am Realise you ve been talking on the Rambla so long it's got light. Hail a cab and fall into it.

Friday night-Saturday morning
10.30pm Convene in **Al Limón Negro** for an innocent *cava* and trancey sounds.
11pm Head over to Plaça George Orwell to eat at the grungy but trendy **Ovisos** (*see also pp142-3*).
12am Set up for the night, walk to **Margarita Blue** to soak up the Latin sounds (*see p161*).
1.30am Needing more elbow space for dancing, speed-walk your way over to **Octopussy**, where big house tunes and an energetic crowd await.
3.30am Jump in a cab to Paral.lel and join the queue for **Nitsaclub** before it gets too long. Get into the thick of it for a few hours of hardcore grooving.
7am Gravitate back towards Plaça de Catalunya and, ravenous, keep the night alive with a trip to **Bar Estudiantil** for a *bocadillo* and a beer.
8.15am Realise your chin is hitting the table and stumble into the street. Hail a cab and call it a day.

Saturday night-Sunday morning
Decide to see a different part of town, Gràcia.
12.30am Discover Plaça del Sol and its busy bars. After checking out some terrible places, pick **Mond** for cool, funky trip hop and lounge.
2am Stop in on **Blue**, where big beats have you bopping on entry.
3am After sizing up the local situation, make a dash for Poble Espanyol in a cab, to dance under the stars to serious house at **La Terrrazza** (or in winter, indoors at **Discotheque** alongside).
6.30am Walk down the mountains and stand in awe at the beauty of the Palau Nacional at dawn. Feel pleased that you've seen a sight.
7am Jump in another cab and enjoy a gorgeous tour of the city before arriving at the beachfront and entering **Tijuana** for an even wilder, sweatier romp.
11am Find your friends and crash on the beach for a few hours. Soak up some sun.
1pm Buy a *Magnum Almendras* ice-cream to give you the energy to find one last cab home.
1.20pm Arrive at *hostal* feeling as though you've done the town.

Catalan/Finnish creation in the heart of the Raval is a charming, dimly-lit venue for sipping mint tea or knocking back vodkas. It's small, but the owners have made the most of the space to fit in plenty of seating, a pair of gleaming Technics, and a minute yet inviting dancefloor. The maroon and gold, pseudo-classical décor lends itself well to late-night groove sessions. Local and foreign DJs play every day of the week, and whether it be smooth east coast rap, Bristol massive, or obscure Spanish electronica, the atmosphere is welcoming and warm. Check out the bizarre eastern theme tapestry behind the bar.

La Confiteria

C/Sant Pau 128 (93 443 04 58). Metro Paral.lel/bus 20, 57, 64, 157, N0, N6. **Open** 10am-2am Tue-Thur; 10am-3am Fri, Sat; noon-midnight Sun. **Map** C6
With murals of rural scenes dating from the 1920's and a mirrored booth offering a curved view of infinity, La Confiteria takes the biscuit among recently renovated bars in the Raval. The clientele is lively, without a defined tendency, englobing local characters, foreigners and normal-looking Catalans. The non-polarizing music is mostly Spanish and Catalan rock/pop, but ethnic sounds also feature. Very good if pricey *bocatas* and other light goodies are served.

Kentucky

C/Arc del Teatre 11 (93 318 28 78). Metro Drassanes/bus 14, 38, 59, N9, N12. **Open** 7pm-3am Mon-Sat. Closed Aug. **Map** C6/**A4**
An old red-light bar left over from the 1960s, when Barcelona was a port of call for US Navy ships. The bar looks essentially unchanged since then: a long, narrow space with an old juke-box, which has a sur-prisingly large selection of music. The Kentucky is popular among an assortment of foreigners, Raval locals and slumming uptowners.

London Bar

C/Nou de la Rambla 34 (93 318 52 61). Metro Liceu/ bus 14, 38, 59, N9, N12. **Open** 7pm-4am Tue-Thur, Sun; 7pm-4.30am Fri, Sat. **Admission** free. **Credit** MC, V. **Map** C6/**A3**
With its 1910 bar and wall mirrors, the London does not look much like an English pub, but is reminis-cent of England in that people tend to arrive and settle in for the rest of the evening. Open since 1910, and more recently a hangout for Catalan hippies, it was taken over a few years back by a livelier man-agement who have kept it popular among young resident expats and a mixed bunch of partying natives. There are regular live gigs, for which there's no entrance fee, but drink prices go up accordingly (*see chapter* **Music: Rock, Roots & Jazz**).

Marsella

C/Sant Pau 65 (93 442 72 63). Metro Liceu/bus 14, 38, 59, N9, N12. **Open** 10pm-2am Mon-Thur; 10pm-3am Fri, Sat. **Map** C6/**A3**
Another survivor of the *Barrio Chino*'s colourful past, a well-loved bar that's been in the same fami-ly for five generations. Dusty, untapped 100-year-old bottles sit in tall glass cabinets (they still have locally-made absinthe, *absenta*), old mirrors line the walls, and motley chandeliers loom over the cheer-ful clientele. It's one for the expat crowd, and attracts many gays too. The bar gets crowded late night on weekends, so come a bit earlier to secure a comfort-able spot at one of the old wooden tables.

Groovy tunes and designer kitsch draw the crowds to **Penúltimo**. *See page 183.*

La Paloma BARCELONA
Fundada el 1903

Modernist Dance Hall

Passion for Dancing, Drinking & Glamour

Evening Sessions
Thurs/Fri/Sat/Sunday
& Holidays
from 6 pm to 9:30 pm

Night Sessions
Thurs/Fri/Sat/Sunday
& Holidays'Eves
from 11:30 pm to 5 am

Tigre 27 · Bookings
Tel. 93 301 68 97 · 93 317 79 94 · Fax 93 317 72 25

Going underground

Scattered among the ruins and renovations of the *Barrio Chino* and Raval are a handful of private, 'underground' spaces where artistico-cultural events are staged, which occasionally bloom into full-grown parties. They're private in the sense that they're not held in a bar or club, but in a space that's been taken over by a group of individuals who every so often open up their uniquely-fashioned environments to anybody who's managed to find out about them. They may not charge admission, but probably need a contribution to the costs.

Some places call themselves 'cultural associations' and have regular programmes – theatre workshops and performances, tai-chi classes, art exhibitions or rummage sales. Others stage imaginatively cool dance parties, with the latest electronic sounds and original visual projections. On a good night, these parties are the places to be. The best way to find out about them is to look out for flyers in nearby bars and restaurants such as **Aurora** (*see page 177*), **Escondite del Pirata**, **Ovisos** (for both, *see page 142*) and the **Bar Fortuny** (*see page 163*).

There's also a select band of semi-legal, clandestine bars in town which, for obvious reasons, can't be listed here. One with a tad more visible existence is the **Marx Bar** near Plaça George Orwell. To find it, ask around in the trendier bars on the plaça, but note that it's a fairly tight underground scene, and not everyone's cup of hemlock.

L'Atelier – Art de Vivre Total

C/Cadena 49 baixos (93 441 07 16). Metro Liceu/bus 14, 38, 59, N9, N12. **Map** C6

A huge, 'life-art' space that seems permanently stalled in the process of 'becoming'. In another era it was a laundry and bath-house, and there are three perfectly preserved, ten-metre-long stone wash basins, which now serve as performance spaces and chill-out rooms whenever it hosts experimental drum'n'bass electro-music parties or DJ sessions.

Conservas

C/Sant Pau 58 baixos (93 302 06 30/e-mail: 10639LA3@teleline.es). Metro Liceu/bus 14, 38, 59, N9, N12. **Map** C6

This medium-sized, well-kept space is run by performance artist Simona Levi. It has excellent, sporadic programmes featuring contemporary theatre performances, poetry readings and up-and-coming comedy acts, and is extremely popular with those in the know.

Las Lolas Club

C/Tiradors s/n (93 268 20 27). Metro Jaume I/bus 17, 19, 40, 45, N8. **Map** D6/**C2-3**

These talented young flamenco promoters and artists currently strut their stuff at Toguna, a cultural association in La Ribera, but watch out for them at other venues. Performances are spontaneous, except on Sunday evenings when there are scheduled pulse-raising gigs of guitar-strumming, handclapping and footstomping gitano genius. *See also chapter* **Music: Rock, Roots & Jazz**.

Mau Mau Bar

C/Fontrodona 33 (606 86 06 17). Metro Paral.lel/ bus 20, 57, 64, 157, N6. **Map** B-C6

This airy warehouse space hosts weekly parties for Barcelona's cool media set. Big sofas and armchairs are provided for chilling out, chatting, and enjoying the projections, and DJs mix up anything from electro and deep house to London techno and drum'n'bass. Entry is tricky (but not impossible), as its underground status means a members-only policy. It's best tried with someone who lives in Barcelona or, at least, by sporting globally trendy footwear. Check flyers for details of DJs.

Paloq'sea

C/Doctor Trueta 186 (93 221 33 71). Metro Llacuna/bus 36.

It's not just the Raval that has its underground scene: out in Poble Nou is Paloq'sea ('For whatever'), a wide open warehouse space normally used for rehearsals by a theatre group, but where raucous, fun-packed parties and concerts are also occasionally held.

Simbiosis

C/Riereta 5 (93 443 10 71). Metro Liceu/bus 14, 38, 59, N9, N12. **Map** C6

Exhibiting original metalwork and sculptures as well as funky wall-paintings and projections, Simbiosis also hosts ocassional theatre performances, live concerts. DJ sessions and more.

Shaft Club

C/Comtessa de Sobradiel 1, baixos (93 317 06 87). Metro Jaume I/bus 17, 19, 40, 45, N8.

Map D6/**B3**

Exactly which shaft we're talking about is made clear by the 1970s dance music at this semi-regular club. Run as a members-only (pay 500ptas at the door to become a Shaftee), it seems to be in a never-ending state of construction, and frankly has the feel of a mine shaft more than a mod TV show. Whatever, the roomy subterranean dance floor is boogie-full on weekends with a cheery, smiley mix of folk.

Dancing on the dock of the bay

No area in Barcelona has more bars per square metre than the **Port Olímpic**. Between Easter and October, the 50 or so bars and restaurants lining the lower level of the port are utterly packed; after 11pm, the pocket-sized dance bars pump up the music and by 1am, most of the restaurants have converted into dance spaces as well. Almost all Port bars are similarly mixed, and differences in décor are minimal. Every bar has a big outdoor *terrassa*. Music runs from Spanish techno to salsa, rock and disco, but the same bar that plays salsa at 1am may play techno at 2am – it depends what the crowd's into.

A few bars, such as **Panini**, **Barlovento**, or **Scandal** are a bit bigger – and so less packed – than the rest, and **¡Oh Tequila!** plays almost only salsa, while **Pachito** of Ibiza fame plays only techno/house. Generally, though, since they're all so close and venues change so often, you're best off just walking along the strip and choosing for yourself. Since it's some way from the centre, most people who start a night out at the Port end up staying there, moving from one bar to another until closing time at 5am. Some after-hours clubs then open up at the beachfront

nearby (*see page 185*). For more on the Port Olímpic's restaurants, *see page 149*.

Still by the water but closer to the centre of things is **Maremàgnum**, the huge entertainment palace in the middle of the Port Vell. All year round, but above all in summer, Maremàgnum-by-night is one massive teen party, and as such has significantly redefined the nocturnal landscape. It offers a strip of Latin-American music bars and clubs on its lower level, where provocatively dressed dancers' hips wiggle to salsa, rumba, and other heated sounds at the **Tropicana Bar** (93 225 80 46), or the club best liked by dedicated *salseros*, **Mojito Bar** (93 225 80 14). Upstairs on the third (top) level, meanwhile, the younger and even more provocatively dressed teen masses squeeze together in the open-air, techno/machine-driven roof-top patio (with a mini-golf course). The deal here is to check out the four clubs that command each side of the square. Techno-pop dominates at all of them, even seeping into **Irish Winds**, a sort of traditional Irish pub with outdoor terrace (*see page 163*). If you've got the stamina, Maremàgnum stays bopping until 5am.

Moog

C/Arc del Teatre 3 (93 301 72 82). Metro Liceu, Drassanes/bus 14, 38, 59, N9, N12. **Open** midnight-5am Mon-Thur, Sun; midnight-6am Fri, Sat. **Admission** (incl one drink) 1,800ptas. **Map** C6/**A4**
Moog expands the Mas family's empire (*see p175* **Jamboree**, *p184* **La Boîte**) to encompass techno and electronic dance. An excellent programme of name DJs keeps this place perennially popular with a happy, young, lively crowd. The dancefloor is smallish and can get tight, but the upstairs '70's dance lounge offers some relief. International DJs usually guest on Wednesday nights.

Sant Pere, La Ribera & the Born

Bass Bar

C/Assaonadors 25 (no phone). Metro Jaume I/bus 17, 19, 40, 45, N8. **Open** 10pm-3am daily. **Map** D-E6/**C3**
A quietly alternative scene clusters in this small, artsy bar. Regular exhibits of local artists and collectives adorn the walls, and the music is anything goes, from Spanish ska or world drumming to Latin.

Colombo

Passeig de Picasso 26 (93 310 75 50). Metro Jaume I/bus 40, 41, 42, 141. **Open** 7am-9pm Mon-Wed; 7am-2.30am Thur-Sat. **Map** E6
A cool oasis in the Born that's resisted conversion

into one more designed-up, pretty place. With a good view of the park, the terrace in summer is a relaxed and funky hangout, with local DJ's playing whatever they like, from Jungle Book music to rare soul-tracks and self-created ambient sounds. Most of this happens at the weekend; other nights it's a quiet, local bar that serves very good *plats combinats*.

Galaxy

C/Princesa 53 (93 310 10 20). Metro Jaume I/bus 40, 41, 42, 141. **Open** 9pm-midnight, Tue, Wed, Sun; 1-4pm, 10.30pm-2am Thur-Sat. *Galaxy* 11pm-3am Sat. **Map** E6/**C3**
Located inside and below the newly opened **Foro** restaurant (*see p147*), Galaxy is a Saturday night club with the sound and feel of groovy London. Dark recesses with comfy chairs, a dim dancefloor with no set territorial limits, and very danceable music by DJ Mark Ryal and others that keeps you in deep house all night, make the Galaxy a very popular place for humans and visiting Americans.

Indeep

Avda Marquès de l'Argentera 27 (93 412 22 94) Metro Barceloneta/bus14, 39, 51. **Open** 11.30pm-4am Fri. **Admission** free. **Map** E6/**C4**
Another cool Born club in a big basement below a restaurant (this time a Greek place called Dionysus). Indeep has an old-school feel, with bare bricks and arched ceilings, that's made bohemian by flickering

candles and funky cloth hangings. It's run by the Galaxy crew, and the strictly deep house music greatly pleases the happy, in-crowd.

Penúltimo (del Borne)

Passeig del Born 19 (93 310 25 96). Metro Jaume I/ bus 17, 19, 40, 45, N8. **Open** 10pm-2.30am Mon-Wed, Sun; 10pm-3am Thur-Sat. **Credit** MC, V. **Map** D6/C3

'Cleopatra's milkbar' might be a better name for this dance-bar, with its bizarre hotchpotch of kitsch and modern design. Dance parties featuring soul, funk, acid jazz, latin and reggae mixes are staged at the weekend by DJ Marta. The atmosphere is infectious, the crowd is an eclectic mix and, on a good night, the place is an oasis of funky fun.

Port Vell & Barceloneta

Distrito Marítimo

Moll de la Fusta (93 221 55 61). Metro Drassanes/ bus 14, 36, 59, 64, N6. **Open** *Café/bar* 11am-3pm, *club* 11pm-3.30am, Wed-Sun. **Map** D7/**B4**

Committed fun-seekers like to start here, at this modern outdoor bar overlooking the old port. At 1am on a Friday or Saturday, the place begins to gear up. Inside, it gets hot and crowded, but there's a good-sized terrace outside where you can walk, let off steam and watch the lights reflected in the water of the harbour. Distrito Marítimo generally serves as a crossroads bar for those heading for further dancing later on at **Woman Caballero**, **Apolo**, **La Terrrazza** or elsewhere.

Octopussy

Moll de la Fusta 4 (93 221 40 31). Metro Drassanes/ bus 14, 36, 57, 59, 64. **Open** midnight-3/4am Fri, Sat. **Credit** V. **Map** D7/**B4**

The most popular spot on the Fusta strip, Octopussy guarantees a waterfront party every weekend. The music is varied, with the emphasis on dance and house, and the smiley, trendy crowd actually remains civilised throughout the night, making it possible to sit outside at a table and enjoy a drink. The terrace is open all year.

Woman Caballero

Estació de França, Avda Marquès de l'Argentera 6 (93 300 40 17). Metro Barceloneta/bus 14, 39, 51, N8. **Open** 1-9am Thur-Sat. Closed some days Aug. **Admission** (incl one drink) 1,500ptas. **Map** E6/**C4**

In the basement of Estació de França, this subterranean darkland consists of three spaces: a very large cement dancefloor, a medium-sized cement dancefloor (both of which cater for the house and techno crowds), and a small, slightly less cementy lounge where drum' n'bass often degenerates into American R&B and disco. Not long ago Woman Caballero was a mecca for the untold numbers of clubbers caught up in international techno-thump. The crowds may have dwindled, but the thump lives on... and on. When you eventually leave, don't forget to stop in at the station's café/bar, **Midnight Express** *(see p188)*.

Tijuana Morning Café

Passeig Maritim 34 (629 36 35 37). Metro Ciutadella-Vila Olímpica/bus 36, 100, N6, N8. **Open** 6-11am Sat, Sun. **Map** E7

By 8am at weekends, this huge dance venue with 800+ capacity (at other times a Mexican restaurant) is a sea of gyrating, pulsating clubbers. The gay and straight clientele is mostly spill-over from the scene at **La Terrrazza** *(see below)*, which finishes when Tijuana starts; both are run by the same promoters. A beautiful wooden bar sweeps through the centre to meet a graceful spiral staircase, while dark curtains act as protection from the fact that day arrived long ago. However, décor is hardly the focus. Music is. The Ibiza influence is undeniable, with its beach front patio and pounding Balearic house sets. It's expensive (a bottle of water, 600ptas), but Tijuana keeps restless party-goers happy till 11am, at which point retirement to the sun-drenched beach is in order. Don't forget your Ray-Bans.

Poble Sec-Montjuïc

Club Apolo/Nitsaclub

C/Nou de la Rambla 113 (93 441 40 01/93 442 51 83). Metro Paral.lel/bus 20, 36, 57, 64, 91, 157, N0, N6. **Open** *disco* midnight-6am Fri, Sat; *gigs* times vary. **Admission** *disco* (incl 1 drink) 1,500ptas; *gigs* prices vary. **Map** C6

This elegant old ballroom has changed hands many times over the years, but has always drawn a crowd. The most recent management has put it to good use with techno-oriented dance parties and concerts. On Fridays, Saturdays and the eves of public holidays, it becomes the **Nitsaclub**, a hugely popular, very young Detroit techno/hard house/electro dance-a-thon. However, two smaller, separate rooms on the balcony level act as chillout rooms with popular downbeat sets from residents Coco, djd!, and Fra, among others. At 4am queues to get in snake to the Paral.lel. On other nights Apolo hosts live concerts *(see chapter* **Music: Rock, Roots & Jazz***)*.

La Terrrazza/Discothèque

Behind Poble Espanyol, Avda Marquès de Comillas (93 423 12 85). Metro Espanya/bus 13, 50, 61E, 100. **Open** (La Terrrazza) *June-Oct* midnight-6am Fri, Sat; (Discothèque) *Oct-June* midnight-6am Fri, Sat. **Admission** (incl one drink) 1,300ptas. **Map** A5

Surrounded by pines and next to a picturesque bridge, this summertime open-air space at the back of Poble Espanyol is one mammoth of a club. Big names in the house world play regularly (John Aquaviva, Sven Vdth, and Eric Morales in 1999), to an enormous crowd of exceedingly happy night owls. Between 3 and 4am is the best time to arrive, when you'll find a scene like something out of a Fellini film: podiums bearing wild-eyed beauties, gold-painted dancers wearing nothing but thongs, and a swathe of arms reaching up to the night sky. Its extreme popularity means that it gets crammed beyond belief, but once a reasonable dancing space is found it's difficult not to enjoy.

Down in one! Preparing to party at **Woman Caballero***. See page 183.*

La Terrrazza also has a wintertime identity, **Discothèque**, which is held from October onwards in two closed areas beside the open-air space. One room hosts DJs from the international house circuit, while the smaller **Night Club Flamingos** is dedicated to more experimental electronic music. To find the venue, just follow the crowd around Poble Espanyol.

Torres de Avila

Poble Espanyol, Avda Marquès de Comillas (93 424 93 09). Metro Espanya/bus 13, 50, 61. **Open** *music bar* 11pm-2am, *disco* 2am-6am, Fri, Sat. **Admission** (includes 1 drink) *disco* 1,500ptas. **Credit** MC, V. **Map** A5

The Torres de Avila is the ultimate product of the 1980-90s Barcelona design-bar phenomenon, and Javier Mariscal's most spectacular creation. There are actually seven bars within this building, inside the main entrance to the **Poble Espanyol** (*see p75*). The entrance is a copy of one of the gates to the medieval city of Avila – hence the name. The main theme of the design, by Javier Mariscal and architect Alfredo Arribas, was day and night, and the whole edifice is full of (tongue-in-cheek) symbols. Only the best materials were used in the construction and fittings, and the whole thing cost millions, in any currency. Whatever you think of that, the result is beautiful, at times magical. For years it was more a monument than a bar, but more recently the stiff drink prices have been lowered to more moderate levels, and it now functions as a trance-techno disco. When the rooftop terrace bar opens in summer, it's a stunning vantage point for views of the city. In July and August, it may also be open on Tuesdays and Wednesdays.

The Eixample

Antilla Barcelona

C/Aragó 141-3 (93 451 21 51). Metro Hospital Clínic/bus 43, 44, N7. **Open** 11pm-5am daily. **Admission** 1,500ptas. **Map** C4

Antilla Barcelona is a friendly yet firey salsa club with a regular live programme (*see chapter* **Music: Rock, Roots & Jazz**). Its new, larger quarters have a sophisticated feel, with a bank of video screens, plenty of room to dance and a raised lounge area where there are comfortable cane chairs for taking a breather from the non-stop action on the floor. Free dance classes are held 11.30pm-12.30am, Monday to Thursday.

La Boîte

Avda Diagonal 477 (93 419 59 50). Bus 6, 7, 15, 27, 32, 33, 34, 63, 67, 68, N12. **Open** 11pm-5.30am daily. **Admission** (incl one drink) *disco* 1,500ptas; *live music* 1,500-3,000ptas. **Map** C3

One of a handful of clubs uptown that pulls in people from across the city, La Boîte is another place owned by the Mas brothers (of **Jamboree** and **Moog**), and is also a good music venue (*see chapter* **Music: Rock, Roots & Jazz**). They work hard to create a good atmosphere: the long bar hugs the curved walls, and mirrored columns make the space surprisingly intimate. The resident DJ usually plays mainly soul, funk and old Motown favourites, but recently some decent progressive house fixtures have started to attract a younger crowd. The rather small dancefloor can get crowded at weekends.

Buenavista Club
C/Rosselló 217 (93 237 65 28). Metro Diagonal/bus 7, 16, 17, 31, 67, 68, N4. **Open** 10.30pm-5am Wed-Sat. **Map** C4
In the center of the Eixample, this is one of the city's most popular *salsotecas*, attracting all sorts of Latin-music fans. At the weekend the dance floor is a seething, energy-charged mass of hip-wiggling bodies. If you haven't perfected your salsa steps yet, there are free dance classes on Wednesday nights.

Costa Breve
C/Aribau 230 (93 414 27 78). FGC Provença/bus 6, 7, 15, 33, 34, 58, 64, N8. **Open** midnight-5.30am Thur-Sat. **Admission** (incl one drink) 1,300ptas. **Credit** V. **Map** C3
Costa Breve has long attracted a varied (largely uptown) clientele. The low ceilings, dim lights and curved bar help create an atmosphere for unwinding, while more energetic visitors really get into it on the dance floor, grooving mainly to funk and popular dance tunes.

La Fira
C/Provença 171 (689 78 10 96). Metro Hospital Clínic/bus 31, 38, 63, N3, N8. **Open** 10pm-3am Tue-Thur; 7pm-4.30am Fri, Sat; 6pm-1am Sun. **Map** C4
Large, airy space that calls itself a 'bar museum' – possibly the wackiest museum in town. It's furnished entirely with old fairground equipment: dodgems, waltzers, or swings provide the seating, and the several bars and food stands are designed like stalls. One of the liveliest of Barcelona's more extravagant bars.

Luz de Gas
C/Muntaner 246 (93 209 77 11/93 209 73 85). Bus 6, 7, 15, 27, 32, 33, 34, 58, 64, N8. **Open** 11pm-4.30/5.30am daily. **Admission** (incl one drink) 2,000ptas. **Credit** AmEx, DC, MC, V. **Map** C3
Red velvet with a touch of kitsch sets the tone for this live venue (*see chapter* **Music: Rock, Roots & Jazz**), which doubles as a disco after 2am. It's popular with an uptown, middle-of-the-road clientele.

Nick Havanna
C/Rosselló 208 (93 215 65 91). Metro Diagonal/FGC Provença/bus 22, 24, 28, N4, N6. **Open** 11pm-4.30am Mon-Thur, Sun; 11pm-5.30am Fri, Sat. Closed sometimes Sun in July, Aug. **Admission** free Mon-Thur, Sun; 1,100ptas (incl one drink) after midnight Fri, Sat. **Credit** AmEx, MC, V. **Map** D4
An emblematic Barcelona design bar, created in 1987 by Eduard Samsó with a bank of TV screens,

After-hours

Barcelona opening hours have become a little more restrictive – a great many clubs close between around 5 and 7am – but it's not compulsory to take to your bed as the sun rises; try **Aurora** (*see page 177*) and especially the **Tijuana Morning Café** by the Vila Olímpica (*see page 183*). Naturally, underground venues have no set hours either (*see page 181*).

bar stools like saddles, and a pendulum swinging over the dancefloor. It's also one of the '80s style bars that has best stood the test of time, although along the way some of the most striking aspects of the original design – the elegant chill-out area, the staff's uniforms – have been discarded. It still packs in a mainly middle-of-the-road crowd: weekends after 1am there's little room to dance, and the DJ plays run of the mill Spanish rock or tekno-pop. In the week it's a more spacious, friendly place.

El Otro
C/València 166 (93 323 67 59). Metro Hospital Clínic/bus 20, 38, 43, 44, 63, N7. **Open** 10.30pm-3am Mon-Sat. Closed Aug. **Map** C4
A lively place, El Otro, unlike some design bars, feels genuinely relaxed, and is regularly packed with a chatty young crowd. In shape, it's the same as most Eixample bars: a long bar on one side with small dancefloor at the end.

La Pedrera de Nit
C/Provença 261-5 (93 484 59 95). Metro Diagonal/bus 7, 16, 17, 22, 24, 28. **Open** July-Sept 9pm-midnight Fri, Sat. **Admission** (incl one drink) 1,500ptas. **Map** D4
The Eixample now has a unique new *terrassa* that shouldn't be missed off any visitor's itinerary: in summer the swerving, rolling roof terrace of Gaudí's visionary **La Pedrera** is opened on Friday and Saturday evenings for drinks, live music, and fine views of the city. *See also p80.*

Ritmos Latinos
C/Provença 43 (93 321 10 75). Metro Entença/bus 43, 44, N7. **Open** midnight-6.30am Thur-Sat. **Admission** 1,000ptas. **Map** B4
This is without a doubt one of the most popular salsa clubs in town. Ritmos is big, with two floors of dancing space and surrounding lounge areas, and seriously fun, even though it has the air of a club not to be messed with (take care with the bouncers at the door). The action begins late, after 1am, and keeps on getting hotter and hotter into the night. The rhythm-frenzied crowd represents a broad cross-section of refugees from the electronic dance scene, with a main core of real-life Latinos and eager neighbourhood locals.

Snooker Club Barcelona

C/Roger de Llúria 42 (93 317 97 60). Metro Passeig de Gràcia/bus 7, 39, 45, 47, 50, 54, 56, 62, N1, N2, N3, N9. **Open** 7pm-4am daily. **Admission** free; *snooker tables* 1,000ptas per hour. **Credit** MC, V. **Map** D5
This novel designer billiard hall, was an early product of the '80s design-bar boom. The open space of the bar areas, in peach and silver grey with an arched roof, is striking. Its tranquility is appreciated by a 30-something clientele. There are pool and Spanish *carambola* tables, but snooker is a main attraction.

Zsa Zsa

C/Rosselló 156 (93 453 85 66). FGC Provença/bus 14, 54, 58, 59, 63, 64, 66, N3, N8. **Open** 10pm-3am Mon-Sat. Closed some days Aug. **Credit** V. **Map** C4
A chic bar patronised by designers, media people and conventional types, who go to talk and sample a sophisticated range of cocktails. An innovation of designers Dani Freixes and Vicente Miranda was the lighting, which changes continuously and subtly, so the mirrored wall may appear completely black, and at other times be ablaze with colour.

Gràcia

Andy Capp

C/Bonavista 13 (93 237 90 63). Metro Diagonal/bus 22, 24, 28, 39, N4. **Open** 7.30pm-2.30am Mon-Thur; 7.30pm-3am Fri, Sat. **Map** D3-4
A shabby, amiable rock'n'roll bar named after Reg Smythe's hero. A picture of Andy covers one wall, a graffiti-like mural another. No dance space, but there is music, from mainstream rock and reggae to occasional heavy metal. Regulars are a mix of old hippies, students and aspiring musicians.

Blue

C/Madrazo 49 (93 415 88 84). FGC Gràcia/bus 16, 17, 27, 31, 32, N4, N8. **Open** 8pm-2.30am Mon-Thur, Sun; 10.30pm-3.30am Fri; 11pm-3.30am Sat. **Map** D3
An uplifting, boogie-inspiring hangout where clubbers about to make a night of it in Gràcia and those merely needing to be immersed in music for a few hours can lounge in the tiny blue chairs or groove to deep house tunes. The sound system is as big a

Cabaret & dance halls

An era came to an end in 1997 when the owners of the **Molino**, last and most famous of the music halls on the Paral.lel, declared bankruptcy and closed down (although efforts are being made to revive it, with Russian capital, for an unknown purpose). Thankfully, other institutions of old Barcelona like **La Paloma** are still going strong.

El Cangrejo

C/Monserrat 9 (93 301 85 75). Metro Drassanes/bus 14, 38, 59, N9, N12. **Open** 7pm-3am Mon-Wed; 11pm-3.30am Thur; 11pm-4am Fri, Sat. **Admission** free. **Map** C6/A4
In the heart of the old *Chino*, 'The Crab' is pure sleaze; a leftover from the neighbourhood's days of fame as a district of forbidden fruits. People come here to be entertained by an over-the-top troupe of drag queens doing Liza Minelli, but the regular clients are ageing (like, over 70), camp barmen are as strange as anything on the small stage. The clientele runs from local devotees who know all the performers, to tourists trying out the *Barrio Chino* experience. An old woman sits in silence by the door. She's probably the one who keeps track of how many drinks you have; beware, because, while there's no cover charge, drink prices are hefty.

La Paloma

C/Tigre 27 (93 301 68 97). Metro Universitat/bus 24, 41, 55, 64, 91, 141, N6. **Open** 6-9.30pm Thur, Sun, public holidays; 11.30pm-5am Fri, Sat and eve before public holidays. **Admission** free

(women), 500ptas (men); Thur; 800ptas Fri, Sat; 500ptas (women), 600ptas (men), Sun. **Map** C5
A complete mix of people frequents this magnificent 1902 dance hall, where clubbers mix with pensioners, many of them practised dancers who have been coming here for years. The band gives you a chance to try anything from cha-cha-cha to jive, passing through tango, *paso doble* and even flamenco-ish *sevillanas*. Anyone who likes kitsch will fall in love with the exuberant, galleried interior, and the atmosphere virtually ensures a fun night out. Go with a group, grab one of the velvet-lined booths, and order a bottle of *cava*.

Sala Cibeles

C/Còrsega 363 (93 457 38 77). Metro Diagonal/bus 20, 39, 45, 47, N6. **Open** 11.30pm-4am Thur; midnight-5am Fri; 6-9.30pm, 11.30pm-5am Sat; 6-9.30pm Sun. Closed Aug. **Admission** (incl one drink) 1,000ptas Thur; 1,500ptas Fri, Sat night; 800ptas (women), 900ptas (men) Sat afternoon, Sun. **Map** D4
Built in the 1940s and revamped in the '80s, Cibeles is a large galleried dance hall similar to La Paloma, but with less rococo decoration. It is usually packed with a friendly, good-humoured crowd that gets younger as the evening progresses. The resident orchestra plays everything from foxtrots to cha-cha-cha, mambo and rock-'n'roll, and on Friday nights Cibeles now welcomes the **Mond Club** (*see* **Mond Bar** *right*), an electro/pop dance and schmooze scene for a brand new band of 20-somethings.

The terminally trendy **Mond Bar**.

feature as the turquoise and silver design; needless to say, this being a cool avant-garde bar, the walls also serve as exhibition space for local artists.

Eldorado Bar Musical

Plaça del Sol 4 (93 237 36 96). Metro Fontana/bus 22, 24, 28, N4, N6. **Open** *café* 6-10pm daily (winter 7-10pm); *bar* 10pm-2.30am Mon-Thur, Sun; 10pm-3am Fri, Sat; *terrace* 6pm-1.30am daily. **Map** D3
A noisy, welcoming Gràcia dance and billiards bar, across from the **Cafè del Sol** (*see p165*). Like other bars on the square it's popular with a variety of ages and types. The walls are painted with comic heroes, while videos flash next to the bar – nothing to do with the music, though, which is mostly mainstream rock.

KGB

C/Alegre de Dalt 55 (93 210 59 06). Metro Joanic/bus 39, 55, N6. **Open** *gigs* 9pm-midnight; *disco* midnight-5am, Thur-Sat. **Admission** *gigs* depends on the band; *disco* (incl one drink) 1,000ptas. **Map** E3
The best time to go to this stark, industrial-style warehouse is 2am or later. The crowd are a lively alternative bunch. Despite its residential Gràcia location, KGB stays open late enough to attract hardcore insomniacs: by 5am, the place is thick and thumping. The drill-hammer house beat gets harder and faster the later it gets. Frenetic live concerts are held here sometimes, and international DJs pass through. *See also chapter* **Music: Roots, Rock & Jazz**.

Mond Bar

Plaça del Sol 21 (670 35 27 22). Metro Fontana/bus 39, N4. **Open** 9pm-2.30am Mon-Thur, Sun; 9pm, 3am Fri, Sat. **Map** D3
The quintessential Gràcia meeting point for fashion-conscious/music press-reading twenty-somethings. A harmonious mix of pop/lounge, downbeat and trip hop emanates from this tiny split-level bar, where calming pastels and happy punters create a brilliant atmosphere. DJs are mostly home-grown talent, many of whom have resident slots elsewhere in town – at **Moog**, **Nitsaclub** or **Malpaso**. A new venture called **Mond Club** at the **Sala Cibeles** (*see p186*) on Friday nights will be worth checking out for electronica in a dance hall setting.

Otto Zutz Club

C/Lincoln 15 (93 238 07 22). FGC Gràcia/bus 16, 17, 25, 27, 31, 32, N4. **Open** 11pm-6am Tue-Sat. **Admission** 1,500-2,000ptas. **Credit** AmEx, DC, MC, V. **Map** D3
A landmark among the city's nocturnal offerings, Otto offers three levels of hard-edged but elegant décor, with galleries overlooking the dancefloor. In times past it was the hottest club in town, but with the years it's moved inexorably towards the mainstream. On an average weekend night the place fills up with wannabes and expensive clothing labels, handsome himbos and their destined mates; door policy can be snooty. Even so, when a good DJ is visiting, it's a great place to dance. The **Hot Club** is a separate space with a softer, funkier tone. There's also live music, usually jazz, on some nights.

Zimbabwe

C/Mozart 13 (696 03 12 51). Metro Diagonal/bus 22, 24, 28, 39, N4. **Open** 7pm-2am Mon-Thur, Sun; 7pm-4.30am Fri, Sat. **Map** D3
In the very bosom of Gràcia, this friendly place plays excellent non-stop reggae and Afro-Latin music. Naturally brewed 'rasta' ginger beer is available, while shawarmas and falafels are served until 3am at the Bar Bosforo, directly across the road.

Tibidabo & Zona Alta

Bikini

C/Déu i Mata 105 (93 322 08 00). Metro Les Corts/bus 15, 30, 43, 59, 66, N0. **Open** midnight-4.30am Tue-Thur; midnight-6am Fri, Sat; 7pm-4.30am Sun. **Admission** (incl 1 drink) free Tue, Wed, Sun; 1,000ptas Thur; 1,500ptas Fri, Sat. **Credit** AmEx, DC, V. **Map** B3
If there were such a thing as a state disco, it would probably be like Bikini. Its institutional feel can be explained from its past: dating from the 1950s, the original Bikini called itself a 'multi-space' and had rooms for concerts and activities. A hub of late-1980s revels, it was closed when a huge mall, L'Illa, was built on the site. In 1996 the new, stately Bikini opened within the mall. It still offers three distinct spaces: a club, a Latin room and a cocktail lounge. *See also chapter* **Music: Rock, Roots & Jazz**.

Dawn munchies

You never know when hunger may strike...

Bar Estudiantil

Plaça Universitat (93 302 31 25). Metro Universitat/bus all routes to Plaça Catalunya. **Open** 6am-2am daily. **Map** C5/A1

From 6am, punters not yet ready to call it a day meander up the Rambla to this big café in Plaça Universitat to watch the commuters go by, chat, and grab a *bocadillo* or a *tapa*. The atmosphere at weekends is buoyant, owing greatly to the staff's clever idea to tune into a local techno station.

Bar-Kiosko Pinocho

Mercat de la Boqueria (93 317 17 31). Metro Liceu/bus 14, 38, 59, N9, N12. **Open** 5am-5pm Mon-Sat. Closed first three weeks Aug. **Map** D6/A2

A bar-stall tucked inside the Boqueria market (take a right turn, if you're coming in from the Rambla) that's a popular breakfast spot for nightbirds on their way home. During the day, it's also good for lunch, if not as cheap as it looks.

Cafè Arnau

Avda Paral.lel 62 (93 329 21 04). Metro Paral.lel/bus 20, 36, 57, 64, 91, 157, N0, N6. **Open** 8am-3am Tue-Sun. **Credit** MC, V. **Map** C6

Next to Teatre Arnau and close to many bars and clubs, this café-restaurant stays open all night

most nights, closing for just a few hours. You can order from a standard Spanish menu, or there are tapas that are unusually good and healthy for the early hours of the morning. After the 'official' closing time, don't be put off by metal shutters; ring the bell beside the door.

Churreria Aguilar

C/de l'Escorial 1 (93 219 35 53). Metro Joanic/bus 39, 55, N6. **Open** Fri-Sun (exact hours vary). **Map** E3

A small *churreria* in Gràcia that caters for the late-night crowd. Snacks and hot chocolate are served to revellers doing the rounds. Opening times are more than usually erratic.

Midnight Express

Estació de França, Avda Marquès de l'Argentera (93 310 16 33). Metro Barceloneta/bus 14, 36, 39, 51, 57, 59, 64, N0, N6. **Open** 6.45am-9pm Mon-Fri; 5am-9pm Sat, Sun, public holidays. **Map** E6/C4

The grand, spacious and early-opening station bar beneath the lofty ceilings of the Estació de França is a breakfast favourite for revellers (especially those coming from the Moll de la Fusta, or turning out of **Woman Caballero** downstairs). A great place for end-of-the-night relaxation.

Partycular

Avda Tibidabo 61 (93 211 62 61). No public transport. **Open** 6.30pm-2.30am Wed-Sun. **Credit** AmEx, MC, V.

Pleasant all year, this enormous bar located in a mansion on the hill up to Tibidabo really comes into its own in summer. It has rambling gardens sprinkled with bars, from where you can look across to the lights of the funfair: there's plenty of space, beautiful people to look at, dance areas, tables for chatting and dark corners to be romantic in. If the weather's cold, the grandeur of the rooms still makes Partycular a good place for an after-dinner drink. All in all, it's a class act. However, we repeat, it's up the hill, so don't bother trying to get there by public transport; take a cab.

Rosebud

C/Adrià Margarit 27 (93 418 88 85). Bus 60. **Open** 9pm-4am Mon-Thur; 7pm-5.30am Fri, Sat. **Admission** usually free. **Credit** MC, V.

On the way up to Tibidabo, in front of the Museu de la Ciència, is this huge two-level bar. The garden and pond area have views over Barcelona that make it worth a visit, even if décor is a tad characterless. It's jammed at weekends; there's no dancefloor, but punters shuffle as much as space allows.

Tres Torres

Via Augusta 300 (93 205 16 08). FGC Tres Torres/bus 30, 66. **Open** 7pm-3am Mon-Thur, Sun; 7pm-4am Fri, Sat. **Credit** MC, V. **Map** B2

As you go up the hill towards Tibidabo, you also go upmarket. Tres Torres is quite a long way up, and its garden is a favourite spot with Barcelona's more affluent citizens. It's worth visiting to see the building, a private house from the nineteenth century, with a courtyard – where there's a palm tree and snack stand – and a small upstairs terrace.

Universal

C/Marià Cubi, 182 bis-184 (93 201 35 96). FGC Muntaner/bus 14, N8. **Open** 11pm-3.30am Mon-Wed; 11pm-4am Thur-Sat. **Credit** AmEx, MC, V. **Map** C3

Divided over two floors, Universal has two distinct atmospheres. Downstairs, the music is loud, the décor dark, and away from the bar there's plenty of space for dancing. Upstairs is a light, high-ceilinged bar-room, big enough to seat diners and quiet enough for conversation. The trendy crowd is no longer the wide cross section of characters it once was: today, it tends towards a happy homogenous band of surburbanites, and as such, the place gets packed at the weekends.

La Pasteleria

C/Lancaster 6 (no phone). Metro Liceu,
Drassanes/bus 14, 38, 59, N9, N12. **Open** 24
hours daily. **Map** C6/**A4**
Right around the corner from **Moog**, this bakery
(*pictured*) is open 24 hours a day: just lean in the
door/window and shout out your order to get
croissants de xocolata (chocolate croissants), *xuxos*
(cream donuts) or just plain croissants, hot and
fresh straight from the oven.

Zoo

C/Escudellers 33 (93 302 77 28).
Metro Liceu/bus 14, 38, 59, N9, N12.
Open 6pm-2am Mon-Thur, Sun; 6pm-2.30am Fri,
Sat. **Credit** MC, V. **Map** C6/**B3**
A central night café with restaurant service.
Endangered animals and their incarcerated mates
are not on the menu, but you will find such dishes
as 'penguin' toast with spinach, pine nuts, raisins,
and cream cheese. Also great salads.

Poble Nou

Texaco

C/Pere IV 164 (93 309 92 64). Metro Llacuna/bus 6,
40, 42, 141, N11. **Open** 11pm-3am Thur-Sat, eves
of public holidays.
An authentic piece of hard-driving rock'n'roll
America, miraculously transplanted to the old and
traditional *barri* of Poble Nou. The walls are littered
with images of American archetypes: cowboys, bik-
ers, rockers. You can even get American-style coffee. There's a small stage where rock bands
sometimes play, but live music or not, the place gets
crowded at weekends.

Underworld

C/Almogàvers 122-C/Pamplona 88 (93 486 44 22).
Metro Marina/bus 6, 40, 42, 141, N6. **Open** 1-5am
Fri, Sat. **Admission** disco 700-900ptas (incl one
drink). **Map** F6
Located in what was the private lounge of **Zeleste**
(*see chapter* **Music: Rock, Roots & Jazz**),
Underworld has plenty of room to dance. Fridays,
it's electronic avant-garde with elements of hard
house and jungle; Saturdays, it's trip-hop and electronic dance. Being out of the centre, it depends on
people in the know and walk-ins from Zeleste.

Downstairs is the **Pop Bar**, administering strictly
to the needs of pop-music fans.

The outer limits

Walden Eight

Avda Indústria 12, Sant Just Desvern (93 499 03
42). Bus 63. **Open** midnight-6am Fri, Sat, eve of
bank holiday. Closed some days Aug. **Admission**
1,000ptas. **Credit** MC, V.
So the design-bar phenomenon isn't quite dead. In
the suburb/town of Sant Just Desvern on the
western edge of metropolitan Barcelona, Walden
Eight is a post-industrial, sci-fi fantasy housed in a
defunct cement factory, with a crystal-ceilinged,
flying-saucer-like restaurant 30m up the factory's
chimney. It was designed by Alfredo Arribas, architect of the **Torres de Avila**, and sits next door to
Ricard Bofill's famous Walden building. In terms of
music style it's a techno/house club, with a wide
range of programming, including concerts by international groups, performances by bizarre circus people and a bevy of very skilled go-go dancers.
At the very top of the chimney, 100m up, there's a
viewing area from where you can gaze down on the
city's twinkling lights. Wow.

Shopping

Giant malls to market stalls, designer workshops, innovative fashion stores or tiny specialists with 300 different herbs: Barcelona's shops cover a very special range.

Tradition and innovation are two elements that characterise Barcelona's shopping scene. They have long coexisted here – up to now, at least – more or less harmoniously, which is one secret of the city's success. Big, everything-under-one-roof mixed spaces were slow to arrive, but since the 1980s Barcelona has taken to them with typical verve (*see page 205*). 'Large spaces' have recently begun to impinge on the city centre, with the opening of **El Triangle** mall and a much-delayed **Marks & Spencer** on Plaça Catalunya as company for the long-established **Corte Inglés**.

Meanwhile, the individual, downright quirky little shops that are one of the glories of Barcelona have been struggling on for years – capacity for survival is one of their characteristics. The biggest concentration of them is in the old city (*see pages 196-7* **Little gems**). Larger fashion stores are mainly on or around Passeig de Gràcia, Rambla Catalunya and Plaça Francesc Macià; many street-fashion outlets are in the old city, especially around C/Portaferrissa and, increasingly, the Raval.

Sunday opening

Sunday and holiday opening has traditionally been closely regulated: the only shops always open on Sundays have been cake shops, *pastisseries* (*see p206*). Most shops have closed for lunch on weekdays as well, and a diminishing number only open until midday on Saturdays. However, 'large spaces' – big stores and malls – are now allowed to stay open through the day in the week, and on eight Sundays each year, including all four Sundays prior to Christmas. The other four 'Sunday shopping' days are spread around the year, and advertised in the local press (special conditions also apply to **Maremàgnum**, open every day). Otherwise, Sunday shopping is associated with outdoor markets (*see pp211-2*). For standby shops always open outside normal hours, *see p195*.

Sales & tax refunds

Sales run from the second week in January to the end of February, and during July and August. Value-Added Tax (IVA) depends on the classification of the product – 7% on food, 16% on most items. In many stores non-EU residents can request a Tax-free Cheque on purchases of more than 15,000ptas, which can be cashed at customs when leaving Spain to reclaim VAT. Stores in the scheme have a 'Tax-Free Shopping' sticker on their doors.

One-stop

See also page 205 **Mall cruising**.

El Corte Inglés

Plaça Catalunya 14 (93 306 38 00).
Metro Catalunya/bus all routes to Plaça Catalunya.
Open 10am-9.30pm Mon-Sat. **Credit** AmEx, DC, JCB, MC, V. **Map** D5/B1

The bulldozer of retailing in Spain, El Corte Inglés provides everything you would expect from a department store, and more: key-cutting, shoe repairs, hair and beauty treatments… plus a rooftop café with a fine view. The recently-opened Portal de l'Angel branch is a leisure megastore specialising in music, audio equipment and books. Should there be anything that you can't find in the main stores (and you have a car) the company also has two giant **Hipercor** hypermarkets, one in Sagrera, on Avda Meridiana on the north side of the city, and another in Cornellà in the southern suburbs.
Branches: Avda Diagonal 471-473 (93 419 20 20); Avda Diagonal 617-619 (93 419 28 28); Avda Portal de l'Angel 19 (93 306 38 00); **Hipercor** Avda Meridiana 350-356 (93 346 38 11); C/Salvador Dalí 15-19, Cornellà de Llobregat (93 475 90 00).

Marks & Spencer

Plaça Catalunya 32 (central number for both branches 93 363 80 90). Metro Catalunya/bus all routes to Plaça Catalunya. **Open** 10am-9.30pm Mon-Sat. **Credit** MC, V. **Map** D5/B1

A fierce pace had to be adopted to get everything finally ready for the late-1999 opening of the world's biggest M&S, on the corner of the Plaça and the Rambla. Its unlikely location is in one of the former central bank offices that used to line the Plaça Catalunya, and the ambitious conversion was dogged by delays. Barcelona already has a two-floor M&S in **L'Illa** mall (*see p205*), but the plans for this six-floor megastore are much, much grander.
Branch: L'Illa, Avda Diagonal 545 (93 363 80 90).

Antiques

The streets around C/de la Palla, in the Barri Gòtic, are crowded with small, idiosyncratic antique shops. Antiques are also found around C/Consell de Cent in the Eixample, and there are some less expensive shops around C/Dos de Maig near **Els Encants** flea market (*see page 212*).

L'Arca de l'Àvia

*C/Banys Nous 20 (93 302 15 98). Metro Liceu/bus
14, 38, 59, 91.* **Open** 10.30am-2pm, 5-8pm, Mon-Fri;
10.30am-2pm Sat. **Credit** MC, V. **Map** D6/**B3**
The beautifully displayed antique cottons, linens
and silks here are not cheap, but the patchwork
eiderdowns, dresses (from 20,000ptas) and antique
beaded bags (from 18,000ptas) are lovely to behold.
Popular with brides looking for something special.

Bulevard dels Antiquaris

*Passeig de Gràcia 55 (93 215 44 99).
Metro Passeig de Gràcia/bus 7, 16, 17, 22, 24, 28.*
Open 9.30am-1.30pm, 4.30-8.30pm, *Sept-May* Mon-
Sat, *June-Sept* Mon-Fri. **Map** D4
Beside the main **Bulevard Rosa** fashion mall (*see
p202*), this arcade houses 73 shops, selling antiques
from fine paintings to religious artefacts and dolls.
In **Turn of the Century**, you'll find miniature
musical instruments from the 1930s, and dolls' fur-
niture; **Trik-Trak** are specialists in old tin toys

Gothsland Galeria d'Art

*C/Consell de Cent 331 (93 488 19 22).
Metro Passeig de Gràcia/bus 7, 16, 17, 22, 24, 28,
63, 67, 68.* **Open** 10am-1.30pm, 4.30-8.30pm, Mon-
Sat. **No credit cards. Map** D4-5
A near-unique specialist in original Catalan
Modernista art, furniture and decoration. Delights
include a spectacular selection of fine furniture
(some pieces by Gaspar Homar), polychrome terracotta sculptures by Casanovas, Pau Gargallo or
Lambert Escaler, alabaster by Cipriani, *Modernista*
vases and mirrors, paintings, and even a marble
sculpture by Frederic Marés. It also hosts exhibitions of painting and other work from the era.

La Llar del Col.leccionisme

*C/Llibreteria 13 (93 268 32 59). Metro Jaume I/bus
17, 19, 40, 45.* **Open** 10am-1.30pm, 4.30-8pm, Mon-
Fri; 10am-1.30pm Sat. **No credit cards. Map** D6/**B3**
More bric-a-brac than antiques, the 'Home of
Collecting' has lots of small items such as old post-
cards, posters, medals and watches. Owner Jesús
Torriente seems to enjoy the company of visitors as
much as doing business.

Botiga de la Virreina

*Palau de la Virreina, La Rambla 99 (93 301 77 75).
Metro Liceu/bus 14, 38, 59, 91.* **Open** 3-8.30pm
Mon; 10am-2pm Tue-Sat; 10am-2pm Sun. **Credit**
AmEx, MC, V. **Map** D6/**A2**
In the city information centre on the Rambla (*see
p295*), this shop has a great selection of all kinds of
books on Barcelona, and attractive souvenirs.

Crisol

*C/Consell de Cent 341 (93 215 31 21). Metro Passeig
de Gràcia/bus 7, 16, 17, 22, 24, 28.* **Open** 10am-
10pm Mon-Sat. **Credit** AmEx, DC, MC, V. **Map** D4-5
A bookshop with a bit of everything, from gifts to
records. It has well-stocked English-language and

Gothsland *has all kinds of rare* Modernista *gems.*

european university
CENTER FOR MANAGEMENT STUDIES

THE CAREER FOR THE NEXT MILLENNIUM

ATHENS

BARCELONA

GENEVA

LISBON

MADRID

MONTREUX

MUNICH

PARIS

PORTO

THE HAGUE

TOULOUSE

ZUG-CHAM

WARSAW

european university
CENTER FOR MANAGEMENT STUDIES

web: www.euruni.edu

In recent years, global competition has been spurring change in Europe, from the factory floor all the way up to the boardroom and to recuitment offices. As companies increasingly expand beyond their borders, they are demanding skills and experience that go beyond the traditional gearhead of sales-and-marketing education.

One business school retaining core courses in finance, marketing and accounting, but offering a stronger accent on international and interpersonal skills is the EUROPEAN UNIVERSITY. It's one of today's leading institutions for Business Management and related fields. Founded 25 years ago, its dynamic and visionary concept of global education with a practical approach has proved its value over time.

The curricula of European University includes undergraduate (Bachelor) 4 years and graduate (Master) and executive MBA programs in:

- Business Administration
- Sports Management
- Communication
  Public Relations
- Food and Nutrition
- Shipping Management
- Leisure and Tourism
- Healthcare
- Finance and Banking
- Information Systems
- Human Resources Management
- Technology Management

International headquarter:
European University Montreux
Villa Les Bosquets
1817 Montreux-Fontanivent
Switzerland
email: eurmon@ibm.net

Campuses in Spain:
Barcelona
Ganduxer, 70
08021 Barcelona
Tel: 93 201 81 71
Fax: 93 201 79 35
email: eubcn@bcn.servicom.es

Madrid
Covarrubias, 23
28010 Madrid
Tel: 91 593 41 33
Fax: 91 593 92 32
email: eumadrid@lite.eunet.es

foreign press sections, and a high-standard photography department. Parts of the Rambla Catalunya branch, including the newsstand, stay open till 1am.
Branch: Rambla Catalunya 81 (93 215 27 20).

Fnac

El Triangle, Plaça Catalunya 4 (93 344 18 00). Metro Catalunya/bus all routes to Plaça Catalunya. **Open** *Sept-May* 10am-9.30pm, *May-Sept* 10am-10pm, Mon-Sat. **Credit** AmEx, DC, JCB, MC, V. **Map** D5/**A1**
This French-owned megastore chain has spread ripples throughout the bookselling world in Spain with its huge stocks of titles (with French and English sections) in modern displays at discount prices. As well as books it has CDs, videos, cameras and games and other software, a very international newsstand and a concert ticket desk (*see p216*).
Branch: L'Illa, Avda Diagonal 549 (93 444 59 00).

Happy Books

C/Provença 286 (93 487 30 01). Metro Diagonal/bus 7, 16, 17, 31, 67, 68. **Open** 9.30am-9pm Mon-Sat. **Credit** AmEx, DC, MC, V. **Map** D4
A big selection of art books – many in English – at discount prices. Housed in a beautiful old mansion, it has the added attraction of a patio café (*see p169*).
Branches: C/Pelai 20 (93 317 07 68);
Passeig de Gràcia 77 (93 487 95 71).

Laie Llibreria Café

C/Pau Claris 85 (93 318 17 39). Metro Urquinaona/bus all routes to Plaça Urquinaona. **Open** *bookshop* 10am-9pm Mon-Fri; 10.30am-9pm Sat; *café* 9am-1am Mon-Fri; 10.30am-1am Sat. **Credit** AmEx, DC, MC, V. **Map** D5/**B1**
An internationally-oriented, arts-based 'bookshop-café' with extremely helpful staff and a very imaginative selection of stock. The splendid and relaxing café is on the floor above (*see p169*).

Llibreria Francesa

Passeig de Gràcia 91 (93 215 14 17). Metro Diagonal/bus 7, 16, 17, 22, 24, 28. **Open** 9.30am-2.30pm, 4-8.30pm, Mon-Fri; 9.30am-2pm, 5-8.30pm, Sat. Closed Sat pm July-mid-Sept. **Credit** AmEx, MC, V. **Map** D4
A long-established bookshop with Catalan, Spanish, French and English books.

El Lokal

C/de la Cera 1 bis (93 329 06 43).
Metro Sant Antoni/bus 20, 24, 64, 91. **Open** 5-9pm Mon; 10am-1.30pm, 5-9pm, Tue-Fri; 5-9pm Sat. Closed some days Aug. **No credit cards. Map** C6
More than a bookshop, this anarchists' hideout has over 1,000 titles on anarchism, anti-militarism, history, ecology, feminism and so on. General books are available in the ground-floor *Amanecer* shop, while in the *Distri* section you can find comics, fanzines, magazines, CDs, videos, pins and T-shirts. Cool.

Ras

C/Doctor Dou 10 (93 412 71 99). Metro Catalunya/bus all routes to Plaça Catalunya. **Open** 10.30am-2pm, 4.30-8pm, Tue-Sat. **Credit** AmEx, DC, MC, V. **Map** C5/**A2**

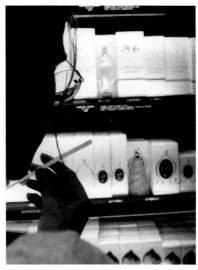

A temple to scent: **Sephora.** *See page 195.*

Opened in 1998, Ras combines a gallery, exhibiting young designers' creations, with a highly stylish bookshop, specialising in recent publications on architecture, photography and design.

Tartessos

C/Canuda 35 (93 301 81 81). Metro Catalunya/bus all routes to Plaça Catalunya. **Open** 10am-2pm, 4.30-8pm, Mon-Sat. **Credit** AmEx, MC, V. **Map** D5/**B2**
Tartessos sells all types of books to survive, but its reason for being is a love of photography, and it has a wonderful range of photographic books from around the world. It also hosts an annual exhibition of work by young Barcelona-based photographers.

Comics

Norma Comics

Passeig de Sant Joan 9 (93 245 45 26).
Metro Arc de Triomf/bus 19, 39, 40, 41, 42, 51, 55, 141. **Open** 10.30am-2pm, 5-8.30pm, Mon-Sat. **Credit** AmEx, MC, V. **Map** E5
The largest comic shop in Barcelona: one floor is dedicated to European and US comics, another to Japanese Manga, and there are special sections for Star Wars, model kits and the like. Next door, Norma has *Tintin Barcelona*, geared exclusively to Hergé's wonderboy. Norma also has a comics gallery.

English-language bookshops

BCN Books

C/Roger de Lluria 118 (93 476 33 43).
Metro Passeig de Gràcia/bus 7, 16, 17, 22, 24, 28. **Open** 9am-2pm, 4-8pm, Mon-Fri; 10am-2pm Sat. **Credit** AmEx, MC, V. **Map** D4

Everything from computer-manuals and teaching materials to the latest best-sellers. BCN also has a big selection of dictionaries and reference books.

Come In

C/Provença 203 (93 453 12 04).
Metro Hospital Clínic, FGC Provença/bus 7, 16, 17, 31, 38, 63, 67, 68. **Open** 10am-2pm, 4.30-8pm, Mon-Sat. Closed Aug. **Credit** MC, V. **Map** C4
Barcelona's largest English bookshop has teaching books and general material, from Chaucer to Joan Collins. Check the notice-board if you're looking for Spanish, Catalan or private English classes.

English Bookshop

C/Entença 63 (93 425 44 66).
Metro Rocafort/bus 9, 27, 50, 56, 109. **Open** 9am-2pm, 4-8pm Mon-Fri; *Sept-June* 10am-1.30pm Sat. Closed three weeks Aug. **Credit** V. **Map** B5
A good stock of educational aids for teacher and student; also, if all you want is a book for the beach, there's also a decent choice of general paperbacks.

Second-hand & rare books

Angel Batlle

C/Palla 23 (93 301 58 84). Metro Liceu/bus 14, 38, 59, 91. **Open** 9am-1.30pm, 4-7.30pm, Mon-Fri. **No credit cards. Map** D6/B2
Despite the old paperbacks in the window, this is a venerable antiquarian bookshop. Inside, there's also an enormous collection of prints (from 2,000ptas).

Travel specialists

Altaïr

C/Balmes 69-71 (93 454 29 66).
Metro Passeig de Gràcia, FGC Provença/bus 7, 16, 17, 63, 67, 68. **Open** 10am-2pm, 4.30-8pm, Mon-Sat. **Credit** AmEx, MC, V. **Map** D4
This travel bookstore publishes an excellent magazine of the same name. It has a fine stock on Catalonia and Spain, plus anthropology, photography, world music, guidebooks and maps. Many titles in English.

Llibreria Quera

C/Petritxol 2 (93 318 07 43). Metro Liceu/bus 14, 38, 59, 91. **Open** 9.30am-1.30pm, 4.30-8pm Mon-Fri; 10am-1.30pm, 5-8pm Sat. **Credit** V. **Map** D6/A2
If you're planning trips to the Catalan countryside and the Pyrenees, this is the ideal place to find good walking maps for every part of the country. Staff also have information on mountaineering and all kinds of outward-bound adventures.

Women

Pròleg

C/Dagueria 13, baixos (93 319 24 25). Metro Jaume I/bus 17, 19, 40, 45. **Open** 5-8pm Mon; 10am-2pm, 5-8pm Tue-Fri; 11am-2pm, 5-8pm Sat. *Aug* 5-8.30pm Mon-Fri. **Credit** MC, V. **Map** D6/B3
Barcelona's only feminist bookshop, Pròleg also organises writing workshops, poetry readings and discussions on literature and cinema.

Children

Clothes

Generally, children's clothes are relatively expensive in Spain. Some adult chains, such as **Zara** (*see page 202*), also have imaginative and quite reasonably priced children's lines.

Cache Cache

C/Valencia 282 (93 215 40 07). Metro Passeig de Gràcia/bus 7, 16, 17, 22, 24, 28. **Open** 10am-8.30pm Mon-Sat. **Credit** V. **Map** D4
Original everyday, casual clothing in natural fibres – mostly cotton – for children aged 0-12. They have 20 shops throughout Barcelona.

Prénatal

Gran Via de les Corts Catalanes 611 (93 302 05 25).
Metro Passeig de Gràcia/bus 7, 16, 17, 22, 24, 28, 50, 54, 56, 67, 68. **Open** 10am-8pm Mon-Sat. **Credit** AmEx, DC, MC, V. **Map** D5
This French-owned chain has everything: good quality prams and pushchairs, cots, feeding bottles, toys, plus clothes for the pregnant mum and for kids up to 8 years old. There are several branches around Barcelona, including a large, central one in **Galeries Maldà** (*see p205*).

Toys

Joguines Foyé

C/Banys Nous 13 (93 302 03 89). Metro Liceu/bus 14, 38, 59, 91. **Open** 10am-2pm, 4.30-8pm, Mon-Fri. **Credit** AmEx, MC, V. **Map** D6/B3
As well as all the usual novelties, Foyé stocks a wonderful collection of tin toys made from original moulds, English and German music boxes, porcelain dolls, furniture for dolls' houses and more oddities. Unusual PVC dolls from eastern Europe are also available.

Joguines Monforte

Plaça Sant Josep Oriol 3 (93 318 22 85). Metro Liceu/bus 14, 38, 59, 91. **Open** 9.30am-1.30pm, 4-8pm, Mon-Sat. **Credit** AmEx, DC, MC, V. **Map** D6/A3
A traditional toy shop that's one of the oldest in Barcelona. The owner tells how she once got rid of 'all those old toys in the back room', only to see them later being sold as valuable antiques.

Cosmetics & perfumes

For **Perfumería Prat**, *see page 197* Little gems.

Regia

Passeig de Gràcia 39 (93 216 01 21).
Metro Passeig de Gràcia/bus 7, 16, 17, 22, 24, 28. **Open** 10am-8.30pm Mon-Fri; 10.30am-2pm, 5-8.30pm, Sat. **Credit** AmEx, DC, JCB, MC, V. **Map** D4
Regia has been serving a very select Barcelona clientele in its main shop and beauty salon on Passeig de Gràcia since 1928. It stocks over 60 types of scent, plus all the best beauty potions, in a world apart where every last detail is attended to. For those inter-

Open all hours

The only fully 24-hour shops in Barcelona are the convenience stores found at many petrol stations (*see page 285*).

Late-night standbys

Depaso *C/Muntaner 14 (93 454 58 46).*
Metro Universitat/bus all routes to Plaça
Universitat. **Open** 6am-2.30am Mon-Thur;
6am-3am Fri-Sun. **Credit** MC, V. **Map** C5
General store for non-sleepers or those in dire
straits. Smaller branches are found at many
petrol stations.
Drugstore David *C/Tuset 19-21*
(93 200 47 30). FCG Gràcia/bus 6, 7, 15, 27,
32, 33, 34. **Open** 7.30am-5am Mon-Sat; 9am-
10pm Sun. **Credit** MC, V. **Map** C3
This pioneer in out-of-hours stores has seen
better days. It now incorporates a tobacco
shop, bookshop, newsstand, and photocopying
service.
7-11 *Plaça Urquinaona (93 318 88 63).*
Metro Urquinaona/bus all routes to Plaça
Urquinaona. **Open** 7am-3am daily. **Credit** MC,
V. **Map** D5/**B1**
The franchise has 50 branches around
Barcelona, many at petrol stations. This is the
most central.
Vip's *Rambla de Catalunya 7-9 (93 317 48*
05). Metro Catalunya/bus all routes to Plaça
Catalunya. **Open** 8am-2am Mon-Thur; 8am-
3am Fri; 9am-3am Sat-Sun. **Credit** AmEx, DC,
$TC, V. **Map** D5/**B1**
Vip's houses a restaurant, a supermarket, a
fairly good bookshop (some books in English), a
newsstand and a toy and gift section.

ested in nasal nostalgia, it also contains the remarkable **Museu del Perfum**, tucked away at the back
of the shop (*see p105*).

Sephora

El Triangle, C/Pelai 13-37 (93 306 39 00).
Metro Catalunya/bus all routes to Plaça Catalunya.
Open 10am-9pm Mon-Sat.
Credit AmEx, MC, V. **Map** D5/**A1**
Truly the most sophisticated of *perfumeries*, this
French mega-shop in the **Triangle** (*see p205*) has
taken Barcelona by storm. The 'perfume street', with
a striking red, black and white colour scheme, occupies almost 2,500 sq m of space in what was once a
dingy underground arcade; all the huge stock is on
display, and you are invited to try out each and
every one, if your sense of smell can stand it.
Shoppers can consult the 'perfume stock market'
wall panel for fluctuating prices of perfumes in capitals around the world, browse through a perfume
and fashion library, or log on to the free Net service.

Crafts & gifts

See also p207 **Art Escudellers**.

Alfar de Arantxa – Ceramica

C/Capellans 3 (93 317 59 41). Metro Jaume I/bus 17,
19, 44, 45. **Open** 10am-2pm, 4-8.30pm, Mon-Sat.
Credit MC, V. **Map** D6/**B2**
Tucked away in a side street opposite the cathedral,
this ceramics shop has an interesting selection ranging from fonts to vases. A great shop for browsing.

Ceràmica Villegas

C/Comtal 31 (93 317 53 30).
Metro Urquinaona/bus 17, 19, 40, 45. **Open**
9.30am-2pm, 4-8.30pm, Mon-Sat. Closed Sat pm July,
Aug. **Credit** AmEx, DC, MC, V. **Map** D5/**B2**
This worldwide distributor of ceramics has everything from one-off art pieces to popular rustic styles,
plus antique water jugs and ceramic jewellery.

Coses de Casa

Plaça Sant Josep Oriol 5 (93 302 73 28). Metro
Liceu/bus 14, 38, 59, 91. **Open** 9.45am-1.30pm, 4.30-
8pm, Mon-Fri; 10am-2pm, 5-8.30pm, Sat. **Credit**
AmEx, DC, MC, V. **Map** D6/**A3**
The rolls of beautiful woven fabric here are traditional, Moorish-influenced Mallorcan work. Cushions, curtains and bedcovers abound, and can be made to order.

2 Bis

C/Bisbe Irurita 2 bis (93 315 09 54). Metro Jaume I/
bus 17, 19, 40, 45. **Open** 10am-2pm, 4.30-8.30pm,
Mon-Fri; 10am-2pm, 5-8.30pm Sat. **Credit** AmEx,
DC, MC, V. **Map** D6/**B3**
Quirky objects for everyone – toys for kids and
adults, tin planes, life-sized Tintin characters, and
lots of other items in wood, paper and papier mâché.

Germanes García

C/Banys Nous 15 (93 318 66 46). Metro Liceu/bus 14,
38, 59, 91. **Open** 4.30-7.30pm Mon; 9.30am-1.30pm,
4.30-7.30pm, Tue-Sat. **Credit** MC, V. **Map** D6/**B3**
There's no name on the shop-front, but it's impossible to miss this wickerwork outlet from the baskets
in the entrance. Inside, there are fruit baskets at
800ptas, laundry baskets for 3,500ptas, and screens
or chests of drawers made in the workshop.

Kitsch

Placeta de Montcada 10 (93 319 57 68). Metro
Jaume I/bus 17, 19, 40, 45. **Open** *Easter* 11am-
3pm, 5-8pm, Tue-Sat; noon-3pm Sun. *Easter-Sept*
11am-3pm, 5-8pm, Mon-Sat; noon-3pm Sun. **Credit**
AmEx, V. **Map** D6/**C3**
Guadalupe Bayona is a lawyer with a passion for papier mâché. Most of her creations are inspired by Klimt,
Botero, Dalí or Picasso, but she also recreates living
personalities. *La Rocío*, a life-sized lady in flamenco
dress who stands at the entrance, is the symbol of the
shop. Prices go from 3,000ptas to 100,000ptas.

Paperona

Plaça Sant Josep Oriol 8 (93 317 15 72). Metro Liceu/
bus 14, 38, 59, 91. **Open** 10am-2pm, 4.30-8.30pm,
Mon-Sat. **Credit** AmEx, DC, MC, V. **Map** D6/**A3**

Little gems

Traditionally, shops in Barcelona kept to a specific trade, and sought to know it well. As a result, the city has an eccentric range of specialists that really is hard to top.

The extraordinary **Herboristeria del Rei**.

Almacenes del Pilar

C/Boqueria 43 (93 317 79 84). Metro Liceu/bus 14, 38, 59, 91. **Open** 10am-2pm, 4.30-8pm, Mon-Sat. **Credit** AmEx, MC, V. **Map** D6/**A3**
This quaint shop exhibits *Mantones de Manila* (fringed and embroidered silk shawls) in its window. Inside there are shawls, *mantillas,* and materials used for traditional costumes in all the regions of Spain. If a red woollen sash is what you've been searching for, look no further.

Aureliano Monge

C/Boters 2 (93 317 94 35). Metro Liceu/bus 14, 38, 59, 91. **Open** 9am-1.30pm, 4-8pm, Mon-Sat. **Credit** AmEx, DC, MC, V. **Map** D6/**B2**
Even if old stamps and coins are not your thing, this *Modernista* shop is worth a look through the window. Designed in 1904 by Calonge, a disciple of Gaudí, it has walls covered in neo-Gothic dark mahogany and four seats that beat classification.

La Casa del Feltre

C/Canvis Vells 8 (93 319 39 00). Metro Jaume I/bus 17, 19, 40, 45. **Open** 9.30am-1.30pm, 4.30-8pm, Mon-Fri; 10am-1.30pm Sat. Closed Aug. **Credit** AmEx, DC, MC, V. **Map** D6/**C4**
A shop that's been selling nothing but felt since 1795, initially mostly for sailors' uniforms. 120 different shades of material can be bought in small squares or by the metre; fancy-dress suits, in felt of course, are on sale from Christmas to Carnival.

Casa Morelli

C/Banys Nous 13 (no phone). Metro Liceu/bus 14, 18, 38, 59. **Open** 5.30-8pm Mon-Fri. Closed Aug. **No credit cards. Map** D6/**B3**
A shop devoted to feathers, wrapped carefully in tissue paper and stored in white cardboard boxes

Develop your fan style: **La Cubana**.

stacked up high around the room. In the window, there are rather dusty but beautifully made feather masks. Take note of the strange opening hours.

Cereria Subirà

Baixada de Llibreteria 7 (93 315 26 06). Metro Jaume I/bus 17, 19, 40, 45. **Open** 9am-1.30pm, 4-7.30pm, Mon-Fri; 9am-1.30pm Sat. **Credit** AmEx, JCB, MC, V. **Map** D6/**B3**
The oldest shop in Barcelona opened in 1761 as a ladies' fashion store, but for many decades has been a candle shop. It's worth a visit for the original décor alone, with steps swirling down from the gallery, and two black maidens holding up torch-like lights at the foot of the stairs.

La Cubana

C/Boqueria 26 (93 317 18 40). Metro Liceu/bus 14, 38, 59, 91. **Open** 9.30am-1.30pm, 4.30-8pm, Mon-Sat. **Credit** AmEx, MC, V. **Map** D6/**A3**
This quaint shop is an institution in the old part of town, where it has supplied ladies with fans, silk shawls, gloves and *mantillas* since 1824. Demand for such things is not what it was, but the shop seems to be holding out in the hope that the fickle winds of fashion might blow back in its direction.

Drap

C/del Pi 14 (tel/fax 93 318 14 87). Metro Liceu/bus 14, 38, 59, 91. **Open** 9.30am-1.30pm, 4.30-8.30pm, Mon-Fri; 10am-1.30pm, 5-8.30pm Sat. **Credit** AmEx, DC, MC, V. **Map** D6/**B2**
The name means rag (dolls), and Drap is the place to find everything related to dolls' houses, with some articles designed and made by owner Maria Elena Admetlla. You can buy a chair for 2,000ptas; an empty house (to your own specifications) is yours for around 50,000ptas.

Herboristeria del Rei

C/del Vidre 1 (93 318 05 12). Metro Liceu/bus 14, 38, 59, 91. **Open** 10am-2pm, 5-8pm, Mon-Sat. **Credit** MC, V. **Map** D6/**A3**
This unique shop was founded in 1818 by Josep Vilà, as *La Lineana*, after the great botanist Linnaeus. It was decorated by the theatre designer Francesc Soler i Rovirosa with an ornate interior, combining a neoclassical structure and Gothic

details. Inside, there is a grand balcony around the shop at second-floor level, while the walls belows are lined with hundreds of tiny specimen drawers all individually worked in marquetry or decorated with miniature watercolours. In 1858 the shop became official herbalist to Queen Isabel II, and changed its name to *Herboristeria del Rei*; it went back to *La Lineana* in the two republican periods. These name changes are still visible in the gold lettering on the door.

El Ingenio

C/Rauric 6 (93 317 71 38).
Metro Liceu/bus 14, 38, 59, 91. **Open** 10am-
1.30pm, 4.15-8pm, Mon-Fri; 10am-2pm, 5-8.15pm,
Sat. **Credit** MC, V. **Map** D6/A3
Ingenio lives up to its name with a truly ingenious collection of paper, cardboard, feather and papier mâché masks and party accessories. There are fancy-dress outfits, carnival clothes, decorations, puppets, tricks and jokes to choose from. Stick-on Dalí moustaches are 200ptas each, and can be twisted into exactly the right shape. The shop, naturally, does booming business at Carnival time.

Merceria i Novetats
– Manel Mogas Puig

C/Llibreteria 5 (93 310 57 46).
Metro Jaume I/bus 17, 19, 40, 45. **Open** 9.30am-
1.30pm, 4.30-8pm, Mon-Fri; 10am-2pm Sat. **No
credit cards. Map** D6/B3
Buttons, lace, tassels and all you might need for sewing, embroidering or decorating in a beautiful old shop by the Ajuntament. The owner seems to sit for hours presiding over the cash register.

Perfumeria Prat

*La Rambla 68 (93 317 71 39). Metro Liceu/bus
14, 38, 59, 91.* **Open** 10am-2pm, 4-8.30pm, Mon-
Sat. **Credit** AmEx, DC, MC, V. **Map** D6/A3
This beautiful perfumery, which until 1997 occupied part of the Liceu building, has been transported pillar by pillar to a new site across the Rambla. This undertaking was justified by its history: the first *perfumeria* established in all Spain, by a certain Renaud Germain in 1847. Its owners never rested on their laurels, and today it continues to thrive, with a fine selection of perfumes and cosmetics.

El Rei de la Màgia

C/Princesa 11 (93 319 39 20).
Metro Liceu/bus 14, 38, 59, 91.
Open 10am-2pm, 5-8pm, Mon-Fri; 10am-2pm Sat.
Credit MC, V. **Map** D6/B-C3
Many a magician's training ground, founded in 1881, this is anything but an ordinary retail outlet. The decoration forms a small stage with a delicately carved counter, behind which is a theatrical black curtain. Walls are covered with autographed photos of magicians. There are no pre-established prices and one doesn't go there to buy a specific item, but rather to develop an idea or concept that might require the use of a special chair, box or mechanism,

Panama-browsing at **Sombreria Obach.**

specially made for the purpose. Ritual is perhaps the key to describing the way everything happens here.

San-Do

C/Cardenal Casañas 5 (93 302 64 33).
Metro Liceu/bus 14, 38, 59, 91. **Open** 10.30am-
2.30pm, 4.30-8.30pm, Mon-Sat. **Credit** AmEx, DC,
MC, V. **Map** D6/A3
Perhaps the smallest shop in Barcelona with the broadest range in different styles of jewellery, from the most traditional pieces in gold, to original designs in silver, some by the owner himself. Small silver boxes for collectors are also available.

Solingen Paris-Barcelona
(Ganiveteria Roca SA)

*Plaça del Pi 3 (93 302 12 41). Metro Liceu/bus 14,
38, 59, 91.* **Open** 9.45am-1.30pm, 4.15-8pm, Mon-
Fri; 10am-2pm, 5-8pm, Sat. Closed two weeks Aug.
Credit AmEx, DC, MC, V. **Map** D6/A2-3
Every cutting instrument under the sun is available here. Knives and scissors for all thinkable purposes, and of all shapes and sizes, are wrapped in green felt and brought forth for inspection by sombre salesmen. Seriously weird.

Sombreria Obach

*C/Call 2 (93 318 40 94). Metro Liceu/bus 14, 38,
59, 91.* **Open** 9.30am-1.30pm, 4-8pm, Mon-Sat.
Closed Sat pm Aug. **Credit** MC, V. **Map** D6/B3
Hats of all varieties, from nylon pom-poms through top-quality felt berets, to formal headgear for men and women.

Vidrieria Grau

C/Vidrieria 6-8 (93 319 40 46).
Metro Jaume I/bus 17, 19, 40, 45. **Open** 9.30am-
1.30pm, 4-8pm, Mon-Fri; 9.30am-1.30pm Sat. **No
credit cards. Map** D6/C4
Behind a façade that looks like a Dickensian old curiosity shop, this is the last *vidrieria*, glass merchant, in the medieval street of *vidrieries*. It was founded in 1837, and is all-but unchanged since. The charming fifth generation of the Grau family, now in charge, can supply a huge variety of bottles, wine glasses, flasks, vases and more, in all sizes – only a small selection is on show on the (very) dusty shelves. Glass items can also be made to order.

Another papier-mâché enthusiast, shopowner Abel offers a curious selection of objects. Choose a Gaudi-inspired shoe for 3,900ptas, or, for a bit more, a Dalí clock. Articles from 1,500ptas to 100,000ptas.

Taller de Marionetas Travi

C/Amargós 4 (93 412 66 92/93 325 46 55).
Metro Urquinaona/bus 17, 19, 40, 45. **Open** 10am-2pm, 4-8.30pm, Mon-Sat. **Map** D5/**B2**
Entering the puppet workshop of Teresa Travieso (whose surname means naughty) is like going back into a world of fantasy and childhood. Hand-made puppets cost from 35,000ptas to 200,000ptas. Opening hours are very unpredictable.

Design/household

Aspectos

C/Rec 28 (93 319 52 85). Metro Jaume I/bus 14, 39, 51. **Open** 4.30-8pm Mon-Fri; 10.30am-2pm Sat. Closed Aug. **Credit** MC, V. **Map** E6/**C3**
A prestigious shop housing work by international furniture and product designers such as Mendini, Kima, Garouste-Bonetti, Lowenstein or Josep Cerdà. It also showcases work by young unknowns.

BD Ediciones de Diseño

Casa Thomas, C/Mallorca 291 (93 458 69 09).
Metro Passeig de Gràcia/bus 20, 39, 43, 44, 45, 47.
Open 10am-2pm, 4-8pm, Mon-Fri; 10am-2pm, 4.30-8pm, Sat. **Credit** AmEx, DC, MC, V. **Map** D4
One of the institutions of Barcelona's design world, BD stocks a sleekly impressive array of (reproduction) furniture by design gurus such as Macintosh and Gaudi, as well as more contemporary designers – Ricard Bofill, Mariscal, Oscar Tusquets – and objects by the Memphis group, Owo and others. The magnificent *Modernista* house, by Domènech i Montaner (*see p77*), is well worth wandering round, even if you can't afford so much as a chair leg.

Dom

Passeig. de Gràcia 76 (93 487 11 81).
Metro Passeig de Gràcia/bus 7, 16, 17, 22, 24, 28.
Open 10am-2pm, 4.30-8pm, Mon-Fri; 10.30am-9pm Sat. **Credit** DC, MC, V. **Map** D4
A fun place to pick up those essential decorative items such as inflatable plastic sofas and a string of blue, fish-shaped lights. Prices are reasonable.
Branch: C/Petritxol 14 (93 318 56 23).

Dos i Una

C/Rosselló 275 (93 217 70 32).
Metro Diagonal/bus 7, 16, 17, 22, 24, 28.
Open 10.30am-2pm, 4.30-8.30pm, Mon-Sat. **Credit** AmEx, DC, JCB, MC, V. **Map** D4
The first design shop in Barcelona (in 1977), and an early patron of Mariscal, Dos i Una has grown up into a high-class gift shop, selling designer crockery, wacky lamps, postcards, earrings and T-shirts.

Gema Povo

C/Banys Nous 5 (93 301 34 76). Metro Liceu/bus 14, 38, 59, 91. **Open** 10am-1.30pm, 4.30-8pm, Mon-Sat. **Credit** AmEx, DC, MC, V. **Map** D6/**B3**

A family-run, artisan shop specialising in beautiful wrought-iron lamps and bedsteads, all designed by the owner. She also sells Mallorcan glass vases, and rustic tables. Well worth a browse.

Gotham

C/Cervantes 7 (93 412 46 47). Metro Jaume I/bus 17, 40, 45. **Open** 10.30am-2pm, 5-8.30pm, Mon-Sat. **Credit** AmEx, DC, MC, V. **Map** D6/**B3**
On a corner of Plaça Sant Miquel, behind the Ajuntament, this hip, off-the-wall shop has a highly original exterior. A second glance reveals that most of its great range of furniture is from the 1930s and '40s, while accessories – lamps, vases, glassware – hail from the '50s or '60s, and there are also completely new, up-to-the-minute items. The owners are interior designers, and can undertake restorations.

Ici et Là

Plaça Santa Maria del Mar 2 (93 268 11 67).
Metro Jaume I/bus 17, 19, 40, 45. **Open** 4.30-8.30pm Mon; 10.30am-2.30pm, 4.30-8.30pm, Tue-Sat. **Credit** MC, V. **Map** D6/**C3-4**
The brainchild of three women – two French, one Spanish – who believe that original furniture and accessories shouldn't be limited to the well-heeled. Wacky ethnic objects and striking contemporary creations are sourced from Barcelona, Europe and the world, and sold at deliberately reasonable prices.

Insòlit

Avda Diagonal 353 (93 207 49 19). Metro Verdaguer/bus 6, 15, 33, 34. **Open** 10am-1.30pm, 4.30-8pm, Mon-Fri; 11am-2pm, 5-8pm, Sat. Closed Aug. **Credit** AmEx, DC, MC, V. **Map** D4
One of few shops to stock entirely original work, since most of the owners' own witty designs are sold only through this outlet. Pick up a star-shaped table in wood and iron for 20,000ptas, or tableware, bizarre lamps and colourful kitsch furniture.

Matarile

Passeig del Born 24 (93 315 02 20). Metro Jaume I/bus 14, 39, 51. **Open** 5-8.30pm Mon, Sat; 9am-2pm, 5-8.30pm, Tue-Fri. **No credit cards**. **Map** D-E6/**C3**
Owner Mauricio sells his own lamps and other light objects. He uses unusual materials, recycled and otherwise, and has some restored lamps from the 1970s.

Vinçon

Passeig de Gràcia 96 (93 215 60 50).
Metro Diagonal/ bus 7, 16, 17, 22, 24, 28. **Open** 10am-2pm, 4.30-8.30pm, Mon-Sat. **Credit** AmEx, JCB, MC, V. **Map** D4
Barcelona's most renowned design palace, with everything for the home down to the smallest accessory. You may find the superbly extravagant furniture a tad expensive, but the lighting, kitchen, bathroom and fabric departments offer affordable alternatives. Each December Vinçon hosts **Hipermerc'art**, an 'art supermarket' where astute buyers can pick up originals by young artists for as little as 9,000ptas. There is a feeling that as it has expanded and become steadily more 'corporate' Vinçon has also become steadily less innovative, but

it's still an attractive place to browse, and for art and architecture buffs there's the consolation that the upper floor is the former apartment of Santiago Rusiñol, one of the greatest *Modernista* artists.

Fashion

Designers

Adolfo Domínguez

Passeig de Gràcia 32 (93 487 41 70). Metro Passeig de Gràcia /bus 7, 16, 17, 22, 24, 28. **Open** 10am-8.30pm Mon-Sat. **Credit** AmEx, DC, MC, V. **Map** D5
One of the foremost names in Spanish fashion, Galician Adolfo Domínguez deserves his reputation as a designer of well-made, timeless clothes for men and women, usually in stylishly austere colours. **Branches**: Avda Diagonal 490 (93 416 17 16); Avda Pau Casals 5 (93 414 11 77); Passeig de Gràcia 89 (93 215 13 39).

Armand Basi

Passeig de Gràcia 49 (93 215 14 21). Metro Passeig de Gràcia/bus 7, 16, 17, 22, 24, 28. **Open** 10am-8.30pm Mon-Sat. **Credit** AmEx, DC, JCB, MC, V. **Map** D4
The flagship shop of this ultra-hip Spanish designer is suitably in the centre of things, and is the only place in town where you can find everything in his men's and women's collections, from body-hugging shirts to more timeless suits, classic knitwear, evening dresses and a wide variety of accessories.

David Valls

C/València 235 (93 487 12 85). Metro Passeig de Gràcia/bus 7, 16, 17, 20, 43, 44, 63, 67, 68. **Open** 10am-2pm, 5-8.30pm, Mon-Fri; 10.30am-2pm, 5-8.30pm, Sat. **Credit** AmEx, DC, MC, V. **Map** D4
David Valls produces original upmarket knitwear for new bohemians, using the latest technology to create unique textures and fabrics. His shop has an extensive collection for women – the dresses are really special – and stylish yet classic sweaters for men.

Museum shopping

Barcelona's museums are becoming ever more enterprising, and several have installed interesting shops that are great places to find unusual gifts and souvenirs. Some star museum shops are listed here; for the museums, *see pages 90-105*. Slightly similar ranges can be found in **Botiga de la Virreina** (*see page 191*) and **Botiga BCN**, attached to the Plaça Catalunya tourist office (*see page 294*).

Botiga Tèxtil

C/Montcada 12 (93 310 74 03). Metro Jaume I/bus 17, 19, 40, 45. **Open** 10am-8.30pm Tue-Sat; 10am-3pm Sun. **Credit** AmEx, DC, MC, V. **Map** D6/**C3**
The **Museu Tèxtil** led the way with its attractive café (*see p166*), and also has one of the best museum shops, a pleasant change from the standard Dalí/Miró/Picasso mug shop. Instead, there are items related to the world of fashion and textiles: designer sweaters (around 16,000ptas), collector's sewing thimbles (1,500ptas), miniature period shoes in ceramics (2,000ptas) and great throws and original textiles by local designers (at good prices). Plus there is also some more of the omnipresent silver designer jewellery.

CCCB

C/Montalegre 5 (93 481 38 86). Metro Catalunya/bus all routes to Plaça Catalunya. **Open** 11am-8pm Tue-Sat; 11am-7pm Sun. **Credit** DC, MC, V. **Map** C5/**A1**
More of a straight bookshop (run by **Laie**, *see p193*) than a souvenir store, but it has an unbeatable selection of books on every kind of urban-related topic, with many titles in English, French and other languages. Plus there are a few T-shirts, diaries and so on. *See also chapter* **Art Galleries**.

MACBA

Plaça dels Angels 1 (93 412 59 08). Metro Catalunya/bus all routes to Plaça Catalunya. **Open** 11am-8pm Mon, Wed-Sat; 10.30am-3pm Sun, public holidays. **Credit** AmEx, MC, V. **Map** C5/**A1**
The bright, white MACBA shop has artist-made items like wacky cups by Ana & Rita (2,300ptas each), many nick-nacky pieces, and original artwork, including signed lithographs by Guinovart (28,000ptas) or Tàpies (300,000ptas) and fine work by young unknowns at very accessible prices. Also occasional shows by young artists, and art books.

Les Muses del Palau

C/Sant Pere Més Alt 1 (93 268 31 95) Metro Urquinaona/bus 17, 19, 40, 45. **Open** 9.30am-8.30pm Mon-Sat; 9.30am-3.30pm Sun. **Credit** AmEx, MC, V. **Map** D5/**B2**
Not a museum shop as such but a gift shop attached to the **Palau de la Música** (*see p67*), although in a separate building. It's a tasteful shop with a sophisticated selection of porcelain, crystal and glassware, some Gaudí inspired, plus silk scarves and silver-plated miniature musical instruments.

Museu d'Arqueologia de Catalunya

Passeig de Santa Madrona 39-41 (93 423 21 49). Metro Poble Sec/bus 55. **Open** 9.30am-7pm Tue-Sat; 10am-2.30pm Sun. **No credit cards. Map** B6
An interesting place to pick up something different: reproductions of Iberian jewellery, Visigothic ceramics and Roman glass vases for anything from 1,500 to 5,000ptas. Tin soldiers are sold for 800ptas.

Giménez y Zuazo
C/Elisabets 20 (93 223 26 84). Metro Catalunya/bus all routes to Plaça Catalunya. **Open** 10.30am-2pm, 5-8:30pm, Mon-Sat. **Credit** MC, V. **Map** C5/A2
This duo won a national competition for young Spanish designers back in 1984, and since then have supplied their limited-edition lines for women to many outlets. They now have their own shop in the Raval. Fabric is the essential starting point of their garments: designs mix and play with different textures, using clean cuts and surprising, original details.

Groc
Rambla Catalunya 100 (93 215 01 80). Metro Diagonal/FGC Provença/bus 7, 16, 17, 20, 22, 24, 28, 43, 44. **Open** 10am-8.30pm Mon-Sat. **Credit** AmEx, JCB, MC, V. **Map** D4
Groc is the place to find men's and women's clothing by one of the most admired of current Catalan designers, Toni Miró. His clothes are designed with a very distinctive flair, in irresistible materials.

Shoes by Miró and jewellery by Chelo Sastre also feature in the range.
Branch: C/Muntaner 385 (93 202 30 77).

Jean-Pierre Bua
Avda Diagonal 469 (93 439 71 00). Bus 6, 7, 15, 33, 34. **Open** 10am-2pm, 4.30-8.30pm, Mon-Sat. **Credit** AmEx, DC, MC, V. **Map** C3
The first, and for many years, the only Barcelona shop to sell avant-garde international designer fashion. Enjoy exclusive selections from Dries van Noten, Yohji Yamamoto and personal friend Jean-Paul Gaultier: this is also the place to go for truly modern bridalwear. Luis and Adolfo make everyone welcome, and it's worth checking for special sales.

Josep Font
Passeig de Gràcia 106 (93 415 65 50). Metro Diagonal/bus 22, 24, 28, 100, 101. **Open** 10am-8.30pm Mon-Sat. **Credit** AmEx, MC, V. **Map** D4
The Mediterranean influence in Josep Font's designs is evident as soon as you walk through the door of

The textile route

The old city of Barcelona, and above all **La Ribera**, was a centre of weaving and textile trades for centuries (*see also page 66*). In the last few years the city authorities have sought to revive this identification by encouraging young designer-makers to move into the area's old workshops. A free guided tour or 'Textile itinerary' of the textile workshops of the Ciutat Vella is available, on the second Saturday of every month, beginning at the district office in Plaça Bonsuccès 3 (**Map** D5/A2) and ending at the **Museu Tèxtil**. A free leaflet with a map and workshop addresses is also available from the museum (note, though, that workshops may not keep consistent hours).

There are workshops all around the Ciutat Vella, but the largest concentration is in La Ribera, especially around **C/Banys Vells**, which runs parallel to C/Montcada (**Map** D6/C3). At **Tela Marinera** at No.5 (93 310 21 34), Olga López produces very attractively original cushions, tablecloths and other items in hand-printed and painted cotton; **Otman**, C/Banys Vells 21 bis (93 319 29 34), is a Moroccan-run shop with unusual, light cotton clothing that's wonderful for a Mediterranean summer. On C/Barra de Ferro, the **Taller Barra de Ferro** (No.8, no phone) is a specialist in lace-making, while **Cocon**, close by at C/Cotoners 8 (93 319 11 79) sells fine Japanese textiles. More original is **L'Intrús**, at No.1 on C/Esquirol (93 310 34 70), a turning off Cotoners, which has strikingly attractive knitwear.

Some workshops are occupied by makers in other fields: **Amulet**, also at C/Esquirol 1 (93 319 26 05) has silver jewellery; **Javier Ubeda**, at

C/Brosoli 3, baixos (93 310 56 65), produces 'useful art', sculptural lamps and other objects in a variety of metals. There are also some textile designers a little further from Banys Vells, notably **Rafael Teja**, at C/Santa Maria 18 (93 310 27 85), by Santa Maria del Mar. He has beautiful hand-printed silk *foulards* and other scarves, from 3,000-15,000ptas. Across Via Laietana at C/Nou de Sant Francesc 17 (93 412 52 67), **Nina Pawlowsky** makes very cool original hats. Overall, the standard of work is very high; prices are reasonable. In addition, of course, workshop-browsing is one more way to explore the charms of La Ribera.

this attractive shop. Particularly outstanding are his minimalist designs in pale colours for women's day suits and evening dresses.

Noténom

C/Pau Claris 159 (93 487 60 84).
Metro Passeig de Gràcia/bus 22, 24, 28, 39, 43, 44, 45. **Open** 4.30-8.30pm Mon; 10.30am-2pm, 4.30-8.30pm, Tue-Sat. **Credit** AmEx, DC, MC, V. **Map** D4
Noténom ('It has no name') is a focal point for all the newest trends and lines, selected from around the world (labels such as Exté, NN Studio, So and D2). The two-level store sells men's and women's wear, and a selection of fashion jewellery and accessories.

Designer bargains

Contribuciones

C/Riera de Sant Miquel 30 (93 218 71 40).
Metro Diagonal/bus 6, 7, 15, 16, 17, 22, 24, 28, 33, 34. **Open** 11am-2pm, 5-9pm, Mon-Sat. **Credit** AmEx, DC, MC, V. **Map** D3
Labels vary according to what's available, but the great bonus-point of this spacious fashion store is that everything is sold at half-price. The in-house designer, Miguel de Otos, also creates a wonderful range of reasonably-priced silks.

Preu Bo

C/Comtal 22 (93 318 03 31).
Metro Urquinaona/bus 17, 19, 40, 45. **Open** 10am-8.30pm Mon-Fri; 10.30am-9pm Sat. **Credit** AmEx, DC, MC, V. **Map** D5/**B2**
For designer clothes Preu Bo ('good price') lives up to names, with up to 65% off end-of-lines by Roberto Verinno, Jordi Cuesta, Purificación García, Joaquim Verdú, María Encarnación and C'est Comme Ça. The staff are very friendly, too.
Branches: C/Balmes 308 (93 414 44 57); C/Craywinckel 5 (93 418 81 74).

Fashion malls

Galeries of individual small shops sprouted apace during the 1980s, some occupying the interiors of whole Eixample blocks, and have stayed among the most popular places for fashion browsing.

Bulevard Rosa

Passeig de Gràcia 55 (93 309 06 50).
Metro Passeig de Gràcia/bus 7, 16, 17, 22, 24, 28.
Open 10.30am-8.30pm Mon-Sat. **Map** D4
A major 1980s success story, this arcade began the *galeria* boom and has attracted some of the most interesting designers of clothes, shoes and jewellery. It has more than 100 shops, including both luxury and more casual outlets for men and women. The Diagonal branch is classier still.
Branch: Avda Diagonal 474 (93 412 32 72).

Gralla Hall

C/Portaferrissa 25 (93 412 32 72).
Metro Liceu/bus 14, 38, 59, 91. **Open** *mall* 9am-8.30pm, *shops* 10.30am-8.30pm (some close 2.30-4.30pm), Mon-Sat. **Map** D6/**B2**

In the middle of the Portaferrissa shopping area, the Gralla is one of Barcelona's favourite places for club-wear and street fashion. For (relatively) expensive club fashion, **Fantasy** and **Loft Avignon** are two of the best in town; **Club** is home to two local talents – you won't find the same design twice. Young clubbers get ready for Saturday night in **Mayday**.

El Mercadillo

C/Portaferrissa 17 (93 301 89 13).
Metro Liceu/bus 14, 38, 59, 91. **Open** 11am-9pm Mon-Sat. **Credit** EC, MC, V. **Map** D6/**B2**
Neon lights and a life-sized fibre-glass camel mean it's hard to miss the entrance to Barcelona's grungier fashion mall. Clothes include PVC jackets, Goth jewellery, tie-dyed jeans, lacy bodices, suede thigh-length boots and nylon bomber jackets. The wonderful bar at the back opens onto an old patio.

Unstoppable chains

Mango

Passeig de Gràcia 65 (93 215 75 30). Metro Passeig de Gràcia/bus 7, 16, 17, 22, 24, 28. **Open** 10.15am-8.30pm Mon-Sat. **Credit** AmEx, DC, JCB, MC, V. **Map** D4
Since its first opening in Barcelona in 1984, Mango has extended into more than 400 branches world-wide, and has become a point of reference for young modern urban women. Well-designed clothes in good-quality fabrics reflect innovative trends at reasonable prices, with ranges for work, free time and party wear. Several branches around Barcelona.

Zara

C/Pelai 58 (93 301 09 78). Metro Catalunya/bus all routes to Plaça Catalunya. **Open** 10am-9pm Mon-Sat. **Credit** AmEx, DC, MC, V. **Map** D5/**A1**
Lately, fashion-watchers and shoppers alike in other countries have become aware of the qualities of Zara, now a real international empire with 200 shops in 17 countries. The secret to its success is a simple, functional formula of reasonable prices, intelligent copies of top designs and an unbelievable capacity to react to changes in consumer taste, enabling them to draw in a clientele running from the very-hip-conscious to those just looking for good, wearable clothes. Several branches around Barcelona.

Street style & second-hand

Most street fashion shops are around C/Portaferrissa and other streets near the Rambla. Malls like **El Mercadillo** and **Gralla Hall** (*see above*) offer a good choice, and C/Avinyó is worth a look to find work by young local designers. In the last couple of years, also, **C/Riera Baixa**, in the heart of the Raval, has become *the* new centre for small, innovative style shops in Barcelona.

An interesting batch of striking second-hand and recycling shops have opened up, several, again, in the Riera Baixa. It's also worth checking out **Els Encants** market (*see p212*), for old and new objects, and some vintage clothes stalls.

Bad Habits

C/Valencia 261 baixos (93 487 22 59).
Metro Passeig de Gràcia/bus 20, 22, 24, 28, 43, 44.
Open 10.30am-3pm, 4.30-8.30pm, Mon-Sat.
Credit AmEx, DC, MC, V. **Map** D4
Mireia Ruiz has always been at the cutting-edge of
the local fashion scene with her label 'Bad Habits'.
She has now opened a shop with the same name and
philosophy: individual, tasteful, comfortable, flexi-
ble – a chic and classy look with a sexy twist. The
shop also stocks shoes by Dorotea for Toni Miró.

Halleluiah

Gran Via de les Corts Catalanes 551 (93 454 26 90).
Metro Urgell/bus 9, 50, 56. **Open** 10.30am-2pm, 5-
9pm, Tue-Fri; 11am-2pm, 5-9pm, Mon, Sat.
Credit AmEx, DC, MC, V. **Map** C5
This shop in the *Gaixample* sells owner-designers
Marco and Alex's own Mark'o and Halleluiah labels.
They're always in search of new international
names, too, and try to stock hip street fashion for
men and women not found anywhere else in the city.

Ho la la

C/Carme 72 (93 441 99 94).
Metro Liceu/bus 14, 38, 59, 91. **Open** 11am-2pm, 5-
9pm, Mon-Sat. Closed some days Aug.
Credit AmEx, DC, JCB, MC, V. **Map** C6
Ibiza favourite Ho la la stocks vintage jeans and
leather jackets, combat trousers, flowery dresses,
hippie shirts and even Indian or Moroccan stuff, plus
scarves, bags and other accessories. Always good
bargains in the 500 and 1,000ptas baskets.
Branch: C/Portaferrissa 17 (no phone).

The Riera Baixa

C/Riera Baixa.
Metro Liceu/bus 14, 20, 38, 59, 64, 91. **Map** C6
This little street has become home to a clutch of
interesting small fashion, music and unclassifiable
shops. This is where you'll find the hottest trends
and the best second-hand bargains, together with
antiques, records, tattoos and piercings, dance
accessories and other urban styles. Going up from
the C/Hospital end, **Cyborg** at No.4 (93 442 66 79)
has techno-inspired street- and clubwear collections,
and **@WC**, Nos.4-6 (93 443 90 11) offers a truly continental selection of sleek new clubwear from Spain,
France, the UK, Italy and further afield. At No.13,
Recicla Recicla (93 443 18 15) has a great selection of second-hand clothing, with around 150 new
pieces each week, including vintage party dresses,
shoes, jewellery and even furniture. The tiny
Triplicat, at No.18 (629 61 07 99) has cute printed
T-shirts, and **Lailo**, No.20 (93 441 37 49), is a delight-
fully quirky second-hand store with everything from
recent designer labels (in perfect condition) to 1920s
or 1960s cocktail dresses and, a speciality, groovy
1970s ski suits. Another speciality of the street is
music shops, with **Edison's** (*see p212*) and others.
Most shops are open roughly 11am-2pm, 5-9pm,
Mon-Sat. In addition, a **Mercat Alternatiu** or
'alternative street market' of fashion, second-hands
and other things is also held in the street, every

Beautiful bargains at Port Vell. See page 212.

Saturday from May to September and in December,
and on the first Saturday of every other month from
October to April.

Tribu

C/Avinyó 12 (93 318 65 10). Metro Jaume I/bus 17,
19, 40, 45. **Open** 10.30am-2pm, 4.30-8.30pm, Mon-
Sat. **Credit** AmEx, DC, MC, V. **Map** D6/**B3**
More than just a fashion store, Tribu is the hippest
place for modern urban trendies to shop. Clothes for
both sexes come from a range of fresh international
and local labels including work by ever-popular
Paulinha Rio. The shop hosts art shows, and local
DJs take turns at the decks on Saturdays.

Zsu-Zsu

C/Avinyó 50 (93 412 49 65). Metro Jaume I/bus 17,
19, 40, 45. **Open** *Sept-June* 11am-2pm, 5-8.30pm,
Mon-Sat. *July-Aug* 5.30-9pm Mon; 11am-2pm, 5.30-
9pm, Tue-Sat. **Credit** AmEx, MC, V. **Map** D6/**B4**
Original, well-designed clothes for younger women,
mainly one-off pieces – especially knitwear. Also a
small but choice selection by young designers.

Fashion accessories
Jewellery

Forum Ferlandina

C/Ferlandina 31 (93 441 80 18). Metro
Universitat/ bus 24, 41, 55, 64, 91, 141. **Open**
10.30am-2pm, 5-8.30pm, Tue-Sat. **Credit** AmEx,
MC, V. **Map** C5

Near the MACBA, this space features all styles of contemporary jewellery. It has exclusively-designed pieces in materials from precious stones to plastic; there are also exhibits by leading jewellery artists.

Hipòtesi
Rambla Catalunya 105 (93 215 02 98).
FGC Provença/bus 7, 16, 17, 20, 22, 24, 28, 43, 44.
Open 10am-1.30pm, 5-8.30pm, Mon-Sat. **Credit** AmEx, DC, MC, V. **Map** D4
A wonderful place to see fine original gold and silver jewellery, and striking costume pieces by Spanish and foreign designers.

Joaquín Berao
C/Rosselló 277 (93 218 61 87).
Metro Diagonal/bus 7, 16, 17, 22, 24, 28. Open 10.15am-2pm, 5-8.30pm, daily. Closed Sat pm Aug. **Credit** AmEx, DC, MC, V. **Map** D4
One of the most avant-garde jewellery designers in Barcelona, Berao works with titanium, aged bronze, gold and silver. Not cheap, but very beautiful.

Magari
C/Horaci 20 (93 418 88 10). Bus 22, 64, 75.
Open 10.30am-2pm Tue-Sat; 5-9pm Tue-Thur. Closed some days Aug. **No credit cards.**
Less a shop than a jewellery gallery, Magari, in a distinctly upmarket location near Tibidabo, has a permanent collection of original and exclusive pieces and hosts exhibitions of international jewellery.

Leather & luggage

There is a clutch of relatively inexpensive shops along C/Ferran that sell all sorts of leather bags, cases, belts and purses.

Calpa
C/Ferran 53/Call 22 (93 318 40 30).
Metro Liceu/bus 14, 38, 59, 91. **Open** 9.30am-8pm Mon-Fri; 10am-2pm, 5-8.30pm, Sat. **Credit** AmEx, DC, JCB, MC, V. **Map** D6/**B3**
Bags for every taste, from 3,000ptas carry-alls to beautifully finished leather cases for 30,000ptas.
Branch: C/del Pi 5 (93 412 58 22).

Casa Antich SCP
C/Consolat del Mar 27-31 (93 310 43 91). Metro Jaume I/bus 17, 19, 40, 45. **Open** 9am-8pm Mon-Sat. **Credit** AmEx, DC, MC, V. **Map** D6/**B4**
This part of the Ribera has dealt in luggage for centuries, and family-owned Antich is one of a clutch of shops that keeps up the tradition, with a vast range of bags, briefcases, suitcases and enormous metal trunks at reasonable prices. If they haven't got what you want, they'll make it for you.

Loewe
Passeig de Gràcia 35 (93 216 04 00).
Metro Passeig de Gràcia/bus 7, 16, 17, 22, 24, 28. **Open** 9.30am-2pm, 4.30-8pm, Mon-Sat. **Credit** AmEx, DC, JCB, MC, TC, V. **Map** D5
The celebrated leather company Loewe has its main Barcelona store in the Casa Morera in the **Mansana de la Discòrdia** (*see p80*). Inside there are high-

priced bags, suitcases, scarves and other accessories of superb quality. Some foreign currencies accepted. **Branches**: Avda Diagonal 570 (93 200 09 20); C/Johann Sebastian Bach 8 (93 202 31 50).

Lingerie & underwear

Casa Ciutad
Avda Portal de l'Àngel 14 (93 317 04 33).
Metro Catalunya/bus all routes to Plaça Catalunya. **Open** 10am-8.30pm Mon-Fri; 10.30am-9pm Sat. **Credit** AmEx, DC, MC, V. **Map** D5-6/**B2**
This charming shop opened in 1892, and sells some of the prettiest women's underwear you can find. The sign at the door says 'manufacturers of combs and articles for the dressing-table'; its collection of combs is something to behold. Opening times vary.

Janina
Rambla Catalunya 94 (93 215 04 21).
Metro Diagonal, FGC Provença/bus 22, 24, 28. **Open** 10am-8.30pm Mon-Sat.
Credit AmEx, DC, MC, V. **Map** D4
A well-established shop that sells its own exclusive silk and satin underwear, nightwear and robes, as well as stockings by Risk and La Perla. A big selection of swimsuits and bikinis is also available.

WC – Susana Riera
C/Avinyó 21 (no phone). Metro Jaume I/bus 17, 40, 45. **Open** 5-8.30pm Mon; 10.30am-2pm, 5-8pm, Tue-Sat. **No credit cards. Map** D6/**B3**
Susi and best mate Raul C are the moving spirits behind this tiny shop selling Susana Riera's pretty, trendy cotton underwear and women's swimwear.

Scarves & textiles
See also page 201 **The textile route**.

Almazul
C/Amargós 15 (93 412 20 45/93 430 01 21).
Metro Urquinaona/bus 17, 19, 40, 45. **Open** 10am-2pm, 4.30-8.30pm, Mon-Sat. **Credit** AmEx, DC, MC, V. **Map** D5/**B2**
Violeta, the owner of this shop near Portal de l'Angel, sells anything from scarves to cushions and rugs, all hand-made from beautiful natural fibres and dyes, and all exquisitely simple but elegant.

Entretelas
Plaça Vicenç Martorell 1 (93 317 76 14/93 318 84 18). Metro Catalunya/bus all routes to Plaça Catalunya. **Open** 10am-2pm, 5-8pm, Mon-Sat. *Aug* Sat only. **Credit** MC, V. **Map** D5/**A1-2**
This small workshop and shop specialises in beautiful and imaginative printed fabrics for the home, accessories with a markedly personal stamp, and an irresistible collection of hand-painted baby clothes.

Shoes

The most traditional Catalan shoe (*espardenyes/ alpargatas*) is a type of espadrille with ribbons attached. It's now used as leisurewear, and by performers of the *sardana* (*see page 10*).

Mall cruising

Although Barcelona acquired its first everything-under-one-roof space as early as 1942, the **Galerias Maldà**, the city was slow to pick up on the idea. In the 1990s it has certainly caught up, as modest local fashion *galeries* have been followed by seriously huge malls at either end of the Diagonal. *See also page 190* **Sunday opening**.

Barcelona Glòries

Avda Diagonal 208 (93 486 04 04).
Metro Glòries/bus 7, 56, 60, 92.
Open *shops* 10am-10pm Mon-Sat.
The largest shopping centre in Spain – a huge, drive-in mall with over 200 shops, including international names such as C&A and Dr Marten's. Located by the Plaça de les Glòries, near **Els Encants** (*see p212*), it's built around an open-air plaça with bars, restaurants and a multiplex cinema. The mall has good coffee shops, and quite high-quality stores specialising in Spanish ham and other food products. For cut-price produce, there's also a hypermarket.

Galeries Maldà

C/Portaferrissa 22 (no phone). Metro Liceu/bus 14, 38, 59, 91. **Open** 10am-1.30pm, 4.30-8.15pm, Mon-Sat. **Credit** AmEx, DC, EC, JCB, V. **Map** D6/**B2**
The first shopping centre in Barcelona, bang in the centre of the old town with access from Plaça del Pi and Portaferrissa, has a bit of everything: from a clothes hanger specialist to shoe shop chains and a big furniture store. The historic building also houses a cinema and a popular cheap *hostal* (*see p127*).

L'Illa

Avda Diagonal 545-557 (93 444 00 00). Metro Maria Cristina/bus 6, 7, 33, 34, 63, 66, 67, 68, 78. **Open** 10am-9pm Mon-Fri; 10am-9.30pm Sat; *supermarkets* 9.30am-9.30pm Mon-Sat. **Map** B3
Thanks to its prime location in the fashionable business area on the upper Diagonal, L'Illa attracts a more upmarket clientele than its Glòries counterpart. It has trendier fashion shops (check out the groovy **Prestige**, 93 444 01 41), and a well-stocked **Caprabo** supermarket, as well as a **Marks & Spencer**, the **Decathlon** sports shop and a **Fnac**.

Maremàgnum

Moll d'Espanya (93 225 81 00).
Metro Drassanes/bus 14, 19, 36, 38, 40, 57, 59, 64, 157, N6, N9, N12. **Discounts** BT.
Open 11am-11pm daily. **Map** D7
A mall, or what? Maremàgnum is intended as an all-round leisure complex, with restaurants, games, cinemas and nightclubs, and has pretty much succeeded. It's unique because of its Port setting, because it was designed by two of the leading architects of the new Barcelona, Viaplana and Piñón, and because you get to it via a bridge linking it with the Rambla. For those who find normal malls claustrophobic, it's a delight, and the giant mirror-wall above the main entrance creates spectacular visual effects. Its shops, though, are mostly better for fun- and souvenir-shopping than clothes-or-other-things-you-really-want-buying. For other facilities, *see chapters* **Restaurants**, **Cafés & Bars** *and* **Nightlife**.

El Triangle

C/Pelai 39-Plaça Catalunya 4 (93 318 01 08).
Metro Catalunya/bus all routes to Plaça Catalunya.
Open *Sept-May* 10am-9.30pm, *May-Sept* 10am-10pm, Mon-Sat. **Map** D5/**A1**
The latest addition to the mall-list is the bunker-like Triangle, opened in 1999. Dominating one side of Plaça Catalunya, it houses a **Fnac**, **Habitat**, and many small, trendy fashion shops including **Camper** for shoes, but its most spectacular store is the **Sephora** perfume mega-space (*see p195*). For the nostalgic, the Triangle has a version of the emblematic **Cafè Zurich** in one corner (*see p158*).

Camper

El Triangle, C/Pelai 13-37 (93 302 41 24). Metro Plaça Catalunya/bus all routes to Plaça Catalunya.
Open *Sept-May* 10am-9.30pm, *May-Sept* 10am-10pm, Mon-Sat. **Credit** AmEx, DC, JCB, MC, V.
Camper is to shoes what Zara (*see p202*) is to clothes – with the same very clever and customer-friendly mix of style, wearability, quality and price. Camper shoes are now becoming known as style items world-wide, but buying them in Spain can still save

you a significant amount of money. There are six more branches in Barcelona; this is the most central.

La Manual Alpargatera

C/Avinyó 7 (93 301 01 72). Metro Liceu/bus 14, 38, 59, 91. **Open** 9.30am-1.30pm, 4.30-8pm, Mon-Sat. **Credit** AmEx, DC, JCB, MC, V. **Map** D6/**B3**
A wonderful old shop dedicated to espadrilles of every possible variety, in business since 1910. Current head of the family sr Tasies continues the tradition of individually-made shoes – he knows

everything about espadrilles, from the types of hemp or jute used for the sole to hundreds of variations in colour and style. Regulars include Michael Douglas, Jack Nicholson and the Pope. Espadrilles can be made to order: your template is stored for future orders. Prices, from 600 to 6,000ptas.

Muxart
C/Rosselló 230 (93 488 10 64).
Metro Diagonal/bus 7, 16, 17, 22, 24, 28. **Open**
10am-2pm, 4.30-8.30pm, Mon-Fri; 10am-2pm, 5-8.30pm, Sat. **Credit** AmEx, MC, V. **Map** D4
Started in the Balearics in the 1980s and now one of Spain's most fashionable shoe brands, Muxart combines design and traditional hand-made manufacturing. Irresistible sandals, bags and accessories, including a small, tasteful range for men.

Noel Barcelona
C/Pelai 46 (93 317 86 38). Metro Plaça
Catalunya/bus all routes to Plaça Catalunya. **Open**
10am-9pm, Mon-Sat. **Credit** MC, V. **Map** D5/**A1**
Funky, trendy shoes in bright colours including knee-high red, green or silver boots with platform soles – Noel Barcelona's footwear is not for the shy.

Flowers

Florists and plant shops can be found everywhere; many offer the Interflora delivery service. As well as the flower stalls on the Rambla, there are stalls at the **Mercat de la Concepció** (corner of C/València and C/Bruc; **Map** E4) open all night.

Food

Chocolate, cakes & bread

Escribà Pastisseries
Gran Via de les Corts Catalanes 546 (93 454 75 35).
Metro Urgell/bus 9, 14, 20, 38, 50, 56, 59. **Open**
8am-9pm Mon-Sun. **Credit** MC, V. **Map** C5
Antoni Escribà, many times champion *pastisser* of Barcelona, is a local celebrity, famous for his victories in the Easter cake competition (*see p7*). At other times, his most delectable cake is the *rambla*, made from biscuit, truffle and chocolate (250ptas). The Rambla branch is in the Antigua Casa Figueras, with a beautiful mosaic façade.
Branch: La Rambla 83 (93 301 60 27).

Forn de Pa Sant Jordi
C/Llibreteria 8 (93 310 40 16). Metro Jaume I/bus
17, 19, 40, 45. **Open** 7am-9pm Mon-Sat; 7am-noon/1pm Sun. **No credit cards. Map** D6/**B3**
There's nearly always a queue outside the Sant Jordi bread shop – testimony to the delicious cakes on sale inside. The bread is good, and the *xuxos/chuchos* (cream doughnuts) are extremely tasty.

La Mallorquina
Plaça de les Olles 7 (93 319 38 83). Metro
Barceloneta/ bus 14, 17, 40, 45, 51, 100. **Open**
8am-2pm, 5-8.30pm, Tue-Sat; 8am-3pm Sun. Closed Aug. **No credit cards. Map** D-E6/**C4**
The smell of baking *carquinyolis* (a Catalan biscuit made with almonds) hits you as you walk past La Mallorquina. The chocolate croissants and cream cakes are also worth tucking into.

Mushrooms, meats & other marvels

Catalonia has as much of a passion for wild mushrooms as any part of the Mediterranean. There's a great deal of culture attached to funghi (*bolets* in Catalan, in Spanish *setas*). Prime season for them is the autumn, when families take to the hills on *bolet* hunts, but there are varieties available at other times of year. Few Catalan *bolets* have English names (or sometimes Spanish ones). Many fruit and vegetable shops sell woodland mushrooms each autumn – especially the highly valued, sweet *rovellons*. Lesser-known but equally tasty are *llenegues*, the nutty *girgoles* and *reig bord*.

If you don't trust in your ability to collect them yourself – many kinds are poisonous, after all – the best bet is to visit *bolet* specialist **Llorenç Petras** at stalls 869 and 870 in the Boqueria (*see page 209*), who stocks nothing but them – up to 30 varieties at any time. While the best season is still autumn, he can provide *bolets* all year round: when a variety is not available locally, he gets them from other parts of Spain, Portugal, Turkey, or even Pakistan or Afghanistan if necessary.

From the baskets displayed at the stall you can choose bitter-tasting Japanese *matsutakes* for about 2,000ptas per kilo, or a mixed kilo of eight to ten varieties of local *bolets* for 1,100ptas. Petras also freezes, dries and tins mushrooms; dried varieties include *ceps* and *moixarnons*, and a mixed assortment, *barretxa*, is available in tins. He even grinds mushrooms to make seasonings for soups and stews. Some tips from the master: break *bolets* up by hand, not with a knife; contact with water should be kept to a minimum, as they get spongy; use olive oil in cooking, and avoid overcooking – if grilling, keep heat low. Chopped garlic, *serrano* ham and parsley can be added to them, but not much else, so as not to drown their natural flavour.

Hams, *embotits* & cheeses
A more widespread favourite, almost a totem of the Spanish diet, is dry-cured ham, *jamón serrano* (*pernil serrà* in Catalan). The very best comes from southwest Spain, but it's found everywhere, and is one thing that unites Catalans with the rest of the

Pastisseria Maurí

Rambla Catalunya 102 (93 215 10 20).
Metro Diagonal, FGC Provença/bus 7, 16, 17, 22,
24, 28. **Open** 8am-9pm Mon-Sat; 9am-3pm, 5-9pm,
Sun, public holidays; Closed Sun pm July-Aug .
Credit MC, V. **Map** D4
Granja Maurí opened in 1885 as a grocery specialising in cakes, and the elaborate painted ceiling is a
relic from that time. Enjoy delicate sandwiches or
cakes in the tea room, or take away a ready-to-eat
meal from what remains of the grocery store.
Branch: Rambla Catalunya 103 (93 215 81 46).

Colmados/general food stores

Colmado Quílez

Rambla Catalunya 63 (93 215 23 56). Metro Passeig de
Gràcia/bus 7, 16, 17, 22, 24, 28. 8.30pm, Mon-Fri; 9am-2pm Sat; *Oct-Dec* 9am-2pm, 4.30-
8.30pm, Mon-Sat. **Credit** AmEx, MC, V. **Map** D4
One of the monuments of the Eixample. The walls
of this fabulous emporium are lined with cans and
bottles from all over the world; there are huge quantities of hams and cheeses, and every type of alcohol: saké, six types of schnapps, a wall of whiskies,
and *cava* from over 55 *bodegas* – one, Cava La
Fuente, is sold exclusively in this shop. The excellent own-brand coffee, Cafe Quílez, is imported from
Colombia, and ground for you on the spot.

Queviures Murrià

C/Roger de Llúria 85 (93 215 57 89). Metro Passeig
de Gràcia/bus 20, 39, 43, 44, 45, 47. **Open** 10am-
2pm, 5-9pm Mon-Sat. **Credit** DC, MC, V. **Map** D4

This magnificent *Modernista* shop, photographed
time and again for its original 1900s tiled decoration
by Ramon Casas and still run by the Murrià family,
is not only an architectural attraction: it also stocks
wonderful food – a superb range of individually-
sourced farmhouse cheeses – and over 300 wines,
including their own-label Cava Murrià. *See also p77.*

Food specialities

Art Escudellers

C/Escudellers 23-5 (93 412 68 01). Metro
Drassanes/bus 14, 38, 59, 91. **Open** 11am-11pm
Mon-Sun. **Credit** AmEx, DC, MC, V. **Map** D6/**A-B3**
A shop that defies all attempts at classification.
From street level it looks likes an exceptionally large
ceramics shop, but descend to the cellar and you'll
find a fantastic selection of wines, olive oil and the
best *jamon serrano* and other meats. There's a small
bar where you can try out some of these delights,
and manager Iván is helpful and knowledgeable.

Cafés el Magnífico

C/Argenteria 64 (93 319 60 81). Metro Jaume I/bus
17, 19, 40, 45. **Open** 8.30am-1.30pm, 4-8pm, Mon-
Fri; 9.30am-1.30pm Sat. Closed 3 weeks Aug. **No**
credit cards. Map D6/**C3**
Since 1919 the Sans family has imported, prepared
and blended coffees from around the world. Prices
vary from 1,200ptas per kilo for a simple blend, to
12,000ptas per kilo for the especially smooth
Jamaican coffee. They also stock over 150 cases of
tea, including blends from Taiwan, Nepal, India, Sri
Lanka, China, Japan and Sikkim.

country. The quality of *jamón* varies a great deal,
and you can expect to pay up to 14,000ptas a kilo
for the best, entirely traditionally cured ham. The
biggest distinction is that between *jamón del país*
(or just generic *serrano*), from conventional pigs,
and *jamón ibérico* or *pata negra* ('black foot'), from
the native Iberian breed of black pig, raised in an
entirely free-range manner, and fed on acorns.
Traditionally, the best *pata negra* ham comes from
Jabugo in Andalusia, which is accordingly usually
the most expensive. Another distinction is that
between *jamón*, hind leg, and *paletilla*, which comes
from the front legs. The sometimes less attractive-
looking, fat-streaked ham is tastier than the leaner
cuts. For expert advice, stop off at **La Pineda** or
Art Escudellers (*see above and p208*).
    As well as *jamón* ham shops offer many other
cold meats such as *chorizo, salchichón*, Catalan
botifarra and spicy Mallorcan *sobrassada*. All
cheese shops in Spain have many kinds of classic
manchego – fans of strong, dry cheeses should try
seco (or even *seco añejo*); *semi* or *tierno* is milder.

Catalan delicacies and Modernista *décor at* **Queviures Murrià**. *See page 207.*

Casa del Bacalao

C/Comtal 8 (93 301 65 39). Metro Urquinaona/bus 17, 19, 40, 45. **Open** 9am-3pm, 5.30-8.30pm, Mon-Sat. **No credit cards. Map** D5/**B2**
The 'house of cod', and the shop sells nothing else – salted and dried, with no chemical additives. Salt-cod features in many Catalán and Spanish dishes, which require different parts of the fish: the cheek (*mejilla*) for *bacalao* with *salsa verde*; broken-up pieces (2500ptas/kilo) for *esqueixada* and small *cocotxes* for Basque *bacalao al pil-pil*. Travellers note – staff can now vacuum-pack your choice piece to take home; don't, though, forget to de-salt it overnight before cooking it.

Casa Gispert

C/Sombrerers 23 (93 319 75 35). Metro Jaume I/bus 17, 19, 40, 45. **Open** 9am-1.30pm, 4-7.30pm, Mon-Fri; 10am-2pm, 5-8pm, Sat; *Aug* 10am-2pm, 5-8pm, Mon-Fri. **Credit** DC, MC, V. **Map** D6/**C3**
Founded in the 1850s, Casa Gispert is a wholesale outlet famous for top-quality nuts, dried fruit and coffee. All are roasted on-site in the magnificent original wood-burning stove. A kilo is the minimum order. Delve into enormous baskets of almonds and hazelnuts, still warm from the oven.

Formatgeria Cirera

C/Cera 45 (93 441 07 59). Metro Sant Antoni/bus 20, 24, 64, 91. **Open** 9am-2pm, 5.30-8.30pm, Mon-Fri; 9am-2pm Sat. **Credit** MC, V. **Map** C6
As well as home-made cheesecakes (suitable for diabetics) this shop has a great selection of cheeses, pâtés, hams, *caves* and fine *sobresada* from Mallorca.

Mantequerías Puig

C/Xuclà 21 (93 318 12 84). Metro Catalunya/bus all routes to Plaça Catalunya. **Open** 8.30am-2pm, 5-8pm, Mon-Fri; 8.30am-2pm Sat. **Credit** MC, V. **Map** D5/**A2**
This traditional cheese shop supplies local hotels and restaurants. If you don't see what you want, ask: there are dozens more cheeses out back.

Mel Viadiu

C/Comtal 20 (93 317 04 23). Metro Catalunya/bus 17, 19, 40, 45. **Open** 10am-2pm, 4.30-8.30pm, Mon-Sat. **Credit** AmEx, DC, MC, V. **Map** D5/**B2**
Founded in 1898 and supplier to Fortnum & Mason, this is the only shop in Barcelona to specialise solely in honey – 14 types from different parts of Spain. Choose honey with ginseng or royal jelly, try honey throat sweets, or buy some of the good local *cava*.

La Pineda

C/del Pi 16 (93 302 43 93). Metro Liceu/bus 14, 38, 59, 91. **Open** 9am-3pm, 5-10pm, Mon-Sat; 11am-3pm, 7-10pm, Sun. **Credit** AmEx, DC, MC, V. **Map** D6/**B2**
La Pineda has specialised in *jamón serrano* since 1930, together with other fine cold meats, and a big choice of cheeses and wines. The shop – a charming Barri Gòtic survivor – also functions as a small local *bodega* (*see p162*), with a few humble tables and stools where you can snack on these delicacies, washed down with a good Rioja.

Tot Formatge 2

Passeig del Born 13 (93 319 53 75). Metro Barceloneta, Jaume I/bus 14, 39, 51. **Open** 7.30am-1.15pm, 4.30-7.30pm, Mon-Fri; 9am-1.15pm Sat. **No credit cards. Map** D-E6/**C3**

Market economy

There are over 40 food markets in Barcelona – every *barri* has its own. **La Boqueria** is deservedly the most famous, but there are others worth visiting. **Santa Caterina**, currently in temporary lodgings on Passeig de Sant Joan while its site off Via Laietana is rebuilt, has some of the best prices. **Sant Antoni**, near the Paral.lel, has a clothes market around the edge and food stands in the middle; **Mercat de la Llibertat** in Gràcia has a village atmosphere. **Mercat del Ninot** at C/Mallorca-C/Casanova has everything you could think of, and **Mercat de la Concepció** at València/Bruc is famous for flowers.

Markets open early (from 8am or earlier) and most close up by around 2-3pm. Monday is not a good day to go, as stocks are low. Don't expect stalls to take credit cards, and for a note on queueing, *see page 295*.

La Boqueria (Mercat de Sant Josep)
La Rambla 91 (93 318 25 84).
Metro Liceu/bus 14, 38, 59, 91. **Open** 8am-8.30pm Mon-Sat. **Map** D6/**A2**
One of the greatest markets in the world, and certainly the most attractive and comprehensive in Barcelona, the Boqueria is always full of tourists, locals and gourmands. Even amid all the bustle, it's

possible to appreciate the orderliness of its structure: fruit and vegetables around the edge, meat and chicken kept apart, and fish and seafood stalls in the centre, arranged in a circle. Enter through the main gates, set back from the Rambla, amid great colourful heaps of red peppers, cucumbers and fruit. Don't buy here, though: the stalls by the entrance are more expensive than those further inside. They do, however, offer delights such as *palmitos* (palm roots), *higos chumbos* (Indian figs) or *caña dulce* (sugar cane sticks). **J Colomines** (stall 477), to the right of the entrance, specialises in fresh herbs, tropical fruit and African food. It's one of the few places selling fresh coriander, tarragon, ginger and okra throughout the year. At the back of the market, there's a stall that's a monument in itself, **Llorenç Petras** (stall 869-870) (*see p206*). On the way, admire the glistening meat and fish stalls, kept firmly in order by perfectly made-up ladies in spotless white overalls. Or stop at one of the cheese stalls offering selections of the 81 types of Spanish cheeses with a *denominación de origen*: try pungent *cabrales*, dry *mahón* from Menorca, or the delicious *garrotxa*, a Catalan cheese made from goat's milk, not to mention the many delicious lamb's milk *manchegos*. Specialised stalls selling over 40 varieties of olives are dotted all over the market.

2 4 2 4 2 3 4 5

Welcome to your shopping island

You won't be surprised if you see an island in the centre of Barcelona. It is called L'illa and you will find it on La Diagonal. It is not a desert island because of its thousands of metres house stores such as Marks & Spencer, Fnac and Decathlon, the 140 best shops in town with the

Open from 10 am to 9 pm. Bus routes: 6, 7, 30, 33, 34, 66, 67, 68, Tomb Bus.

L'iLLA

DIAGONAL

557, Diagonal Avenue

most up-to-date fashion and prestigi international brands, as well as the tast Mediterranean cooking and a varied marke fresh products. Come to L'illa Diago a paradise where you will find the gifts you looking for and make unforgettable purcha

Underground: Reina Maria Cristina, Les Co

The shopping island in Barcelona

Probably the most comprehensive cheese specialist in Barcelona, with cheeses from all over Catalonia and Spain, France, Italy and many other parts of Europe. The goats' cheeses from Extremadura are excellent; if you prefer something milder, try the Catalan *mató* (cream cheese).

Health & herbs

See also page 196, **Herboristeria del Rei**.

Herbolari Ferran

Plaça Reial 18 (93 304 20 05).
Metro Liceu/bus 14, 38, 59, 91. **Open** 9.30am-2pm, 4.30-8pm, Mon-Sat. **Credit** MC, V. **Map** D6/A3
Herbolari Ferran has been serving a faithful public since the 1940s. Its large new basement area is a combination of an old-fashioned herb shop, a modern self-service store, a coffee/teashop, a bookshop and an exhibition area, to provide a very allround health store service. The branch nearby has special gift-wrapped products.
Branch: **El Regal de l'Herbolari** Passatge Bacardí 1 (Plaça Reial) (93 301 78 39)

Macrobiòtic Zen

C/Muntaner 12 (93 454 60 23). Metro Universitat/bus 9, 14, 24, 41, 50, 55, 56, 59, 64, 91, 141. **Open** 9am-8pm Mon-Fri; *Aug* times vary.
Closed two weeks Aug. **No credit cards. Map** C5
All kinds of cheeses suitable for macrobiotic, diabetic and vegetarian diets, with a self-service canteen at the back of the shop.

Supermarkets

Caprabo and **Dia** are small chains with at least one branch in every district; another, **Champion**, has a branch on the Rambla (No.113, **Map** D5/**A2**). Big hypermarkets such as **Hipercor** (*see page 190*) or **Pryca** (near the north and south exits to Barcelona on the *Rondes*) are designed to be visited by car, but the **Glòries** mall has a **Continente** hypermarket that is accessible by Metro.

Cheese! **Mantequerías Puig**. *See page 208.*

Markets: flea, art & antique

Barri Gòtic antique/art markets

Antique Market
Avda de la Catedral 6 (93 291 61 00).
Metro Jaume I/bus 17, 19, 40, 45. **Open** *Jan-Nov* 10am-10pm Thur. **No credit cards. Map** D6/**B2**
Art Market
Plaça Sant Josep Oriol (93 291 61 00).
Metro Liceu/bus 14, 38, 59. **Open** *first weekend each month* 11am-10pm Sat; 10am-3pm Sun. **No credit cards. Map** D6/**A3**
Bric-a-brac and antique stalls are spread in front of the Cathedral every week. There are few bargains, but it's always enjoyable to rummage through the religious artefacts, pipes, watches, lace hankies and old telephones. Before Christmas, the market transfers to the Portal de l'Àngel. An **art market** of variable quality is held in Plaça del Pi/Plaça Sant Josep Oriol one weekend each month throughout the year.

Book & Coin Market

Mercat de Sant Antoni, C/Comte d'Urgell 1 (93 423 42 87). Metro Sant Antoni/bus 20, 24, 38, 64, 91.
Open 9am-2pm (approx) Sun.
No credit cards. Map C5
This Sunday second-hand book market is an institution in Barcelona. Struggle through the crowds to rummage through boxes of dusty tomes, old magazines and video games, and whole collections of old coins. If it gets too much, sit at **Els Tres Tombs** bar (*see p165*) to watch the bargain-hunters pass by.

Nutty delights: **Casa Gispert**. *See page 208.*

Brocanters del Port Vell

Moll de les Drassanes. Metro Drassanes/bus 14, 36, 38, 57, 59. 64, 100, 157. **Open** 11am-9pm Sat, Sun. **No credit cards. Map** C7/A4

A relatively new bric-a-brac and antique market, held in a prime position by the bottom of the Rambla and the Maremàgnum bridge . The only antiques market on Sundays, it's proving popular with locals on the look-out for ceramics, china, coins, collectors' records, costume jewellery, *mantillas* and old lace, toys, or even old fountain pens. Prices are more reasonable than at the Barri Gòtic market.

Els Encants (flea market)

C/Dos de Maig, corner C/Consell de Cent (93 246 30 30). Metro Glòries/bus 62, 92.
Open 9am-8pm Mon, Wed, Fri, Sat; *auctions* 9am-5pm. **No credit cards. Map** F5

Despite modernisation all around it, Els Encants (also known as the **Mercat de Bellcaire**) remains the most authentic of flea markets – from its fringes, where old men lay out battered shoes and toys on cloths on the ground, to the centre, where a persistent shopper can snaffle up bargains to furnish a whole flat: earthenware jugs and country furniture from La Mancha, second-hand clothes, new textiles, and loads of fascinating junk. If possible avoid Saturdays, when it's very crowded, and watch out for short-changing and pickpockets. The market is officially open in the afternoons, but many stalls

All kinds of books at Sant Antoni. See p211.

pack up at midday; for the best stuff and real bargains, get there early in the morning. To avoid problems with the police, illegal stall holders sometimes move into the nearby Bosquet dels Encants park by the Teatre Nacional.

Stamp & Coin Market

Plaça Reial (no phone). Metro Liceu/bus 14, 38, 59. **Open** 9am-2.30pm (approx) Sun.
No credit cards. Map D6/A3

This somewhat incongruous gathering for enthusiasts blends surprisingly well with the goings-on in Plaça Reial. Having inspected the coins, stamps and rocks, take an aperitif in the sun and watch the experts poring over each other's collections.

Music

The Portal de l'Angel branch of the **Corte Inglés** (*see page 190*) and the **Fnac** (*see page 193*) also house comprehensive mainstream music stores.

La Casa

Plaça Vicenç Martorell 6 (93 412 33 05).
Metro Catalunya/bus all routes to Plaça Catalunya.
Open 11am-2pm, 4.30-8pm, Tue-Sat.
Credit MC, V. **Map** D5/**A1-2**

Probably the most respected record shop for the dance music scene. Its owners are mines of information on dance music across the board, and the vinyl selection never disappoints.

Casa Luthier

C/Balmes 73 (93 454 15 78).
Metro Passeig de Gràcia/bus 7, 16, 17, 20, 43, 44, 63, 67, 68. **Open** 9.30am-1.30pm, 4.30-8pm, Mon-Fri; 10am-2pm Sat. **Credit** MC, V. **Map** D4

Superb guitars, in all shapes and sizes, books and magazines on the subject, and guitar classes.

Discos Castelló

C/Tallers 3 (93 318 20 41).
Metro Catalunya/bus all routes to Plaça Catalunya.
Open 10am-2pm, 4.30-8.30pm, Mon-Sat. **Credit** AmEx, DC, MC, V. **Map** D5/**A2**

A chain of small shops, each with a different emphasis. This one specialises in classical; Nou de la Rambla is good for ethnic music and flamenco.
Branches: C/Nou de la Rambla 15 (93 302 42 36); C/Sant Pau 2 (93 302 23 95); C/Tallers 7 (93 302 59 46); C/Tallers 9 (93 412 72 85); C/Tallers 79 (93 301 35 75).

Edison's

C/Riera Baixa 9 & 10 (93 441 96 74). Metro Liceu/bus 20, 64, 91. **Open** 10am-2pm, 4.30-8.30pm, Mon-Sat. **Credit** AmEx, DC, MC, V. **Map** C6

C/Riera Baixa now has music specialists to cater for all tastes (*see p203*). Edison's buy and sell unlisted vinyl LPs and singles, and CDs of every persuasion.

Ethnomusic

C/Bonsuccés 6 (93 301 18 84).
Metro Catalunya/bus all routes to Plaça Catalunya.
Open 5-8pm Mon; 11am-2pm, 5-8pm, Tue-Sat.
Credit MC, V. **Map** D5/**A2**

This ethnic music shop in the Raval has music from all over the planet, although most foreign visitors seem to be hunting for rare flamenco. Staff know their business and are extremely helpful.

Sports

La Botiga del Barça
Maremàgnum, Moll d'Espanya (93 225 81 00).
Metro Drassanes/bus 14, 19, 36, 38, 40, 57, 59, 64,
157. **Open** 11am-11pm daily.
Credit AmEx, DC, MC, V. **Map** D7
If you feel a visit to Barcelona would be incomplete without acquiring some FC Barcelona paraphernalia, look no further. The Botiga del Barça has every permutation of *Barça* merchandise imaginable, from scarves, towels and hats through (of course) shirts to an appalling range of claret-and-blue clocks. Barça being a club that fancies itself, there are also 'classy' items like champagne glasses, or silver spoons. Why go to any other souvenir shop?
Branches: Gran Via de les Corts Catalanes 418 (93 423 59 41); Museu del FC Barcelona, Nou Camp (93 496 36 00).

Esports Mañanes
C/Canuda 26 (93 318 45 00/fax 93 318 44 34).
Metro Catalunya/bus all routes to Plaça Catalunya.
Open 10am-1.30pm, 4.30-8.30pm, Mon-Sat.
Credit AmEx, DC, MC, V. **Map** D5/**B2**
Very centrally located just off Portal del Angel, Esports Mañanes offers a wide range of top brands in sports clothes, shoes and other equipment.

Kaotik.o
C/Cucurulla 4 (93 412 13 22). Metro Catalunya/bus
all routes to Plaça Catalunya. **Open** 10am-9pm Mon-Sat. **Credit** DC, MC, V. **Map** D6/**B2**
Kaotik.o is smaller but trendier than Mañanes, and more label-conscious. Staff and shoppers are very young, and live up to the shop's name – 'chaotic'.

Tobacco & cigars

L'Estanc de Laietana
Via Laietana 4 (93 310 10 34).
Metro Jaume I/bus 17, 19, 40, 45. **Open** 8.30am-2pm, 4-8pm, Mon-Fri; 9am-2pm Sat. **Credit** (for gifts, not cigarettes) MC, V. **Map** D6/**B4**
The busiest and most famous of the tobacco shops in Barcelona, run with zest and enthusiasm by sr Porta. Over 100 brands of cigarettes and 100 types of rolling tobacco are on sale; he also has a *humidor* at sea level in his underground cellar to store his exceptional range of fine cigars.

Gimeno
Passeig de Gràcia 101 (93 237 20 78).
Metro Diagonal/ bus 7, 16, 17, 22, 24, 28.
Open 10am-2pm, 4-8.30pm, Mon-Sat. **Credit** AmEx, DC, JCB, MC, V. **Map** D4
Gimeno has anything and everything to do with smoking, with hundreds of pipes and lighters. Plus, an interesting collection of ornate walking sticks.

Liquid assets

The prime Catalan wine area, the Penedès, produces good reds, whites and rosés: the Torres and René Barbier labels are reliable, and Bach whites have a great dry tang. The most famous of Spanish wines, Rioja, can be found everywhere, but quality is pretty variable; in recent years the Ribera del Duero and Navarra regions have been as highly regarded as Rioja for reds.

Catalan *cava*, sparkling wine, is also from the Penedès. *Caves* are labelled, according to quality and sweetness, Brut Nature, Brut, Seco and Semi-Seco – the latter may be not *seco* at all but very sweet, and is the cheapest. For more on wines, *see pages 270-1.*

El Celler de Gèlida
C/Vallespir 65 (93 339 26 41). Metro Plaça del
Centre or Sants Estació/bus all routes to Estació
de Sants. **Open** 9am-2pm, 5-8.30pm Mon-Fri;
9.30am-2.30pm, *Oct-June* 5-8.30pm Sat. Closed Aug. **Credit** MC, V. **Map** A4
A little way off the beaten track in Sants, this modern cellar has over 3,000 labels and an unbeatable selection of Catalan wines. Staff are very knowledgeable, and advise many restaurants on their wine lists.

Lafuente
C/Johann Sebastian Bach 20
(93 201 25 21). FGC Bonanova/bus 14.
Open 9am-2pm, 4.30-8.30pm, Mon-Fri; 9am-2pm Sat. **Credit** MC, V. **Map** C2
Smart wine store with another huge stock of wines, *caves* and spirits. A good selection of non-Spanish wines.

Vila Viniteca
C/Agullers 7-9 (93 310 19 56/93 268 32 27).
Metro Jaume I/bus 17, 19, 40, 45.
Open 8am-3pm, 5-9pm, Mon-Sat. **Credit** AmEx, DC, MC, V. **Map** D6/**B4**
Joaquim Vila carries on the work of his grandfather, who opened the shop in 1932. From outside it looks like a grocery store, but inside there's a huge range of wine and *cava*, explained in a monthly leaflet.

Vins i Caves La Catedral
Plaça de Ramon Berenguer el Gran 1
(93 319 07 27). Metro Jaume I/bus 17, 19, 40,
45. **Open** 4.30-8.30pm Mon; 10.30am-2.15pm, 4.30-8.30pm ,Tue-Sat. **Credit** AmEx, DC, JCB, MC, V. **Map** D6/**B3**
La Catedral has a good supply of wines from all over Spain, and a particularly ample choice of Catalan wines and fine *caves*.

Services

Ticket-selling operations, shoe repairers, places to hire an outfit – you never know when you might need them.

The contrast between old-world and ultra-modern characteristic of so much in Barcelona also applies to the world of services. A recent trend is the growth of all-day services, with stores, supermarkets and malls offering same-day cleaners, shoe repairers, opticians and other chain businesses. However, there are still plenty of quirky old businesses around too, so Barcelona now offers a very wide choice.

Body & hair care

Beauty treatments

Gòtic Maquillatges
C/Comtessa de Sobradiel 6 (93 310 00 64). Metro Liceu/bus 14, 18, 38, 59, 91. **Open** 10.30am-8pm Mon-Fri. **Credit.** **Map** D6/B3
A specialist in make-up for day, night-time, theatre, TV or carnival, with advice and beauty kits for each customer's specific needs. No makeovers on site, but visits by specialists to your home or hotel can be arranged. Make-up courses are offered at C/Tuset.
Branch: Galerias David, C/Tuset 19-21 (93 200 74 44)

Instituto Francis
Ronda de Sant Pere 18 (93 317 78 08). Metro Catalunya/bus all routes to Plaça Catalunya. **Open** 9.30am-8pm Mon-Fri; 9.30am-4pm Sat. **Credit** DC, MC, V. **Map** D5/B1
Eight floors dedicated to making you look and feel great; from make-up and make-overs on the first floor, up through hairdressing, waxing, facials, slimming and massages. Not cheap, but a real treat.

Hairdressers

Clear
C/del Pi 11, pral 10 (93 317 08 22). Metro Liceu/bus 14, 38, 59, 91. **Open** 10am-8pm Mon-Sat. **Credit** MC, V. **Map** D6/B2
Welcome to the hair salon for the year 2000: the place where the stylish go for minimalist cuts or the craziest extensions. Even if you're not after a makeover, the all-white futuristic décor is worth a visit.

Llongueras
C/Balmes 162 (93 218 61 50). Metro Diagonal, FGC Provença/bus 7, 16, 17, 31, 67, 68. **Open** 9.30am-6.30pm Mon-Sat; July, Aug 9.30am-6.30pm Mon-Fri; 9.30am-2pm Sat. **Credit** AmEx, DC, MC, V. **Map** D4
Best-known hairdressing chain in Spain, with over a dozen city branches. Expensive, but the Balmes shop's hairdressing school offers cheaper cuts.

La Pelu
C/Argenteria 70-72 (93 310 48 07). Metro Jaume I/bus 17, 19, 40, 45, N8. **Open** 11am-8pm Mon-Wed, Sat; 11am-9pm Thur, Fri. **Credit** MC, V. **Map** D6/C3
Groovy cuts for all: men's wash and cut from 2,500ptas; women's from 3,900ptas. On the night of the full moon each month La Pelu is open 11pm-2am, with magic and other entertainments to keep you amused while you have your midnight trim.
Branches: C/Tallers 35 (93 301 97 73); C/Rauric 8 (93 302 29 76).

Peluquería Vicente
C/Tallers 11 (no phone). Metro Catalunya/bus all routes to Plaça Catalunya. **Open** 9am-1pm, 4-8pm, Mon-Fri; 9am-1pm Sat. **No credit cards.** **Map** D5/A1
Gentlemen: for a no-nonsense haircut and one of the closest shaves in the world, try out this small traditional barber's shop.

Polo-pelo
Gralla Hall, C/Portaferrisa 25 (93 412 38 42). Metro Liceu/bus 14, 38, 59, 91. **Open** 3-8.30pm Mon; 10.30am-8.30pm Tue-Sat. **Credit** MC, V. **Map** D6/B2
A hip hairdressers in the Gralla Hall (*see chapter* **Shopping**), run with flair by French-Argentinian Eric. One of the best places in town for fun highlights or a different style.
Branch: Passeig del Born 14 (93 268 18 45).

Clothes & accessories

Cleaning, repairs, shoe repairs

There are still many old street-corner repairers in Barcelona who will alter or restore virtually any piece of clothing. Look for the signs '*Arreglos*' or '*Brodats/Bordados*'. **Jaimar**, C/Numància 91-3 (93 322 78 04), is an excellent example. To have your shoes repaired, look for the sign '*Ràpido*'. There is also a range of services available at **El Corte Inglés** (*see chapter* **Shopping**).

5 a Sec
L'Illa, Avda Diagonal 545-557 (93 444 00 34). Bus 6, 7, 33, 34, 63, 66, 67, 68, 78. **Open** 9am-9pm Mon-Fri; 9.30am-9.30pm Sat. **Credit** AmEx, MC, V. **Map** B3
This efficient, modern dry cleaners offers a one-hour service at reasonable prices. There are several branches throughout the city.

Mr Minit
Centre Barcelona Glòries, Avda Diagonal 208 (93 486 03 52). Metro Glòries/bus 7, 56, 60, 92. **Open** 10am-10pm Mon-Sat. **Credit** V.
On-the-spot shoe repairs (heels, 700ptas) and key cutting (from 150ptas) at many points around town.

Qualitat Servei
C/Amargós 10 (93 318 31 47/93 301 36 87). Metro Urquinaona/bus 17, 19, 40, 45. **Open** 8am-10pm Mon-Sat. **No credit cards. Map** D5/**B2**
Near the Barri Gòtic, this shop will wash and iron or dry-clean clothes and deliver them to you within 24 hours (although there's no pick-up service). Also minor repairs.

Dress & costume hire

Casa Peris
C/Junta de Comerç 20 (93 301 27 48) Metro Liceu/bus 14, 38, 59, 91. **Open** 9am-2pm, 3.30pm-6.30pm, Mon-Fri. **No credit cards. Map** C6/**A3**
A flourishing family firm since 1840, which has supplied the Liceu and Madrid operas, and stocks close to one million theatrical costumes. A walk through the warehouse reveals a Don Giovanni outfit from the opera and many film costumes. More mundanely, men's formal wear can be hired for 8,000ptas.

Menkes
Gran Via de les Corts Catalanes 642 & 646 (93 412 11 38). Metro Passeig de Gràcia/bus 7, 16, 17, 22, 24, 28, 50, 54, 56, 62. **Open** 9.30am-1.30pm, 4.30-7.45pm, Mon-Fri; 10am-1.30pm, 5-8pm, Sat. **Credit** AmEx, DC, MC, V. **Map** D5

Kit yourself out for Carnaval at this magnificent costumier and dress-hire store. No.646 has sale stock, with a vast array of ballet shoes; No.642 has over 800 hire costumes, from Catalan peasant outfits to Carnival queen regalia. Any design can be made to order. There are jokes, false noses and other silly things, and dinner jackets for the more discreet.

Faxes & photocopies

A great many local *papereries* (stationers) have photocopiers, and also fax machines.

Central Fotocopia
C/Pelai 1, pral (tel/fax 93 412 61 02). Metro Universitat/bus all routes to Plaça Universitat. **Open** 9am-2.30pm, 4-8pm, Mon-Fri. **Credit** MC, V. **Map** C5/**A1**
Good-value photocopiers much used by students: excellent rates for multiple copies, but long queues in term time. Also a fax sending/receiving service.

Copisteria Miracle
C/Dr Joaquim Pou 2 (93 317 12 26/fax 93 412 18 12). Metro Jaume I/bus 17, 19, 40, 45. **Open** 9am-1.30pm, 4-7.30pm, Mon-Fri; *July-Sept* 8am-1.30pm, 4-7.30pm, Mon-Fri. **Credit** MC, V. **Map** D6/**B2**
This store is the best in the city for high-quality copying of all kinds, at reasonable prices. Again, be prepared to wait around, as queues are long. The other branches do not close at midday.
Branches: C/Rector Ubach 6 (93 200 85 44/ fax 93 209 17 82); Passeig Sant Joan 57 (93 265 53 54/fax 93 265 30 70).

Tickets: try a *caixa*

Catalonia's savings banks (*caixes d'estalvis*) are among its most omnipresent institutions. Lately, they have eagerly embraced electronics to expand into ticket sales. Most theatres and many other venues release tickets through one or other *caixa*: to find out which tickets are currently sold by each one, check at any branch or in a listings magazine (*see chapter* **Media**). No booking fees are charged.

Servi-Caixa – la Caixa
Phoneline 902 33 22 11. **Credit** MC, V.
Next to the cash machines in branches of the biggest of them all, the Caixa de Pensions, better known just as *la Caixa*, you find a machine called a *Servi-Caixa*, through which you can with a Caixa account or a credit card obtain T2 and T50/30 travel cards, (free) local information and tickets to a great many attractions and events, including **Port Aventura**, the **Teatre Nacional** and the **Liceu**, 24 hours a day. You can

also order tickets by phone (many of the staff speak reasonable English) or Internet.
Website: www.lacaixa.es/servicaixa

Tel-entrada – Caixa Catalunya
Phoneline **902 10 12 12**. **Central desk** *Plaça Catalunya (no phone).* **Open** 9am-9pm Mon-Sat. **Credit** MC, V. **Map** D5/**B1**
La Caixa's eternal competitor sells tickets through its Tel-entrada system for many theatres (never the same as the Servi-Caixa), over the counter at all its branches and at this desk, next to Plaça Catalunya tourist office (*see p294*). You can also reserve tickets by phone with a credit card (many staff speak handlable English); you will be given a reference number, and then must collect the tickets at the venue. You can call from outside Spain (on 93 479 99 20), and buy tickets on the Net. Also, you can get tickets half-price by buying them (cash only) within three hours of a performance at the Plaça Catalunya Tel-entrada desk.
Website: http://cec.caixacat.es

Food delivery

Few places specifically offer takeaway meals, but many restaurants will provide a takeaway service if you make an arrangement in advance.

Pizza World

C/Diputació 329 (93 487 85 85). Metro Girona/bus 7, 47, 50, 54, 56, 62, N1, N2, N3, N9. **Open** 1pm-midnight daily. **No credit cards.** **Map** D5
Pizza delivery from 16 branches, all of which can give you the 'phone number of your nearest outlet. From 7-11pm daily, call 902 30 53 05 with the address where you're staying for the same information.

Musical instrument rental

La Lonja del Instrumento

C/Gran de Gràcia 206 (93 415 77 77). Metro Fontana/bus 22, 24, 25, 28. **Open** 10am-2pm, 4-8pm, Mon-Sat. **Credit** AmEx, MC, V. **Map** D3
A rare service for renting, selling, exchanging or repairing musical instruments, particularly second-hand ones. Renting an electric guitar for a weekend costs from 1,500ptas plus deposit (10% of the guitar's value). A saxophone costs around 20,000ptas.

Opticians

Grand Optical

El Triangle, Plaça Catalunya 4 (93 304 16 40). Metro Catalunya/bus all routes to Plaça Catalunya. **Open** *Sept-May* 10am-9.30pm, *May-Sept* 10am-10pm, Mon-Sat. **Credit** AmEx, MC, V. **Map** D5/**A1**
English-speaking staff at Grand Optical offer eye-tests and can provide new glasses within two hours, or one hour if you have your prescription. Lens prices begin at about 4,500ptas.
Branch: Centre Barcelona Glòries, Avda Diagonal 208 (93 486 02 77).

Optipolis

Centre Barcelona Glòries, Avda Diagonal 208 (93 486 04 28). Metro Glòries/bus 7, 56, 60, 92. **Open** 10am-9.30pm, Mon-Fri, 10am-10pm Sat. **Credit** AmEx, DC, MC, V.
The same type and price of service as Grand Optical, also with English-speaking staff, but less central.

Photographic

Arpi Foto Video

La Rambla 38-40 (93 301 74 04/fax 93 317 95 73). Metro Drassanes, Liceu/bus 14, 38, 59, 91. **Open** 9.30am-2pm, 4.30-8pm, Mon-Sat (section opening times vary). **Credit** AmEx, DC, MC, V. **Map** D6/**A3**
This giant specialist camera store has a wide range of professional-standard cameras and accessories and a good basic repair department. Although service has improved, it can still be snail-like at times, but the staff do know what they are doing. Stock ranges from happy-snappers to studio Hasselblads.

Fotoprix

C/Pelai 6 (93 318 20 36/information 93 451 10 43). Metro Universitat/bus all routes to Plaça Universitat. **Open** 9.30am-2.30pm, 3.30-8.30pm, Mon-Sat. **Credit** V. **Map** C5/**A1**
Over 100 branches in the city, offering one-hour film developing, photocopying and fax services.

Ticket agents

Tickets for many concerts and events are sold through savings banks (*see page 215* **Tickets:** **try a *caixa*)**. The best places to get advance tickets are often the venues themselves; concert tickets for smaller venues may be sold in record shops (*see chapter* **Shopping**); look out for details on posters. The bullring has its own ticket office (*see page 81*) and football tickets can only be bought from the clubs (*see chapter* **Sports & Fitness**).

Fnac

El Triangle, Plaça Catalunya 4 (93 344 18 00). Metro Catalunya/bus all routes to Plaça Catalunya. **Open.** *Sept-May* 10am-9.30pm, *May-Sept* 10am-10pm, Mon-Sat. **Credit** AmEx, DC, JCB, MC, V. **Map** D5/**A1**
The Fnac has an efficient ticket desk to compete with the *caixes*. Mainly good for rock/pop concerts.

Taquilles Gran Via/Aribau

Plaça Universitat, corner Gran Via de les Corts Catalanes & C/Aribau (no phone). Metro Universitat/bus all routes to Plaça Universitat. **Open** 10am-1pm, 4.30-7.30pm, Mon-Sat. Closed public holidays and some weeks in summer. **No credit cards.** **Map** C5/**A1**
This booth mainly has tickets for events in the city's sports arenas, especially Olympic venues (stadium, Palau Sant Jordi, Velòdrom). This includes Espanyol football games, and stadium-scale pop concerts.

Travel services

Travel agents have become more competitive here, and it pays to shop around to find good deals.

Halcón Viajes

C/Aribau 34 (93 454 59 95/902 30 06 00). Metro Universitat/bus all routes to Plaça Universitat. **Open** 9.30am-1.30pm, 4.30-8pm, Mon-Fri; 10am-1.30pm Sat. **Credit** AmEx, DC, MC, V. **Map** C5
This chain travel agency is part of a group that also owns the airline Air Europa, and so often has exclusive bargain deals on its Spanish domestic and European flights. Also a hotel booking service, and good deals on car rental (*see also p115*).

Nouvelles Frontières

C/Balmes 8 (93 304 32 33/reservations 902 21 21 20). Metro Universitat, FGC Plaça Catalunya/bus all routes to Plaça Catalunya. **Open** 9.30am-8pm Mon-Fri; 10am-6pm Sat. **Credit** AmEx, DC, MC, V. **Map** D5
A no-nonsense agency with very competitive prices, sometimes offering savings of over 10,000ptas on European flights compared to larger agencies.

Arts & Entertainment

Children

Big fun for small fry.

Much of what makes Barcelona so appealing to adults is also inherently appealing to children. Gaudí's fairy tale-like buildings, the daily chaos of the Rambla and the city's streetlife are ageless pleasures, making sightseeing with kids in tow an enjoyable prospect. Cobbled streets in the old city can prove tricky with pushchairs, but Barcelona's compact layout also means you don't have to travel far to reach child-oriented attractions.

The birth rate may be dropping, but family bonds are strong in Catalonia, and children play an active role in everyday life. They are often treated very much like little adults; it's not unusual to see very young kids out for dinner with their parents at 11pm, and on summer evenings they fill city squares, playing impromptu football matches or charging around on rollerblades and bicycles. Your children will be made welcome wherever you go, and the most boisterous behaviour or worst temper tantrum will be met with patient smiles.

Practicalities

Unfortunately, the relaxed attitude toward kids also means a lack of child-specific concessions and facilities. Public transport is only free for children under four and a half, and few places have baby-changing facilities. Barcelona restaurants rarely offer children's menus, but will often supply small portions or simple dishes on request. Similarly, most hotels do not offer special services, although more upmarket establishments often have family suites and a child-minding service. Some (but not enough) even have pools (*see chapter* **Accommodation**).

To avoid frustration, adapt to the local timetable: most restaurants don't serve lunch before 2pm and dinner before 8pm. In summer, too, an afternoon siesta makes a lot of sense for over-heated children.

Attractions

Children's attractions cluster around Montjuïc, Tibidabo and the Port Vell, and there's a host of fun ways to get around them: funiculars, trams, cable cars and *golondrines* (swallow boats), as well as the open-top **Bus Turístic** (for all *see pages 58-9*). The **Poble Espanyol** is a bit of a tourist trap, but popular with kids, with a resident glassblower, arts and crafts demonstrations and magic and circus shows most summer weekends (*see page 75*). On a rainy day a good (expensive) standby can be the **IMAX** giant-format cinema (*see page 225*). For advance ticket outlets, *see page 215*.

L'Aquàrium de Barcelona

Moll d'Espanya, Port Vell (93 221 74 74). Metro Barceloneta/bus 14, 19, 36, 40, 57, 59, 64, 157, N6. **Open** *Sept-June* 9.30am-9pm Mon-Fri; 9.30am-9.30pm Sat, Sun, public holidays. *July, Aug* 9.30am-11pm daily. **Admission** 1,400ptas; 950ptas 4-12s; over-65s; group discounts; free under-4s; *advance sales* Tel-entrada. **Discounts** BC, BT. **Credit** MC, V. **Map** D7

One of the most attractive of its kind, the aquarium reproduces Mediterranean habitats in 21 tanks. The highlight is naturally the 80-metre glass tunnel through a shark tank, allowing you to walk through with scary sharks' teeth inches from your face. Little kids prefer the upstairs area, with a touching pool. *Disabled: wheelchair access. Multilingual staff.*

New Park

La Rambla 88 (93 412 51 78). Metro Liceu/bus 14, 38, 59, 91, N9, N12. **Open** 10am-11pm Mon-Thur, Sun; 10am-1am Fri, Sat. **No credit cards.** **Map** D6/A2-3

One for if you're desparate: this charmless amusement arcade offers three floors of video games and high-tech simulation games, for 100-200ptas each.

Nits hípiques a Barcelona (Horse shows)

Pista Hípica de la Foixarda, Avda Montanyans 1, Parc de Montjuïc. Metro Espanya/bus 9, 13, 38, 61, 65, 91. **Performances** *late June-Sept* 9pm Fri. **Tickets** tourist offices & Tel-entrada. **Admission** 700ptas; 500ptas under-10s. **Credit** MC, V. **Map** A5

Every Friday during summer the city police's ornately-uniformed display team presents an appealingly dainty show on their Andalusian horses, strutting their fancy footwork to music.

Tibidabo funfair

Parc d'Atraccions del Tibidabo, Plaça del Tibidabo 3-4 (93 211 79 42). FGC Av Tibidabo/bus 17, 22, 58, 73, 85, then Tramvia Blau and Funicular to park. **Open** *end-Mar-June, late Sept-early Oct* noon-early eve Sat, Sun, public holidays; plus *May* 10am-6pm Thur, Fri; *June* 10am-6pm Wed-Fri. *July, Aug* noon-10pm Mon-Thur, Sun, public holidays; noon-1am Fri, Sat; ; *early Sept* noon-8pm Mon-Thur; noon-10pm Fri-Sun, public holidays. **Admission** *entrance & 5 rides* 1,200ptas; free children under 1m 10cm tall. *Pass & unlimited number of rides* 2,400ptas; 600ptas under 1m 10cm. **Discounts** BC, BT. **Credit** MC, V.

Make a day of it by catching the **Tramvia Blau** up the hill to then the **Funicular**, which takes you through the woods to the top of the mountain and the funfair. Few amusement parks can compete with this spectacular mountain-top view. The park has lots of

Fun for all the family at **Tibidabo funfair.**

good old fashioned attractions (bumper cars, Ferris wheel, and so on), as well as the infamous house of horrors, **Hotel Krueger**. Also worth a visit is the **Museu d'Automates**, a wonderful collection of old fairground machines (*see p104*). If you've still got some energy, ramble back through the woods to the tram stop on the well sign-posted path.

Zoo de Barcelona
Parc de la Ciutadella (93 225 67 80). Metro Barceloneta, Ciutadella/bus 14, 39, 40, 41, 42, 51, 100, 141. **Open** *Nov-Feb* 10am-5.30pm; *Mar, Oct* 10am-6pm; *Apr, Sept* 10am-7pm; *May-Aug* 9.30am-7.30pm, daily. **Admission** 1,500ptas; 950ptas under-12, over-65s; group discounts; free under-3s. **Discounts** BC, BT. **Credit** MC, V. **Map** E6
The cramped concrete enclosures are not ideal for the animals, but small humans often enjoy the green, shady picnic areas, the regular shows at the Dolphinarium, the cuddly creatures in the farm area, and the chance to meet *Copito de Nieve* (Snowflake), the only albino gorilla in captivity.

Museums

In July and August many museums take part in the **Estiu als Museus** (Summer in the Museums) programme, with fun educational activities for kids. Details can be found at tourist offices and **La**

Virreina centre (*see pages 294-5*). The **Museu de Zoología** will delight budding zoologists, and has good children's exhibitions; the big, bold paintings at the **Fundació Miró** are a perfect introduction to the joys of art. The biggest hit with kids, though, is very often the **Museu del FC Barcelona**. For details *see chapter* **Museums**.

Museu de Cera (Wax museum)
Passatge de la Banca 7 (93 317 26 49).
Metro Drassanes/bus 14, 38, 59, 91. **Open** *mid Sept-mid July* 10am-1.30pm, 4-7.30pm, Mon-Fri; 11am-2pm, 4.30-8pm Sat, Sun, public holidays; *mid-July mid-Sept* 10am-10pm daily. **Admission** 900ptas; 550ptas over-65s, 5-11s; free under-5s.
No credit cards. Map D6/A4
Not a patch on Madame Tussauds, but worth a trip on a rainy day, the museum is home to over 300 wax figures, with good costumes. In the square outside is a bar, El Bosc de les Fades, with fairy-grotto décor. *Café. Disabled: toilets, wheelchair access.*

Museu de la Ciència
C/Teodor Roviralta 55-C/Cister 64 (93 212 60 50). FGC Tibidabo, then Tramvia Blau/bus 17, 22, 73, 85, 158. **Open** 10am-8pm Tue-Sun, public holidays. **Admission** 500ptas; 350ptas students under-25, over-65s; free under-7s, *additional exhibits* 200-250ptas extra. **Discounts** BC. **Credit** (shop only) V.
The science museum seeks to teach everything from mechanics to the layout of the human body through hands-on fun and gadgetry. It also runs a series of children's workshops in Castilian or Catalan that are touchy-feely enough to be enjoyed by foreign children. Contact the museum for details. *See also p103. Disabled: wheelchair access.*

Museu Marítim
Avda de les Drassanes (93 342 99 29). Metro Drassanes/bus 14, 20, 36, 38, 57, 59, 64, 91, 157. **Open** 10am-7pm daily. **Admission** 800ptas; 400ptas students, over-65s, under-16s; free under-7s. **Discounts** BC, BT. **Credit** MC, V.
Map C6/A4
The maritime museum is fab for kids: it offers life-sized models of boats and cabins, an oared galley and an audio-visual exhibit on life at sea through the ages. *See also p103.*

Museu d'Història de Catalunya
Plaça Pau Vila 3 (93 225 47 00). Metro Barceloneta/ bus all routes to Barceloneta. **Open** 10am-7pm Tue, Thur-Sat; 10am-8pm Wed; 10am-2.30pm Sun, public holidays. **Admission** 500ptas; 350ptas under-15s, students under 25, over-65s; group discounts; free under-7s, disabled. *Temporary exhibitions & combined tickets* prices vary. **Discounts** BC, BT. **Credit** (shop only) MC, V. **Map** D7/C4
Labels may be mostly Catalan-only, but kids enjoy this hands-on museum. At Museu d'Història de Catalunya they can mount a medieval horse, explore air raid shelters or step into a 1950s bar and a Franco-era schoolroom. See also p102. *Café. Disabled: wheelchair access. Shop.*

Beaches

As well as safe swimming and pretty clean sands, Barcelona's beaches offer lifeguards, showers and play areas, but few toilets, and no baby-changing facilities. From March to May the city council organises children's sports on the beaches, culminating in May with the **Festa de la Platja**, a fun-packed day of activities and games. Tourist offices (*see page 294*) have details. *See also page 70.*

Parks & playgrounds

Many of the city's most beautiful parks are outside the centre, and those in the old town are often disappointing paved squares. The exception is lush, green and fun **Ciutadella**. The bright ceramic sculptures in **Parc Güell** appeal to kids, and, further away, **Parc del Laberint** has a fun maze. For park details, *see pages 82-3.*

Parc del Castell de l'Oreneta

Camí de Can Caralleu & C/Montevideo (93 424 38 09). Bus 60, 66. **Open** *Nov-Feb* 10am-6pm; *Mar, Oct* 10am-7pm; *Apr, Sept* 10am-8pm; *May-Aug* 10am-9pm, daily. One of Barcelona's largest parks, not far from the **Monestir de Pedralbes** (*see pp86, 92*). Attractions include a pony club, a model steam train, a play area, a sports circuit and a snack bar.

Turó Parc

Avda Pau Casals. Bus 6, 7, 14, 15, 27, 32, 33, 34, 63, 67, 68. **Open** *Nov-Feb* 10am-6pm; *Mar, Oct* 10am-7pm; *Apr, Sept* 10am-8pm; *May-Aug* 10am-9pm, daily.* **Map** C2 Near the Diagonal, this park is a little uninspiring but pleasantly shady, and has a play area and a mini-theatre that hosts children's shows on Sundays.

Entertainment

Film

The **Verdi** has one screen that shows children's films undubbed, and the **Filmoteca** has a children's session Sundays at 5.30pm. For details, *see p226.*

Music

The auditorium of the **Fundació la Caixa** (*see chapter* **Art Galleries**) presents top-notch family concerts complete with entertainers, usually on Saturday mornings or Sunday afternoons from September to May. On June and July evenings, orchestras play in the city's parks for the **Classics als Parcs** cycle, and, for a really special outing, the **Liceu** season will include some shows for children. *See also chapter* **Music: Classical & Opera**.

Theatre

Barcelona hosts some excellent children's theatre, but basic understanding of Catalan or Spanish is essential. Plays and puppet shows can be seen at the **Jove Teatre Regina**, C/Sèneca 22 (93 218 15 12); **Teatre Goya**, **Teatre Malic** and **Artenbrut**

(*see chapter* **Theatre**). On Sundays there are children's shows at **Casa Elizalde** (*see chapter* **Music: Classical & Opera**), **Turó Parc**, **Poble Espanyol**, **Fundació Miró** and the **CCCB**. For English-language theatre check ads in English bookshops (*see pp193-4*) and *Metropolitan* magazine.

Festivals & seasons

See also pages 5-12 **Barcelona by Season**.

December: Christmas

In the run-up to 25 December Barcelonans flock to **Santa Llúcia** market in the Cathedral square, to buy Christmas trees and crib figures. Children traditionally get presents on 6 January, **El Dia dels Reis**. Excitement begins on the evening of the 5th with the *Cavalcada* (parade). Visit the life-sized crib in the Plaça Sant Jaume, and the exhibition of beautifully crafted cribs at the **Monestir de Pedralbes**.

February: Carnaval

Carnival week sees the streets of Barcelona filled with miniature Batmen, fairies and bumble bees. Colourful parades are held along the Rambla, with King Carnestoltes as the star of the show.

March, April: Easter

Treat them to a *mona*, an elaborate chocolate traditionally bought by godparents for their godchildren.

May: La Tamborinada

For a whole Saturday the Ciutadella is taken over by performers, puppets, magicians and circus acts.

June: Sant Joan

Sant Joan enters with a bang on 23 June, Midsummer Night's Eve, when bonfires are lit and fire crackers are set off all over the city. Hectic for small children, but very much a teen favourite.

August: Festa Major de Gràcia

Street parties are held in each area of Barcelona for a week during the summer. The best by far is in Gràcia. Beside enjoying the decorated streets, kids can join in the games, rides and competitions.

September: La Mercè

A huge street party: for a whole week, squares fill with clowns, puppets, concerts and theatre.

Out of town

For a day at the seaside, **Sitges** is easy-going and pretty, with pleasant, safe beaches; for a more hectic experience you can't beat **Port Aventura**, one of Europe's best theme parks. *See pages 258-60.*

Catalunya en Miniatura

Can Balasch de Baix, Torrelles de Llobregat (93 689 09 60). By Bus Oliveras from Plaça d'Espanya/by car N-II to Sant Vicens dels Horts, then left (10km/6 miles). **Open** *Oct-Mar* 10am-6pm, *Apr-Sept* 10am-7pm, daily. **Admission** 1,000ptas; 800ptas over-65s; 600ptas under-14s; free under-3s. **No credit cards.**

Apparently the largest model village in Europe, with over 170 miniatures of Catalonian monuments and buildings, and a mini train to take you around.

Parc de les Aus

Carretera de Vilassar de Mar a Cabrils, Vilassar de Mar (93 750 17 65). By car A19 or N-II north to Vilassar, then left (24km/15 miles)/by train RENFE from Sants or Plaça Catalunya to Vilassar, then taxi. **Open** *Sept-June* 10am-8pm, *July, Aug* 10am-9pm, Tue-Sun, public holidays. **Admission** 750ptas-1,100ptas; free under-3s. **Credit** AmEx, DC, MC, V.
Enjoy over 300 local and exotic bird species, extensive gardens, picnic spots and play areas.

Vintage trains

Steam trains **Information & reservations** *(93 205 15 15).* **Dates** Sept-June. **Tickets** 1,800ptas return; 1,000ptas return 3-14s; free under-3s. **No credit cards.**
An FGC steam train departs from Abrera (near Martorell) to Monistrol de Montserrat every Sunday at 11.30am, returning at 13.30pm. To reach Abrera, catch the 10.17am FGC train from Plaça d'Espanya. If you prefer a 1920s electric train, vintage rolling stock is in action, with live jazz on board, from Plaça Catalunya to Reina Elisenda on the first Sunday of each month. Railway buffs also enjoy the **Museu del Ferrocarril** (railway museum) in **Vilanova i la Geltrú** (Plaça Eduard Maristany, 93 815 84 91). *Booking well in advance essential.*

Waterparks

For fun cooling off, Catalonia has six waterparks. Other options further afield include **Aqua Brava** (Roses), **Aquadiver** (Platja d'Aro) and **Water World** (Lloret de Mar) along the Costa Brava, and **Aqua Park** near **Port Aventura**.

Aqualeón Safari

Finca les Basses, Albinyana (977 68 76 56). By car A2, then A7 via Vilafranca, or N340 to El Vendrell, then right to Albinyana (65km/40 miles). **Open** (safari park) *Easter-June, mid-Sept-Oct* 10am-6pm daily; *July-mid-Sept* 10am-7pm Mon-Fri, 10am-8pm Sat, Sun. (Water park) *mid-May-June* 11am-5pm daily; *July-mid-Sept* 11am-7pm Mon-Fri, 11am-8pm Sat, Sun. **Admission** *Easter-mid May, mid-Sept-Oct* 1,675ptas; 925ptas under-12s; free under-3s. *mid-May-mid-Sept* 2,200ptas; 1,200ptas under-12s; free under-3s. **Credit** AmEx, DC, MC, V.
An all-in-one water and safari park between Barcelona and Tarragona, with tigers, birds of prey and parrots as well as giant water slides, fun pools and wave machines. Captive dolphins too.

Illa de Fantasia

Finca Mas Brassó, Vilassar de Dalt (93 751 45 53). By car A19 or N11 north, left at Premià de Mar (24km). **Open** (waterpark) *June-mid-Sept* 10am-7pm Mon-Fri, Sun; 10am-7pm, 9pm-4am, Sat; (disco) *all year* 10pm-6am Sat. **Admission** *waterpark* 1,500ptas; 1,000ptas 2-10s; free under-2s. **No credit cards.**
In the evenings this park becomes a water disco.

A miniature Superman at **Carnaval.**

Babysitting & childcare

The agencies below employ qualified childminders, and can supply an English-speaker if necessary. Supervised daycare centres offer parents the chance of a few child-free hours.

Cangur Serveis

C/Aragó 227, pral (93 487 80 08/24-hour mobile 639 66 16 06). Metro Passeig de Gràcia/bus 7, 16, 17, 22, 24, 28. **Open** (office) *Sept-June* 9am-6pm Mon-Fri; July, Aug 9am-2pm Mon-Fri. **No credit cards. Map** D4
This specialist agency provides babysitters at two hours' notice any day of the year. Charges begin at 850ptas per hour, or 6,000ptas for an all-night service, with discounts for longer-term arrangements.

Cinc Serveis

C/Pelai 11, 5C (93 412 56 76/24-hour mobile 639 36 11 11/609 80 30 80). Metro Catalunya/bus all routes to Plaça Catalunya. **Open** *office* 9.30am-1.30pm, 4.30-8.30pm, Mon-Fri. **No credit cards. Map** D5/A1
The basic babysitting rate at Cinc Serveis, after 9pm, is 1,100ptas per hour; day and longer-term rates are less, phone for details.

Happy Parc

C/Comtes de Bell-lloc 74-78 (93 490 08 35). Metro Sants-Estació/bus all routes to Estacio de Sants. **Open** 5-9pm Mon-Fri; 11am-9pm Sat, Sun; 11am-2pm, 5-9pm, public holidays. **Rates** 500ptas per hour Mon-Thur; 550ptas per hour Fri-Sun, public holidays; 125ptas each subsequent 15mins. **No credit cards. Map** A3
An indoor fun park and drop-in daycare centre for kids from 2-12.
Branch: C/Pau Claris 97 (93 317 86 60).

Xiqui Park

C/Manuel de Falla 31 (93 205 46 76). FGC Les Tres Torres/bus 34, 66. **Open** 4.30-9pm Mon-Fri; 11am-2.30pm, 4.30-9pm, Sat, Sun. **Rates** 500ptas per hour. **No credit cards. Map** B2
Xiqui Park caters for children aged 1 to 12 with a range of fun activities, and also organises birthday parties. Phone for further details.
Branch: C/Marina 228 (93 231 40 59).

Dance

Enthusiasm and invention keep contemporary dance alive and kicking in Barcelona.

In Spain, while Madrid is the centre of traditional Spanish dance and has the most solid ballet programme, Barcelona has established itself as the most vibrant centre for contemporary dance. There are no big, institutional companies that preside over the scene, but the city is the base for a diverse range of small- to medium-sized groups consistently producing exciting and original work.

This situation emerged out of the cultural exuberance of the late 1970s, when new freedoms encouraged new departures in all the arts. Experimentation was especially evident in dance, since previously Barcelona had never really had any recognised dance groups, nor a classical ballet school. Unhindered by tradition, young dancers were free to try anything and everything. Much the same is true today, as a new generation of young dancers tests the limits of what their elders have left them. Meanwhile, some of the companies that first appeared in the '70s-early '80s have matured into contemporary dance powerhouses with international reputations, such as Angels Margarit's **Mudances** and Cesc Gelabert and Lydia Azzopardi's **Companyia Gelabert-Azzopardi**.

There is now a solid core of young dancers and companies in Barcelona, but, as ever, they often have to scramble for resources. Enthusiasm remains essential to keeping the dance scene going, for it still lacks funding and a central location where dancers can study and practise. Apart from the Institut del Teatre dance school, only a few private schools nurture serious dancers, although **La Caldera** (the Boilerhouse) in Gràcia, serves as a joint rehearsal space for several younger companies. Things have improved with regard to places for dancers to perform: many Barcelona venues now feature dance fairly regularly, and the **Teatre Nacional** (*see p253*) includes a varied dance menu in its seasons, providing a completely new venue for contemporary dance with first-rate facilities.

The Generalitat supports dance, to the tune of around 150 million pesetas (£600,000/$1 million) each year. Most of this goes into performances rather than development of new talents, and dance groups can't prevent young stars from going abroad to further their careers. This concentration on performance over preparation can result in well-dressed, but hurried pieces; nevertheless, it's still common to see fine performances in which the power of imagination makes lack of resources a minor consideration.

NON-CONTEMPORARY DANCE

If contemporary dance has become an integral part of the local arts scene, opportunities to see other kinds of dance (except folk dancing, for which *see pages 5-12* **Barcelona by Season**) are relatively few. Barcelona still does not have a classical ballet school, and while it has often been suggested that one should be included in the rebuilt Liceu, nothing has been decided, even though the opera house was re-inaugurated in October 1999. The new Liceu will host some prestigious international dance companies – William Forsythe and the Frankfurt Ballet appeared in the first season – but also seems likely to continue its dubious pre-1994-fire tradition of importing ballet productions by tired touring companies from eastern Europe (*see chapter* **Music: Classical & Opera**).

As for Spanish dance and flamenco, the best of the genre is not permanently in residence here, but high-quality flamenco companies such as those of Sara Baras or Antonio Canales do pass regularly through Barcelona on national tours, and the major Madrid companies are, again, likely to visit the Liceu. Performers at the city's flamenco *tablaos* are rarely first-rate, although even middling flamenco can provide a memorable evening, and since the mid '90s there has actually been a vogue for flamenco in Barcelona, with venues like **Tarantos** sprucing up décor and programmes. For venues, *see chapter* **Music: Rock, Roots & Jazz**.

Information

Associació dels Professionals de Dansa de Catalunya *Via Laietana 52, entresol 7 (93 268 24 73/dansa_catalunya@ols.es). Metro Urquinaona/bus 17, 19, 40, 45.* **Open** 10am-2pm Mon, Wed, Fri; 10am-2pm, 4.30-7.30pm, Tue, Thur.
Acts as a clearing-house for the dance companies, with information on who is doing what at any time. For programme information, check the *Guia del Ocio* and the free *Barcelona en Música*, available in record shops and at venues. These and other venue leaflets are also available at **La Virreina** (*see page 295*).
Website: www.dancespain.com

Dance groups

Other groups to look out for include **Búbulus, Erre Que Erre**, the contemporary/flamenco **Increpación Danza, Hamilton/Renalias, Las Malqueridas** and **Nats Nus**.

Mudances *performs L'Edat de la Paciència.*

Danat Dansa

This ever-experimental company first performed in 1985. Choreography is by Sabine Dahrendorf, from Germany, and Alfonso Ordóñez, from León, in collaboration with a core group of five dancers. The extensive research behind each piece and the varied backgrounds of the directors ensure works with complex content and an original, dynamic language. In 1999 they presented an eight-dancer piece called *L'ull esbalaït* (The Astonished Eye), a homage to filmmaker Luis Búñuel, at the Teatre Nacional.

Gelabert-Azzopardi Companyia de Dansa

Cesc Gelabert studied at the Cunningham School in New York and on his return became the most influential figure in Catalan contemporary dance, helping develop a particular style concentrating more on form than emotion, and forming a crop of new dancers at his school, La Fàbrica. Lydia Azzopardi, previously at The Place in London, has contributed a sophisticated level of traditional dance knowledge. Current projects include a work 'dedicated to Buster Keaton', *Useless Information Meets Boy*, to be presented at the Teatre Nacional in April 2000.

Lanònima Imperial Companyia de Dansa

Juan Carlos García, who founded and choreographs Lanònima Imperial Companyia de Dansa, benefited from time with Galotta in France and Cunningham in America. Since 1986 he has used his extensive training to develop a rich and very physical language, with philosophical content. In 1999 Lanònima premiered Transfigured Night, to music by Schoenberg, and Alçada, with music by Xavier Maristany and Alex Polls. A new piece, Liturgia de Somni i Foc (Liturgy of Dream and Fire), is in preparation for the National Theatre.

Mal Pelo

The name means 'bad hair' implying a rebellious spirit, and its choreography combines abstract dance with a strong storyline. Formed in 1989 by two well-respected dancers, Pep Ramis and María Muñoz, this group has performed across Europe and the US, where it received excellent reviews for *Dol* in 1995. Mal Pelo's most recent performance piece,

El Alma del Bicho (The Soul of the Beast), directed by María Muñoz and danced by Pep Ramis and Enric Fábregas, was presented at L'Espai in 1999.

Mudances

Angels Margarit has been gaining in stature as a choreographer through the last decade, producing highly structured, complex work. Mudances features two male dancers and four women, and has had many international successes, beginning in 1991 with *Atzavara*. Margarit's work has a strong sense of female-ness: the highly praised 1999 *L'Edat de la Paciència* (The Age of Patience) dealt very originally with the ageing process in the female body.

La Porta

This collective performs more or less monthly at the **Sala Beckett** or the **Metrònom** gallery (*see chapter* **Art Galleries**), and represents an all-star team drawn from Barcelona's best young dancers.

Roseland Musical

Formed in 1983 by Marta Almirall to bring exciting, original dance to children, Roseland produces work that can easily satisfy adults as well. Storylines and choreography are original, and the style combines theatre, dance and music. The company has won international acclaim when on tour, and will be performing a new piece, *1,001 Nights* during 2000.

Venues

L'Espai is the only venue with a permanent slot for dance, but the **Teatre Nacional** has provided a new main stage for Catalan dance companies, usually in its *Sala Tallers* (Workshop Space). The **Teatre Lliure** and **Teatre Adrià Gual** present dance with reasonable frequency, and **Sala Beckett** hosts small-scale, fringe events (for all, *see pages 252-4* **Theatre**). There are dance seasons at the **Casa Elizalde** (*see chapter* **Music: Classical & Opera**), and experimental dance shows at the **CCCB** (*see chapter* **Art Galleries**).

An officially-promoted dance season, **Dansa + a prop** (roughly, 'Dance closer to you') features performances by well- and lesser known companies from April to June, in a wide range of venues, often civic centres away from the city centre. Information is available at **La Virreina** (*see page 295*).

L'Espai

Travessera de Gràcia 63 (93 414 31 33). FGC Gràcia/bus 16, 17, 27, 31, 32, N4. **Box office** 6-10pm Mon-Sat; 6-7pm Sun; *advance sales* box office & Servi-Caixa. **Performances** *Sept/Oct-June* usually 10pm Mon-Sat, 7pm Sun. **Tickets** 1,000-2,000ptas (subject to change). **No credit cards.** **Map** C3
The full title of this Catalan government showcase is 'L'Espai de Dansa i Música de la Generalitat de Catalunya', and it combines dance programmes (nearly always contemporary) with contemporary, experimental and (sometimes) other music.

Film

Could movie-mad Barcelona soon become a favoured film location?

Movies never have trouble finding an audience in Barcelona – this is a city of film-lovers, where lines for the latest Hollywood sensation stretch around the block. Moviegoing, moreover, has actually been increasing in popularity through the '90s. A string of new cinemas with first-rate facilities has opened in recent years to meet a booming demand, including multiplexes such as the six-screen **Renoir** in Les Corts or the 15-screen **Icària** in Vila Olímpica.

Most first-run films are still shown dubbed into Castilian Spanish, or sometimes Catalan. Fortunately for outsiders, however, there is a growing number of people in the city who want to see films in the language in which they were made, with Castilian (or occasionally Catalan) subtitles. There are currently about 22 screens regularly showing films undubbed, and the closure of old-favourite art cinemas such as the Capsa and the Arkadin has been balanced by new additions such as the delightful two-screen **Méliès** or the newly-renovated **Boliche** on the Diagonal.

The biggest crowds still turn out for Hollywood movies, and pictures like *The Matrix* or a new *Star Wars* fill cinema lobbies. However, Spanish and Catalan films are not shunned by Barcelona audiences, and one consequence of the current boom in cinemagoing in Spain has been to give a new boost to domestic production. The central government provides substantial subsidies and tax breaks to encourage the home film industry, and lately it has seemed this effort is finally bearing fruit. In 1998, 15 per cent of film tickets bought in Spain were for Spanish productions, up from 13 per cent in 1997, and a lowly 9.3 per cent in 1996.

Spain's best-known director is still Pedro Almodóvar, who after a few years in the doldrums was named Best Director at the 1999 Cannes Festival for *Todo Sobre Mi Madre* (All About My Mother). One of his strongest films, it was also shot in Barcelona, the first ever of his 17 features not to be filmed in Madrid. This could, maybe, signal a new chic for Barcelona as backdrop. The Mediterranean, and the city's *Modernista* architecture, stand out strongly in Almodóvar's tale of two women with crossed lives, played by Cecilia Roth and Penelope Cruz.

Some of the best films currently being made in Spain, and among the most successful at the box office, are set in gritty urban *barrios*, and offer a window into a kind of everyday Spanish life rarely seen on television or in the press. Two examples

are Fernando León de Aranoa's Madrid-based *Barrio*, from 1998, and 1999's *Solas* by Benito Zambrano, set in an unidentified Andalusian city.

CATALAN CINEMA

In the first part of this century, Barcelona itself was a major film centre. By the 1960s, though, Madrid exerted its influence more and more, and became the unquestioned centre of Spain's film industry. Today, the Catalan government offers its own subsidies to local productions, on condition that the film be shown in Catalan inside Catalonia. Two films released in 1999 under these terms were *Saïd*, a low-budget story of a Moroccan illegal immigrant in Barcelona's *Chino*, and *Amic/Amat*, by Ventura Pons. One of the most long-awaited of Catalan productions, *La Ciutat dels Prodigis* (The City of Marvels), based on Eduardo Mendoza's renowned Barcelona novel and directed by Mario Camus, was finally shot in 1998. However, it received almost universally (and wholly justified) bad reviews when it opened the following spring.

After years without any organisation to promote it as a place to make films, recently Barcelona finally acquired a film commission, **Barcelona Plató**. In addition to maintaining location files and helping crews shoot here, they have spearheaded an effort to bring the **Women's Film Festival** and several other small film festivals and events under one administrative umbrella.

In 1998, also, Catalan President Jordi Pujol threatened to impose quotas on the screening of Hollywood films, if studios did not pay for a percentage of their work to be dubbed in Catalan for exhibition here. Distributors in Spain set up a howl, while Hollywood just shrugged its shoulders and made it clear it had no intention of complying. The Generalitat necessarily backed down; sr Pujol, though, had the headlines to savour.

Films undubbed: VO

Independent movies are nearly always shown in their original language, and it's also now common for Hollywood releases to be shown in English on at least one screen in the city. Films shown undubbed with Spanish/Catalan subtitles are called *versió original* or *VO* films, and identified by the letters VO. We list specialised VO cinemas below.

Tickets & times

Current programme details are found in the *Guía del Ocio* and daily papers (*see chapter* **Media**). Like most things in Barcelona, filmgoing tends to happen later

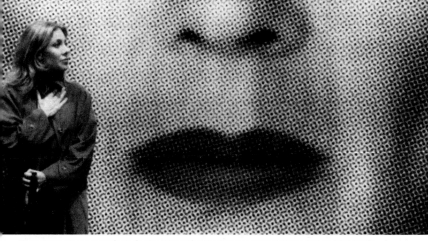

Barcelona on screen: from Pedro Almodóvar's Cannes-winner Todo Sobre Mi Madre.

than in northern countries, and the most popular sessions are those that start around 10.30pm, when there are big queues at weekends. On Sundays, it's advisable to buy tickets in advance, or at least arrive at the cinema in very good time for 8pm and 10.30pm shows. Real 'late' shows are after midnight on Fridays and Saturdays. There are good VO weekend late shows at the **Icària**, **Renoir**, and **Verdi**.

All cinemas have a cheap day (*dia del espectador*), usually Monday or Wednesday. A few take phone bookings, and some sell advance tickets via *Servi-Caixa* (*see p215*), but getting a ticket at the door is rarely a problem except on weekend evenings. For information on films for kids, *see chapter* **Children**.

All cinemas listed have air-conditioning.

Mega-screen movies

IMAX Port Vell

Moll d'Espanya (902 33 22 11). Metro Barceloneta/ bus 14, 36, 57, 59, 64, 100, 157, N6. **Open** *box office* 30 min before first performance, until 1am. *Advance sales* through Servi-Caixa, and at box office until one hour before performance time. **Tickets** *early shows* 1,000ptas; *afternoon/evening shows* 1,400ptas, *night shows* 1,500ptas, daily. **Discounts** BT. **Credit** MC, V. **Map** D7

Like one city after another, Barcelona has an IMAX. Opened in 1995, it has drawn big audiences, but how many filmgoers bother to see 'large format' cinema more than once is unknown. It offers a choice of mega-formats, with films on a wrap-around, dome-like OMNIMAX screen and on a towering flat IMAX screen in 3-D, with polarised glasses provided. The problem is that there aren't many films made for these screens, so programmes rarely stray from a repetitive round of nature films like *Life in the Deep*, and other documentaries like *New York-3D* and the IMAX chestnut *The Rolling Stones live at the Max*. *Disabled: toilet, wheelchair access.*

VO cinemas

Boliche

Avda Diagonal 508 (93 218 17 88). Metro Diagonal/bus 6, 7, 15, 27, 32, 33, 34. **Open** *box office* from 3.30pm daily. *Advance sales* box office & Servi-Caixa. **Tickets** 650ptas Mon; 725 ptas Tue-Fri; 750ptas Sat, Sun, public holidays. **Map** D3

A four-plex that opened in 1998 and shows Hollywood and mainstream features, usually in VO on at least one screen. The smallest *sala* only seats 64, and feels almost like a big living room, while the largest has 190 seats and is a full-scale movie theatre. Sound and sight-lines are excellent in all four.

Casablanca

Passeig de Gràcia 115 (93 218 43 45). Metro Diagonal/bus 22, 24, 28, 100, 101, N4. **Open** *box office* 15 min before first performance. **Tickets** 600ptas Mon; 725ptas Tue-Fri; 775ptas Sat, Sun, public holidays. **No credit cards. Map** D4

Two-screen art cinema mostly showing US and European non-mainstream films. The bar has decent food, and its occasional revivals are very popular. *Bar/café.*

Icària Yelmo Cineplex

C/Salvador Espriu 61 (information 93 221 75 85/ bookings 93 221 79 12). Metro Ciutadella-Vila Olímpica/bus 36, 41, 71, 92, 100, N6, N8. **Open** *box office* 11am-11pm Mon-Thur, Sun; 11am-1am Fri, Sat. *Advance sales* box office & ServiCaixa. **Late shows** 12.50am Fri, Sat. **Tickets** 600ptas Mon, before 2.30pm Tue-Sun; 775ptas after 2.30pm Tue-Sun, late shows. **No credit cards. Map** F7

This 15-screen modern mega-cinema opened in 1996 in the Olympic Village shopping centre, across from the beach. Often as many as half of the films showing at any given time are in English, with a good mix of mainstream and independent work. Weekend late shows (in all 15 screens) are often interesting, too. *Disabled: toilet, wheelchair access.*

Maldà

C/del Pi 5 (93 317 85 29). Metro Liceu/bus 14, 38, 59, N9, N12. **Open** *box office* 15 min before first performance. **Tickets** 500ptas Mon; 700ptas Tue-Fri; 750ptas Sat, Sun, public holidays. **No credit cards. Map** D6/B2-A3

A much-loved place, this is the only cinema housed in an eighteenth-century palace, with a grand staircase for its entrance, just inside the Galeries Maldà arcade near Plaça del Pi. It shows a double-bill VO repertory programme that changes each week, with classics and recent movies you may have missed.

Méliès Cinemes

C/Villaroel 102 (93 451 00 51). Metro Urgell/bus 14, 20, 38, 59, N12. **Open** *box office* 30 min before first performance. **Tickets** 400ptas Mon; 600ptas Tue-Sun, public holidays. **No credit cards. Map** C5

This two-screen Eixample cinema opened in 1997, and quickly developed a faithful audience. It shows mainly Hollywood classics, leaning towards film noir, in a frequently-changing programme. It's a comfortable place, and is run both for film buffs and for those who just like a movie that stands the test of time.

Disabled: toilet, wheelchair access.

Renoir-Les Corts

C/Eugeni d'Ors 12 (93 490 55 10). Metro Les Corts/bus 15, 43, 59, 70, 72. **Open** *box office* 3.45-11pm Mon-Thur, Sun; 3.45-11pm, midnight-1am, Fri, Sat. *Advance sales* box office & ServiCaixa. **Late shows** from 12.30am Fri, Sat, eves of public holidays. **Tickets** 575ptas Mon; 750ptas Tue-Fri; 800ptas Sat, Sun, public holidays. **No credit cards. Map** A3

In a nondescript street a short walk from Les Corts Metro, this six-screen complex shows non-Spanish films exclusively in VO. There are usually at least two films in English, and a separate programme for late shows. Sound quality and comfort are of a high standard, and there are also unusually good facilities for disabled people.

Café. Disabled: toilet, wheelchair access.

Verdi

C/Verdi 32 (93 237 05 16). Metro Fontana/bus 39. **Open** *box office* 15 min before first performance. **Late shows** (Verdi only) 12.45am Fri, Sat. **Tickets** 600ptas Mon; 750ptas Tue-Fri; 800ptas Sat, Sun, public holidays. **No credit cards. Map** D3

This is the great success story of Barcelona's VO film houses. In 1992, the Verdi had three screens; in 1993, it added two more, and in 1995 the four-screen **Verdi Park** opened just around the block. All the venues are popular as meeting-places as well as movie-houses. Classic revivals are shown alongside contemporary international releases. Moreover, the Verdi has gained an international reputation for its willingness to screen new independent films. There's a separate late-show programme, and one screen dedicated to showing children's films, also usually in VO (*see chapter* **Children**).

Disabled: toilet, wheelchair access at Verdi Park only.
Branch: Verdi Park C/Torrijos 49 (93 238 79 90).

The Filmoteca

Filmoteca de la Generalitat de Catalunya

Cinema Aquitania, Avda Sarrià 31-3 (93 410 75 90). Metro Hospital Clínic/bus 15, 27, 32, 41, 54, 59, 66, N3, N12. **Open** *box office* 1 hour before first performance. Closed some public holidays & Aug. **Tickets** 400ptas; 300ptas students and over-65s; 5,000ptas block ticket for 20 films; 10,000ptas for 100 films. **Credit** *for block tickets only* MC, V. **Map** C3

The official Filmoteca film theatre shows a changing slate of three films each day, nearly always in VO, usually in short seasons on themes, countries or directors. The eclectic mix is often fascinating. In the past the *Filmo* has been a virtual school for aspiring directors and producers, providing the only opportunity in the city to see classics from other countries. A children's programme is shown at 5pm on Sundays.

Bar. Disabled: toilet, wheelchair access.

Events

Mostra Internacional de Films de Dones de Barcelona (Women's Film Festival)

Venue *Filmoteca de la Generalitat de Catalunya.*
Dates first half of June.

Held since 1993, this highly successful event, organised by Dracmàgic (93 216 00 04) is an exhibition (not a competition) of women's cinema, past and present. Directors also speak about their work in lively debates.

Festival Internacional de Cinema de Catalunya, Sitges

Information *Avda Josep Tarradellas 135, esc A, 3er 2a, 08029 Barcelona (93 419 36 35/fax 93 439 73 80).* **Dates** first half of Oct.

The current handle of the very popular Sitges Festival of Fantastic Cinema, which began as a small-scale event specialising in all kinds of cinema roughly classed as 'fantastic', from sci-fi to pure fantasy or horror movies. This definition became everlooser over the years (to the irritation of real schlock buffs), and in 1997 was dropped from the title. Fantasy and horror still feature, but alongside other sections such as retrospectives, and the *Gran Angular* for new international independent productions, whether by Jean-Luc Godard (with *For Ever Mozart*, his film on Bosnia) or complete unknowns. This section also has its own prize which, as an original touch, is voted by the viewing public: in 1998 it went to *Lluvia en los Zapatos* (UK title *If Only*), a whimsical comedy filmed in London, in English, by Catalan director Maria Ripoll. The main critics' prize was for Canadian Vincenzo Natali's brilliantly constructed *Cube*. The festival is aimed at the industry and the public, and this is a key to its success. Films are shown in several venues around Sitges, and many of the town's restaurants and bars join in the spirit and stay open through the night. Tickets can be bought in Barcelona through **Tel-Entrada** (*see p215*). *See pp258-9* for details of how to get to Sitges, and where to stay and eat once there.

Gay & Lesbian Barcelona

Cafés, clubs, cabaret and Carnaval keep Barcelona's gay scene lively all year round – and if that's not enough there's fun in the sun at Sitges, just down the coast.

Barcelona is gay in both senses of the word. It is merry for all and, at the same time, the city has seen an explosion of new gay bars, clubs, shops and restaurants in the last couple of years. There are now more than 75 establishments catering specifically for the gay and lesbian market. Moreover, the city is nestled on the Catalan coast, with the beautiful beach town and gay mecca of **Sitges** a few kilometres away.

The city hosts a lively gay community that flexes its economic muscle even on the political scene. One area of the Eixample, roughly in the blocks around the junction of C/Muntaner and C/Consell de Cent (**Map** C4-5), has acquired such a concentration of gay venues that it has been labelled the *Gaixample*, and is rapidly becoming the Soho or West Hollywood of Barcelona. It's no surprise that Barcelona is one of the few Spanish cities to recognise the rights of gay domestic partners. At the

same time, however, while it's true that things are changing rapidly, it is also still not uncommon to meet young *guapos* (good-looking men) who cannot invite you back to their place because they live with their parents. So, be prepared.

The visitor should also keep in mind that some of the best places to have 'a gay old time' are not strictly gay. Nightlife here brings many different types of people together to *pasarlo bien* (have a good time). The gay scene, sometimes called *el ambiente* – which can equally be translated just as atmosphere – is quite gender- and persuasion-mixed. Don't worry about dress codes – you can wear just about anything or almost nothing. Like most things in Spain, gay nightlife goes on long and late, so make the most of it; you can always rest on your return from your trip. If you like to stroll and/or you're an eye-candy addict, then this is your town. Cruising and sightseeing combine

House and garage get the crowd going at the happening **Arena**. *See page 229.*

fluidly. Try the top of Montjuïc for stunning views of the city; it's one of Barcelona's gems.

A *Gay Barcelona* map and answers to questions are available in **Sextienda** and **Zeus** (*see page 232*). In addition, there are several free city gay rags that you can pick up for more information about current events and updated listings. The local magazine *Nois* is comprehensive, accurate, has a great map, and offers information on gay-owned and/or -friendly places throughout Catalunya. *Nois* also has a related website (www.revistanois.com).

The biggest concentration of gay venues may be in the Eixample – making it easy to wander from one to the next – but even venues located in other areas are never too far from the centre of town. Naturally, spring and summer are the best times to visit the city, but don't underestimate the surprisingly fun time to be had at *Carnaval* in mid-February (*see pages 12, 278*).

Cafés & bars

It's worth mentioning here that, although **Cafè de L'Opera**, **Schilling**, the **Tèxtil Cafè** (*see chapter* **Cafés & Bars**) and the **Marsella** (*see chapter* **Nightlife**) are not gay per se, they are regularly well-frequented by gays and lesbians.

Acido Oxido
C/Joaquín Costa 61 (93 412 09 39). Metro Universitat/bus 24, 41, 55, 64, 91, 141, N6. **Open** 6pm-2.30am daily. **Map** C5
A trendy oblong industrial-style venue with a panoramic view of the main floor from the men's urinal. Tattoos and piercings are accessories for much of the clientele. A different sort of place to have a drink before **Metro**.

Café de la Calle
C/de Vic 11 (93 218 38 63). Metro Diagonal/bus 16, 17, 22, 24, 28, N6, N9. **Open** 6pm-2.30am Tue-Sun. **Map** D3
Where does one go for light-hearted, intimate conversation with someone special or in a small group? Café de la Calle is a well-lit, cosy and orderly environment where there's pleasant music and good sandwiches. Women like it just as much as men.

Café Dietrich
C/Consell de Cent 255 (93 451 77 07). Metro Universitat/bus 14, 54, 58, 64, 66, N3. **Open** 10.30pm-2.30am daily. **Map** C5
This was once the most popular gay place in BCN, and still holds it own against the other major contenders. The elegant deco entrance leads to a small dance floor and good music. Well-done short drag performances are put on at regular intervals each night for the good-looking crowd.

The Eagle
Passeig de Sant Joan 152 (93 207 58 56). Metro Verdaguer/bus 15, 55. **Open** 8pm-2.30am daily. **Map** E4

On the rough side: the Eagle has a moustached and bearded clientele, and subdued lighting to enhance that rustic darkroom effect. The dress code stipulates jeans and leather, and some nights only underwear.

Frivolité
C/Casanova 71 (93 323 10 00). Metro Urgell/bus 9, 50, 54, 56, 58, 64, 66, N1, N2, N3. **Open** 6pm-3am daily. **Map** C5
The newest up-and-coming place in the *Gaixample* is very large with cutting edge design, wall projections and good house sounds. It is next door to, and acts as an escape valve for, **Medusa**. All are welcomed with a smile, even on the busiest nights.

Medusa
C/Casanova 75 (93 454 53 63). Metro Urgell/bus 9, 50, 54, 56, 58, 64, 66, N1, N2, N3. **Open** 10pm-3am daily. **Map** C5
This is the most popular of the recently-opened nightspots for a youthful, trendy crowd. Minimalist décor leaves space for browsing and/or dancing (good grooves). It also has furnished corners and wall sofas for chatting or taking the load off. Boys have preference for entry on busy nights.

New Chaps
Avda Diagonal 365 (93 215 53 65). Metro Diagonal or Verdaguer/bus 6, 15, 33, 34, N4, N6. **Open** 9pm-3am daily. **Map** D4
The cowboy bar atmosphere still lingers, but times have changed. New Chaps mostly attracts the mature and manly, and regular theme nights as well as the downstairs darkroom draw an ample crowd.

Ouí Café
C/Consell de Cent 247. (no phone). Metro Universitat/bus 14, 54, 58, 59, 64, 66, N3. **Open** 5pm-2am daily. **Map** C5
Situated near several popular bars, Ouí Café is a pleasant, stylish place for the first cocktail of the night.

Punto BCN
C/Muntaner 63-65 (93 453 61 23/93 451 91 52). Metro Universitat/bus 14, 54, 58, 59, 64, 66, N3. **Open** 6pm-2.30am daily. **Map** C5
Punto BCN is one of few places to open in the early evening. Plenty of seating upstairs offers full view of the entrance and the main floor bar, and the friendly air and pleasant décor lend themselves to the comingling of people of all sizes, shapes, ages and types.

Clubs

As with bars in general, there are several locales that are not strictly gay but which have a big and established gay following, especially among the young and hip: the waterside **Distrito Marítimo**, **Octopussy** and **Tijuana Morning Café** to name but three of the most popular (for all, *see chapter* **Nightlife**).

Arena

C/Balmes 32 (no phone). Metro Passeig de Gracia, Universitat/bus 7, 16, 17, N1, N2. **Open** midnight-5am Tue-Sun. **Admission** 600ptas (incl beer or soft drink). **Map** D5

In the tradition of **Martins** and **Metro**, this large spacious dancefloor with lighting and special effects, and pounding house and garage sounds, attracts a younger crowd with energy to burn.

Arena VIP

Gran Via de les Corts Catalanes 593 (93 487 83 42) Metro Universitat/bus all routes to Plaça Universitat. **Open** midnight-5am Tue-Sun. **Admission** 600ptas (incl beer or soft drink). **Map** D5

Even the latest hot spots haven't diminished this club's drawing power. A cross-section of gays, lesbians and straights make it an interesting place to move the feet. Great new and not-so-new music on tap.

Martins

Passeig de Gracia 130 (93 218 71 67) Metro Diagonal/bus 22, 24, 28, N4, N6. **Open** midnight-5am daily. **Admission** 1,500ptas (incl one drink). **Map** D3-4

Martins is now experiencing a comeback after many years in waiting. Three floors give plenty of room to roam about, and the music gets you like dancing. **New Chaps** and **Eagle** empty into here as they close, especially on co-operative theme nights.

Metro

C/Sepúlveda 158 (93 323 52 27). Metro Universitat/bus 24, 41, 55, 64, 91, 141, N6. **Open** midnight-5am daily. **Admission** 1,500ptas (incl one drink). **Map** C5

Surprisingly, this club is yet to lose its hold on BCN gay nightlife. It's unbearably packed at the weekend, but the punters keep coming back for more. Women are always welcome, and there are regular mid-week party nights. The backroom can be an entertaining labyrinth, but take care with valuables.

Salvation

Ronda Sant Pere 19-21 (no phone). Metro Urquinaona/bus 16, 17 18, 19, 40, 45. **Open** midnight-5am daily. **Admission** 1,500ptas. **Map** D5

Two large dance floors, decent music and handsome, muscular, bareback personnel are fast making this newcomer a popular night stop on the gay circuit.

Castro

C/Casanova 85 (93 323 67 84). Metro Universitat/bus all lines to Plaça Catalunya. **Open** 1-4pm, 9pm-midnight, Mon-Fri; 9pm-midnight Sat. **Average** 3,500ptas. **Set menu** 1,200ptas. **Credit** DC, MC, V. **Map** C4

A new, modern mix of industrial and elegant decor entertains the eye while you enjoy one of the best Mediterranean-style menus available in gay BCN, with truly excellent food. The place is very popular, so book ahead.
Booking advisable.

Ovlas

C/Portaferrissa 25 (93 412 38 36). Metro Plaça Catalunya/bus 14, 16, 17, 38, 41, 59, N6, N9. **Open** 9.30am-8.30pm Mon-Sat. **Set menu** 1,250ptas. **Credit** AmEx, MC, V. **Map** D6/B2

A new if rather antique-style accompaniment to the **Ovlas Men's Store** chain (*see p229*), serving varied Italian dishes, pastas and salads.

Roma

C/Alfons XII 39-41 (93 201 35 13). Metro Fontana/bus 14, 17, 24, 25, 30, 31, 58, 64. **Open** 1-4pm, 9pm-midnight, Mon-Sat. **Set lunch** 1,200ptas. **Set dinner** 2,100ptas. **Credit** DC, MC, V. **Map** D3

This long-time uptown favourite continues to serve a more-than-decent Mediterranean-style meal at a reasonable price. You can't help but be pleased with the congenial staff, warm setting and the after-dinner cocktails at its well populated bar.

Silver

C/Consell de Cent 257 (no phone). Metro Universitat/bus 14, 54, 58, 64, 66, N3. **Open** noon-2am. **Average** 1,050ptas day menu; 1,750ptas night menu. **Credit** MC, V. **Map** C5

Offers interior or exterior seating (weather permitting) and a fine meal at good value for money.
Tables outdoors.

Cabaret-restaurants

In all three of these gilded, lushly decorated venues dining is really secondary to the highly professional (each in its own way) and very entertaining drag shows on offer. Opinions vary, but word is out that one eats better in **Miranda** and **Diva**. Try them all and judge for yourself.

Café Miranda *C/Casanova 30 (93 453 52 49). Metro Universitat/bus all routes to Plaça Catalunya.* **Open** 9pm-1am daily. **Average** 3,000ptas. **Credit** DC, MC, V. **Map** C5. Weekend booking essential.

La Diva *C/Diputació 172 (93 454 63 98). Metro Universitat/bus all routes to Plaça Catalunya.* **Open** 1-3.30pm, 9pm-midnight Tue-Sun. **Average** 3,500ptas. **Set b** 1,750ptas. **Credit** MC, V. **Map** C5 Weekend booking essential.

Eternal *C/Casanova 42 (93 453 17 86). Metro Universitat/bus all routes to Plaça Catalunya.* **Open** 1-3.30pm, 9.30pm-midnight. **Average** 4,000ptas. **Set menu** (lunch only) 975ptas. **Credit** DC, MC, V. **Map** C5. Weekend booking essential.

Accommodation

Hostal Qué Tal

C/Mallorca 290 (93 459 23 66). Metro Passeig de Gracia, Verdaguer/bus 6, 15, 33, 34, 45, N4, N6. **Rates** *single* 4,800ptas; *double* 7,200ptas,-(with bath) 9,500ptas. **No credit cards. Map** D4

What a nice place to spend the night. The 'Hostal How Are You' is exceptionally clean, with very attractive simple décor and fantastically helpful staff

The Sitges ambience

Gay men from around the world agree that it's hard to beat the offerings of this little gay home from home. The mediterranean climate and beautiful beaches seduce even the most city-hardened. A good deal of its enchanting old fishing village atmosphere remains, but the night comes alive with song, dance and rowdy camaraderie. Sitges attracts many other people as well as the gay crowd, but tolerance makes it an easy place to relax and be yourself. Even if you don't stay overnight, Sitges is a must for the gay traveller to Barcelona.

The gay scene in Sitges is at its height from June to September, when gay males from just about every country converge here. However, perhaps the most emblematic event is **Carnaval** in the middle of February (*see page 278*). If you've ever wanted to dress up in drag, this extravagant celebration is your chance to join in the parade of thousands on the climax night. Although most gay venues in the town close up at the end of summer, they reopen for this very special week. For more on Sitges, including how to get there, *see pages 258-9*.

Accommodation

If you really want to take advantage of the nightlife in Sitges you should stay overnight in one of its abundant hotels and *hostals*, most of which welcome gay clients. Just remember to book ahead. The **Hotel Romàntic** *C/Sant Isidre 33* and **La Renaixença** *C/Illa de Cuba 7 (93 894 83 75/fax 93 894 81 67)* are two of Sitges' most popular places – the Romàntic is in a beautifully restored nineteenth-century house with palm-filled patio – managed by the same people and very gay-friendly. The Renaixença is not quite as architecturally or historically distinctive, but they both offer well-kept, attractive gardens and very reasonable prices (around 11,000ptas, a double, breakfast included.

The **Hotel Liberty** *C/Illa de Cuba 35 (93 811 08 72)* is another option that's less attractive yet still popular, and is currently undergoing complete renovation. According to its owner it'll be the tops in 2000, with double rooms for 13,500ptas. In the hills ten kilometres (six miles) inland from Sitges, **La Masia Casanova** *Passatge Casanova 8 (93 818 80 58)* offers luxury suites with all the trimmings, a pool, a bar and lots of tranquility. Book well in advance for the minimum three-day stay (single or double, 15,000ptas). If all else fails, **RAS** *(607 14 94 51/fax 93 894 71 35)* is a recently-founded agency that can find rooms in Sitges or Barcelona.

Bars

There is no lack of bars in Sitges, whatever your style. **Trailer** is still about the only one that charges admission, and you can forget about using your credit cards in any of them. Crowds move around, and venues change hands and names from season to season, so it's best to refer to the free Gay Maps of Barcelona and Sitges (available from **Sextienda** or Zeus, *see p232*) for orientation. The year-round pub **Bar 7** *C/Nou 7 (no phone)* makes an interesting stop early in the evening. **Bourbons** *C/Sant Bonaventura 9 (no phone)* and **El Horno** *C/Juan Tarrida 6 (93 894 09 09)* are mature men's hangouts that could be included as stopping-off points, especially in high season, and the two-floored **Mediterraneo** *C/Sant Bonaventura 6 (no phone)* is still an international happening spot; an appearance here is obligatory before going on to Trailer. Go to **Parrot's Pub** *Plaça de l'Industria (93 894 81 78)* for a cool drink on the streetside terrace after a hard day at the beach. **Play Boy** *C/Bonaire 15 (no phone)* is an all-gay disco, but it can't outdo the long-running **Trailer** *C/Angel Vidal 36 (no phone)*. Absolutely everybody generally ends up here. The international DJs and scene are hot and heavy until its closing time of 5am.

Restaurants

Sitges is loaded with places to have a good meal. Moreover, the number of gay-owned and/or gay-friendly restaurants has more than tripled recently. The garden environment at **Flamboyant** *C/Pau Barrabeitg 16 (93 894 58 11)* still appeals to the gay clientele, with set menus at 2,500ptas. It would be difficult to be displeased, equally, with a meal at the Catalan-French **Chez Jeannette** *C/Sant Pau 23 (93 894 00 48)*, **El Trull** *Passeig Mossèn Fèlix Clarà 3 (93 894 47 05)*, the more apparently traditional **Can Pagés** *C/Sant Pere 24-26 (93 894 11 95)*, **Gabriel** *C/España 6 (93 894 46 50)* or **Sucre Salé** *C/Sant Pau 39 (93 894 23 02)*.

*The popular **La Renaixenca**.*

in the person of Carlos. This combination will make your stay comfortable and memorable, and it's close to everything, so you won't get lost on the way home.

Hotel California
C/Rauric 14 (93 317 77 66/fax 93 317 54 74). *Metro Liceu/bus 14, 18, 38, 59, N6, N9.* **Rates** *single* 6,000ptas; *double* 9,500ptas. **Credit** AmEx, EC, MC, V. **Map** D6/**A3**
California is very comfortable and centrally located, in the heart of the Ciutat Vella. All 31 rooms have individual bathrooms; there's no bar, but breakfast and drinks can be had.
Hotel services *Air-conditioning. Laundry. Multilingual staff. Safe.* **Room services** *Minibar (some). Radio. Room service (24hours). Telephone. TV.*

Bookshops

Antinous
C/Josep Anselm Clavé 6 (93 301 90 70). Metro Drassanes/bus 14, 18, 36, 38, 57, 59, 64. **Open** 10am-9pm Mon-Fri; 11.30am-9pm Sat. **Credit** AmEx, DC, MC, V. **Map** D6/**A4**
Bright natural lighting and ample space make this a great place to browse and cruise or to have some refreshment in the cute little café at the back. It stocks a wide range of gay literature (books, magazines and the press) and announcements of cultural events of interest to the gay community abound.

Complices
C/Cervantes 2 (93 412 72 83). Metro Jaume 1/bus 17, 40, 45. **Open** 10.30am-8.30pm Mon-Fri; noon-8.30pm Sat. **Credit** MC, V. **Map** D6/**B3**
Complices was Barcelona's first gay bookshop, run by a largely female group. Although its stock in English is limited, it does have a very ample selection of materials in Catalan and Spanish.

Fashion & accessories

B Free
Plaça Vila de Madrid 5 (93 412 27 59). Metro Plaça Catalunya/bus 14, 16, 17, 38, 41, 59, N6, N9. **Open** 10.30am-8pm Mon-Fri; noon-8.30pm Sat. **Credit** MC, V. **Map** D5-6/**B2**
This place is a godsend for those who've forgotten their disco or work-out drag in the rush to catch the plane. It also has accessories, gift items and cards.

M69
C/Muntaner 69 (93 453 62 69). Metro Universitat/bus 14, 54, 58, 64, 66, N3. **Open** 10.30am-2pm, 5pm-8.30pm, Mon-Sat. **Credit** MC, V. **Map** C5
M69 is the newest and probably the best gay-owned men's shop in the city, with a great many eye-catching lines of fine clothing, accessories, books and gift items on hand.

Ovlas
C/Porteferrissa 25 (93 412 52 29). Metro Plaça Catalunya/bus 14,16, 17, 18, 38, 41, 59, N6, N9. **Open** 9.30am-8.30pm Mon-Sat. **Credit** AmEx, V. **Map** D6/**B2**

*Have a pleasant cruise in **Antinous**.*

There is chic, trendy, provocative menswear on the rack; not to mention the underwear on offer.

Ritual
C/Consell de Cent 255 (93 451 91 68). Metro Universitat/bus 14, 54, 58, 59, 64, 66, N3. **Open** 11am-2pm, 5-9pm, Mon-Sat. **Credit** AmEx, DC, MC, V. **Map** C5
Fine fashions for the more modern and adventurous of us. Check out the urban streetwear before you count yourself out of that group.

Zona Intima
C/Muntaner 61 (93 453 71 45). Metro Universitat/bus 54, 58, 64, 66, N3. **Open** 10am-2pm, 5-8.30pm, Mon-Sat. **Credit** MC, V. **Map** C5
High-priced designer (Calvin Klein and others) jeans, underwear and accessories. Worth a look-see.

Saunas

There are at least eight gay saunas in the city; here you have the most popular. All have showers, open bar, porno lounge and cubicles. You get a locker, towel and shower sandals, and everything is charged to your locker/key number. **Casanova**, **Thermas** (lots of rent boys) and **Condal** are the most visited, especially after-hours and on their 'Client's (Discount) Day'.
Sauna Casanova *C/Casanova 57 (93 323 78 609). Metro Urgell/bus 9, 50, 45, 56, 56, 58, 64, 66, N1, N2, N3.* **Open** 24hours daily. **Admission** 1,300ptas Mon, Wed, Fri-Sun; 1,700ptas Tue, Thur. **Credit** MC, V. **Map** C5
Sauna Condal *C/Espolsa Sacs 1, off C/Comtal (93 301 96 80). Metro Urquinaona/bus 16, 17, 18, 19, 40, 45, and all nightbuses to Plaza Catalunya.* **Open** 11am-5.30am Mon-Thur; 11am Fri-5:30am Mon. **Admission** 1,300ptas Mon, Wed; 1,700ptas Tue, Thur-Sun. **Credit** MC, V. **Map** D5/**B2**
Galilea *C/Calabria 59 (93 426 79 05). Metro Rocafort/bus 9, 27, 50, 56, 109, 127, N1, N2.* **Open**

noon-midnight Mon-Thur; noon Fri-midnight Sun.
Admission 1,400ptas Mon, Tue, Fri-Sun; 1,000ptas
Wed, Thur. **Credit** MC, V. **Map** B5
Thermas *C/Diputació 46 (93 325 93 46). Metro
Rocafort/bus 9, 27, 50, 56, 109, 127, N1, N2.* **Open**
noon-2am Mon-Thur; noon Fri-2am Mon.
Admission 1,500ptas. **Credit** V. **Map** B5

Sex shops

Two exclusively gay sex shops with very friend-
ly and helpful staff. Both produce free gay maps
of Barcelona and Sitges, updated annually.
Sextienda *C/Rauric 11 (93 318 86 76). Metro
Liceu/bus 14, 16, 38, 59, N6, N9.* **Open** 10am-
8.30pm Mon-Sat. **Credit** MC, V. **Map** D6/A3
Zeus *C/Riera Alta 20 (93 442 97 95). Metro San
Antoni/bus 24, 64.* **Open** 10am-9pm Mon-Sat.
Credit V. **Map** C5

Gay & lesbian groups & info

Groups/centres

Actua *C/Gomis 38, baixos (93 418 50 00/fax 93
418 89 74). Bus 22, 73, 85.* **Open** 9am-2pm, 4pm-
7pm, Mon-Fri.
Similar to Act-Up in the UK and US, it provides
counselling and information to people living with HIV.
Ca la Dona *C/Casp 38, pral (tel/fax 93 412 71 61).
Metro Urquinaona/bus all routes to Plaça Catalunya.*
Open *office* 10am-2pm, 4-8pm, Mon-Thur. Closed
Aug. **Map** D5
Barcelona's main women's centre. It houses a variety
of women's groups, dedicated to all related issues.
See also p298.
Casal Lambda *C/Ample 5 (93 412 72 72/fax 93
412 74 76). Metro Drassanes/bus 14, 18, 36, 38, 57,
59, 64.* **Open** 5-9pm Mon-Thur; 5pm-midnight Fri;
noon-10pm Sat. **Map** D6/A4
Gay cultural organization that regularly hosts a wide
range of activities and publishes the monthly
magazine, LAMBDA. It has a nice interior
patio that's used more by men than women, but all
are welcome.
Coordinadora Gai-Lesbiana *C/Buenaventura
Muñoz 4 (900 601 601/fax 93 218 11 91). Metro
Arc del Triomf/bus 39, 41, 51.* **Open** 5pm-9pm Mon-
Fri. **Map** E6
'The' gay umbrella organization in BCN works
with the Ajuntament on all issues of concern to the
gay community.
**Front d'Alliberament Gai de Catalunya
(FAG)** *C/Verdi 88 (93 217 26 69). Metro
Fontana/bus 22, 24, 28, ND, NG.* **Open** 5pm-8pm
Mon-Fri. **Map** D-E3
Vocal multi-group that produces the *Barcelona Gai*
information bulletin.

Phone Lines

AIDS Information Line *(900 21 22 22).*
9am-5.30pm, June-mid Sept 8am-3pm, Mon-Fri.
Official city freephone service. Some english spoken.
Teléfon Rosa *(900 60 16 01).* **Open** 6-10pm
daily.
The phoneline of the Coordinadora Gai-Lesbiana is at
your service if you need help or advice.

Lesbian Barcelona

The lesbian lifestyle doesn't stand out as much in
Barcelona as the gay male's, but don't be fooled
by surface appearances. Women may always
have been more discreet, but they aren't hiding in
the closet. Gay women's idea of social life is less
tied to the bar scene: instead, there are regular
weekly and monthly special events and women-
only dances, organised by a whole variety of collectives and groups: **Complices** – as much a gay
women's as a men's bookshop – and **Ca La Dona**
(see also page 298) are good places to get information on current venues. Of other gay venues,
Café de la Calle is one that's almost as popular
with lesbians as with gay men (*see page 228*).
Films on Lesbian-themes are enthusiastically
received at the **Women's Film Festival** in June
(*see page 226*).

Cafés, bars, restaurants, clubs

Bahia

*C/Sèneca 12 (no phone). Metro Diagonal/bus 6, 7,
15, 22, 24, 27, 28, 33, 34, N4, N6.* **Open** 10pm-3am
daily. **Map** D3
Pleasant laid-back Gothic bar with a friendly ambience and good music. It is especially popular as a
place to go with a group of friends.

Café Bar Aire

*C/Enric Granados 48 (93 451 84 62). Metro Passeig
de Gracia/bus 7, 16, 17, 54, 58, 64, 66, N3.* **Open**
10pm-3am Tue-Sun. **Map** C4
This former gay men's café-bar has recently become
the current hot spot for women. The colourful décor
and light environment put you at your ease, and
there's lots of space and intimate tables for chatting
up. Gay men are not turned away at the door.

Free Girls

*C/Marià Cubí 4 (no phone). FGC Muntaner/bus 58,
64, N8.* **Open** 10pm-2am daily. **Map** D3
Once known as Imagine, this is an interesting little
'70s-style dance bar that attracts a younger set.

La Rosa

*C/Brusi 39, passatge (93 414 61 66). FGC Sant
Gervasi/bus 16, 17, 27, 58, 64, 127, N8.* **Open**
10pm-3am daily. **Map** C2
A little on the tacky side, but this veteran bar still
draws a crowd of mature women on weekends.

La Singular

*C/Francisco Giner 50 (93 237 50 98). Metro
Diagonal/bus 22, 24, 28, N4, N6.* **Open** 1pm-
midnight Mon, Tue, Thur, Sun; 1pm-1.30am Fri, Sat.
Average 2,000ptas. **Set menu** (lunch only)
1,100ptas. **Credit** MC, V. **Map** D3
This place offers very good tapas and home-cooked
meals for your pleasure, and the women who run it
are very friendly and attentive. Don't miss out on
their desserts.

Media

Political skullduggery, wall-to-wall football, more and more TV: quite normal, really.

Barcelona's media world is characterised by a contrast between a few fixed points amid a panorama of constant change. All the main print and broadcast media have been created or totally transformed since the 1970s. In the press, the major newspapers – *El País, El Periódico, La Vanguardia* – have their established niches in local life, but other projects are noticeably volatile, as this year's success turns into next year's closure.

The pace of change has been greatest in television. Spaniards watch more television than anyone else in Europe (after the British). The monopoly of state broadcaster TVE was broken in the 1980s, first by the arrival of separate channels for autonomous regions, beginning with the Catalan TV3 in 1983, and then by private channels, in 1989. This transformed viewing habits, and around the same time satellite dishes first began to be seen on Barcelona's balconies. Now cable has arrived, and in the last few years people willing to pay for the pleasure have had a steadily increasing number of channels to zap into.

Volatility of a kind also characterises the politics of the media, with a disquieting overlap between the worlds of politics and journalism. This has became especially marked since the *Partido Popular* (*PP*) of José María Aznar came to power in Madrid in 1996. Matters have come to a head precisely over the expansion of TV, as moves to change the regulatory framework in broadcasting have precipitated tremendous struggles for control of digital, satellite and pay television, and for the revenues they are expected to generate.

In Catalonia there is another important element in the scene, in the expansion of Catalan-language broadcasting. Bidding head-to-head for mass audiences with Spanish media, Catalan TV and radio have won healthy, and often top, ratings – in fact, in 1998 TV3 had the highest viewing numbers in Catalonia of any network. This too has its political aspect, for TV3 is also publicly owned, by the Catalan regional government, and, in the same way that TVE is accused of being the instrument of whoever is in power in Madrid, TV3 is rarely seen to challenge the wishes of Jordi Pujol and his party. This provides balance, of sorts.

Nevertheless, whatever the political background, the growing popularity of Catalan-language media is undeniable. The strength of broadcasting in Catalan has so far contrasted with the weakness of print media in the language, but the situation has changed somewhat with the introduction of *El Periódico*'s edition in Catalan.

Newspapers & magazines

All the main dailies are locally-produced – El País is Spain's closest thing to a 'national' paper – and there are no true mass-appeal popular newspapers. In contrast to the limited range of papers, newsstands offer a vast range of magazines.

Avui

The *Avui* was launched in 1976 as the first Catalan-language newspaper published openly for 40 years, and its appearance was heralded as a great national event. However, it set a reputation for stuffiness, and failed to win more than a limited readership. A 1990s redesign made it a bit more lively, but it's known as the mouthpiece of the Gerneralitat, which supports it with heavy subsidies. It's often said its days are numbered, particularly with the arrival of the Catalan edition of *El Periódico*, which in 1998 far outdistanced *Avui's* circulation of 34,000.

El Mundo de Catalunya

In Madrid, *El Mundo* is the main rival of *El País*, and won its reputation through its exposure of the scandals of the previous Socialist government of Felipe González. However, with its PP allies in power the paper's appetite for investigative reporting on government seems very diminished. In 1995 it launched a separate Catalan edition, which so far has survived in a difficult market, and in 1998 had a circulation in Catalonia of about 17,500.

El País

Spain's premier daily, the only one that could claim to be a national paper. It still has to adapt: its Barcelona edition, which sells 63,000 copies, has a 16-page local section. With Friday's *País* comes the *Tentaciones* supplement, with arts features and listings, and Saturday's includes the *Babelia* literature and arts section. Politically it has been sympathetic to the Socialists, and critical of the Pujol administration in Catalonia. Jesús Polanco, president of the Prisa group that owns *El País*, was the target of criminal charges brought by the Aznar government in 1997, trying to force Prisa out of its satellite TV partnership with Canal +.

El Periódico de Catalunya

The closest local paper to a tabloid, with big headlines, colour and lots of photos, which have enabled it to build up a circulation of about 208,000 across Catalonia. It's still more wordy than a true popular tabloid would be; in politics it's more or less leftwing and sympathetic to the Socialists. Since 1997 it has had an edition in Catalan (the one with a blue masthead), with completely the same editorial content as its Spanish one. With its breezy style and design, it is providing stiff competition for *Avui*.

Sport & El Mundo Deportivo

Two papers in straight competition with one another, both devoted to sports. The ongoing melodrama of Barcelona FC usually takes up half their pages. Highlights are the vox-pops, when fans-in-the-street have their say on last weekend's game plan. In recent years, both papers have had colourful redesigns.

La Vanguardia

The old guard of Barcelona's newspapers, it was founded in 1881 and, with a circulation of 206,000, has only recently lost its traditional position of topselling paper in Catalonia to *El Periódico*. It's the only paper to have survived from the Franco era (and well before that), and did so by revamping itself with a redesign into a lively, imaginative paper; its correspondents, especially in Latin America and the Middle East are excellent. It has an enterprising local section, in pink, with interesting Barcelona news and features. Politically, *La Vanguardia* has always been conservative and generally sympathetic to the Pujol government (dull Pujol stories have been a front-page staple), but one reason why it has survived so long is that it never commits itself too strongly to any position. Very good for listings (*Cartelera*), especially for Catalonia outside Barcelona.

¡Hola!, Semana, Lecturas, Diez Minutos...

Checking up on what's going on in the *prensa del corazón* ('heart press') is an essential part of being in Spain, for after all, as its nationalities move apart, knowing who of these celebs are marrying, splitting up, or just showing off their new furniture could be one of few things that gives the place a common culture. Regulars include international paparazzi-fodder like Pamela Anderson or Monte Carlo royalty, but there's also a stream of home-grown Spanish attention-grabbers, some of whom seem to do very little *except* appear in the magazines.

Classified ads

For general classifieds the best paper is *La Vanguardia*, especially on Sundays. There are three small-ad magazines: *Primeramà*, published Tuesdays and Thursdays (93 321 40 40), carries general ads, as does *Los Clasificados* (906 30 61 60), every Wednesday, which has a large job section. *Mercat Laboral*, out Friday (93 321 65 56), is dedicated to job ads. Placing ads in all three is free.

BTV, *sometimes the best viewing in town.*

English-language press

Best places to find foreign papers are the kiosks on the Rambla and Passeig de Gràcia. For more specialised press try **Fnac** or **Crisol** (*see pages 191-3*).

Barcelona Business

A monthly newspaper launched in 1998 with a wide range of news, business and general articles on Catalonia. It's on sale at some newsstands, and is available by subscription (fax 93 443 04 40) or for free through some schools and other institutions.

Barcelona Metropolitan

A free monthly magazine launched in 1996 aimed at English-speaking Barcelona residents, with classifieds, advice, features and extensive listings. Available in cinemas, bars, consulates and a variety of locations around the city.

Listings magazines

The weekly *Tentaciones* supplement of *El País* and *La Vanguardia*'s *Què Fem* (both with Friday editions) are good extra sources of information, and there are several free broadsheets that add to the sometimes limited scope of *Guía del Ocio*. For titles, *see chapter* **Music: Rock, Roots & Jazz.**

Guía del Ocio

Published weekly, on Thursdays, with basic what's-on information. Good for cinema and theatre, less so for music, it sells for 125 pesetas.

TV & radio

TV

The coming of private TV in 1989 led to a scramble for audiences, with channels going straight for the mass market. In the mid-'90s, the next big audience-grabber was live football, to the extent of overkill. However, satellite networks are gobbling up broadcasting rights, and now more and more matches are vanishing to pay-per-view.

Some films are shown in the original language with subtitles, particularly on TVE 2 and Canal+. With the right type of set (with the dual system) it's also possible to see otherwise-dubbed films in the original language on TV3 and Canal 33.

TVE 1 (La Primera)

The state television's flagship network has lost great chunks of its audience to private channels, and in

Catalonia to TV3. TVE 1 in Catalonia, is mostly in Spanish, with a few programmes in Catalan. As far as news goes, since the PP victory in 1996 the entire top echelon of the station has changed; news programmes have become heavily pro-government, and the network's credibility suffers as a result.

TVE 2 (La 2)

TVE's second channel shows slightly more intellectual programming than TVE 1, and more sports, particularly at weekends. In Barcelona, many of its programmes are in Catalan. Late-night classic movies, quite often in English, are a highlight.

TV3

Set up by the Generalitat in 1983, this all-Catalan-language channel has won healthy audiences with programmes such as 1999's wacky and satirical late night *Cosa Nostra*, amid more routinely conventional material. Original Catalan-language soap operas have also proven extremely popular, but TV3 also produces some quality documentaries. One of the main channels for live football on Saturday nights, and European Barça games on Wednesdays. Programmes shown dubbed on TV3 can be seen in English on sets with a NICAM stereo system.

Canal 33

Opened in 1989 as a second Catalan-language complement to TV3, showing slightly more 'quality' programming, documentaries, movies and sports.

Antena 3

The first and now most successful of the private channels, its programmes (the same throughout Spain, and normally all in Spanish, but with the recent addition of a midday news broadcast in Catalan) are a fairly bland mix of game shows, football, endless chat, and some good-quality films.

Tele 5

Tele 5 started off as pace-setter in the ratings war, grabbing itself an audience with a non-stop stream of prizes, soaps and entertainment extravaganzas, but in the mid-1990s the formula seemed to pale. Recently it's picked up with some lively chat shows, and can be counted on for at least one violent Hollywood film per night. The Sunday afternoon *Caiga Quien Caiga*, hosted by El Gran Wyoming, often has some riotous send-ups of political figures.

Canal +

Associated with the similar French channel, Canal+ is only available to subscribers, but many hotels, cafés and bars receive it. It's primarily a movie and sports channel, showing recent films (often undubbed), and paid out huge sums to win exclusive rights to most live league football games. It also has the best football show on TV, *El Día Después* on Monday nights, with former Liverpool man Michael Robinson. Also strong news slots, documentaries, music and comedy. The news division has formed an operating alliance with CNN, called CNN +.

BTV

Launched in 1994, the Ajuntament's local public-access channel. It's on-air daily, and material runs from concerts and theatre to talk, sports, general information and occasional film classics. It relies heavily on student broadcasters, but even so its 9pm newscast has won considerable respect. Revamped in 1997 as BTV, it's sometimes the best viewing in town, although the signal is weak in some *barris*. At night, when it's off the air, there's a single camera trained on the fish at the Aquàrium, with music.

Satellite & cable

Cable is just beginning here, and only a small part of the city has been wired, but the principal provider, Menta Cable i Televisió de Catalunya, hopes to have access to 100,000 Barcelona homes by the year 2000. Satellite TV, though, is going strong. There are two providers: Via Digital, majority-owned (53.7%) by the national phone company Telefónica, and Canal Satélite, owned by Sogecable, made up of Canal + and Prisa, among others. Both offer a basic programme package for around 3,000 pesetas a month; whether there will be enough subscribers to support them both, or they will merge into one super satellite-provider, remains to be seen. As of July 1999, Canal Satélite claimed 714,000 members, Via Digital, 280,000. That month Sogecable became the first communications group to trade on the Spanish stock market.

Radio

There's a healthy underground radio scene, but stations have irregular hours and can be hard to pick up in some areas. **Ràdio Contrabanda** (91.3 FM), has an English-language slot at 6pm on Saturdays; **Ciutat Vella** (106.8 FM), has multi-varied music; and **Ràdio Pica** (91.8 FM) a bit of everything. On the aboveground dial, good music stations are **Catalunya Música** (101.5 FM), mainly for classical music, with some jazz, while **Ràdio Associació de Catalunya** (105 FM) plays rock, jazz, world music and R&B.

The **BBC World Service** can be picked up on 15070, 12095, 9410 and 6195 KHz Short Wave, depending on the time of the day.

Barcelona online

The Barcelona Ajuntament has an information-packed website, *www.bcn.es*, and the tourist authority has *www.barcelonaturisme.com*, both of which have links in English. The Catalan regional government's *www.gencat.es* is a great mine of sometimes dry information, but the site of the Generalitat information office in the Palau Robert, *www.gencat.es/probert*, is far more interesting. On a less official note, *www.barcelonareview.com* is the Barcelona Review, a Barcelona-based online literary magazine; *www.diaridebarcelona.com*, a local online newspaper, has an engaging English page, 'BCN in 5 Minutes'. Vilaweb (*http://vilaweb.com*) is a Catalan links page, and more links can be found on the Barcelona page of *www.timeout.com*.

Music: Classical & Opera

A resurrected opera house and a brand new concert hall have given Barcelona some serious musical space to play with.

Classical music in Barcelona enters a new era in 1999-2000. The **Liceu** opera house has risen from the ashes of its predecessor; the new concert hall, **L'Auditori**, is enjoying its first full season, having opened to a fanfare of different styles and genres in May 1999; and the **Palau de la Música Catalana**, seen by many as the spiritual home of orchestral and choral music in Catalonia, is embarking on a three-year renovation programme which will add a 650-seat chamber music hall on the site of the church next door. All reasons for the city's music-lovers to be in an excited mood.

A question arises, though, over how this space will be filled, as it seems doubtful whether traditional audiences of classical music will be able to do the job on their own. Over the next few years the administrations responsible for these spaces will be forced to develop strategies for attracting a new clientele, by extending the range of music available, lowering ticket prices or catering for less mainstream tastes. The next few seasons will show if the city can rise to the challenge.

Traditionally, classical audiences in Barcelona have tended to be fervent, conservative and partisan. Both at the Liceu and at concerts by the **Orquestra Simfònica de Barcelona i Nacional de Catalunya (OBC)** at the Palau de la Música, music has sometimes taken second place to the social aspect of concert-going. At both the repertoire has rarely strayed far from the classical canon.

The audience at the Palau de la Música has been particularly uncritical, supporting the OBC much like a football team, with particular applause for composers who are male, generally Germanic and definitely dead. To its credit, the OBC also regularly inserts new works by young (living) Catalan and Spanish composers into its more usual repertoire, although the audience tends to greet these variations to their regular programme with muted applause and a lack of interest.

Before the move, many people saw the OBC and the Palau de la Música as part of the same administration, when, in fact, the orchestra was a mere tenant, albeit a favoured one. If nothing else, the Auditori has corrected the anomalous situation of a city with its own orchestra but without its own publicly-owned concert hall. The OBC will still give concerts at the Palau de la Música, but it has now found its own home in the Auditori. While this will simplify the administration of the orchestra, it could have a more profound effect on the music itself, and not just because of the technical superiority of the new venue. With the move, the audience are faced with a test of their loyalty, and while the majority have happily followed the OBC, the more reactionary elements prefer to stay in the comfortingly familiar surroundings of the Palau. Faced with a unique opportunity to revamp its programming, the orchestra's new season, while still strong on Beethoven and the boys, has an encouraging range of more modern work by Bartok, Schoenberg and Poulenc.

Apart from the OBC and the Liceu orchestras, and their poor country cousin, **L'Orquestra Simfònica del Vallès**, regular large-scale orchestral work in Barcelona relies on touring orchestras brought here by private promoters, **Ibercamera** and **Euroconcert**. The former specialises in major international names, the latter in less well-known groups and performers. Concerts are held in both the Palau and the Auditori, as well as other venues around the city, and both cycles of concerts have developed a reputation for quality performances. The Palau de la Música also promotes a concert series, Palau 100, featuring major performers and orchestras, such as the Chicago Symphony Orchestra under Daniel Barenboim, the Israel Philharmonic Orchestra under Zubin Mehta or the BBC Symphony Orchestra under Andrew Davis.

At the other end of the scale, music for anything from duos to chamber orchestras flourishes, though lack of financial support has made it difficult for most ensembles to survive long enough to gain an established audience base. The one exception is the OBC again, which runs a series of free weekly concerts featuring quartets and quintets made up of its members. Apart from this, there are innumerable performances every week by professional and semi-professional groups at various venues around the city.

Information

Apart from the venues themselves, the best source of information is the monthly leaflet *Informatiu Musical*, detailing concerts across all genres. You can pick a copy up at tourist offices, record shops or at the cultural information centre in the **Palau de la Virreina** (*see page 295*), or at the Generalitat's bookshop almost opposite. Both *El Pais* and *La Vanguardia* carry small ads for larger venues, and on most days also publish details for that day's concerts. The free what's-on magazine in English, *Barcelona Metropolitan*, features extensive listings information for music, dance theatre. The Ajuntament's web page (*www.bcn.es*) also provides full listings of events.

BUYING TICKETS

Technology has made buying a concert ticket very much easier. Tickets for most major venues can be bought by phone or in person via **Tel-Entrada**, or at La Caixa's **Servi-Caixa** machines (*for both, see page 215*).

Venues

L'Auditori

C/Lepant 150 (93 247 93 00). Metro Marina/bus 6, 7, 10, 56, 62, N2, N3. **Open** *information* 8am-3pm, 4-6/7pm, Mon-Fri; *box office* 10am-9pm daily; *performances* from 8pm daily, plus 11am-1pm Sun. **Tickets** prices vary. **Discounts** (OBC concerts) BC. **Credit** MC, V. **Map** F5

When Cerdà (*see p23*) conceived of his blue-print for Barcelona, Plaça de les Glóries Catalanes was designed to be at its centre. At last, 150 years later, the focus of the city is subtly beginning to change in accordance with his plan, as people head for the Auditori, the **Teatre Nacional de Catalunya** (*see p253*) or the huge new Glóries shopping centre nearby. Much like London's South Bank a decade ago, the area is something of a no-man's land once the theatre and concert audiences have chattered their way home, though with property prices ever increasing, the character of the area is gradually changing. In the meantime, a special bus service whisks you swiftly back to the civilisation of Plaça Catalunya after a performance. Looking rather like a top-secret toothpaste factory on the outside, the Auditori, by Madrid architect Rafael Moneo, boasts the latest sound technology. Its excellent acoustics make up for the stark, sterile interior of its 2,300-seat main hall, the Sala Simfonica. For smaller scale work, there is the Sala Polivalente, which seats 400.

Palau de la Música Catalana

C/Sant Francesc de Paula 2 (93 268 10 00). Metro Urquinaona/bus 17, 19, 40, 45, N8. **Open** *box office* 10am-9pm Mon-Sat; 1hr before concert Sun (concert days only); *advance sales* box office, phone & Servi-Caixa or Caixa de Catalunya. **Ticket** prices vary. **Credit** MC, V. **Map** D5/**B-C2**

Commissioned and paid for by the Orfeó Català in 1908, Domènech i Montaner's modernist masterpiece has long been seen as the spiritual home of Catalan music. It is a wedding cake of a concert hall, its stage jealously watched over by the busts of Beethoven and local composer Anselm Clavè. Above them soar the Valkyrie's chariots, while performers are encircled by a ring of musical muses. The effusive detail and florid decoration both complement and are complemented by music in performance. Despite being conceived with very populist intentions, the narrow shape of the auditorium means the majority of seats are rather distant from the stage. Acoustically, the hall is not ideal, although since the renovation of 1989 extraneous street sounds are at least muffled, if not always entirely absent. A further renovation, due to take about three years, will add a smaller space for chamber orchestras. With the OBC no longer in regular attendance, alternative income is provided by an increase in guided tours of the building, though the experience does not really compare with seeing a concert there.

Gran Teatre del Liceu

La Rambla 51-59 (93 485 99 00). Metro Liceu/bus 14, 38, 59, 91, N9, N12. **Open** 9am-2pm, 4-7pm, Mon-Fri; *summer* 8am-3pm Mon-Fri. **Ticket sales** *box office* 10am-1pm, 3-7pm, Mon-Fri; *summer* may open 8am-3pm Mon-Fri; Servi-Caixa. **Map** C-D6/**A3**

Though it might be heretical to say so, the welder's spark that burnt the original Liceu down in 1994 was a blessing in disguise. Plans for expansion had already been afoot for some time before that fateful morning, and the fire provided a useful excuse to relocate the tenacious inhabitants of adjoining flats and expand the building. In place of a creaking, dusty, wooden wreck, the theatre is now a spanking new building of three times the size, equipped with the latest technology. The backstage systems are fully automated, in theory allowing various productions to be performed in rotation. Lovers of the original will be pleased to know that the auditorium has been recreated in all its red-velvet and gold-leaf glory, for that authentic nineteenth-century-opera feel, but with the addition of extraordinary ceiling paintings by Catalan artist Perejaume, (*see p112*).

Auditori Winterthur

Auditori de l'Illa, Avda Diagonal 547 (93 290 10 90). Metro Maria Cristina/bus 6, 7, 33, 34, 63, 66, 67, 68, N12. **Open** *information* 8.30am-4.30pm Mon-Fri. **Tickets & credit** arrangements vary according to production. **Map** B3

The huge, cream-coloured shopping centre of L'Illa, on the Diagonal is the last place one would expect to find a concert hall. But tucked in behind Marks and Spencer, the Auditori Winterthur is a small, modern hall whose size, intimacy and acoustics make it an excellent venue for chamber music concerts. However, it is also often used as a private function space, and the music programme is both limited and sporadic.

Casa Elizalde

C/València 302 (93 488 05 90). Metro Passeig de Gràcia/bus 7, 16, 17, 22, 24, 28, 39, 43, 44, 45, 47, N4, N6, N7. **Open** *information & box office* 10am-2pm, 5-9pm, Mon-Sat; 10am-2pm Sun. **Tickets** 450ptas; *shows & concerts for children* 300ptas. **No credit cards. Map** D4

Most districts in Barcelona have local cultural centres that hold courses and give occasional concerts of all types. The Casa Elizalde is unusual in its range of activities, which include regular dance performances and poetry readings. Music is performed on Wednesdays and Fridays, either in its own auditorium, or on the interior patio.

Sala Cultural de la Caja de Madrid

Plaça Catalunya 9 (93 301 44 94). Metro Catalunya/ bus all routes to Plaça Catalunya. **Open** *information* 11am-1pm, 6-9pm, Tue-Sat; 11am-1pm Sun. **Tickets** free. **Map** D5/**B1**

This small, idiosyncratic space hosts a programme of recitals, duos and quartets, plus the occasional important international act. The free concerts start at 7.30pm, but you have to be in the queue by 6pm to pick up your numbered ticket, and then again at 7.15pm as your number is called out. Seats are either uncomfortable, Franco-era cinema seats or folding chairs at 45° to the stage, often behind pillars. The Sala attracts pensioners who are liable to doze or shuffle off at key moments in the performance.

Churches

Churches around Barcelona, particularly in the old town, hold concerts from time to time. The most beautiful is probably **Santa Maria del Mar** (*see page 67*), whose tall, ghostly interior exemplifies the gothic intertwining of music, light and spirituality. Recent concerts have included everything from Renaissance music to Gospel singers. Other venues include the main **cathedral**, **Santa Maria del Pi**, **Sant Felip Neri** and **Santa Anna**.

Orchestras & Ensembles

Orquestra Simfònica de Barcelona i Nacional de Catalunya (OBC)

C/Lepant 150 (93 247 93 00). Metro Marina/bus 6, 10, 62. **Open** 9am-3pm, 4-6pm, Mon-Fri. **Map** F5

The orchestra started life as the plain *Orquestra Municipal de Barcelona* in 1944, under the baton of Catalan composer Eduard Toldrà, changed its name to the *Orquestra Ciutat de Barcelona* in 1967, and acquired its current cumbersome title in 1994. The title is heavy with political significance since, if Catalonia is a country, it should have a national orchestra. The marketing bods do what they can to style it *L'Orquestra*, but most people just call it the *OBC*. Under the baton of conductor Lawrence Foster, and principal guest conductor Franz-Paul Decker, the orchestra performs weekly concerts on Friday and Saturday evenings and Sunday mornings from October to May. On Thursday evenings members of

the orchestra also perform quartets and quintets, free, in the Sala Polivalente of the Auditori (*see p237*). It also hosts an annual Mozart festival in September, under the direction of Christopher Hogwood.

Despite regular appearances by guest conductors and soloists, including Daniel Barenboim and Barbara Hendricks in 1999, the orchestra is yet to develop a strong reputation beyond Catalonia. It is more a steady workhorse, delivering the classics with confidence, if without great flair. At the same time it provides an outlet for young Catalan composers. Works by Salvador Brotons, Xavier Boliart, Albert Guinovart and Antoni Besses received their first public performance this year.

Orquestra Simfònica i Cor del Gran Teatre del Liceu

Information *see* **Gran Teatre del Liceu**.

After dragging their sorry basses and bassoons around Barcelona for the last five years, the Liceu orchestra and choir have at last returned home, starting the new season with *Turandot*, the work they had been due to play when the fire struck. The inaugural season throws up few surprises: Puccini, Donizetti, Verdi, Mozart and Wagner send the message of business as usual down at the opera house, although Ferrari's Sly is one less well-known work. And the great and good from the Liceu's recent past will be giving recitals, among them Catalonia's favourite opera diva, Montserrat Caballé, Jaume Aragall, Joan Pons, and several international names. The season also includes concerts (Strauss, Mahler, Verdi, Wagner) plus a series of foyer performances to complement the main productions.

Orfeó Català

Information *Palau de la Música, C/Sant Francesc de Paula 2 (93 268 10 00).* **Map** D5/**B-C2**

The Orfeó Catala had its origins in the patriotic and social movements at the end of the nineteenth century, and was just one of over 150 choral groups that sprang up in Catalonia at this time. It was sufficiently successful to be able to commission the Palau de la Musica, with which it is inseparably identified. Though no longer enjoying the strongest moments of its history, it still offers around 25 performances a year, giving a cappella concerts as well as providing a choir for the OBC and other Catalan orchestras when necessary. The Orfeó Català is largely non-professional, though it includes a small professional nucleus, the Cor de Cambra del Palau de la Música, which gives around 50 performances a year.

La Capella Reial de Catalunya, Le Concert de Nations, Hèsperion XX

All three of these ensembles come under the baton of Jordi Savall, one of the most respected figures in early and baroque music in Europe today and the genius behind the music for the film *Tous les matins du monde*. Hespèrion XX specialises in early music (*see also* **Festival de Música Antiga**, *right*), while the repertoire of the other two focuses largely on Romantic and Renaissance work.

Orquestra Simfònica del Vallès

Information *C/Narcis Giralt 40, Sabadell (93 727 03 00). FGC Sabadell Rambla/RENFE Sabadell Centre.* **Open** 9am-2pm, 3-5pm, Mon-Fri.

One of the main beneficiaries of the OBCs departure from the Palau de la Music, this orchestra, founded in 1987, continues to enjoy an increasingly healthy reputation thanks largely to its dynamic young conductor/composer Salvador Brotons. Based in the nearby town of Sabadell, where it performs regularly at the Teatre Municipal La Faràndula, it also gives a series of eight Saturday evening concerts between October and June at the Palau de la Música.

Orquestra de Cambra Teatre Lliure

Information: Teatre Lliure (*see p253*).

Despite giving only a handful of concerts a year, and without a fixed membership, under the guidance of Josep Pons this ensemble has acquired a reputation for retrieving and revitalising twentieth-century work by both Catalan and non-Catalan composers, and for a short but successful series of recordings.

Festivals

Aside from the main orchestras and ensembles, much of the music in Barcelona is organised into festivals and seasons, from ancient to modern. The **Grec** and the **Mercè** (*see pages 9, 11*) both feature classical and contemporary work, while outside the city, summer festivals in Cadaqués, Perelada and Torroella de Montgrì take off when the regular season ends.

Festival de Música Antiga

Information *Centre Cultural de la Fundació la Caixa, Passeig de Sant Joan 108 (93 458 89 07).* **Dates** Apr-May. **Tickets** 500-1,500ptas; some concerts free. **Map** E4

The early music festival in May is the highpoint in Fundació La Caixa's admirable series of cultural events, bringing ensembles from all over Europe to perform in several of the most beautiful spaces of the old town. Recent performers have included La Real Cámera, The King's Noyse, Emma Kirkby and Mala Punica. At the same time, the fringe offers young performers the chance to practise and perform alongside more established musicians.

Classics als Parcs

Information *Parcs i Jardins, Avda Marques de Comillas 16-36 (93 424 38 09/fax 93 423 84 60). Metro Espanya/bus 13, 50, 100.* **Open** *information* 8am-3pm Mon-Fri. **Dates** June-July. **Tickets** approx 700ptas. **No credit cards**. **Map** A5

This relatively new series offers a variety of concerts in Barcelona's more attractive parks. There are two or three alternatives to choose from every Thursday, Friday and Saturday night throughout June and July, at venues such as Gaudí's Parc Güell, the Ciutadella and the Laberint parks, as well as the Espigó de Bac de Roda, the pier along the beach from Poble Nou.

Contemporary Music

The contemporary classical music scene is noticeably healthy in Barcelona, playing to a small but loyal crowd whose fidelity has been rewarded by an increase in venues and concert cycles.

Nick Havannah

C/Rossello 208 (93 215 65 91). Metro Diagonal/FGC Provença/bus 7, 16, 17, 31, 67, 68. **Open** 11pm-4.30am Sun-Thur; 11pm-5.30am Fri, Sat. *July, Aug* sometimes closed Sun. **Admission** free Sun-Thur; 1,100ptas (incl. 1 drink) after midnight Fri, Sat. **Discounts** BC. **Credit** AmEx, MC, V. **Map** D4

Against the old-Baghdad-meets-*Blade-Runner* aesthetic of this carpet-lined cocktail bar, Albert Sardá started carving out a niche for small-scale performances of contemporary music long before the rest of the city had caught on.

Avuimusics

Associacio Catalana de Compositors, Passeig Colom 6, space 4 (93 268 37 19/fax 93 268 12 59/ acc@accompositors.com). Metro Jaume I/bus 14, 36, 57, 59, 64, 157, N6. **Open** *information* 9.30am-1.30pm Mon-Fri; *box office* 30mins before concert. **Concerts** Oct-May 8.30pm Thur. **Tickets** 800ptas; 400ptas students; season tickets also available. **Credit** Auditori only. **Map** D6/B4

This increasingly successful series offers concerts each month from October to July. Run by the Association of Catalan Composers, the repertoire is approximately half by living Catalans, and half by international twentieth-century heavyweights. Some concerts are held at the **Auditori** (*see p237*). *Website: www.accompositors.com*

Festival de Músiques Contemporànies

Information *Centre de Cultura Contemporania de Barcelona, C/Montalegre 5 (93 306 41 24/fax 93 301 41 04/fmcb@cccb.org). Metro/FGC Catalunya/ bus all routes to Plaça Catalunya.* **Open** *information* 9am-2pm, 4-7pm, Mon-Fri. **Concerts** times & locations vary. **Tickets** 1-2,000ptas; sometimes free. **Sales** *box office* from 30min before concert; *in advance* Tel-Entrada. **No credit cards**. **Map** C5/A1

With a wider brief than the Avuimusics series, the Festival of Contemporary Musics has a more international makeup, and a less rigid definition of classical music. Organised jointly by the **CCCB** (*see p107*) and the **MACBA** (*see p93*), concerts take place in locations all over the city.

Fundació Joan Miró

Parc de Montjuïc (93 329 19 08). Metro Paral.lel, then Funicular de Montjuïc/bus 50. **Open** *box office* from 7.30pm Thur. **Sales** *box office* & *Tel-Entrada* (902 10 12 12). **Tickets** 800ptas; 2,000ptas for three concerts; 4,500ptas for seven concerts. **Credit** MC, V. **Map** B6

It may not be the world's best auditorium, nor the easiest to reach, but the brief series of concerts at the Fundació Miro that run from July to September feature an eclectic and interesting selection of contemporary music from around the world.

Music: Rock, Roots & Jazz

DJs may rule the club scene in Barcelona, but the excitement of live jazz, rock, salsa and flamenco is never far away.

There's a certain momentum in Barcelona's live music scene as the city approaches the new millennium. You can measure it in the number of mid-1990s musical initiatives that, five or six years later, have matured into important elements of the local scene. Festivals such as **BAM** and **Sonar** have become key dates, and Barcelona-based free music papers *Mondo Sonoro* and *AB* are so successful they've gone national.

However, it's not a clear-cut energy boom: the number of live venues hasn't increased, even if a few of them are working more. And the key musical genre that's packing in the punters is actually the DJ-based dance scene. This is a two-edged sword as far as live music goes: club culture gets young people out on the town, with an eclectic, open attitude on how they get their fun; but even if some clubbers are also into live performances, these gigs become a kind of optional extra, and for the venues, of course, a DJ is cheaper than a band.

Nevertheless, there is now a wide variety of rock-based music around. Well-known international acts keep rolling in, joined these days by a steady stream of more obscure foreign groups at venues like **Magic**, **Garatge** and **Sidecar**. Meanwhile, Spanish indie rock has come of age in the '90s. Granada's Los Planetas are its uncrowned kings, but there are many others worth noting, among them award-winning Barcelona bands Fang and Fromheadtotoe. Outsiders might hear a thousand Anglo-American influences in some of this music, but they will also hear some very good sounds – the self-confident local rap of Solo Los Solo; reggae and latin rhythms woven into the rock mestizo sound; more theatrical approaches, from Astrud's posey electro-pop to the loopy cover versions of the Azucarillo Kings; and Spanish-produced dance music from the Minifunk label.

Rock català is another important part of the local mix, defined by (and receiving institutional support for) its Catalan lyrics. Musically, it tends toward the mainstream, but groups like Sopa de Cabra have huge followings in Catalonia. Mature solo albums by Quimi Portet (ex-Último de la Fila) and Adrià Puntí (formerly of Umpah Pah) have also made waves lately.

JAZZ, LATIN, GYPSY RHYTHMS

Jazz is a scene apart, although venues like **La Boîte** and **Jamboree** have for years been combining their jazz or blues concerts with packed-out after-show dance sessions. Jazz in Barcelona has a traditionally strong base, with competent musicians and an established festival calendar, but clubs can have problems pulling a crowd. Some say the scene needs to breathe a little and find its own *jazz mediterráneo* voice, perhaps following the creative lines of local pianist Lluís Vidal or saxophonist Perico Sambeat. Barri Gòtic venue the **Harlem Jazz Club** keeps the audiences coming with bold programming that mixes jazz, Brazilian and African performers, and other venues have also diversified. The same inclusive approach is exemplified by the **Taller de Músics**, the 20-year-old Barcelona music school that runs the **Jazz Sí Club** (*see page 243*), which started out concentrating on jazz, but is now a musical melting pot with jazz, flamenco, rock, and Latin genres all energetically taught and promoted.

Latin rhythms and a diversity of African music styles also have a strong presence in Barcelona. Salsa and merengue move bodies from Maremàgnum to the top of town, and bigger venues often feature visiting Caribbean groups or expatriate talent like local Cuban star Lucrecia. Come the festival season, the living legends arrive – everyone from Brazil's Marisa Monte and Cape Verde queen Cesària Evora, to Algerian *raï* stars such as Khaled and Cheb Mami. The flavour of Buenos Aires also features in the city's musical melange; the Barcelona-based Trio Argentino de Tango and jazz/tango artist Emilio Solla are frequent performers.

Two other genres, both related to gypsy culture, have firm enough roots in Barcelona soil for critics to claim that new local hybrids have emerged: the infectious sound of *rumba catalana*, exemplified by groups like Sabor de Gràcia, and *flamenco catalán*,

Smooth vibes at the **Harlem Jazz Club**. *See page 245.*

born in the city's Andalusian communities and with a reputation for excellence thanks to leading 1990s *cantautores* (singer-songwriters) such as Duquende and Maite Martín. Flamenco now has a sufficient following here for festivals and one-off gigs to bring the very biggest names to the city. There's regular flamenco at the tourist-oriented *tablaos* too, although they're also a reminder of the ever-present threat that local flamenco will become a purely commercial phenomenon.

One more, very Catalan genre is the local folk music that was labelled *nova cançó* when it appeared in the '60s and '70s, led (then and now) by much revered singers such as Joan Manuel Serrat, Raimón and Maria del Mar Bonet. Folky *cantautores* have also been back in vogue throughout Spain in the '90s; among the most popular are Pedro Guerra and Rosana, while locally there's the duo Silvia Comas and Lidia Pujol, and Paul Fuster, a Catalan-American who sings in English.

SEEING STARS...

All this richness, yet the local charts are still dominated by the global top 40, plus a few Spanish *mega-estrellas* like heart-throb Alejandro Sanz, Enrique Iglesias or the ballady guitar of Jarabe de Palo. When the hitmakers and the ultra-famous come to Barcelona they usually play at either the **Palau d'Esports** or the infinitely preferable **Palau Sant Jordi**, both on Montjuïc (*see chapter* **Sports & Fitness**). Another often-used sports barn is the **Palau d'Esports** in Vall d'Hebron. Barcelona's new, acoustically-superb **Auditori**

also hosts non-classical music, and the venue it ostensibly replaces, the **Palau de la Música**, has a great atmosphere, although not such a brilliant sound (*see chapter* **Music: Classical & Opera**). Medium sized bands keep **Bikini** heavily booked, with **Zeleste** a slightly bigger option.

Many smaller venues shut down for August. Summer outdoor spaces are important in this festival-oriented town: get to a concert in the magical **Plaça del Rei** if you can, and the **CCCB** and its Pati de les Dones provide great atmosphere for all kinds of music. There's no completely foolproof gig listings guide; the *Guia del Ocio*'s main advantage is that you can get it weekly in any newsstand, while in bars and shops you can pick up the monthly giveaways *Mondo Sonoro* (the complete rock chronicle), *AB* (dance/style/bands), and *Barcelona Metropolitan* (in English). Local papers publish entertainment supplements on Fridays; *El País* has the best one for music, *Tentaciones*.

Rock/pop & other

Bikini

C/Déu i Mata 105 (93 322 08 00). Metro Les Corts/ bus 15, 30, 43, 59. **Open** midnight-4.30am Tue-Thur; midnight-6am Fri, Sat; 7pm-4.30am Sun. **Admission** (incl one drink) free Sun, Tue, Wed; 1,000ptas Thur; 1,500ptas Fri, Sat. **Credit** AmEx, DC, V. **Map** B3

The original, legendary Bikini was torn down in 1990 to make way for L'Illa shopping mall. Re-opened by the same management within the new building, it now looks a bit like a cinema multiplex, but its eclectic musical policy survives; from Venezuelan dance fiends Los Amigos Invisibles to dour post-rockers Labradford, the variety is incredible and quality is high. With good acoustics and the flexibility of one large space or two smaller ones, Bikini reigns supreme in city music venues. *See also chapter* **Nightlife**.

La Boîte

Avda Diagonal 477 (93 419 59 50). Bus 6, 7, 15, 27, 32, 33, 34, 63, 67, 68, N12. **Open** 11pm-5.30am daily; *live music* midnight-1.30am daily. **Admission** (incl one drink) *disco* 1,500ptas, *gigs* 1,500-3,000ptas. **No credit cards. Map** C3
Barcelona's live music scene owes a lot to the dynamic Mas siblings, who have restored and reinvented venues such as **Jamboree** and **Los Tarantos**, and proved to the sceptics that you can maintain musical credibility while also attracting the bigger-spending dance crowd. La Boîte, an uptown basement club, was their first music venue, and has featured everything from blues, kitschy cabaret and South American *cantautores*, to a month-long residency by The Supremes. *See also chapter* **Nightlife**.

Club Apolo/Nitsaclub

C/Nou de la Rambla 113 (93 441 40 01). Metro Paral.lel/bus 36, 57, 64, 91, N6, N9. **Open** *disco* midnight-6am Fri, Sat; *gigs* times vary. **Admission** *disco* (includes one drink) 1,500ptas; *gigs* prices vary. **No credit cards. Map** C6

As well as being one of the best clubs in town, this ex-music-hall hosts top live acts of the world music/reggae, pop/rock and salsa varieties, and more avant garde events like the weekly Cine Ambigú, an alternative film night. A balcony ensures a good view even for big-name acts. After the gig, the **Nitsaclub** takes over and the crowds pour in. *See also chapter* **Nightlife**.

Garatge Club

C/Pallars 195 (93 309 14 38). Metro Llacuna/bus 40, 42, 92, N11. **Open** midnight-5.30am Fri, Sat; *June-Sept* outdoor terrace 11pm-3am. **Admission** depends on band. **No credit cards**.
If rock'n'roll is the devil's music, then his satanic majesty would be right at home in Garatge, with a Stratocaster hanging off his shoulder and belting out one hell of a noise. The Poble Nou 'garage' is one of Barcelona's hotbeds of harder-edged guitar and home-made pop, taking in a range of styles from ska to speed metal to psychodelia. Performers at the club include some of the better Spanish indie groups and foreign visitors.

Jamboree

Plaça Reial 17 (93 301 75 64). Metro Liceu/bus 14, 38, 59, N9, N12. **Open** 10.30pm-5.30am daily; *gigs* 11pm-12.30am daily. **Admission** (incl one drink) 1,500ptas. **No credit cards. Map** D6/A3
Inaugurated in 1959, this cellar was the first jazz 'cave' in Spain, re-opened by the Mas brothers (*see*

The festival round

Barcelona's cosmopolitan atmosphere, clement weather and great street venues create perfect conditions for a string of music festivals each year. In summer, especially, music and other arts performances, enjoyed in the open air, are among the essential ways in which the city shows it's alive.

Going from the beginning of the year, the first festival that comes up is the **Festival de Guitarra**, in the Palau de la Música in March (information 93 232 67 54; *see chapter* **Music: Classical & Opera**). During May, the CCCB (*see chapter* **Art Galleries**) showcases the best in flamenco in the **Festival de Flamenco**.

The big opener to the summer season is **Sonar** in June – Barcelona's 'Festival of Advanced Music and Multimedia Art', which has grown into one of the most prestigious gatherings of its kind in the world, attracting crowds from across Europe. Prominent artists in musical, audio-visual and multimedia production come together in a unique three-day event that's a must for anyone interested in innovative electronic art forms. Over 200 activities – exhibitions, concerts, audio-visual presentations, a record and publishing fair – take

place by day at the **CCCB**, while by night the **SonarClub** at the Pavelló de la Mar Bella, a shortish walk from the beach, hosts DJs and concerts (information 93 442 29 72).

The **Grec**, Barcelona's main official summer culture festival (*see page 9*), takes advantage of outdoor venues such as the Greek theatre itself and squares like the **Plaça del Rei** to present a varied programme of music ranging from classical to flamenco, blues and Brazilian, with concerts every night throughout July. The last big musical event of the summer is **BAM**, the alternative music festival that takes place as part of **La Mercè** in September (*see page 11*). For three days and three nights stages throughout the Barri Gòtic host the newest in pop, hip-hop, rock and dance music, with performances by local bands and international big names (information 93 401 97 16).

As summer ends, festivals take on a more intimate flavour. The **Festival de Músiques Contemporànies** begins alongside BAM during the Mercè, but runs on into November. The CCCB, the MACBA and the Auditori (*see chapter* **Music: Classical & Opera**) offer an *above* **La Boîte**) in 1993. Barcelona-based and visiting names in jazz, blues, funk, and hip-hop all play at this enormously popular venue. The Sunday night blues sessions are an institution, and a club is held after the gigs. *See also chapter* **Nightlife**.

Jazz Sí Club/Café

C/Requesens 2 (93 329 00 20). Metro Sant Antoni/bus 20, 24, 38, 41, 55, 64, N6. **Open** 9am-11pm daily. **Admission** varies. **No credit cards. Map** C5
This quirky club/café in a tiny street in the Raval is run by the pro-active Barcelona contemporary music school, **Taller de Músics** at C/Requesens 5, and is a meeting point for musicians. There's live music every night of the week catering, like the school, for diverse interests, with music from the experimental vanguard on Mondays; a jazz jam on Tuesdays; single artist nights on Wednesdays; salsa on Thursday; rock on Fridays and Saturdays, and a rock/blues jam session on Sundays. Good, reasonably-priced snack food is also available.

KGB

Alegre de Dalt 55 (93 210 59 06). Metro Joanic/bus 25, 31, 32, 39, 55, 74, N4, N6. **Open** *gigs* 9pm-midnight, *disco* midnight-5am, Thur-Sat. **Admission** *gigs* depends on band; *disco* (incl one drink) 1,000ptas. **No credit cards. Map** E3
Unlike its namesake, KGB still exists, but this long-standing venue has also seen less real action lately. Once a famous after-hours joint, it now features live

gigs at the weekend, mostly from young local bands playing pop, punk or ska. When the live music stops, it's a big black box with a dancebeat inside. *See also chapter* **Nightlife**.

London Bar

C/Nou de la Rambla 34 (93 318 52 61). Metro Liceu/bus 14, 38, 59, 91, N9, N12. **Open** 7pm-4am Tue-Thur, Sun; 7pm-4.30am Fri, Sat.
Admission free. **Credit** MC, V. **Map** C6/A3
A Barcelona institution and a relic from the heyday of the Barrio Chino, the bohemian-ish London is usually packed at weekends, mainly with young foreigners. Music tends to be on the blues/boogie/be-bop side, played by local and resident-foreign bands – fun if you don't mind a noisy, smoky atmosphere. And although it's been thoughtlessly renovated at times, it's managed to save a touch of its original 1910 *Modernista* décor. *See also chapter* **Nightlife**.

Luz de Gas

C/Muntaner 246 (93 209 77 11/93 209 73 85). Bus 6, 7, 15, 27, 32, 33, 34, 58, 64, N8. **Open** 11pm-4.30/5.30am daily; Closed Sun in July, Aug. **Admission** (incl one drink) 2,000ptas. **Credit** AmEx, DC, MC, V. **Map** C3
This beautiful *belle époque* music hall usually maintains a regular weekly live programme: soul/funk artist Monica Green has a Thursday spot, and there's jazz, salsa, pop and stand-up comedy on other nights. The club sometimes suffers from uptown snootiness,

interesting overview of twentieth-century music, from concerts by the Liceu orchestra to electro-acoustic and multimedia shows (information from the CCCB, 93 306 41 00). In October, the Fundació la Caixa (*see chapter* **Art Galleries**) hosts a **Festival de Músiques del Món** (Musics of the World) that truly journeys through the earth's cultures; the 1999 edition included Mexican, Gospel, Tunisian and Jewish Kletzmer performers (information 93 458 89 07).

Winter is the time for lovers of jazz. The long-running **Festival Internacional de Jazz**, from October to December, and the **Festival de Jazz de Ciutat Vella** within it are opportunities to enjoy an intense jam session at the **Harlem Jazz Club** or some some jazz legend in the **Palau de la Música** (information 93 232 67 54).

Finally, and though not proper festivals in themselves, there are interesting regular events such as the **Electric Café**, a monthly programme of music and cinema at the CCCB (information 93 442 29 72) and activities organised by **Gràcia Territori Sonor**, a contemporary music collective (information 93 237 37 37).

Electrified masses at **Sonar.**

but its atmosphere changes when an international guest passes through: recent guests include Egyptian artist Natacha Atlas, punk poet Lydia Lunch, and Kool and the Gang. *See also chapter* **Nightlife**.

Magic

Passeig Picasso 40 (93 310 72 67). Metro Barceloneta/bus 14, 39, 51. **Open** 11pm-6am Thur-Sat and eves of public holidays. Closed sometimes Aug. **Admission** *gigs* 500-1,200ptas; *disco* (incl one drink) 1,000ptas. **No credit cards. Map** E6

Despite a slightly odd, claustrophobic layout, over the last few years Magic has been an important venue for independent music in the city. Acts vary from young, green and noisy local bands, to somewhat unlikely (but often wonderful) tourists, such as US surf band Man or Astroman, ex-Minuteman Mike Watt, and a steady stream of northern European guitar groups.

Penúltimo (del Borne)

Passeig del Born 19 (93 310 25 96). Metro Jaume I/bus 17, 19, 40, 45, N8. **Open** 10pm-2.30am Mon-Wed, Sun; 10pm-3am Thur-Sat. **Credit** MC, V. **Map** D6/**C3**

This eclectically-decorated downstairs bar/dance club in the current-place-to-be Born district holds live performances several nights a week before the DJ starts. The imaginative programming features small formations playing tango, Brazilian sounds, flamenco, jazz, and frequently fringe theatre. *See also chapter* **Nightlife**.

Savannah

C/Muntanya 16 (93 231 38 77). Metro Clot/bus 33, 34, 35, 43, 44, N7, N9. **Open** midnight-5am Thur-Sat; *gigs* midnight Thur. **Admission** (incl one drink) 1,000ptas; *gigs* free. **No credit cards.**

A spacious and attractive rock and blues venue out in Clot, pulling in some lesser-known international players and bigger names from the national scene. Live gigs are not too regular.

Sidecar Factory Club

C/Heures 4-6 (93 302 15 86). Metro Liceu/bus 14, 38, 59, N9, N12. **Open** 10pm-3am Tue-Sat; *gigs* normally 10/11pm. Closed Aug. **Admission** depends on band. **No credit cards. Map** D6/**A3**

A basement club tucked into a corner of the Plaça Reial, Sidecar offers all genres of pop-rock most nights of the week, performed by local and touring independent bands. On Tuesdays, the G's Club takes over, offering 'alternative' performances by a local arts collective – everything from theatre and poetry readings to video art and experimental music. The 'underground' crowd are friendly. *See also chapter* **Nightlife**.

Zeleste

C/Almogàvers 122/Pamplona 88 (93 486 44 22). Metro Marina/bus 6, 40, 42, 141, N11. **Open** *gigs* normally from 9pm; *club* 1-5am Fri, Sat; 7pm-1am Sun. *July, Aug* also 11pm-4.30am Thur. **Admission** *gigs* 1,500-3,500ptas; *club* (incl one drink) 700-900ptas. **No credit cards. Map** F6

The best medium-sized rock venue in Barcelona. If they're too big for Bikini, and not big enough, or don't want to fill a stadium, first-rank acts perform here: recent headliners include PJ Harvey, Manic Street Preachers and Spain's fab five Los Planetas. On the city-side of Poble Nou, Zeleste has three halls and hosts club nights each weekend, when the late-night bar is open to all with no admission fee. *See also* **Underworld** *in chapter* **Nightlife**.

Flamenco

Las Lolas Club

C/Tiradors s/n (93 268 20 27). Metro Jaume I/bus 17, 19, 40, 45, N8. **Open** 10pm Sun. **Admission** 1,000ptas (incl 1 drink). **Map** D6/**B4**

A friendly night run by young local flamenco-lovers, Las Lolas takes over the Toguna club on Sundays (sometimes other nights too) with live flamenco gigs. The same group runs a flamenco academy, **Las Lolas Local** at C/Pinzón 3-5 (93 319 89 88) in Barceloneta, with classes in dance, guitar, *cante* and *cajón* (percussion). From time to time they run one-week intensive courses for visitors to the city, and also organize accommodation. *See also chapter* **Nightlife**.
Website: www.personal5.iddeo.es/laslolaslocal

La Macarena

C/Nou de Sant Francesc 5 (93 317 54 36). Metro Liceu/all routes to Plaça Catalunya. **Open** 11pm-4am Mon-Sat. **Map** D6/**A4**

With an interior like an Almodóvar film set and an owner who could be one of the extras, La Macarena is a once-in-a-lifetime experience. It's totally unpredictable: you could be treated to anything from a thrilling, spontaneous session from visiting flamenco artists or a cursory ten-minute spot from the regulars who hang around the bar. Whatever, you'll be expected to pay. There's no cover charge, but be warned: if they ask you after the show if you would 'like to buy a drink for the artists', it could empty your wallet. An acceptable way out is to leave a tip as you go; the amount should depend on the length and quality of the 'show'. Go late (2am onwards) and, if possible, with somebody who lives in the city.

El Tablao de Carmen

C/Arcs 9, Poble Espanyol (93 325 68 95). Metro Plaça d'Espanya/bus 13, 50, 61. **Open** approx 8pm-2am Tue-Sun; *flamenco shows* 9.30pm, 11.30pm, Tue-Thur, Sun; 9.30pm, midnight Fri, Sat. **Admission** *Poble Espanyol* 950ptas; 525ptas students, over-65s, groups; *El Tablao de Carmen copa-espectacle* 4,200ptas (incl one drink & Poble Espanyol); *sopar-espectacle* 7,800ptas (incl dinner & Poble Espanyol). **Credit** AmEx, DC, JCB, MC, TC, V. **Map** A5

A high-quality supper/flamenco show venue in the Poble Espanyol (*see p75*), with a full *tablao* of guitarists, singers and dancers, frequented by locals and tourists alike. It's great fun, and if you book in advance you don't have to pay the Poble entry fee.

Los Tarantos

Plaça Reial 17 (93 318 30 67/tablao 93 389 16 61).
Metro Liceu/bus 14, 38, 59, 91, N9, N12. **Open**
9.30pm-5.30am daily; *flamenco show (tablao)* 10-
10.30pm (sometimes 11-11.30pm, too) Mon-Sat.
Admission *disco* (incl one drink) 1,500ptas; *tablao*
(incl two drinks) 4,000ptas; *other performances*
depends on the artist. **Credit** MC, V. **Map** D6/A3
When Mas i Mas (*see p242* **La Boîte**) took over
Los Tarantos on Plaça Reial, they retained the long-
established flamenco *tablao* for tourists, but also
began booking straight concerts, too. The concerts
often feature the best Catalan flamenco artists, as
well as tangos, Latin, salsa, and *cantautores*, complementing the music on offer at the **Jamboree**
next door (*see p242*). When the live gigs finish, the
door between the two clubs opens, to give a choice
of two dancefloors.

Folk

L'Espai (*see page 223*) acts as a showcase for
mostly-Catalan musicians. There are no specific
criteria; performances can be anything from flamenco to folk or experimental, but the aim is to
give unknown performers a space to display their
talent. Folk, Celtic music and other mainly-
acoustic sounds are also on offer in many of the
city's British or Irish-style pubs (*see page 163*),
although the standard can vary considerably.

Centre Artesà Tradicionarius (C.A.T.)

Travessera de Sant Antoni 6-8 (93 218 44 85).
Metro Fontana/bus 22, 24, 28, 39, N4.
Open *bar* 5pm-midnight Mon-Fri; *gigs* about 10pm
Mon, Fri. **Admission** 500-2,000ptas.
No credit cards. Map D3
This centre is dedicated to the teaching and exposure of indigenous music from Catalonia, Spain and
occasionally the rest of Europe. Performances usually take place on Friday nights in the centre's hall,
with classes and workshops during the week. From
January to March the annual **Tradicionarius** folk
festival offers at least three concerts and dances a
week, featuring visiting musicians from countries
all over the world.

Jazz-based

An important gap has been left in the live jazz
scene by the city-council-enforced prohibition of
live gigs in Plaça Reial's **Pipa Club** (93 302 47
32/www.bpipaclub.com). Concerts are currently
continuing in temporary venues while Pipa look
for a new home. Consult their website for the
latest information.

La Cova del Drac

C/Vallmajor 33 (93 200 70 32). Metro Muntaner/
bus 14, 58, 64, N8. **Open** usually 6.30pm-5am Tue;
10pm-5am Wed-Sat. Closed Aug. **Admission** (incl
one drink); 500-1,500ptas (midnight show).
No credit cards. Map C2

Few echoes remain of the days when this swish
uptown jazz club was a bohemian/intellectual hangout in the final years of Francoism. The current club
has live acts (with bigger names at weekends) at
11.30pm Thursday to Saturday, preceded by 'new
talent' gigs at 9.30pm – usually folk, pop or jazz
fusion; and followed by the 'Classic Plastics Disco'
from 1.30am. On Tuesday nights there are poetry
readings at 6.30pm, followed by a jam session.
Drinks are on the pricey side, but La Cova has a
reputation for excellence.

La Filharmònica

C/Mallorca 204 (93 451 11 53). Metro Hospital
Clínic/bus 54, 58, 64, 66, 67, 68, N3, N8.
Open 10.15pm-2am Mon-Sun. **Admission** varies.
No credit cards. Map C4
Run by a local jazz pianist and his English wife, this
new venue in the Eixample is a café/restaurant all
day before the gigs kick in later on. Jazz, country,
rock and Latin variations all feature, and very popular country-and-western dance classes are held in
the large wood-grained lounge out back.

Harlem Jazz Club

C/Comtessa de Sobradiel 8 (93 310 07 55). Metro
Jaume I/bus 17, 19, 40, 45, N8. **Open** 8pm-4am
Tue-Thur, Sun; 8pm-5am Fri, Sat. *Gigs* 10.30pm,
midnight, Tue-Thur, Sun; 11.30pm, 1am, Fri, Sat.
Closed some weeks Aug. **Admission** free (but you
must have a drink). **No credit cards. Map** D6/B3
This intimate Barri Gòtic club has a wonderful
atmosphere and is a real favourite with Barcelona
jazz aficionados. Creative programming mixes jazz
and blues with sounds that hail from Cuba,
Senegal, or other points of the compass. In the past,
the club has also hosted popular story-telling
sessions (for adults).

Latin

Antilla Barcelona

C/Aragó 141 (93 451 21 51). Metro Hospital
Clínic/bus 43, 44, N7. **Open** 11pm-3am Mon-Thur,
Sun; 11pm-5am Fri, Sat. **Admission** 1,500ptas; *salsa*
classes free. **Map** C4
Great live bands get the crowd moving and
grooving from Sunday to Thursday in this very
popular salsa/Latin venue. There are free dance
classes of the 'follow the leader' variety on Thursday
and Friday at 11.30pm, almost until the band starts.
On Fridays and Saturdays there's a 'salsoteca'. *See*
also chapter **Nightlife**.

Quinta Avenida

C/Tarragona 141-7 (93 426 84 44). Metro
Tarragona/bus 10, 30, 44, 109, N7. **Open** midnight-
4.30am Tue-Sun. **Admission** 1,500ptas. **Map** A-B4
A big new club for Latin rhythms, 'Fifth Avenue' is
not far from Sants station, and has a large dancefloor, three bars and lots of chrome. The club
manages to book big names in salsa, merengue and
son – among them Cuban legends Los Van Van – to
entertain the well-dressed, cosmopolitan crowd.

Sport & Fitness

Barça *may sometimes look like the only game in town, but there are plenty of places around the city where you can swim, bowl, swing a club or sail a boat.*

Barcelona has not rested on its sporting laurels since the 1992 Olympics; if anything, there has been a further upsurge in interest, and another improvement in facilities. Some 500,000 people make regular use of the Ajuntament's sports services, and 300,000 take part in events such as the **Mercè** fun-run (*see page 11*).

However, the foremost sporting interest for visitors – and many locals – is football, and more precisely FC Barcelona, *Barça*, which dominates the city's sporting life to a very special degree (with teams in many other sports as well as football). On Monday mornings groups of men huddle together over the sports dailies analysing whether *Barça* are doing better than eternal rivals Real Madrid.

Spectating

Tickets can often be bought by credit card through **Servi-Caixa** or **Tel-entrada** (*see page 215*).

Major sports venues

Estadi Olímpic de Montjuïc *Avda de l'Estadi.*
Palau Sant Jordi *Passeig Olímpic 5-7.*
Both (93 426 20 89). Metro Espanya, then escalators, or Paral.lel then Funicular de Montjuïc/bus 61. **Map** A6
Palau dels Esports *C/Lleida (93 423 15 41). Metro Espanya, Poble Sec/bus 55.* **Map** B5-6
Velòdrom d'Horta *Passeig Vall d'Hebron (93 427 91 42). Metro Montbau/bus 27, 73.*

This glut of large-scale multi-purpose sports venues left to Barcelona by the 1992 Games has been pretty much under-used, but the Estadi Olímpic has taken on the more consistent life since it became home to **Espanyol** football club and the **Barcelona Dragons** (*see below*). As well as sport, all the venues are used for concerts and other events (*see chapter* **Music: Rock, Roots & Jazz**). The beautiful Velodrom, in Vall d'Hebron, tends to be the least used. The **Palau d'Esports** at the foot of Montjuïc is older than 1992, but was rebuilt for Olympic year. A booth in Plaça Universitat provides information and tickets for events at all four venues (*see p216*).

American football

Barcelona Dragons
Estadi Olímpic de Montjuïc, Avda de l'Estadi (93 425 49 49). Metro Espanya, then escalators, or Paral.lel then Funicular de Montjuïc/bus 61. **Ticket office** *match days* from two hours before kick-off. **Tickets** 1,600-3,500ptas; *VIP ticket* (incl refreshments) 8,000ptas. **Credit** MC, V. **Map** A6
Runners up in the NFL European final in 1999, the Dragons have been surprisingly successful in gaining support in a city with very little experience of the game (average attendance is around 8-10,000). They play in the Estadi Olímpic, usually on Sundays at 7pm from April to June. The promoters try to make it a full day out, with cheerleaders and all the razzle-dazzle Americana attached to the sport. Most players are American, but there are a few locals in the squad. Tickets can be bought at the stadium on the day or in advance from the ticket booth at Plaça Universitat (*see p216*) or via Servi-Caixa.

Basketball

Second only to football in popularity. The season runs from September to May, and league games are usually on Sunday evenings; European and Spanish Cup matches mid-week.

FC Barcelona
Palau Blaugrana, Avda Arístides Maillol s/n (93 496 36 00). Metro Maria Cristina, Collblanc/bus 15, 52, 53, 54, 56, 57, 75. **Ticket office** from the day before match, 10am-1pm, 4-8pm, or Servi-Caixa. **Tickets** 500-2,700ptas. **No credit cards**.
The basketball arm of *Barça* is fanatically well supported, and it's advisable to book in advance. League games are mainly on Sundays at 6/6.30pm; Cup and European games 8/8.30pm during the week. In *Barça*'s centenary year the club won the Spanish league in play-off finals against Real Madrid.

Pinturas Bruguera (Joventut)
Avda Alfons XIII-C/Ponent 143-161, Badalona (93 460 20 40). Metro Gorg/bus 44. **Ticket office** from one hour before match times. **Tickets** 1,600-3,000ptas. **No credit cards**.
Badalona's standard-bearers stand head-to-head with their wealthier neighbours, and unlike them have actually won the European Basketball Cup. A recent controversy has been over the changing of the club name to 'Pinturas Bruguera', under pressure from its sponsor. Most Sunday games are at 6pm; fans can be even more passionate than at Barcelona.

Football

The city's two first-division clubs are **FC Barcelona** and **RCD Espanyol**. Such is the all-absorbing power of *Barça* that lower-division teams tend to be reduced to semi-pro status through lack of support, but fans of Brentford or Raith Rovers might want to commune with **Hospitalet**, or **Jupiter**, from Poble Nou. The season runs from late August to May, and league games have traditionally been played at 5pm or 7pm on Sundays. Due to pressure from TV at least one game a week is played at 8.30-9pm on Saturday; mid-week cup games are usually at 8.30pm, while European matches are as late as 10pm, again at the behest of TV. *See also page 248.*

FC Barcelona

Nou Camp, Avda Aristides Maillol (93 496 36 00). Metro Maria Cristina, Collblanc/bus 15, 52, 53, 54, 56, 57, 75. **Ticket office** 10am-1pm, 4-8pm, Mon-Fri; tickets available two days before each match. **Tickets** 2,500-14,300ptas. **No credit cards.** **Map** A3

Barça now has more season-ticket holders than seats to go round, so it has become very difficult to get into even the most mundane of games. However, there are various options. The best bet is to phone the club about two weeks in advance and ask exactly when tickets will go on sale, then get to the ground an hour beforehand and queue. Alternatively, you can try your luck with the ticket touts (scalpers), generally found in front of the ticket office on Travessera de Les Corts. Rather than look to 'professionals' it's often better to look for someone with a spare season ticket, who may be willing to bargain. Finally, you can always try asking at the entrance gates if anyone has a spare ticket – '*si us plau, li sobra un carnet?*' – it does work. There's a range of ticket prices, but, since the *entrades generals* areas (for non-members) are very high up, it's worth spending more for a decent view. Barcelona also has teams in the Spanish second (the old third) division and at amateur level. The second-division *Barça-B* plays in the *Mini-estadi*, a 16,000-seater ground connected to the main stadium. Tickets cost about 1,000-2,000ptas, and games are at 5pm on Saturdays. If A and B teams are both at home, a joint ticket allows you to see both games. There is also the option of watching a training session (usually at 10am) or visiting the ultra-popular club museum *(see p105).*

RCD Espanyol

Estadi Olímpic (93 424 88 00). Metro Espanya or Paral.lel, then Funicular de Montjuïc/bus 61 (special buses on match days). **Ticket office** 10-1.30pm, 5-8pm, Fri; 10am-2pm Sat; *match days* 10am-match time.* **Tickets** 3,000-7,000ptas. **No credit cards.** **Map** A6

Getting a ticket to see an Espanyol game is a lot easier than at the Camp Nou, and the Olympic athletics stadium lacks the atmosphere of a real football ground. On match days free buses go up Montjuïc from a special stop at Plaça Espanya 1½ hours before kick-off. There is a ticket booth at the right hand side of the stadium entrance.

Ice hockey

FC Barcelona

FC Barcelona Pista de Gel, Avda Aristides Maillol (93 496 36 00). Metro Maria Cristina, Collblanc/bus 15, 52, 53, 54, 56, 57, 75. **Admission** free.

Once again, it's *Barça* that sponsors the only professional ice hockey team in town. The rink, open to the public on non-match days, is part of the club's vast sports complex. A match schedule is available by phone or from the arena.

Roller hockey

FC Barcelona

Palau Blaugrana, Avda Aristides Maillol (93 496 36 00). Metro Maria Cristina, Collblanc/bus 15, 52, 53, 54, 56, 57, 75. **Ticket office** two hours before match times. **Tickets** prices variable. **No credit cards.**

Roller hockey is extremely popular in Catalonia. The game follows ice hockey regulations, with one notable exception – body-checking and most other forms of contact are prohibited. Matches are played at the *Palau Blaugrana* indoor arena; for match times, see the local press, or phone the above number.

Other events

Barcelona Marathon (Marató de Catalunya-Barcelona)

Information & entry forms *C/Jonqueres 16, 15°, 08003 (93 268 01 14/fax 93 268 43 34).* **Office** 5.30-8.30pm Mon-Fri. **Date** mid-March. **Map** D5/B1

Barcelona's Marathon celebrates its 23rd anniversary in 2000. The race begins north along the coast in Mataró, and ends in Plaça d'Espanya. Prospective participants should apply to the above address between October and the end of February. The city also holds two half-marathons, and the **Cursa de la Mercè** during the Mercè *(see p11)*. The sports information centre *(see* **Servei d'Informaciò Esportiva**, *p249)* has details.

Motor sports

Circuit de Catalunya *Carretera de Parets del Vallès a Granollers, Montmeló (93 571 97 00/fax 93 572 27 72). By car A7 or N152 to Parets del Vallès exit (20km/13 miles).* **Times & tickets** vary according to competition; also from Servi Caixa. **Credit** MC, V.

This motor racing circuit at Montmeló, north of Barcelona, was inaugurated in 1991. Motor sports have become extremely popular here in the last few years, mainly due to the success of Catalans Alex Crivellé and Carles Checa in 500cc motorbike competitions. The Spanish Formula-1 Grand Prix is held here in late May, and a motorcycle Grand Prix in mid-June. For details of events call the circuit, or check with the **RACC** in Barcelona *(see page 284).*

A tale of two centenaries

FC Barcelona, one of the contenders for the status of biggest football club in the world, and their more humble city rivals Espanyol have both been wrapped up in their respective footballing centenaries in 1999-2000. Both clubs exist inadvertently through British influences. Barcelona's first president, contrary to popular myth, was not the Swiss Hans Gamper but an Englishman, Arthur Witty; Espanyol came into being because a group of British seamen arrived in Barcelona in 1900 looking for a game of football. They played a friendly against a team called Català FC, and a couple of students in the crowd were so taken by the spectacle that they decided to start their own club, which became Espanyol.

Over the years Espanyol have always been branded with being pro-Spanish and anti-Catalan. This has to some extent been true in the past, but in recent years the club has tried to rectify this by Catalanising its name (with a *y*, instead of *Español*), and it does have a core of Catalan supporters, bloody-minded souls who like to resist the *Barça* bandwagon. One other way they can certainly justify their Catalan credentials is by pointing to the fact that they have several more locally-bred players in their side than Barcelona.

THIS GREAT INSTITUTION

On the other side of town *Barça* are finally winding down their centenary celebrations in 2000, having been founded one year before Espanyol, in 1899. After a whole year of concerts, exhibitions, football and fireworks, the club is again trying to win its elusive second European Champions' Cup, and so at last banish the ghost of Cruyff.

It is difficult to talk about *Barça* without mentioning Johan Cruyff, their most charismatic player and their most successful manager. His testimonial at the ground probably outshone the rest of the centenary celebrations, including the flagship game against Brazil, much to the disgust of Josep Lluís Núñez, the club president, Cruyff's former mentor and now arch enemy. Núñez is said to be the second most important man in Catalonia after Generalitat president Jordi Pujol, and like him has been in power for 20 years. He has the perfect club chairman's background – he made his millions in the building industry – but unlike many has had the savvy to ride all the intrigues that have passed through the constantly argument-ridden club

during his reign. His latest plan is to create a sporting Disneyland in the grounds, 'Barça 2000' (*see page 86*), to the consternation of local residents, who are fighting the project tooth and nail.

The main reason for this new venture is to find a way to pay the ever-escalating wage bill. Barcelona can field two international class teams at any one time, but there is a price to pay for such talents as Rivaldo, Figo, the De Boers et al. The club has also come under a wave of criticism since the signing of 'charismatic' manager Louis Van Gaal from Ajax a couple of seasons ago. Having won the Spanish league twice in a row you might expect the fans to be content, but Catalans are a hard lot to please, especially when it comes to football. Many bemoan the fact that instead of nurturing home-grown talent – as Cruyff did – the new Dutchman in charge seems to have the sole aim of creating a bizarre clone of his earlier Ajax side, buying in a whole block of fellow Dutchmen, many of whom played for him at his old club.

It can be confusing for visitors to the stadium to see the home side winning and yet being booed by their 'supporters'. Local cartoonists and wags refer to the current Barcelona side scathingly as *Barçajax*, and, no matter how well Van Gaal does in future, it's hard to imagine him ever being loved.

Barça-mania, however, is a habit that runs deep here, irrespective of disenchantment with this year's manager. It expresses itself, though, in odd ways: even more surprising than fans booing their own side is the deathly silence that sometimes engulfs the ground in a normal league game. Catalans may be passionate about their football, but they sometimes seem to express it more strongly in reading or talking about it – or acquiring *Barça*-junk – than actually at the game.

For those who are unable to get a ticket or have an interest in giant concrete structures, the **Nou Camp** stadium and **Museu del FC Barcelona** can make a good day out (*see pages 86, 105*), and for the first half of the year 2000 the club's centenary exhibition will still be at the **Fundació la Caixa**'s **Casaramona** centre on Montjuïc (*see chapter* **Art Galleries**). Plus, there's the club's unmissable shops, **La Botiga del Barça** (*see chapter* **Shopping**), and website, www.fcbarcelona.com, both worth checking out.

Tennis

Reial Club de Tennis Barcelona-1899 *C/Bosch i Gimpera 5-13 (93 203 78 52/fax 93 204 50 10). Bus 63, 114.* **Open** *club* (members only except during competitions) 8am-10pm daily. *Ticket office* 9am-6pm daily during competitions.

The city's most prestigious tennis club hosts a major international tournament, the ten-day **Trofeig Comte de Godó**, part of the men's ATP tour, generally in mid-April. Tickets, available through Servi-Caixa or the club, cost 2,300-9,000ptas; *bono* tickets give you admission on all ten days (60,000ptas). A women's invitation event, the **Open de Catalunya**, is usually in late June at the **Club de Tenis Hispano-Francés** (93 428 12 36) in Vall d'Hebron.

Centre Municipal de Tennis Vall d'Hebron.

The Ajuntament runs an extensive network of *Poliesportius* or sports centres: some have basic gyms and indoor halls suitable for basketball and five-a-side; others a lavish range of facilities including pools and running tracks. Charges are low, and you don't have to be a resident to use them. For cycle hire, *see page 285.*

Servei d'Informació Esportiva

Avda de l'Estadi 30-40 (information phoneline 93 402 30 00). Metro Espanya, then escalators, or Paral.lel then Funicular de Montjuïc/bus 61. **Open** *July-Sept* 8am-3pm Mon-Thur; *Oct-June* 8am-2.30pm Mon-Fri, 4-6.15pm Mon-Thur. **Map** A6

The Ajuntament's sports information service is based alongside the **Piscina Bernat Picornell** (*see p251*). It has leaflets listing district sports centres, or you can phone to ask which is the one nearest to you. Staff are helpful, but only some speak English.

Billiards, snooker, pool

Many bars have tables for Spanish billiards (*carambolas*, blue, and without pockets) or American pool, and a few full-size snooker tables. A favourite bar for *billar* is the **Velòdrom** (*see page 169*), and **Snooker Club Barcelona** (*see chapter* **Nightlife**) has full-size English snooker tables.

Club Billars Monforte

La Rambla 27 (93 318 10 19). Metro Drassanes/bus 14, 18, 38, 59, 64, 91. **Open** 10am-11pm daily. Closed 1 Jan. **Rates** *membership* 1,000ptas per month; *members* 200ptas per hour per person; *non-members* 800ptas per hour. **No credit cards. Map** C6/**A4**

Men of a certain age play cards, dominoes and billiards in this old-fashioned club in a room of faded glory. Officially Club Billars Monforte is members only, but non-members are usually welcome, although you need to knock after 10pm, and it doesn't hurt to phone ahead. Make a point of going to the toilet, as there is a fantastic ballroom with an amazing domed roof to see.

Bowling

Bowling Barcelona

C/Sabino Arana 6 (93 330 50 48). Metro Maria Cristina/ bus 7, 59, 67, 68, 70, 72, 74, 75, 114. **Open** 11am-2am Mon-Thur; 11am-3am Fri; 11am-4am Sat; 11am midnight Sun. Closed 1 Jan. **Rates** *per game* 200-600ptas per person, depending on day and time. *Shoe hire* 150ptas. **Credit** MC, V. **Map** A2

This centre has added extra facilities in a bid to keep up with the nearby Pedralbes bowl. Lunchtime is a good time to go, to take advantage of cheaper rates.

Bowling Pedralbes

Avda Dr Marañón 11 (93 333 03 52). Metro Collblanc/bus 7, 54, 67, 68, 74, 75. **Open** 10am-1am daily. *Aug* open from 5pm only. **Rates** *per game* 220ptas per person until 5pm Mon-Fri; 400ptas from 5pm Mon-Thur; 550ptas from 5pm Fri, all day Sat, Sun. *Shoe hire* 100ptas. **Credit** MC, V.

A well-equipped operation, with bar and dining area, where you can hire gloves and shoes, and play snooker, pool or darts. Best time is early afternoon, but if it's full, leave your name at reception and they will page you at the bar when a lane becomes free.

Football

Barcelona International Football League

Information *(93 218 67 31/nicksimonsbcn@ yahoo.co.uk).*

How do expats bond? By starting a football league, that's how. The BIFL was formed in 1991 and is made up of 16 teams with international players who play from September to June. If you're new in town, league president Nick Simons will help you find a team. Games can also be set up for visiting teams.

Gyms/fitness centres

If you want to keep fit on a visit here, a good bet are the sport centres run by the city – they are cheaper and generally more user-friendly than private clubs. Check with the **Servei d'Informació Esportiva** (*see above*) for centres with the right facilities.

Califòrnia Look

Plaça Ramon Berenguer el Gran 2 (93 319 87 25). Metro Jaume I/bus 17, 40, 45. **Open** 7.30am-

10.30pm Mon-Fri; 10am-4pm Sat. Closed Sun, public holidays. **Rates** *non-members* 1,200ptas per day; 5,000ptas one week; 6,500ptas two weeks; 9,500ptas per month; *membership* 7,944ptas per month. **No credit cards. Map** D6/B3
One of few fitness centres in Barcelona to offer daily, weekly or monthly rates for the short-term visitor. Basic rates give you access to all sports facilities; a higher rate includes UV and beauty treatments.

Centres de Fitness DIR
C/Casp 34 (901 30 40 30). Metro Catalunya/bus all routes to Plaça Catalunya. **Open** 6.30am-12.30am Mon-Fri; 8am-9pm Sat, Sun, public holidays. **Rates** from 2,875ptas five days; 4,025ptas seven days. **No credit cards. Map** D5/B1
Centres de Fitness DIR is a chain of seven centres in Barcelona, all with excellent facilities (weights machines, pools, saunas, and more) and flexible rates for non-members. Call the central number for information on the one nearest to you.

Golf

Club de Golf El Prat
El Prat de Llobregat (93 379 02 78). By car Carretera de l'Aeroport (21km/13 miles). **Open** 8am-10pm daily; *Oct-May* members only Sat, Sun. Closed 25 Dec. **Rates** *non-members* 12,380ptas Mon-Fri; 24,840ptas Sat, Sun, public holidays. **Credit** MC, V.
Due to close down in two or three years time to make way for Barcelona airport's third runway, this is a premiere 36-hole course that has hosted the Spanish Open six times. Equipment is available for hire, but you must be a member of a federated club to play. Best chance of a game is very early on a weekday.

Club de Golf Sant Cugat
C/de la Villa s/n, Sant Cugat del Vallès (93 674 39 58). By car Túnel de Vallvidrera (E9) to Valldoreix/by train FGC from Plaça Catalunya to Valldoreix. **Open** 7.30am-9pm Tue-Sun. Closed 25 Dec, 1 Jan. **Rates** *non-members* 9,000ptas Tue-Fri; 20,000ptas Sat, Sun, public holidays. **Credit** MC, V.
This attractive and well-equipped 18-hole course was built in 1919, and saw the professional debut of the young Seve Ballesteros. A drawback for visitors is that you cannot hire clubs or trolleys, but green fees allow access to facilities such as the bar, restaurant and pool.

Horse riding

Hípica Severino de Sant Cugat
Passeig Calado 12, Sant Cugat del Vallès (93 674 11 40). By car Carretera de l'Arrabassada (exit 5 from Ronda de Dalt). **Open** 8am-8pm daily. Closed 25 Dec. **Rates** *lessons* 1,600ptas per hour; *rides* by arrangement. **No credit cards**.
This school takes groups riding through the pretty countryside around Sant Cugat and along Collserola. All-day rides include a lunch stop on the way. Book weekend rides at least two days in advance.

The Olympic **Piscina Municipal de Montjuïc**.

Hípica Sant Jordi
Carretera de Sant Llorenç Savall, km. 42, Cànoves i Samalús (93 843 40 17). By car A18 or N150 to Sabadell, then B124 to Sant Llorenç Savall. **Rates** from 3,000ptas per 1½ hours. **No credit cards**.
A child-friendly riding establishment in the hills near the Montseny, which offers varied programmes for beginners and experienced riders. One of the owners is English, so there are no language problems. Call ahead to book, and get directions.

Ice Skating

The skating rink in the *Barça* complex, **FC Barcelona Pista de Gel** (93 496 36 30) is open to the public whenever it's not needed for ice-hockey games (*see p247*; usually, any time except early Saturday evenings). The rink is quite functional, but prices are low (1,000ptas, weekdays, including skate hire).

Skating Roger de Flor
C/Roger de Flor 168 (93 245 28 00). Metro Tetuan/bus 6, 19, 50, 51, 54, 55, N1, N3, N4, N5. **Open** 10.30am-1.30pm Tue-Sun; 5-10pm Wed, Thur, Sun; 5pm-midnight Fri, Sat. **Rates** (incl skates) 1,400ptas; *glove hire* 125ptas; group discounts. **No credit cards. Map** E5
The modern rink with bar and restaurant facilities offers group discounts if you arrange your visit at least a day in advance.

Jogging & running

The best place for jogging is the **seafront**, from Barceloneta past the Vila Olímpica, or in the other direction along the breakwater. Away from the water, the next best spot is **Montjuïc**: run up from Plaça d'Espanya, or start at the top. **Tibidabo** and **Collserola** are also good spots, and from Plaça Dr Andreu, at the top of the tramline, fairly level, quiet roads lead along the hillside, with great views. Traffic makes street running in the city unpleasant.

Sailing

The Port Olímpic has brought completely new sailing opportunities to the city. For sailing facilities outside Barcelona, *see pages 262-3*.

Base Nàutica de la Mar Bella
Espigó del Ferrocarril, Platja de Bogatell, Avda Litoral s/n (93 221 04 32). Bus 36, 41, 92.
Open 9.30am-5.30pm daily. **Rates** *membership* 21,000ptas per year; *boat hire & courses* rates vary. **Discounts** BC. **No credit cards.**
Base Nàutica de la Mar Bella, on the third beach after the Port Olímpic, hires out windsurfing and snorkelling facilities, and many classes of boat for experienced sailors. The well-trained staff run courses for beginners.

Centre Municipal de Vela
Moll del Gregal, Port Olímpic (93 221 14 99). Metro Ciutadella-Vila Olímpica/bus 10, 36, 45, 59. **Open** 9am-9pm daily; *office* 10am-8pm daily. Closed 25, 26 Dec. **Rates** *individual sessions* from 3,500ptas per hour; *17½ hour course* 26,000ptas; 14,000ptas children. **Credit** MC, V. **Map** F7
A relaxed city sailing club offering courses at reasonable prices. The five-day programme is the same price in whatever class of boat, and for the complete novice Centre Municipal de Vela offers a sea-christening session.

Sport climbing
Barcelona boasts several indoor climbing-walls or *rocodroms*, many in municipal *Poliesportius* (inquire at the **Servei d'Informació Esportiva**, *see page 249*). Climbers should bring proof of national federation membership or climbing credentials.

Unió Excursionista de Catalunya
C/Jocs Florals 51 (93 331 10 12). Metro Mercat Nou/bus 70. **Open** 7-10pm Mon-Fri. **Rates** *membership* 2,500ptas plus 810ptas per month. 125ptas per hour. **No credit cards.**
The premises are open to anyone who can prove membership of their national climbing federation, and foreign visitors are welcomed with a rugged handshake. You can borrow the club's ropes, but bring your own appropriate clothing.

Squash
Squash 2000
C/Sant Antoni Maria Claret 84-6 (93 458 22 02). Metro Joanic/bus 15, 20, 45, 47. **Open** 7.30am-11.30pm Mon-Fri; 8am-10pm Sat; 8am-3pm Sun. Closed public holidays. **Rates** *non-members* from 675ptas per half-hour. **Credit** AmEx, MC, V. **Map** E3
Squash 2000 has 12 courts (advance booking necessary), a sauna, bar and restaurant areas.

Swimming pools
There are 27 municipal pools in Barcelona; for a full list contact the **Servei d'Informació Esportiva** (*see page 249*). The most spectacular of the 1992 pools, the **Piscina Municipal de Montjuïc** (93 443 00 46) used for the diving events, is only open from June to August.

Club de Natació Atlètic Barceloneta
Plaça del Mar (93 221 00 10). Bus 17, 45, 57, 59, 64. **Open** *June-mid-Sept* 7am-11pm Mon-Sat; 8am-8pm Sun, public holidays. *Mid-Sept-June* 7am-11pm Mon-Sat; 8am-5pm Sun, public holidays. **Admission** *non-members* 1,000ptas per day; 1,400ptas per day with sauna/jacuzzi. **No credit cards. Map** D7
Three indoor pools, plus the usual bar and restaurant, are supplemented by the **Banys de Sant Sebastià** (Passeig Joan de Borbó 93), where the Passeig meets the beach, which has indoor and outdoor pools, massage/sauna area and a gym.

Piscina Bernat Picornell
Avda de l'Estadi 30-40 (93 423 40 41). Metro Espanya, then escalators, or Paral.lel then Funicular de Montjuïc/bus 61. **Open** 7am-midnight Mon-Fri; 7am-9pm Sat; *Oct-May* 7.30am-4pm, *June-Sept* 7.30am-8pm, Sun, public holidays. **Admission** *open-air pool* 700ptas; 475ptas under-15s; free under-6s. *All facilities* 1,300ptas; 700ptas under-15s; free under-6s. **Discounts** BT. **Credit** MC, V. **Map** A6
Built in 1969, this pool was lavishly renovated for the 1992 games. There are two Olympic size pools, one outdoor (heated in winter), the other indoor. You can also tone up in a gym/weights room. During the Grec festival (*see p9*), the pool hosts a joint swimming/film session, from around 10.30pm, and on Saturday, 9-11pm, there is a session for naturists.

Piscina Municipal Folch i Torres
C/Reina Amalia 31 (93 441 01 22). Metro Paral.lel/bus 20, 36, 57, 64, 91, 96. **Open** 7am-11.30pm Mon-Fri; 8am-7.30pm Sat; 8.30am-1.30pm Sun, public holidays. Closed public holidays, two weeks Aug. **Admission** *non-members* 900ptas; 500ptas children aged 6-14; 250ptas under-6s. **No credit cards. Map** C6
This city complex on the edge of the Raval has three covered pools, and a sauna and weights room.

Tennis
Club Vall Parc
Carretera de l'Arrabassada 97 (93 212 67 89). Bus A6/ By car Carretera de l'Arrabassada. **Open** 8am-midnight daily. **Rates** *courts* 2,200ptas per hour; 600ptas for floodlights. **No credit cards.**
On Tibidabo, near Vall d'Hebron, this club offers 14 outdoor courts and two open-air pools. Racquets can be hired, but you must bring your own tennis balls.

Centre Municipal de Tennis Vall d'Hebron
Passeig de la Vall d'Hebron 178-196 (93 427 65 00). Metro Montbau/bus 27, 60, 73, 76, 85, 173. **Open** 8am-11pm Mon-Sat; 8am-7pm Sun, public holidays. Closed 25 Dec, 1 Jan. **Admission** *non-members* 1,700-2,200ptas; 650ptas for floodlights. **No credit cards.**
The city tennis centre, purpose-built for the Olympics, is some way from the centre of town. It has 17 clay courts, and a full-size court for *pelota*. You need your own racquet and balls.

Theatre

With lavish new venues, theatre in Barcelona is booming, even though commercial pressures muddy the waters.

Catalan has been a literary language since the middle ages, but dramatic texts did not appear until the modern era. Public venues bent on promoting a national theatre fall back on a few so-called classics – rarely very memorable – from the late nineteenth century. Contemporary writers include Josep Maria Benet i Jornet, who squanders his talent on soap operas for Catalan TV, and Sergi Belbel and Jordi Galceran, who tend towards lightish comedies. As compensation for the scarcity of Catalan texts, theatre professionals have taken to defending a universal theatre, translating works from many countries and bringing foreign companies to perform here, often in their own language.

Great texts may be lacking, but theatre is booming here. Its vitality has not been dependent on literary dialogues so much as on an extraordinary capacity to blend music, choreography, multimedia resources and spectacular production values into a distinctive Catalan style, accessible even if you're unable to follow the language. This crowd-pleasing Catalan approach to theatre has drawn ecstatic reactions from critics and audiences around the world for groups like Els Comediants and La Cubana, and is continued by new, cabaret-inspired companies like Chicos Mambo Boys.

The vibrancy of this kind of theatre, added to Barcelona people's love for music hall and vaudeville – revived as cabaret and home-grown musicals – has aided a spectacular growth in theatre attendances during the '90s. One consequence of this is that private promoters and producers now surpass public ones in prestige and power; more theatres are dedicated to unabashedly commercial shows, with little or no dependence on public support.

Not even the opening of the Generalitat-sponsored **Teatre Nacional de Catalunya (TNC)** in 1997 has altered the balance much. At the first clash between public and private sectors the complaints of local theatre bosses were enough to ensure the firing of TNC head Josep Maria Flotats. A counterpoint to the Teatre Nacional is a city-sponsored project to create a **Ciutat del Teatre** ('City of Theatre') on Montjuïc, around the existing **Mercat de les Flors**. This converted flower-market, and summer festival programmes, are where English-language productions usually appear in Barcelona. Also, a new Barcelona-based English-language company, Escapade, presented Steven Berkoff's *Metamorphosis* in late 1999.

Seasons & festivals

The main theatre season runs from September to June, and by tradition theatres have closed in summer. However, the success of the **Festival del Grec** (*see p9*) and influx of tourists has convinced promoters to present programmes in July and early August. The Grec is the best time to catch visiting theatre and dance companies, both international and from other parts of Spain. There's no fringe festival per se in Barcelona (Catalonia's best experimental showcase is in **Tàrrega**, in Lleida, in September), but worth watching out for are the **Opera de Butxaca** series at the **Artenbrut** and **Malic**, and the **Marató del Espectacle** in May (*see p8*).

Tickets & times

Main shows at most theatres start late, around 9-10.30pm. Many theatres also have earlier (cheaper) performances at 6-7pm, often on Wednesday and Saturday or Sunday; weekend nights there are also late shows. Most theatres are closed on Mondays. Advance bookings are best made through the ticket sales operations of savings banks, **Servi-Caixa** or **Tel-entrada** (*see p215*). Which Caixa handles the tickets of a particular theatre is indicated below. Theatre box offices often take cash sales only. Best places to find current programmes are the *Guia del Ocio*, newspapers and, for Tel-entrada theatres, the *Guia del Teatre* free at Caixa Catalunya branches.

Major companies

Els Comediants

Over 25 years, around the figure of director/guiding light Joan Font, Els Comediants have developed a unique style of performance based on street theatre, mime, circus, music and Mediterranean traditions of folklore, *festa* and celebration. A Comediants show, often presented in open-air venues such as parks or squares, is as much an event as a piece of 'theatre', with structure but no real script, which makes them particularly appealing to international audiences. Comediants have been accused of being adolescent, and lately what had seemed so fresh and innovative has sometimes begun to look repetitious and complacent, but their best effects are still startling. Their last project has been for the Millennium, a 'millennial clock' on the façade of Gaudí's **La Pedrera**, amid their usual festive paraphernalia.

The **Teatre Nacional de Catalunya.**

contemporary drama by Catalan and international authors, in Catalan. The company is part of the Ciutat del Teatre project, and has a fine chamber orchestra (*see chapter* **Music: Classical & Opera**).

Mainstream theatres

The boom in commercial theatre in Barcelona has meant that some theatres have lost their identification with any one genre or company. Big central theatres like the **Borràs** (Plaça Urquinaona 9, 93 412 15 82) or **Tivoli** (C/Casp 10-12, 93 412 20 63) are used for big-draw productions. The **Villaroel** (C/Villaroel 87, 93 451 12 34) is a semi-fringe theatre that sometimes hosts interesting work; **Teatre Victòria** (Avda Paral.lel 67, 443 29 29) has excellent acoustics and sightlines, which make it a good venue for opera, classical music and dance.

La Cubana

Perhaps the Catalan company with the widest appeal, La Cubana has thrived on a dazzling mix of satire, gaudy showbiz effects, camp music and audience participation. Its productions ¡*Còmeme el Coco, Negro!* and *Cegada de Amor* (Blinded by Love) were huge successes; the latter, exploiting and inter-mixing film and theatre conventions, blew audiences away at the 1997 Edinburgh Festival. A new production is awaited for 2000, and meanwhile group members such as Mont Plans keep busy with their own extravagant shows.

Dagoll Dagom

Under the direction of Joan Lluís Bozzo this company has honed a Catalan musical genre almost of its own, with striking use of colour and comedy. Its productions *Mar i Cel* and *Flor de Nit* – inspired by the anarchist 1920s – were box-office hits, and DD have wowed audiences around Europe.

La Fura dels Baus

With their primitivist rituals, industrial music and latent threat of danger, La Fura burst onto the international scene in the 1980s with provocative productions like *Suz-O-Suz* ('85) and *Tier Mon* ('88), in which water, fire, and raw meat formed part of the messy recipe, treating audience members like shipwreck victims in a sea of noise, power-tools, naked men, shopping trolleys, mayhem and constant motion. Later productions like *Noun* (1991), *MTM* (1994) and *Manes* (1996) have featured more text and narrative; in 1998 they produced a version of *Faust* for the TNC, and have recently worked as production designers for operas in prestigious settings like the Salzburg Festival. La Fura also generates satellites such as CDs, videos and interactive CD-Roms.

Els Joglars

A company that revolves around Albert Boadella, its founder, ideologist and leader, who was imprisoned for his political stances under Franco. With sardonic humour and text as well as the customary Catalan mime and dance skills, Boadella has kept to a line of caustic satire, with creations such as *Yo tengo un tío en América* (I've got an uncle in America), on the Columbus commemorations of 1992. A bit reiterative in their spoofs of Church, state and nationalist clichés, Joglars have recently produced *Daaali*, a sympathetic portrait of Figueres' famous eccentric, to rave reviews.

Teatre Lliure

Probably Barcelona's most reputable theatre company, since 1976 the Lliure has presented classic and

Mercat de le Flors

Plaça Margarida Xirgu, C/Lleida 59 (93 426 18 75). Metro Espanya, Poble Sec/bus 55. **Box office** one hour before performance; *advance sales* Tel-entrada & Centre de la Virreina. **Tickets** prices variable. **No credit cards. Map** B6

A huge converted flower market with three halls of different sizes, the Mercat is due to become part of the Ciutat del Teatre project, and was partially closed for work to begin in 1999. It has become the usual venue for multidisciplinary performances like those by La Fura dels Baus, and major visiting productions such as those of Peter Brook, La La La Human Steps and Cheek by Jowl. Also a major venue for the Grec festival (*see p9*).

Teatre Goya

C/Joaquín Costa 68 (93 318 19 84). Metro Universitat/bus all routes to Plaça Universitat. **Box office** from 5pm Tue-Sun; *advance sales* Tel-entrada. **Tickets** from 2,500ptas. **Credit** MC, V. **Map** C5

Founded in 1917 and dedicated to modern Spanish theatre, the Goya saw the premières of many works by García Lorca, often starring his favourite leading lady, Barcelona actress Margarida Xirgú. Nowadays it hosts anything from Noël Coward to the Iliad.

Teatre Lliure

C/Montseny 47 (93 218 92 51). Metro Fontana/bus 22, 24, 28, 39, N4. **Box office** from 5pm Tue-Sun; *advance sales* box office (5-8pm Tue-Sat) & Tel-entrada. **Tickets** 2,000ptas Tue-Thur; 2,500ptas Fri-Sun. **No credit cards. Map** D3

Long the most prestigious venue in Catalan theatre, a breeding ground for fine actors and directors such as Lluís Pascual, who went on to run companies in Madrid and Paris before taking charge of the Ciutat del Teatre project. The Lliure is due to move to the Ciutat too, but when this will be is an open question.

Teatre Nacional de Catalunya (TNC)

Plaça de les Arts 1 (93 306 57 00//info@tnc.es). Metro Glòries/bus 7, 18, 56, 62, N3, N9. **Box office** noon-3pm, 4-9pm Mon; noon-9pm Tue-Sat; noon-6pm Sun; *advance sales* box office & Servi-Caixa. **Tickets**

2,500-3,000ptas; discounts students, over-65s, groups; 50% discount on standby tickets from 50min before performance. **Credit** MC, V. **Map** F5

Ricard Bofill's Parthenon-like TNC is by far the most impressive theatre building in the city, standing alone on a grand lot near the Plaça de les Glòries. Yet, ever since prestigious actor/director Josep Maria Flotats was brought back from France to design the project for the Generalitat in the 1980s, the TNC has been enveloped in controversy. Flotat's unyielding personality and identification with one political party gave rise to intense jealousy and criticism in the rest of the theatre world. The infighting lead to his sacking just after the theatre opened in 1997, and his vision for an independent, entirely public theatre has largely gone with him. Still, the TNC's hefty budget allows it to bring in major productions from elsewhere in Spain and Europe, as well as promoting Catalan theatre in all its variety. It also hosts a substantial dance programme.
Website: www.tnc.es

Teatre Poliorama

La Rambla 115 (93 317 75 99). Metro Catalunya/bus all routes to Plaça Catalunya. **Box office** 5pm to performance Tue-Sun; *advance sales* box office & Servi-Caixa. **Tickets** 1,500-3,500ptas; some discounts for students, over-65s. **Credit** MC, V. **Map** D5/A2

This theatre was acquired by the Catalan government in 1984 to house the Flotats company, genesis of the future National Theatre. Since the opening of the TNC it has been used by commercial producers 3X3, run by groups like Dagoll Dagom. George Orwell was holed up on the roof during the fighting between anarchists and Communists, in 1937.

Teatre Principal

La Rambla 27 (93 301 47 50). Metro Drassanes/bus 14, 38, 59, 91, N9, N12. **Box office** from 4.30pm on day of performance Wed-Sun; *advance sales* box office & Servi-Caixa. **Tickets** *plays* 2,000-4,000ptas; *opera* 2,000-4,500ptas; *recitals* 2,000ptas; some discounts under-14s, over-65s, groups. **No credit cards. Map** C6/A3

The Principal stands on the site of Barcelona's first theatre, the Teatre de la Santa Creu, opened in 1597. Destroyed by fire in the eighteenth century, it was rebuilt and renamed in the 1850s. It has been recently refurbished, and offers everything from classical and popular music to opera and serious drama.

Teatre Romea

C/Hospital 51 (93 317 71 89/93 301 55 04/group enquiries 93 309 76 00). Metro Liceu/ bus 14, 38, 59, 91, N9, N12. **Box office** from 4.30pm Tue-Sun; *advance sales* box office & Tel-entrada. **Tickets** 1,500-3,000ptas; group discounts. **No credit cards. Map** C6/A2

Now another theatre of the Generalitat's Centre Dramàtic, the Romea has been a centre of the Barcelona theatre world for over a century. It offers classical and contemporary theatre, almost always in Catalan, and continues as a public theatre in spite of the tendency of the TNC to usurp its role.

Alternative & fringe

Artenbrut

C/Perill 9-11 (93 457 97 05). Metro Verdaguer/bus 6, 15, 20, 33, 34, 39, 45, 47, N6. **Box office** 8pm till performance Wed-Sun; *advance sales* box office & Tel-entrada. **Tickets** 1,600-2,000ptas. **No credit cards. Map** D4

Artenbrut is a small venue with great intentions, and a double bill at weekends usually split between text-based works and the Opera de Butxaca (pocket opera) series, from real mini-operas to drag-queen cabaret.

La Cuina & Teatre Adrià Gual

C/Sant Pere Més Baix 7 (93 268 20 78). Metro Jaume I/bus 17, 19, 40, 45, N8. **Box office** two hours before performance Mon-Sat; one hour before performance Sun; *advance sales* box office & Tel-entrada. **Tickets** 1,700-1,900ptas; 25% discount students, over-65s; free Mar, May-June (student productions). **No credit cards. Map** D6/B2

Two stages that serve as outlets for Barcelona's Theatre Institute, in interesting (and cheap) productions. Student and professional productions are staged, often by prestigious visiting directors. The school should move to the Ciutat del Teatre in 2000.

Espai Escènic Joan Brossa

C/Allada Vermell 13 (93 310 13 64/93 315 15 96). Metro Jaume I/bus 17, 19, 39, 40, 45, 51, N8. **Box office** two hours before performance; *advance sales* Tel-entrada. **Tickets** 1,500-2,000ptas. **No credit cards. Map** E6/C3

One of Barcelona's most curious theatre projects is dedicated to poet and artist Joan Brossa, who wrote wonderful, performance art-like pieces in the 1960s. The space reflects his obsessions: magic and sleight of hand, *commedia dell'arte*, the circus and cabaret. Many shows are accessible to non-Catalan speakers.

Sala Beckett

C/Alegre de Dalt 55 bis (93 284 53 12). Metro Joanic/bus 24, 25, 31, 32, 39, 55, 74, N6. **Box office** two hours before performance; *advance sales* box office (10.30am-2pm, 4-6pm, Mon-Fri) & Tel-entrada. **Tickets** 1,500-2,000ptas. **No credit cards. Map** E3

Founded by the Samuel Beckett-inspired Teatro Fronterizo group, whose guiding light José Sanchis Sinisterra is one of Spain's best modern playwrights, this small Gràcia space offers varied new theatre, and also contemporary dance.

Teatre Malic

C/Fusina 3 (93 310 70 35). Metro Jaume I/bus 39, 51. **Box office** two hours before performance; *advance sales* box office (10am-2pm, 4-6pm, Mon-Fri) & Tel-entrada. **Tickets** 1,500-2,000ptas. **Credit** MC, V. **Map** E6/C3

A tiny (60-seat) theatre in a Born basement, the Malic has jumped on the mini-musical bandwagon. It also hosts minimalist readings, contemporary music, and kids' shows, on weekend mornings.

Trips Out of Town

Getting Started

Orientation and resources to take you beyond the city streets.

Catalonia is a small triangle of plenty. Each of its borders is within a day's drive of Barcelona, but depending on the direction you take scenery and climate vary remarkably. North and east are the Pyrenees and the coastal mountains; to the west, the country slopes into a broad, hilly plain. It's possible (with just a little racing around) to wake up amid cold, fresh mountain air, and later the same day siesta on the coast in temperatures over 35°C. The Catalan 'costes' – Brava, Maresme, Garraf and Daurada – have their high-density tourist towns, but there are plenty of lesser-known beach villages too, and inland the countryside is a goldmine of beautiful towns, villages and scenery.

The Catalan government information centre in the **Palau Robert** (*see page 295*) and local offices have brochures (many multi-lingual) on areas (*comarques*), parks, topics (*Modernisme*, or Roman sites) and activities. Some places around Barcelona make easy day trips, but others are best visited with a stopover. Exploring the countryside is now easier thanks to the Generalitat's farmhouse accommodation scheme (*see page 269*), a guide to which (*Residències – Casa de Pagès*) is available at the Palau Robert, local offices and bookshops. Other Generalitat guides include *Hotels Catalunya* and *Catalunya Campings*, and a good website (*www.gencat.es/probert*). For travel agents, *see page 216*.

By bus

Coach services around Catalonia are operated by several private companies, concentrated mostly (but not entirely) at the **Estació d'Autobusos Barcelona-Nord**, C/Ali Bei 80 (Metro Arc de Triomf/**Map** E5). General information is on **93 265 65 08**, but each company has its own phone lines. Two areas better served by buses than trains are the high Pyrenees (with the Alsina-Graëlls company) and the central Costa Brava (with Sarfa).

By road

For many locals the greatest of Barcelona's 1992 acquisitions was the *Rondes*, the ring road built to ease traffic into, around and out of the city. The **Ronda de Dalt** runs along the edge of Tibidabo, and the **Ronda Litoral** along the coast, meeting north and south of the city. They intersect with several motorways (*autopistes*): from north to south, the A19 (from Mataró), the A17/A7 (Girona, France)

and **A18** (Sabadell, Manresa, Puigcerdà), which both run into Avda Meridiana; **A2** (Lleida, Madrid), a continuation of Avda Diagonal, which connects with the **A7** south (Tarragona, Valencia); and the **A16** (Sitges), reached from the Gran Via. These are toll roads. Where possible, toll-free alternatives are given in the pages that follow. The **Túnel de Vallvidrera**, the continuation of Via Augusta that leads out of Barcelona under Collserola to Sant Cugat and Terrassa, also has a high toll. Further north, the **C25** (*Eix Transversal*) highway between Girona and Lleida is a means by which long-distance traffic can avoid the Barcelona hub.

Post-*Rondes*, traffic on main roads runs fairly freely most days, but journeys into Barcelona on Sunday evenings are always to be avoided. For more on driving and car hire, *see pages 284-5*.

By train

Spanish Railways (**RENFE**) has an extensive network within Catalonia – particularly useful for the coast, Girona, the Montseny and the Penedès. All trains stop at **Barcelona-Sants** station (Metro Sants-Estació/**Map** A4). Tickets for local and suburban (*Rodalies/Cercanías*) services are sold at separate, well-labelled windows. In the city centre, some routes (the coast north, the Penedès) pass through **Plaça Catalunya**; others (the coast south, Girona), **Passeig de Gràcia**.

Regional trains are *Regulars*, stopping at every station, *Deltas*, at nearly all of them, or *Catalunya Exprés*, stopping less often and costing a bit more. Long-distance (*Largo Recorrido*) services also stop at main stations, but supplements are paid for high-speed services. RENFE fare structures are complicated, but special deals include the *Bonotren* and *Bono-Exprés* tickets, valid for ten trips on *Rodalies* and regional trains respectively; *Abono 1, 3, 5* tickets, for unlimited travel on *Rodalies* trains for from one to five days; and off-peak days (*dias azules*, blue days, and usually midweek) when long-distance services are cheaper. For **RENFE information**, call **93 490 02 02** (English spoken); the RENFE website is at *www.renfe.es* (partly in English).

Catalan Government Railways (**FGC**) serves some destinations from its two stations: **Plaça d'Espanya**, for Montserrat and Manresa, and **Plaça Catalunya** for the line within Barcelona and trains to Sant Cugat, Sabadell and Terrassa. **FGC information** is on **93 205 15 15**.

City Limits

To find a quick change of air in Barcelona, look just over the hill.

You don't have to go far to discover a different side to Barcelona: pine forests and hill villages are no more than a half-hour train ride away. The areas around the city's fringes also hold many striking examples of Catalan *Modernista* architecture.

The Vallès

Just behind Tibidabo, on the other side of the great ridge of Collserola from Barcelona, extends the hilly plain of the Vallès. A little way further along from the road and rail tunnels, **Les Planes** is a picnic area on the edge of Collserola, with cheap restaurants and a *merendero*, an area with tables and charcoal grills where Sunday visitors bring their own food for long, leisurely barbecues. There's an attractive walk or cycle ride from Les Planes towards **El Papiol**, a town with a medieval castle and the remains of an Iberian settlement.

A little further north is **La Floresta**, a leafy suburb of houses scattered between pines up and down steep hillsides. It was once called 'La Floresta Pearson', after the Canadian engineer who brought mains electricity to Barcelona in 1911, and planned the village. In the 1970s it was Barcelona's hippy haven – legendary 'Fat Freddy's Cat' cartoonist Gilbert Shelton even lived here for a while – and the influence survives in the friendly Bar Dada. La Floresta is a great place for an easy, short walk, with beautiful views. For Collserola walks within Barcelona, *see page 87*.

Below Collserola stands **Sant Cugat**, a fast-growing town with a Romanesque **monastery** and, on the Arrabassada road back towards Barcelona, the **Casa Lluch**, a striking 1906 Modernist creation with superb tiling. The main towns of the Vallès are two of Catalonia's historic industrial hubs. **Terrassa** is rarely seen as a tourist attraction, but has at its centre three very ancient Visigothic-Romanesque churches, **Santa Maria**, **Sant Miquel** and **Sant Pere**, with sections from the sixth century. The town also has a host of *Modernista* buildings, such as the extraordinary **Masia Freixa**, a blend of mosque and Disneyland palace, and the Aymerich i Amat factory, home to Catalonia's science museum, the **Museu de la Ciència i de la Tècnica**.

Terrassa's eternal rival, **Sabadell**, also has its Modernist buildings: an unmissable covered market, the **Torre de les Aigües** (water-tower) and **Caixa d'Estalvis de Sabadell** savings bank.

Information

Getting there: **Les Planes**, **La Floresta**, **Sant Cugat** *By car* A7 via Túnel de Vallvidrera (exit 8 off Ronda de Dalt, toll), or the winding but scenic Carretera de l'Arrabassada (exit 5 off Ronda de Dalt) for free. *By train* FGC from Plaça Catalunya, Terrassa or Sabadell trains. Journey time 15-25min. **El Papiol** *By car* A7, then B30 from Molins de Rei. *By train* RENFE from Plaça Catalunya. **Terrassa**, **Sabadell** *By car* A18 or N150 (exit 1 off Ronda de Dalt). *By train* RENFE or FGC from Plaça Catalunya. **Where to eat**: Sant Cugat has a very good grilled-meat restaurant, **Braseria La Bolera** *C/Baixada de l'Alba 20 (93 674 16 75)*. In Terrassa, **Casa Toni** *Carretera de Castellar 124 (93 786 47 08)* has an fine range of wines. In Sabadell, **Forrellat** *C/Horta Novella 27 (93 725 71 51)* is pricey but top quality. **Museu de la Ciència i de la Tècnica** *Rambla d'Ègara 270, Terrassa (93 736 89 66)*. **Open** 10am-7pm Tue-Fri; 10am-2.30pm Sat, Sun, public holidays. Closed Mon. **Admission** 400ptas, 275ptas students, over-65s; free under-7s and first Sun of the month.

Colònia Güell

The Colònia Güell in the small town of **Santa Coloma de Cervelló**, on the western edge of Barcelona's sprawl, was one of the most ambitious projects on which Gaudí worked for his patron Eusebi Güell. It was intended to be a model industrial village around a textile factory, with a complete range of services for Güell's workers. Like their park in Barcelona, it was never finished.

Nevertheless, the Colònia's crypt – begun in 1898, and the only part of the church to be completed before Güell died in 1918 – is one of Gaudí's most extraordinary and architecturally experimental works. The interior combines great sobriety with a look irresistibly like a giant fairy grotto, with parabolic vaults and tree-like, inclined columns that pre-date their use by modern architects by at least half a century. All the fittings, stained glass and pews are the originals, by Gaudí. The other buildings of the 'colony', most of them by Francesc Berenguer, are also interesting.

Colònia Güell

Santa Coloma de Cervelló (93 640 29 36). By car A2 to Sant Boi exit, and turning to Sant Vicenç dels Horts (8km/5 miles). *By train* FGC Plaça d'Espanya to Molí Nou; Colònia is a 10min walk from the station. **Open** 10am-1pm, 4-6pm (*May-Sept* 4-7pm), Mon-Wed, Fri, Sat; 10am-1.15pm Thur, Sun, public holidays. **Admission** 100ptas.

Beaches

Sun, sea, sand, scuba diving... and even beaches where you don't have to search for space amid the crowds.

Barcelona's triumphant return to the sea, with kilometres of redesigned beaches a mere hop from the city centre, has lessened the need to catch a train to some sandy haven further along the coast. Catalonia's coastal towns have other attractions, though, and despite a highly developed tourist industry many are surprisingly unspoilt.

In addition to the places to stay listed here, check out the Generalitat's *Residències – Casa de Pagès* guide (*see page 269*) for low-price farmhouse accommodation, particularly in remoter areas.

South

To Sitges & Vilanova

Used in summer by generations of Barcelonans, **Castelldefels** has now become a year-round suburban residence. Just 20km (12 miles) south of Barcelona, the town has kilometres of windswept, uncrowded beaches (used more by locals than foreigners) and fine seafood restaurants. Perched on one of the hills just inland are the romantic ruins

of a Templar castle, and on the west side is an attractive marina development, **Port Ginesta**. A few minutes' ride further is **Garraf**, a tiny village with a small beach served by a couple of beach bars, and the **Celler de Garraf**, a *Modernista* gem designed by Gaudí for the Güells, in 1895.

Just on the other side of the Garraf mountains, **Sitges** is one of Catalonia's most famous resorts. First 'discovered' in the 1890s by writer/artist Santiago Rusiñol (whose circle included Manuel de Falla, Ramon Casas and Picasso) it has a character many other Mediterranean resorts lack. Since the 1960s, Sitges has also become a favourite international gay destination (*see chapter* **Gay & Lesbian Barcelona**). There are nine beaches along the seafront, and quieter beaches at the (artificial) port of **Aiguadolç** – to get there, turn left out of the station. For nudist beaches, get to the seafront, turn right, and keep going (it's quite a walk). For a walk into the Garraf hills behind Sitges, *see page 276.*

Even when crowded, Sitges is charming, with a long promenade, the Passeig Marítim, curving along the beaches. Beautiful buildings cluster around the

*Style crisis hits the beach at **Sitges**.*

The tourist has landed.

town's most visible monument, the seventeenth-century church of **Sant Bartomeu i Santa Tecla**. Almost adjacent are the old market, the Ajuntament and the **Museu Cau Ferrat** on C/Fonollar (93 894 03 64), Santiago Rusiñol's old home, bequeathed to the town as a ready-made museum, chock-full of paintings, archaeological finds, *Modernista* iron-work and other fascinating objects. Opposite is the **Palau Mar i Cel**, a delightful old residence with a finely crafted door, unusual interior and eclectic collection of medieval and baroque artwork. The **Museu Romàntic** in Casa Llopis, C/Sant Gaudenci 1 (93 894 29 69), has a valuable collection of antique dolls. There is a joint ticket for all three museums. Sitges hosts a string of events through the year, including the spectacular Carnaval in February (*see page 278*), a theatre festival in June, and the **Film Festival** in October (*see page 226*).

Vilanova i la Geltrú is the largest port between Barcelona and Tarragona, and has some good beaches. It also has several museums, including the important **Biblioteca-Museu Balaguer** on Avda Víctor Balaguer (93 815 42 02), with some El Grecos and many other artefacts, and a distinguished main square, the *Plaça de la Vila*. The town is known for its Carnaval, and its seafood, especially served with *xató* – a spicy variant of *romesco* sauce.

Information

Getting there: *By car* A16 to Castelldefels, Garraf, Sitges (41km/25 miles) and Vilanova (extra tunnel toll between Garraf and Sitges); or C246 via a slow, winding drive around the Garraf mountains. *By train* RENFE approx. every 20min from Sants or Passeig de Gràcia to Platja de Castelldefels, Sitges (30min) and Vilanova (40min); not all stop at Castelldefels and Garraf.

Tourist offices: **Castelldefels** *Plaça Rosa dels Vents (93 664 23 01)*; **Sitges** *Passeig de Vilafranca (93 894 12 30)*; **Vilanova i la Geltrú** *C/Torre de Ribarroges/Platja. (93 815 45 17)*.

Where to eat:

Castelldefels: Cheap seafront paella places, or more upmarket **Nàutic** *Passeig Marítim 374 (93 665 01 74)*. **Sitges**: The **Sitges** *C/Parellades 61 (93 894 34 93)* and **La Salseta** *C/Sant Pau 35 (93 811 04 19)* are good value. Worth the extra expense, **Chez Jeanette** *C/Sant Pau 23 (93 894 00 48)* serves Catalano-French seasonal cuisine in the evenings, Mon-Fri and for lunch and dinner Sat, Sun. For really good seafood at a price, go to **La Nansa** *C/Carreta 24 (93 894 19 27)*. **Vilanova i la Geltrú**: **Avi Pep** *C/Llibertat 128 (93 815 17 36)* is cheap and cheerful; **Peixerot** *Passeig Marítim 56 (93 815 06 25)* gets the pick of the day's fish; and excellent grilled meat can be had at **Can Pagès** *C/Sant Pere 24-6 (93 894 11 95)* or **El Celler Vell** *C/Sant Bonaventura 21 (93 894 82 99)*.

Where to stay:

Sitges: **Celimar** *Passeig de la Ribera 18 (93 811 01 70)*. Comfortable seafront hotel (about 12,000ptas a double room); **Hotel Romàntic** *C/Sant Isidre 33 (93 894 83 75)* is a Sitges classic, an almost over-the-top hotel in a delicately restored set of nineteenth-century villas; doubles cost about 11,000ptas. **Hostal Maricel** *C/d'en Tacó 11 (93 894 36 27)* weighs in at 7,000ptas/double, while the **Parellades** *C/Parellades 11 (93 894 08 01)* is a good cheaper option. *See also chapter* **Gay & Lesbian Barcelona**.

Cubelles (4km/2.5 miles west of Vilanova): **Llicorella** *(93 895 00 44)*. Comfortable upscale (20,000ptas a double) hotel with pool and sculptures in the garden, and a very highly regarded restaurant.

Tarragona & the Costa Daurada

If you're looking for castles and sand, **Altafulla**, between Vilanova and Tarragona, has both, plus one of the best-preserved medieval centres on the coast. The modern section is close to the seafront, where there are fine white sand beaches between rocky outcrops, and a picturesque seaside castle at nearby **Tamarit**. The old walled town – crowned by the imposing **Castell d'Altafulla** and floodlit at night – is ten minutes' stroll inland. One of Catalonia's best-preserved Roman villas lies between the old and new towns at **Els Munts.**

Tarragona, a busy city of over 100,000 people, is overlooked by most foreign visitors, despite the fact that as Roman *Tarraco* it was the capital of half the Iberian peninsula, and so contains the largest ensemble of Roman buildings and ruins in Spain, an extraordinary architectural legacy: the original town walls, an amphitheatre, circus, aqueduct and forum. Much later, Catalan colonisers spent 61 years constructing the majestic **Catedral de Santa Maria**, which dominates the beautiful *ciutat antiga* (old city). A walkway around the Roman walls, the **Passeig Arqueològic**, provides a breathtaking view of the sea and the flat hinterland, the *Camp de Tarragona*. Below are a busy modern boulevard, the Rambla Nova, and an attractive fishermen's district with good seafood restaurants. The **Platja del Miracle** ('Beach of the Miracle') lies just beyond the amphitheatre.

Further southwest is **Salou**, resort hub of the Costa Daurada, with sand, sea, hotels, discos, bars, calamares'n'chips and sun cream all on tap. It also has some Modernist buildings, and, on another note, **Port Aventura** theme park is just nearby.

Port Aventura

(977 77 90 90). **Open** *Mar-late June, mid-Sept-late Oct* 10am-8pm, *late June-mid-Sept* 10am-midnight, daily. **Admission** *One day* 4,100ptas; 3,100ptas 5-12s, over-65s; free under-5s. *Two consecutive days* 6,250ptas; 4,850ptas 5-12s, over-65s; free under-5s. *Three consecutive days* 8,200ptas; 6,400ptas 5-12s, over-65s; free under-5s. *Night ticket (7pm-midnight, late June-mid-Sept only)* 2,500ptas; 1,900ptas 5-12s, over-65s. **Credit** AmEx, DC, JCB, MC, V.
Getting there: *By car* A2, then A7 to exit 35, or N340 (108km/67 miles). *By train* RENFE from Sants or Passeig de Gràcia (1hr 15min). The park has its own station, on the Barcelona-Tarragona-Tortosa line; in season seven southbound and ten northbound trains stop there daily.

Port Aventura has drawn in the crowds from the day it opened in 1995. Top attraction is the stomach-crunching Dragon Khan, largest roller-coaster in Europe, with eight 360° loops; there are also special rides for little kids, and all sorts of floor shows. Theme-park fans rate Port Aventura very highly; non-addicts might note that it's more authentic than most, in the design of buildings and the goods on sale in the shops. Admission gives you unlimited rides. Facilities include video and buggy hire, and

wheelchairs and other disabled services. Food and drink cannot be taken into the park, but there are food outlets (serving alcohol) on every corner.

Information

Getting there: *By car* A2, then A7 via Vilafranca (Tarragona 98km/60 miles); or toll-free N340 (Molins de Rei exit from A2). *By train* RENFE from Sants or Passeig de Gràcia to Altafulla (55min), Tarragona (1hr 6min) and Salou (1hr 18min). Trains hourly approx 6am-9.30pm.
Tourist offices: Altafulla *Plaça dels Vents (977 65 07 52);* **Tarragona** *C/Fortuny 4 (977 23 34 15);* **Salou** *Passeig Jaume I 4 (977 35 01 02).*
Where to eat:
Altafulla: Faristol *C/Sant Martí 5 (977 65 00 77).* Well-priced bar-restaurant in an eighteenth-century house, with a pleasant outdoor terrace.
Tarragona: Bufet el Tiberi *C/Martí d'Ardenya 5 (977 23 54 03),* is enjoyable and cheap; **Sol-Ric** *Via Augusta 227 (977 23 20 32)* is famous for seafood *romesco* and its fine wine list (average 5,000ptas).
Salou: Eating here is pricey. **Goleta** *C/Gavina-Platja Capellans (977 38 35 66)* has good salt-baked fish.
Where to stay:
Altafulla: Yola *Via Augusta 50 (977 65 02 83).* Clean, modern place with brand-new swimming pool, around 13,000ptas/double. To rent rooms in the old town, ask at **El Corral** bar *(977 65 04 86).*
Tarragona: Imperial Tarraco *Rambla Vella 2 (977 23 30 40),* is luxurious; the **Forum** *Plaça de l'Ajuntament (977 23 17 18)* is pleasant and cheap.
Salou: El **Racó** *Platja del Racó (977 37 02 16)* has doubles for 6,500 ptas; there are 53 other places in town.

The Ebro Delta

About an hour down the coast from Tarragona is the **Delta de l'Ebre** nature reserve, an ecologically remarkable 320 square km (125 square mile) area that's home to almost 300 species of birds (60 per cent of all the species found in Europe) including flamingoes, great crested grebes, herons, marsh harriers and a huge variety of ducks. The towns of the delta are nothing special, but the natural beauty of the place – the immense, flat, green expanse of wetlands, rice fields, channels and dunes – makes it fascinating all year round.

The town of **Deltebre** is the base for most park services. From there it's easy to make day trips to the bird sanctuaries, especially the remote headland of **Punta de la Banya.** The delta's flatness makes it ideal for walking or cycling (for bicycle hire, check at the information office in Deltebre). Small boats offer trips along the river from the north bank about 8km (5 miles) east of Deltebre. It's a good two-hour train ride from Barcelona, so plan on at least a weekend in the Delta.

Information

Getting there: *By car* A2, then A7 via Vilafranca, or N340 (Molins de Rei exit from A2). Barcelona-Amposta 172km/107 miles. *By train and bus* RENFE from Sants or Passeig de Gràcia to L'Aldea-Amposta (2 hrs), then bus (HIFE 977 44 03 00) to Deltebre.

Tourist office: Deltebre *Park Information Centre, C/Ulldecona 22 (977 48 96 79).* Alongside is a small museum about the different Delta habitats.

Where to stay & eat:
Deltebre: El Buitre *Carretera de Riumar (977 48 05 28)* is a box-style hotel with low-budget James Bond undertones (about 4,000ptas a double); the restaurant serves very good Delta rice dishes. Another excellent restaurant is **Galatxo** *Desembocadura Riu Ebre (977 26 75 03),* at the mouth of the Ebro. There are two official campsites between Deltebre and the river mouth, **L'Aube** *Urbanització Riumar (977 44 57 06),* and **Riomar** (with pool) *Urbanització Riumar (977 26 76 80),* and a youth hostel, **Alberg Mossèn Batlle** *Avda de les Goles de l'Ebre (977 48 01 36).*

The Costa del Maresme

The Maresme coast, immediately north-east of Barcelona, is close enough for easy day-tripping. Of the string of small towns along the shoreline, **Caldes d'Estrac,** also known as **Caldetes,** and **Sant Pol de Mar** both have good beaches (some nudist), and plenty of tourists, local and foreign. Caldetes has some interesting *Modernista* houses, a spa, and a recently restored park with fine views, and Sant Pol is a tranquil, mostly unspoilt, if yuppified, fishing village. In contrast to many places along this coast, where railway tracks run close to the beach, some of Sant Pol's beaches are separated from roads and rail by rocky cliffs.

Information
Getting there: *By car* N II from Barcelona to Caldes d'Estrac (36km/22 miles), Sant Pol (48km/30 miles). *By train* RENFE from Sants or Plaça Catalunya. Trains every 30min, journey time approx 35min.
Where to stay and eat:
Caldetes: **Emma** *Baixada de l'Estació 5 (93 791 13 05)* is one of the town's best middle-priced restaurants (open Apr-Oct). If you want to stay over, **Pinzón** *C/El Callao 4 (93 791 00 51)* has double rooms for about 5,500ptas a night.

Sant Pol: **Hostalet I** *C/Manzanillo 9 (93 760 06 05)* and **Hostalet III** *C/Antonio Soleda 1 (93 760 02 51),* are pleasant hotels (doubles 5,000ptas). Good paella restaurants on the main street.

The Costa Brava

The area best-known internationally as the Costa Brava consists of a clutch of towns around the local hub of **Blanes,** which have been given over to big-scale package tourism since the 1960s. For the sake of simplicity, over the years different towns along the stretch have really come to specialise in different nationalities: **Calella de la Costa** is known as the coast's German burg – with bratwurst available at all times of day; **Lloret de Mar** there are more British and Dutch, and so pubs and places selling chips with mayonnaise. If you're looking for the full disco-blow-out-fall-asleep-on-the-beach experience, head for Lloret.

Oddly enough, this is not really the Costa Brava proper at all, which actually lies 50km (30 miles) further north in Baix Empordà. This rocky peninsula was the original 'rugged coast' for which journalist Ferran Agulló dreamt up the name 'Costa Brava' in the early 1900s. It is still the Costa's most unspoilt section: there are no big sandy beaches, and public transport is limited, so the area has largely escaped mass tourism. Accommodation facilities are also relatively small-scale (it's essential to book in high season), as are nightlife and organised activities for children and families. This does not mean the area is undiscovered, though: it's a favourite holiday and second-home location for prosperous Catalans, and in summer it's best to visit midweek to avoid the crowds.

The first town of interest in the *comarca* is **Sant Feliu de Guíxols,** for centuries the principal port for Girona (*see page 273*) and the cork industry. Sant Feliu has a charming Passeig Marítim, and a treasure trove of ancient ceramics in the town museum. The curved sandy beach gets crowded, but offers respite from an otherwise rocky coast.

*The endless horizontals of the **Ebro Delta**.*

Making the most of the coast

SCUBA DIVING

Scuba diving is hugely popular in Catalonia. The coastal waters are relatively deep, and the effects of mass tourism are often easy to see, but there is some very decent diving to be had, especially among the rocky coves and caves of the Costa Brava. Wetsuits, tanks, regulators and guides can be hired at diving clubs in towns along the coast (masks, fins, and snorkels are also available, but it's even more common to bring your own). Prices generally run from about 5,000 to 8,000ptas per dive, including equipment and guide. A valid diver's certificate is required. Scuba clubs in Barcelona also arrange trips up the coast, but inevitably charge a bit more.

The **Illes Medes** near Estartit are an official underwater reserve, with some of the last beds in the western Mediterranean of the sea's native red coral. Unfortunately, this means that diving areas at the Medes are often uncomfortably crowded, with bunches of 50 divers being dumped into the sea every half-hour or so.

If you've never dived before it's also possible to try a simple baptismal dive with a guide, or sign up for a course. Courses usually last from a few days to a week, and cost around 50,000ptas.

Diving clubs, north to south

Cadaqués: Sotamar *Avda Caritat Serinyana 17 (972 25 88 76).* **Open** all year. Ten dive routes.
Roses: Poseidon *C/Bernd i Barbara Mörker (972 25 57 72/25 44 07/929 58 15 06).* **Open** all year.
L'Estartit (for Illes Medes): **Diving Center La Sirena** *C/Camping La Sirena (972 75 09 54).* **Open** all year; **Unisub** *Carretera Torroella de Montgrí 15 (972 75 17 68).* **Open** Mar-Nov.

Quim's Diving Center *Carretera Torroella de Montgri, km 4.5 (972 75 01 63).* **Open** all year.
Begur: Aqualògik *Cala d'Aiguafreda (972 62 42 47).* **Open** all year. Ten dive routes.
Barcelona: **Aquamarina** *C/Castillejos 270 (93 455 29 62).* **Open** all year. **Map** F4
Guided tours in Catalonia, and equipment for sale and rent.

SAILING/WINDSURFING/KAYAKING

Nearly every coastal town has a *Club Nàutic* (boat club) that rents small sailboats or windsurf-boards by the hour. Yachts (with or without a captain) for day trips or longer adventures are also available, as are sea kayaks – a great means of exploring the *cales* of the Costa Brava. Other rental places specialise in one or another type of boat, catamarans being the most common. Coastal campsites also sometimes have boats or windsurfing equipment for rent. Prices range between 1,500ptas and 3,500ptas an hour for smaller class craft, and

A less-visited beach lies 3km (1.8 miles) north at **Sant Pol**. Nearby is **S'Agaró**, a private village of luxury beach houses built when tourist facilities were scarce on this coast. It's worth visiting for its spectacularly ritzy architecture – the cliffside balconies are favourites for perfume ads.

Heading north about 20km (12 miles) and avoiding the more crassly touristy areas of **Platja d'Aro** and **Palamós**, you arrive at the main inlets on the peninsula. The northern ones (**Sa Riera**, **Sa Tuna**, **Aiguablava**) are most accessible from Begur, those further south (**Tamariu**, **Llafranc** and **Calella**) are best reached from Palafrugell.

Begur is an attractive old town dominated by the remains of a fourteenth-century castle. It's set just inland on a rocky hillside commanding magnificent views. From there it's a steep 3km (2 mile) walk down to the coast (no public transport). A little further inland is the very carefully preserved

medieval village of **Pals**, now seemingly converted almost entirely into second homes. It is nonetheless a remarkable survivor, with a core of fine twelfth- to fifteenth-century buildings, and beautiful views over the surrounding countryside.

Sa Riera, at the end of the road from Pals to the coast, is the northernmost cove of the peninsula, with one of its largest sandy beaches and good views of the Medes islands to the north. There's a popular nudist beach, the **Illa Roja**, between Sa Riera and La Platja del Racó. From Sa Riera a road leads south to **Sa Tuna**, a picturesque fishing village with a stony beach. Its one *hostal*-restaurant has a great position on the seafront. From there a 40-minute walk along a coastal path takes you northwards through **Aiguafreda**, a small wooded cove, to a spectacular building cut into the promontory beyond. Steps lead down to swimming pools cut into the precipitous cliff-face.

anywhere from 25,000ptas up per day for yachts. For boat hire within Barcelona, *see chapter* **Sports & Fitness**.

Barcelona and further south

Barcelona: Jack London Charters *C/Riera Alta 10 (tel/fax 93 442 08 69/639 35 89 92/ jalondon@teleline.es)*. **Open** all year. The 40ft sloop *Northwind* sleeps six people, and can be hired with English-speaking captain for trips along the coast, to the Balearics, or the Caribbean, if need be. **Map C5**
Castelldefels: Catamaran Center *Port Ginesta, Local 324 (93 665 22 11)*. **Open** all year. All sizes and classes of catamarans for rent, including a 53ft cat-yacht. Sea kayaks also available.
Sitges: Club Nàutic Sitges *Espigon s/n (93 894 09 05)*. **Open** all year. Catamarans for rent.
Calafell (south of Vilanova i la Geltrú):
Windcat House *Passeig Marítim 51 (Mas Mel) (977 69 30 72)*. **Open** all year.
Catamarans and kayaks; courses also available.

North of Barcelona

Sant Andreu de Llavaneres (near Arenys de Mar): **Motyvel Yacht Charter** *Port El Balís s/n (93 792 73 06)*. **Open** all year.
Fleet of ten Dufour sailing yachts, for hire with or without captain.
Calella de la Costa: Club Nàutic Calella *Passeig Platja s/n (93 766 18 52)*
Open all year. Cats, *estells*, kayaks and windsurf equipment for rent.
L'Escala: Kayaking Costa Brava *Passeig Lluís Albert 11 (972 77 38 06)*.
Open all year. Kayak hire, guided group trips (full or half-day) from Tamariu to Aiguablava, and courses. Half-day trips, 6,000ptas.
Sant Pere Pescador: La Ballena Alegre *C/Despoblat Sector Sud (972 52 03 02)*.
A campsite on the Costa Brava that rents windsurf equipment.

Heading south via Begur, you'll reach **Fornells** and **Aiguablava**, both in a larger bay. Aiguablava has a beach with beautiful white sand, a small yacht harbour, and an old, luxurious hotel. **Tamariu**, in an intimate bay, is slightly larger, with hotels and bars known for excellent seafood. You can swim from the rocks, and hire boats for exploring, water skiing or fishing (call Paco Heredia on 972 30 13 10 or 907 29 25 78). **Llafranc** is a more developed resort, thanks to its main road connection with Palafrugell. From here, walk south to the beachside village of **Calella de Palafrugell**. Tamariu and Llafranc are the only places on this stretch easily accessible by public transport, with regular buses from **Palafrugell**, the peninsular's transport hub, which also hosts a lively Sunday market.

Leaving the Costa Brava outcrop, further up the coast is the small town of **Estartit**, a water-sports centre situated opposite the **Illes Medes** under-

water nature park. Glass-bottomed boats leave Estartit every hour (June to September; in April, May, October, according to demand) to tour the now rare coral deposits for which the rocky islets are renowned. The more adventurous can go scuba-diving (*see left*). A little inland is the **Castell de Montgrí**, an unfinished but imposing twelfth-century castle with fine views.

Information

Getting there: *By bus* Sarfa (93 265 11 58), 15 buses daily to Sant Feliu de Guíxols from Estació del Nord (1hr 20min); nine daily to Palafrugell (2hrs), some continue to Begur. Change in Palafrugell or Torroella for Estartit. *By car* A7 north to exits 9 or 7 onto C253 or C250 for Sant Feliu de Guíxols, then C255 for Palafrugell (123km/76 miles); or A7 exit 6 for Palafrugell and Begur via La Bisbal. A slower option is the coastal N-II, then C250, C253, C255.
Tourist offices: Sant Feliu de Guíxols *Plaça Monestir s/n (972 82 00 51)*; **Begur** *Plaça de l'Església 8 (972 62 40 20)*; **Pals** *C/Aniceta Figueras 6 (972 68 78 57)*; **Palafrugell** *C/Carrilet 2 (972 30 02 28)*; **L'Estartit** *Passeig Marítim (972 75 89 10)*.
Where to eat:
Sant Feliu de Guíxols: Nàutic *Passeig Marítim (972 32 06 63)*, in the Club Nàutic sailing club, has great port views and top-notch seafood. Eight set menus are available, from 1,500ptas
Begur: Can Torrades *(972 62 28 82)* has good but pricey Catalan home cooking; **Fonda Platja** *(972 62 21 97)* is also quite expensive, but excellent. Much cheaper pizzas can be found at **La Pizzeta** *(972 62 38 83)*. On the road toward Palafrugell is **Mas Comangau** *(972 62 32 10)*, a popular traditional restaurant. In **Pals**, **Alfred** *C/La Font 7 (972 63 62 74)* has home-cooking for 3,000ptas.
Aiguablava: Hotel Aiguablava (*see below*) has a top-class restaurant. The **Parador** *(972 62 21 62)* enjoys panoramic views, as does the simple restaurant at the **Hostal Sa Tuna** (*see below*).
Tamariu: There's not much to choose between the restaurants on the seafront, but family-run **Snack Bar Es Dofí** *(972 61 02 92)* is open all year.
Llafranc: Hotel Llafranc *Passeig de Cipsela 16 (972 30 02 08)* and **Hotel Llevant** *C/Francesc de Blanes 5 (972 30 03 66)* both have fine restaurants.
Where to Stay:
Sant Feliu de Guíxols: Hotel Les Noies *Rambla del Portalet 10 (972 32 04 00)*. 50 reasonably-priced rooms in town (5,000ptas a double). More intimate (6,000ptas a double) is the **Florida** *Plaça del Monestir 7 (972 32 03 79)*; **Casa Rovira** *(972 32 12 02)* is a rambling old bohemian-style *hostal* run by an English family. Booking essential (6,000ptas a double, meals extra; website: *www.aphobos.net/casarovira*).
Camping Sant Pol is at *Carretera de Palamós km 0.8 (972 32 10 19)*.
S'Agaró: the luxury choice is **Hostal de la Gavina** *(972 32 11 00)*. Five-star-plus, prices to match, real antiques; but don't go expecting a funky atmosphere.
Begur: Hotel Begur *C/De Coma i Ros 8 (972 62 22 07)* is centrally placed and open all year (10,700ptas, double); **Hotel Rosa** *C/Forgas i Puig 6 (972 62 30 13)* is less expensive (5,200ptas). **Pals** has the **Barris** *C/Enginyer Algarra 51 (972 63 67 02)*, for 4,800ptas.

Port de la Selva: *less hip than Cadaques, but full of charm.*

There are two campsites near Begur: at Sa Riera, **El Maset Platja de Sa Riera** *(972 62 30 23)*; and on the Palafrugell road, **Begur** *Carretera de Begur a Palafrugell (972 62 32 01)*.

Sa Tuna: **Hostal Sa Tuna** *Platja Sa Tuna (972 62 21 98)* five rooms in a perfect spot (12,500ptas/double).

Aiguablava: The four-star, family-run **Hotel Aiguablava** *Platja de Fornells (972 62 20 58)*, is one of the coast's grand hotels. Choose from standard rooms or almost self-contained villas (13,700ptas double).

Tamariu: **Hotel Hostalillo** *C/Bellavista 28 (972 30 01 58)* is the largest hotel in town (14,200ptas double; open June-Sept only); **Sol d'Or** *C/Riera 18 (972 30 04 24)* is open all year (6,000ptas double).

Llafranc: **Hotel Llafranc** *(see above)* charges around 11,000ptas/double, or try two-star **Hotel Casamar** *C/de Nero 3-11 (972 30 01 04)* for 9,000ptas a double. The campsites near Calella are: **La Siesta** *C/Chipitea 110-20 (972 61 51 16)*; and **Moby Dick** *C/Costa Verda 16-28 (972 61 43 07)*.

L'Estartit: **Santa Clara** *Passeig Maritim 18 (972 75 17 67)* is pleasant (6,500ptas per double).

Figueres to France

The centre of the northern Costa Brava and the *comarca* of **Alt Empordà** is **Figueres**. From here it's possible to travel to every other place of interest in the area. The *tramontana* wind regularly sweeps this area, allegedly leaving the locals slightly touched (read, crazy), a fact apparently borne out by two of Figueres' most famous sons: Narcís Monturiol, the utopian socialist and inventor (some say) of the first submarine, and Salvador Dalí. The Empordà is also known for fine *mar i montanya* dishes combining meat and seafood.

Figueres is an attractive town, with a lively Rambla, and boasts one of Catalonia's most visited attractions, the **Teatre-Museu Dalí** *(see right)*. Also worth visiting is the **Museu de l'Empordà** *(972 50 23 05)* on the Rambla, for a well-presented overview of the area's art and history.

East of Figueres, **Roses** was once a major port and is now the area's largest tourist town. It has a glut of hotels, discos, and (often overpriced) restaurants, but also some good beaches and a sixteenth-century citadel, the **Ciutadella**. To the south are the **Aiguamolls de l'Empordà**, a nature reserve

in the wetlands at the mouth of the Fluvià river that's a bird-watcher's paradise. Some 300 species of birds winter or rest here, and fish and amphibians (and mosquitos, so take bug repellent) are also plentiful. The information centre at Mas Cortalet *(972 45 22 22)* has guides to walks in the reserve.

From Roses the road climbs through spectacular switchbacks with fabulous views to take you to **Cadaqués**, in splendid isolation at the end of the Cap de Creus peninsula. This once remote fishing village was first brought to outside attention by Dalí and friends in the 1920s, and later became the favourite summer resort of Barcelona's cultural élite. In the tourist-boom years high-rise hotel-building was barred from Cadaqués, so it has kept its narrow streets and whitewashed houses. The village's cultural season includes a summer classical music festival. Due to its chic-rating Cadaqués is relatively expensive, but still strikingly beautiful. The peninsula around it is an extraordinary mass of rock, lined by tiny coves (many reachable only by boat) offering the chance for complete relaxation. Cadaqués natives, whose ancestors lived for centuries in total isolation from anywhere inland, are well-known for their lack of interest in outsiders.

A short walk and you're in **Port Lligat**, the tiny bay where Dalí built his main home *(see right)*. Beyond it a road continues to **Cap de Creus** ('Cape of Crosses'), with its lighthouse, nature reserve and unique, pock-marked rock formations used as a location in many science-fiction movies.

Port de la Selva, on the cape's north side, has never received the accolades showered on Cadaqués, yet is similarly unspoilt, quieter, and closer to the magnificent Romanesque monastery of **Sant Pere de Rodes**, often lost in clouds on the mountain above the town. Sant Pere was founded in 1022, and large sections of it are still intact. A little further north is **Llançà**, an appealing fishing village with several beaches, a beautiful old centre and good transport links to the French border.

Alternatively, south of Figueres are the well-preserved remains of the ancient city of **Empúries**, founded in 600 BC by the Phoenicians, re-colonised by the Greeks and finally by the Romans, in the year AD 2. Ruins from all three periods, and the line of the original Greek harbour, are clearly visible. It's a picturesque and atmospheric ancient site, and right next to a beach. The nearest town, **L'Escala**, has an attractive beach and port. It is noted for its fine anchovies, and as the birthplace of Catarina Albert, author of the classic Catalan novel *Solitud*.

Sant Pere de Rodes

Open *Oct-May* 10am-1.30pm, 3-5pm, *June-Sept* 10am-7pm, Tue-Sun. **Admission** 300ptas; 150ptas students. **No credit cards**.

Information

Getting there: *By bus* Barcelona Bus (93 232 04 59), several buses daily to Figueres from Estació del Nord (2hrs 30min); Sarfa (93 265 11 98) has two buses daily direct to Roses and Cadaqués (2hrs 15min). The easiest way to get anywhere on the coast is by train to Figueres, then Sarfa bus from the depot next door. Sarfa has services to Llança, Roses, Port de la Selva, Cadaqués and L'Escala. *By car* A7 or N-II to Figueres (120km/74 miles). From Figueres, C260 to Roses. *By train* RENFE from Sants or Passeig de Gràcia to Figueres (1hr 45min) or Llançà.

Tourist offices: Figueres *Plaça del Sol (972 50 31 55)*; **Roses** *Plaça de les Botxes (972 25 73 31)*; **Cadaqués** *C/Cotxe 2A (972 25 83 15)*; **Llançà** *Avda d'Europa 37 (972 38 08 55)*; **L'Escala** *Plaça de les Escoles 1 (972 77 06 03)*.

Where to eat:
Figueres: Most restaurants are in the old town. The ones in C/de la Jonquera are cheapish, with tables outside in summer. **Presidente** *Ronda Firal 33 (972 50 17 00)* offers good Catalan food (about 3,000ptas). **Roses: El Bullí** *(972 15 04 57)*, one of Catalonia's very best, is a must (*see chapter* **Restaurants**).

Hello, Dalí

Figueres had an on-off relationship with its most famous son while he was alive, but since Salvador Dalí's death the town has become an obligatory visit for anyone curious about the great masturbator's special universe. The **Teatre-Museu Dalí**, in Figueres' former theatre, was designed by Dalí complete with music, optical illusions and bizarre installations, and also contains his tomb. From July to September, the museum stays open later, with Dalí's own choice of lighting and music and a free glass of *cava*. The **Torre Galatea**, Dalí's egg-topped Figueres residence, is next door.

Since 1998 the two other Empordà properties associated with the great man have been opened to the public, forming a new 'Dalí Triangle' (*triangle dalinià*) for aspiring surrealists to disappear into. Dominating the cove of **Port Lligat** just outside Cadaqués is his own favourite house (*pictured*), a Dalí image in itself with two giant cracked heads on the top wall seen against the rocky hillside and azure sea. The house, designed for Dalí with many strange features, was all but abandoned for years and is in poor condition. Only eight people are allowed in at a time, so reservations are essential. In **Púbol**, about 35km (22 miles) south of Roses in the Baix Empordà, is the twelfth-century castle that Dalí bought for his wife and 'muse' Gala. Here she entertained a string of young men, while Dalí himself was not allowed to visit without an appointment. Today, reservations are only obligatory for groups of over 30 people.

The Dalí tour

Casa-Museu de Port Lligat *(reservations 972 25 80 63)*. **Open** *14 Mar-14 June, 16 Sept-1 Nov* 10.30am-6pm, *15 Jun-15 Sept* 10.30-8.10pm, daily. Closed Nov-Mar. **Admission** 1,200ptas. **No credit cards**.

Castell de Púbol *(enquiries to Teatre-Museu Dalí, 972 51 18 00)*. **Open** *14 Mar-14 June, 16 Sept-1 Nov* 10.30am-6pm, *15 Jun-15 Sept* 10.30-9pm, daily. Closed Nov-Mar. **Admission** 600ptas. **No credit cards**. Púbol is best reached via Girona. by Figueres: by train to Girona or Flaçà, and then by Sarfa bus from either to La Bisbal, which stops at Púbol village. With a car, take the N-II north from Girona, and then the C255 towards La Bisbal.

Teatre-Museu Dalí *Plaça Gala-Salvador Dalí 5, Figueres (972 51 18 00)*. **Open** *Oct-June* 10.30am-5.15pm Tue-Sun; *July-Sept* 9am-7.15pm daily; *12 July-12 Sept* also 10pm-1.30am, daily. **Admission** *Oct-June* 700ptas; 400ptas students, over-65s; *July-Sept* 1,000ptas; 700ptas students, over-65s. **Credit** AmEx, MC, V.

Cadaqués: Best-known restaurant is **La Galiota** *C/Narcís Monturiol 9 (972 25 81 87*; average 5,000ptas). **Casa Anita** *C/Miguel Roset (972 25 84 71)* is a long-running, very popular family-owned place with excellent seafood; cheaper but also good is **Pizzeria Plaza** *Passeig Marítim 10 (no phone)*.
Where to Stay:
Figueres: Hotel Duran *C/Lasauca 5 (972 50 12 50)* is a comfortable hotel with doubles for 9,500ptas; **Hostal Bon Repòs** *C/Villalonga 43 (972 50 92 02)* is a good budget option.
Roses: There are dozens of places in the town. **Nautilus** *Platja Salatar (972 25 62 62)* facing the beach costs 5,700ptas per double; **Hostal Can Salvador** *C/Puig Rom 43 (972 25 78 11)* is one of the cheaper *hostals* at 5,500ptas for a double room.
Cadaqués: There are not many hotels for the summer demand, and smaller *hostals* may be closed out of season, so always book. The tourist office has lists of hotels and of families who rent rooms. Try

Hostal Marina *C/Frederic Rahola 2 (972 25 81 99)* at 7,000ptas a double, and the **Pension Vehí** *C/de l'Església 6 (972 25 84 70)* at 3,900ptas a double.
Port de la Selva: **German** *C/Poeta Sagarra 11 (972 38 70 92)* is a reasonably-priced small hotel (6,400ptas, double); **Porto Cristo** *C/Major 48 (972 38 70 62)* is the luxury option (17,000ptas, double).
Llançà: Try **Casa Narra** *C/Castella 5 (972 38 01 78)* for 5,000ptas/double, or the **Colomer** *C/Puig d'Esquer 4 (972 38 02 70)* at 3,800ptas a double room. For greater comforts there is the **Berna** *Passeig Marítim 13 (972 38 01 50)* at 10,175ptas.
Empúries: If you have a car, the best place to stay is the village of Sant Martí d'Empúries, which has the comfortable, beautifully situated **Riomar** *Platja del Riuet (972 77 03 62*; 8,000ptas a double), or the cheaper **Can Roura** *Plaça de l'Església 12 (972 77 03 05*; 4,800ptas per double). The **youth hostel** *(972 77 12 00)* is on the beach by the ruins, but often full. An IYHF card is required.

The Balearic beat

Due to their status as Europe's number-one holiday patch, it's nearly always cheaper and easier to reach **Mallorca**, **Menorca**, **Eivissa** (aka **Ibiza**, in Spanish) or **Formentera** by direct flight from northern Europe than via Barcelona. Even so, the islands are only a short hop away, and fast shuttle ferries have made getting to them much easier.

Despite millions of visitors each year, the islands still retain their individual characters. Ibiza, legendary hub of international club culture, is a desert island that burns yellow each summer, while small Formentera alongside it is more desert-like still. Go in February and you can have large bits of them to yourself. Mallorca has remote, mountainous areas, an attractive capital in **Palma**, and a big difference in atmosphere between the chic north coast and the mass tourist-runs of the south. Green Menorca has beautiful coves and pine forests, and was held by Britain for 70 years in the eighteenth century. This occupation left strange traces: door latches, sash windows, and some of the world's best gin – result of a happy encounter between Navy grog and a Mediterranean skill with herbs. Unknown to most visitors, the inhabitants of the Balearics have produced a rich literature in Catalan, the islands' main language. Mallorca is also home to a considerable colony of artists, who keep Palma's many galleries well-stocked.

Information

Getting there by air: Over ten flights daily, Barcelona-Mallorca, and three daily to Ibiza and Menorca. Three companies – Air Europa, Spanair

and Iberia/Aviaco – compete on prices: return flights to Mallorca cost about 22,000ptas for a weekend or 16,000ptas if you stay a bit longer, but this may vary.
Getting there by sea: **Trasmediterránea** *Estació Marítima de Balears, Moll de Barcelona (902 45 46 45)* is the main ferry operator to the islands. Ferries leave from the Estació Marítima at the foot of the Rambla (Metro Drassanes/**Map** C7). Standard ferries leave daily for Mallorca at 11.30pm (journey time 8hrs), plus a 1pm sailing on Sundays. There are also 'fast ferries' (journey time 4hrs); schedules vary, but there is normally one daily, Mon-Thur, two a day (usually 7am, 5.30pm) Fri, Sat, and two (usually 9am, 8.30pm) Sun. One-way fares to Palma in summer are around 6,600ptas (standard) or 7,500ptas (fast), seat-only, or 15,000ptas per person for a cabin shared by two, with a 15% discount for return tickets. Ferries to Menorca or Ibiza (all standard) also leave at 11-11.30pm (both 9hrs), but only on some days of the week.
Buquebus *Estació Marítima 1, Moll de Barcelona Nord (902 41 42 42/reservas@buquebus.es)* is a superfast hydrofoil service that now competes with Trasmediterránea on the Mallorca route (journey time 3hrs), with four departures to and from Palma daily *(July-15 Sept)*, and two a day in other months. A one-way ticket costs from about 8,100ptas; in summer there's also a half-price fare for night travel. Check for further discounts. Prices for taking a **car** on both companies begin around 18,000ptas one-way (plus passenger fares), but vary by size of vehicle.
Tourist offices: **Ibiza & Formentera** *Paseo Vara del Rey 13, Ibiza (971 30 19 00)*; **Mallorca** *Avda Jaime III, Palma (971 71 22 16)*; **Menorca** *Plaça de la Esplanada 40, Mahón (971 36 37 90)*.

Inland

Pine-clad crags, mountain lakes, ancient towns, cava cellars, stone farmhouses hunkered down into steep hillsides: the Catalan countryside offers a wonderful mix of lushness and ruggedness.

Catalonia's climate and coastline attract millions to its shores, but comparatively few explore the country's insides. Those who do discover striking beauty: Mediterranean colours and rugged hills mix with lush verdure, merging into alpine landscapes in the Pyrenees. The Pyrenean valleys are also one of the birthplaces of Romanesque architecture, with exquisite early-medieval buildings in every town and village.

In addition to the places to stay listed here, it's worth checking the Generalitat's *Residències – Casa de Pagès* guide (*see page 269*) for farmhouse accommodation, particularly in remoter areas.

Montserrat

Geologically distinct from anything else around it, **Montserrat** (the literal translation, 'saw-tooth mountain', describes it accurately) gropes up out of the land with striking visual force. Perched half-way up this dramatic ridge are the monastery and hermitages that form the traditional spiritual centre of Catalonia. The fortress-like atmosphere is emphasised by difficult access – the road meanders hair-raisingly, and the only other way up, more spectacular still, is by cable-car.

Hermits were attracted to this isolated place as early as the fifth century, a Benedictine monastery was founded here in 1025 and the so-called 'Black Virgin', a small wooden figure of the Madonna and child, was installed here in the twelfth century. All kinds of legends and traditions have grown up around the statue over the centuries. It is the patron virgin of Catalonia, and Montserrat is still the most common name for Catalan women. In the Middle Ages, the monastery became an important place of pilgrimage. It grew rich and powerful, its remote position helping ensure its independence. In the Franco era, the monastery was a lonely bastion of Catalan nationalism.

The **shrine of the Black Virgin**, inside the sixteenth-century basilica, can be visited and touched by queuing to the right of the main door and up behind the altar. The museum houses liturgical gold and silverware, archaeological finds and gifts presented to the virgin, including some Old Master paintings and three Picassos. The monastery itself is not particularly interesting, and the cafeterias and souvenir shops tend to take the

edge off the place's spirituality, although fans of religious kitsch might feel this justifies the whole trip.

It's the walks and views around the site that are truly spectacular. The whole mountain, 10km (6 miles) long, is a reserve, and the monastery occupies a very small part of it. As well as the cave where the virgin was discovered (20 minutes' walk from the monastery) there are 13 hermitages, the most accessible of them **Sant Joan**, reached by funicular from beside the monastery or a 20 minute walk with superb views. There are also longer walking routes (*see page 276*), including a circuit of all the hermitages and the (relatively easy) trek to the peak of **Sant Jeroni**, at 1,235m (4,053ft). Rock climbing is popular amid the unique geology, and enthusiasts can find several thrilling climbs on well-marked routes (inquire at the tourist office).

By the southern foot of the mountain is **Collbató**, which has caves (*les coves de Salitre*) open to visitors.

Information

Getting there: *By bus* Julià-Via 9am from Sants bus station (journey time approx 80min). Julià also run guided tours to Montserrat (*see p58*). *By car* N-II to exit km 59; or A2 to Martorell exit, then through Abrera and Monistrol (60km/37 miles). The road to the monastery is often crowded and very slow, especially at weekends and on holy days. *By train* FGC from Plaça d'Espanya, every 2hrs from 7.10am daily, to Aeri de Montserrat (journey time approx 1hr); then cable car to the monastery, every 15min. Return fare (including cable car) is 1,770ptas.
Tourist office: Montserrat *(93 877 77 77)*.
Where to eat: Restaurants on Montserrat are expensive and unimpressive. The café at the top of the Funicular de Sant Joan is better, but only open in summer. Best bet is to take a picnic lunch.
Where to stay: There are two hotels run by the monks – the recently renovated **Hotel Abat Cisneros** (16,540ptas double; reductions mid-Nov-mid-Mar) and the lower-category **Hotel-Residència Monestir** (8,335ptas double; no singles; closed mid Nov-mid-Mar). To book a room at either, phone *(93 877 77 01)*. There is a **campsite** *(93 835 02 51)* beyond Sant Joan funicular; look for the sign.

The Royal Monasteries

Montblanc, 112km (70 miles) due west of Barcelona and inland from Tarragona and the Costa Daurada, is one of the most beautiful towns in western Catalonia, yet all but unknown to foreign visitors. Around it, roughly forming a triangle, are three exceptional Cistercian monasteries: **Poblet, Santes Creus** and **Vallbona de les Monges**.

In the Middle Ages Montblanc was a substantial and prosperous town with an important Jewish community, a past that is reflected in its *Carrer dels Jueus* ('Jews' Street'), the magnificent thirteenth-century town walls (two-thirds of which are intact), the churches of **Santa Maria la Major, Sant Miquel** and **Sant Francesc**, the **Palau Reial** (Royal Palace) and the **Palau del Castlà** or chamberlain's palace.

The great monasteries of the region enjoyed a uniquely close relationship with the Catalan-Aragonese monarchs, and were all built partly to house royal tombs. **Poblet**, a few kilometres west of Montblanc, was founded as a royal residence as well as a monastery in 1151 by Ramon Berenguer IV, who created the joint Catalan-Aragonese monarchy and gave generous grants of land to the Cistercian order. The remarkable complex includes a fourteenth-century Gothic royal palace, the fifteenth-century chapel of Sant Jordi and the main church, housing the tombs of most of the Count-Kings of Barcelona. The monastery can be seen by guided tour only, conducted by a monk.

Santes Creus, founded in 1158 and perhaps still more beautiful than Poblet, grew into a small village when families moved into abandoned monks' residences in 1843. Fortified walls shelter the **Palau de l'Abat** (abbot's palace), a monumental fountain, twelfth-century church with more royal tombs, and superb Gothic cloister and chapterhouse. Visits to Santes Creus now include an audio-visual presentation.

Vallbona de les Monges, third of these Cistercian houses, was unlike the others a convent of nuns, and was particularly favoured by Catalan-Aragonese Queens, especially Violant of Hungary (wife of Jaume I), who is buried here. It has a fine part-Romanesque cloister, but is less grand than the other two. A small village was built around it in the sixteenth century. All three monasteries still house religious communities.

The Monasteries

Monestir de Poblet *(977 87 02 54)*. **Open** *Mar-Sept* 10am-12.30pm, 3-6pm, Mon-Fri, 10am-12.30pm, 3-5.30pm, Sat, Sun; *Oct-Feb* 10am-12.30pm, 3-5.30pm, daily. **Admission** 500ptas; 300ptas students, over-65s.
Monestir de Santes Creus *(977 63 83 29)*. **Open** *Oct-May* 10am-1.30pm, 3-6pm, Tue-Sun; *June-Sept* 10am-1.30pm, 3-7pm, Tue-Sun. **Admission** 600ptas; 500ptas under-21s, over-65s.

Watery splendour in the hills of the Guilleries near **Rupit**. *See page 271.*

Rural pleasures

Until recently, opportunities for spending time in the Catalan countryside and mountains were limited by a shortage of suitable places to stay. Unless you happened to know someone with a house up a hillside, the only choices in many areas were often a few plain hotels, or camping. Recently, however, the rapid expansion of *turisme rural* ('rural tourism') has opened up a whole range of new possibilities.

The characteristic house found across the Catalan countryside is the *masia*, a manor-farmhouse with massive stone walls and sloping roof. First conceived as a combination fort, farm, home, and a holding area for livestock, as a basic structure it dates back well over 1,000 years. Many *masies* are still working farms; others are now second homes. Between these two extremes there are a few hundred *masies* that are now open to visitors. Some can be rented complete as self-catering accommodation, while others have introduced the farmhouse bed-and-breakfast principle into the Catalan countryside.

The Catalan Generalitat has made the job of locating these houses easier with an annual guide, *Residències – Casa de Pagès* (500ptas), available from bookshops or the **Palau Robert** information centre *(see page 295)*. This is a fairly barebones affair, with no real description, but just a picture, prices and basic details for over 500 houses around Catalonia. Facilities vary enormously: some are very simple farm b&bs, others offer real hotel service and luxuries such as pools; some give a choice of rooms or self-catering annexes around the farm; some are on remote mountainsides, some are near a beach. There is no central booking service, nor does the guide indicate how much *masia* owners can handle any language other than Catalan or Spanish (although several houses are actually foreign-owned). The thing to do is get on the phone, find out as much as you can from the owner and take the plunge. There are idyllic spots to be found.

Three especially attractive *masies* are described here. Exploring villages is, predictably, easier with a car, but many can be reached by public transport with a little effort. The Generalitat also sponsors **GITES-**Catalunya (93 412 69 84/93 238 40 00), listing more upscale self-catering houses for rent in rural Catalonia. The Palau Robert has details.

Masia Can Cardús

08775 Torrelavit, Alt Penedès (93 899 50 18)
Getting there: *By car* A2, A7 to Sant Sadurní d'Anoia, then north-west to Torrelavit village. *By bus/train* the nearest are at Sant Sadurní (4km/2.5 miles). **Rates** *doubles with breakfast* 4,500ptas.

This giant earth and stone *masia*, in the Penedès wine country north of Sant Sadurní *(see p270),*is a former Benedictine monastery and dates from the eleventh century. Six rooms sleep two, three or four people. A working farm and vineyard, Can Cardús has information on eight more *masies* nearby.

Mas la Garganta

17814 La Pinya (La Vall d'en Bas), La Garrotxa (972 27 12 89). **Getting there**: *By car* N-II to Girona, then C150 to Olot: then C153 Vic road, and before reaching Les Presses turn right to La Pinya. Nearest buses Olot, Les Presses (3km/2 miles). **Rates** *doubles* 6,000ptas; *self-catering* 8,000ptas per cabin.

A *masia* offering b&b or self-catering in the hills of La Garrotxa, with magnificent views. The eighteenth-century building, with seven double rooms, has been finely maintained. B&B and home-cooked dinner comes to 6,000ptas per person, and local and home-grown produce can be bought from the house. The *masia* also organises walking tours with two *masies* nearby, so you can stay a night or two in one place and spend a day walking (without bags) to the next.

El Molí

17569 Siurana d'Empordà, Alt Empordà (972 52 51 39). **Getting there**: *By car* A7 to Figueres (exit 4), then C252 toward L'Escala and right turn to Siurana. *By bus* local service from Figueres. Nearest stop 2km/1.2 miles. **Rates** *doubles* 6,000ptas.

Amid a delicious, 10,000-square-metre garden full of medicinal herbs, this is a beautifully restored large *masia* with six rooms about 7km (4.4 miles) from Figueres, and slightly further from the Costa Brava. Meals are available. This is also a working farm, and homemade produce can be sampled and bought. The owners speak English and French, and can provide ready-prepared cycle and walking routes in the area.

On the grapevine: *cava* & wines

Catalonia's most famous wines and all of its *cava* or sparkling wine come from the **Alt Penedès** west of Barcelona, one of the most respected wine-producing areas in Spain. **Vilafranca del Penedès**, capital of the *comarca*, has a **Museu del Vi** (wine museum) in the middle of town, with a fascinating display of equipment from across the centuries (93 890 05 82; closed Mon). The region's largest winemaker, **Bodegues Torres**, offers guided tours daily (93 817 74 87; booking essential) at its Vilafranca headquarters.

Sixty per cent of the Alt Penedès is given over to vineyards. Vilafranca is the main centre for table wine and brandies, but neighbouring **Sant Sadurní d'Anoia** is the capital of *cava*. **Codorniu** was the first company to begin production. Manuel Raventós, heir to the estate, worked in the Champagne region in the 1870s, and reproduced the *méthode champenoise* in his native land. The Can Codorniu building with its vast cellars is a beautiful *Modernista* work by Josep Puig i Cadafalch, from 1896-1906. **Caves Freixenet** was established in the 1920s. Several other companies in Sant Sadurní offer tours, tastings and sometimes food; the tourist office has a full list.

Catalonia has several other *denominació d'origen* wine regions. The small **Alella**, just east of Barcelona, is best known for whites. More important are **Priorat** and **Terra Alta**, either side of the Ebro west of Tarragona and renowned for powerful, heavy reds – **Falset** and **Gandesa**, respectively, are their capitals. The better Priorat reds, in particular, have become quite coveted (try Scala Dei or Rocafort de Queralt); Gandesa rosés are also worth looking for. Local tourist offices have information on visits and tastings; look out too for the **Bodega Cooperativa** in Falset, by Gaudi's disciple César Martinell, and the **Cooperativa Agrícola** in Gandesa, two more great Modernist contributions to the wine trade.

Cava cellars

Canals i Domingo *Carretera de Sant Sadurni a Vilafranca (C243) km 1, Sant Sadurni d'Anoia (93 891 03 91)*. **Open** 10am-5pm Sat, Sun.
A small *cava* producer that gives tastings and tours at weekends (English spoken), followed by a meal in the cellars: Catalan country classics (chargrilled lamb, rabbit or *botifarra* sausages, salads, huge *torrades*, masses of *all i oli*), accompanied by *cava* and/or the vineyard's own Cabernet red.

Monestir de Santa Maria de Vallbona
(973 33 02 66). **Open** 10.30am-2pm, 4.30-6.30pm, Tue-Sat; noon-2pm, 4.30-6.30pm, Sun. **Admission** 250ptas; 200ptas over-65s.
Hours can vary according to times of services.

Information

Getting there: *By bus* Hispano Igualadina *(93 430 43 44)* runs daily services to Montblanc from C/Europa (behind the Corte Inglés on Avda Diagonal; Metro Maria Cristina). More buses from Valls and Tarragona. *By car* A2, then A7, then again A2 to exit 9, or N340 to El Vendrell then C246 for Valls and Montblanc (112km/70 miles). For Poblet, take N240 west from Montblanc and turn left in L'Espluga de Francoli. Santes Creus is connected by a slip road to the C246. For Vallbona de les Monges, take the C240 north from Montblanc towards Tàrrega and turn left onto a signposted side road. *By train* RENFE from Sants or Passeig de Gràcia to Montblanc, five trains a day (journey time approx 2hrs).
Tourist office:
Montblanc & Poblet *(977 86 00 09)*.
Where to eat: Montblanc has an inn, **Fonda Colom** *C/Civaderia 3 (977 86 01 53)*, behind the Plaça Major. Five-courses for around 3,000ptas. You can also eat well at **Els Àngels** *(see below)*.
Where to stay: Highly recommended in Montblanc is **Els Àngels** *Plaça dels Angels 1 (977 86 01 73)*. The **Colom** *(see above)* also has a few rooms.

L'Espluga de Francoli, on the way to Poblet, has **Hostal del Senglar** *Plaça Montserrat Canals (977 87 01 21)*, a country hotel known for great Catalan food, and **Masia del Cadet** *(977 87 08 69)*, a restored farmhouse. Poblet's neighbouring village of Vimbodi has the **Fonoll**, *C/Ramon Berenguer IV 2 (977 87 03 33)*. Santes Creus has the equally cheap **Hostal Grau** *C/Pere III 3 (977 63 83 11)*. The only accommodation near Vallbona is at **Cal Cabestany** *(973 33 02 69)*, a farmhouse with a few b&b rooms.

Montseny to the Pyrenees
Vic, Rupit & Les Guilleries

Vic, an easy day-trip from Barcelona, is surrounded by the wonderful mountain nature reserves and ideal walking territory of Montseny, Les Guilleries and Collsacabra. It began life as the capital of the Ausetian tribe, became a Roman city, and later fell briefly to the Moors, who lost it to Wilfred the Hairy (*see page 13*) in the ninth century. Since then it has remained a religious, administrative and artistic centre. In the nineteenth century it produced the great Catalan poet Jacint Verdaguer, and the philosopher Jaime Balmes.

Vic has many late-medieval houses, and its **Plaça Major** is one of the finest and liveliest in

Can Soniol del Castell *Masia Grabuac, Carretera de Vilafranca a Font Rubi (BV2127) km 6, Font Rubi (93 897 84 26)*. **Open** by appointment.
A limited quantity of very fine *cava* is produced at this vineyard, centred on a historic *masia*. Tours (English spoken) are followed by a tasting.
Caves Codorniu *Avda Codorniu, Sant Sadurní d'Anoia (93 818 32 32)*. **Open** 8am-12.30pm, 3pm-4.30 pm, Mon-Fri; 10am-1.30pm Sat, Sun.
Admission Mon-Fri free; Sat, Sun 200ptas.
All visits include a short film, a mini-train ride through the cellars and a tasting.
Caves Freixenet *C/Joan Sala 2, Sant Sadurní d'Anoia (93 891 70 00)*. **Tours** 9am, 10am, 11.30am, 3.30pm, 5pm, Mon-Thur; 9am, 10am, 11.30am, Fri. **Admission** free.

Wine Festivals

Most of the main wine-towns have festivals in autumn to celebrate the grape harvest (*verema*).

In **Alella** it takes place very early, around the first weekend in September. Much larger are events in **Vilafranca** on the first Sunday in October, and **Sant Sadurní**, usually a week later, featuring concerts, dances, exhibitions, tastings and more. The *Reina del Cava*, the Cava Queen, is crowned in Sant Sadurní, and the crowd are treated to several free glasses of the product as well. Smaller towns have their own events; ask at the **Palau Robert** (*see p295*) and local offices for details.

Information

Getting there:
Alella: *By bus* Autocars Casas (93 798 11 00) from corner of Gran Via and C/Roger de Flor. *By car* N-II north to Montgat, left turn to Alella (15km/9 miles).
Alt Penedès: *By car* A2 then A7 to Sant Sadurní (44km/27 miles) and Vilafranca (55km/34 miles), or A2 then N340 from Molins de Rei, which is much slower. *By train* RENFE from Sants or Plaça Catalunya, trains hourly 6am-10pm (45min).
Falset & Gandesa: *By car* A2, then A7 to Reus, and right onto N420 for Falset (143km/89 miles) and Gandesa (181km/112 miles). *By train* RENFE from Sants or Passeig de Gràcia to Marçà-Falset. Six trains daily (approx 2hrs). For Gandesa continue to Mora d'Ebre (another 20min) and catch local bus.
Tourist offices:
Sant Sadurní d'Anoia *Plaça de l'Ajuntament 1, baixos (93 891 12 12);* **Vilafranca del Penedès** *C/Cort 14 (93 892 03 58);*
Gandesa *Avda Catalunya (977 42 06 14).*

Catalonia, particularly on Saturdays (market day) and during the *Mercat del Ram* (livestock market), held the week before Easter. Monuments worth seeing are the **Temple Romà** (Roman temple), now an art gallery, and the neo-classical **Catedral de Sant Pere**, which has a perfectly-preserved eleventh-century bell tower, and a set of sombre twentieth-century murals painted by Josep Lluís Sert. The **Casa de la Ciutat**, in a corner of the Plaça Major, dates from the fourteenth century. Vic is also famous for its *embotits* (charcuterie), and shops selling *botifarres*, *llonganisses* and other sausages can be found in almost every street.

The district of Osona, of which Vic is the capital, is full of interesting villages, and can be recommended to anyone with limited time who seeks a taste of the Catalan countryside at its best. The most rewarding route is up the C153 road towards Olot into Les Guilleries, stopping at **Rupit**, an extraordinarily beautiful and ancient village built against the side of a medieval castle. An eleventh-century sanctuary, **Sant Joan de Fàbregues**, and massive farmhouses such as **El Bac de Collsacabra** and **El Corriol** (which has a collection of ceramics and historical artefacts), are all within walking distance. Back towards Vic, another right turn off the C153 leads to **Tavertet**, a

perfectly preserved seventeenth-century village with panoramic views of the *Ter* valley.

Information

Getting there: *By bus* Empresa Sagalès *(93 231 27 56)* from the corner of Passeig Sant Joan-C/Diputació (Metro Tetuan) to Vic. There is no direct bus to Tavertet and Rupit from Barcelona, so get a train or bus to Vic and then a Pous company *(93 850 60 63)* local bus. *By car* N152 from Barcelona, signed for Puigcerdà, to Vic (65km/40 miles). For Tavertet and Rupit, take C153 out of Vic (signposted to Olot). *By train* RENFE from Sants or Plaça Catalunya to Vic, approx two trains per hour (journey time 1hr).
Tourist office: Vic *Plaça Major 1 (93 886 20 91)*.
Where to eat: Vic has good medium-price restaurants. **Basset** *C/Sant Sadurní 4 (93 889 02 12)*, has great seafood (2,500-5,500ptas); **Ca l'U** *Plaça Santa Teresa 4-5 (93 889 03 45)*, is a more traditional inn with pork specialities. For something special, take the N152 Ripoll road and before Sant Quirze de Besora turn onto a 2km (1.2 mile) signposted road to the **Rectoria d'Oris** *C/Rectoria (93 859 02 30)*, one of the best restaurants in the area, with a great view.
Where to stay: The luxury option is the **Parador de Vic** *(93 812 23 23)* – relatively modern and in a fabulous location overlooking the Ter gorge (around 19,000ptas double; offers often available). Vic's own top-range hotel is the **Ciutat de Vic** *C/Jaume el*

Conqueridor *(93 889 25 51)*, at 13,000ptas a double; **Can Pamplona** *(93 883 31 12)* is cheaper (8,000ptas a double). In Tavérnoles, just off the C153 from Vic, **Mas Banús** *(93 812 20 91)* is a giant old *masia* with rooms and self-catering. The delightful *hostal*-restaurant **Estrella** *Plaça Bisbe Font 1 (93 852 20 05)* in Rupit has rooms for 5,500 or 6,500ptas.

Ripoll to the Vall de Núria

Ripoll, north of Vic, grew up around the unique church and monastery of **Santa Maria de Ripoll**. Known as the 'cradle of Catalonia', the church has a superb twelfth-century Romanesque stone portal. This valley was the original fiefdom of Hairy Wilfred, Guifré *el Pilós*, before he became Count of Barcelona *(see page 13)*. He is buried in Santa Maria, which he founded in 879.

Wilfred the Hairy also founded the monastery and town of **Sant Joan de les Abadesses**, 10km (6 miles) up the C151 road east, and worth a visit for its Gothic bridge as well as the twelfth-century monastery itself. The monastery museum (972 72 00 13) covers a thousand years of local life.

From Sant Joan the road leads to **Camprodon**, on the river Ter, known for a crunchy biscuit called a *carquinyoli*. It has a fine Romanesque church. From here a local road veers left up the main Ter valley to the tiny mountain village of **Setcases**, a famous beauty spot now taken over by second homes. By now you are well into the Pyrenees; the valley road comes to an end at **Vallter 2000** (972 13 60 75), the easternmost ski station in the mountains. As with all ski resorts in the area, the best way to stay there is to book a package, available at any travel agent in Barcelona.

Ribes de Freser, the next town on the N152 north of Ripoll, is an attractive base from which to travel to the pretty if gentrified villages of **Campelles** and **Queralbs**. Ribes is also the starting point for the *cremallera*, the FGC's narrow-gauge 'zipper train', which runs via Queralbs along the Freser river up to the sanctuary of **Núria**. Núria itself nestles by a lake on a plateau at over 2,000m (6,500ft). Home to the second-most-famous of Catalonia's patron virgins, a wooden statue of the Madonna carved in the twelfth century, it was a refuge and place of pilgrimage long before then. The mostly nineteenth-century monastery that surrounds the shrine is not especially attractive, but its location is spectacular. The zipper-train makes it an accessible place to try relatively light high-mountain walking (the tourist office has maps). It's also a winter sports centre (972 73 07 13), suited to novice skiers.

Information

Getting there: *By bus* TEISA *(972 20 48 68)* from the corner of C/Pau Claris-C/Consell de Cent to Ripoll, Sant Joan de les Abadesses and Camprodon. *By car* N152 direct to Ripoll (104km/65 miles). For Sant Joan de les Abadesses and Camprodon, C151 out of Ripoll.

By train RENFE from Sants or Plaça Catalunya, approx two trains each hour (to Ripoll approx 1hr 30min). For Queralbs and Núria change to the *cremallera* train in Ribes de Freser.
Tourist offices: **Sant Joan de les Abadesses** *(972 72 01 00)*; **Ribes de Freser** *(972 72 71 84)*; **Núria** *(972 73 07 13)*.
Where to eat: **El Racó del Francés** ('The Frenchman's Corner') *Plà d'Ordina 11 (972 70 18 94)* in **Ripoll** serves French dishes (average 4,500ptas). In Sant Joan de les Abadesses, **Sant Pere** *C/Mestre Andreu 3 (972 72 00 77)* offers local food at reasonable prices; in Queralbs the one good place is **De la Plaça** *Plaça de la Vila 5 (972 72 70 37)*.
Where to stay:
Ripoll: Decent rooms are available at **Ca la Paula** *C/Berenguer 8 (972 70 00 11)*, for 4,820ptas/double (no private bathrooms); **La Trobada** *Passeig Honorat Vilamanya 4 (972 70 23 53)*, is more comfortable (7,500ptas).
Sant Joan de les Abadesses: **Janpere** *C/Mestre Andreu 3 (972 72 00 77)*, is the best, at 6,000ptas per double. There is little accommodation at Vallter; most people stay in towns further down the valley.
Ribes de Freser: **Catalunya Park Hotel** *Passeig Salvador Mauri 9 (972 72 71 98)* is very comfortable (7,000ptas a double); **Traces** *C/Nostra Senyora de Gràcia 1 (972 72 71 37)* is cheaper.
Queralbs: **L'Avet** *C/Major (972 72 73 77)*, is tiny; slightly larger is **Sierco** *C/Major 5 (972 72 73 77)*.
Núria: There's a three-star hotel, the **Vall de Núria** *C/Santuari Mare de Dèu de Núria (972 73 20 00)*, for 10,050ptas a double, and a youth hostel, **Alberg Pic de l'Aliga** *(972 73 20 48)*.

Berga & Puigcerdà

Some 50km (31 miles) west of Ripoll on the C149 (or on the C154, from Vic) is **Berga**, capital of the *comarca* of the Berguedà. Just north the giant cliffs of the **Serra del Cadí**, one of the ranges of the 'Pre-Pyrenees' or Pyrenees foothills, loom impressively above the town. Berga also has a medieval castle, **Sant Ferran**, to provide a suitably storybook air, and a charming old centre, with a Jewish quarter from the thirteenth century. It's famous for a frenzied festival of devils, drink and drums each May called **La Patum** *(see page 278)*, and for its mushroom-hunting competition on the first Sunday of October in the Pla de Puigventós. Great basketloads of different *bolets* (wild mushrooms) are weighed in before an enthusiastic public. Prospective participants should contact the tourist office, which has information on where to hunt.

Heading north along the C1411, uphill into the Cadí, you'll come to the small town of **Bagà**, with partially preserved medieval walls and a central square with Romanesque porticoes. It marks the beginning of the **Parc Natural del Cadí-Moixeró**, a gigantic mountain park of 41,300 hectares (159 square miles) containing wildlife and forest reserves and some 20 or so ancient villages. All retain some medieval architecture, and many offer stunning views. Picasso stayed and painted

Girona's Arab Baths. See page 274.

in one village, **Gósol**, for several weeks in 1906. Rugged and austerely beautiful, the Cadí is rich in wildlife, and can feel more like the American West than the Mediterranean. Chamois and roe and red deer roam the slopes. There are also golden eagles, capercaillies, and black woodpeckers.

Above Bagà the C1411 road enters the Túnel del Cadí, to emerge into the wide, fertile plateau of the **Cerdanya**. Described by writer Josep Pla as a 'huge casserole', the Cerdanya has an obvious geographical unity, but since a treaty of 1659 the French/Spanish frontier has run right across its middle, with one Spanish village, **Llívia**, left stranded in French territory. The Cerdanya is also crossed by the Segre, a famous trout-fishing river.

The snow-capped peaks that ring the valley are laced with ski resorts, including **La Molina** (972 89 20 31), and **Masella** (972 14 40 00). The capital of the area (on the Spanish side), **Puigcerdà**, is a sizeable town heavily touristed by Catalans and French, where discos and après-ski bars mix with remnants of things medieval. Other places of interest in the Cerdanya are the cross-country ski centre of **Lles**, with a Romanesque church, and **Bellver de Cerdanya**, a hilltop village on the edge of the Cadí-Moixeró that was the unlikely scene of a battle during the Civil War. The village has a park information centre.

Paragliding

Espais Parapent del Berguedà
Berga (93 823 01 31).
Price *beginner's course* 48,000ptas.
Four-day courses in the Cadí, with a solo flight up to 1,000m (3,200ft) on the last day.

Information

Getting there: *By bus* ATSA *(93 873 80 08)*, five buses daily to Berga from corner of C/Balmes-C/Pelai (journey time approx 2hrs). Alsina Graëlls *(93 265 68 66)* daily to Puigcerdà from Estació del Nord (3hrs). *By car* C1411 via Manresa to Berga (118km/73 miles) and Bagà. For Gósol turn off before Bagà onto B400. From Bagà continue on C1411 through Túnel de Cadí (toll) for Puigcerdà; a scenic alternative is the N152 through Vic and Ripoll. Lles and Bellver are both off the N260 west from Puigcerdà. *By train* RENFE from Sants or Plaça Catalunya to Puigcerdà, about two trains each hour (approx 3hrs).
Tourist offices: Berga *(93 822 15 00)*; **Puigcerdà** *C/Querol, Baixos (972 88 05 42)*; **Bellver de Cerdanya** *(973 51 02 29)*.
Where to eat:
Berga: La Sala *Passeig de la Pau 27 (93 821 11 85)* has good if pricey local dishes (great mushrooms).
Puigcerdà: Good regional food, moderately priced, is served at **El Galet** *Plaça Santa Maria 8 (972 88 22 66)*. A pizzeria that also offers good regional dishes is **La Tieta** *C/Dels Ferrers 20 (972 88 01 56)*. In Bolvir, 5km/3 miles outside Puigcerdà, the **Torre del Remei** *C/Camí Reial s/n (972 14 01 82)*, has the best and most expensive restaurant in the area (and perhaps one of the best in Spain).
Where to stay:
Berga: Estel Hotel *C/Sant Fruitos 39 (93 821 34 63)* is modern and well-run (5,000ptas a double); in the medieval centre is **Queralt Hotel** *Plaça de la Creu 4 (93 821 06 11)*, with doubles at 4,700ptas.
Bagà: La Pineda *C/Raval 50 (93 824 45 15)*, is inexpensive (5,200ptas/double) and has a restaurant.
Gósol: Triuet *Plaça Major 4 (973 37 00 72)* in the central square of the village is cheap (2,600ptas a double; 5,000ptas, meals included).
Puigcerdà: Plenty of places in the town centre: **Avet Blau** *Plaça Santa Maria 14 (972 88 25 52)* charges 13,000ptas/double, **Hotel Alfonso** *C/Espanya 5 (972 88 02 46)* is more moderate (6,000ptas/double). A little further out, the **Torre del Remei** *(see above)*, is sumptuous (26,000ptas).
Lles & Bellver: In Lles, **Domingo** *C/Travessera 8 (973 51 50 87)* is an inexpensive *pensió* at 3,600ptas. A private farmhouse, **Casa Barber** *C/Major s/n (973 51 52 36)*, has doubles for 3,400ptas. Bellver has the **Pendis** *Avda Cerdanya 4 (973 51 04 79)*, at 4,000ptas a double, or the larger **Mesón Matias** *Carretera Puigcerdà s/n (973 51 00 39)*, at 5,200ptas.

Girona, Besalú & Olot

The most interesting and vibrant Catalan city after Barcelona, **Girona** was one of the first paleolithic communities in the region, a major trading town under the Romans, and a flourishing centre throughout the Middle Ages. Its spectacular **cathedral**, built from the eleventh to the fifteenth centuries, has a Romanesque cloister, a soaring Gothic nave and a five-storey tower. From the cathedral's main façade, 90 steep steps lead down to the main street and the river Onyar, where the

*Stunning Pyrenean scenery in the **Aigüestortes** nature reserve. See page 275.*

buildings packed along the side of the river have been attractively renovated.

Back at the top, Carrer de la Força, just off the cathedral square, leads to the uniquely atmospheric **Call**, the medieval Jewish quarter. The centre for Jewish studies here is run by the last surviving native Jewish community in the peninsula. Add to this the **Banys Àrabs** – a thirteenth-century Moslem/Jewish bathhouse; the **Passeig Arqueològic**, a walk around the old city wall; seven other impressive churches; an iron bridge designed by Eiffel; and the **Palau Episcopal**, with a fine art museum, and you have some idea of the beauty of Girona. The city today is also a highly active artistic and literary centre.

Banyoles, 16km (10 miles) north of Girona, is an attractive town divided into the **Vila Vella** (Old Town) and **Vila Nova** (New Town), both of which contain medieval buildings. Its main attraction, though, is the **Estany de Banyoles**, a huge, peculiarly placid lake in an ancient volcanic crater, surrounded by smaller lakes and containing rare species of fish. It is a very delicate environment, and only eco-friendly watersports are permitted; it hosted rowing events in the 1992 Olympics.

Besalú, another 14km (9 miles) north, is a gem: a small, wonderfully peaceful medieval town founded in the tenth century. The whole town centre has been declared a monument and, with few modern buildings, seems suspended in time. Of special interest are the streets of the old Jewish

Call and the *mikveh* (Jewish baths), the two main squares and the church of **Santa Júlia**, but most eye-catching of all is the entirely intact twelfth-century **fortified bridge** over the Fluvià.

The N260 road continues west past extraordinary villages, such as **Castellfollit de la Roca**, perched atop a precipitous crag, to **Olot**. The medieval town was destroyed in an earthquake in 1427, but it has imposing eighteenth-century and *Modernista* buildings. In the last century it was home to a school of landscape painters; the local **Museu de la Garrotxa** (972 27 91 30) has works by them and Casas, Rusiñol and other Modernist artists. Olot's most unusual feature, though, is its 30-odd extinct volcanoes and numerous lava-slips, sometimes no more than green humps in the ground, that surround it to form the **Parc natural de la zona volcànica de la Garrotxa**. Just south of the town on the Vic road there is a museum and information centre, the **Casal dels Volcans** (972 26 67 62). On the pretty back road south-east to Banyoles (GI524) is a delightful beech forest, **La Fageda d'en Jordà**, made famous by poet Joan Maragall, grandfather of Barcelona's former mayor (for walks, *see page 277*).

Information

Getting there: *By bus* Barcelona Bus *(93 232 04 59)* to Girona from Estació del Nord; TEISA *(972 20 48 68)* runs to Banyoles, Besalú, Olot from the corner of C/Pau Claris-C/Consell de Cent (more frequent services from Girona). *By car* A7 or toll-free N-II to

Girona. For Banyoles, Besalú, Olot, take C150 from Girona (direction Besalú). *By train* RENFE from Sants or Passeig de Gràcia to Girona, hourly approx 6am-9.15pm (1hr 15min, Catalunya Exprés).
Tourist offices: Girona *Rambla Llibertat 1 (972 20 26 79).* Banyoles *(972 57 55 73).* Olot *C/Bisbe Lorenzana 15 (972 26 01 41).* Offices also have information on farmhouse lodgings in the area.
Where to eat:
Girona: Albareda *C/Albareda 7 (972 22 60 02),* in a historic building, has high-quality fare for around 4,000ptas. Cheaper (3,000 ptas) and simpler is **Casa Marieta** *Plaça Independència 5 (972 20 10 16).*
Banyoles: La Rectoria *C/Espinavesa (972 55 35 31),* a famous gourmet restaurant (around 5,000ptas).
Besalú: Best in town is **Fonda Siqués** *Avda Lluís Companys 6-8 (972 59 01 10);* **Cúria Reial** *Plaça de la Llibertat 15 (972 59 02 63)* is cheaper.
Olot: **Ramón** *Plaça Clarà 10 (972 26 10 01),* is best value. With transport, **La Deu** *(972 26 10 04),* on the Vic road, is worth a visit – not least for its view.
Where to stay:
Girona: Europa *C/Juli Garreta, 21 (972 20 27 50),* is comfortable, for about 6,500ptas/double; for a similar price, **Pensión Bellmirall** *(972 20 40 09)* is an unusually charming *hostal.*
Banyoles: Can Xabernet *C/Carme 27 (972 57 02 52)* has doubles at 6,000ptas; **L'Ast** *Passeig Dalmau (972 57 04 14)* has a pool and garden (9,000ptas/double).
Besalú: Venència *C/Major 8 (972 59 12 57),* is cheap at 4,250ptas a double, or try the riverside **Siqués** above Fonda Siqués restaurant (*see above*).
Olot: The **Borrell** *C/Nònit Escubós 8 (972 26 92 75)* has wheelchair access (8,000ptas); **Garrotxa** *Plaça de Móra 3 (972 26 16 12)* is a bargain (3,750ptas a double).

The High Pyrenees

The *comarques* of the High Pyrenees, to the west of Andorra, reach altitudes of well over 3,000m (9,800ft), and contain some of the most spectacular scenery in the whole mountain range. These high valleys and crags form Catalonia's main districts for real mountain walking, climbing, adventure sports and skiing. Too far from Barcelona to be comfortably visited in a couple of days, they are wonderful places to explore over a week or a long weekend.

The Pallars Sobirà

The Pallars Sobirà runs up to the French frontier alongside Andorra, a region of steep-sided valleys and flashing rivers, snow-covered in winter and idyllic in summer, with centuries-old villages of stone and slate that seem encrusted into the mountain sides. The capital of the *comarca* is **Sort**, the centre for organised sports in the area. Several companies in Sort organise rafting and kayaking trips, caving and other adventure sports, and hire out equipment (*see below*; the tourist office has details of others in the area).

For winter, the area has two ski stations: **Super Espot** (973 62 40 15), a large, fully equipped resort near the village of **Espot**, 24km (14 miles) north of Sort on a turn to the left after **Llavorsí**, and the smaller **Port Ainé** (973 62 03 25), near the town of **Rialb**, just to the north of Sort. A special attraction of Super Espot is a blue run that allows even the most inexperienced skiers to descend from the highest point on the mountain all the way to the base. As at Vallter (*see page 272*), stays at these resorts are best booked direct from Barcelona, at any travel agency.

From spring to autumn there are different attractions. The same road that leads to Espot continues to the nature reserve of **Aigüestortes** (winding waters), with a network of paths through alpine wilderness. Its centre is the **Estany de Sant Maurici**, a fabulously beautiful, crystal-clear mountain lake beneath the peaks of **Els Encantats**, popular with serious rock climbers. There are several smaller lakes dotted all through the mountains. In the park there are mountain shelters with full-time wardens. Given the remoteness of most areas, you are advised to contact the well-organised park information centre in Espot (973 62 40 36) and equip yourself with good walking maps before embarking on any long hikes.

Rafting Llavorsí
Carretera Vall d'Aran s/n, Sort (973 62 21 58).
One of Sort's most established adventure sports companies, offering white-water rafting trips 15km (9 miles) down the Noguera Palleresa, from around 4,000ptas per person. Also kayaks, canoeing, bungee jumping from bridges (ponting), a do-it-all river tour called 'barranking' and guided mountain treks on horseback (from around 2,000ptas an hour).

Information
Getting there:
By bus Alsina Graëlls *(93 265 68 66),* one bus daily to Sort from Estació del Nord, leaves 7.30am and arrives 12.20pm. *By car* For Sort (approx 250km/155 miles), take A18 to Manresa, C1410/C1412 to Tremp, then N260 north-east via Pobla de Segur.
Tourist office: Sort *(973 62 11 30).*
Where to eat:
Sort: There are plenty of traditional *fondes* in the old town. **Hotel Pessets II** *C/Diputació 3 (973 62 00 00),* specialises in high-quality local cuisine, with a rich wild boar stew (*civet de porc senglar*).
Espot: Casa Palmira *C/Únic (973 62 40 72).*
Where to stay:
Sort: Pey *Avda Montserrat 3 (973 62 02 54)* by the river, charges 7,000ptas per person (breakfast and lunch or dinner included); **Pessets II** *C/Diputació 3 (973 62 00 00),* offers a bar, pool, tennis courts and restaurant for 10,700ptas a double.
Espot: The luxury hotel is **Saurat** *C/Sant Martí (973 62 41 62),* costing 14,000ptas for a double room; **La Palmira** *C/Marineta s/n (973 62 40 72),* is cheaper and simpler (4,600ptas a double). There are also a few farmhouses with rooms in the village.

Taking to the hills

Barcelona is surrounded by easily-accessible mountain regions with spectacular landscapes, many now national parks, and hiking and hill-walking are hugely popular. The mountains are mostly low- to medium-height, and in many places walking is made easier by GR (*gran recorregut*) long-distance footpaths, indicated with red and white signs.

If you try any walking take local walking maps, suitable clothing and light walking boots, water and food supplies. Best shops for buying maps are **Llibreria Quera** and **Altair** (*see chapter* **Shopping**); as usual, **Palau Robert** (*see page 295*) is also a good source of information. The selection of possible walks given here is ordered in a rough west-east arc around Barcelona. There are many more.

Organised walks

Several clubs and companies organise guided walks around Catalonia and further afield. They include:
Centre Excursionista de Catalunya (CEC)
C/Paradís 10 (93 319 01 00).
Unió Excursionista de Catalunya (UEC)
Gran Via de les Corts Catalanes 580 (93 453 11 65).
These clubs plan walks for members only, normally at weekends and lasting one or two days, but can be good information sources.
Spain Step by Step
C/Casp 55, 3° 1ª (93 245 82 53)
Tailor-made accompanied or unaccompanied group walking tours all over Spain, by arrangement only.

Garraf

This arid, stony, almost desert-like park in the hills above Sitges is fascinating to geologists. Karst outcrops abound, cliffs fall sharply to the sea, and the margallo palm – the only native European palm – and African plant species are common.

Olesa de Bonesvalls to Sitges

(4hrs 30min). Leave Olesa village along the road past the medieval Hospital d'Olesa. Take the GR5 towards Sitges, traverse the deep Avenc de l'Esquerrà, past an ancient *masia*, Can Grau, and carry on through Jafre and past the Maset de Dalt. Cross over the cols at Pota de Cavall and La Fita and drop down the old paths of La Fita and Dels Capellans to walk into Sitges.
Getting there: *By bus* Mohn bus from Plaça d'Espanya to Olesa de Bonesvalls. *By car* A16 or C246 to Gavà and Sitges, BV2411 from Gavà to Olesa de Bonesvalls.

Sant Llorenç del Munt i l'Obac

A wild craggy landscape cut with narrow ravines hosting a huge range of flora. Its highest point is **La Mola**, crowned by the eleventh-century monastery of **Sant Llorenç del Munt.**

Circular route from Matadepera via Sant Llorenç del Munt

(4hrs). From Matadepera village, follow the Les Arenes stream, before bearing right towards Can Prat. Pick up a signposted track that runs left off a sharp bend to connect with the *Camí dels Monjos* (C31). Walk along this marked track and climb, zig-zagging at times, to the peak of **La Mola** (1,104m/3,622ft), with an information centre. Continue north to a rocky outcrop, the *Morral del Drac* (Dragon's Snout), and drop down into the ravine of Canal de Santa Agnès, until a path on the right marked with an X, the *Camí de la Font Soleia*. Follow this until it meets the *Camí dels Monjos*, to return to Matadepera by the same route.
Getting there: *By car* A18 and N150 to Terrassa, then BV1221 to Matadepera. *By train and bus* RENFE or FGC from Plaça Catalunya to Terrassa, then Thireo bus to Matadepera.

Montserrat

The most emblematic and most visited massif in Catalunya. For the monastery and information on how to get there, *see page 267.*

Circular route from the monastery via Sant Jeroni

(4hrs 30min). Walk up the steps from the **Font el Portal** by the monastery to the Via Crucis, and cross the stream, the Torrent de Santa Maria. Follow this to its source, through several passes. Continue up to the hermitage of **Sant Jeroni** on the col at Pou de Calaç; this is about 15 minutes below the peak of Sant Jeroni. Return to the monastery down the steep ravine of Sant Jeroni, turning right on to the GR72 (also called the *Camí de l'Arrel*), which skirts the north-east face of the main massif, before you reach the road. Continue to the monastery via the Pla de la Trinitat.

The 'Hermitage Route'

(3hrs). Leave the main monastery the same way as the previous route and follow the path to the **Plaça de Santa Anna.** Turn right here towards the hermitage of **Sant Benet** (now a refuge) and the cave-hermitage of **Sant Salvador.** Continue on over a less steep stretch and turn left when you reach the Pla dels Ocells. Traverse the small peak of **Trencabarrals** to pick up the *Camí Nou de Sant Jeroni.* From this path you can take in the cir-

cuit of panoramic views and hermitages, including **Sant Jaume, Sant Onofre, Sant Joan, Santa Caterina** and **Santa Magdalena**. Return to the monastery via the *Camí de Les Ermites* and *Camí de Sant Miquel*, along the top of the main ridge.

Montseny

The Montseny massif north of Barcelona is sacred to Catalan ramblers, and has been a reserve since 1978. Several of its peaks top 1,700m (5,577ft), and woodland covers about 60 per cent of the area.
Getting there: *By bus* Sagalès from corner of Passeig de Sant Joan-C/Diputació to El Figueró and Aiguafreda. Also A7 or C251 to Sant Celoni and BV5301 to Montseny. *By train* RENFE from Sants or Plaça Catalunya to El Figueró and Sant Martí de Centeller-Aiguafreda, Vic line (approx two trains hourly).

Circular route from El Figueró via Tagamanent

(5hrs). From the station in **Figueró** walk along the track towards Vallcárquera, until you reach the *Font del Molí* and church of **Sant Pere**. Continue, leaving the Vallcárquera stream on your right, and pick up another track signposted Tagamanent via Sant Martí col. Climb up the promontory from here to the hermitage of **Santa Maria de Tagamanent**. From the peak, drop down again to the col and go on to Can Bellever and L'Agustí. Turn right along a path through woods to La Roca Centella, which you leave on your left. Drop down, bearing right, towards the hermitage at **San Cristòfol** and a col at Creu de Can Plans. Follow a power line to the Vallcárquera stream to return to Figueró.

Circular route from Aiguafreda via Serra de l'Arca

(4hrs). From **Aiguafreda** village take the track along a stream called the *Riera de l'Avencó*. After crossing bridges at Pere Curt and La Bisbal (by a *masia* at Casa Nova de Sant Miquel), you come to a third bridge at Picamena. Don't cross it, but continue along the track to the left through holm oaks to Pla de la Creu, a beautiful mountain pasture

above the Serra de l'Arca. There is a neolithic dolmen nearby at Pla del Boix. Go on south-west to the GR92 path, and follow it left to reach another dolmen. At a fork soon after that, go right past two dolmens to the dolmen at **Cruïlles**. Pass an abandoned *masia* at Can Serra and return to Aiguafreda.

Montnegre & El Corredor

The Montnegre and El Corredor massifs run north-east of Barcelona between the Tordera valley (with the A7 motorway) and the sea. Fields, farmhouses, medieval churches, Iberian remains and neolithic dolmens are scattered among the area's natural Mediterranean woodlands.

Sant Celoni to Canet de Mar

(6hrs). From Sant Celoni, on the south side of the Montseny, walk via Pertegas towards Vilardell, and continue until you see signs for the GR5 path. Cross the Boscos de Montnegre woods, following the signs, to **Sant Martí de Montnegre**. Follow the path to the right, now the GR92, and skirt Turó d'en Vives peak. Drop down to the hermitage of **Sant Iscle de Vallalta**, and walk on to Safigueras col. The route finishes by the sea in the attractive seaside town of **Canet de Mar**, by the castle of Santa Florentina.
Getting there: *By bus* Barbà from Pla del Palau to Sant Celoni. *By car* A7 to Granollers, C251 to Sant Celoni (49km/30 miles). A19/N-II to Canet de Mar. *By train* RENFE from Sants or Passeig de Gràcia to Sant Celoni (Girona line) or Canet (Blanes line).

Olot & La Garrotxa

There are over 20 old larva flows and 30 volcanic cones around Olot. **El Croscat** was the last to erupt, about 11,500 years ago. The forms, textures and colours of the lava contrast strongly with the leafy, damp forests. For Olot town and information on how to get there, *see page 274.*

Circular route from Olot via Fageda d'en Jordà & the volcanoes of Santa Margarida & El Croscat

(7hrs). From the Park Information Centre (**Casal dels Volcans**), follow itinerary three (green) through the beech forest of Fageda d'en Jordà, on an old lava flow from El Croscat. When you reach the junction with itinerary two (red), take this path to the right. Pass the Romanesque church of **Sant Miquel de Sacot** and walk up the southern slope of **Santa Margarida**. There is a hermitage in the centre of the crater. Drop down the northern slope until you reach the car park at Santa Margarida, cross the GI524, and continue round El Croscat to the information centre at Can Serra. Pick up itinerary three here to return to Olot. Local maps and ideas for many other itineraries are available from the Casal dels Volcans.

Festa: every town should have one

Every village and town in Catalonia has at least one major *festa* (*fiesta*, in Spanish). Most include Catalan traditions such as *sardanes* and *castells* (*see pages 5-12*), alongside entirely local features. The only festivity shared by the whole country is **Sant Joan**, the celebration of the summer solstice, with bonfires and fireworks on the night of 23 June. The following is only a tiny selection, as there are hundreds more. Information on most of them is available at the **Palau Robert** (*see page 295*).

Carnaval

Catalonia's most spectacular pre-Lent **Carnaval** is in **Sitges**, usually in mid-February and attracting some 300,000 revellers – one of the biggest bashes on the peninsula. There's a major gay element, and all-night parties are further enlivened by outrageous costumes and a 50-float parade. Carnaval in nearby **Vilanova** is a little more sedate. *See pp258-9.*

Easter

In general less important than in other parts of Spain, but still the occasion for numerous traditional festivals. Passion plays are performed open-air in **Cervera** (Lleida) and **Olesa de Montserrat** (Barcelona). In **Vergés** in the Empordà, north-east of Girona, the mysterious 500-year-old *Dansa de la Mort* ('Dance of Death') is re-enacted on the night before Good Friday. A procession of people dressed as skeletons moves through the village in an eerie, meandering dance, swaying to a mesmeric drum beat.
Getting there: Cervera *By bus* Alsina Graëlls (93 265 68 66) from Estació del Nord, four daily. *By car* A2 to Martorell, then N-II (106km/66 miles). *By train* RENFE from Sants, two trains daily. **Olesa de Montserrat** *By car* A2 to Martorell, N-II (40km/25 miles). *By train* FGC from Plaça d'Espanya, two or more trains each hour. **Vergés** *By car* A7 or N-II to Girona, C255 east, and left to Vergés (120km/74 miles). *By train & bus* RENFE to Girona, then Sarfa bus.

La Patum

Catalonia's wildest and most berserk *festa* is **La Patum** in **Berga**. It has been held on Corpus Christi, 60 days after Easter (so usually in May), since 1394, but the *Patum* folklore is very pagan in origin. Celebrations go on for days, to reach a peak on Corpus Thursday. The town's streets fill with fantastic figures – dwarfs, the Angel-knight, the dragon-like *guites*, the magic eagle – which career through the crowds amid deafening noise, throwing out sparks and fireworks. *Patum* revellers get very drunk (but rarely aggressive), and crowds get more enormous by the year. For how to get there, *see pp272-3.*

The Val d'Aran

North of Sort the old C142 road begins to wind ever more tightly up to one of the most spectacular mountain passes in Europe, the **Port de la Bonaigua** at 2,072m (6,800ft), which makes it very clear that the valley you are entering, the **Val d'Aran**, is on the north side of the Pyrenees, the source of the river Garonne, which meets the sea at Bordeaux. This is a district with an architectural style, administration and even language (Aranese, a dialect of Provençal) all of its own, and that it is Spanish territory is purely an accident of history.

Vielha e Mijaran (usually just called Vielha), the valley's capital, is a fascinating mountain town with very distinctive medieval houses such as **Çò de Rodés**, and slate churches such as **Sant Pèir d'Escunhau** and **Sant Miquèu**. The Val d'Aran is a great walking area, but is best known for winter sports, at its two big ski stations: **Tuca-Malh Blanc** (973 64 10 50), not far south of Vielha near Betren, and the giant **Baqueira-Beret** (973 64 44 55), one of the largest and smartest winter sports complexes in the Pyrenees, and patronised by the Spanish royal family.

Information

Getting there: *By bus* Alsina Graëlls (93 265 68 66), two buses daily from Estació del Nord, at 6.30am and (via Sort) 7.30am (journey time 5hrs 45min, more if via Sort). *By car* From Sort (*see above*), C147 and C142 continue to Port de la Bonaigua (55km/34 miles, allow over an hour). Most direct route from Barcelona is A18 to Manresa, C1410/ C1412 to Tremp and N260 north-east from Pobla de Segur, to enter Val d'Aran by the Vielha tunnel at the western end of the valley.
Tourist office: Vielha *C/Sarriulera 6 (973 64 01 10).*
Where to eat:
Vielha: Good and cheap is **Nicolàs** *C/Castèth 10 (973 64 18 20),* while **Era Mola** *C/Marrec 8 (973 64 24 19),* is the most typically Aranese restaurant.
Betren: La Borda de Betren *C/Major (973 64 00 32)* is a rustic-style restaurant near Tuca-Malh Blanc
Where to stay:
Vielha: The town is expensive, but **Aran** *Avda Castiero 5 (973 64 00 50)* is decent at 14,700ptas a double. Cheaper (4,000ptas double) is the small **Busquets** *C/Major 9 (973 64 02 38).*
Baqueira: The ski resort has the two-star **Val de Ruda** *Carretera de la Bonaigua (973 64 58 11),* dwarfed by two very expensive luxury hotels nearby.
Betren: The only hotel, **Tuca** *Carretera Salardú s/n (973 64 07 00)* has doubles at 7,100-15,500ptas.

Directory

Directory

Getting Around

Getting your bearings in Barcelona is helped, firstly, by its gently sloping topography, from the sea up to the mountain of Collserola looming up just inland, and then by the city's distinctive street geometry, clearly visible on any map.

Down by the port is the lozenge-shaped mass of narrow streets that is old Barcelona, divided through the middle by the great avenue of La Rambla (*Ramblas*, in Castilian Spanish). At the top of the Rambla is the city's central hub, Plaça Catalunya. This marks the transition from the old town to the right-angled grid of the *Eixample*, the nineteenth century 'extension' to the city, with a street plan only varied by even wider boulevards such as Gran Via de les Corts Catalanes (better known as just *Gran Via*) and Avinguda Diagonal. Beyond the Eixample there are districts that were once separate villages – Sants, Gràcia –, more recent creations like the new beaches , the Port Olímpic and uptown suburbs; and the mountains of Tibidabo and Montjuïc.

It's a compact city. Much of Barcelona is easy to explore on foot; for longer journeys, a fast, safe Metro (underground/subway) system and buses will get you to most places within half an hour during daytime. Motorbikes or mopeds can be handy in the traffic; a car is usually more of a liability, and only comes into its own for trips out of town. For more details of transport outside Barcelona, *see page 256.* **Note: all local transport and taxi fares are subject to revision each January.**

Before arriving

Visas & immigration

Spain is one of the European Union countries covered by the Schengen agreement, with many shared visa regulations and reduced border controls (the others are Portugal, France, Belgium, Holland, Luxembourg, Germany, Austria and Italy). To travel to Schengen countries British and Irish citizens need full passports; most EU nationals only need carry their national ID card. Passports, but not visas, are needed by US, Canadian, Australian and New Zealand citizens for stays of up to three months. Citizens of South Africa and some other countries also need visas to enter Spain, obtainable from Spanish consulates and embassies in other countries (or from those of other Schengen countries you plan to visit).

EU citizens intending to work, study or live long-term in Spain are required to obtain a residency card, which has to be done after you have arrived here; non-EU nationals aiming to work here, or study for more than three months, should officially have a special visa before entering the country. For more on the formalities of living in Spain, *see pp290-1.*

Customs

EU residents do not have to declare goods imported into Spain for their personal use if tax has been paid on them in the country of origin.

Customs can still question whether large amounts of any item really are for your own use, and random checks are also made for drugs. Quantities accepted as being for personal use are as follows:

• up to 800 cigarettes, 400 small cigars, 200 cigars and 1kg of loose tobacco
• 10 litres of spirits (over 22% alcohol), 90 litres of wine (under 22% alcohol) and 110 litres of beer.
   Non-EU residents can bring in:
• 200 cigarettes or 100 small cigars or 50 cigars or 250 grams (8.82 ounces) of tobacco
• 1 litre of spirits (over 22% alcohol) or 2 litres of fortified wine or other alcoholic drinks with under 22% alcohol
• 2 litres of wine
• 50 grams (1.76 ounces) of perfume
There are no restrictions on cameras, watches or electrical goods, within reasonable limits for personal use, and visitors can carry up to 1 million ptas in cash. without having to declare it. Non-EU residents can also reclaim Value-Added Tax (IVA) paid on some large purchases when they leave Spain. For details, *see p190.*

Insurance

EU nationals are entitled to make use of the Spanish state health service, provided they have an E111 form, which in Britain is available from post offices, Health Centres and Social Security offices. This will cover you for emergencies, but for short-term visitors it's usually simpler to avoid the bureaucracy and take out private travel insurance before departure, which will also normally cover you in the case of theft or other expenses. Some non-EU countries have reciprocal health-care agreements with Spain, but, again, for most travellers it will be more convenient to have private travel insurance. For more on health services, *see p288.*

Arriving & leaving
By air

Barcelona's **Aeroport del Prat** is 12km (7 miles) south of the city in Prat de Llobregat.

Terminal **A** is used by non-Spanish airlines and all arrivals from non-EU countries; Terminal **B** takes most flights by Spanish companies; Terminal **C**, many domestic flights and the air shuttle to Madrid. In A and B there are tourist information desks, cash machines that take credit cards, and exchange offices (open 7am-11pm daily). From the airport there are three ways of getting into town: bus, train or taxi. For airport information, call **93 298 38 38**.

Aerobús

This special bus service is usually the most convenient means of getting to central Barcelona, although not the cheapest. Buses run from stops outside each terminal, via Gran Via, to a stop in Plaça Catalunya near the Corte Inglés store. Buses to the airport go from Plaça Catalunya via C/Aragó, and also pick up at Sants railway station and Plaça Espanya. Buses leave the airport every 15 minutes, 6am-midnight Mon-Fri (6.30am-midnight Sat, Sun, public holidays); in the opposite direction from Plaça Catalunya, 5.30am-11.15pm Mon-Fri (6am-11.20pm Sat, Sun, holidays). The trip takes about 30 minutes; a single ticket costs 485ptas (*see also p282*). Two local buses, the **EA** and **EN**, also run between the airport and Plaça d'Espanya; they are slow and infrequent but cheap (145ptas), and the EN runs late (last departure from the airport 2.40am, from Plaça d'Espanya 3.15am).

Airport trains

To catch the airport train into town, walk out of the terminal and cross the long overhead bridge (with moving walkway) between terminals A and B. All trains to and from Prat stop at four stations in Barcelona: Sants, Plaça Catalunya, Arc de Triomf and Clot-Aragó, all of which are also Metro stops. Trains leave El Prat at 13 and 43 minutes past each hour, 6.13am-10.43pm Mon-Fri; from the city, trains leave Plaça Catalunya at 8 and 38 minutes past the hour, 5.38am-10.08pm Mon-Fri (five minutes later from Sants). At weekends and on public holidays, timings vary slightly but there are still trains every half-hour. The journey takes 23 minutes, or 18 minutes to/from Sants. A single ticket is 310ptas (355ptas Sat, Sun, public

holidays), but you can now also pay using some of the *targeta* multi-trip transport tickets (such as the T-1, *see p282*), which works out far cheaper.

Taxis from the airport

The taxi fare to central Barcelona should be about 2,000-2,500ptas (depending very much on traffic), including a 300ptas airport supplement. Fares are about 20% higher after 10pm and at weekends (*see pp283-4*). There is a minimum charge for trips to/from the airport of 1,500ptas, and a 100ptas supplement for each large piece of luggage placed in the car boot. It's best to ignore any cab drivers who approach you inside the airport; take only the next cab in line at the ranks outside each terminal.

Airlines

British Airways *Passeig de Gràcia 16, 6° (93 301 02 86/information & reservations 902 11 13 33). Metro Diagonal/bus 7, 16, 17, 22, 24, 28, 42, 47.* **Map** D5/**B1** *Airport office (93 379 44 68/ baggage enquiries 902 13 10 24).*
Delta Airlines *Airport Terminal A (93 478 23 00/93 478 28 00).*
Iberia *C/Diputació 258 (24-hour information & reservations 902 40 05 00). Metro Passeig de Gràcia/bus 7, 16, 17, 22, 24, 28.* **Map** D5
TWA *C/Consell de Cent 360, 5° (93 215 81 88). Metro Metro Girona/bus 39, 45, 47.* **Map** D5
Airport office (93 298 33 21).

By bus

Most long-distance coaches (national and international) stop or terminate at **Estació d'Autobusos Barcelona-Nord** at C/Ali Bei 80, next to Arc de Triomf rail and Metro station (**Map** E5; general information 93 265 65 08). The **Estació d'Autobusos Barcelona-Sants**, by Sants rail station and Sants-Estació Metro, is only a secondary stop for many coaches, but some international **Eurolines** services (information 93 490 40 00) stop only at Sants. Some services to rural Catalonia have their own stops elsewhere in the city (*see pages 256-78*).

By sea

All Balearic Islands ferries (*see page 266*) dock at the **Moll de Barcelona** quay, at the bottom of Avda Paral.lel (Metro Drassanes; **Map** C7).

There is also a ferry three times a week between Barcelona and Genoa in Italy, from the **Moll de Ponent**, 400m further south (Grimaldi Lines; for information phone their agents Condeminas, 93 443 98 98). Cruise ships use several berths around the harbour; when cruisers are in port, a **PortBus** shuttle service transports passengers to the foot of the Rambla.

By train

The giant **Barcelona-Sants** station (**Map** A4) is the stop or terminus for most long-distance trains run by Spanish state railways, RENFE. It's about 3km from the centre, but has a Metro stop (Sants-Estació), on line 3 (green, the most direct for the centre) and line 5 (blue). Currency exchange, tourist information, hotel booking and other services are available at Sants. Some international services from France do not go to Sants but terminate at the 1920s **Estació de França**, near Ciutadella park and Barceloneta Metro (**Map** E6/**C4**). Other trains stop at both stations, and many also stop between the two at **Passeig de Gràcia** (**Map** D4), which can be the handiest for the city centre. *See also page 256.*

RENFE information

General information, reservations & sales **93 490 02 02**.
Open 7.30am-10.30pm daily. **Credit** AmEx, DC, JCB, MC, V.
This number is often very hard to get through to. RENFE tickets can be bought by phone and delivered to an address or hotel for a small extra fee. *International info. & reservations (93 490 11 22).* **Open** 8am-8pm Mon-Fri.

Left luggage

All have automatic, coin-operated luggage lockers.

Luggage lockers

Aeroport del Prat *Terminal B.*
Open 24 hours daily. **Rates** 635ptas per day.
Estació d'Autobusos Barcelona-Nord *C/Ali Bei 80. Metro Arc de Triomf/bus all routes to Arc de Triomf.*
Open 24hrs daily. **Rates** 300, 400, 600ptas per day. **Map** E5.

Estació Marítima (Balearics
Ferry Terminal) *Moll de Barcelona.*
Metro Drassanes/bus 18, 36, 38, 57,
64, N4, N6. **Open** 8am-11.30pm daily.
Rates 300, 500ptas per day. **Map** C7
Train Stations.There are lockers at
Sants and Passeig de Gràcia (both
open 5.30am-11pm daily) and França
(6am-11pm daily), but not at the
smaller Barcelona stations. **Rates**
400, 600ptas per day.

Maps

Metro and central area street
maps are included at the back
of this guide. Tourist offices
provide a reasonably detailed
free street map, and the City
tourist offices also have a better
map for 200ptas. Metro maps
are available free at all Metro
stations (ask for '*una Guia del*
Metro') and city transport

information offices (*see right*),
which also have free bus maps.
Metro and bus maps also
indicate access points for the
disabled onto public transport.

Public transport

The Metro is generally the
quickest, cheapest and most
convenient way of getting
around the city, although buses
give you a view and cover some
'holes' in the underground
network – notably around
Plaça Francesc Macià – without
a convenient Metro station.
Buses also run later at night.

   Public transport, although
now pretty integrated, is still run
by different organizations. Local
buses and the Metro are run by

the city transport authority
(TMB). Two more underground
lines (from Plaça Catalunya to
Reina Elisenda, Les Planes, or
Avda Tibidabo; and from Plaça
d'Espanya to Cornellà) connect
with the Metro but are run by
Catalan government railways,
the *Ferrocarrils de la Generalitat*
de Catalunya (FGC, often just
called '*els Ferrocarrils*') which
also has suburban services.

   For transport information call
the **010** information line (*see*
page 295). Barcelona also offers
a choice of sightseeing services
and rides, one of which, the
Barcelona Card, gives unlimited travel on public transport; for
these, and organised tours, *see*
page 58. For facilities for
disabled people, *see page 288*.

Paying your way: take a *targeta*

The basic fare for a single ticket on the Metro,
FGC and buses is the same, currently 145ptas,
and each trip costs the same no matter how far
you travel. Unless you plan to make just a few
journeys, however, it's much cheaper and more
convenient to buy one of the different types of
multi-journey tickets or *targetes*. The basic all-
purpose *targeta* is the T-1, valid on all three
systems, and which can be shared by two or
more people, so long as one unit is cancelled on
the card for each person travelling. The T-1
and some other *targetes* can also now be used
on local RENFE trains within the city, and,
notably, on the airport train.

   You can change freely between Metro lines;
between Metro and FGC, you can change
without paying again, but you must go through
the Metro exit gates and then re-insert the card
in the FGC ticket machine, which will not deduct
the extra unit if less than an hour has passed. If
you combine a bus trip with Metro or FGC, you
have to pay twice with a T-1, but not with the T-
10x2 *targeta*, designed for this eventuality,
so long as the change is made within 1 hour
15 minutes. With the 'unlimited travel' *targetes*
valid for a certain period you can obviously
travel, and change, as much as you like.

   T-1, T-10x2 and T-50/30 cards can be bought
at ticket desks and automatic machines in Metro
and FGC stations, at transport offices, by credit
card from *Servi-Caixa* machines (*see page 215*)

and at many newsstands and lottery shops.
Outlets for other cards are listed below. You
cannot buy *targetes* on buses. The **Barcelona**
Card discount scheme (*see page 58*) also gives
unlimited travel for one, two or three days.

Targeta varieties

T-1 Valid for ten trips on Metro, FGC, buses
and some trains. Can be shared by two or more people,
and costs 795ptas.
T-10x2 Valid for ten trips on Metro, FGC and buses,
with free transfer between all three (except from one bus
to another). It too can be shared, and costs 1,300ptas.
T-50/30 Gives 50 trips within any 30-day period
on Metro and FGC (not buses). It can be shared,
and currently costs 3,175ptas.
T-Mes One month's unlimited travel on all three
systems for one person only, costing 5,450ptas.
Note, though, that this means a calendar month, not 30
days from date of purchase. With your first month's
card you must obtain an identity card (which costs
200ptas and requires a photograph), available only at
the TMB and FGC offices. In succeeding months you
can renew your card at any Metro/FGC station.
T-Dia Unlimited travel for one person on Metro,
FGC and buses for one day (600ptas).
Sold at transport offices and Metro/FGC stations.
3 Dies Unlimited travel for one person on Metro and
buses (not FGC) for three days, for 1,450ptas.
Available from the same outlets as the T-Dia, and the
Plaça Catalunya and Sants tourist offices.
5 Dies The same, but valid for five days' travel,
for 2,150ptas.
Aerobús+Bus+Metro The same as the previous two,
but also including a return bus trip from and to the
airport. Valid for three (1,900ptas) or five days
(2,400ptas) and bought on board the Aerobús.

Directory

Information Offices

TMB *Main vestibule, Metro
Universitat (93 318 70 74).* **Open**
8am-8pm Mon-Fri. **Map** C5/**A1**
Branches: Vestibule, Metro Diagonal
(open 8am-8pm, Mon-Fri); Vestibule,
Metro Sagrada Família (open 7am-
9pm daily); Vestibule, Metro Sants-
Estació (open 7am-9pm daily).
Website www.tmb.net
FGC *Vestibule, Catalunya FGC
station (93 205 15 15).* **Open** 7am-
9pm Mon-Fri; *July, Aug* 8am-8pm
Mon-Fri. **Map** D5/**B1**
Branches: Vestibule, FGC Provença
(open 9am-7pm, Mon-Fri);
Vestibule, FGC Plaça d'Espanya
(open 9am-2pm, 4-7pm, Mon-Fri).

Metro & FGC

The five Metro lines are
identified by a number and a
colour on maps and station
signs. At interchanges, lines in a
particular direction are indicated
by the names of the stations at
the end of the line, so you should
know which they are when
changing between lines. On FGC
lines, note that some suburban
trains do not stop at all stations.

Metro hours

Mon-Thur 5am-11pm
**Fri, Sat & days preceding public
holidays** 5am-2am
Sun 6am-midnight; **Public holidays
midweek** 6am-11pm
The FGC has similar hours, but weekday trains on some routes start slightly later, and may run later at night.

Boarding the train

At Metro and FGC stations, insert your
ticket or *targeta* into the machine next
to the turnstile (to your left on the
Metro, to your right on the FGC).
Retrieve the card, and the turnstile will
let one person pass: the machine cancels
one unit for each trip, and will reject
expired tickets. Keep your ticket in case
of inspections. Trains run about every 5
minutes on weekdays, and every 7-9
minutes after 9pm and at weekends.
Outside peak hours (7.30-9.30am, 6-
8.30pm), trains are not usually too full.

Buses

City bus stops are easy to find: a
great many routes originate in or
pass through Plaça Catalunya,
Plaça Universitat and/or Plaça
Urquinaona. Because of the
many one-way streets buses
often do not follow exactly the
same route in both directions,
but run along parallel streets.

Taking the bus

Most bus routes function between
6am and 10.30pm, Mon-Sat, although
many begin earlier and finish later,
sometimes after midnight. There are
usually buses on each route about
every 10-15 minutes, but frequency is
lower before 8am or after 9pm. On
Sundays and public holidays a few
routes do not run at all, and buses are-
less frequent on most routes. You
board buses at the front, and get off
through the middle or rear doors.
Only single tickets can be bought on
board; if you have a *targeta*, insert it
into the machine just behind the
driver as you board, which will
register it and return it. If you change
buses you must pay again, except
with an unlimited-travel *targeta*. On
suburban services fares increase on a
zone system outside the city limits,
and tickets must be bought on board.

Useful routes

Buses that connect Plaça Catalunya
with popular parts of town include:
22, via Gràcia to the *Tramvia Blau* on
Tibidabo and the Pedralbes
Monastery; **24**, the best way to get to
Parc Güell; and **41** and **66**, to Plaça
Francesc Macià, an area not served
by the Metro; in the opposite
direction, the 41 goes to Ciutadella
and the Vila Olímpica.
45 through Plaça Urquinaona and
down to the beach near Port Olímpic.
50 from north-east Barcelona past
Sagrada Família and along Gran Via
to Montjuïc; **61** climbs Montjuïc from
Plaça d'Espanya to Miramar.
Two more crosstown routes: **64**, from
Barceloneta beach, past Colom, Avda
Paral.lel, Plaça Universitat to Sarrià
and Pedralbes; and **7**, connecting the
upper Avda Diagonal and the
university with the centre (Gran Via,
Passeig de Gràcia) and Glòries.

Night buses

There are 16 *Nitbus* (night bus)
routes, most of which run 10.30pm-
4.30am nightly, with buses every 20-
30 minutes. Most of these **N** bus
routes pass through Plaça Catalunya,
and some also run out of town to
Badalona, Castelldefels and the
airport. Standard *targetes* are not
valid on night buses; instead, you
must buy single tickets (160ptas) or
the special 10-trip night bus *targeta*
(1,015ptas), both of which are
available only on board.

TombBus

A special shoppers' bus service (the
spooky-sounding name actually
means 'round trip') that runs only
between Plaça Catalunya and Plaça
Pius XII on the Diagonal, 7.30am-
9.38pm Mon-Fri; 9.10am-9.20pm Sat.
Again, normal *targetes* are not valid
on the bus, and single tickets cost
175ptas.

Local trains

For trips into the suburbs and
surrounding towns there are, as
well as buses, regional rail lines
run by the FGC and RENFE.
From FGC **Plaça Catalunya**
(the same station as for the
Sarrià and Tibidabo lines)
trains go to Sabadell, Terrassa
and other towns beyond
Tibidabo, and from FGC **Plaça
d'Espanya**, to Hospitalet and
Montserrat. All trains on the
RENFE local network (signed
Rodalies/Cercanías at mainline
stations) stop at **Sants**, but
many lines also converge on
Plaça Catalunya (for Vic and
the Pyrenees, Manresa, the
Penedès, the Maresme coast to
the north) or **Passeig de
Gràcia** (for the southern
coastal line to Sitges, and the
Girona-Figueres line north).
Fares vary according to zones.
For more on rail services, *see
page 256*; for a map of local
RENFE lines, *see page 321.*

see page 256; for a map of local
RENFE lines, *see page 321.*

Taxis

Barcelona's 11,000 black-and-
yellow taxis are among its most
distinctive symbols, and at most
times easy to find. Fares have
been rising, but are still
reasonable. Taxis can be hailed
on the street when they show a
green light on the roof, and a
sign saying *Lliure/Libre* ('Free')
behind the windscreen. There are
also ranks at railway and bus
stations, main squares and other
locations throughout the city.
When giving instructions to the
driver, it's a good idea to know
the name of the district you are
heading for and maybe a local
landmark, as well as just the
address. *See also page 281.*

Fares

Current official rates and supplements
are shown inside each cab (in
English). The current minimum fare
is 300ptas, which is what the meter
should register when you first set off.
After the first couple of kilometres (or
minutes) the fare begins to increase at
a rate per kilometre, or on a time rate
at slow speeds. The basic rates apply
6am-10pm, Mon-Fri; at all other times

(including midweek public holidays) the rate is about 20% higher, although the initial charge remains the same. There are also supplements for each item of luggage larger than 55cm x 35cm x 35cm (100ptas), and for animals (125ptas). If you require a taxi to wait, you will be charged 2,200ptas per hour. Note also that taxi drivers are not officially required to carry more than 2,000ptas in change, and that very few accept credit cards.

Receipts & complaints

To get a receipt, ask for '*un rebut, si us plau/un recibo, por favor'*. It should include the fare, the taxi number, the driver's *NIF* (tax) number, the licence plate and the date; if you have a complaint of any kind about a cab driver insist on all these, and the more details the better (driver's signature, time, route). Call transport information on *010* to explain your complaint, and follow their instructions.

Phone cabs

The companies listed below take phone bookings 24 hours daily. Only some operators speak English, but if you are not at a specific address give the name of a street corner (ie *Provença/Muntaner*), or a street and a bar or restaurant where you can wait. You'll be asked your name. Phone cabs start the meter as soon as a call is answered.
Barnataxi *(93 357 77 55)*; **Fono-Taxi** *(93 300 11 00)*; **Ràdio Taxi** *(93 225 00 00)*; **Ràdio Taxi Verd** *(93 226 39 39)*; **Servi-Taxi** *(93 330 03 00)*; **Taxi Groc** *(93 490 22 22)*; **Taxi Miramar** *(93 433 10 20)*; **Taxi Ràdio Móvil** *(93 358 11 11)*.

Driving

Driving in Barcelona can be wearing. There's seldom enough driving space, let alone parking space. Within the city limits a car is rarely a time-efficient form of transport, and it's only out in the country where one becomes an asset (*see pages 256-78* **Trips Out of Town**). If you do drive here, bear these points in mind:
• You can drive in Spain with a valid licence from most other countries. An international driving licence can be useful as a translation/credibility aid.
• Keep your driving licence, vehicle documents and insurance Green Card with you at all times.
• It is compulsory to wear seat belts at all times (more seriously enforced on highways than in cities) and have with you two warning triangles, a spare tyre, spare lightbulbs and tools to fit them.
• Legal alcohol limits for drivers are low, similar to those in most EU countries.

• Children under 12 may not travel in the front of a car.
• Do not leave anything of value, including a car radio, in your car, nor bags or coats in view on the seats. Take all your luggage into your hotel when you park your car. Foreign number-plates can attract thieves.
• Many drivers ignore speed limits, and it's common to race through traffic lights changing from amber to red (so don't brake suddenly in this situation, or you may be hit from behind).
• When oncoming drivers flash lights at you this means they will **not** slow down (contrary to British practice). On main highways, the flashing of lights is usually a helpful warning that there is a speed trap ahead.

Spanish residents

If you become resident in Spain you must make some changes to your driver's licence within six months to continue driving legally. EU citizens need only register as local drivers at the Prefectura Provincial de Trànsit. Non-EU citizens (except Swiss and European Economic Area citizens) have to pass a Spanish driving test, which means enrolling at a driving school, and will probably cost at least 40,000ptas, even if you already drive.
Prefectura Provincial de Trànsit
Gran Via de les Corts Catalanes 180-4 (93 331 16 16/93 331 13 66). FGC Magòria-La Campana/bus 9, 38, 109.

Car & motorbike hire

Car hire is relatively expensive here, but price structures vary, so it's worth shopping around. Check what's included: unlimited mileage, 16 per cent IVA (VAT) tax, and especially full insurance cover, rather than the third-party minimum (*seguro obligatorio*). You will need a credit card, or have to leave a large cash deposit. Most companies also have a minimum age limit and require you to have had a licence for a year, or sometimes longer.

Hertz

C/Aragó 382 (93 270 03 30). Metro Girona, Tetuan, Verdaguer/bus 6, 19, 50, 51, 55. **Open** 8am-2pm, 4-7pm, Mon-Fri; 9am-1pm Sat. **Credit** AmEx, DC, JCB, MC, V. **Map** E4.
Renault Clio or similar, 11,500ptas per day, 17,100ptas a weekend, 48,510ptas per week; Ford Mondeo 77,900ptas per week (all prices incl tax, full insurance, unlimited mileage). With the big agencies you often get a better deal if you book from your home country. Minimum driver age, 25.
Branch: Airport *(93 298 36 36)*. **Open** 7am-midnight daily.

Laser

Avda Roma 15 (93 322 90 12). Metro Sants-Estació/bus 30, 32, 43, 44, 78, 112. **Open** 8.30am-2pm, 4-8pm, Mon-Fri; 9am-2pm Sat. **Credit** AmEx, DC, MC, V. **Map** B4.
Small car rental at good rates: a weekend (pick-up Fri, return Mon am) for 19,000ptas, all inclusive. You must have had a licence for two years.

Vanguard

C/Londres 31 (93 439 38 80/93 322 79 51). Bus 15, 27, 32, 41, 54, 59. **Open** 8am-2pm, 4-8pm, Mon-Fri; 9am-1pm Sat, Sun, public holidays. **Credit** AmEx, DC, MC, V. **Map** B3.
Good rates for small cars, especially at weekends, and scooter and motorcycle hire. All-inclusive weekend rates from 9,280ptas (50cc Honda) to 29,000ptas (Yamaha 600); you must be 18 to hire a moped and have had a licence a year, 25 and three years for larger bikes.

Breakdown services

If you are taking a car to Spain it is advisable to join a motoring organisation such as the AA or RAC in Britain, or the AAA in the US. They have reciprocal arrangements with the Catalan equivalent, the **RACC**.

RACC (Reial Automòbil Club de Catalunya)

Avda Diagonal 687 (93 495 50 00/ 24-hour breakdown assistance & medical emergencies 902 10 61 06/ 24-hour information 902 30 73 07). Metro Zona Universitària/bus 33, 54, 67, 68, 74, 75. **Open** *office* 9am-2pm, 4-7pm, *Aug* 9am-2pm, Mon-Fri.
The RACC has English-speaking staff and will send immediate assistance if you have a breakdown. Outside Barcelona the emergency number is the same, but you may be referred to another local number. Non-members can also get breakdown attention , but will be charged. The RACC also provides a range of other services.

Midas

Via Augusta 81-83 (93 217 81 61). FGC Gràcia/bus 16, 17, 22, 24, 25, 28. **Open** 8am-8pm Mon-Fri; 9am-2pm Sat. **Credit** AmEx, DC, MC, V. **Map** D3.
While-you-wait exhaust, brakes and filter repairer. 13 local branches; call freephone 900 10 13 41 for the nearest.

Neumáticos Roger de Flor SA

C/Roger de Flor 133 (93 231 66 16). Metro Tetuan/bus 6, 7, 19, 50, 51, 55, 56, 62. **Open** 9am-2pm, 4pm-8pm, daily. **Credit** V, MC, EC. **Map** E5.
A quick-service tyre repair workshop. Also, general mechanical services.

Vidrauto

C/Mallorca 342 (93 458 36 44/93 459 03 64). Metro Verdaguer/bus 6, 15, 19, 33, 34, 43, 44, 50, 51, 55. **Open** 9am-1.30pm, 3.30-8pm, Mon-Fri; 9am-1.30pm, 4-7.30pm, Sat. **Credit** AmEx, MC, V. **Map** E4.
Can replace all kinds of autoglass.

Parking

Parking is never easy in central Barcelona. The Municipal Police readily give out tickets (which many people never pay), or tow cars away, which leaves you no option. Be careful not to park in front of doorways with the sign *Gual Permanent*, indicating an entry with 24-hour right of access. In some parts of the old city, notably La Ribera and the Barri Gòtic, not just parking but also entering with a car is banned to non-residents for much of the day. Large signs indicate when this is so.

Pay & display areas (Zones Blaves)

Many streets in the central area and the Eixample are pay-and-display areas (*Zones Blaves*, Blue Zones), with parking spaces marked in blue on the street. Ticket machines will be nearby. Parking restrictions in the zones apply 9am-2pm, 4-8pm, Mon-Sat. During these times you are allowed to park for a maximum of two hours; the basic charge rate is 5ptas/minute, or 255ptas for one hour and 510ptas for two hours. If you overstay by no more than an hour you can cancel the fine by paying an additional 500ptas; to do so, press *Anul.lar denúncia* on the ticket machine, insert 500ptas and take the receipt that comes out. Machines accept credit cards (MC, V) but do not give change.

Car parks

Car parks (*parkings*) are signalled by a white 'P' on a blue sign, beside which *Lliure/Libre* or a green light means there's space, a red light and *Complet/Completo* or *Ple/Lleno* means full. The city parking company SMASSA has 28 underground lots, charging 220-240ptas per hour. You can get pre-paid cards usable in any SMASSA lot, for periods of 25 hours (4,700ptas) and up. Many car parks are run by the SABA company; minimum charge is 245ptas, for the first hour. SABA also offers overnight parking (9pm-9am) for 1,470 ptas. You are especially advised to use a car park if your car has foreign plates.
Central car parks: SABA *Plaça Catalunya, Plaça Urquinaona, Arc de Triomf, Avda Catedral, Passeig de Gràcia, C/Diputació-C/Pau Claris;*

SMASSA *Plaça dels Àngels-MACBA, Moll de la Fusta, Avda Francesc Cambó.* **Open** 24 hours daily.

Metro-Park

Plaça de les Glòries.
Open 24 hours daily.
Credit AmEx, DC, MC, V. **Map** F5.
A park-and-ride facility recommended for anyone coming in to Barcelona with a car for the day and not needing it while here. For 675ptas you can leave your car the whole day, and the ticket gives unlimited travel for one person for one day on Metro and city buses (but not the FGC). For 2,800ptas you get the same deal for a week (but not overnight parking). The car park is in the middle of Plaça de les Glòries, at the key junction of the Diagonal, Meridiana and Gran Via, a short Metro ride (Metro Glòries, line 1) from the centre.

Towing away & car pounds

(93 428 45 95).
Credit AmEx, DC, MC, V.
If your car has been towed away by the Municipal Police they will leave a triangular sticker on the pavement near where you left it. Call the number on the sticker or the one above (open 24 hours) and quote the car number to be told which of the city car pounds it has gone to. Staff do not normally speak English. It will cost 14,875ptas to recover the vehicle during the first four hours after it was towed away, plus 270ptas for each additional hour (or fraction of an hour) after that, and very likely an extra fine which can vary according to where you were illegally parked.

Petrol

Most *gasolineres* have unleaded fuel (*sense plom/sin plomo*), regular (*super*) and diesel (*gas-oil*).

24-hour petrol stations

Several have round-the-clock shops.
Raval/Poble Sec: Campsa *Avda Paral.lel 37, corner of C/Palaudaries.* **Credit** V. **Map** C6
Poble Sec/Plaça d'Espanya: Total *Avda Paral.lel 140, corner of C/Parlament.* **Credit** MC, V. **Map** B6
Eixample: Cepsa *C/Casanova 89, corner of C/Aragó.* **Credit** MC, V. **Map** C4
Near Plaça Francesc Macià: Cepsa *C/Comte d'Urgell 230, junction with Avda Sarrià.* **Credit** AmEx, MC, V (no shop). **Map** C3
Arc de Triomf: Cepsa *C/Roger de Flor 58, near Estació d'Autobusos.* **Credit** AmEx, MC, V. **Map** E5
Clot: BP *C/Clot 2, junction with Avda Meridiana heading north.* **Credit** AmEx, MC, V (no shop).
Ronda de Dalt: Repsol *Plaça Karl Marx, south side, exit onto Passeig Vall d'Hebron.* **Credit** MC, V.

Cycling/rollerblading

Recreational bike-riding in Barcelona is on the up, and there is an incomplete but growing network of bike lanes (*carrils bici*) along major avenues and the seafront. Mass bike commuting is a long way off, though, for in weekday traffic cyclists still face daunting risks. Rollerblading is also popular. Tourist offices (*see pages 294-5*) have route details.

Bike & skate hire

Most bike rental shops are near the sea, from the old town to the Port Olímpic. At weekends, some shops also open by the Ciutadella to rent bikes and *bicicars*, four-wheelers with side-by-side seats, just for use in the park. Many shops also rent rollerblades. Be sure to get a bike lock, and use it, as theft is increasingly common.

Un Cotxe Menys

C/Esparteria 3 (93 268 21 05). Metro Barceloneta/bus 14, 17, 39, 40, 45, 51, 100. **Open** 10am-2pm Mon-Fri; pm Mon-Fri & Sat, Sun by arrangement.
No credit cards. Map D-E6/**C3-4**
The name means 'one car less'; at this La Ribera shop bike hire costs 600ptas per hour; 1,500ptas per half day; or 2,000ptas per full day. They also run guided cycle tours (*see p58*).

...al punt de trobada

C/Badajoz 24 (93 225 05 85). Metro Llacuna/bus 36, 41, 92. **Open** 8am-2pm, 3.30pm-9pm, Mon-Fri; 8am-8pm Sat, Sun, holidays. **No credit cards.**
Near the beach: mountain bikes and rollerblades cost 500ptas per hour, 1,500ptas a half-day, 2,500ptas a whole day. Also tandems, bikes with baby chairs, bike tours, and other services.

Pedestrian tips

Advice for cyclists and those on foot: take special care at pedestrian crossings. After the green 'cross' signal lights up, a couple more cars will usually come speeding through to beat the red light, so look very carefully. Be careful too of vehicles turning onto the street you are crossing, as they will often speed up or veer to avoid a pedestrian rather than actually give way, green pedestrian light or not.

Directory A-Z

Communications

Internet & e-mail

To check or send e-mail, ready options are cybercafés (*see page 158*) and coffee-less Net centres. Some libraries (*see page 292*) and institutions offer free web access, but not usually e-mail. For other computer services, *see right*.

E-Mail from Spain

La Rambla 42/Passatge Bacardi 1 (93 481 75 75/info@emailfromspain.es). Metro Liceu/bus 14, 38, 59, 91. **Open** 10am-8pm Mon-Sat. **Map** D6/A3
Traveller-oriented net centre that also offers Spanish courses (*see p298*). Access is from the passage between the Rambla and the Plaça Reial. 600ptas for 30 e-minutes.
Website: www.emailfromspain.es

Realnet

C/Perla 28 (93 218 98 61/ reservas@realnet.es). Metro Fontana/bus 22, 24, 28, 39. **Open** 11am-3pm, 4-11pm, Mon-Fri; 11am-11pm Sat; 4-11pm Sun. **Map** D3
One of several well-priced net centres in Gràcia. Half-hour on the Net, 400ptas; games, office programmes cheaper still.
Website: www.realnet.es

La Web a Ciutat Vella

C/Sant Pere Més Baix 14 (93 295 40 07/webciutatvella@worldonline.es). Metro Urquinaona/bus 17, 19, 40, 45. **Open** 11am-10pm Mon-Sat; 5-10pm Sun. **Map** D6/B2
In Sant Pere, not far from the Cathedral, this net-and-games space offers on-line time at 450ptas for the first 30 minutes.

Mail

Normal-rate stamps for cards or letters can most easily be bought in any *estanc* or tobacco shop (*see page 295*). Postal information is on 902 19 71 97.

Correu Central

Plaça Antoni López (93 310 04 04). Metro Jaume I/bus 14, 17, 19, 36, 40, 45, 57, 59, 64, 157. **Open** 8.30am-9.30pm Mon-Sat; *some services only* 9am-1pm Sun. **Map** D6/B4
In the imposing main post office, there is an information desk in the middle of the hall; most services are available at any of the *Admissió Polivalent* windows straight ahead of you as you enter. There's a separate window for the fax sending and receiving service, offered at all post offices (more expensive than

private fax shops, but with the option of courier delivery within Spain). Letters sent Poste Restante (General Delivery) to Barcelona should be addressed to *Lista de Correos, 08070 Barcelona, Spain;* to collect them go to the windows to the left, with your passport. To send something express post, say you want to send it *urgente*. Note that within the general opening hours not all services are available at all times; also, some post offices close in August.

Other city centre post offices:
Open 8.30am-2.30pm Mon-Fri; 9.30am-1pm Sat.
Plaça Urquinaona 6. Metro Urquinaona/bus all routes to Plaça Urquinaona.
C/Aragó 282. Metro Passeig de Gràcia/bus 7, 16, 17, 22, 24, 28.
C/València 231. Metro Passeig de Gràcia/bus 7, 16, 17, 20, 43, 44, 63, 67, 68.

Postal rates & post boxes

Letters and postcards weighing up to 20gm cost 35ptas within Spain; 70ptas to the rest of Europe; 115ptas to the US, Canada, Africa and much of Asia; 155ptas to Australasia and South-East Asia. Mail to other European countries generally arrives in three-four days, to North America in about a week. Aerogrammes (*Aerogramas*) cost 85ptas for all destinations. Normal post boxes are yellow. There are also a few special red post boxes for urgent mail, with collections about every two hours.

Postal Exprés

Available at all post offices, an express post system with guaranteed next-day delivery to provincial capitals, and 48-hour delivery elsewhere in Spain. The most convenient and reliable way of sending small packages within Spain.

Telephones

With several telecom companies (*Retevisión, UNI2, Jazztel, BT* and more) now competing with the (privatised) former state monopoly *Telefónica*, the Spanish phone scene is changing rapidly, and prices are coming down. Normally, though, calls from public phones and all local calls still go through *Telefónica*, whose basic rates are quite high. International calls cost less from 8pm to 8am, and all day at weekends; other timings for lower rates vary. Some phone cards (*see right*) give cheaper rates than *Telefónica*.

Phone numbers

All normal Spanish phone numbers now have nine digits, as the area code (*93* in Barcelona and its province) must be dialled with all calls, local or long-distance. This is sometimes still not indicated on stationery, leaflets and so on. If you're ever given a Barcelona number with only seven digits, chances are you simply need to add the *93* in front of it. Spanish mobile phone numbers begin with *6*. Numbers beginning *900* are freephone lines; *902* numbers are special-rate services.

Public phones

The most common model of pay phone accepts coins, *Telefónica* phonecards and credit cards, and has a digital display with instructions in English and other languages. Minimum charge for a local call is currently 20ptas; for a mobile phone in daytime, 100ptas; for a 902 number, 60ptas. This type of phone also gives you credit to make further calls without having to reinsert money. Most bars and cafés also have phones for public use, but they often cost 50% more than regular phone booths.

International & long-distance calls

To make an international call, dial 00 and then the country code: **Australia** 61; **Canada** 1; **Irish Republic** 353; **New Zealand** 64; **United Kingdom** 44; **USA** 1, followed by the area code (omitting the first zero in UK numbers) and number. To call Barcelona from abroad, dial the international code (00 in the UK), then 34 for Spain. To call Barcelona from anywhere else in Spain the number is now the same as the local number, beginning with 93.

Phone cards

Post offices, newsstands and *estancs* sell 1,000 and 2,000ptas *Telefónica* phone cards, which save on money and inconvenience if you're making several calls. Also on sale at newsstands are cards from other companies (*UNI2, BT* and *Universal*) which currently give you cheaper rates than *Telefónica* on all but local calls. The cards give you a toll-free number to call; an operator then connects you with the number you want and, at the end of the call, tells you how much you have left on the card.

Phone centres

Phone centres (*locutorios*) offer greater convenience for long-distance calls: you call from a booth and pay at the counter when you've finished. Many private *locutorios* in the old town make use of the new phone companies' cheaper rates – but add their own mark-up as well. Some also offer international money transfer and exchange.

Telefónica *Main vestibule, Estació de Sants. Metro Sants-Estació/bus all routes to Estació de Sants.* **Open** 8am-9.30pm daily. **Map** A4. **Branch: Estació d'Autobusos del Nord** *C/Ali Bei 80. Metro Arc de Triomf/bus all routes to Arc de Triomf.* **Open** 9am-9pm Mon-Fri; *July, Aug* also 10am-1pm Sat; 5-9pm Sun. **Map** E5.
Cambios Sol *La Rambla 88 (93 318 97 53). Metro Liceu/bus 14, 38, 59.* **Open** 8am-9pm daily. **Map** D6/A3
Europhil *C/Corders 13 (93 268 12 07) Metro Jaume I/bus 17, 19, 40, 45* **Open** 10am-10pm Mon-Fri; 10am-11pm Sat, Sun. **Map** D6/**C3**
Branch: *C/Joaquim Costa 12 (93 442 71 18).* **Map** C5

Operator services

Normally in Catalan & Spanish only.
National directory enquiries 1003
International directory enquiries 025
National operator 1009
International operator *Europe & North Africa* 1008; *Rest of World* 1005
Telephone breakdowns 1002
Telegrams 93 322 20 00.
Time 093
Weather information for Spain 906 305 53 65
Alarm calls 096
Once the message has finished (when it starts repeating itself), key in the number you are calling from, followed by the time at which you wish to be woken, in four figures, ie. 0830 if you want to be called at 8.30am.
General information 098
A local information service provided by Telefónica, with information particularly on duty pharmacies in Barcelona. Otherwise, generally less reliable than the 010 line (*see p295*).

Computer services

To find a Net terminal quickly, *see left*. Options for putting your own computer on-line are changing as the telecom market evolves. Local Net server Arrakis (902 22 21 22/ *www.arrakis.es*) is introducing services using BT instead of *Telefónica*'s *Infovía Plus* data lines; many companies (such as *Retevisión*, tel 015/ *www.alehop.es*) now offer 'free' Internet – no sign-up charge, but there's still your phone bill.

Cinet

Passeig Lluís Companys 23 (93 268 26 40/fax 93 268 07 00/ info@cinet.es). Metro Arc de Triomf/ bus 39, 40, 41, 42, 51, 141. **Open** 9am-2pm, 4-7pm, Mon-Fri. **Map** E5.

Internet service provider who can connect you directly or via a phone company data system. Also consultancy services.

Data Rent

C/Muntaner 492, 5° 4ª (93 434 00 26/fax 93 418 78 83). FGC Pàdua/ bus 16, 58, 64, 74. **Open** *Oct-June* 9am-2pm, 4-7pm, Mon-Fri; *July-Sept* 8am-3pm Mon-Fri. **Map** C2.
PCs and laptops, printers and presentation equipment for hire.

Microrent

C/Provença 385-387, 3°,1ª (93 459 26 86/fax 93 459 09 79). Metro Verdaguer/bus 15, 55. **Open** 9am-2pm, 4-7pm, Mon-Fri; *July-mid Sept* 8am-3pm Mon-Fri. **No credit cards. Map** E4.
Computer equipment of all kinds for rent: PCs, Macs, laptops, peripherals, faxes and photocopiers.

Consulates

A full list of consulates in Barcelona is in the phone book under *Consolats/Consulados*. Outside office hours most have answerphones that give an emergency contact number. For more on what to do if you lose a passport, *see page 294.*

Consulates

American Consulate *Passeig Reina Elisenda 23 (93 280 22 27/fax 93 205 52 06). FGC Reina Elisenda/bus 22, 64, 75.* **Open** 9am-12.30pm, 3-5pm, Mon-Fri. **Map** A1
Australian Consulate *Gran Via Carles III 98 (93 330 94 96/fax 93 411 09 04). Metro Maria Cristina/ bus 59, 70, 72.* **Open** 10am-noon Mon-Fri. Closed Aug. **Map** A2-3
British Consulate *Avda Diagonal 477 (93 419 90 44/93 405 24 11). Bus all routes to Plaça Francesc Macià.* **Open** *end Sept-mid-June* 9.30am-1.30pm, 4-5pm, Mon-Fri; *mid-June-mid-Sept* 9am-2pm Mon-Fri.* **Map** C3
Canadian Consulate *Passeig de Gràcia 77 (93 215 07 04/fax 93 487 91 17). Metro Passeig de Gràcia/bus 7, 16, 17, 20, 22, 24, 28, 43, 44.* **Open** 10am-noon Mon-Fri. **Map** D4
Irish Consulate *Gran Via Carles III 94 (93 491 50 21/ fax 93 411 29 21). Metro Maria Cristina/bus 59, 70, 72.* **Open** 10am-1pm Mon-Fri. **Map** A3
New Zealand Consulate *Travessera de Gràcia 64(93 209 03 99/fax 93 202 08 90). FGC Gràcia/ bus 16, 17, 27, 31, 32, 58, 64.* **Open** 9.30am-1.30pm, 4.30-7.30pm, Mon-Fri; *July, Aug* closed Fri afternoon. **Map** C3

Courier services

Estació d'Autobusos Barcelona-Nord

C/Ali Bei 80 (93 232 43 29). Metro Arc de Triomf/bus all routes to Arc de Triomf. **Open** 7am-7.45pm Mon-Fri; 7am-12.45pm Sat. **No credit cards. Map** E5
Inexpensive service at the bus station for sending parcels on scheduled buses to towns within Spain.

Missatgers Trèvol

C/de la Verneda 18 (93 266 07 70). Metro Clot/bus 33, 43, 44, 92. **Open** 8am-7pm Mon-Fri. **No credit cards.**
Bike-based courier company, which also has motorbikes and vans. Price for delivering a 2kg package by fast bike within the central area is 430-495ptas, plus IVA (15% more, non-account holders). Non-urgent deliveries are cheaper.

UPS

C/Miguel Hernández, corner of C/Industria, Polígon Industrial Zona Franca, L'Hospitalet de Llobregat (freephone 900 10 24 10/fax 93 263 39 09). **Open** 7am-8pm Mon-Fri. **Credit** AmEx, MC, V.
Reliable international couriers. Call by 5pm for pick-up at your door by 7pm and next-day delivery. The city depot is at Avda Diagonal 511 (open 8.30am-8.30pm Mon-Fri); parcels dropped there before 7.30pm leave that evening.

Disabled travellers

Transport facilities and access in general for the disabled still leave a lot to be desired, despite steady improvements. For wheelchair users, buses and taxis are usually the best public transport options. There is a special transport information phoneline (*see page 288*), and transport maps, available from transport information offices (*see page 283*), indicate wheelchair access points and adapted bus routes.

New museums like the **MACBA** have good access, but the process of converting older buildings is slow and difficult – the Picasso Museum, for example, now has a lift, but still has internal stairs as well. Phoning ahead before a visit is always a good idea even if a building is listed as accessible to disabled people; this may depend, for example, on getting a lift key in advance.

Thanks to ONCE (Spain's lottery-funded organisation for the blind) more has been done on behalf of blind and partially sighted people. Most street crossings in the city centre are identifiable by knobbled paving, and low kerbs.

Institut Municipal de Persones amb Disminució *C/Llacuna 161 3r (93 291 84 00/fax 93 291 84 09). Metro Glòries/bus 56, 60, 92.* **Office hours** 8am-8pm Mon-Fri; *mid-June-mid-Sept* 9am-3pm Mon-Fri. The city's organisation for the disabled has information on building access (theatres, museums, restaurants, and more) and other facilities.

Transport information for the disabled *(93 486 07 52/fax 93 486 07 53)*. **Open** 9am-9pm Mon-Fri; 9am-3pm Sat. *Aug* closed Sat. English-speakers sometimes available; if not, call the 010 information line.

Buses

All **Aerobús** buses from the airport and most on the **Bus Turístic** route are fully accessible to wheelchair users. Similar fully adapted buses also alternate with standard buses on about a third of daytime city routes and all *Nitbus* services – currently 7, 9, 10, 14, 17, 19, 20, 22, 24, 27, 30, 32, 33, 34, 41, 44, 47, 54, 56, 57, 59, 63, 64, 65, 67, 68, 72, 74, 78, 96, 212, B20, B21, B22, B25, B28; night buses N0-N15, EN, 53N.

Metro & FGC

Access is limited. Only line 2 (Paral.lel-La Pau) has lifts and ramps at all stations; some line 1 stations have lifts. FGC stations at Provença, Muntaner and Av Tibidabo are accessible, as are many FGC stops further out of town: Sant Cugat, Sabadell and others.

RENFE trains

Sants, França, Passeig de Gràcia and Plaça Catalunya stations are accessible to wheelchairs, but the trains are not. If you can get through to RENFE (information 93 490 02 02), a ramp or help on the platform can be arranged.

Taxis

All taxi drivers are officially required to transport wheelchairs (and guide dogs) for no extra charge, but their cars can be inconveniently small, and in practice the willingness of drivers to cooperate varies widely. Special minibus taxis adapted for wheelchairs can be ordered from two companies: **Barnataxi** (93 357 77 55) and **Taxi Ràdio Móvil** (93 358 11 11); say you want a *Taxi Amic* when ordering. Fares are the same as for standard cabs, but the numbers of such taxis in Barcelona are limited, so call well in advance to get one for a specific time.

Emergencies

All services are on call 24 hours daily.
For information on police forces, *see p293.*
Ambulance/*Ambulància 061/93 300 20 20.*
Fire Service/
Bombers/Bomberos 080.
Municipal Police/*Policia Municipal 092.*
National Police/*Policia Nacional 091.*
Catalan Government Police/*Mossos d'Esquadra 93 300 22 96/93 300 91 91.*

Guardia Civil 062.

Emergency repairs

All lines are open 24 hours daily; *900* numbers are freephone lines. Which electricity company you need to call will be shown on your electricity meter.
Electricity: *Enher/ Hidroelèctrica de Catalunya 900 77 00 77; Fecsa 900 74 74 74.*
Gas/*Gas Natural 900 75 07 50.*
Water/*Aigües de Barcelona 93 265 11 11.*

Health

All visitors can obtain emergency health care through the local public health service (*Servei Català de la Salut*, often just referred to as the *Seguretat Social/Seguridad Social*). EU nationals are entitled to basic medical attention for free if they have an E111 form (if you can get an E111 sent or faxed within four days, you are still exempt from charges). Many medicines will be charged for. In non-emergency situations short-term visitors will usually find it quicker to use private travel insurance rather than the state system. Similarly, non-EU nationals with private medical insurance can also make use of state health services on a paying basis, but other than in emergencies it will usually be simpler to use a private clinic.

If you are a resident registered with the *Seguretat Social* (*see page 290*) you will be allocated a doctor and a local health clinic. Information on health services is available from the 010 line (*see page 295*).

Emergencies

In a medical emergency the best thing to do is go to the casualty (*Urgències*) department of any of the main public hospitals. All those listed are open 24 hours daily. In the central area, go to the **Clínic** or the **Perecamps**. If necessary, call an ambulance on **061**.

Hospitals

Centre d'Urgències Perecamps *Avda Drassanes 13-15 (93 441 06 00). Metro Drassanes/ bus 14, 36, 38, 57, 59, 64, 91, 157, N6, N9, N12.* **Map** C6/A4
Near the Rambla, this clinic specialises in primary attention for injuries and less serious emergencies.
Hospital Clínic *C/Villarroel 170 (93 227 54 00). Metro Hospital Clínic/bus 14, 31, 38, 54, 59, 63, 66, N3, N12.* **Map** C4
The main city-centre hospital, in the Eixample. The Clinic also has a first-aid centre for less serious emergencies two blocks away at C/València 184 (93 451 79 22). **Open** 8am-9pm Mon-Fri.
Hospital de la Creu Roja de Barcelona *C/Dos de Maig 301 (93 433 15 51). Metro Hospital de Sant Pau/bus 15, 19, 20, 25, 35, 45, 47, 50, 51, 92, N1, N4, N7.* **Map** F4
Hospital del Mar *Passeig Marítim (93 221 10 10). Metro Ciutadella/bus 45, 57, 59, 157, N8.* **Map** E7
Hospital de la Santa Creu i Sant Pau *C/Sant Antoni Maria Claret 167 (93 291 90 00). Metro Hospital de Sant Pau/bus 15, 19, 20, 45, 47, 50, 51, N1, N4.* **Map** F3

Local clinics (*Centres d´Assistència Primària*)

A CAP is a lower-level local health centre where you can be seen by a doctor and, if necessary, sent on to a hospital. They are open 8am-9pm Mon-Fri; 9am-5pm Sat.
Central area:
Raval/Plaça Universitat *C/Torres i Amat 8 (93 301 24 82/93 301 24 24). Metro Universitat/bus all routes to Plaça Universitat.* **Map** C5/A1

Raval/Drassanes *Avda Drassanes 17-21 (93 329 44 95/93 329 39 12). Metro Drassanes/bus 14, 36, 38, 57, 59, 64, 91, 157.* **Map** C6/A4
La Ribera *C/Rec Comtal 24 (93 310 14 21/310 50 98). Metro Arc de Triomf/bus 39, 40, 41, 42, 51, 141.* **Map** E6/C2
Esquerra de l'Eixample *C/Manso 19 (93 325 28 00). Metro Poble Sec/bus 13, 38, 57, 157.* **Map** B5
Vila Olímpica *C/Joan Miró 17 (93 221 37 85). Metro Ciutadella-Vila Olímpica/bus 14, 41, 71, 92.* **Map** F6

Private health care

Centre Mèdic Assistencial Catalonia (Dr Frances Lynd)
C/Provença 281, baixos (93 215 37 93). Metro Diagonal, FGC Provença/bus 6, 7, 15, 16, 17, 22, 24, 28, 33, 34, 39, 100, 101. **Open** 8am-8pm Mon-Fri. **Credit** V. **Map** D4
Dr Lynd is a British doctor who has practised in Barcelona for many years. She is at this surgery 3.30-6.30pm Wed; at other times, call for an appointment and she will ring you back.

Dr Mary McCarthy
C/Aribau 215, pral 1ª (93 200 29 24/mobile 607 220 040). FGC Gràcia/bus 27, 31, 32, 58, 64. **Open** by appointment. **No credit cards.** **Map** C3
An internal medicine specialist from the US; she also treats general patients.

AIDS/HIV

Spain's HIV infection rate is falling, but is still among the highest in the EU. Many local chemists take part in a needle-exchange and condom-distribution programme for intravenous drug users. For the AIDS (*SIDA*) information phoneline, *see right*.

Alternative medicine

Centre de Medicina Integral
Plaça Urquinaona 2, 3er 2na (93 318 30 50). Metro Urquinaona/bus all routes to Plaça Urquinaona. **Open** *information* 10am-1pm, 4-8pm, Mon-Fri. Closed Aug. **Map** D5/**B1**
Acupuncture, homeopathy, chiropractics and several other forms of complementary medicine are available at this clinic. There are some English-speaking practitioners on the staff.

Contraception & women's health

Women's health programmes are run in most CAPs (*see left*). Condoms (*condons/condones*) and other forms of contraception are available in all pharmacies. Condom vending machines can also be found in the toilets of many night-time bars and clubs, and in petrol stations.

Specialised clinics
Ambulatori les Drassanes/ Centre de Planificació Familiar *Avda Drassanes 17-21 (93 329 44 95). Metro Drassanes/bus 14, 36, 38, 57, 59, 64, 91, 157.* **Open** 9am-2pm Mon-Fri. **Map** C6/A4
Specialised family planning clinic within the large Drassanes CAP, but run separately by an all-women staff.
Centre Jove d'Anticoncepció i Sexualitat *C/La Granja 19-21 (93 415 10 00). Metro Lesseps/bus 24, 31, 32, 74.* **Open** *approx Oct-May* 10am-7pm Mon; noon-7pm Tue-Thur; 10am-2pm Fri; *June-Sept* 10am-5pm Mon-Thur; 10am-2pm Fri. Closed Easter, Aug. **Map** E2
A family planning centre aimed at young women with very friendly staff and a tolerant attitude towards social security status and residency papers.

Dentists

Not covered by EU reciprocal agreements, so private rates, which can be costly, apply.

Centre Odontològic de Barcelona
C/Calàbria 251, baixos (93 439 45 00). Metro Entença/bus 41, 54. **Open** 9am-9pm Mon-Fri; 9am-2pm Sat; *Aug* 9am-1pm, 3pm-8pm, Mon-Fri. **Credit** DC, MC, V. **Map** B4
Well-equipped clinics providing a complete range of dental services. Several of the staff speak English. **Branch:** Institut Odontològic de la Sagrada Família *C/Sardenya 319, baixos (93 457 04 53). Metro Sagrada Família/bus 10, 19, 33, 34, 43, 44, 50, 51, 101.* **Open** 9am-1pm, 3-8pm, Mon-Fri. **Map** F4

Pharmacies

Pharmacies, *farmàcies*, are signalled by large green or red crosses, often in flashing neon, and are plentiful throughout the city. They are normally open 9am to 1.30pm, 4.30 to 8pm, Monday to Friday, and 9am to 1.30pm on Saturdays.

At other times a duty rota operates: every pharmacy has a list of *farmàcies de guàrdia* (duty pharmacies) for that day posted outside the door. Those listed as *diürn*, marked in **green**, are open all day 9am-10pm (sometimes only till 1.30pm on Sundays); those in the *nocturn* list (marked **red**) are open all night 10pm-9am, and often for the full 24 hours. This list is also given in local newspapers, and on the 010 and 098 phonelines. Note that at night duty pharmacies often appear to be closed, and it's necessary to knock on the shutters to be served.

A growing number of city pharmacies also keep extended hours all year round.

Out-of-hours pharmacies
Farmàcia Vilar *(93 490 92 07). Metro Sants-Estació/bus all services to Sants-Estació.* **Open** 7am-10.30pm Mon-Fri; 8am-10.30pm Sat, Sun, public holidays.
In the vestibule of Sants train station. The following pharmacies are all open 24 hours, every day of the year.
Farmàcia Alvarez *Passeig de Gràcia 26 (93 302 11 24). Metro Passeig de Gràcia/bus 7, 16, 17, 22, 24, 28, N4, N6.* **Map** D5
Farmàcia Cervera *C/Muntaner 254 (93 200 29 57). FGC Gràcia/bus 6, 7, 15, 27, 32, 33, 34, 58, 64, N8.* **Map** C3
Farmàcia Clapés *La Rambla 98 (93 301 28 43). Metro Liceu/bus 14, 38, 59, 91, N9, N12.* **Map** D6/**A3**
Farmàcia Laguna *C/Provença 459 (93 455 12 05). Metro Sagrada Família/bus 10, 19, 33, 34, 43, 44, 50, 51, 101, N1, N7, N9.* **Map** F4

AIDS Helpline
(900 21 22 22). **Open** 9am-5.30pm, *June-mid Sept* 8am-3pm, Mon-Fri.
Official health service freephone line, with some English-speaking staff.

Alcoholics Anonymous
(93 317 77 77). **Open** 11am-1pm, 5-8pm, Mon-Fri; 7-9pm Sat, Sun; answerphone at other times.
There are several English-speakers among the local AA groups.

Telèfon de l'Esperança
(93 414 48 48). **Open** 24 hours daily.
Privately-funded local helpline that caters for a wide range of needs, from psychiatric to legal. English sometimes spoken, but not guaranteed.

Living & working in Barcelona

Barcelona's many pleasures attract ever-growing numbers of foreign residents and working visitors. Not many from developed countries, though, are drawn here just by filthy lucre – sometimes the reverse is the case, for Barcelona can be a difficult place to find well-paying work, and yet is still a not-too-painful place to live (relatively) cheaply.

A great many foreigners, however – especially from EU countries –, have found niches in Barcelona in the last decade. Many are brought by companies, or have a job lined up before arriving; this is more and more possible, if you have a specialist skill. In general, of course, employability also depends on Spanish (and sometimes Catalan) language ability.

Other common recourses for English-speakers are tourist-sector jobs (often seasonal and outside the city), translation, and language teaching – probably still the best chance of finding work quickly. For the typical October-June contract in a school, a recognised English-teaching qualification is near-essential (*see page 298* for teaching centres). There is also demand for private classes, for which a serious teacher can ask at least 2,000ptas/hour; due to the sheer number of people offering classes, though, there is steady downward pressure on rates. Prime places to advertise are the **Escola Oficial d'Idiomes** (*see page 298*), and **Come In** bookshop (*see chapter* **Shopping**). Also, talk to established teachers or schools, who often receive enquiries about private classes.

With undeclared, under-the-table wage payment still quite common in Spain, some people manage to ignore the complicated process of becoming formally resident, but this becomes very limiting after a while, even if you're lucky enough not to get caught. Free advice can be had from the union-run **Centre d'Informació per a Treballadors Extrangers**, (*see right*); many, however, find it worthwhile to pay for a *gestor*, a combination of lawyer, consultant and accountant who can sometimes show a path through bureaucratic tangles. For *gestories, see page 296*.

Getting legal

Spain's *ley de extranjería*, the 'law of foreign-ness', is currently being redrafted, but things are unlikely to change much before 2001. The Interior Ministry has a freephone for immigration enquiries, 900 15 00 00, and some information is on their website, *www.mir.es*

EU citizens

All EU citizens have the right to live, work and study in Spain, but must become legally resident if they stay for more than three months. If you have a job or study course lined up, you are ready to make an appointment to present your residency application. In Barcelona, you do this at the foreigners' office (*Oficina de Extranjeros*) at the **Delegación del Gobierno** (*see right*). They will give you a date several weeks away, so it's best to make the appointment straight away by phone on *93 482 05 60* (8am-3pm Mon-Fri; often engaged, but persist). You will also need to get down to the Delegación a little later to queue up for your application forms. Be sure to also pick up the list saying exactly what other documents you need to bring to your interview.

If you are going to work as an employee (*trabajador de cuenta ajena*), you will need to present a work contract, which can be part-time and of no fixed duration. Other necessities: your passport; three passport photos; a receipt to show you have paid a fee into a government bank account (around 1,000ptas); and possibly some other documents, such as proof of address, a medical certificate and evidence of suffcient funds. Take originals and photocopies of all documents (especially copies of the information pages of your passport) to the interview. The residency card, normally valid for five years for EU citizens and automatically renewable, will take more long weeks to come through.

A self-employed person (*trabajador autónomo* or *trabajador de cuenta propia*), has to attend to some other matters before presenting his or her application – basically tax-related – and on these the help and advice of a *gestor* is almost indispensable. First of all you need to get a tax number or *NIF* (*Número de Identificación Fiscal*), essential if you're going to do any consistent business. For foreigners, this is the same as the *NIE* (*Número de Identificación de Extranjero*) that will later appear on your residency card; ask for a *NIF/NIE* at the Delegación del Gobierno. Then, take your number to the nearest office of Hacienda, the tax department (in the phone book). At the *Actividades Económicas* desk fill in forms 845, specifying the sector you wish to work in, and 036, the *Declaración Censal*, and keep copies of both.

Thirdly, visit the local Social Security office (*Delegació de Seguritat Social*) to say you want the *alta como autónomo* – meaning that you are about to start working (and paying contributions) as a freelance; the payments

Holidays

On public holidays (*festes/fiestas*) virtually all shops, banks and offices, and many bars and restaurants, are closed. Public transport runs a Sunday service,

or a very limited service on Christmas and New Year's Day; some museums are open, but for shorter-than-usual hours. When a holiday falls on a Tuesday or Thursday, some people take the intervening day before or after

the weekend off as well, in a long weekend called a *pont/puente* (bridge). Few offices now close the whole of Easter Week, but activity diminishes greatly from the Wednesday on. For more on city festivals, *see pages 5-12*.

demanded can be huge, and here particularly a *gestor* can often give money-saving advice. If you've done all this you're ready to present your residency application, with the same other documentation (passport and so on) as in a *cuenta ajena* case (*see left*).

Non-EU citizens

While there's still red tape for EU citizens moving to Spain, things are in another league for people from outside the Union. White-skinned foreigners from developed countries face much less police hassle than Africans or Asians, but if your papers are not in order, it only takes one unexpected encounter with the law and you could find yourself on a plane; deportations do happen.

Officially, non-EU residency applicants need to enter Spain with a special visa, for which you must apply at a Spanish consulate in your home country, although if you're in Spain you can start the ball rolling – later you'll need to make at least one trip home. With this need for travel and the length of the process (up to a year), good legal advice is essential. The magic document required is a contract or firm offer of work from a registered Spanish company. This is then presented to the consulate back home, along with (usually) a medical certificate, a certificate of good conduct from your local police force, translated copies of relevant qualifications, your passport and some photos. Your application is passed to Madrid, and if approved, the consulate will issue your special visa. If you apply to work freelance or start your own business procedures are slightly different and you will also be asked for proof of income. Once back in Spain you apply for residency in the same way as EU citizens, but you'll only get a one year residency card at first; each subsequent renewal will be a year longer.

Recognition of qualifications

Professionals who need their qualification in order to work should check on whether it is recognised in Spain. If not, the ratification process or *homologación* can take months.

Students

Students who stay in Spain over three months, including EU nationals, also officially require a residence permit, and those enrolled on full-time courses might find it creates difficulties if they do not get one. To do so, you will need to show the Delegación del Gobierno a confirmation of enrolment on a recognised course; confirmation of income for the duration of the course (estimated at around 800,000ptas for a year); and confirmation of health insurance status, private or public.

Delegación del Gobierno – Oficina de Extranjeros

Avda Marqués de l'Argentera 2 (93 482 05 44/appointments 93 482 05 60). Metro Barceloneta/bus 14, 17, 39, 40, 45, 51, 100. **Open** 9am-2pm Mon-Fri. *Appointments phone* 8am-3pm Mon-Fri. **Map** D-E6/C4

Often still referred to by many people by its historic title as the *Gobierno Civil*. There are various queues; make sure you're in the right one before you start. Shorter waits on Fridays.

Centre d'Informació per a Treballadors Extrangers

Avda Paral.lel 202 (93 202 40 77). Metro Espanya/bus 13, 38, 50, 57, 65, 91, 141, 157. **Open** 10am-2pm Mon, Wed, Thur; 4-7pm Tue. **Map** B5

Run by the *Comissions Obreres* trade union, this centre gives free advice and guidance to immigrants on work and residency issues. You have to queue here too, but at least there's some real help at the end of the wait.

Renting a flat

Property prices boomed in Barcelona in the late '90s, but rental costs, surprisingly, remained relatively stable. Good places to look for flats are *La Vanguardia* (under *alquileres*), and the small-ad magazines (*see chapter* **Media**), but be aware that many ads are placed by agencies, who charge a (sometimes exploitative) fee for access to their (sometimes unreliable) listings. Look out too just for signs headed *es lloga* or *se alquila* in apartment-block doorways.

Individual rental contracts (*contracte de lloguer/contrato de alquiler*) between you and your landlord can vary a great deal, and before signing it's important to be clear on the exact conditions in the contract, particularly regarding responsibility for repairs; if in doubt, have it checked by a *gestor*. The city council's consumer information office recommends one-year contracts; by law they will be automatically extendable to five years' rental, during which the landlord cannot ask you to leave, and can only raise the rent each year in line with inflation as measured by the retail price index, (*Índice de Precios de Consumo, IPC*). For residents rent paid is tax-deductible, provided you have all the necessary receipts.

Oficina Municipal d'Informació al Consumidor

C/Ferran 34 (93 402 77 30). Metro Liceu/bus 14, 38, 59, 91. **Open** 9am-2pm Mon, Wed, Fri; 9am-2pm, 4-6pm, Tue, Thur. *July-Sept* mornings only. **Map** D6/B3

This Ajuntament office can answer queries about rental contracts, as well as other consumer matters.

Usual official holidays include: **New Year's Day (Cap d'Any)** 1 January; **Three Kings (Día de Reis)** 6 January; **Good Friday (Divendres Sant); Easter Monday (Pasqua Florida); May Day (Festa del Treball)** 1 May; **Whit Monday (Dilluns de Pasqua Granada);**

Saint John/ Midsummer's Day (Sant Joan) 24 June; **The Assumption (L'Assumpció)** 15 August; **Catalan National Day (Diada Nacional de Catalunya)** 11 September; **Our Lady of Mercy (La Mercè)** 24 September; **Discovery of America (Día de la Hispanitat)**

12 October; **All Saints' Day (Tots Sants)** 1 November; **Constitution Day (Día de la Constitució)** 6 December; **Immaculate Conception (La Immaculada)** 8 December; **Christmas (Nadal)** 25 December; **Boxing Day (Sant Esteve)** 26 December.

Libraries

Barcelona has over 20 public libraries; call 010 for the address of the nearest. Some have children's sections, novels in English, and Internet access.

Ateneu Barcelonès

C/Canuda 6 (93 318 86 34). Metro Catalunya/bus all routes to Plaça Catalunya. **Open** 9am-10.45pm daily. **Map** D5/**A2**
This venerable cultural and philosophical society has the best private library in the city, open nearly every day of the year, plus a deliciously peaceful interior garden patio and bar. Initial membership costs 20,000ptas (payable in instalments), and the subsequent fee is 2,100ptas per month.

Biblioteca de Catalunya

C/Hospital 56 (93 317 07 78). Metro Liceu/bus 14, 38, 59. **Open** 9am-8pm Mon-Fri; 9am-2pm Sat. **Map** C6/**A2**
The largest of the city's libraries, the Catalan national collection, housed in the medieval **Hospital de la Santa Creu** and with a wonderful stock reaching back centuries. Reader's cards are required, but one-day research visits are allowed (take your passport). The library has Net terminals, and the catalogue is on-line (*www.gencat.es/bc*). On the ground floor is the city's most central public library, the **Biblioteca de Sant Pau i Santa Creu**.

British Council/ Institut Britànic

C/Amigó 83 (93 241 97 11). FGC Muntaner/bus 14, 58, 64. **Open** *Oct-June* 9.30am-9pm Mon-Fri; 10.30am-1.30pm Sat; *July, Sept* 9.30am-2pm Mon-Fri, 4-8.30pm, Mon-Thur. Closed Aug-early Sept. **Map** C2-3
UK press, English books, satellite TV and a big multi-media section oriented towards language learning. Access is free; borrowing cost 8,000ptas a year (16,000ptas, Net access included).

Institut d'Estudis Nord-americans/Institute of North American Studies

Via Augusta 123 (93 240 28 58). FGC Sant Gervasi/bus 14, 58, 64. **Open** 11am-2pm, 4-9pm, Mon-Fri. **Map** C2
Down the road from the British Council, the IEN library is a trans-Atlantic equivalent, but is members-only, just to go in; members can borrow materials as well (5,000ptas a year, take a photo).

Institut Municipal d'Història/Ca de l'Ardiaca

C/Santa Llúcia 1 (93 318 11 95). Metro Liceu, Jaume I/bus 17, 19, 40, 45. **Open** 9am-8.45pm Mon-Fri; 9am-1pm Sat. *Aug* 9am-7.30pm Mon-Fri. **Map** D6/**B2-3**

The city newspaper archive, with extensive document and book collections as well. It occupies the Ca de l'Ardiaca in front of the Cathedral, with one of the prettiest patios in the Barri Gòtic. Reader's cards are required, for which you need two photos and 200ptas, but one-day visits are permitted.

Mediateca

Centre Cultural de la Fundació la Caixa, Passeig de Sant Joan 108 (93 458 89 07). Metro Verdaguer/bus 6, 15, 33, 34, 55. **Open** 11am-8pm Tue-Fri; 11am-3pm Sat. Closed Aug. **Map** E4
A high-tech art, music and media library in the arts centre of Fundació la Caixa, housed in a *Modernista* mansion by Puig i Cadafalch (*see chapter* **Art Galleries**). This remarkable facility lets you explore the latest technologies (CD-Rom, Internet), watch satellite TV or videos, listen to (and borrow) CDs, check out contemporary art slides, and browse among a whole array of print and non-print references on contemporary culture. Most materials are open-access; borrowing rights cost 1,000ptas (for ever), for which you will need to show your ID or passport. A *User Guide* in English is available. *Website: www.lacaixa.es/fundacio*

Lost property

Airport & rail stations

If you lose something land-side of check-in at Prat Airport, report the loss immediately to the *Aviación Civil* office in the relevant terminal, or call airport information on 93 298 38 38. There is no central lost property depot for the RENFE rail network: if you think you have mislaid anything on a train, look for the *Atención al Viajero* desk or *Jefe de Estación* office at the nearest main station to where your property has gone astray, or call ahead to the destination station of the train. To get information by phone on lost property at main rail stations call their general information numbers and ask for *Objetos Perdidos*.

Municipal lost property office

Servei de Troballes *Ajuntament, C/Ciutat 9 (93 402 31 61). Metro Jaume I/bus 17, 19, 40, 45.* **Open** 9am-2pm Mon-Fri. **Map** D6/**B3**
All items found on public transport and taxis in the city, or picked up by the police in the street, should eventually find their way to this office, with an entrance on the C/Ciutat side of the city hall. Within 24 hours of the loss you can also try ringing the city transport authority (93 318 70 74), or for taxis, the Institut Metropolità del Taxi (93 223 40 12).

Money

Euro? What euro? Although the new common European currency is already the official monetary unit of Spain, and euro-prices appear on many receipts next to the old ones, until 1 January 2002 the only notes and coins in circulation will be Spanish *pesetas*, the usual abbreviation for which is *ptas* (*pesseta, ptes*, in Catalan). There are coins for 1, 5, 10, 25, 50, 100, 200 and 500 pesetas. A 5ptas coin is called a *duro*. Notes begin with the green 1,000ptas, and continue through 2,000 (red), 5,000 (brown) and 10,000ptas (blue).

The 11 euro-zone currencies have fixed exchange rates with the euro and one another; one euro equals 166.386ptas. The big changeover will come in the first half of 2002, when euro notes and coins will circulate alongside the old currencies. After 30 June 2002, your pesetas, marks, punts and so on will be worthless. For euro-information in Spain, call 901 11 20 02 or 902 44 15 44.

Banks & foreign exchange

Banks and savings banks readily accept travellers' cheques (you must show your passport), but are less keen to take personal cheques with a Eurocheque guarantee card. Commission rates vary a good deal, and it's worth shopping around before changing money. Given the rates charged by Spanish banks, the cheapest way to obtain money is often through an ATM machine with a credit card rather than with travellers' cheques, despite the fees charged for cash withdrawals. It is always quicker and more trouble-free to change money at larger bank offices rather than at local branches.

Bank hours

Banks are normally open 8.30am-2pm Mon-Fri, and from 1 Oct to 30 Apr most branches also open 8.30am-1pm Sat. Hours vary a little between banks: some open slightly earlier or later. Savings banks (*Caixes d'Estalvis/Cajas de*

Ahorros), which offer the same exchange facilities as banks, open 8am-2pm Mon-Fri, and from Oct to May they also open 4.30-7.45pm Thur. They never open on Saturday. Banks and *caixes* are closed on public holidays.

Out-of-hours services

Outside normal hours there are bank exchange offices open at the **airport** (Terminals A and B, open 7am-11pm daily) and **Barcelona-Sants station** (open 8am-10pm daily). There's a private bureau de change (*cambio*) at the **Estació d'Autobusos Barcelona-Nord** (open 8.30am-10pm Mon-Fri; 8.30am-4pm Sat, Sun), and many more in the city centre. Some in the Rambla are open until midnight, or 3am in July-Sept. *Cambios* do not charge commission, but their exchange rates are usually less favourable than bank rates. At the airport, Sants and outside some banks there are automatic cash exchange machines that accept notes in major currencies, so long as they are in good condition.

American Express

C/Rosselló 261 (93 217 00 70). Metro Diagonal/bus 22, 24, 28, 33, 34. **Open** 9.30am-6pm Mon-Fri; 10am-noon Sat. **Map** D4
All the usual AmEx services, and an ATM for AmEx cards. 24-hour money transfers anywhere in the world (charges paid by the sender).
Branch: *La Rambla 74 (93 301 11 66).* **Open** *Oct-Mar* 9am-8.30pm Mon-Fri; 10am-2pm, 3-7pm, Sat. *Apr-Sept* 9am-midnight daily.

Western Union Money Transfer

Loterías Manuel Martín *La Rambla 41 (93 412 70 41). Metro Drassanes/bus 14, 38, 59, 91.* **Open** 9.30am-midnight Mon-Sat; 10am-midnight Sun. **Map** C-D6/**A3**
The quickest, if not the cheapest, way of having money sent from abroad.
Branches: Mail Boxes *C/València 214 (93 454 69 83).* **Open** 9am-2pm, 4.30-8pm, Mon-Fri; closes earlier in Aug; also at Avda Meridiana 316.

Credit cards

Major credit and charge cards are widely accepted in hotels, shops, restaurants and many other services (including Metro ticket machines, and pay-and-display parking machines in the street). With major cards you can also withdraw cash from most bank cash machines, which provide instructions in different languages at the push of a button. Exchange rates and handling fees are often more

favourable than with cash or travellers' cheque transactions. Banks also advance cash against a credit card, but prefer you to use the machine.

Card Emergencies

All lines have English-speaking staff and are open 24 hours daily.
American Express *(card emergencies 91 519 60 00/travellers' cheques freephone 900 99 44 26).*
Diner's Club *(93 467 01 45/24-hour helpline 91 547 40 00).*
MasterCard *(900 97 12 31).*
Visa *(91 519 60 00).*

Police & street crime

There are two sides to street crime in Barcelona: on the one hand, the general atmosphere on the street is relaxed, and violent crime still uncommon. On the other hand, bag-snatching and pickpocketing are a problem, with tourists the prime target. The constant increase in visitor numbers in the last few years has also been accompanied by a (relative) increase in street crime, after years in which it had stabilised or fallen in frequency. Favourite spots for thieves are the Rambla, Barri Gòtic and the old town in general; public transport, especially the Metro; and, sometimes, quieter areas such as Parc Güell or the beach.

Most street robberies, though, are aimed very much at the unwary, and could be avoided with a few simple, common-sense precautions:
• Whenever you put your bag or coat down in a public place, indoors or out, keep it right in front of you, clearly visible to you but inaccessible to passers-by. When sitting in a café, especially outdoors, **never** leave a bag on the back of a chair, on the floor or on a chair where you cannot see it clearly. If in doubt, keep it on your lap.
• In crowded spaces be aware, in a relaxed way, of people moving around you. Don't carry wallets or valuables in back pockets of trousers or backpacks. Keep shoulder bags closed, pulled to the front (not at your back) and keep a hand on the bag.
• Avoid pulling out big-denomination notes or bulging wallets in public places; try not to get stuck with large notes when changing money.
• Be aware that street thieves often work in pairs or groups: one may ask

you the time, or attempt to start a conversation, while his friend hovers behind you and then grabs your bag. This is often done very crudely, so it's not hard to recognise. Sudden requests to shake your hand, or 'helpful' passers-by who say you've got something spilt on your back and offer to clean it off, should likewise be ignored, as they may be part of the same game. A more subtle scam is that of the people (mostly other foreigners) who approach you speaking English, German or other suitable tongue, give you a hard-luck story about how they themselves have been ripped off, and ask for a loan of 6,000ptas or so which they will send you once they get back to Zurich, Amsterdam or wherever. They won't.

Police forces

Barcelona has several police forces. Most numerous are the local *Guàrdia Urbana*, who wear navy and pale blue, and are concerned with traffic, local regulations, and general law and order in the city. The *Policia Nacional*, in darker blue uniforms and white shirts (or blue combat-style gear) also patrol the street, and have primary responsibility for dealing with more serious crime. The Catalan government's police, the *Mossos d'Esquadra*, in navy and light blue with red trim, are gradually expanding their role, and during 2000 will begin to share responsiblity for traffic control in the city. A fourth body is the *Guardia Civil*, who wear military green, and watch over inter-city highways, customs posts, and some government buildings, but are not often seen within Barcelona.

ID checks

Passports or, for most EU residents, national identity cards are supposed to be carried at all times when you're in Spain, and police can ask to see your ID (*documentación*) at any time. 'Random' checks aimed at catching illegal immigrants are often made on an overtly racial basis, and people with black or brown skin may find themselves stopped while their pale-skinned friends are left alone. There's not a lot you can do about this, short term; carrying valid ID and producing it if requested is the best advice.

Reporting a crime

If you are robbed or attacked report the incident as soon as possible to the *Turisme-Atenció* station on the Rambla, a special police service to assist foreign visitors in difficulties. Officers on duty can speak French, German, Italian and English. If you report a crime you will be asked to make an official statement (*denuncia*). It is frankly unlikely that anything you have lost will be recovered, but you need the *denuncia* to make an insurance claim. At other times or in other areas report the incident to the nearest *Policía Nacional*

station (*Comisaria*), which will be listed in the phone book. For emergency phone numbers, *see p288*.
Turisme-Atenció *La Rambla 43 (93 301 90 60/93 317 70 16). Metro Liceu/bus 14, 38, 59, 91.* **Open** 7am-midnight Mon-Thur, Sun; 7am-2am Fri, Sat. **Map** D6/**A3**

Lost passports

The loss or theft of a passport must be reported immediately to the police and your national consulate (*see p287*). If you lose a passport over a weekend and have to travel immediately, consulates will charge for opening specially to issue an emergency passport. Spanish authorities and airlines may be prepared to let you out of the country without one if you do not look suspicious and have other documents, including a police *denuncia* confirming the loss of the passport, but in such cases it's advisable to be at the airport in plenty of time. You will also have to explain your situation at the other end.

Religious services

Anglican & Protestant

Saint George's Church *C/Horaci 38 (93 417 88 67). FGC Av Tibidabo/bus 14, 22, 64, 70, 72, 75.* **Main service** 11am Sun.
A British church with a multi-cultural congregation.

Catholic Mass in English

Parròquia Maria Reina *Carretera d'Esplugues 103 (information 93 203 41 15). Bus 63, 75, 78.* **English mass** 10am Sun. **Map** A1

Jewish

Sinagoga de Barcelona *C/Avenir 24 (93 200 61 48). FGC Gràcia/bus 14, 27, 32, 58, 64.* **Prayers** 7.30am Mon-Thur; 8am, 9pm Fri; 9am, 8.30pm Sat; 8.30am Sun. **Map** C3

Moslem

Centre Islàmic *Avda Meridiana 326 (93 351 49 01). Metro Sagrera/bus 62, 96.* **Prayers** 5-8pm daily; 2.45pm Fri.

Removals

AGS

C/Albert Einstein 21, Polígon Santa Margarida de Dos, Terrassa (902 10 08 08). **Open** 9am-2pm, 4-8pm, Mon-Fri. **No credit cards.**
Door-to-door service anywhere in the world, plus storage.

Gil Stauffer

C/Pau Claris 176 (93 215 55 55). Metro Diagonal/bus 6, 7, 16, 17, 22, 24, 28, 33, 34, 39. **Open** 9am-7pm Mon-Fri. **Credit** AmEx, V. **Map** D4
Reliable national and international movers with worldwide links.

Seasons & climate

Barcelona sees a lot of blue sky all year round, and temperatures are rarely extreme, although there can be surprises (midsummer downpours, or cold snaps in mid-spring).
Spring *Average temperatures 9-18ºC (48-64ºF).* Often the most unpredictable season, when warm sunny days alternate with cold winds and showers, but generally by Easter locals are casting off winter coats, and May is one of the most enjoyable of all times to be in Barcelona, warm enough to sit out through the night but never oppressive.
Summer *Average temperatures 18-27ºC (64-80ºF).* In early summer the weather is delicious, and Barcelona's street life is at its most vibrant. The real heat hits from late-July to mid-August; more of a problem than the temperature is humidity. Many locals escape the city altogether, leaving visitors to explore a tranquil, partly-closed Barcelona with an atmosphere of its own; the biggest event is the *Festa Major* in Gràcia. As August goes on there's more chance of thunderstorms – intense but refreshing.
Autumn *Average temperatures 13-21ºC (55-70ºF).* September weather is again beautiful, warm and fresh, although autumn is also the wettest season, with sporadic downpours. In October the weather can visibly 'break': temperatures drop, and there may be torrential storms. Pavement tables mostly go in by November, although some remain out all year.
Winter *Average temperatures 5-14ºC (41-57ºF).* Crisp winter sunshine is common, although where it doesn't reach the cold can be damp and penetrating. Snow is rare. A busy time for business and the arts, with major festivities at Christmas and Carnival.

Tipping

There are no fixed rules, nor any expectation of a set ten per cent or more, and many locals tip very little. It is common to leave around five per cent for a waiter in a restaurant, up to and rarely over 500ptas, and people may also leave something in a bar, maybe part or all of the small change, according to how much they have had and the level of service. It's also usual to tip hotel porters, and toilet attendants. In taxis, the usual tip is around five per cent, but more is given for longer journeys, or if the driver has helped with luggage.

Tourist information

The city council (*Ajuntament*) and Catalan government (the *Generalitat*) both run tourist information offices, and the City also has an efficient information service for local citizens that's useful to visitors. Information on what's on in music, theatre and so on is found in local papers and listings magazines (*see chapter* **Media**). For youth and student agencies, *see page 297*.
City tourist offices sell multi-journey transport tickets, tourist bus (*Bus Turístic*) tickets and the *Barcelona Card* discount card. For details, *see pages 58, 282*. City and Generalitat also have useful websites (in English).

Oficines d'Informació Turística

Main office *Plaça Catalunya (general info. 906 30 12 82/hotel info. 93 304 32 32). Metro Catalunya/bus all routes to Plaça Catalunya.*
Open 9am-9pm daily. **Map** D5/**B1**
The city tourist board (*Turisme de Barcelona*) main office is underground beneath the Corte Inglés side of the plaça (look for big red signs with *i* in white). It has a full information service, money exchange, a souvenir and book shop, a hotel booking service, and coin-in-slot Net access.
Branch offices: Plaça Sant Jaume (*in Ajuntament). Metro Jaume I/bus 17, 40, 45.* **Open** 10am-8pm Mon-Sat; 10am-2pm Sun, public holidays. Closed 25 Dec, 1 Jan. **Map** D6/**B3**
Barcelona-Sants station *Metro Sants-Estació/bus all routes to Sants-Estació.* **Open** *Oct-May* 8am-8pm Mon-Fri; 8am-2pm Sat, Sun, public holidays; *June-Sept* 8am-8pm daily. Closed 25 Dec, 26 Dec, 1 Jan. **Map** A4
Palau de Congressos (**Trade Fair office**) *Avda Reina Maria Cristina. Metro Espanya/bus all routes to Plaça d'Espanya.* **Open** during trade fairs only, hours variable. **Map** A-B5
Websites: City of Barcelona, www.bcn.es; City tourist authority, www.barcelonaturisme.com

Temporary office & 'Red Jackets'

Information Booth *located at Sagrada Família.* **Open** late June-late Sept 10am-8pm daily. **Map** F4
In summer *Turisme de Barcelona* opens this temporary booth (no hotel booking service). 'Red Jacket' information officers (in red uniforms) also roam the Barri Gòtic and Rambla, ready to field questions in a heroic variety of languages, 10am-8pm daily.

Palau Robert

*Palau Robert, Passeig de Gràcia 107
(93 238 40 00). Metro Diagonal/bus
6, 7, 16, 17, 22, 24, 28, 33, 34.*
Open 10am-7pm Mon-Sat; 10am-
2pm Sun. Closed public holidays.
Map D4

The Catalan government's lavishly-
equipped information centre is in the
Palau Robert, a grand mansion at the
junction of Passeig de Gràcia and the
Diagonal. It doesn't have as much on
Barcelona itself as City offices –
although it still has maps and other
essentials – but has a huge range of
information in different media on other
parts of Catalonia, activities and so on.
It also hosts interesting exhibitions on
different aspects of the country.
Branches: Airport Terminal A
(93 478 47 04). **Open** 9.30am-8pm
(mid-June-mid-Sept 9.30am-8.30pm)
Mon-Sat; 9.30am-3pm Sun.
Terminal B *(93 478 05 65).* **Open**
9.30am-8pm Mon-Sat. Both branches
close on some public holidays.
*Websites: Generalitat, www.gencat.es;
Palau Robert, www.gencat.es/probert*

Centre d'Informació de la Virreina

*Palau de la Virreina, La Rambla 99
(93 301 77 75). Metro Liceu/bus 14,
38, 59, 91.* **Open** 10am-2pm, 4-8pm,
Mon-Fri. *Ticket sales* 11am-7pm
Tue-Sat. **Map** D6/**A2**

Not a tourist office as such, but the
information office of the City culture
department, with details of exhibitions,
concerts, theatres and so on. Also the
best place to buy tickets for events in
the **Grec** summer festival *(see p9),*
and some other city-sponsored events
and venues. In the same building is the
Botiga de la Virreina bookshop,
which has a wide choice of books
on Barcelona, some of them in
English editions.

010 phoneline

Open 8am-10pm Mon-Sat.
City-run information line that's again
mainly aimed at local citizens, but does
an impeccable job of answering all
kinds of queries. Calls are taken in
French and English as well as Catalan
and Spanish, but you may have to wait
for an English-speaking operator. From
outside Barcelona, call 93 402 70 00.

Addresses

Most apartment addresses consist of a
street name followed by a number, floor
level, and flat number. So to go to
C/València 246, 2n 3a, find number 246;
go up to the *segon pis/segundo piso* –
second floor – and the *tercera porta/
puerta,* the third door. Ground-floor
flats are usually called *baixos* or *bajos*
(often abbreviated *bxs/bjos);* one floor
up is usually the *entresòl/entresuelo*
(*entl.),* and the next is often the *principal*
(*pral.).* Numbered floors start here, first,
second, up to the *àtic/ático* at the top.

Electricity

The standard current in Spain is today
220v. A diminishing number of old
buildings still have 125v circuits, and
it's advisable to check before using electrical equipment in old, cheap hotels.
Plugs are all of the two-round-pin type.
The 220v current works fine with
British-bought 240v products, with a
plug adaptor (available at **El Corte
Inglés**). With US 110v equipment you
will also need a current transformer.

Estancs/Estancos (tobacco shops)

The tobacco shop, usually known as an
estanc/estanco and identified by a
brown-and-yellow sign with the words
tabacs or *tabacos,* is a very important
Spanish institution. First and foremost,
as the sign suggests, they supply
cigarettes and every other kind of
tobacco, but they are also the main
places to buy postage stamps, as well
as many official forms demanded by
Spanish state bureaucracy in all kinds
of minor procedures. They also sell
sweets, postcards and phonecards.

Opening times

Most shops open 9/10am to 1-2pm and
4.30/5 to 8/9pm, Mon-Sat, but many do
not reopen on Saturday afternoons.
Markets open earlier, at 7/8am, and
most smaller ones are closed by 3pm.
Major stores, malls and a growing number of shops open all day, 10am-9pm,
Mon-Sat. Larger stores are also allowed
to open some Sundays and holidays,
mostly around Christmastime.

Staggered holidays are more
common these days, but many

restaurants and shops still close up for
all or part of August. Most (but not all)
museums are open at weekends, but
close one day each week, usually
Monday. They do not close in summer.
For restaurant times, *see p133.*

Public toilets

Not common: the main rail stations
have clean toilets, and in some
places there are pay-on-entry
cubicles that cost 25ptas. Generally,
when in need, you're best advised to
pop into a bar or café; proprietors
usually don't mind. Major stores or
fast food restaurants are, of course,
staple standbys.

Queuing

Catalans, like other Spaniards, have a
highly developed queuing culture. In
small shops and at market stalls
people may not stand in line, but they
are generally well aware of when it is
their turn. Common practice is to ask
when you arrive, to no one in
particular, *'Qui es l'últim/la última?'*
('Who's last?'); see who nods back at
you, and follow after them. Say *'jo'*
('me') to the next person who asks the
same question.

Smoking

People in Barcelona still smoke – a lot.
Non-smoking areas are rare in bars or
restaurants, although smoking bans in
cinemas, theatres and on trains are
generally respected. Smoking is
banned throughout the Metro and
FGC, but many people take this to
mean on trains only, not station
platforms. For places to buy tobacco,
see chapter **Shopping.**

Time

Local time is one hour ahead of British
time (changes to or from summer time
are now on the same nights). So, when
it's 6pm in Barcelona it's 5pm in
London and, usually, noon in New York.

Water

Barcelona tap water is entirely safe
and drinkable, but has a minerally
taste. By preference most people drink
bottled water, and if you ask for water
in a restaurant you will automatically
be served this unless you specifically
request otherwise.

Business

In the 1990s Barcelona
reaffirmed its reputation as the
Spanish city most open to the
world – in trade, tourism, the
adoption of new ideas and
projects – even if Madrid is still
'Head Office'. Yet, business
people still have a formidable

four-headed bureaucracy to grap-
ple with: all the machinery of the
Spanish state; the growing
power of Catalonia's autonomous
government, the Generalitat; the
mass of regulations emanating
from the EU; and a very
assertive city council.

It's a waste of time trying to
deal with this system single-
handed. A visit to the **Cambra
de Comerç** is a must; consulates
can also refer you to English-
speaking professionals, and a
good *gestoria* will probably save
you time and a lot of frustration.

Institutions & info

Government

EU office: Patronat Català Pro-Europa *C/Bruc 50, 2° (93 318 26 26). Metro Urquinaona/bus 7, 47, 50, 54, 56, 62.* **Open** 9am-2pm Mon, Fri; 9am-2pm, 4-6pm, Tue-Thur. *June-Sept* 9am-2pm Mon-Fri. **Map** D-E5/**C1**
Information on EU regulations and their effect on Spain, and EU grants.
Central government: Delegación de Hacienda
Your business will need a tax number (*Número de Identificación Fiscal* or *NIF/NIE*), issued by the local tax office. There are several district offices (*see p290*, **EU citizens**). It is very advisable to obtain this via a *gestoria*.
Catalan Government: Generalitat de Catalunya
(general information 012/business development 93 476 72 00/new businesses 902 20 15 20).
The Generalitat provides a range of consultancy and other services.
City council: Ajuntament de Barcelona *Plaça Sant Miquel 4-5 (93 402 70 00). Metro Jaume I/bus 17, 19, 40, 45.* **Open** 8.30am-6pm Mon-Fri; *July, Aug* 8.15am-2.15pm Mon-Fri. **Map** D6/**B3**
Permits for new businesses are issued by the ten municipal districts.

Other institutions

Borsa de Valors de Barcelona (Stock Exchange) *Passeig de Gràcia 19 (93 401 35 55). Metro Passeig de Gràcia/bus 7, 16, 17, 22, 24, 28, 42, 47.* **Open** *visits* 9am-6pm, *library* 9am-noon, Mon-Fri; *departments* 9am-2pm, 4-6.30pm, Mon-Fri. **Map** D5
British Society of Catalunya *Via Augusta 213 (tel/fax 93 209 06 39). FGC Bonanova/bus 14.* **Map** C2
Keep in touch with fellow ex-pats in monthly get-togethers and other events. Membership 1,500ptas a year.
Cambra de Comerç, Indústria i Navegació de Barcelona (Chamber of Commerce) *Avda Diagonal 452-454 (93 416 93 00). Metro Diagonal/bus 6, 7, 15, 16, 17, 33, 34.* **Open** *Sept-June* 9am-5pm Mon-Thur; 9am-2pm Fri; *July-Aug* 8.30am-3pm Mon-Fri. **Map** D4
The most important institution for business people, offering databases and a wealth of other information and advice.

Business services

Conference services

Barcelona Convention Bureau
C/Tarragona 149 (93 423 18 00). Metro Tarragona/bus 27, 30, 109, 215. **Open** *Sept-June* 9am-2.30pm, 4-7pm, Mon-Thur, 9am-3pm Fri; *July, Aug* 8am-3pm Mon-Fri. **Map** D4

Specialised arm of the city tourist authority to assist organisations or individuals holding conferences or similar events in the city.

Centre de Relacions Empresarials

Aeroport del Prat (93 478 67 99). **Open** 8.30am-8.30pm, *July, Aug* 8am-3pm, Mon-Fri.
The Cambra de Comerç provides this 'meeting point' at the airport, with six meeting rooms. The Chamber can also provide conference halls in the historic medieval Stock Exchange, the **Llotja** (*see p67*). For information, call 93 416 93 00.

Fira de Barcelona

Avda Reina Maria Cristina (93 233 20 00). Metro Espanya/bus all routes to Plaça d'Espanya. **Open** 9am-2pm, 4-6pm, Mon-Fri; *mid-June-mid-Sept* 9am-2pm Mon-Fri. **Map** A5
The Barcelona trade fair is one of the largest permanent exhibition complexes in Europe. In addition to the main area at Plaça d'Espanya it includes a huge state-of-the-art new site, **Montjuïc-2**, in the Zona Franca towards the airport, and administers the **Palau de Congressos** conference hall in the Plaça d'Espanya site, which can be let separately (93 233 23 71/93 233 23 41).

Gestories – administrative services

The *gestoria* is a very Spanish institution, the main function of which is to lighten the weight of local bureaucracy by dealing with it for you. A combination of bookkeeper, lawyer and business adviser, a good *gestor* can be very helpful in handling paperwork and pointing out shortcuts foreigners are usually unaware of. Unfortunately, local *gestoria* employees rarely speak English.

Forteza Asesoría y Gestión

C/Aribau 256, pral, 2° (93 200 79 25). FGC Gràcia/bus 27, 32, 58, 64) **Open** 9am-7pm, *July, Aug* closed Fri pm. Mon-Fri. Closed 1-15 Aug. **Map** C3
Full range of *gestoria* services. Some staff speak English.

Gestoría Tutzo

C/Aribau 226 (93 209 67 88/ stutzoro@aranzadi.es) Metro Diagonal/bus 27, 32, 33, 34. **Open** 8.30am-2pm, 4-7pm, Mon-Fri; *July, Aug* closed Fri pm. **Map** C3
With years of experience, Tutzo offers legal, fiscal, accounting, social security, contracts and other services. Some English is spoken.

LEC

Travessera de Gràcia 96, 2° 2ª (93 415 02 50). FGC Gràcia/bus 16, 17, 22, 24, 27, 31, 32. **Open** 9am-2pm, 4-7pm, Mon-Fri. Closed Aug. **Map** D3
Lawyers and economists as well as a *gestoria*. English speakers on the staff.

Office services

Office space & facilities

Centro de Negocios *C/Pau Claris 97, 4° 1ª (93 301 69 96). Metro Passeig de Gràcia/bus 7, 22, 28, 39, 45, 50, 54, 56.* **Open** 8am-9pm Mon-Fri; Aug 9am-3pm Mon-Fri. **Map** D5
Office space, desk space in shared offices, mail boxes, meeting rooms, secretarial services and a wide range of administrative services for hire.
Offiten *C/Galileu 303-305, 4° (93 321 08 12). Metro Les Corts/bus 15, 43, 59.* **Open** 8.30am-8pm, *Aug* 8.30am-2.30pm, Mon-Fri. **Map** A3
Furnished offices with secretarial, fax, Internet and translation services.
Picking Pack Megaservice *C/Consell de Cent 276 (93 487 61 31/mega-bcn1@pickingpack.es). Metro Passeig de Gràcia/bus 7, 16, 17, 63, 67, 68.* **Open** 9am-9pm Mon-Sat. **Credit** AmEx, MC, V. **Map** D5
Computers, Net, fax, design, printing, mail-outs, meeting rooms and more.
Website: www.pickingpack.es

Temp agencies

Adar Solutions *C/Balmes 245, 6° 1ª (93 415 21 61).* **Open** 9am-7pm Mon-Fri. **Map** D3
Manpower *C/Aragó 277 (93 487 68 68).* **Open** 9am-7pm Mon-Fri. **Map** D4

Translation agencies

BCN Consultores Lingüísticos *C/Balmes 67, 1° 1ª (93 454 51 12/ fax 454 35 46). Metro Passeig de Gràcia/bus 7, 16, 17, 63, 67, 68.* **Open** 8am-8pm Mon-Fri. **Map** D4
Professional translators/interpreters in 40 languages; prices are quite high.
DUUAL *C/Ciutat 7, 2° 4ª (93 302 29 85/fax 93 412 40 66). Metro Jaume I/bus 17, 19, 40, 45.* **Open** 9am-2pm, 4-7pm, Mon-Thur; 9am-2pm Fri; *June-Sept* 8.30am-3pm Mon-Fri. **Map** D6/**B3**
Good rates and excellent DTP facilities.

Traductores Jurados (Official translators)

Many official bodies demand foreign documents be translated by legally-certified translators. Rates are higher than for conventional translators.
Teodora Gambetta *C/Escorial 29-31, escala C, àtic 2ª (tel/fax 93 219 22 25). Metro Joanic/bus 39, 55.* **Open** by appointment. **Map** E3
Luís Pérez Pardo *C/Dr August Pi Sunyer 11, 6° 1ª (tel/fax 93 204 43 27). Metro Maria Cristina/bus 6, 7, 16, 33, 34, 63, 67, 68, 74, 78.* **Open** by appointment. **Map** A2

Students

Catalonia is ardently Europhile, and its universities lend enthusiastic support to EU student exchange programmes. Of the 3,000 students studying in Spain under the EU's Erasmus scheme, around 90 percent are enrolled at Catalan universities.

Barcelona's own students, though, are a stay-at-home lot. The Spanish system obliges them to take a course at a local university, if possible, which, added to economic factors and family ties, means that it's the norm for young people to study as close to home as possible.

The main teaching language in universities is usually Catalan, although lecturers (and students) are often relaxed about using Castilian in class for the first few months with non-Catalan speakers. Foreign students who stay for over three months, including EU nationals, are officially required to have a residence permit (*see page 291*).

Information centres

Centre d'Informació i Assessorament per a Joves (CIAJ)

C/Ferran 32 (93 402 78 00). Metro Liceu/bus 14, 38, 59, 91. **Open** 10am-2pm, 4pm-8pm, Mon-Fri; *Aug* 10am-2pm only. **Map** D6/**A-B3**
City council youth information centre, with advice and information on work, study, travel and more; also small-ads, noticeboards and a free Web terminal.

Secretaria General de Joventut – Punt d'Informació Juvenil

C/Calabria 147-C/Rocafort 116 (93 483 83 83/93 483 83 84). Metro Rocafort/bus 9, 41, 50, 56. **Open** 9am-2pm, 3-5.30pm Mon-Fri; *June-mid-Sept* 9am-2pm Mon-Fri. **Map** B5
Generalitat-run centre hosting a range of services: a 'youth information point' with information on travel, work, and study, Net access, and others, including: **Habitatge Jove** (93 483 83 92). **Open** 10am-1.30pm, 3.30-5pm, Mon-Fri; *Aug 1-15* 9am-2pm Mon-Fri.
Youth accommodation service: Erasmus students can use the website to find a place to live before they arrive in Barcelona.

Viatgeteca (93 483 83 81). **Open** 9am-2pm, 3-7pm, Mon-Fri. Travel information centre, where you can consult guidebooks and the Web, and book youth hostels.
Websites:
www.gencat.es/joventut/index_3x.htm
www.habitatgejove.com
www.gencat.es/catalunyajove

Universities

EU Programmes: Socrates, Erasmus, Lingua

The **Erasmus** student exchange scheme and **Lingua** project (specifically concerned with language learning) are the most important parts of the EU's **Socrates** programme to help students move between member states. Barcelona's universities have exchange arrangements with many British and Irish colleges, covering a wide range of subjects. Erasmus is open to students from their second year onwards; anyone interested should approach the Erasmus coordinator at their home college. General information is available in Britain from the *UK Socrates & Erasmus Council, R & D Building, The University, Canterbury, Kent CT2 7PD (01227 762 712/fax 01227 762 711/ erasmus@ukc.ac.uk)*.
Website:
www.ukc.ac.uk/ERASMUS/erasmus/

Universitat Autònoma de Barcelona

Campus de Bellaterra, 08193 (93 581 10 00/student information 93 581 11 11). FGC to Universitat Autònoma (Sabadell line). **Open** *information Sept-June* 9.30am-2pm, 3-8pm, *July, Aug* 9.30am-2pm, Mon-Fri.
The Autonomous University occupies a rambling 1960s campus outside the city at Bellaterra, near Sabadell, but with frequent FGC train connections.
Website: www.uab.es

Universitat de Barcelona

Gran Via de les Corts Catalanes 585 (93 403 54 17). Metro Universitat/bus all routes to Plaça Universitat. **Open** *information: Servei d'Atenció a la Comunitat Universitària (Pati de Ciències entrance)* 9am-6pm, *July, Aug* 9am-2pm, Mon-Fri. **Map** C-D5
Faculties in the main building on Plaça Universitat, in the Zona Universitària and other parts of town.
Website: www.ub.es

Universitat Internacional de Catalunya

C/Inmaculada 22 (93 254 18 00) FGC Sarrià/bus 22, 60, 64, 75. **Open** *information* 9am-8pm, *Aug* 9am-2pm, Mobn-Fri. Closed Christmas, Easter.

New private university with English as main teaching language. Expensive.
Website: www.unica.edu

Universitat Politècnica de Catalunya

C/Jordi Girona 1-3 (93 401 62 00/ student information 93 401 73 96). Metro Zona Universitària/bus 33, 54, 60, 75. **Open** *information* 9am-6pm Mon-Thur; 9am-3pm Fri; *mid-June-end July, Christmas* 9am-3pm Mon-Fri. Closed Easter & Aug.
Specialises in technical subjects. Most of it is in the Zona Universitària, but it has faculties in other towns.
Website: www.upc.es

Universitat Pompeu Fabra

Plaça de la Mercè 10-12 (93 542 20 00/ information 93 542 24 00). Metro Drassanes/bus 14, 36, 57, 59, 64, 157. **Open** *office* 8am-9.30pm, *July, Aug* 7.30am-8.15pm, Mon-Fri; *information phoneline* 9am-2pm, 4-6pm, Mon-Fri. Closed Aug. **Map** D6/**B4**
Social-sciences-based university with faculties in central Barcelona, many in the old city. Founded only in 1991.
Website: www.upf.es

Universitat Ramon Llull

Central office C/Sant Joan de la Salle 8 (93 253 04 50). FGC Tibidabo/bus 22, 58, 64, 73, 75, 85. **Open** *information* 9am-2pm, 4-7pm, Mon-Fri. Closed Easter, first half Aug.
Private university bringing together a number of previously-separate institutions owned and/or run by the Jesuits, although there is no strong religious presence in teaching. Fees are high.
Website: www.url.es

Language learning

Catalan-language use is always expanding, but Barcelona is also a popular location for studying Spanish. For full lists of course options, try youth information centres (*see left*).

American-British College

C/Guillem Tell 27 (93 415 57 57) FGC Plaça Molina/bus 22, 24, 25, 27, 28, 31, 32. **Open** 9am-9pm, *Aug* 9am-7.30pm, Mon-Fri. **Map** D2
An established school with reasonably-priced intensive Spanish courses. Accommodation can be arranged with families or in student residences.
Website: www.ambricol.es

Bla Bla & Company

C/Muntaner 82 (902 12 12 16). Metro Universitat/bus 54, 58, 64, 66. **Open** 8am-10pm Mon-Fri; 10am-2pm Sat. **Map** C4

Directory

A multi-media-based language school, offering Spanish courses, drop-in facilities and flexible, personalised tuition.
Website: www.blabla.es

Centres de Normalització Lingüística

Central office C/Pau Claris 162 (93 272 31 00/ cnlb@mx2.redestb.es).
Metro Passeig de Gràcia/bus 20, 39, 43, 44, 45. **Open** *Sept-June* 9am-2pm, 3-5.30pm, *15 June-15 Sept* 8am-3pm, Mon-Fri. **Map** D4
The official Generalitat organisation for the support of the Catalan language has centres around the city offering Catalan courses at low prices from beginners' level upwards, with intensive courses in summer, and self-study centres.

E-Languages

La Rambla 42/Passatge Bacardi 1 (93 481 75 75). Metro Liceu/bus 14, 38, 59, 91.* **Open** 10am-8pm Mon-Sat. **Map** D6/A3
Spanish courses from a 'superintensive' 30 hours a week to just three hours each week. Methods include on-the-street practice and new technologies (it is linked to a Net centre, *see p286*)
Website: www.spanishinbarcelona.com

Escola Oficial d'Idiomes

*Avda Drassanes (93 329 24 58).
Metro Drassanes/bus 14, 36, 38, 57, 59, 64, 91, 157.* **Open** 10.30am-12.30pm, 4.30-5.30pm, Mon-Thur; 10.30am-12.30pm Fri. **Map** C6/A4
The 'official school' has semi-intensive three-month courses at all levels in Catalan, Spanish and other languages. They're cheap, and classes are big, but

the Escola has a good reputation and demand is very high. To enrol you go on a set day in September or January, and do a level test; but, since demand outstrips supply they often resort to a lottery draw to decide who gets a place. There are also summer courses, a self-study centre, and a good library.
Website: www.xtec.es/centres/a8038570 **Branch:** Avda del Jordà 18, Vall d'Hebrón (93 418 74 85/93 418 68 33; website *www.pangea.org/org/EOI2*)..

Instituto Mangold de Idiomas

Rambla Catalunya 16 (93 301 25 39). Metro Catalunya/bus all routes to Plaça Catalunya. **Open** *offices* 9am-9pm Mon-Thur; 9am-8pm Fri. *Aug* 9am-6pm Mon-Fri. **Map** D5/B1
Well-regarded, centrally located school with intensive Spanish courses from July to September. Non-intensive Catalan courses are also offered.

International House

C/Trafalgar 14, entresol (93 268 45 11). Metro Urquinaona/bus all routes to Plaça Urquinaona. **Open** 8am-9pm Mon-Fri; 9.30am-1.30pm Sat. **Map** D5/C1
Intensive Spanish courses all year; IH is also the leading Barcelona centre for TEFL teacher training (*see right*).
Website: www.ihes.com/bcn

Universitat de Barcelona

Gran Via de les Corts Catalanes 585 (93 318 42 66). Metro Universitat/bus all routes to Plaça Universitat. **Open** *language course information* 9am-1pm Mon-Fri. **Map** C-D5

The university runs reasonably-priced courses for foreigners in Catalan and Spanish, some of which also include higher-level studies in literature, culture and so on. Ask for the *Servei de Llengua Catalana (403 54 77/e-mail slc@slc.ub.es)* for information on Catalan courses; *Estudios Hispánicos (403 55 19/e-mail est-hispa@d1.ub.es)* for Spanish. Courses are held throughout the year, and there are intensive language courses in July and September.
Website: www.ub.es

Other courses

TEFL Teacher Training

Recognized training courses for teachers of English are offered at several centres in Barcelona. Most important for the RSA/Cambridge CELTA (better known as 'the TEFL') is **International House** (*see left*), while the equally-respected TESOL is offered by several other schools. Both CELTA and TESOL certificates require four-week full-time courses.
Oxford House College *Avda Diagonal 402, pral 1ª (93 458 01 11/ ohc@mx4.redestb.es) Metro Verdaguer/bus 6, 15, 33, 34.* **Open** 9am-9pm Mon-Fri. **Map** D-E4
TESOL certificate and diploma courses are available.
Next Training *C/Rocafort 241-243, 6º 5ª (93 322 02 00). Metro Entença/bus 41.* **Open** 8am-9pm, *Aug* 10am-6pm, Mon-Fri. **Map** B4
TESOL courses and the diploma, with distance-learning option.
Website: www.next-training.es

Women

The Catalan capital is in many ways a female-friendly city. Sexism can certainly be found, but a woman can have a drink in a bar or go out alone without anyone making much of it, and generally feel quite safe.

The position of women in Spanish society has been utterly transformed in the last 25 years. One major index is the birth rate: from second-highest in Europe (after Ireland) in 1975, it's now one of the lowest in the world; at work, there are nearly as many women as men – and universities have more women students.

On the other hand, a feminist movement *per se* is small. There is a feminist bookshop, **Pròleg** (*see chapter* **Shopping**).

Organisations

Associació Catalana de la Dona

C/Providència 42, 2º 2ª (93 213 34 40). Metro Fontana/bus 39. **Open** by appointment. **Map** E3
Independent association for the defence and promotion of women's rights.

Ca La Dona

C/Casp 38, pral (93 412 71 61/ caladona@pangea.org). Metro Catalunya/bus all routes to Plaça Catalunya. **Open** *office* 10am-2pm, 4-8pm, Tue-Thur. Closed Aug, Christmas, Easter. **Map** D5/B1
Women's centre hosting a range of groups, among them the *Coordinadora Feminista de Catalunya*, the most important local feminist organisation, video groups and a lesbian group. A good place to get general information. It also has a magazine (of the same name, in Catalan) with event listings. *See also* chapter **Gay & Lesbian Barcelona**.

Centre Municipal d'informació i Recursos per a Dones

C/Llacuna, 161, 2ª (93 291 84 92/93 291 84 93/CIRD@mail.bcn.es). Metro Glòries/bus 56, 60, 92. **Open** *Sept-May* 4-7pm Tue, Thur; *25 June-23 Sept* noon-2pm Mon-Fri.
The Ajuntament's women's resource centre. Its publications include a monthly events guide, *Agenda Dona*.
Website: www.cird.bcn.es

Institut Català de la Dona

Head office *C/Viladomat 319, entresol (93 495 16 00/ icd@correu.gencat.es).* **Map** B3
Information centre *C/Portaferrissa 1-3 (93 317 92 91/icdcentredoc @correu.gencat.es). Metro Liceu/bus 14, 38, 59, 91.* **Open** *16 Sept-31 May* 9am-2pm, 4-8pm, *1 June-15 Sept* 8am-3pm, Mon-Fri. **Map** D6/A2
The women's affairs department of the Catalan government.
Website: www.gencat.es/icdona

Further Reading

Several useful books on Barcelona are produced locally in English-language or bilingual editions, both by the city council (Ajuntament de Barcelona) and independent publishers, especially the Editorial Gustavo Gili. Places to find them are the **Botiga de la Virreina** city bookshop and the main **tourist office** (*see p191 and p294*).

Guides & walks

Amelang, J, Gil, X & McDonogh, GW: *Twelve Walks through Barcelona's Past* (Aj. de Barcelona).
Well thought-out walks by historical themes. Original, and better-informed than many walking guides.

García Espuche, Albert:
The Quadrat d'Or (Aj. de Barcelona).
Building-by-building guide to the central Eixample, the 'Golden Square' of *Modernista* architecture.

González, A & Lacuesta, R: *Barcelona Architecture Guide 1929-1994* (Ed. Gustavo Gili)
Thorough paperback guide to all of Barcelona's contemporary architecture.

Güell, Xavier: *Gaudí Guide* (Ed. Gustavo Gili)
Handy, with good background on all his work.

Pomés Leiz, Juliet, & Feriche, Ricardo:
Barcelona Design Guide (Ed. Gustavo Gili)
An eccentrically wide-ranging but engaging listing of everything ever considered 'designer' in BCN.

History, art, architecture, culture

Burns, Jimmy: *Barça: A People's Passion*
The first full-scale history in English of one of the world's most overblown football clubs.

Elliott, JH: *The Revolt of the Catalans*
Fascinating, highly detailed account of the Guerra dels Segadors and the Catalan revolt of the 1640s.

Fernández Armesto, Felipe:
Barcelona: A Thousand Years of the City's Past
A solid, straightforward history.

Fraser, Ronald: *Blood of Spain*
A vivid oral history of the Spanish Civil War and the tensions that preceded it. It is especially good on the events of July 1936 in Barcelona.

Hughes, Robert: *Barcelona*
The most comprehensive single book on Barcelona: tendentious at times, erratic, but beautifully written, and covering every aspect of the city up to the 1900s.

Kaplan, Temma: *Red City, Blue Period – Social Movements in Picasso's Barcelona*
An interesting book, tracing of the interplay of avant-garde art and avant-garde politics in 1900s Barcelona.

King, Jeff: *High Noon: A Year at Barcelona*
A blow-by-blow account of Bobby Robson's year in charge at FC Barcelona.

Orwell, George: *Homage to Catalonia*
The classic account of Barcelona in revolution, by an often bewildered, but always perceptive observer.

Paz, Abel: *Durruti, The People Armed*
Closer to its theme, a biography of the most legendary of Barcelona's anarchist revolutionaries.

Richardson, John:
A Life of Picasso, Vol. I, 1881-1906
The definitive biography: volume I covers the whole of Picasso's Barcelona years among the *Modernistes*, and his later important visits to Catalonia.

Solà-Morales, Ignasi: *Fin de Siècle Architecture in Barcelona* (Ed. Gustavo Gili)
Large-scale and wide-ranging description and evaluation of the city's *Modernista* heritage.

Tóibín, Colm: *Homage to Barcelona*
Evocative and perceptive journey around the city: good on the booming Barcelona of the 1980s, but also excellent on Catalan Gothic, Gaudí and Miró.

Vázquez Montalbán, Manuel: *Barcelonas*
Idiosyncratic but insightful reflections on the city by one of its most prominent modern writers.

Zerbst, Rainer: *Antoni Gaudí*
Lavishly illustrated and comprehensive survey.

Literature

Calders, Pere: *The Virgin of the Railway and Other Stories*
Ironic, engaging, quirky stories by a Catalan writer who spent many years in exile in Mexico.

Català, Victor: *Solitude*
This masterpiece by woman novelist, Caterina Albert, shocked readers in 1905 with its open, modern treatment of female sexuality.

Marsé, Juan: *The Fallen*
Classic novel of survival in Barcelona during the long *posguerra* after the Civil War.

Martorell, Joanot, & Joan Martí de Gualba:
Tirant lo Blanc
The first European prose novel, from 1490, a rambling, bawdy shaggy-dog story of travels, romances and chivalric adventures.

Mendoza, Eduardo:
City of Marvels and *Year of the Flood*
A sweeping, very entertaining saga of Barcelona between its great Exhibitions, 1888 and 1929, and a more recent novel of passions in the city of the 1950s.

Oliver, Maria Antònia:
Antipodes and *Study in Lilac*
Two adventures of Barcelona's first feminist detective.

Rodoreda, Mercè: *The Time of the Doves* and *My Cristina and Other Stories*
A translation of *La Plaça del Diamant*, most widely-read of all Catalan novels. Plus a collection of similarly bitter-sweet short tales.

Vázquez Montalbán, Manuel: *The Angst-Ridden Executive* and *An Olympic Death*
Two thrillers starring Vázquez Montalbán's detective and gourmet extraordinaire, Pepe Carvalho.

Food & drink

Andrews, Colman: *Catalan Cuisine*
A mine of information on food and much else besides (but also with usable recipes).

Casas, Penelope: *Food and Wines of Spain*
A useful general handbook.

Index

Advertisers' Index

Maps

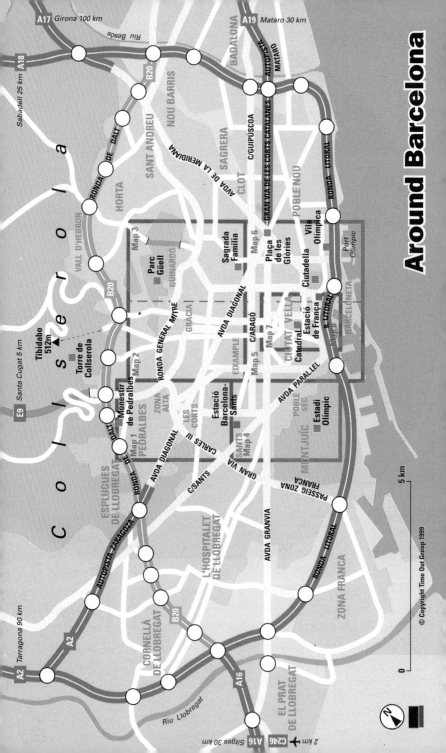

Around Barcelona

A17 Girona 100 km
A19 Mataro 30 km

Sabadell 25 km A18
A2 Tarragona 90 km
E9 Santa Cugat 5 km

Riu Besòs
Riu Llobregat

BADALONA
AUTOPISTA MATARO
NOU BARRIS
SANT ANDREU
SAGRERA
CLOT
POBLE NOU
C/GUIPÚSCOA
GRAN VIA DE LES CORTS CATALANES
AVDA DE LA MERIDIANA
RONDA DE DALT
B20

HORTA
VALL D'HEBRON
Parc Güell
GUINARDÓ
Map 3
GRÀCIA
Sagrada Família
Map 6
Plaça de les Glòries
Vila Olímpica
Ciutadella
Port Olímpic
BARCELONETA
RONDA LITORAL
R. LITORAL

Tibidabo 512m
Torre de Collserola
Collserola
B20
RONDA GENERAL MITRE
AVDA DIAGONAL
C/ARAGÓ
Map 7
EIXAMPLE
Map 5
CIUTAT VELLA
Catedral
Estació de França
R. LITORAL

Monestir de Pedralbes
Map 2
ZONA ALTA
LES CORTS
PEDRALBES
Map 1
RONDA DE DALT
AVDA DIAGONAL
CARLES III
GRAN VIA
C/SANTS
SANTS
Map 4
Estació Barcelona-Sants
AVDA PARAL·LEL
POBLE SEC
MONTJUÏC
Estadi Olímpic
PASSEIG ZONA FRANCA

ESPLUGUES DE LLOBREGAT
AUTOPISTA ZARAGOZA
RONDA DE DALT

L'HOSPITALET DE LLOBREGAT
AVDA GRANVIA
RONDA LITORAL
ZONA FRANCA

CORNELLÀ DE LLOBREGAT
B20
A2
A16
EL PRAT DE LLOBREGAT

Riu Llobregat

C246 Sitges 30 km A16 2 km

5 km
0

© Copyright Time Out Group 1999

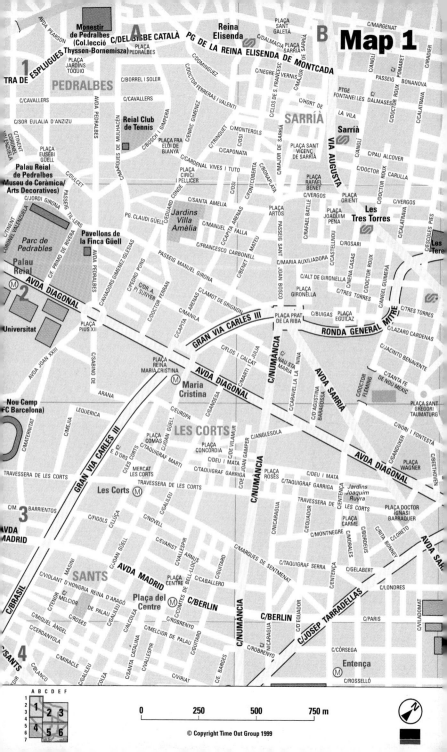

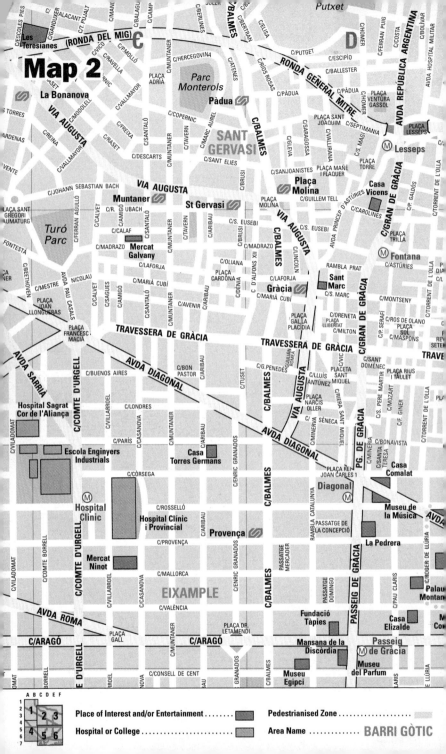

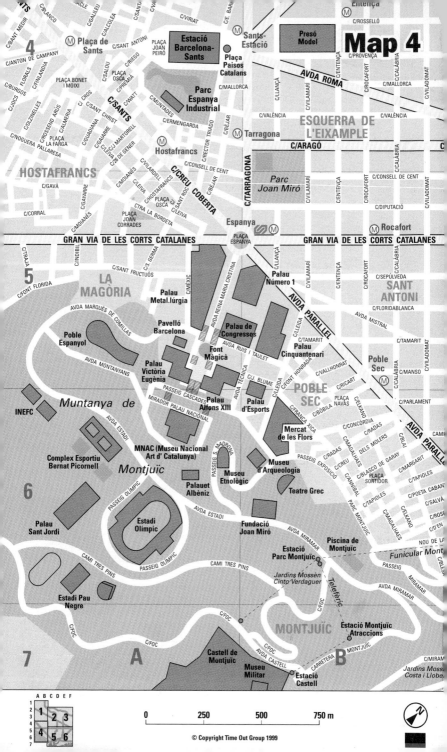

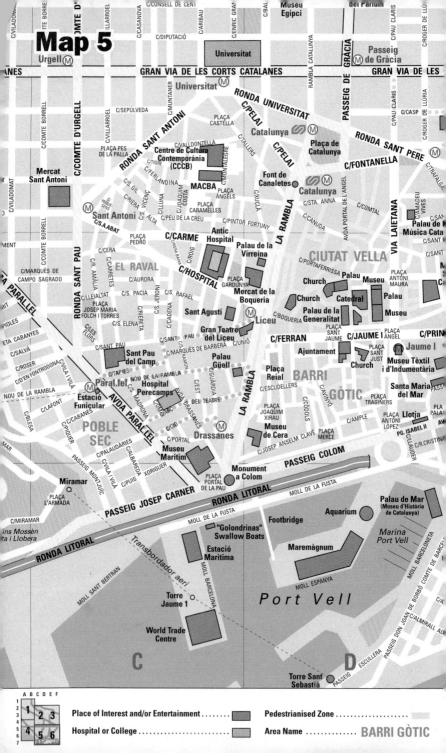

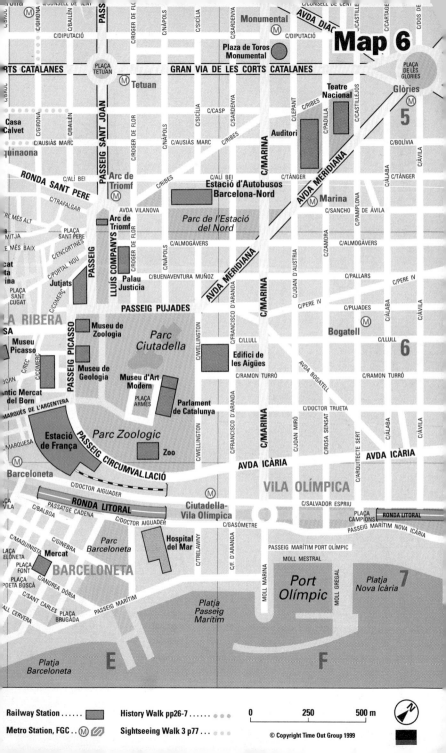

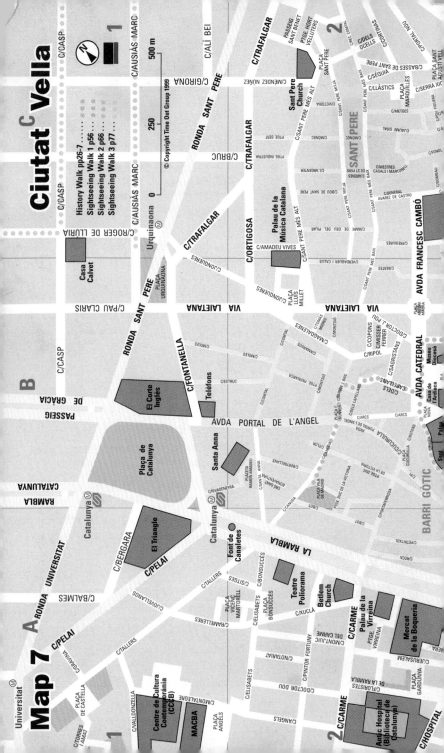

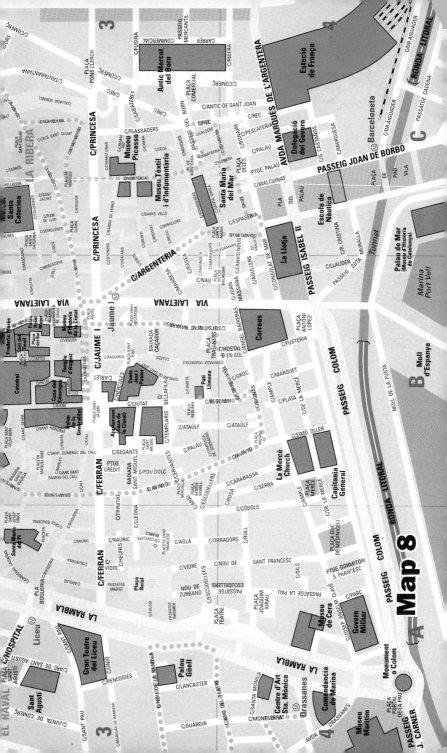

Map 8

3

C/COMERÇ
C/SABATERET
C/BLANQUERIA
PLAÇA
PONS CLERCH
C/COMERÇ
C/REC
C/FUSINA
PASSEIG MERCANTIL
CARRER COMMERCIAL
C/RIBERA

Antic Mercat
del Born

PLAÇA
COMMERCIAL
C/BORN
C/ANTIC DE SANT JOAN
C/REC

Estació
de França

RONDA LITORAL
COR AIGUADER
PASSATGE CADENA
COR AIGUADER

AVDA MARQUÈS DE L'ARGENTERA

Barcelona **C**

LA RIBERA
C/PRINCESA

Museu
Picasso

Museu Tèxtil
i d'Indumentària

C/MONTCADA

Santa Maria
del Mar

C/COMERÇ
C/REC
C/CALDERS
PASSEIG DEL BORN
C/BONAIRE
C/PESCATERIA
C/PALAU

Delegació
del Govern

PASSEIG JOAN DE BORBÓ

C/G CASTANOS
C/MARQUESA
PLAÇA DE PAU VILA

Santa
Caterina

C/PRINCESA

C/ARGENTERIA

Escola de
Nàutica

Palau de Mar
(Museu d'Història
de Catalunya)

La Llotja

PASSEIG ISABEL II

Marina
Port Vell

VIA LAIETANA
Jaume I
VIA LAIETANA

Palau
Reial

Museu
d'Història
de la Ciutat

C/JAUME I

Temple
d'August

Catedral

Casa de
l'Ardiaca

Palau de
la Generalitat

Ajuntament
Casa de
la Ciutat

Correus

MOLL DE LA FUSTA

B
Moll
d'Espanya

PASSEIG COLOM

La Mercé
Church

Capitania
General

PASSEIG COLOM

RONDA LITORAL

C/FERRAN

Sant
Just i
Pastor

Pati
Llimona

Sants
Justi i
Pastor

3

Santa Maria
del Pi

Plaça
Reial

C/FERRAN

PASSATGE ESCUDELLERS

Museu
de Cera

Govern
Militar

LA RAMBLA
Liceu

Gran Teatre
del Liceu

Palau
Güell

EL RAVAL

Sant
Agustí

Centre d'Art
Sta. Mònica

Comandancia
de Marina

Museu
Marítim

LA RAMBLA

Monument
a Colom

PASSEIG
J. CARNER

Drassanes

4

A

PLAÇA
PORTAL
DE LA PAU

Street Index

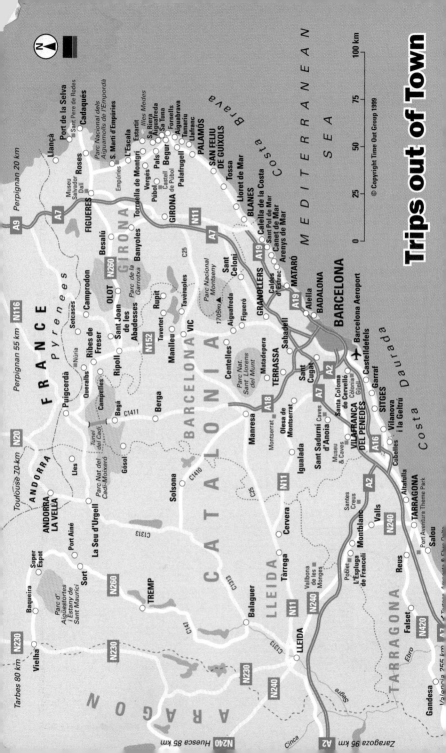

Trips out of Town

© Copyright Time Out Group 1999

RENFE local trains

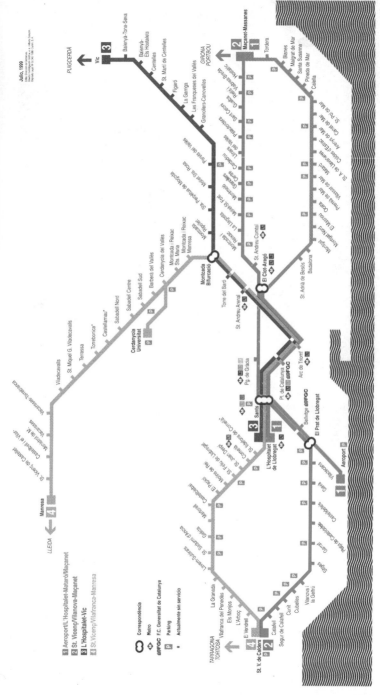

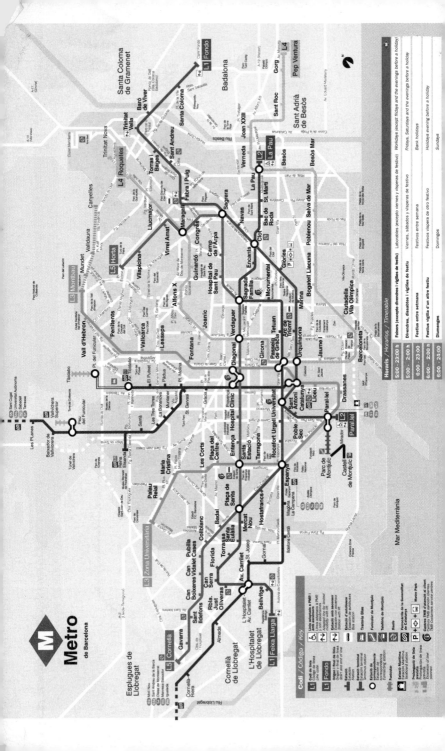